Freedom's Empire

Freedom's Empire

Race and the Rise
of the Novel in
Atlantic Modernity,
1640–1940

Laura Doyle

DUKE UNIVERSITY PRESS : DURHAM AND LONDON 2008

© 2008 Duke University Press
All rights reserved
Printed in the United States of America on acid-free paper ∞
Designed by April Leidig-Higgins
Typeset in MinionPro by Copperline Book Services, Inc.

Library of Congress Cataloging-in-Publication Data appear
on the last printed page of this book.

For my mother
and
for Nick,
without whom
nothing

These waters were unfathomably deep.
Into them had spilled so many lives . . .
—Virginia Woolf, *To the Lighthouse*

Mention "lap of wave"
and the sea becomes a monument
of bones walking backward
and we, the skin of the waves.
— Danielle Legros Georges, "Maroon"

Contents

Acknowledgments

WRITING THIS BOOK has been a working-through of something old and deep, a shared political unconscious that has also been personal. I am delighted finally to thank the people who have inspired, read, and shaped this work and the institutions that have supported it. Although it is impossible to name everyone, I want to single out a few people who very pointedly kept the project alive.

I would like especially to thank Peter Agree. It so happened that, long ago, in his role as an unofficial, generous advisor, he told me to follow the path that has led to this book — to follow it all the way. I needed to hear that. Over subsequent years I needed to hear it again and again, and Peter helpfully, patiently repeated it. At one level, I owe the completion of this book to Peter.

This project was begun long ago during my year as a Rockefeller Fellow in Intercultural Studies in the Afro-American Studies Program at Princeton University. Without that year, I might never have seen or gotten hold of the thread that led to this book. Thank you particularly to Arnold Rampersad, Tricia Rose, and Kevin Gaines for the fertilizing dialogue and collegiality of that year; and to the Rockefeller Foundation for generous support. Since that year, I have been fortunate to work in an English department that cultivates the peace, shuns the jockeying, and, more than that, brings to Bartlett Hall at the University of Massachusetts, Amherst a ready spirit of camaraderie in our common projects of teaching, learning, and desiring a good world. This spirit has supported every aspect of my life in Amherst — the book-writing included.

I am deeply indebted to the readers for Duke University Press, who undoubtedly spent many hours with the manuscript and who offered detailed, incisive suggestions for revision. I cannot convey my profound sense of gratitude (not to mention relief) on reading those reports! I thank Reynolds Smith for giving me a place to put the book, once written — for accepting its heft and believing in it with full gusto from beginning to end. I am grateful as well to the staff at Duke University Press, with special thanks to Lynn Walterick for her careful copyediting of these many pages and to Katharine Baker for coordinating that effort.

The book has also benefited from the generosity of several colleagues who read chapters in draft, gave trenchant advice, and encouraged me to press forward —

most especially Nancy Ruttenburg, Kevin Gaines, Richard Millington, Deborah Nord, Shirley Samuels, Nicholas Bromell, Leo Damrosch, and Stephen Clingman. My thanks as well to the members of the Atlantic Studies Seminar (including my co-facilitator Michelle Stephens) for your thoughtfulness in all of our conversations, as well as your salutary comments on this project as I entered its last phases. Our discussions about transatlantic work helped me better imagine an audience for this book. And I thank Five Colleges, Inc., which has generously supported our work together. Any errors in the book are my own, while any virtues must be attributed to this large circle of scholars and friends that supported my work on it.

I was fortunate to have, at different times over the last five years, three excellent research assistants; my thanks to Elizabeth Keller, Mary Wilson, and Ethan Bresner. All were astute, able, and wonderfully reliable researchers. I couldn't have faced the endnotes without them. In the case of Ethan I thank Commonwealth Honors College at the University of Massachusetts, Amherst for the funding they provided to support his work. Thank you, too, to Nancy Doherty and Michelle Fredette, who provided crucial clerical and editing support in the final stages of the project.

Last but not least, I thank my close friends and my family (both Doyle and Bromell) who at least pretended to have faith that I would one day be able to answer "Finished" to the question, "How's the book?" And finally, the inexpressible, for which the following sentences will stand in. Thanks to my mother and two fathers, for the ways they lived and faced race and thereby unconsciously planted the seeds for this book. Thanks to Sam and Leon, for being, and for being joyous. Thank you most profoundly to Nick, for all that happens between us, which has shaped this book and everything else I am and do.

Introduction

IN *THE SOCIAL CONTRACT* (1762), Jean-Jacques Rousseau likens revolution in the state to the rupture of a person's memory — and so gives a hint of the novel's work in Atlantic modernity:

> just as certain afflictions unhinge men's minds and banish their memory of the past, so there are certain violent epochs and revolutions in states which have the same effects on peoples . . . ; only instead of forgetting the past, they look back on it in horror, and then the state after being consumed by civil war, is born again, so to speak, from its own ashes, and leaps from the arms of death to regain the vigour of youth.[1]

Published before the American and French revolutions, Rousseau's reflections would have recalled for his contemporaries the English Revolution and its aftermath. For in the preceding century all of Europe had stood witness as the English fought a bloody civil war, beheaded their king, swerved from republic to Protectorate to Restoration to "bloodless" revolution and finally fashioned themselves as a youthful "people" of vigorous free spirit, destined to win colonies from their European rivals and build the next western empire. The immensely popular eighteenth-century histories of England written by the Frenchman Paul de Rapin-Thoyras, the Scot David Hume, and the Englishwoman Catharine Macaulay had both intensified and reflected the eighteenth-century Anglo-European preoccupation with English revolutionary history.

It is this revolutionary history, I argue, that the English-language novel most deeply encodes and that, in turn, racializes its plots. The kind of radical un-hinging that, in Rousseau's account, follows both violent revolution and personal trauma creates the turning point in many English-language novels. Overwhelmed by force or betrayal, protagonists swoon into dissociation or seeming death, fall under threat of utter forgetting, yet rise (sometimes) into their full (e)state. This story tells not only a person's but also a people's history — and not just a people's but, more specifically, a race's. It makes race history out of violent ruin. For in what later became known as the Whig narrative of English history, the nation's ruptures and revolutions were explained as the effects of a uniquely Saxonist legacy of freedom; and in complex, implicit ways, the English-language novel from *Oroonoko* to *Quicksand* has taken up this racial legacy.

Rousseau may in fact have borrowed his trope of the reborn state from a liter-ary text that helped to define this Saxonist narrative: the enormously popular eighteenth-century narrative poem *Liberty* (1736), penned by that poet of the Brit-ish nation, James Thomson, and read on both sides of the Channel as well as the Atlantic. Telling the story of Britain's revolutionary turn toward freedom, Thom-son's poem contributed both to the racializing of this revolutionary "people" and to the novel's emergent "phoenix" plot of ruin and rebirth which would inscribe that racialization.[2] He gives an epic account of liberty's migration from Greece to Rome and then, triumphantly, to the northern climes, where the "yellow-haired, the blue-eyed Saxon" (4. 670) of "the Gothic nations" (4. 742) cultivated liberty and carried it to England and the world. And he conjures the same phoenix image of rebirth, using it to mark the turning-point crisis in the progress-story of a free, Gothic-descended (if Briton-blended) people.[3] The narrator, Liberty herself, ex-plains that in the English Revolution of the early seventeenth century, "There was a flame/ Broke out that clear'd, consum'd, renew'd the Land," a "Conflagration" in which "KINGS, LORDS, COMMONS, thundering to the Ground,/ Successive, rush'd — Lo! From their Ashes rose, / Gay-beaming radiant Youth, the *Phoenix-State*" (4. 1020 – 21, 1041 – 45).

Thomson's narration of freedom as a racial inheritance and of revolution as racial renewal later finds its most influential elaboration in the work of G. W. F. Hegel. Hegel likewise invokes the phoenix in his vision of a racialized, dialectical "spirit" that realizes the state's freedom telos. In his account, "the German Spirit is the Spirit of the new World" whose "absolute Truth" is the "self-determination of Freedom."[4] And it is by way of the Germanic Spirit of Freedom that the state "arises rejuvenated from the ashes of its embodiment, . . . exalted" (59). Here, too, the phoenix image representing the cataclysmic origins of the free state emblema-tizes the modern racial refashioning of identity, a refashioning in which novels have played a key part.[5] Together, race and liberty fire both the revolutions and the fictions that remake citizens from the inside out, as Rousseau suggests in his analogy between the person's psyche and the nation's history. Herein lie the deepest ideological (as opposed to economic) roots of what we now call whiteness, whose purported superiority rests on its racially inherited, mastering capacity for freedom. To be white is to be fit for freedom, and the white man's burden is to lead others by forging the institutions and modeling the subjectivities required to practice proper freedom, even if along the way this requires enslaving, invading, or exterminating those others who may not (yet) be fit for freedom.

That is to say, in Atlantic modernity, freedom is a race myth. The project of this book is to understand how, why, and to what effect — and so to take seriously Saidiya Hartman's suggestion that we scrutinize "the vexed genealogy of freedom" as it is structured by race.[6] In a way, novels tell the whole story, but to gather the light we need to read them, we must begin by uncovering the ways race first takes shape as a *revolutionary* formation in seventeenth-century England. In other words, the task entails a fundamental revision of our histories of race in the West. While it is true, as Hartman establishes so incisively and David Brion Davis's work also explores, that the interproduction of freedom and bondage on the Atlantic meant that freedom's individualist meanings rested utterly on slavery's (de)meanings of individuals, it is also crucial to consider the prehistory of the rhetoric of freedom.[7] This prehistory supplements our understanding of how and why racialization came so readily to hand as slavery's explanatory ideology. In the different history of race that I propose here, the Atlantic economy plays a crucial part, but not strictly along the lines that historians of race have drawn.[8] For, although the racialization of freedom was fed by the Atlantic slave trade and exploitive encounters with American Indians, this racialization and these contact-zone conditions are only part of the picture — and, initially, not the most important *racial* part.

The original fashioning of race in English-language culture, at least, develops in an emergently transatlantic England in the 1620s through 1640s as what can rightly be called a postcolonial discourse — whether it was pure ideology or not — of Anglo-Saxon rights. It was an insurgent discourse, and, as long as the Stuart kings were in power, to speak it was to be stripped of privileges, put in the Tower, or have one's ears cut off. In this ideology as it eventually was embellished, "outlandish" Norman conquerors had invaded England in 1066 and trampled, without utterly destroying, her Anglo-Saxon traditions. These traditions, brought to England by the fierce Gothic Saxons who had displaced the Rome-weakened Britons, included participatory government through the *witenagemot*, zealous protection of land and rights, and a populace of "freeborn" men. These were the purportedly native traditions and common laws that in the first decades of the 1600s the Society of Antiquaries worked to translate, print, and reassert — until this society was banned by the Stuart king James I in 1614. This early, insurgent history of Anglo-Saxonism can teach us much about its long racist aftermath.

The society's work of unearthing pre-Conquest or Anglo-Saxon legal and parliamentary traditions first found subscribers among members of the English Parliament claiming the "ancient" right to participate in state decision making against the divine-right claims of James I; its discourse of native rights then got taken up in the later 1620s by a transatlantic coalition of merchants and Puritans who used it to challenge royal monopoly rules and justify religious and colonial dissent —and who by the 1640s, with their new, unregulated wealth, helped to fund civil war and behead the king; and finally, especially with the civil-war lapse of censorship controls, this Saxonist discourse found vociferous and widespread expression among a war-weary populace who went so far as to assert—in print— an inherent God-given freedom for all English souls, including those of women, Quakers, and the landless. Among such groups as the Diggers, this claim to freedom even threatened to turn universalist and leave race behind. But exactly because freedom's far-reaching implications were unthinkable and, furthermore, threatened both landed and mercantile wealth, the idea of freedom was ultimately recontained, I argue, within an exclusionary Saxonist narrative. Revolution in England was, as all kinds of agitators put it, decreed from within, in conformity to an Anglo-Saxon, Protestant conscience and habit of independence, now laudably "manifested" in print and bravely being recovered, in phoenix fashion, after generations of a Norman-Catholic oppression (perpetuated by Stuart tyranny and eventually the Puritan Protectorate). The Protestant and Saxonist vocabularies of tender conscience and native birthright worked in this way to position liberty as an interior, racial inheritance, planted in the individual and constituting an irrevocable principle for the government of the state.

Thomson, Rousseau, and Hegel thus express what I propose is an Atlantic imaginary structured by this narrative in which the state, phoenix-like, falls into revolution, dissolves, reclaims its racial birthright to liberty, and is reborn into the freedom of a modern nation. What makes this narrative "Atlantic" is that the Anglo-Saxon race's entry into a "state" of liberty is from the beginning associated with an Atlantic crossing and trauma of exile that, moreover, resonates richly with Old Testament narratives of sea-crossing by another, affiliated, freedom-seeking race. The phoenix fall and rise entails, that is, a deracinating but ultimately racialized and triumphant Atlantic crossing. The pattern constitutes a central chronotope in English-language texts—in other words, a vehicle for the cultural reorganization of space, time, and subjectivity. In the earliest incarnations of this Atlantic imaginary, there is something that we can call racialism or nativism that is not immediately *racist*, even though it soon provides the infrastructure for a racist and imperial "white" subjectivity in transatlantic culture. This revolutionary racialism that formed around the notion of liberty eventually comprises the "ancient" ballad structure, so to speak, for the full orchestral and eugenic racist symphonies of the nineteenth and twentieth centuries.

Only by recognizing this revolutionary understory of race can we fully appreciate its later force in transatlantic modernity and in the English-language novel. Attending to it, we can more cogently answer Paul Gilroy's call in *Black Atlantic* to "take the Atlantic as one single, complex unit of analysis" and "use it to produce an explicitly transnational and intercultural perspective."[9] We can also more fully interpret the racialized Atlantic performances catalogued by Joseph Roach in *Cities of the Dead*. Most structurally, we can see how a racialized pattern of narrative participates in the emergent differentiation between modernity and barbarity; for these texts work along or move against what Walter Mignolo calls the modernity/coloniality border, a border that is not so much geographical as ontopolitical, inflecting language, sorting persons, and creating divergent bodily and social experiences through a racialized liberty discourse. Although the fullest picture of Atlantic literature and its involvement in these dynamics would be translingual as well as transnational and transcultural, for feasibility's sake I have limited this study to literature published in the United States and Britain, in English, by African-Atlantic and Anglo-Atlantic authors, as I call them here.[10] Nonetheless, even to consider this circumscribed set of materials opens up a much broader perspective on English-language narratives' imagining of modernity than has usually been visible. Most specifically, from this perspective, we can begin to understand the regularity with which, in authors from Behn to Defoe to Equiano to Sedgwick to Hawthorne to Melville to Jacobs to Hopkins to Stein to Larsen to Woolf, the troubled entry into modernity, race, and freedom takes the form of a cataclysmic crossing of the Atlantic Ocean.

Anglo-Atlantic and African-Atlantic narratives in English diverge radically, of course — as determined exactly by the racialization of liberty that deems one group free and the other not yet capable of freedom — even while the narrative of a sea-crossing and an experience of exilic self-loss underlies both sets of stories. Indeed, by the end of the eighteenth century Anglo-Atlantic and African-Atlantic authors were writing back and forth to each other in a vexed dialectic centering on this chronotope. Anglo-Atlantic authors do so less consciously. Their narratives frequently register the presence and sometimes the "freeing" work of African-Atlantic (and in some cases Indian-American) persons in the service of whites, yet then, in habitual gestures, subordinate and elide this presence. Think, for example, of the labors of Xury and Friday in Robinson Crusoe's two escapes from captivity, reframed by Crusoe as his liberation of them. That is, Anglo-Atlantic novels from the beginning practice what Toni Morrison calls Africanism, unwittingly manifesting how the production of white identity, articulated as free and modern, depends on an African-Atlantic presence and labor.[11] And in the case of authors such as Nathaniel Hawthorne and Catharine Maria Sedgwick, an analogous practice of "Indianism" shapes their characters and their narratives.

Meanwhile, however, the narratives' logic of liberty and their muffled acknowledgment of an African presence create an opening for the articulation of the black experience in English-language texts. Although, not surprisingly, given language differences and racist literacy laws, the trope of an Atlantic trauma first found *printed*, English-language expression in Anglo-Atlantic texts, African-Atlantic authors such as Olaudah Equiano, Harriet Jacobs, Pauline Hopkins, and others directly rewrite these Atlantic stories so as to inscribe African-Atlantic subjects' experience and highlight their enabling role. The project of these authors is not strictly one of postcolonial mimicry, or even only of signifying on the liberty narrative. They do more than ventriloquize the dominant liberty narrative with a subversive différance. They implicitly generate an African-Atlantic archeology of it, installing themselves as its absent origin.

And yet, in another twist, since the founding logic of freedom decrees that it can be claimed only under the sign of race, African American writers must adopt the *race* plot of freedom, extending its genealogical idea to African peoples. Thus do African-Atlantic counternarratives at once resist and embrace the racial order of Atlantic modernity. In this vexed dialectical way, a diverse range of Atlantic narratives develop an allegorical structure for the advent of an unanchored modern self who finds a steadying current, however, in the idea of race. They record the (re)patriation of the liberated individual within a racialized national or international community.

Within all these narratives, the trope of an Atlantic crossing correlates with what I call a swoon moment—the phoenix fall—involving a bodily "undoing" or "ruin" that is often sexual or coded as feminine. The swoon appears as a tableau-moment in narrative after narrative, from Behn's *Oroonoko* to Richardson's *Clarissa* to Pauline Hopkins's *Of One Blood:* a character faints or momentarily collapses in the wake of violation by a terrorizing or tyrannizing force, whether seducer, slaver, or swallowing sea storm. As a primal, symbolic scene operating by way of displacement and condensation like Freudian dreamwork, the collapse distills the "undoing" effects of the Atlantic crossing and economy. That is, the fainting swoon marks the crossing of a social and ontological threshold, symbolizing the person's entry into the supposedly free republics of Atlantic modernity; it signals that this entry entails a radical remaking of the subject, psychically and bodily, for it supplants the subject's familiar temporal, spatial, and intersubjective coordinates. Thus the self in an Atlantic swoon moment faces an abyss, losing its old social identity as it faints — only to reawaken, uprooted and yet newly racialized, "born again" from its own ashes, as Rousseau and Hegel say of the state. Because this bodily violation occurs within a colonial horizon of captivity or opportunity, the narratives merge the notion of "entry" as transatlantic arrival in a new society with "entry" as coercive physical or sexual violence.

For African-Atlantic writers, the origin of the association between an Atlantic crossing and this scene of bodily ruin is, of course, the middle passage. The violent unmaking and remaking experience of the middle passage is heralded when Equiano faints as he arrives on the Guiney slave ship.[12] This middle-passage origin for the swoon scene in African-Atlantic texts finds repeated enactment in Pauline Hopkins's novels, in faintings that unveil rape as the most brutal racial event of the Atlantic and the Americas. By the time that Nella Larsen writes *Quicksand* and narrates Helga Crane's final, parodic swoon into the arms of Reverend Pleasant Green in the midst of a storm (a fall already prepared by her Scandinavian mother's ocean-crossing and race-mixing sexual fall), Larsen joins a tradition of African-Atlantic authors crafting a palimpsest of the ruinous, racialized liberty story of the Atlantic. Indeed, in her later short stories "Freedom" and "Sanctuary," as I argue in the penultimate chapter of this study, Larsen wryly reframes the whole long Atlantic history expressed in this ruinous scene in both traditions.

This swooning scene appears from the seventeenth century forward in the work of Anglo-Atlantic writers as well, most recognizably in sentimental or gothic seduction plots such as *Charlotte Temple, Clarissa,* or *The Monk* (whose Atlantic horizons I'll detail) but likewise in mariners' stories such as *Billy Budd* and traumatic immigrant narratives like Charles Brockden Brown's *Wieland*. As in African-Atlantic texts, in these novels the fainting marks the protagonist's self-losing movement from an Old World order into a new one, a crossing-over whereby the person is at once exiled and made native. The swoon in these narratives often operates more sentimentally or metaphorically, and its displacements work more coyly, especially regarding the correlative ruin of racialized others. Nonetheless, at the same time it encodes the seventeenth-century Anglo-Atlantic experience of migration, civil war, kidnapping, forced overseas labor, and radical public challenges to class and gender assumptions, all of which forged an association between an Atlantic crossing and a psychological and corporeal "unhinging," to borrow Rousseau's word. The growth of American colonies particularly threatened to create the experience of freedom as aporia, insofar as, economically, geographically, and viscerally, the colonies put new stress on the contours of English identity. What Gordon Wood observes about "the precariousness of society" in the new nation of the United States was already beginning to be felt in the trans-atlantic seventeenth century — that is, "the loosening and severing of the hierarchical ties of kinship and patronage that were carrying them into modernity only increased their suspicions and apprehensions" since "they could not know then what direction the future was taking."[13]

The trope of the swoon thus condenses the Atlantic economy's bodily, psychic, and socioeconomic uprootings for all kinds of subjects — in texts as different as Equiano's *Interesting Narrative*, Defoe's *Robinson Crusoe*, Susanna Rowson's *Charlotte Temple*, Hawthorne's *The Scarlet Letter*, Melville's *Billy Budd*, Pauline Hopkins's *Contending Forces*, and Virginia Woolf's *The Voyage Out*. The swoon sometimes conflates diverse histories and subjects, as with the lynched Billy Budd, who stands in for an African while also becoming victim of the "yearning" of Claggart — a yearning which must be suppressed if races are to be reproduced, and yet which returns in the form of a deadly Atlantic martial law. Or the swoon may be distilled into the forced kiss from an English gentleman that ultimately catapults a young woman like Woolf's Rachel Vinrace into colonial fever. Then again, it may come closer to baring the core formation of race and liberty on the Atlantic, as in the painfully chosen "fall" of Harriet Jacobs, who sleeps with a white congressman instead of her white master so as to seize the form of ruin that might move her toward freedom. My readings aim to move flexibly through these different conditions and symbolizations of the ruinous swoon, all the while staying alert to the larger surround of Atlantic coercion they inscribe.

Ultimately, all the swoons in the Atlantic literary and political narratives of freedom carry the shadow of events like those aboard the *Zong* in 1783, when the captain ordered 132 purchased Africans thrown overboard in order to win the insurance money for their value. As Ian Baucom points out in *Specters of the Atlantic*, his book-length meditation on this event, the economy that calculated these enslaved persons' value at forty pounds each is the same economy that valued the limb of a Lieutenant John Willis ("who had the misfortune to lose his right thigh in actions against the French and Spanish Fleets," as the Lords Commissioners' remark in their budget notes), at the rate of five shillings a day and half pay.[14] These calculations are *not* comparable — the lieutenant gains some of the profit, so to speak, of his wounds, while the slave suffers death by horror and drowning, which profits someone else. These losses are *not* comparable, yet they work in combination: historically, the military actions and violent "afflictions" of the lieutenant operated in tandem with the slave's trauma. African-Atlantic authors undertake the work of wresting back into view this mass-murderous frame for Anglo-Atlantic power, and for the trope of the swoon in English-language literature.

At the same time, the placing of the swoon at the origin of the Atlantic political order also implicitly references an older history and discourse: a classical set of associations between rape and the founding of republics. To recall this point is to recover yet another layer of the faded yet felt palimpsest that makes up the Atlantic imaginary. For the link between rape and republics reaches back, of course, to the story of Tarquin's rape of Lucretia as catalyst for the founding of Rome's republic.[15] In Livy's account, the final threat that Tarquin makes to Lucretia before he rapes her involves a slave, and all elitist assumptions about the slave are kept in place throughout the story. As Livy tells it, in order to persuade Lucretia to submit to his rape, Tarquin threatens to kill her and lay the body of a slave next to hers so that it appears she was killed after committing "foul adultery."[16] This is the threat that finally convinces her to submit—she would rather befoul her body than her family's name. Lucretia's submission to rape, followed by her spectacular suicide before Brutus, which fires him to fight the tyranny of the ruling Tarquins and leads to the famous founding of the Roman republic, thus takes shape as much against the threat of mingling with slaves from "below" as it does against the coercions of brute power from "above."

Modern Atlantic narratives tap into this classical story—including its logic of a submission that frees, or a death that, phoenix-like, gives birth to a republic—but they also encounter certain unclassical stumbling blocks. In modernity, slaves and women appear on the scene not only as catalysts but also as *potential* republican subjects. Because the ideology of the English Revolution has made the principle of liberty interior, and also because of the dissent enabled by print literacy, both the woman and the slave potentially have the means for claiming rights in a free society. Anglo-Atlantic women can draw on their claim to race membership to authorize their freedom to write—so that female historians such as Catharine Macaulay and Mercy Otis Warren argue precisely that, as women of a free race, they *must* speak and write freely. "Fortunate" men like Olaudah Equiano (as he deemed himself) can find a way to write and therefore to send a written account of the crimes committed on the *Zong,* for example, as Equiano does to Granville Sharp. Yet, again, to do so, Equiano and other African-Atlantic writers must find ways to renarrate the story of "their race" so as to establish a naturally free interiority for the black subject. This pressure gives rise to an author like Hopkins, who narrates the rapes that collapse her women and then makes those rapes the catalysts for visions of African American noble domesticity or for the recovery of an ancient racial genealogy—in other words, for racial "uplift" within the order of the free republic.

One more aspect of the racial republic needs mention here. The swoons of Atlantic narrative mark the entry not only into a raced republic but also into what Juliet Flower MacCannell calls the "regime of the brother." As many scholars have explored, the early modern shift from strict monarchy to "republics" founded on participatory government in many ways challenged the paternal order of patriarchy.[17] And yet somehow this shift did not wholly undo the subordination of women. Following the clues of political and literary texts (including those of Rousseau, Stendhal, Freud, Lacan, Duras, Rhys, and Jhabvala), MacCannell suggests that, under republican rule, the order of the father is replaced by the order of the brother. Here, competition among brothers drives the narrative and demands either exclusion or proper marriage of sisters. In opening her analysis, MacCannell mentions Samuel Richardson's story of Clarissa and her jealous brother James as a paradigmatic example.

I agree and will later elaborate on the ways that Richardson's novel offers a cautionary tale of the birth of a republic that, in effect, botches the task of emplacing yet subordinating the sister within it. I emphasize the fused discourses of race and freedom that provide the terms of this sibling competition; this fusion shapes the pattern of "ruin" that emerges as a necessary pivot or condition within republican modernity. In this new order, men and women both vie for power by way of race. When we note that Clarissa challenges the violations of James and Lovelace precisely by way of a nativist claim to a "birthright" of freedom, we see how race enters the republican regime of the brother at its inception and, by giving the woman as well as the man a point of entry, trips up the brother's aim to rule in place of the father. Indeed, the incest plot that circulates in many novels expresses the trouble in this new "sibling" political relation, announcing the dangers to normative heterosexuality lurking within women's new claim to freedom under the sign of race "birthrights." As I read it, the repeatedly fictionalized scandal of brother-sister incest is the scandal of a claim to overly "intimate" sibling relations within this free, racial order — that is, an uncomfortably side-by-side position within the sphere of power. In texts as different as *Moll Flanders, Charlotte Temple, Wieland, Our Nig, Daniel Deronda, Of One Blood,* and *The Waves,* brothers and sisters symbolically or literally endure ocean crossings only to find themselves "too close" or somehow at odds on the competitive and racially staked ground of freedom.

Ultimately, however, these English-language liberty narratives that pivot on ruin offer an object lesson for all subjects and all readers, even those who are apparently most secure — readers who identify with Arthur Dimmesdale or Daniel Deronda as well as those who are most like Clarissa Harlowe, Olaudah Equiano, Hester Prynne, or Helga Crane.[18] Narratives on both sides of the Atlantic, both sides of the color line, and both sides of the gender divide grapple with the revolutionary dispersal of community into an aggregate of independent individuals. In turn they reconstruct community as an interior, racial, bodily sensibility, which offers a stay against the centrifugal forces of individualist freedom and the corollary condition of wage labor. At the same time these narratives strenuously negotiate, each one differently, with both the race-authorized liberation of white women and the entrenched unfreedom of non–Anglo-Saxon persons in the lands of freedom.

It is not so much that these stories express "anxiety about consent as an adequate expression of the individual," as Gillian Brown puts it,[19] as that they express a social and bodily destabilization experienced in the very making of this racialized, contractual, and possessive individuality.[20] For if, in a laissez-faire, individualist, contract-based, and geographically dispersed social order, freedom — theoretically — is the right of the racial "everyman," by the same token failure is also a possibility for everyone. Everyone is a *contingent* member of this race-empire of freedom. Everyone is free to rise, and free to fall, to rule or be ruined, financially and bodily. Even as the reach of this modern Atlantic society expands powerfully through colonies and commerce, the potential for falling symbolically and materially outside of it also oddly increases, for all it takes is a failure to be responsible for oneself as a wage-earning or property-owning, autonomous, "free" individual (or failure to be a woman married to such a one). Failure to be autonomous can mark one as a member of an inferior race, or it can authorize expulsion from the dominant race, or at least threaten loss of race protection and privilege. Conversely, the enactment of self-supporting, individual *autonomy* ratifies one's membership in the race community, as Theo Goldberg has also argued.[21] Strangely, individual freedom can only be had by way of a race group. Desiring freedom, and fearing a ruinous fall, modern selves bind themselves to race as a source of security, history, and identity.

In *The Social Contract*, Rousseau offers a reading of this social logic when he lays out the necessary "alienation entailed by the social contract" (67). He labors earnestly to make sense of the apparently freely chosen self-deracination entailed in this making of oddly group-dependent individuals. To do so, he reverses the "before" and "after" of the historical process, positioning free individuality as the "natural" and earliest human condition, before sociality. Overlooking the fact of infant dependency on adults (despite his aggrandizement of motherhood), he theorizes that the social contract "replace[s] the physical and independent existence we have all received from nature with a moral and communal existence" (84). In this community "each man must be stripped of his powers, and given powers which are external to him, and which he cannot use without the help of others" (84). That is, this society that exposes and maximizes the vulnerability of each person in this way encourages their allegiance to the (racial) nation. Despite this allegiance's effect of dependency, Rousseau argues that participation in such a state still expresses freedom, for "obedience to a law one prescribes to oneself is freedom" (65). Thus, although the contract with a society based on freedom entails "the total alienation by each associate of himself and all his rights to the whole community" (60), those rights are understood to be held in trust. They are the citizen's, only via the laws of the community.

In thinking through the paradoxical relation between freedom and law within the republican state, Rousseau wrestles with the same questions that troubled the English Revolution and that came to propel the plots of novels: how can freedom be the founding principle of community? How can liberation from social bonds — from "subjecthood" under a king — create a bonded community of citizens? How can "a people" be "a people" by virtue of their individual autonomy? Like the English revolutionaries, and in tandem with novels, Rousseau, too, taps race as the notion that will cohere these contraries and naturalize this volatile, dispersed, and apparently voluntary socius. When he tells his readers, echoing Montesquieu, that "Freedom is not the fruit of every climate, and it is not therefore within the capacity of every people" (124), he enacts modernity's contradictory harnessing of freedom to race, re-establishing the very organic community that his notion of contractual community has undone, or made anonymous and abstract. He dramatizes the impulse by which the threat of alienation calls forth a compensatory racialization. And he then articulates the turn by which this racialization becomes racist and colonialist when he excludes Africans and Native Americans from consideration — the latter of whom, he says, never developed farming or technology and "therefore always remained savages" — apparently outside the purview of the contract (quoted in Goldberg 46). The "capacity" for freedom distinguishes a people and concentrates, it seems, in certain peoples of the North.

Rousseau's turns of thought parallel those of Atlantic memoirs and novels, which likewise ameliorate and naturalize, by way of the racialization of freedom, the alienations and elisions entailed in the contractual republic. They reveal, without fully intending to, how a contractual society positions everyone as a lone outsider who *must join a race* if he or she wants security. The undoing quest for freedom is the necessary ritual for racial membership. In tracking this ideology as it unfolds in novels, we begin to see how race, that backward myth, came to drive modern revolutions and bind modern communities.

OF COURSE THE racialization of power and community is nothing new. Myths of noble races or ancient lineages are as old as the hills. What is new, and what comes to dominate after the seventeenth century, is a myth in which the capacity for *liberty* places the ruling "races" above others. *Freedom's Empire* recovers this racialization of liberty in English-language modernity, a racialization that has at once fostered revolutionary claims and justified violent slavery and colonization, even as it has buffered the existential aporia of an individualist and capitalist notion of freedom. While the shift from Anglo-European bonded labor to African slavery in American colonies encouraged a distinction between "white" and "black" persons, the idea of liberty as a racial inheritance infused the discourse and provided both a principle of interiority and a quest plot for the "white" person — and for Anglo-Atlantic culture as a whole. This racialization of liberty has, I would add, helped to constitute subaltern coloniality as the alter-ego of the first-world nation-state. In tracking these formations I offer an account not only of racism but specifically of liberty's powerful intertwining of racialism and racism within the English-language transatlantic novel and, in turn, the English-language discourses of modernity.

This discussion brings together a set of English-language conversations about Atlantic modernity, race history, and the nation, including both Britain and the United States, that have for too long proceeded in parallel lines. Historians of Britain have long considered the pamphlets and debates of the English Civil War the first articulation of democratic ideas of liberty, and, more recently, historians of the seventeenth century have clarified the role, which I recount in chapter 1, of a new transatlantic, mercantile network in the eruption of that civil war. At the same time, scholars of race have traced the rise of Saxonism in England in this period. But no work that I am aware of has considered the tight bonding of these elements. And yet it is their profound co-formation that has intensified their powerful effects in Atlantic history — and created English-language stories of racial destiny.

Likewise, in recent studies of republicanism on both sides of the Atlantic, scholars have considered many elements of the emerging, English-language nation-state: ancient constitutionalism, the turn to documentary history, the pitting of commoner against aristocrat, the religious rhetoric of dissent, and, within both family and state, the redefinition of authority, contract, virtue, and independence.[22] Yet with the exception of Reginald Horsman, recent historians have overlooked or misunderstood the racial strain within these debates. American scholars in particular have made little of the abundant evidence of American Saxonism gathered by earlier historians.[23] Overlooking the earliest transatlantic genealogies of the rhetoric of liberty, which manifest its embeddedness in notions of birthright and race, this scholarship often casts the modern republic, and especially the American republic, as one of "political membership based on consent" by contrast to the Anglo-European ones "based on birthright."[24] This false contrast reduces race in the United States to an interloping ideology that illogically skews the formation of the liberal, contract state. But transatlantic seventeenth-century history reveals that race is of a piece with the discourses of consent and freedom. From their first articulation, the vocabularies of liberty, consent, birthright, and Saxonism were tightly intertwined—by way of the idea that liberty itself was a birthright—and they continued to be so throughout the founding of the United States.

The story I tell about the ways that modern nations implicitly racialize their individualist political identities is thus informed by and yet also diverges—in its emphasis on seventeenth-century, revolutionary racialism—from the accounts of political theorists who have addressed questions of race and citizenship, from C. L. R. James and Hannah Arendt to Etienne Balibar, Ann Laura Stoler, David Theo Goldberg, Theodore Allen, and Homi Bhabha. Likewise with my understanding of ideologies of race and whiteness as they emerge in the Atlantic Triangle: I am indebted to the work of W. E. B. Du Bois, Ralph Ellison, David Brion Davis, Winthrop Jordan, Paula Giddings, Nancy Stepan, Toni Morrison, Robert Young, and David Roediger as well as many others, but ultimately I offer a different framework for understanding race on the Atlantic.[25] For, instead of treating Anglo-Saxonism only in terms of what it became—a form of racism—I study how it began—as a form of racialism. Here I build on the work of scholars of Anglo-Saxonism, such as Leon Poliakov, Samuel Kliger, Eleanor Adams, Roberta Brinkley, and Trevor Colbourn, who document—without foregrounding—the link between Saxonism and freedom.[26] Although my account of the transatlantic co-formation of Saxonism and liberty certainly corroborates Etienne Balibar's and Theo Goldberg's arguments that the modern liberal nation-state has from the start been a racial state, it also rewrites the story of how this came to be by showing that, at least on the Atlantic, the state's earliest and most long-lived "racial contract" began as an equivocally revolutionary one, written under a broad range of pressures in which Africans and Native Americans initially had an important economic but incipient racial part. Similarly, *Freedom's Empire* provides the revolutionary back story for recent studies of Atlantic narrative by such scholars as Michelle Stephens, Alys Weinbaum, and Alan Rice.[27]

It needs saying that the history of religious, political, and scientific race thinking since the medieval period defeats any attempt to codify the meanings of race, especially in relation to the overlapping notions of nation, ethnicity, and class. The historian and theorist both trip over race's status as a cultural fiction and its susceptibility to the manipulations of the moment. From medieval German Catholic claims to superiority over the Romans, to Victorian and contemporary Anglo-Saxon presumptions of superiority over Africans, that is, race distinctions have taken the shape required by the political surround. Moreover, in the eighteenth and nineteenth centuries in Europe, the word "nation" served sometimes as a synonym for, and sometimes as a subcategory of, race, even while it also named the official, political entity ruled by a single government within guarded borders. Eighteenth-century English writers, for instance, spoke of the "nations" of the Gothic "race," and they entered into heated debate, as I discuss in chapter 2, about the best way to distinguish European "races," not strictly aligned with nations, from one another. They, too, found themselves negotiating with the migrations and histories of conquering that so muddle distinctions not only between races but also among the categories of race, nation, and class. Later, in the Victorian period, social commentators conveniently began to think of Britain's lower classes as distinct races, while Americans and Britons both assumed (and often still do) that their "original" citizens share an Anglo-Saxon "stock" bridging the two nations and the Atlantic—and creating their alliance as world leaders. These more recent conflations of race and nation indicate their co-development in Atlantic modernity within an imperial, world-system economy. Race has sustained the imperial reach of the nation, providing both temporal continuity and socio-spatial integrity—in the face of rupture in both dimensions. That is, race articulated a genealogy for the nation (including as expressed in discursive skirmishes over which lineage was the true one), which in turn ennobled its imperial projects, profits, invasions, and enslavements as part of a people's world-historical freedom struggle. At the same time, exactly against the distensions and dissensions—the loosening of the center—created by this imperial reach, race provided a principle of cohesion among "the English" or "Anglo-Saxons," in the process justifying the exclusion or forced labor of all "Others" and generating oppositions between primitive and modern peoples (a sorting of fit and unfit that may well continue even under the kind of postmodern empire that Michael Hardt and Antonio Negri describe in the twenty-first century).[28]

Within this shifting history of race discourses, I sound the depths of one specific but enduring, important, and overlooked strain of race thinking: the one organized around the liberty plot and the notion of free subjectivity, explicitly linked to Anglo-Saxonism supported by African-Atlantic and Indian bodies; the one adapted by African-Atlantic writers who counter the racist turn of Anglo-Saxonism by reframing its race-liberty plot; and the one, as I consider next, that English-language readers and scholars have so deeply internalized.

THE LIBERTY PLOT so infiltrates our selves and stories that literary criticism has often reiterated it, especially in relation to the novel. It is crucial to develop some self-consciousness about our literary-critical absorption of the liberty plot and its racial subtexts so that the works I discuss in the following chapters appear not as misguided attempts to join liberty and race but rather as articulations of the conundrums and phantasms that we still, in the twenty-first century, share with these texts.

As the critic Judith Kegan Gardiner noted in 1989, "the traditional history of the novel has been 'Whig history'—progressive, enlightened, and focused around values of freedom and rationality."[29] Long before the Russian literary theorist Mikhail Bakhtin argued that the novel was from its beginnings an open-ended, comic form written to deflate epic and tragedy, the novel had been understood as the genre that airs suppressed voices, frees individual natures, and embraces "real" people and history against the tyranny of artifice and orthodoxy. Implicitly, as William Warner has noted, most novel criticism follows the line laid out by William Hazlitt, who remarked in 1841 that novels illustrate how the "Protestant Ascendancy" has "given a more popular turn to our literature and genius, as well as to our government" ever since the eighteenth century, when "[i]t was found high time that the people should be represented in books as well as in Parliament."[30] Again and again since the nineteenth century, critics have implicitly invited a community of novel readers to adopt this Whig attitude toward novels—as does Ian Watt when he fashions Clarissa as the "heroic representative of all that is free and positive in the new individualism."[31] Margaret Doody admires Richardson's epistolary form as itself "an image of freedom; the characters are on their own" and she echoes an eighteenth-century, race-inflected rhetoric of the organic growth of culture in praising his recognition that freedom "is the soil from which all authentic actions grow."[32] "Love requires freedom to work itself out," she explains, although the "other aspect of this freedom is loneliness" since "[t]he inner consciousness is all one can fully know" (11). Implicitly Doody retells the history that blends organic freedom, interiority, and the work of the novel.

Other novel critics have emphasized political struggle over free knowing, but they nonetheless assume our identification with the protagonist's "individual will" as it "grappl[es] with forces . . . which would deny it political, economic, and emotional freedom," as Steven Cohan describes it.[33] We, too, can join the project John Richetti understands as Defoe's "attempt to imagine a radical individualist who cannot be contained by any totality."[34] We can identify with Defoe's libertine protagonist Roxana as she "achieves freedom" even at the expense of social bonds, and we are encouraged to experience the random events of Defoe's plots as "liberating irrelevancies."[35] Even in Michael McKeon's measured, dialectical account of the novel, one of his tasks is to track the ways that an emergent "anti-romance" strain of fiction "liberates itself" from the aristocratic, romance conventions of narrative.[36] Similarly, decades of Americanist scholars of the U.S. novel regularly deem freedom "a characteristic, almost obsessive American theme."[37] Like Walter Wenska and Leslie Fiedler in their genealogies of the American novel, in his *The American Novel and Its Tradition,* Richard Chase influentially celebrates what he deems "that freer, more daring, more brilliant fiction" of the U.S. novel "that contrasts with the solid moral inclusiveness and massive equability of the English novel."[38] Yet in fact this celebration of freedom in both theme and form, although nationalized in political discourses, is a transatlantic phenomenon.

Although feminist critics recovering early British women's fiction speak more often of ambivalence and compromised freedom, they nonetheless position their authors' works as part of the "struggle for autonomy and authority" in the public sphere.[39] Terry Castle interprets eighteenth-century masquerade fiction as fascinated with those sites where "individual behavior was freer . . . than at virtually any other public occasion where the classes and sexes met openly," while Catherine Craft-Fairchild dissents from this fully positive reading yet keeps the liberatory ideal intact when she reads masquerade fiction's liberties as only "apparent freedoms."[40] Among Americanists, feminist readers have celebrated such novels as Catharine Maria Sedgwick's *Hope Leslie* because it "sets conscience, innocence, and individual liberty against the needs of community or the state."[41]

While in the African American tradition, the fact of slavery has made the pursuit and narration of freedom a fundamentally necessary practice, the encoding of the liberty vocabulary in recent criticism may still warrant consideration for its complicated appropriations of the Atlantic tradition. In light of liberty's long and vexed discursive history, we can begin to reconsider, for instance, the black aesthetic theorist Stephen Henderson's seizing back the theme of freedom: he argues that a distinctively black expressivity arises from an "inner dynamism" by which "the idea of liberation" creates black literature's structure and tone as well as theme. Writing in 1973, Henderson is creating a new literary-intellectual platform for his generation, and yet necessarily, within Atlantic history and its American legacy, he racializes it.[42] Or, turning to more recent feminist discussions we can notice that, when critics argue that Nella Larsen's fiction "marks the beginning of greater freedom for self-examination and narrative experimentation in the writing of black American women," this narrative accrues to the critic (white or black) as well as to the author, and yet vexedly in the case of Larsen the rhetoric attributes a racial quest to this author whose fictions deconstruct race and whose life belies the power of race to support the subject's desire for freedom.[43] In *Color and Culture,* Ross Posnock studies black intellectuals who, he explains, "believe in the promise of aesthetic freedom — that art and culture can be practices resistant to race identity." He glimpses the conundrum of this promise when he further remarks, "Struggling to assert the freedom of art while laboring for racial uplift, they enact 'two unreconciled strivings.'"[44] This Du Boisian double striving of black writers had been prepared by a long history. Posnock himself is forced into engagement with it as he seeks to harken to the call of freedom while challenging the call of race.

In all of these discussions, as we internalize liberating accounts of art and literature, we implicitly fashion ourselves in the terms that Roger Chartier theorizes in *The Order of Books*. Chartier claims that the "book always aims at installing order" but "the multi-faceted order is not all-powerful . . . when it comes to annulling the reader's liberty" for "liberty knows how to distort and reformulate the significations that were supposed to defeat it."[45] We are reader-dissidents, as made evident in our critical affiliation with the dialogical text.

Yet a striking moment in Ian Watt's Whiggish reading of *Clarissa* hints at the scene of colonial ruin that stands behind literary critics' trajectory toward freedom via literature and in particular the novel. In characterizing what Richardson must encounter as he moves (freely) into Clarissa's interior so as to track all dimensions of her struggle against tyranny, Watt quotes Richardson's admiring contemporary, Diderot. Watt approves of the way in which Diderot imagines what Watt calls the "frightening reality of [Clarissa's] unconscious life," particularly Diderot's image of a dark cavern presided over by a "hideous Moor" who metaphorically "lies hidden in the most virtuous heart" (235). Here is the complete passage from Watt, worth quoting not so much to critique Watt as to dredge up the materials of a collective political unconscious — *our* unconscious as English-language novel readers:

> It was Richardson, Diderot said, "qui porte le flambeau au fond de la caverne; c'est lui qui apprehend à discerner les motifs subtils et déshonnêtes qui se cachent et se dérobent sous d'autres motifs qui sont honnêtes et qui se hâtent de se montrer les premiers. Il souffle sur le phantôme sublime qui se présente à l'entrée de la caverne; et le More hideux qu'il masquait s'aperçoit." Such certainly is the nature of the voyage of discovery which we take in *Clarissa;* and the hideous Moor is surely the frightening reality of the unconscious life which lies hidden in the most virtuous heart. (235)

Watt's account outlines the unconscious colonial plot especially as it takes shape in the hands of key Anglo-Atlantic authors: a sublime voyage of discovery that the free and bold author narrates as the entry into a woman whose accessibility, however, is preempted or somehow haunted by the dark body of a foreign man. We can read this from a Sedgwickian angle, so that the woman stands as a homoerotic conductor and mediator between dark and light men.[46] But it's important to note that the story centers on the woman's struggle to be free. If we look again at Diderot's "Moor," we can see that this figure actually stands as a kind of sentinel at the "entrée" into the woman, blocking the way of the author.

By contrast to the strict homoerotic reading, this angle of vision aligns the woman and the Moor as obstacles to the Englishman's authorial freedom, and to his free penetration of dark places. This scenario in fact retells the Atlantic situation encountered by "freeborn Englishmen." As women and "Moors" both took up the discourse of freedom, the liberty struggle threatened to turn against him, to hinder his preeminence. The whole drama is made "sublime" only by the "white" man's assumption that he will surpass these obstacles. And, historically, for a time, he does, by figuring his entry *into* the Englishwoman as an identification *with* her, subsuming her freedom struggle into his own, and implicitly racializing her "virtue" in contrast to the "hideous" (read "leering") Moor from whom he rescues her. The author's entry into her interior is recast as the Moor's threatened rape from which the author rescues her by writing her story, which is then subsumed within his own triumph as free author. This instrumentality of the woman in the man's racial freedom-story perhaps constitutes an aspect of what Alice Jardine calls "gynesis"; and the parallel maneuver in relation to African-Atlantic persons certainly exemplifies the practice that Morrison calls Africanism.[47]

Under the influence of accounts of the novel like Watt's, readers can unconsciously bond over their experience of the unnerving sublime that ultimately stands as testimony to their brave freedom. For to manage this sublime expedition into this heart of darkness, Richardson, Watt tells us, had to "pacify his inner censor and thus leave his imagination free" (235). In a sublime turn, he had to overcome his own fear and resistance. "This is Richardson's triumph," Watt concludes his chapter on Richardson (238). Indeed, "the tremendous imaginative expansion which Richardson gave his theme" led him into "so profound a penetration of his characters that their experience partakes of the terrifying ambiguity of human life itself" (238). Expansion, penetration, terror: these are the materials of the colonial and sexual plot of freedom. Such an imagination peopled by dark "Moors" does indeed create the surround of *Clarissa* and many other novels in a similarly ambiguous way, as we will see. The gothic sensationalizes these elements, the Victorian race epic recontains them, and the modernist novel mockingly deflates or melancholically mourns them.

Even those critics who claim to escape this Whig plot of the novel reiterate it. William Warner, on the one hand, has fully "outed" this plot. In *Licensing Entertainment,* he argues that, after its formulation among nineteenth-century literary historians, the "Whiggish interpretation of the free golden age of the Whig mid-eighteenth century . . . is embedded in every subsequent version of the rise of

the novel thesis."[48] He usefully draws attention, furthermore, to the nationaliza-
tion (or what I would call nativism) of this account. He points to Walter Scott's
celebration of the "English Genius" of Fielding and to William Hazlitt's story
(quoted earlier) of the "popular turn" in "our literature and genius" understood
as an expression of "the general spirit of sturdiness and independence, which
made the English character more truly English."[49] He likewise tracks the way
that Hippolyte Taine reconfigured this idea in the more organic vocabulary of
Romanticism, which, we can further observe, highlights the interiority of characters in English novels as their distinguishing trait: the novel's expression of
the "more reflective" character of Englishmen is for Taine the emergence of "the
voice of a people buried underground."[50] Warner establishes this tradition in
order to challenge it, including its latest expression in Marxist and feminist readings of the novel.[51] Yet Warner himself revives this "Whig" narrative in casting
his scholarship as a liberating dissent from the feminist/Marxist tradition. Now
he will free the past from its capture by constricting orthodoxy. In arguing that
the early novel should be understood within a history of "media culture" rather
than high culture, he points to the ways that early fiction, like the market it arises
within, "incites desire and promotes the liberation of the reader as the subject of
pleasure" (*Licensing* 93). Echoing the language of political freedom, he insists,
"This culture of, by, and for a print market is more polyvalent and promiscuous in its address and effects than feminist and Marxist readings have allowed"
(*Licensing* 93). Warner "allows" those readings that the tyranny of feminism and
Marxism has excluded, and in doing so he interestingly echoes the sexualization
of freedom in the novels. He will liberate the reader into his or her "polyvalent"
pleasure as these novels do. Accordingly, he titles one subsection of his book
"Roxana's Freedom" and the conclusion of it "The Freedom of Readers" (where
he determines that Richardson and Fielding share a "consensus about the essential freedom of readers" but "Richardson reins in this liberty, while Fielding
sanctions it" [*Licensing* 290]). It is fitting that Warner's own career was initially
propelled into visibility by Clarissa's swoon moment — that is, by his provocative first book on Richardson's *Clarissa,* in which he reads the rape against the
grain of feminist liberation versions.[52] He attributes agency to Clarissa in her
predicament and thereby makes her less innocent. In the process, on the pivot of
a culturally fraught rape plot, he releases himself into a profession of print and
seems to free us from its tyranny. Once more, history moves forward by way of
a sexualized rupture moment. Another independent citizen, and critical state, is
born into print from the scene of rape.

My point is that the liberty plot is nearly impossible to escape and so is its organization around sexual, colonial rupture. Gardiner's seminal essay on Whiggish

novel criticism takes its own whiggish turn when she concludes that "[Aphra] Behn is a pioneer in championing autonomous female desire, in speaking through an assertive, desiring, changing female voice, and in showing women's choices in a constrained social world."[53] *Freedom's Empire* is itself organized around this liberty plot, the only difference being that I have come to see how this scholarship that includes my own signals my membership in rather than my dissent from the normative discourse. My goal is simply to trace the palimpsest of our collective novelistic unconscious and to bring its historical force into view. Although no readers will be freer when this book is published, perhaps it will make a few historical and discursive patterns clearer, including patterns of scholarly narrative, with implications for our reading and scholarly practices that I will consider in the book's conclusion.

To capture the dialectical force of these patterns, *Freedom's Empire* offers a genealogy of the English-language novel that is as epic and abruptly juxtapositional as some of the tradition's novels. As I discuss in the book's conclusion, my method has been to combine two kinds of literary-critical practice. On the one hand, I juxtapose dissimilar texts from different nations and time periods in order to throw into relief the Atlantic patterns they share. In reading *Moll* Flanders beside *Charlotte* Temple beside *Our* Nig, as I do in chapter 6, for example, I partly displace these works from their different traditions so as to understand the traditions' dialectical relation to each other within the Atlantic world. On the other hand, I do not generally follow the new-historical method that offers brief elliptical readings of texts, moving quickly among them so as to highlight their common rhetoric. Instead, in both the multi-text chapters and those chapters that develop extended readings of a single text, I dwell carefully within each work, since only in this way can the extent of each text's cultural labor be simultaneously weighed and deconstructed—and in turn guide my reading of the larger field of texts with which it interacts. This double method of relocation within the field and attentive tracking within the text has enabled me to resituate these many narratives within an Atlantic constellation.

This form of genealogical practice makes for a long book—even excluding, as I have had to do, Irish, Scottish, and Caribbean materials as well as the Latin American corpus of the Atlantic world. To create a framework for these constellated materials, I have organized the book into five parts. Part I establishes how Protestantism, privatization, print, and mercantile colonialism together gave rise to an intimate mingling of the vocabularies of freedom and race, initially in the English Revolution and then later in the form of national histories and literary histories, which position the Saxonist will to freedom as the alpha and omega of both historiography and art. This liberty telos reaches from James Harrington's

Oceana (1656) through the multivolume works of David Hume and Catharine Macaulay on English history and David Ramsay and Mercy Otis Warren on U.S. history; and, in literature, it finds voice as early as the Third Earl of Shaftesbury's *Characteristics* (1711) and extends through Sir Thomas Percy's "Ancient Reliques of English Poetry" (1765) to the writings of Walt Whitman and Ralph Waldo Emerson that position American literature as the apotheosis of this long history of freedom.

Part II juxtaposes a series of English-language novels and memoirs, from both sides of the Atlantic, to highlight their shared matrix of racialized liberty plots—including texts by Aphra Behn, Eliza Haywood, Samuel Richardson, Daniel Defoe, Susanna Rowson, William Hill Brown, Harriet Wilson, Olaudah Equiano, and Herman Melville. Parts III, IV, and V focus respectively on three influential, transatlantic narrative styles—the gothic, the epic, and the modernist—as they unfold within the strained coupling of race and liberty. When Atlantic modernists more jadedly take up the liberty plot, they narrate the drama of ruin not so much as a loss of chastity or natality but rather as the loss of errant, erotic possibilities, for persons and communities. In particular they bring into view—though only fleetingly—a queer sexuality that strays from race's reproductive mandate. Because race holds freedom captive, however, and at the same time requires this reproductive mandate, the possibility of freeing a queer sexuality sinks as well, and so these modernist writers add their own ruined protagonists to the many generations of bodies lost on the Atlantic.

From *Oroonoko* to *Quicksand,* then, the Atlantic swoon and its encoding of violence remain in place. In approaching this pattern I have aimed to follow flexibly its peculiar formation in each text, yet I nonetheless find in its repetitive appearance an allegorical expression of selves lost and remade, of communities deracinated and re-racialized, across three centuries of Atlantic history.

BY TRACING HOW racial ideas of an English "birthright" of liberty first gave limits to the extraordinary idea of freedom, and by studying how sexual plots embody the crises of "free" yet racialized individuals and communities, *Freedom's Empire* pieces together a genealogy of liberty in Atlantic modernity. While along the way it attends to the existential dimensions of freedom, and the puzzle of how humans, as Rousseau says, may be born free but are everywhere in chains, it is more centrally concerned with the historical contingency and specificity of such conundrums of freedom on the Atlantic, including the particular ways that freedom has been imagined. It broods on the ways Atlantic freedom functions as a tar baby because it is offered on terms that are not free and not universally shared, terms whose conception and institutionalization reflect a long, compromised, and greedy history. It wonders, in light of freedom's continuing enlistment in empire's missions, whether the notion of freedom should remain the light by which communities guide their ships or whether it might be time for other principles (mutuality? dignity? equality? radical cooperation?) to usurp freedom's rallying power. And finally it meditates on the past and future of racially defined community, especially race's confusing ability to limit or cripple its members even as it launches or supports them.

This last question of race's value and power haunts this book as it does the narratives. It remains unresolved for me. My experiences and my research have taught me that historically formed, yet racially identified cultural communities promise, compellingly, to give circumference to what might otherwise be an utterly atomistic and materialistic modernity. Especially when understood culturally, race *has* in fact been a binding force for community, organizing necessary political struggles, supplying us a place and a time, a historical ontology, even if "merely" imagined. Yet, in answer to the question, "do race beliefs inevitably engender inequality and violence?" I am largely persuaded by the modernists and cultural critics who answer yes. These writers offer neither exit from nor hope for race as a freeing embrace. At the same time, while I am inclined to share this pessimism about race, the writing of this book also reflects my immersion in race — historically, personally, ontosocially. Growing up white, Irish-Catholic American in Mayor Daly's 1960s Chicago, in a neighborhood bordered by the railroad tracks that divided whites and blacks, I was witness to the blood on the tracks, yet I also attended the public high school that was roughly 50 percent white and 50 percent black, where there was some separateness but no racial violence (probably because most of the Irish Americans attended Catholic schools!). Race defined everything, even the seeming transcendence of race at my high school. So this book expresses my own involvement in the paradox — a critical study of race and liberty ostensibly written from outside these legacies yet undoubtedly compelled by my own life within them. I, too, work within the narrative, adopting the fiction of a narrator who seeks insight from outside, in quest of better freedom, but whose every written word is testimony to tarred hands.

I | Race and Liberty in the Atlantic Economy

Atlantic Horizon, Interior Turn

1 | Seventeenth-Century Racial Revolution

"THERE IS NO MAN that understands rightly what an Englishman is," the revolutionary Civil War pamphleteer John Hare proclaims in 1647, "but knows withal, that we are a member of the Teutonick nation, and descended out of Germany: a descent so honourable and happy, if duly considered, as that the like could not have been fetched from any other part of Europe." Indeed, he continues, "in England the whole commonalty, are German, and of the German blood; and scarcely was there any worth or manhood left in these occidental nations, after their long servitude under the Roman yoke, until these new supplies of freeborn men from Germany reinfused the same." Contributing to the shift from a Briton to a Saxon origin story for the English, Hare argues that it is the Germanic Anglo-Saxons whose free traditions his nation has inherited, for while the Britons were utterly defeated by the Romans (who were then routed by the Anglo-Saxons), the Normans, when they arrived in 1066, did not wholly conquer the Anglo-Saxons. Therefore, the Norman king William "sirnamed the Conqueror, [should] be stripped of that insolent title," and the association between kingship and the unbounded claims of a conqueror should be ended, while the language and laws of England should be purged of any Normanisms — hence Hare's title for this tract, *St. Edward's Ghost or Anti-Normanism*. Aiming to rally his compatriots against the tyranny of King Charles I, who (though a Scot) operates on Normanish presumptions of absolute power, he beseechingly asks, "Did our ancestors, therefore, shake off the Roman yoke [. . . .] that the honour and freedom of their blood might be reserved for an untainted prey to a future conqueror?" Then, in a move that will become paradigmatic, Hare adds a touch of pathos by remarking that, after all, the key characteristic of the Anglo-Saxon "mother nation" is "her unconquerableness, her untainted virginity and freedom from foreign subjection, which from her first foundation and cradle she hath so conserved and defended, that none can truly boast to have been her ravisher."[1] For Hare, England is unravished even now — though her virginity faces a tyrant's threat — and this fantasy limned with fear organizes novels and histories in English for centuries hereafter.

That is, by way of this dissident narrative, the story of "ravishment" became an implicit race plot for the novel in English, beginning with Aphra Behn's *Oroonoko,* and finding its first epic expression in Samuel Richardson's *Clarissa.* In Richardson's novel, Belford condemns Lovelace's rape of Clarissa, the novel's paragon of "*native* dignity," and he laments, "Hadst thou been a king, and done as thou hast done by such a meritorious innocent, I believe in my heart it would have been adjudged a *national* sin."[2] Challenging Lovelace, Clarissa herself pinpoints the racialized national drama encoded in her predicament when she demands to know "whether it be, or be not, your intention to permit me to quit [this house]? — To permit me the *freedom* which is my *birthright* as an English subject?" (934, emphasis added).

While white Anglo-Atlantic readers rallied around Clarissa's brave challenge, making the novel a transatlantic success, these same readers insisted on setting racial boundaries on such liberty claims. As one *London Chronicle* writer pointed out in 1765, commenting on black servants and settlers in England, "there can be no just plea for [black Britons] being put on an equal footing with natives whose birthright, as members of the community, entitles them to superior dues."[3] And yet, as we will see in chapter 7, an African-Atlantic writer such as Olaudah Equiano assumes exactly this "equal footing" in his autobiography, not only by telling the story of his own freedom quest but also in imagining his sister's ruin at the hands of tyrannical slave traders within the Atlantic circuit. Equiano, too, lays claim to a birthright of freedom, by way of a story of threatened sexual ruin and a genealogy linking "his people" to ancient Hebrews. He shrewdly enters the culture of freedom through its race narratives.

Bound together and yet divided by such racialism, Atlantic writers of all kinds participated in the making and remaking of this narrative of ravished liberty. Only by returning to the early-seventeenth-century crises that shaped this story can we begin to fathom the profound cultural work such writers undertook. Attending to this history, we better understand how their writing aims to articulate and stabilize the disruptive — freeing yet racializing, enlarging yet isolating, enslaving yet modernizing — conditions of Atlantic modernity. Thus this chapter traces how what began as the Reformation "recovery" of the "Anglo-Saxon roots" of the "true church" developed into the parliamentary claim to ancient native rights of governance and then, dramatically, in the context of new transatlantic circuits of power and the violence of civil war, became the kind of revolutionary, popular renarrating of a racial and free English identity epitomized in Hare's pamphlet. This discourse's dangerous extension of liberty's meanings — inward to the very soul and downward to the laboring classes — appears most starkly in the Putney Debates of 1647 between Oliver Cromwell and the restive Army representatives. Turning to those debates at the end of this chapter, I suggest that they display how, as the notion of liberty began to challenge all hierarchies of property and power, nativism was redeployed to establish the proper limit of liberty's reach and property's distribution. The Putney Debates laid the template for the novel's equivocally dissenting transatlantic plots, which over three centuries consolidate the interior racialization of nations and persons.

Saxonism Made Secular

In the early decades of the 1600s, no commercially printed novels or grand race epics of righteous liberty were yet conceivable. Bankruptcy, absolutism, fierce censorship, and popery threatened the kingdom. Although in 1603, the Stuart and Scot king James I had been joyously embraced by both the English Parliament and the broader population, hailed as the new Arthur prophesied by Merlin who would combine the Tudor and Stuart as well as Briton and Roman lineages even as he unified Scotland and England, the welcome quickly faded when James showed his absolutist will. He openly pitted the divine right of kings against parliamentary process, disingenuously invoking the rhetoric of freedom to do so, in such proclamations as the "Trew Law of Free Monarchies or the Reciprock and Mutuall Duetie Betwixt a Free King and his naturall Subjects." Asserting that "the King is above the law" and going so far as to claim that "Kings are not onely Gods Lieutenants upon earth [. . .] but even by God himselfe they are called Gods," he boasted that kings "can make and unmake their subjects [. . .] like men at the Chesse."[4] This highhandedness was an affront to Parliament. Exacerbating the insult — and perhaps partly explaining his need to press the point so insistently — were James's perpetual shortage of funds and attempts to extort money from Parliament, his increasing dependence on and alignment with city merchants against landed parliamentary members, and finally his friendliness with Spain, which raised fears of a Catholic resurgence and interfered with some members' Atlantic trade ambitions. Throughout the first four decades of the seventeenth century, under both James and his son Charles I, England witnessed active parliamentary resistance to the principle of Divine Right, to which the Stuart kings responded with imprisonment of parliament members and dissolutions of parliamentary proceedings.

Most important, this face-off between king and Parliament gave a secular, insurgent turn to what had been an emergent religious discourse of ancient Saxonism.[5] Under the Tudor kings of the sixteenth century, the Society of Antiquaries had been founded and its scholars were directed "to serche after England's antiquities and to peruse libraries of all cathedrals, abbyes, priories, colleges, & co" (Brinkley 32) so as to reveal "the obscured Truth of the Church and reprove Popish Tyranny."[6] In other words, these researchers were enlisted to authorize the Reformation by establishing evidence of a pre-Roman, Saxon church, native to England, and Christian, but without ties to Rome. Henry VIII had begun the process by employing Matthew Parker to gather from England and abroad all documents revealing the Germanic and Anglo-Saxon origins of the "true and primitive" church that predated popery (Adams, 11). As Parker's secretary, John Jocelyn, explained, Parker "was verie carefull and not without some charges to know the religion off the ancient fatheres and those especially were off the English Church. Therefore in seeking upp the Chronicle of the Brittones and the English Saxones [. . .] "he indevored to sett out in printe certaine of those aunciente monuments [. . .] which he thought would be most profitable for the posterytye to instruct them in the faythe and religion of the elders" (quoted in Adams 20 – 21). Parker determined to put in print as many of these documents as he could, furnishing the printer John Day with the first Anglo-Saxon type and sponsoring the first Anglo-Saxon book, a collection of sermons, epistles, and prayers called *A Testimonie of Antiquities* (1566 – 67). As in his tract *A Defense of Priests' Marriages* (written in exile under Queen Mary), in his preface to this volume, Parker drew on Saxon materials to authorize specific changes in church practice, including that of the communion ceremony: so that "thou mayest knowe (good Christian reader) how this [sacrament] is advocated more boldly than truely, [. . .] here is set forth unto thee a testimonye of verye auncient tyme, wherein is plainly showed what was the judgement of the learned men in thys matter, in the days of the Saxons before the Conquest" (quoted in Adams 24 – 25). Such prefaces were typical, as in John Fox's address to Queen Elizabeth in the preface to his Old English version of the Gospels (*The Gospels of the former Evangelistes translated in the olde Saxons tyme out of Latin*), where he explains that his book shows "how the religion presently taught & professed in the Church at thys present, is no new reformation of things lately begonne, which were not before, but rather a reduction of the Church to the Pristine State of olde conformitie" (quoted in Adams 32 – 33). This notion of a return to the ancestors' primitive simplicity would soon begin to encompass the idea of return to England's true and free Anglo-Saxon laws.

For, by the early years of the seventeenth century, as scholars unearthed information about Anglo-Saxon law-making councils and the Magna Carta, Parliament began to draw on this historical research to defend its "ancient" liberties against the encroachments of James I — in the process and perhaps unwittingly shifting the genealogy of English identity away from a Briton and classical lineage and toward a Germanic, Anglo-Saxon one. This research provided fuel for the arguments of Sir Edward Coke and other parliamentary lawyers, and in response, James I banned the Society of Antiquaries, "lest it should be the source of plots" (quoted in Kliger 126). When the society attempted to reconvene in 1614, they were again forced to disband, despite their conciliatory resolution not to "meddle with matters of State or religion" (Brinkley 32).

Throughout the early seventeenth century all publication on Anglo-Saxons was censored — important to recall if we are to appreciate the initially subversive nature, and the complicated genealogy, of Saxonist mythologies, and in turn understand how this prehistory of Saxonism provides one point of origin for modern liberation movements that rest on "native" claims. The prominent lawyer and admired scholar John Selden, a close friend of Ben Jonson, was twice imprisoned by the High Court even though his account of the Saxons evenhandedly avoided any notions of a post-Briton, Anglo-Saxon watershed, instead acknowledging that "the Saxons made a mixture of the British customes with their own."[7] Yet his suggestion that the "original of our English Laws" derived from the pre-Conquest era was apparently bad enough, especially since he treated history not as a revelation of absolute truths or the eternally divine rights of conquerors and kings but rather as a complicated matter of change and custom (quoted in Adams 67). After the publication of his controversial *History of Tithes* (1618), he was called before the High Court to apologize and the king forbade him to publish any responses to the royalist rebuttals of his work (Woolf, *Idea* 231–32). A few years later he was arrested for providing services to the Commons in their search for legal precedents for Parliamentarian prerogative (Brinkley 32–33). Bishop Laud, though a supporter of some Anglo-Saxon research, interfered with the publication of Sir Henry Spelman's Glossary, offended by its comments about the rights outlined in the Magna Carta (Brinkley 33). More widely, sermons that even hinted at the need for constraints on the king's power were burned in public and one preeminent Anglo-Saxon scholar, Dr. Dorislaus, lost his university post. In short, throughout the first two decades of the seventeenth century, James I repeatedly silenced challenges to his power in part by censoring this antiquarian legal scholarship and at the same time disseminating the doctrine of divine right, for instance by sponsoring the schoolbook *God and the King* (1615) to teach children about the divine sources of kingly power (Brinkley 37; Kliger 125).

Matters reached an early crisis point — and the rhetoric of ancient rights found its legs — when in 1620 the king issued a proclamation restricting Parliament's right to discuss high matters of state. Parliament responded directly, coining a language that would not only become the basis of the 1628 Petition of Right but would also create the heart of the Whig politics and Saxon myth well into the twentieth century: "The privileges and rights of Parliament are an ancient and indubitable birthright and inheritance of the English, and all important and urgent affairs in Church and State as well as the drawing up of laws and the remedying of abuses, are the proper subjects of the deliberation and resolutions of the Parliament. The members are free to speak upon them in such order as they please, and cannot be called to account for them" (quoted Brinkley 38). In further exchanges with the king, the Parliament reasserted its "Ancient and Undoubted Right, and an Inheritance received from our Ancestors," until the king "publicly tore these protests from the Journal of the House of Commons and dissolved Parliament" (quoted in Brinkley 38).

Throughout the 1620s and 1630s Parliament and the Stuart kings reached several such impasse moments, until finally James's son, Charles I, again dissolved Parliament in 1629 — and it did not reconvene until 1640. Meanwhile, however, other forces were gathering.

Atlantic Liberty

Across the Atlantic, a group of men was building a new commercial and religious network that would eventually help to break the impasse. Ultimately, this development would make the racialized rhetoric of rights and liberty a transatlantic phenomenon, embedding it deep in the structures of English-language narrative. Attending to this rhetoric helps us to see that, although the British empire would turn east by the end of next century, the American colonies crucially served as its crucible and in some ways remained the root of its liberty and race ideologies. In a sense the Civil War and its aftermath, from Cromwell's Commonwealth to Queen Victoria's empire, find their necessary cause in the years between 1610 and 1630 in American colonies, in the form of a group of "new men": these middling class and eventually Puritan-affiliated men who initiated activities and alliances that would reshape the economic balance of power. With the parliamentary crisis of 1628–29, culminating with Charles I's eleven-year dissolution of Parliament and renewed persecution of Puritans, the network of Atlantic merchant relations that had been spun throughout the 1620s attached itself to those interested in creating colonies as safe havens for religious refugees—and together (to put it oversimply) these men overthrew the king. The details of this development shed crucial light on the Atlantic conditions for the emergence of a nativist rhetoric of liberty and so deserve attention here.

WHILE THE FIRST PERMANENT English Atlantic settlement in Jamestown was initially underwritten by landed gentry and crown-allied merchants encouraged by the king (as its name indicates), its returns were minimal compared with those flowing in from the East through the East India, Levant, Muscovy, French, Somers Island, and other such companies. Launching a trading post in Virginia required significant investment under tenuous settlement conditions, whereas the Eastern trades moved within established infrastructures and required no building of settlements or importation of labor. Hence, although initially the Virginia Company was dominated by the same aristocratic men who ran the Eastern import companies (such as Sir Thomas Smythe, who at one time or another was governor of several of the companies named above), these adverse conditions weakened the investors' commitment, provoked in-fighting, and ultimately led to the Virginia Company's dissolution, permanently disrupted by the death of James in 1625.[8]

This is the point at which most histories of American colonization turn the colonizing narrative north to the great wave of Puritan immigration to Massachusetts. But some historians, most notably Robert Brenner, have tracked the fortunes of those "lesser" men who remained in Virginia and who ultimately made the settlement profitable. These men built up both wealth and social networks that supported the "refugee" American colonization during the crisis years in the twenties and thirties. They expanded their reach both south to the West Indies and north to the Massachusetts Bay Colony, financially backing the settlement of Massachusetts and helping to organize provisions for colonies both north and south. Most important, during the Civil War they forged a powerful coalition with the Puritan leadership in Parliament that eventually beheaded the king.[9]

Like other royal-merchant companies, the original Virginia Company was also explicitly a monopoly that divided planters and shopkeepers from gentlemen traders and excluded new traders from entering the field, restricting all profits from trade to the traders. Their bylaws included the standard "mere-merchant" provision that prohibited all "shopkeepers, sea captains, and artisans from becoming company members so long as they maintained their domestic businesses" in England (Brenner 114). After the dissolution of the Virginia Company, however, none of these rules was in place in Virginia, so the middling men who stayed on accrued tremendous wealth by manipulating all sides of the transatlantic trading/planting economy. That is, many of these men maintained overseas trading as well as domestic selling businesses in England or in the colonies (or both) without the cost of the middleman and outside the purview of the monopolies. Meanwhile, their promises of land and profits attracted a new wave of tobacco planters, supplied with laborers who were often coerced, kidnapped, or deported for crimes, so that the colony grew from a thousand members in 1624 to eight thousand in 1640, and between 1622 and 1638 tobacco imports to England grew exponentially (from sixty-one thousand to two million pounds per year). The "new" men organizing this growth derived profits not only from tobacco sales but by serving the needs of these new planters in what is called the colonial "provisions" trade, which brought supplies from England and resold them to other colonists at high prices (Brenner 113). As Brenner explains, "[p]aradoxically, then, the collapse of company organization for the Americas, and the consequent withdrawal from the trade of London's leading overseas traders, may actually have facilitated the colonizing process" (106).

From this profitable mixture of conditions there emerged in Virginia what Brenner calls the "colonial entrepreneurial leadership," including such men as Maurice Thomson and his brothers, Thomson's brother-in-law, Captain William Tucker, Elias Roberts (whose son of the same name married another of Thomson's sisters), Ralph Hamor, and William Claiborne. All of these men rose from "middling sorts" of backgrounds or lower, usually the younger sons of minor gentry or prosperous yeomen, sometimes from borough commercial families; and many became active in Virginia government during the 1620s. Both Tucker and Thomson had been involved in the Virginia colony's activities early on, emigrating there as very young men — Tucker at age twenty-one in 1610 and Thomson at age sixteen in 1617 (Brenner 118–20). Both began their rise as sea captains, transporting passengers and goods between Virginia and England. By 1619 Tucker had set up a plantation, was doing business with Londoners Roberts and Hamor, and was elected as a representative to the first meeting of the Virginia House of Burgesses; he would later become a powerful appointee to the trade-controlling body of the Virginia Council.

It's striking to note how these few men and their extended families dominated the center of this network and in this sense played a decisive founding role in the project we now call the United States of America. By the early 1620s Tucker had married one of Thomson's sisters and paid for the transport of Thomson's three younger brothers. As marriage connections among these men tightened and their wealth accrued, they emerged as a formidable monopoly. They used their transatlantic business operations and their colonial government positions to give themselves exclusive rights in fur trading and provisions trading. And in the end, crucially, they fostered the "transatlantic network of Puritan religio-political opposition to the crown" that included Massachusetts, Connecticut, Rhode Island, and, in the West Indies, Bermuda Island and Providence Island, all of which drew investors for religious as well as economic and political reasons and all of which served as both "ports of exile and staging posts for revolt" (Brenner 113, 110). The accretion of power and money that eventually built and supported this network began in Virginia with these men.

This network came into its own during the critical years following the king's dissolution of Parliament in 1628. As the king grew increasingly tolerant of Catholics and intolerant of Puritans, allowed the imprisonment of Parliament members, seized goods when merchants refused to pay newly imposed taxes, and pursued friendly relations with Spain that interfered with the new merchants' trade ambitions in the East, these Virginia men formed strong alliances with the emergent Puritan leadership in Parliament. Sir Nathaniel Rich, the Earl of Warwick, Lord Sele, and Lord Sayre launched several colonizing ventures in Bermuda, Massachusetts, and Providence Island, which the new merchants both supported and profited from. Thus did the interests of Puritans and entrepreneurs dovetail, even when religious motives were paramount, since economic "freedoms" were requisite (as Karen Kupperman shows) to make the colonial settlements viable.[10] Starting in 1638, Thomson was the key provisioner for the Puritan Bermuda colony founded by the Earl of Warwick, from which vantage point he led the way (which Warwick soon followed) in organizing and financing a series of bold and profitable raids on the Spanish West Indies (Brenner 158), eventually forming the vanguard of southward expansion. Also in 1638, it was to Thomson that Warwick, John Pym, Lord Mandeville, and Benjamin Rudyerd turned when they sought to exploit a silver mine in the Bay of Darien — an adventure that was part of this Puritan group's aggressive entrepreneurship in the Central American mainland. Conversely, when faced with obstacles to their scheme to claim Kent Island as a provisioning base for New England and Nova Scotia, Maurice Thomson, William Claiborne, and other new Virginia merchants called on the support of the Puritan leadership of the Bermuda Company, which co-signed the former's petition to the Privy Council.

It was thus together with Puritan leadership that Thomson built "a veritable commercial empire in the Caribbean in the space of two decades" (Brenner 125). From this Caribbean base, and for this base, Thomson and his circle began to interlope in the slave trade and the East Indies trade, enabling the colonies' shift from indentured English and Irish labor to African slaves, which in turn served to make the West Indies the "model" of profitability in the Western world (Brenner 161–65).[11] This rapidly accruing wealth encouraged and funded the "growing ties between the American merchant leadership and the great Puritan aristocrats who ran the Bermuda and Providence Island companies, as well as the lesser gentry who governed the New England colonies" (Brenner 149). These relationships became a "crucial element within an ongoing Puritan opposition network" that challenged the Stuart kings (Brenner 149).

When Parliament finally reconvened in 1641, in effect the so-called Puritan Revolution began. A new coalition of members, including Pym and other Puritans, succeeded in abolishing the Star Chamber (which had handled licensing and press censorship since 1586), purging those members they considered popish or unlawful, and exerting powerful resistance to the king's demands, eventually declaring war. These men and their supporters spoke a liberty rhetoric that loosely blended religious and economic referents. In this phase, the rhetoric of liberty was turned not just against the king but also against those merchants of the East that the king had sponsored and depended on — thus serving the interests of the new merchants who had been working with the Puritan leaders overseas.

That is, many of the petitions to Parliament during the mid-1640s cultivated the language of freedom and rights mainly to argue against monopolies and the old proprietary forms of ownership and control. Such was the case with one of the petitions organized by the Thomson group which called for "freehold" conditions in the West Indian colonies (Brenner 166), and the petition challenging the Royalist Calverts who controlled Maryland, also signed by Thomson and associates (Brenner 166–67). During the meeting of the Long Parliament in 1641, for example, the courtier-merchant Sir Nicholas Crispe, who had been granted a patent for the Guinea trade by Charles I in 1631, was labeled as a monopolist trampling on freedom and was forced from the trade. Most ambitiously, in "The Humble Petition of Divers Citizens" (1645) presented to the London City Council, the writers enumerate twenty pages of economic grievances and at the same time remark the contradictions in Parliament's policies: "Seeing the Parliament ordained, that none should be accepted to be a Parliament-man, that had been a Monopolizer to the Kings Councell, and false judges against the Liberties of the free-men of *England,* is it not as unjust to imploy any man in a place of Trust, Credit, or profit now in Parliament . . . that have been known to be a Monopolizer in any place or Office to or for the Parliament, to the prejudice of the Free-men of *England?*"[12] Likewise, "A Remonstrance of Many Thousand Citizens, and other Free-Born People of England to theire own House of Commons" complains of "the oppression of the Turkey Company, and the Adventures Company, and all other infringements of our Native Liberties [which] yee seemed to abominate, are now by you complyed withall, and licensed to goe on" (Haller 358). Such rhetoric served the new Atlantic merchants well, enabling their interloping efforts to break the Turkey and other companies' hold on the eastern trade, while the honorable parliamentary and reverent religious language of liberty dignified their aims.

After the capture of the king Charles I, as the city government and the Presbyterians allied against the political and religious independents, and each side maneuvered to come to a separate settlement with Charles, the network linked to Maurice Thomson came to the fore in London as spokespersons for the Independents. At this point, the intertwining of religious and economic goals became even more tightly drawn and more pointedly expressed within the language of liberty. Independent minister Hugh Peters was a key spokesperson; his mastery of this discourse was distinguished by an instinct to shape it within a larger imperial vision for England. Peters had been involved with Thomson and Pennoyer since the 1630s, participating with them initially in fishing ventures in Massachusetts Bay and serving as chaplain in the new merchants' privately backed incursions into Ireland—a mission, as he phrased it, "to teach the peasants liberty" (Brenner 507). He emerged as "perhaps the key political link between the army officers and London's political independent leadership" and as such he worked closely with parliamentary committees as they sought ways to block the king's supplies arriving from the Continent while at the same time soliciting private individuals who might provide ships or carry out privateering raids on ports held by the Royalists around Amsterdam and Rotterdam (Brenner 500–501). (Notably, the twelve-person committee that oversaw the sale of prizes from these raids included Maurice Thomson and Thomas Andrews.) Peters served in the parliamentary navy under the Puritan earl of Warwick as it conducted these raids, and he was chaplain for the Model Army, rousing troops to righteous anger against "the mountains to be overcome [of] slavery and tyranny" in order to win "liberty for tender consciences" (Brenner 501). Apparently, after the Presbyterians went on the offensive in building links with the king and suppressing religious Independents, it was Peters who drew up the political Independents' petition in June 1646—with its reported twenty thousand signatures. Among the leaders of the delegation that presented the petition was Samuel Warner, whose niece was a sister-in-law of Maurice Thomson (Brenner 505).

It was perhaps his lynchpin position between the merchants, the religious dissidents, and the Puritan parliamentary leaders that allowed Peters to apprehend the future imperial riches promised by this convergence of forces under the sign of liberty. He first of all advocated renewed conquest and colonization of Ireland, in part to build support through economic incentives (the plan originally included the promise to give supportive Londoners tracts of Irish land) and perhaps in part to continue building the power of the New Model Army. At the same time he called for an international Protestant coalition fostered by England through diplomacy with the Swiss, the Swedish, and the Dutch, and led by England with a well-financed navy. Then, once "our back-door were well-shut at home," Peters predicted, the English would find that "the West Indies and the East [would] offer themselves to our devotion" (quoted in Brenner 507). He goes on to voice a view that would become ubiquitous by the early eighteenth century when he admonishes: "Let us still remember the support of trade is the strength of the island; discountenance the merchant and take beggary by the hand" (quoted in Brenner 507). The very soul of Maurice Thomson must have smiled at this warning against "discountenanc[ing] the merchant." The rhetoric had turned in his favor. The Atlantic economy had joined the nation, and, in turn, native liberty bridged the vast Atlantic.

A Native Public Is Born

Meanwhile, during the 1640s, because of the abolition of the Star Chamber, the growth of an uncensored press, and the unregulated preaching of ministers, liberty rhetoric spread "downward." The very Army forces Peters had stirred began to take the language of liberty further, so that it reverberated through those lower "chains of being" that included women and the landless—forces that, through print, could threaten the new merchants from below, as Edward Sexby anticipated when he urged the Army to acquire a printing press for their cause or "wee shall be at a losse."[13] Because the Long Parliament had not immediately replaced the Star Chamber with any equivalent censorship organ, there circulated increasing numbers of polemical newspapers, pamphlets, and petitions that eventually made it impossible for Cromwell or Parliament or the new merchants to maintain control of the liberty discourse.[14] Parliamentary leaders and their merchant allies could no longer contain their recruits' application of liberty principles within the political and religious boundaries that would serve their purposes.

This is the moment when a nascent and dissenting Habermasian public sphere appears briefly in England—temporarily, chaotically, and yet influentially.[15] The first newspaper had appeared in 1620 (published in Holland and exported) and, with its coverage of the Thirty Years War, had provided a model for readership and a stimulus to conversation about current events which, especially during the English Civil War, led to an intense "public demand for up-to-date news of domestic political affairs" (Thompson 67). Between November 1641 and April 1642, there appeared eleven domestic weekly papers; by 1645, fourteen more regular newspapers were available in London (Thompson 67). At the same time pamphlets and petitions spread like fire, readily accessible to a broad segment of what now became a "publick" literate enough through their Bible reading to comprehend such texts. Especially as Parliament gained the upper hand in the war, numerous petitions were presented to the House of Commons, expressing the protests of soldiers, soldiers' wives, tradespeople, religious sects, and landless laborers against their exclusion from both trade and political power, their forced exportation to colonies, and the widespread poverty arising from tithes and enclosure of the commons.

But relief and representation were not forthcoming, and so the public sphere swelled with complaints and new coalitions. By 1647, the failure to hold new parliamentary elections with an expanded electorate, to pay soldiers their arrears, to finance support for widows and orphans or for citizens who quartered the soldiers, to break up monopolies of trade in an already debilitated postwar economy, to allow for full religious toleration instead of new preferential treatment of the Puritans, to repeal the tithes and taxes that weighed heavily on the poorest — all of these fed widespread disenchantment among a people who had sustained years of war for the sake of "liberty" and better living conditions. Given the threat that royalists would regain the field, the newly powerful Puritans and Atlantic entrepreneurs were temporarily forced to align themselves with these more democratic groups, at least until the absolute securing of their power in 1649, after which they discredited all democratic platforms and began to imprison and persecute these groups' spokespersons.

This period of crisis provoked political activism among women as well as men; it thus encouraged the association between political and sexual scandal that would become so apparent in novels and that in this moment found expression in political publications.[16] Women wrote petitions, held meetings, and joined or led public protests to address economic, religious, and civic injustices. Early in 1641, four hundred women gathered at Parliament to demand a response to a petition on the loss of trade. When they received no satisfactory attention, they penned the "Humble Petition of many hundreds of distressed women, Tradesmens wives, and widdowes" in which they claimed that "we have an interest in the common Privileges with them [who have petitioned for the] Liberty of our Husbands, persons, and estates."[17] In August 1643, some five to six thousand women (as numbered by their critics) marched on the Commons for peace. By 1647, it seems that women frequently appeared on the steps of Parliament to petition or demand responses to petitions, for the House of Commons enacted an ordinance against loitering and a directive to guards to clear away "those clamourous women, which were wont to hang in clusters on the staires" (quoted in McEntee 96). The women must have kept returning for, later in the year, the Commons issued an order to apprehend and jail all such loiterers.

Significantly, these new groups took up the same Saxonist rhetoric of liberty that the Parliamentarians and merchants had come to use. The Levellers led by Lieutenant Colonel John Lilburne, Thomas Rainborough, and others spoke continually of "native rights," "the people's just rights and liberties," the "Nation's freedoms," "the free-born people of England," and the "free-born People's freedoms or rights."[18] "The Women's Petition" (1651) laments that "[O]ur expectation of freedom (the fruits of our bloudshed, and expence of our estates) is removed far away; yea the hope of our Liberty is cut off like the Weavers thrumb. . . . the Norman laws of the oppressors still bear Dominion over us."[19] Like John Hare, Nathaniel Bacon elaborately laid out the Saxonist historical narrative underlying this rhetoric which would become Whig orthodoxy by the eighteenth century. In his *Historical and Political Discourse of the Laws and Government of England,* which addressed the "Debate concerning the Right of an English King to Arbitrary Rule over English Subjects, as Successor to the Norman Conqueror" (1647), Bacon at first traces some form of assembly to the Britons, before the Saxons, though in rude form. When he turns to the Saxons, he reveals how pivotal and popular their role had become. He remarks that it is "both needless and fruitless to enter into the Lists, concerning the original of the Saxons. . . . They were a free people, governed by Laws, and those made not after the manner of the Gauls (as Caesar noteth) by the great men, but by the people; and therefore called a free people, because they are a law unto themselves; and this was a privilege belonging to all the germans, as tacitus observeth. . . . The Saxons fealty to their King, was subservient to the publick safety; and the publick safety is necessarily dependant upon the liberty of the Laws." The Norman Conquest "trenched not upon the fundamental Laws of the people's Liberty"; and thus those laws still had validity as precedents (quoted in Kliger 139 and 140). Here we can glimpse the incipient widening of the liberty language as it moves beyond Parliament's "ancient rights" to "the fundamental Laws of the people's Liberty" and finally to the realm of "publick safety."

Such pronouncements opened the way to more radical thinkers, who nonetheless invoked the same nativist rhetoric. The Diggers, for instance, mounted one of the most communistic economic platforms of the Revolution, and yet also employed the opposition between native and Norman. In "The True Levellers' Standard Advanced" (1649), Gerard Winstanley (identified as a Digger by others while he himself embraced the "levelling" of all hierarchy that the more moderate Levellers like Lilburne explicitly rejected) claimed that "the last enslaving conquest which the enemy got over Israel was the Norman over England" (Prall 179). Thus even now, he argues, "when any trustee or state officer is to be chosen . . . who must be chosen but some rich man who is the successor of the Norman colonels or high officers? And to what end have they been chosen but to establish that Norman power the more forcibly over the enslaved English, and to beat them down again whereas they gather heart to seek for liberty? For what are all those binding and restraining laws . . . what are they but the cords, manacles, and yokes that the enslaved English, like Newgate prisoners, wear upon their hands and legs as they walk the streets; by which those Norman oppressors, and their successors from age to age, have enslaved the poor people ?" (Prall 179). Similarly in his "Law of Freedom" letter to Cromwell, Winstanley argues, "When the Norman power had conquered our forefathers, he took the free use of our English ground from them."[20]

In *Manifestoes,* Janet Lyon studies the political manifestoes of this period as precursors, especially, to modernist manifestoes that name "the breach between modernity's promissory notes and their payment."[21] She astutely notices the Levellers' and Diggers' unprecedented use of a narrative "we" to name that breach — that is, to establish "a new civic voice making demands" which begins to instantiate, she argues persuasively, "a new kind of political subject" (21). Yet this "we" appropriated to itself a historical and native identity, not in most cases a universal one. At the very moment of its emergence, this insurgent "we" was being defined as Anglo-Saxon, as distinctively English.

Thus we have the co-emergence of three elements that form the racialist liberty narrative: an Atlantic colonialism in the hands of the new merchants, a coalition of these men with dissenting Puritans and other religious Independents within Parliament, and the entry of increasingly radical political dissenters into a nascent public sphere, galvanized by the Army and including women and the poor. All of these groups use the language of native liberty, and although they use it to make different, sometimes conflicting, economic or political claims, they also share underlying interests — mainly economic — that allow them to tolerate their divergent priorities with respect to liberty.

It is worth noting that the cry for broader economic rights and justice did momentarily if unsuccessfully point the way beyond the nativist rhetoric. Winstanley, for instance, bemoaned the greedy history that gave rise to these racialized oppositions between Normans and "the English people." And even the relatively moderate Army protestors began to formulate a "natural rights" vision that transcended race. In fact a deeper panic arose when pamphleteers began to denigrate the Magna Carta and the "English birthright" tradition, as Lilburne eventually did, probably under the influence of the powerful merchant and outspoken religious Independent William Walwyn. In an ostensibly private letter to Lilburne titled "Englands lamentable Slaverie" (1645), Walwyn praised Lilburne's "undaunted resolution in defence of the common freedome of the People" but went on to explain that "Magna Charta hath been more precious in your esteeme than it deserveth" (Haller 315): "MAGNA CHARTA (you must observe) is but a part of the people's rights and liberties, being no more but what with much striving and fighting, was by the blood of our Ancestors, wrestled out of the pawes of those Kings, who by force had conquered the Nation" (Haller 314). Furthermore, subsequent kings, he says, with the "unnatural assistance of Parliaments" have continually striven to diminish rather than enhance the few rights granted in the charter: "see how busie they have been about the regulating of petty inferiour trades and exercises, about the ordering of hunting, who should keep Deere and who should not . . . most of them put on purpose to divert [the people] from the very thoughts of freedome" (314). Thus "when by any accident or intollerable oppression they were roused out of one of those waking dreames, then whats the greatest thing they ayme at? . . . MAGNA CHARTA . . . calling that messe of pottage the birthright, the great inheritance of the people, the Great Charter of England" (314). Consequently, the English have come to "call bondage libertie, and the grants of Conquerors their Birth rights" (315). Soon thereafter Lilburne helped to pen a document averring that Magna Carta "itself being but a beggarly thing, contain[s] many marks of intollerable bondage" (Haller 365, "Remonstrance of Many Thousands"). Others, too, began to suggest that "it is ridiculous for private men to build hopes upon rotten titles of ages long passed, upon weak maxims of law" (Kliger 262).

For some of those involved, this dismissal of Magna Carta and the notion of ancient birthright proved too disruptive, casting aside as it did all loyalty to a specifically English tradition of culture and freedom. It incensed William Prynne, for instance. After their publication of these attacks on the Magna Carta, he denounced the Levellers as "desperately impudent" in their claim that "the Freemen and People have no such unalterable Fundamental Laws and Liberties left them by their forefathers" (quoted in Kliger 153). In effect, Prynne wrestled with the Levellers for control of the liberty discourse, implicitly using "Freemen" in its economic-status sense and "People" in its more traditional sense, that is, as embodied by Parliament. When he charges that these agitators aim "to establish a *meere popular* Tyrannie, which they will *assure unto themselves under the Notion of a People,* to the destruction of *our* Laws and Liberties," he registers the newly divergent — populist vs. Parliamentarian — meanings for "people," and he labors to affiliate the populist version with "tyranny" (quoted in Kliger 155, emphasis in original).

The widening of liberty claims also prompted sympathetic yet pragmatic moderates, aware of the way the king and royalists could use such radical claims to slander the cause of Parliament, to advise the Levellers that "[a]bove all you must not be anti-Parliamentary" (quoted in Kliger 262). Implicitly this was an admonition to cleave to the rhetoric of Anglo-Saxonism and the nativist principle of freedom. Sensing the potential undoing not just of the old monarchical order but also of the emergent Anglo-Saxonist, Puritan, and mercantile one, contemporaries began to observe that "[t]he greatest powers in the kingdom have been shaken."[22] They bemoaned the "wounds of the kingdom," and they expressed "a great expectation of sudden destruction" (Woodhouse 46, 42). These fears explain the important tempering part eventually played by Anglo-Saxonism.

Yet even as a nativist discourse, the call to liberty threatened to reach not only downward and outward across social boundaries but also inward, weakening mental and religious habits of obedience. For, as I'll next discuss, this discourse also drew authority from the Protestant emphasis on private conscience, an influence encouraged by the lineage that attributed an Anglo-Saxon origin to Protestantism. Such were the manifold effects and powers of the Anglo-Saxonist idea of freedom and the legacy of the Magna Carta. Ultimately this legacy would serve to replace historical rupture with ancient continuity, to gloss religious dissent as native subjectivity, to fashion colonial adventurism as national patriotism — and so to forestall the atomization of society into a fractious collection of dissenting selves of the kind Thomas Hobbes theorized. In providing this coherence, Saxonism racialized the very heart, mind, and soul of the English and their colonial descendants.

The Interior Turn

While economics often motivated the talk of native liberty in this period there emerged another dimension of the notion of liberty that has become equally essential to its role in Atlantic modernity: its articulation as an interior principle planted in the breasts of all persons. The Leveller pamphleteer John Warr signaled this turn when he claimed that "Justice was in men, before it came to be in Laws" (Kliger 269). Lilburne named the implications for the new public sphere when he asserted that "the Lawes of this nation are unworthy a Free-People, and deserve from first to last, to be considered, and seriously debated, and reduced to an agreement with the common equity, and right reason" (Kliger 267). As Lilburne hints in his phrase "right reason," the basis for law was being relocated within, and public practices would now be called to account — and "seriously debated" — in accordance with those interior standards. Insofar as it opened the way to a universalization of the liberty principle, this interiorizing of liberty had radical potential — a potential that would be variously tapped and contained over the subsequent three centuries of Atlantic history.

In the late sixteenth and early seventeenth centuries, the Protestant promotion of Bible reading, the publication of vernacular Bibles, and the accompanying encouragement of literacy — all of which initially served a project of uniformity and obedience — returned to haunt the Protestant hierarchy by feeding the sects' claims to conscience-driven dissent. Bible reading had indeed led the flock to turn inward and assess their relations with God individually, and of course the Puritans took this notion with full and literal seriousness. Furthermore, because the Reformation had created ongoing religious upheaval, entailing severe codes of repression and horrific punishment, the conditions were created for a discourse of dissent, and among the sects, especially an inward justification and secret articulation of dissent.[23] Thus Prynne spoke for many when he proclaimed, "The elect can't resist the inward powerful and effectual call or working of God's spirit in their hearts" — and, for his vision of an interior that must dictate public actions, he was twice imprisoned by Charles with the further punishment of having his ears cut off.[24]

Eventually, in the era of civil war, democratic and communitarian thinkers applied this notion of an interior source for ethical duty to questions of economic right. Lilburne and friends preface their *Manifestation* and their political claims by insisting that "we cannot be thereby any whit dismayed in the performance of our duties, supported inwardly by the Innocency and evenness of our Consciences," and they go on to explain that, in order to counteract the political manipulations of others, they will "open our breasts and show the world our insides" (Prall 165, 167). Although he came to be a key antagonist of Cromwell's, Lilburne's statement reveals his participation in the very dream of transparency between inside and outside that Cromwell would aim to institute both at home and abroad in the city on a hill. He goes on to insist that "the world may clearly see what we are, and what we aim at: We are altogether ignorant [of] and do from our hearts abominate all ["levelling"] designs and contrivances of dangerous consequence. ... Having no men's person in hatred, and *judging it needful that all other respects whatsoever are to give way to the good of the Commonwealth, and this is the very truth and inside of our hearts*" (*A Manifestation*, 1649 written jointly by Lilburne, Walwyn, and Thomas Overton from the Tower, Prall 174, emphasis added).

In this articulation of the "inside of our hearts," there emerges, then, the unforeseen consequence of the underlying relationship between Protestantism and print. Just as Bible reading had been understood as the true basis of a private relation with God, now publication in print began to be cast as the vehicle of a true interior, so that print provides the medium for the complete congress of private and public spheres. The deepest inside — of hearts — finds its expression in print, which in turn should all at once serve, constitute, and guide the outside — the Commonwealth. Such notions articulate an ideal wherein the inner laws of conscience or reason adjudicate the external laws and actions of government, challenging the more traditional, hierarchical model in which the external laws of property and obedience govern the behavior of subjects. As the frequent use of the word "manifestations" suggests, that is, these printed documents advocate the interior founding of an exterior state. This new paradigm no doubt helped to generate much of what Michel Foucault later observed about the interiority of modern power, its channeling through discourse, and the circuit of power linking psyche and social setting. Certainly the vision of a perfect alignment of inside and outside ultimately comes to characterize sentimental culture and novelistic narration, insofar as it offers readers a "transparent window" that makes manifest the characters' hearts and souls, as Leo Damrosch and, more recently, John Bender have explored.[25]

In the 1640s and 1650s, the radical Winstanley most fully theorizes the interior as a source for exterior, political relations, and his writings serve to indicate how the nativist framework infiltrates this interior turn. He argues, first of all, that a person should be controlled by "Reason, his Maker, . . . his teacher and ruler within himself, . . . the indweller of the five senses," and he asserts that "[i]n the beginning of time, the great Creator, Reason, made the earth to be a common treasury" ("The True Leveller's Standard," quoted in Prall 174). Winstanley repeatedly casts "reason" and "selfish imagination" as psychological qualities generating good and evil in the world; in his vision, both reason and liberty are expressions of the divine as it dwells within humans: the "great Creator, who is the Spirit Reason" (Prall 175), engenders "the Spirit of Christ, which is the Spirit of universal community and freedom" (Prall 180), and so it is "the spreading power of righteousness that gives liberty to the whole creation" (Prall 176). Winstanley implicitly places this psychology of freedom within a Saxonist historical narrative, suggesting that there was a conquering moment, when "selfish imaginations" came to "rule as king in the room of Reason" and thereafter "man was brought into bondage and became a greater slave to such of his own kind than the beasts of the field were to him. . . . And thereupon the earth, which was made to be a common treasury of relief for all, both beasts and men, was hedged into enclosures by the teachers and rulers, and the others were made servants and slaves. . . . whereby the Creator is mightily dishonoured" (Prall 175). Reading within the context of his other writings, we can infer that Winstanley is suggesting that the Normans who conquered the humble English were ruled by "selfish imaginations" and so enchained this interior principle of divine reason, eventually forcing the "enclosure" of the common treasury which current rulers, he implies, are extending. He urges the English to recall that "indwelling" principle, reclaim their common land, and reassert their freedom. And his printed call apparently manifests a decree already written within: "all the prophecies of *scriptures and reason* are circled here in this community, and mankind must have the law of righteousness once more *writ in his heart,* and all must be made of one heart and mind — then this enmity on all lands will cease" (Prall 176, emphasis added).

We glimpse the generative influence of such seventeenth-century ideas when we scroll briefly forward to the work of G. W. F. Hegel, perhaps the single most important Anglo-European philosopher of race as it intertwines with a subjectivity founded on freedom. Winstanley's theosophy strikingly anticipates Hegel's abstraction of God into a principle of interiority embroiled in a play of "forces" in which the life of Spirit and the freedom of a race are at stake. Hegel will speak of the primal battle between lord and bondsman as well as the dialectic between spirit and matter, just as Winstanley had imagined that "proud imaginary flesh . . . gets dominion to rule over others, and so forces one part of the creation, man, to be a slave to another. And thereby the Spirit is killed in both" (Prall 175). Winstanley imagines liberty as a divine principle, and in Hegel, the energy of "Spirit" finds its expression in "Reason," so that Reason drives the "Universal History" of the world toward "Freedom."[26] Hegel states what Winstanley implies: that "the History of the World is nothing but the development of the Idea of Freedom" (Hegel, *Philosophy of History* 456).

Of course, for Winstanley, the rhetoric of native Saxonism remains a revolutionary, domestic discourse, while in Hegel, two centuries later, it becomes imperial and racist. Hegel (once famously, now infamously) locates Indian Americans and Africans outside the universal history of freedom, and he announces, "The German spirit is the Spirit of the new World. Its aim is the realization of absolute Truth as the unlimited self-determination of Freedom. . . . The destiny of the German peoples is to be the bearers of the Christian principle . . . of Spiritual Freedom" (Hegel, *Philosophy of History* 341). Winstanley could not have predicted this arrogant, racist turn in the nativist liberty discourse. Yet exactly by positioning Winstanley as a precursor of Hegel, we can chart the path by which his anti-capitalist, revolutionary racialism became a nationalist and imperial racism.

Equally important to subsequent history and the Atlantic plot of ruin and liberty — and more immediately threatening in the 1640s than Winstanley's metaphysical meditations — was women's use of the interior turn to justify their participation in the public sphere.[27] Women's public demonstrations, printed petitions, and open-air preaching clearly provided a threatening spectacle, and these activities signaled the deeper ideological threat — that women could lay claim to a free interior. Katherine Chidley, for example, makes the inner call of God the basis for challenging the prerogatives of fathers and husbands. An Independent preacher from 1630 to 1653 (who also spearheaded the 1653 petition appealing for the release of John Lilburne), Chidley appeals to "tender conscience" and "liberty of conscience" to unveil gender trouble in the spiritual order, wondering "what authority [the] unbelieving husband hath over the conscience of his believing wife."[28] Although she concedes that "he hath authority over her in bodily and civil respects," she argues that he is "not to be a lord over her conscience" (B. Hill 20). Other women were similarly bold in pursuing the implications of this dissenter's logic for women.[29] In "the Daughter of Sion Awakened" (1677), Margaret Fell-Fox cites Samuel Torshell's claim that "[t]he soul knows no difference of sex" before proposing that Christ "Hath made no difference in this Work between Male and Female." Asking "May not the spirit of Christ *speak* in the female as well as the male?" she built on the emergent connection between private godly inspiration and public expression.[30] Female as well as male preachers embellished the notion of an interior source for action in characterizing themselves as vessels of Christ, wives of Christ, and nurturing mothers of their communities — taking an imagery which was quite old and reshaping it to serve a discourse of dissent and liberty (Trubowitz 120 – 21). The Levellers allied themselves with such women no doubt for strategic reasons without exactly promoting feminist ideas, yet such alliances helped to publicize the women's innovative interior claims.

Some women applied their religious insights directly to political events. As one writer put it, "We are assured of our Creation in the image of God, and of an interest in Christ, equall unto men, as also a proportionable share in the freedoms of the Commonwealth" (McEntee 102). Meanwhile female preachers and prophets of all political sympathies openly drew on their revelations to shed light on the political turmoil, most famously in the case of Elizabeth Poole, who was summoned by Parliament in December 1649 to describe her visions concerning the pending execution of the king (Trubowitz 112). Of course the Puritan elite who led the country and the American Puritan colonies for a decade after the Revolution in the long run had no more tolerance than the Royalists for this feminist interpretation of "liberty of conscience," as reflected perhaps in the fact that a considerable portion of the women burned as witches in the 1640s and 1650s were Quaker women — that is, members of the sect that most openly promoted women's inner visions and political equality. If the notion of liberty for all men threatened to "destroy all distinctions of degrees" until "nothing at all" of civil constitution would be left, women's claims to liberty of conscience and speech no doubt threatened to destroy the very conception of "constitution."

This set of gender disruptions sparked by the English Revolution undoubtedly swells the symbolic force of the plot of sexual ruin that would become pivotal in so many Atlantic liberty narratives. That is, the seduction plot not only serves as an *allegory* for all kinds of political violation but it also signals the specifically gendered origins and effects of this trope of violation. Uppity, early modern women suffered abuse and violation, while their transgressions at the same time created a sense of rupture in the social world. Gender transgressions thus joined those other pressures — religious, economic, and civic — that were shaping a new kind of interiorized political being: one centered in the interiority of a racialized, propertied self and imagined through printed literature. As fashioned in memoir and fiction over the next three centuries, this self threatened with ruin appears as the violated yet reborn embodiment of a people seeking free expression. By the middle of the twentieth century, however, in the wake of the long history of violations and failures undergone by this freedom-seeking self, and in the face of a virulent, genocidal racism, authors begin to deflate this idealization of ruin, rob the seduction plot of its redemptive, phoenix force, and obscure the operations of the interior self. When we witness James Joyce's Dedalus, Jean Toomer's Kabnis, and Djuna Barnes's Nora making their sexually ruinous, midnight descents into self and race, and hear Gertrude Stein's narrator weeping in *The Making of Americans* because she has failed to know everyone right down to their racial "bottom nature," we encounter the shattering of a freedom dream born in the seventeenth century.

Interior Liberty Meets Native Property: The Putney Debates

The Putney Debates dramatize, as if on a stage, the tensions that would implode three centuries later in the texts of Atlantic modernism. In these debates, the elements of nativist liberty, new mercantile economics, and interior-founded, print polis all come into volatile play — exposing their as-yet unstable interdependence. As such, the debates constitute one of the most far-reaching and purely political events of the Revolution. In them, the foundation of a political order is laid bare — prompting the racial coverup that would function triumphantly for three subsequent centuries. To study the Putney Debates is therefore to better understand the logic of Atlantic modernity.

Held in response to Cromwell's terms for a settlement with the Army's demand for more representation and in resistance to his plans to remove forces to Ireland (in part, some suspected, to break up their political maneuverings at home while reinstating colonial rule over the Irish), the debates were specifically meant to take up the Army's objections as laid out in "The Case of the Army Truly Stated" and "An Agreement of the People." These documents expressed the notion that the Representatives' power is "inferior only to theirs who choose them" and they enumerated what the writers considered their "native rights," such as a more representative electorate and a biennial parliamentary election.[31] They announced resistance to any curtailment of these rights, resistance which they threatened to undertake in accord with "the examples of our ancestors" who often fought for "the recovery of their freedoms" (Woodhouse 445). This rhetoric quietly references the new narrative of free Englishness that surrounded the event of the debates, and although the debaters themselves seldom invoke the narrative directly, their concern with questions of contract and property reveals that a whole new social and political economy is at stake within that freedom narrative.

From the opening moments, the debaters' strenuous attempt to speak freely and to make manifest the private conscience in the public sphere threatens to overwhelm the procedures. The participants initially get so entangled in the question of whether everyone has arrived with the interests of the Commonwealth utmost in their hearts, and ready to speak transparently with clear conscience in favor of those interests, that on the first day they discuss very little of the substance of the Army's petitions. Cromwell first of all insists, "I shall offer nothing to you but that I think in my heart and conscience tends to the uniting of us," and urges others to do the same: "he that meets here not with that heart [invested above all in unity], and dares not say he will stand to that, I think he is a deceiver" (Woodhouse 8). Ostensibly establishing the ideal of transparency, yet practicing his typical doublespeak, Cromwell on the one hand avers that he is "confident that there sits not a man in this place" who is interested in anything but "the good of the kingdom," but on the other hand hints that indeed he suspects such men are present, warning again that "God will discover whether our hearts be not clear in this business" (Woodhouse 17). Under the guise of this concern, he applauds the suggestion by a member of his council that they adjourn for the day — before they have really begun — so that all can spend the next morning in prayer. In this way, "that Spirit that is the only searcher of hearts . . . can best search out and discover to him the errors of his own ways and of the workings of his own heart" (Woodhouse 21). He predicts that all participants will return to the debate in a transparent condition; each individual heart will shine forth its commitment to dissolve its dissent and difference in "the uniting of us." By means of such proclamations of transparency, Cromwell duplicitously stalls the progress and dynamics of the debate.

But the adjournment itself is delayed, tellingly, by the intervention of other voices in this new public sphere, and in particular by questions about the right of people to dissent from authority — which seems to justify Cromwell's earlier complaint that the terms of the debate must be clearly circumscribed because "How do we know if, whilst we are disputing these things, another company of men shall [not] gather together, and put out a paper as plausible as this? . . . And not only another, and another, but many of this kind?" (Woodhouse 7). He had initially attempted to limit the discussion to only the first and more moderate document ("The Case of the Army"), because, he says, the second was published after the agreement to debate had been made and, furthermore, in its radical proposals seems not to put the "unity" of the Commonwealth above all other considerations. And in any case such a proliferation of ideas calling for "alterations of the very government of the kingdom" would be "utter confusion" (Woodhouse 7). His comments give evidence of how destabilizing the "putting out of papers" had become. Despite Cromwell's attempts to contain the topics of debate, the discussion after all turns to the underlying question of whether, first of all, the Army can break its agreement with the Parliament because they find the original terms of that contract unjust and, secondly, whether it can accordingly shift the terms it first proposed for Parliament in its negotiations with the king.

In their attempts to lay grounds for the debate, the participants thus stumble on the absent-center question at its heart: what is the origin of authority and law? Whose interests does the law represent and protect? They labor to establish the founding terms of the social contract. As the discussion develops, Cromwell and his son-in-law Colonel Ireton work to deny the Army's right to withdraw from their contract and from their promise to remain loyal and obedient to Parliament. But, prefiguring the circularity of Clarissa's conflict with Lovelace, the Army speakers contend that their contract with Parliament was broken first by Parliament when it violated the a priori right underlying the contract — the right to be heard.

In the fascinating discussion that follows, the debaters probe this question of a social contract. They explore the basis of their social obligations to each other and the conditions under which any party can withdraw from them. Ireton concedes that "where a performance of an engagement might be expected from another, and he could not do it because he thought it was not honest to be performed . . . it is possible there might be some reason for it"; thus "honesty" can adjudicate and nullify the contract if that contract turn false. But he objects to the assertion of a general principle that unjust engagements can or should be broken for "this is a principle that will take away all commonwealths" (Woodhouse 11). The representatives of the Army and the "freeborn people" gloss this problem differently, however, explaining that once the state breaks its compact, the people are likewise freed of their obligations to the state. Although the demands in the Army's proposals have not yet been explicitly taken up, their underlying question has inevitably surfaced. They are implicitly asking, what is the nature of the obligation men have to a government over and above their sense of right or rights? From whence do "rights" arise? Are rights *conferred* by the government, encompassed a priori and wholly by this national entity? If so, what room or basis is there for dissent? Aren't rights and autonomy a priori and natural, and preparatory to sociality? If not, from whence arises the agency of one who breaks or withdraws from the contract? These questions threaten the perfect alignment of public and private. Their unanswerability, the aporia they represent, may well be one cause of the sense of a communal swoon — that feeling of confusion, incoherence, and dissociation — that then gets staged in English-language narratives.

Nativism eventually steps in to restabilize the social world. Ultimately, in his refutations of the Army representatives' claims, Ireton reveals how a new racialized and interiorized discourse of freedom, even as it loosened the ties binding the position of the obedient and duty-bound monarchical subject, could reinstall around this free subject certain limits and hierarchies founded on property. He is prompted to move in this direction, first of all, by the Army's claims to a universal right to dissent. After making clear, defensively, that he is "far from holding" that "if a man have engaged himself to a thing that is not just . . . that man is still bound to perform what he hath promised," Ireton goes on to question, however, the basis of the claim for the *innate* rights of all men that might, in all manner of situation, justify their disobedience to authority and their dissent from government (Woodhouse 25–26). He distinguishes between that which is just before God and that "which is just according to the foundation of justice between man and man"; and then he confesses:

> There is no other foundation of right I know, of right to [any] one thing from another man, no foundation of that [particular] justice or that [particular] righteousness, but this general justice and this general ground of righteousness, that we should keep covenant one with another. Covenants freely made, freely entred [*sic*] into, must be kept one with another. Take away that, I do not know what ground there is of anything you can call any man's right. I would very fain know what you gentleman, or any other, do account the right you have to anything in England. . . . For matter of goods, that which does fence me from that [right] which another man may claim by the Law of Nature, of taking my goods, that which makes it mine really and civilly, is the law. . . . This is the foundation of all the right any man has to anything but to his own person. This is the general thing: that we must keep covenant one with another when we have contracted with another. (Woodhouse 26)

We can sense the socio-epistemological crisis within this fledgling public sphere in Ireton's emphasis on what he doesn't know — "There is no other foundation of right I know," "I do not know what ground there is" — and his wish to reach a point of understanding — "I would very fain know what you gentleman do account." He goes on to express his anxiety more directly when he explains that "when I hear men speak of laying aside all engagements to [consider only] that wild or vast notion of what in every man's conception is just or unjust, I am afraid and do tremble at the boundless and endless consequences of it" (Woodhouse 27). He finds himself face to face with the "vast notion" of an absolute freedom — including the freedom to question the very idea of state authority and, by extension, the property order its laws protect.

In exasperation, Ireton openly names the property stakes of the matter and works to preserve property's uneven distribution by taking it as a foregone conclusion that a "constitution" by its nature "founds property": "The Law of God doth not give me property, nor the law of Nature, but property is of human constitution. I have a property and this I shall enjoy. Constitution founds property" (Woodhouse 69). Yet, we might ask, how can it be that men both constitute themselves to protect property and that the process of constituting "founds" property? Ireton would apparently make "property" both cause and effect, eliding the question of property's legitimacy in the first place. His moment of pure assertion — "I have a property and this I shall enjoy" — fleetingly exposes the simple will-to-power that "founds" this circular logic.

What Ireton evades, as the Levellers and especially the Diggers understood, is the question of how "freely made, freely entred into" this covenant is — given initial conditions of inequality. That is, if you have some property and I have none, how "freely" do I enter into a contract with you to obtain the goods necessary for my survival? More fundamentally, why would I even agree to conceive of "ownership" as an original principle? Montesquieu will later pose the question quite pointedly: "Why should I be forced to labour for a society to which I refuse to belong? Why in spite of myself should I be held to an agreement made without my consent?"[32] Although Montesquieu supported a noble class and contributed to racialism's turn toward racism, he was honest enough to expose this economy's logic: "that one man may live delicately, a hundred must labour without intermission" (*Esprit* 107).

Ireton's tone almost of desperation and certainly of defensiveness is not surprising given that he is glimpsing both the logical extension into democracy (if not communism) of the Army's principles and furthermore the circular logic of any contract theory of the state. He scorns those who "fly for refuge [for their arguments] to an absolute natural right" which is "no right at all" because it imperils both civil rights and property. With deft but telling sophistry, he pushes the challenge to its worst-case incarnation, arguing that natural right would mean that a man "hath the same [equal] right in any goods he sees — eat, drink, clothes, to take and use them for his sustenance" (Woodhouse 58). In other words, he suggests that natural right licenses broadscale theft and anarchy.

In insisting finally that "we must keep covenant one with another when we have contracted with another," Ireton invokes a spiritual language to dignify his property argument, in the process giving early expression to the merging of materialism and religion in the Protestant ethic that Max Weber later analyzed. As David Zaret shows, the concept of covenant (like that of liberty) had been undergoing a range of appropriations and revisions throughout the early seventeenth century. The core meaning of a bond with God had been widened by ministers to include the relation between dissenting ministers and parishioners, as ministers sought to secure the loyalty of their congregations and authorize their *own* right to preach.[33] At the same time, by the middle of the century, political agitators began to characterize Parliament's actions as a violation of covenant, invoking Isaiah: 10, for instance: "Woe unto to them that decree unrighteous decrees, . . . To turn aside the needy from judgment, and to take away the right from the poor of my people" (Haller 305). In one of his pamphlets, Lilburne directly compares "our freedoms restrained" to "our Covenants slighted" (Haller 258). Working in the same vein, the Cromwellian "republic's" first real constitution is called the "National Covenant." As does the language of nativism, the spiritual language of covenant helps to suture the kingdom's "wounds" and supply a principle of unity amid the sense of upheaval created by an emergent, individualizing, and laissez-faire contract polis.

Yet even the language of covenant cannot fully calm the anxiety expressed in Ireton's confession that "there is no other foundation of right I *know*." When one debater refers to "this Oedipus riddel" and "this Gordian knot" that entangles the participants, he acknowledges the deconstruction of the origins of authority that is underway and hints at its entanglement with sexuality, which finally calls forth the romance of a covenanted nativism (Woodhouse 35). For, like Oedipus, these men must elide the origin of authority, sexual and propertied, in order to assume it for themselves. They must self-blindingly assume the place of the king.

Having just registered the political aporia faced by the debaters, this same speaker then begins to evade it when he suggests, in a conciliatory spirit, that after all the Council and the Army share the same goals (Woodhouse 35). He is, of course, right. They both have an interest in slurring over the untraceable authority for their rights and property claims. For it is true, as Lilburne insisted (in contrast to the Diggers) that many of the Army representatives sought no economic leveling. They sought a basis for accruing property—as reflected in the fact that critiques of commercial monopoly and tariffs were always a part of their "remonstrances" — and they demanded the rights of representation and commercial freedom that would support this pursuit. While the Putney Debates deserve their reputation as an event that marks a historical crossroads, as Linebaugh and Rediker understand it, for the battle between propertied and communal visions, the Diggers were not at this debate and those dissenters who were present expressed a range of political views that stopped short of democracy or communism.[34] The Diggers' communal vision probably creates the background pressure that brought Cromwell to the table at all, and against which the Army debaters' representation and property demands can appear relatively moderate; but no communal vision of a propertyless society finds expression at Putney Hall.

On the contrary, both debating parties invoked nativism to protect the property principle. First, when the Army representatives openly suggest that "every man is naturally free" (Woodhouse 61), Ireton shrewdly recalls the nativist principle. He conjures the threat of foreign control of English property as the final disastrous effect of liberty understood as a universal interior right. He argues that if a man need not have any land and so no "real or permanent interest in the kingdom" underlying his bid for representation, there is nothing to stop "a foreigner coming in amongst us — or as many as will coming in amongst us, or by force or otherwise settling themselves here" and claiming rights of representation. Tellingly, his contestants quickly reiterate that they speak only of "birthright" — that is, the rights of those born in England. And so we glimpse the pressure toward nativism that the struggle for property exerts.

At one point, the Army representatives explicitly attempt to disentangle birthright from property, observing, "There are many thousands of us soldiers that have ventured our lives; we have had little propriety in the kingdom as to our estates, yet we have had a birthright. But it seems now, except a man hath a fixed estate in this kingdom, he hath no right in this kingdom" (Woodhouse 69). And yet one can sense their concern not to seem to challenge the very idea of property, for they also assert that the principle of universal natural freedom is "the only means to preserve property" (Woodhouse 61) especially given that "[o]ur very laws were made by conquerors" (Woodhouse 65). They are working hard to retain the elements of the Anglo-Saxonist discourse that will enable their entry into the propertied order of things. Here, an incipient coupling of race and liberty work in tension and yet also in tandem to manage the question of what founds and what protects property.

Meanwhile the very event of the Putney Debates testifies to the political potential of this coupling of race and liberty. Invocations of native liberty had already enabled the accumulation of property in new hands — had in effect made possible this "putting out of papers" and this public debate in which subjects could more openly demand rights and liberties. As William Guthrie was to put it in his *New Geographical, Historical, and Commercial Grammar* (1770) which went through thirty editions and became a standard text in both England and the United States, it was "the vast increase of property through trade and navigation which enabled the English at the same time to defend their liberties."[35] And, I suggest, even to imagine them in the first place.

At the close of his important study of Saxonism, *The Goths in England,* Samuel Kliger touches on the foundational questions precipitated by the English Civil War. He suggests that "[t]he fiction of freedom and the duplicity which may underlie the grant of liberal laws were [. . .] standing exposed in the cold light of anti-Normanism" so that some revolutionaries began to ask, "Where is the source of equitable government if parliaments fail? Is Freedom only a fiction? Are liberal laws the supremely clever contrivances of tyrants?" (264–65). Certainly the question of whether freedom is only a fiction haunts the Putney Debates as well as the founding of American colonies and later the United States. But, in contrast to Kliger, I suggest that "anti-Normanism" shed a warm rather than a cold light on this question. Its racialist principle offered an origin-story for social bonds that averted the exposure of freedom as a rhetorical fiction, even as it yielded a principle for circumscribing freedom's leveling reach. It gave a romantic glow to the investment in property by nativizing and spiritualizing it, casting it as a God-given and ancient covenant.

When the Scotsman Charles Tisbet visited the United States shortly after the American Revolution, he saw a "new world . . . unfortunately composed . . . of discordant atoms, jumbled together by chance, and tossed by inconstancy in an immense vacuum"; and he concluded that the society "greatly wants a principle of attraction."[36] What Tisbet did not see — and nor could Ireton as he too conjured the specter of a "discordant" world without principles of hierarchy or attachment — was the way that the Anglo-Atlantic dissenters, founders, and entrepreneurs were fashioning race to provide exactly this principle. Ralph Waldo Emerson later celebrated the discordant world of modernity, pronouncing his "the age of severance, of dissociation, of freedom, of analysis, of detachment. Every man for himself." Yet he also noted that, under these conditions, "People grow philosophical about native land and parents and relations" (quoted in Wood, *Radicalism* 365). Emerson names the ways that the dissociative laws of a "free" modernity call forth the associative laws of nativism.

Modern nativism served to generate a mode of historicity as well as sociability, as we will see in the next chapter. For it provided a narrative, a story of ancient peoples. To put it more abstractly, insofar as the notion of race posits that characteristics are passed down through generations, it emplaces individuals in time as well as space; it yields an ontosocial situatedness spanning generations as well as oceans. Just so, very concretely, race identity had allowed a set of "new" men — who occupied a world outside the political center and far from the island of England — to redefine and reorient that center. And thereafter, the narrative of racial freedom worked, in historiography and novels, to explain dispersion and severance as effects of the forward-moving, history-making force of a native liberty. This narrative has helped to quell and contain what Amy Kaplan, following W. E. B. Du Bois, has called the anarchy of empire.[37]

In this way, the idea of racial freedom has both propelled and made mythic the "westward transatlantic movements of peoples" that Bernard Bailyn has called "one of the greatest events in recorded history."[38] "From 1500 to the present," Bailyn points out, this movement "has involved the displacement and resettlement of over fifty million people, and it has affected indirectly the lives of uncountable millions more" (5). And, as recent historians have shown, it has also provoked the peasant insurrections, slave revolts, mass riots, and radical visions of justice in the Atlantic world — whose spokespersons often share with their persecutors, however, a nativist rhetoric of liberty. In the hands of writers on both sides of the struggle, race liberty has provided the ideology that gave this massive displacement of people a past and future — that is, an English-language legacy in Atlantic modernity.

2 | Liberty's Historiography
James Harrington to Mercy Otis Warren

IN *THE PHILOSOPHY OF HISTORY*, Hegel not only articulates the liberty telos of history; he explicitly locates its vanguard in modern England. He praises the "Constitution of England" for its dialectical balancing of individual interests and general laws, which allows the "principle of Freedom" to "realize itself" (454). Hegel may well have in mind what came to be called the "Gothic balance" between people and king in the English parliamentary monarchy, formulated by the early modern historian James Harrington and touted by eighteenth-century thinkers from Jonathan Swift to Catharine Macaulay, as we will see. In Macaulay's account, England still lives by the "Gothic constitution" that "our ancestors founded . . . in which the liberty of the subject is as absolutely instituted as the dignity of the sovereign."[1] For Hegel, by way of this constitution, "Liberty" thrives because the "particular interests are . . . determined in view of that common interest," an arrangement that epitomizes for Hegel the achievement of the "German Spirit" of Protestantism. He concludes that now, "in the Protestant world . . . [t]his is the point which consciousness has attained, and these [dialectics] are the principal phases of that form in which the principle of Freedom has realized itself, — for the History of the World is nothing but the development of the Idea of Freedom" (454–56). For Hegel, history *is* the story of freedom's unfolding, driven originally by a German spirit and finding its contemporary material form in England. English-language novels craft their own versions of this race epic of freedom; they extend the work of history into the realm of the imaginary. In other words, if the way "to the novel lies through the historical study of historiography," as Robert Mayer suggests of the British novel, then the path is marked out by the liberty story that novels and histories develop together.[2]

Hegel's casting of freedom as the motor of history raises to the level of metaphysics a cultural paradigm that had long been in formation. Over a century earlier, in 1692, his theory had been anticipated in England by the editors of *State Tracts, 1660–1687*, an unprecedented collection of original government documents. Their text supports, they announce, a new kind of history: in this "enlightened era," history's proper story is no longer "of Battels and Sieges, Births, Marriages, and Deaths of Princes, which are temporary and momentary things." Rather, as they hope is evident in the documents they present, history is the story "of the Legal Government of a Nation, Struggling with Arbitrary Power and Illegal Proceedings" (quoted in Brinkley 41). In other words, history is a freedom struggle. The editors imply that the very availability of these documents — an availability enabled by the Glorious Revolution and the final uprooting of Stuart tyranny — is one gain of such a struggle, and in turn the writing of history based on these materials will enable the nation's full entry into an enlightened era of law and freedom, into true history. Opening the way to Hegel as well as to historians, these annalists implicitly fashion historiography itself as a form of participation in liberty's battle against tyranny.

Historiographers typically identify this late-seventeenth-century period as the era of modern history's birth — the moment when it openly began to reject the mode of chronicle and passed-down anecdote and instead embraced documentary research — but they pay little attention to the political tropes of liberty shaping this new form of history. Writing in 1932, Roberta Brinkley was one of the earliest students of this moment to recognize that its "study of original sources ... establish[es] the much-desired authentic past of the nation" and entails a "new conception of history," but her point can be taken further (40–41). As hinted in her phrase "much-desired authentic past," this documentary project did not so much establish an authentic past as establish and pursue a desire to unearth such a past. It successfully sought to naturalize, through historiography, a nativist liberty-myth that in 1649 had nearly been exposed as a political fiction protecting property and hierarchy. And this history writing developed a transatlantic life. As Trevor Colbourn remarks in his seminal study of the influence of Saxonist history on the American Revolution, not only in England but also in the minds of the rebellious colonists "English history had been the history of freedom."[3]

When Robert Mayer argues that we best understand the late-seventeenth-century rise of the novel in light of contemporary developments in seventeenth-century history, he focuses mainly on historical memoirs as precursors to the individualist stories of novels, similarly overlooking the content common to the memoirs and the novels. But it is this content — the story of liberty's battle with tyranny — that propels both the memoirs and the novels and that encourages the novelistic forms Mayer most emphasizes. In this chapter I establish this point, first of all, by briefly depicting the world of Anglo-Atlantic politics in the late seventeenth century, so as to clarify the conditions under which this liberty-driven historiography emerged, for it was within a vacillating, violent, and newly distended social world that modern historiography took up liberty as a narrative and genealogical principle. This principle — the very principle that undermined English hierarchies and dispersed English people — paradoxically came to bestow power and a sense of ancient community, in significant part because it was fashioned as native and racial. Recalling the volatile conditions of seventeenth-century Anglo-Atlantic history, we better appreciate the historians' achievement in transforming the rhetoric of freedom from a splintering force into a centering force. After briefly recollecting these conditions, I consider the early national histories of Britain, including those of David Hume and Catharine Macaulay; and then I turn to their counterparts in the United States, especially those of David Ramsay and Mercy Otis Warren — noting how, for the women historians, the race principle of liberty authorizes their transgressive acts of history writing. The women historians particularly display the ways that race-liberty at once licenses dissent from communal norms and establishes membership in a "native" community. Their maneuvers clarify, in turn, the means by which, as I discuss in chapter 3, literary men and women likewise come to mark out a "romantic" place for themselves, as dissidents within modernity who are simultaneously the most native voices of the culture for that very reason. With these elements in place, we can best see how novels and histories become partners in the project of narrativizing racial liberty, of institutionalizing it as a mode of story.

Liberty at Large

Early modern historians had their cohering work cut out for them, for the Civil War legacy of revolution and dissent exerted its agitating force on transatlantic England throughout the seventeenth century. In the wake of war and regicide came the repressive Protectorate, sternly policing religion, censoring the theater and all kinds of publications, and brutally suppressing any populist movement while failing to ameliorate economic hardship. Not surprisingly, then, in 1660 many English people welcomed the restoration of a Stuart king. But this apparent return to order was haunted by restive ghosts — as might be expected when the son of a beheaded father ascends the throne. Although for some it initially raised hopes that authority, order, and tradition were returning, the unpredictability and raucous sexuality of the court and culture of Charles II made it difficult to sustain this hope. Then, when Charles II's son James II took the throne, his affiliation with Catholicism threatened, in the Exclusion Crisis (1678–81), to force a replaying of Civil War issues as the Whigs worked to sidestep inherited succession. To exacerbate matters, Dutch wars were proving expensive and unprofitable while the Catholic French showed ambitions to a "universal monarchy."

At the same time, during the Restoration, "unfree" economic and religious conditions continued to stoke bottom-up, political discontent—and the precedent of the Civil War lingered in memory as a model of resistance. David Underdown argues that Monmouth's Rebellion of 1685 above all "shows how violently the civil war had intensified the politicization of many of the English people" (127).[4] It seems that the legacy of the 1640s did not die so easily, although James II did his part, for example, in pressing for the 1683 decree at Oxford (that hive of Saxonism) against all "false, seditious, and impious" books, including any "deriving civil authority from the people, upholding the idea of a contract between king and people, or supporting the right of deposition" (Brinkley 84–85). Milton's works made the list. Concerning religion, as one contemporary lamented in 1661, "The liberty of the late times gave men so much light, and diffused it so universally amongst the people . . . that the clergy aught to be very wary before they go about to impose upon [the people's] understandings, which are grown less humble than they were in former times."[5]

The same problem apparently troubled men's attempts to "impose" on women's "understandings," as late-seventeenth-century drama testifies. In these plays we see how the contract notion that in the 1640s and again in the 1680s justified Parliament's rebellion against the king circulates with the farcical force of the repressed. As the unhappily married Lady Brute in John Vanbrugh's *The Provok'd Wife* (1697) asks herself as she considers taking a lover: "Let me see — What opposes? — My matrimonial vow — Why, what did I vow? I think I promised to be true to my husband. Well; and he promis'd to be kind to me. But he han't kept his word. Why then I'm so absolved from mine. Aye that seems good to me. The argument's good between the king and the people, why not between the husband and wife?"[6] Aphra Behn puts it more succinctly in *The Younger Brother* (1696) when Olivia points out, "When parents grow arbitrary, tis time we look into our Rights and Privileges."[7] The liberty notion that gave so much light made visible the possibility of subversion in every corner.

The North Atlantic colonies proved this point most strikingly. For what Gordon Wood says of the mid-eighteenth-century United States was already evident in transatlantic discourses of dissent at the end of the seventeenth century — that "[e]very cause, even repression itself, was wrapped in the language of English liberty."[8] It's crucial to establish this point at some length so as to begin to dismantle, first of all, the pattern of American exceptionalist historiography and literary study that forgets this history whenever it takes the period of the American Revolution as the first institutionalization of the liberty discourse. Tracing these earlier phases of native liberty's political life on the Atlantic clarifies the deeply transatlantic nature of the discourse and in turn lays firmer ground for interpreting Aphra Behn's *Oroonoko* and the novels that follow it.

When the newly crowned Charles II began demanding the colonists' "entire submission and obedience" to his decrees and "strict acknowledgment of his sovereignty," the Massachusetts Assembly immediately began issuing statements "concerning our liberties."[9] In the long run, Charles II's main aim was to return the colony's government to terms originally granted by his father, Charles I, and to make null the terms under which, during the 1630s, it was allowed to become a self-governing joint-stock company. More immediately, as Charles II discovered that the Massachusetts colonists were openly trading with other European powers and "freely declar[ing] . . . that the lawes made by your Majestie and your parliament obligeth them in nothing . . . and that your Majestie ought not to retrench their liberties" (Hall et al. 19), he formulated the Navigation Acts. These decreed that "no commodities Shall be imported into or exported out of this Colony" except by ships belonging to English dominions and "whereof the Master and three fourths of the Mariners at least are English" (21). Although eventually in 1682 the Massachusetts Assembly begrudgingly supported the Acts, the House of Deputies made the symbolic gesture of writing their own version of the Acts so as to claim that they were instituting them for themselves rather than by decree from the king (19–20).

In 1683 when Charles demanded that Massachusetts surrender its charter for revision, for the first time the official government openly defied the king. Here again, Puritanism and mercantilism came together under the banner of ancient English liberties to resist the throne — foreshadowing and preparing the rhetoric of the American Revolution. In a nice emulation of Oliver Cromwell's rhetorical maneuvers, Increase Mather argued that the colonies "could not without sin make such a Resignation" because "God forbid that I should give away the Inheritance of my Fathers" (Hall et al. 23–24). Mather chastises the other American colonies (which had closer ties to the crown) for giving in to royal pressures, arguing that as godly men they should have "abode by their liberties longer" (24). But in fact both New York and Maryland raised open objections to Restoration policies, including a series of insurrections against Lord Baltimore's nepotism and Catholic favoritism, and loud challenges to Governor Andros's violations of "free government and our ancient libertyes" (Hall et al. 143, 127). At this juncture,

English identity began to split into the colonial and the metropolitan, and each side aimed to affiliate with the true native tradition in order to stake its claim within the empire.

Indeed, throughout these years, both the monarchy and the colonies bandied the rhetoric of native liberty in protection of rights, and ironically it was the monarch's men who galvanized it, although self-servingly, on behalf of American Indians and slaves — as they would later do again during the American Revolution. Just as Thomas Jefferson would complain in that liberty document, the Declaration of Independence, that the king had attempted to arm and offer freedom to the slaves against the revolutionary colonists, so earlier the Massachusetts colonists had complained of the way the king's men trampled on *colonists'* liberties when they "release[d] and [set] at liberty sundry Indians that were in hold, some of them known enemies to the English," for the colonists considered their landholdings as "honestly purchased from [the Natives]" (Hall et al. 36; 33 – 34). Sir Edmund Andros, the man Charles II made governor of Massachusetts when he revoked the colony's charter, and who was of course deeply resented by the Boston leaders, further provoked their ire by siding with the Indians in land and legal disputes and speaking the language of liberty to do so. Repeatedly, the monarchy and its colonial bureaucracy in this way played Native Americans and African Americans against the colonial leaders, who monopolized land and trading rights and resisted the monarchy's taxes and trade restrictions.

Additionally, the king's men used liberty rhetoric to play less powerful English colonists against the colonial elite and entrepreneurs. Thus one of Charles II's royal commissioners to New England took up the cause of the people of New Hampshire, who complained of the "oppression and usurpation of the magistrates of Boston" for excluding them from office (and therefore power and wealth) because they were not members of Puritan congregations. Likewise, in the New York colony, the citizens of Albany resented the leaders in New York City who attempted to monopolize trade with the Indians and exclude the citizens of Albany, leading those citizens to proclaim — ridiculously — that it "is the ancient privilege of the inhabitants of this city to trade overseas" (Hall et al. 87). These manipulations would later be repeated in Southerners' use of liberty rhetoric to condemn all attempts to prohibit slavery. Thus do we see that an earlier era had laid the precedent for the eighteenth-century American Revolution as well as for the pro-slavery discourse in which "even repression itself was wrapped in the language of English liberty" (Wood 13).

The Glorious Revolution temporarily eased the emergent split between colony and metropole, yet this turn of events, too, was glossed within the nativist liberty discourse. A transatlantic English birthright seemed to be restored by it.

Celebrating the accession of William and Mary and enumerating what they suffered under the Stuarts, whose "Illegal Subversion of our Ancient Government" amounted to a "Treasonable Invasion" of the rights of "every true English-man" (Hall et al. 48), colonists announced themselves grateful to his Majestie for "restoring to them the undoubted Rights and Privileges of Englishemen . . . soe necessary and soe much esteemed by our Ancestors" (Hall et al. 121). In reviewing Stuart crimes, "The Boston Declaration of Grievances" explained how "we have been treated with Multiplied Contradictions to Magna Charta, the rights of which we laid claim unto" (Hall et al. 43). As Samuel Mather later narrated events: "It was in April [1689] when we had news by the Edges concerning a Descent made upon England by the Prince of Orange for the rescue of the nation from Slavery and Popery; Then a strange Disposition entred the Body of our People to assert our Liberties against the Arbitrary Rulers that were fleecing them" (Hall et al. 39). Thus did the old rhetoric continue to find new confirmation — even as it also found new grievances of which to complain. For within a few years the colonists felt equally "fleeced" by the new monarchy, and so once again they would overcome their differences to rally around their "auncient priviledges," as Increase Mather put it in his later appeal to the crown (Hall et al. 76). As Michael Hall argues, although in the course of these many disputes colonial government became regularized into a form that combined representative assembly with monarchical control through royal governors, this rallying of colonists around shared interests and a shared language of dissent laid the basis for intracolonial coalitions and, in turn, for the American Revolution.

The American "founders," that is, took up *this* well-established Saxonist rhetoric of liberty. They spoke continually of the "constitutional rights inherited from their Saxon ancestors," an affiliation epitomized in the bestowing of the name "Alfred" on their first revolutionary warship, in honor of the first Anglo-Saxon king (Colbourn, 147, 100). As we will see, when later Americans came to write national histories and fashion literary genealogies, they likewise were guided by this notion of free Anglo-Saxons making history.

The Gothic Balancing Act of British National History

In England, national history writing from the beginning tapped the rhetoric of native liberty to create a coherent story for the nation — to fashion continuity out of rupture. Paradoxically, at the turn into the eighteenth century, historians often understood themselves to be in a pitched partisan battle between Whigs and Tories (and so have later histories of their writing understood them to be), but they were simultaneously developing a shared ethos. On one hand, the histories of England that began to proliferate in this period, often funded by Whig or Tory "societies" for the writing of history, were indeed partisan and polemical, and they took opposing views of the sins of king and Parliament in the seventeenth century. Consistently, their main focus and their sharpest points of contention were the early Stuart era and the English Revolution, with Whigs condemning the Stuarts, and Tories the regicides. As Laird Okie notes, "The upheaval of the Stuart era engendered continuous historical debate in Hanoverian England" (Okie 2).

Yet, on the other hand, on close reading it becomes clear that all these histories narrate English history as a liberty story, a point overlooked by later scholars of these works. These early modern histories transformed liberty's threatening centrifugal, colonial effects into a centripetal, "modern" magnet. And in the more ambitious, multivolume works, historians implicitly narrated their texts as "manifestations" and culminations of this modern freedom-seeking history.

That is, whether these histories bemoan or justify the fate of Charles I, whether (accordingly) they celebrate the Britons or the Saxons, and whether they see the king or Parliament as protector of the inherited English birthright, they subscribe to liberty as the principle at stake in history. In Whig histories, the Saxons received high praise for their parliamentary legacy, while in more royalist histories, the Britons and the legends of Arthur and Brutus were celebrated for their heroic tradition of independence. But the fact is that the Britons were increasingly honored for the most part only insofar as they, too, could be said to have held councils or shown a spirit of freedom, as we'll see is the case in Hume. This implicit settling on a common idea was reinforced by the consolidation of English sea power, the Act of Settlement (1701), and the Union with Scotland.

In other words, the polemics themselves, and the contest for control of English government, reflected new degrees of wealth and consolidation of power across differences, including the ability to sustain an uncensored, commercial press championing liberty. We might say, then, that the first half-century of modern history writing in England polishes the narrative "Englishing" of liberty that the 1640s had begun. Significantly, it does so by the practice of documentation — the print logo-centering of liberty — that the Reformation and later antiquarian lawyers had initiated, and that was indeed renewed through the resurrected Society of Antiquaries in the first two decades of the eighteenth century. These histories were fed by both the late-seventeenth-century "profluvium of Saxonists" at Oxford (quoted in Adams 75–76) that included George Hickes, Edward Thwaites, and William and Elizabeth Elstob, and the "profusion of documentary collections" of parliamentary debates, diplomatic conventions, and treaties, put in print for the first time (Okie 17). The various "natural histories" and ethnographies of the New World together with colonial histories documenting their economies and their governments further swelled the momentum of historical writing, all under the banner of liberty.

By the middle of the eighteenth century, the compromise-ideal embraced by writers across the political spectrum regarding the British historical legacy was that of the "Gothic balance" in Britain's constitution, a distorted version of an idea borrowed from one of the first histories of the revolutionary era, James Harrington's *Oceana* (1656). Harrington crucially, if unintentionally, helped to create the notion of a balanced monarchy as the true English legacy of liberty, and he was taken to offer a genealogy for that tradition beginning with the "Gothic" Saxons. Although for Harrington, the "Gothic balance" in government introduced by the "Teutons" was irrevocably undone by the redistributions of land under Henry VII and Henry VIII, so that in his view the balance was a thing of the past, the idea had deep appeal as a compromise-formation that gave the English parliamentary government historical authority while also limiting the sway of both king and people.

Yet Harrington did provide the terms for this genealogy of English parliamentary tradition, including its legal basis. In Harrington's account, the Goths ("deriving their roots from the northern parts of Germany") effected the "transition of ancient into modern prudence" by way of "*feudum* [. . .] a Gothic word of diverse signification" but involving "lands, distributed by the victor unto such of his captains and soldiers as had merited in his wars, upon condition to acknowledge him to be their perpetual lord."[10] This land distribution created "three kinds or orders," each one beholden both to the king and to the preceding order. "And this" Harrington says, "is the gothic balance, by which all kingdoms this day in Christendom were at first erected" (*Oceana* 47). Thus Harrington puts Gothicism in place as a point of legal, proto-contractual origin for Anglo-Protestant kingdoms.

Harrington goes on to conclude that in England this balance was superseded by a wider distribution of property through the Commons and the mercantile class, but others from Sidney to Thomas Jefferson ignored this point and developed the Gothic balance as a present and future ideal—although in *Common Sense* the more unruly Thomas Paine rejects exactly this "Gothic balance" as too conservative, too likely to serve a "race of Kings."[11] Harrington's friend Henry Neville first popularized the idea, explaining in *Plato Redivivus* (1681) that "Limited Monarchies" were "first introduced by the Goths, and other Northern People" (quoted in Kliger 175). Algernon Sidney further disseminated the idea of a "Gothic polity" in his *Discourses Concerning Government* (1698), which of course had a powerful influence on the organizers of the American Revolution. He notes that the Britons were "a fierce people, zealous for liberty" but, more important, the Saxons "from whom we chiefly derive our original and manners, were no less lovers of liberty, and better understood the ways of defending it."[12] Sidney describes the "Gothic polity" as a combination of "king, lords, commons, dyets, assemblies of states, cortex, and parliaments" and deems it, as was becoming commonplace, the source of "our original and government" (477, 376). In particular, "the Saxons, coming into our country, retained to themselves the same rights" for they had "no kings but such as were set up by themselves, and they abrogated their power when they pleased" (376). Sidney finally concludes that no matter which lineage one emphasizes, it is clear that "our ancestors were perfectly free" (513). Via the idea of liberty, it became possible to reintegrate the Briton lineage into English history while also promoting the Gothic lineage to special prominence.

Sidney's language continued to surface in pamphlets and histories throughout the century. A decade later, the anonymous pamphlet *Vox Populi, Vox Dei* (1709), reissued ten times in the course of the eighteenth century, including to great effect in the American colonies just before their revolution, repeats Sidney's words: "The Saxons, or Angli, were no less Lovers of Liberty and understood the Ways of defending it" (quoted in Kliger 202). Despite his conservative political views, the same idea finds expression in Jonathan Swift, who echoes Sidney in his "Abstract of the History of England" (1719) when speaking of the "great councils" held by the "Saxon princes who first introduced them into this island, from the same original with the other Gothic forms of government" and then goes on to consider the perils of "the destruction of the Gothic balance" in governments.[13] Certainly by this second decade of the eighteenth century, the notion of a Gothic balance in English government was becoming a cliché, as Addison hints in a 1716 *Freeholder* essay when he refers to "an old Justice of the peace who [. . .] will talk to you from Morning till Night on the Gothic Balance" (quoted in Kliger 203).

Among political players, Lord Bolingbroke's Country-Tory platform, integrating a "Whig" emphasis on Saxon principles into a Tory position, best exemplifies the infusion of Saxonism across the wide stream of English politics and the use of a liberty language to bridge factionalism. Apparently Bolingbroke understood what David Hume more explicitly articulated in "Of the Parties in Great Britain," where Hume argued that, in order to succeed, the Tories needed to use "the language of their adversaries" and speak "in the republican stile."[14] Bolingbroke's historical analysis integrated into one vision Harrington's attention to landed wealth and economics, Rapin's framework of political parties and factions, *and* a Saxonist emphasis on liberty: "Though the Saxons submitted to the yoke of Rome, in matters of religion, they were far from giving up the freedom of their Gothic institutions of government" (quoted in Kliger 20). The Glorious Revolution, Bolingbroke argued, had achieved a reclamation of those liberties descended from the Anglo-Saxons, but those liberties were now under threat again as landed wealth lost its authority and the corrupt government of Walpole bred factionalism. In according Saxonism a settled place of honor in his Country-Tory formulations, Bolingbroke made it palatable in all manner of history thereafter.

Meanwhile, by this time national history writing was becoming an institution, itself manifesting the "Gothic balance" in its relatively nonpartisan and broad perspective — best displayed in the epic, multivolume works of Paul de Rapin-Thoyras, David Hume, and Catharine Macaulay in England (all of them published and influential in America as well), and, in the United States, David Ramsay and Mercy Otis Warren. These historical works played a powerful role in forming British and later American communities around the Saxonist idea of liberty. Not only do they make liberty the *theme* of Anglo-Atlantic history but also, in their very form — and especially their serialized, multivolume publication — they help to create a reading community organized around that theme. Hinting at this performative, culture-building function of history, Hume implicitly traces the documentary impulse underlying his history back to the Saxons, while Macaulay and Warren emphasize liberty as an interior principle of dissent and they explain their own boldness as women historians by way of it.

Rapin's *Histoire d'Angleterre* (published in English 1721 – 31) opened the way to these later works.[15] Once translated, Rapin's *History* was read remarkably widely by all kinds of English-language readers on both sides of the Atlantic (Jefferson read it in his father's library), and indeed, for a decade he became "cited and quoted more than any other historian" (Okie 62). His work reached both the intelligentsia and the lay literate public as it provoked much of the "historical debate conducted in party newspapers during the 1730's" and finally emerged as one of "the most popular scholarly works of the century" among the general public (Okie 52). Reports had it that as many as fifteen thousand copies of each volume were in print by 1732 (Okie 57 – 62). Rapin's work gained immediate respect for its relatively balanced account of England's revolutionary history. Here was a history that didn't simply align itself with Tory or Whig; it endeavored to explain the rise of these parties and of factionalism in English society and so offered British readers a basis for self-reflexivity about their history. At the same time (although he designated a late, post – Anglo-Saxon origin for the House of Commons), Rapin invoked Tacitus's *Germania* and identified the Anglo-Saxons as the descendants of those fierce yet assembly-holding German tribes, thus putting in place the Germanic, Tacitean element that would appear in many Anglo-Atlantic histories to come (Okie 57; Colbourn 27).

Yet I suggest that what Rapin's incredibly popular work generated above all was a newly dramatic, transatlantic experience of history, via print, which in turn helped to create a shared, interiorized Saxonist identity; and it is this internally and historically rooted Saxonist identity that became so influential in shaping the modern/colonial Atlantic order. The serial multivolume *form* of this history's content was crucial, for first of all it introduced a method that encouraged a broader base of buyers. Rather than being announced, published, and then slowly fading from center stage, this serial work remained alive over a period of ten years (in the case of the English translation), with new installments and new occasions for subscription and advertisement. The popularity of Rapin's *History* demonstrated the commercial potential of serial publication and in turn encouraged the continuous publication of such histories from his day to ours.

Second, this serial form also helped to install a new readerly simultaneity — crucially organized around a story of liberty that was consistently rendered as Saxon or Gothic in origin. That is, from the serial yet communally simultaneous reading of national history there emerged the kind of imagined community Benedict Anderson discusses in relation to novels and newspapers, and yet in the case of serial histories it had a powerful diachronic aspect. Reading became something lived over time, and suspensefully, with others. Moreover, in a serial *history*, in particular, the reading community's sense of living in historical time would have been mirrored in and enhanced by the historical events narrated in the history. In the act of reading, citizens would experience themselves and their historically authorized native kinship *as* historical, in this way proudly entering the epic story of freedom, through race, and through print.

Thus Rapin's *History* begins to reveal the ways that the private, interior event of reading could newly emplace Anglo-Atlantic subjects in a public, racial history. The combination of diachronic longevity and synchronic reach in the readership would reinforce the experience of group suspense and group identification at the same time that it countered readers' geographical distension and economic isolation (not unlike television serials today). This epic and transatlantic seriality could begin to resolve the paradox whereby independence, distant colonial wealth, and liberty formed the basis of community. Readers could experience their dispersed independence from each other *together*. This is an effect to which the early novels of Behn, Haywood, Manley, and Defoe also aspired, and that Fielding and Richardson, under the tutelage of historians, extended into an epic form of fiction.

Hume's multivolume *History of England* continued this centering accretion of Saxonism, despite Hume's Royalist sympathies. At first slow to sell, by the time that all of the volumes of Hume's *History* (1754–62) appeared, it had become "the most popular history of England ever written" (Okie 195), outrunning Rapin's. And liberty operates as a key word, perhaps the key word, in Hume's *History*.

While Rapin's *History* is widely accepted as moderately "Whig" in orientation (that is, Saxon- and Parliament-sympathetic), Hume's is most often cast as conservative, so a good look at its Saxonist liberty discourse is in order.

Although for Thomas Jefferson's Tacitean sympathies, Hume's moderating liberty vision was too tame, Hume quietly wrote his own version of the Saxon myth. At first glance, Hume *seems* to diminish the Saxonist influence by referring to the Britons' "relish for liberty" and averring that "[t]heir governments, though monarchical, were free, as well as those of the Celtic nations" for "the common people seemed to have enjoyed more liberty among them than among the nations of Gaul."[16] (This emphasis was perhaps influenced as well by his Scottish identity, although he is later utterly racist about the Irish and none too easy on the Scots.) Yet in fact Hume adapts his account of the Britons to the terms of the Anglo-Saxon ideal of liberty. Indeed, he shortly denigrates the Britons for their weakening devotion to liberty, and in the process he helps to fashion what would become a standard account of how the Britons became "an enervated race" (1:9) with "effeminate," slavish habits under the Romans.

Hume proceeds to praise the Saxons much more highly, for they descended from the Germans, who "seem to have been the most distinguished both by their manners and political institutions, and to have carried to the highest pitch the virtues of valour and love of liberty" (1:14). The Anglo-Saxons' "manners and customs were wholly German" and they displayed "a fierce and bold liberty [which] gave rise to those mutual jealousies between them and the Normans" (1:141). He deems the Anglo-Saxon state "one of the freest nations of which there remains any account in the records of history" (quoted in Okie 175), though he qualifies his praise by insisting that any state of freedom was, at first, offset by the barbarism of the age and by the time of the Norman Conquest was eroded by the elitism of the landed. These Anglo-Saxons also embraced Christianity, establishing the "Independence of English churches" (1:53), and, under Alfred, developed institutions of learning. In one of his appendices, Hume explains further that "[t]he government of the Germans, and that of all Northern nations, who established themselves in the ruins of Rome, was always extremely free" (1:appendix I).

And it is this superior liberty legacy that Anglo-European nations have inherited: "The free constitutions then established, however impaired by the encroachments of succeeding princes, still preserve an air of independence and legal administration, which distinguish European nations, and if that part of the globe maintain sentiments of liberty, honour, equity, and valour, superior to the rest of mankind, it owes these advantages to the seeds implanted by those generous barbarians" (1:appendix I). This is the same emergent-imperial story that Humes's contemporary, James Thomson, versified in his poem *Liberty*, [17] and that Edward

Gibbon later and more boldly fashioned as the Goths' gift to all nations when he wrote that "the invincible Goths . . . issued in numerous swarms from the neighborhood of the Polar circle, to chastise the oppressors of mankind."[18] The key moment for these early British historians, when their Royalist or republican sympathies most register, is always the period of Stuart crisis in the first half of the seventeenth century. When Hume arrives at this moment, he explicitly characterizes it as a struggle over liberty. Following Bolingbroke and others, Hume has learned to appropriate the discourse. Thus he can say that those who stayed loyal to Charles I in the 1640s "breathed the spirit of liberty" (5:124) for they wished fervently to "restore [the king] to liberty" (5:255), while the Parliament's excessive "zeal for liberty" (5:50) unfortunately led to Cromwell's attempt "by arbitrary power to establish liberty" (5:255). Thus does Hume display his own ability to speak "in the republican stile." And his widely read work further fostered the growth of a transatlantic community that turned a legacy of acrimony into a legacy of liberty.

Perhaps Hume's most shrewd and important contribution is his equation not only between history and liberty but also between historiography and liberty — or between the preservation of "records" and the free state. And here, too, in Hume's account the Saxons take pride of place over the Britons. In turn Hume's written history takes *its* place as part of the Anglo-Saxon legacy. Early in his first volume, one of his hardest blows to the Briton origin-myth accompanies an implicit privileging of historical records, which are lacking for the Britons. On his opening page, he announces that he considers all information passed down merely through oral tradition to be beyond the bounds of proper history and open to questions about its veracity. Accordingly, he puts in doubt the existence of Arthur, a central figure of heroic claims about the Britons, due to the lack of supporting written records. Mentioning that the Britons are said to have enlisted the help of Arthur in their battles with the Romans, Hume remarks, "This is that Arthur so much celebrated in the songs of Thaliessin . . . and whose military achievements have been blended with so many fables, as even to give occasion for entertaining a doubt of his real existence" (1:21). Hume thus subordinates the merely legendary Briton genealogy and implicitly places the Saxons at the origin of English history "proper." Despite his Tory leanings, in his role as public historian-scribe Hume affiliates himself within the lineage of the Anglo-Saxons. The turn to Saxonist documentation as the basis of authority begun in the Reformation and irrevocably made central in the 1640s Revolution has come full circle here, in an act of documentation that considers documentation a heroic Saxon act.[19]

In her eight-volume *History of England from the Accession of James I* (1765 – 83), Catharine Macaulay differently makes her work an embodiment of native liberty.

It is not just that she takes an unapologetically Whig position on the "pretensions" of Stuarts (preface ix). Rather Macaulay's distinctive contribution is her rhetorical interiorization of the liberty legacy, which she naturalizes and racializes in part by way of an organic imagery of roots and soil. After explaining in her preface that she aims to tell the story of "the exalted patriots" who "attacked the pretensions of the Stewart [sic] family, and set up the banner of Liberty" (viii-ix), she remarks that these struggles reveal how "noble principles had taken deep root in the minds of the English people" for these were principles that "the people had preserved from the ruins of the Gothic constitution" which "had in it many latent resources to preserve Liberty" (273). This notion that liberty takes "deep root" in the people carries an echo of the eighteenth-century racial theory that equated a people and their climate, and Macaulay joins it here with the more political vocabulary of the "Gothic constitution," suggesting an interior, natural source for the workings of the English polis. Her formulation gives a bucolic cast to the dream of alignment between conscience and contract, soul and state, which was more sternly and urgently expressed in the Putney Debates. Macaulay is working out a new, romantic language by which liberty can suture the very wounds it opened between person and polity as well as past and present.

Macaulay also embellishes the organicism of this native story of inheritance with the language of sensibility — of excited hearts and imaginations — which by the middle of the eighteenth century had begun to characterize the nativist attitude toward liberty and to complete its interior turn. In Macaulay, the vocabulary of sensibility both propels and authorizes her history; as does Hume, she implicitly makes a self-reflexive move in which her writing itself displays the sensibility it historicizes. Naming "love of freedom" as the source of her inspiration for undertaking this history, she explains that she had from "early youth . . . read with delight those histories that exhibit Liberty in its most exalted state, the annals of the Roman and the Greek republics" and that "Liberty became the object of a secondary worship in my delighted imagination" (vii). Her "delighted imagination" loves to ponder an exalted Liberty and to read books that "excite the natural love of Freedom which lies latent in the breast of every rational being" (ix). And so, she modestly concludes in her preface, even "if the goodness of my head may be justly questioned [on the basis of any flaws in the book], my heart will stand the test of the most critical examination" (ix). Delight, exalt; breast, heart: these emotional states and parts are the interior channels through which the history of liberty flows.

Macaulay mingles her organic and nativist language with an apparently universalist conception of liberty — "the natural love of Freedom which lies latent in the breast of every rational being." Yet her comments, like those of many of her contemporaries, leave room for the implication that the English propensity for liberty and freedom exceeds that of others — others in whom it may be "stifled by prejudice," as Macaulay goes on to say. For such prejudice also signals the lack of that "rationality" that Macaulay implicitly makes a condition of liberty, which inhabits the breast of "every *rational* being." Clearly, this leaves open the possibility that irrational or less rational others will be incapable of true liberty.

This possibility appears a bit more clearly in Macaulay's remarks on the role of history in education, and in accordance with her attempt to balance rational education with organic inheritance. She begins her *History* by advocating a program of history reading that will "cultivate" in future generations the English "birthright" of liberty (xv). As with her reference to the "deep roots" of liberty in the English "mind," Macaulay implies that the seeds of liberty are planted in English breasts and minds, yet need cultivation through reading. She laments the fact that "the study of history is little cultivated . . . , and not at all those fundamental principles of the English constitution on which our ancestors founded a system of government, in which the liberty of the subject is as absolutely instituted as the dignity of the sovereign" (xv). Instead, she complains, the English send their youth on tours of the Continent, which she considers the "finishing stroke that renders [these youth] useless to all the good purposes of preserving the birthright of an Englishman" (xv). Thus "English youth" are inadequately educated to any "inward principle of love to their country and of public Liberty" (xv). In this critique, "public liberty" is at once an "inward" principle and a public project that must be "instituted." It is natural and yet needs "cultivation" by the study — and we might add, the writing — of history, especially in the face of unfree, foreign influences. In these ways, throughout Macaulay's discussion, history and body become organically interlocked: the race-d interior becomes the seed of the national community.

Catharine Macaulay particularly needed to tap into this interiorized, racial conception, for she was a woman writing history. She was quite conscious of her transgression in undertaking this project, as her references to her "sex" show (x; xviii). In the most prominent instance, after speaking of her conscientiousness in fulfilling her "duties" as a "historian" obligated to give "facts" and "just information," she comments: "The invidious censures which may ensue from striking into a path of literature rarely trodden by my sex, will not permit a selfish consideration to keep me mute in the cause of Liberty and Virtue" (x). What lovely sophistry: her private interest as a woman will not stand in the way of her public duty to liberty. Some might say, of course, that it is her public duty as a woman to remain a private woman quietly protecting a private virtue. But in her account, her very enthusiasm for liberty, her delighted imagination, her freedom-loving breast, her *English inheritance of this sensibility* impels this transgressive movement. Reenacting the logic inscribed in Cromwell's Commonwealth Seal (of "freedom *restor'd*"), in which revolution is recast as recovery of ancient precedent, Macaulay can claim that loyalty to ancient principles of liberty underwrites her gender transgression. Liberty lifts her across the gendered divide between private and public, as an organic rhetoric can naturalize culture. Macaulay's move became paradigmatic: as we will see, it was repeated by Anglo-American women historians as well as in the transatlantic sagas of heroines who pursue freedom by associating themselves with an ancient and superior freedom-loving race.[20]

Mirroring the Myth in America: Early U.S. National Histories

In an odd way, American colonists were the first British documentary historians, or at least the colonies encouraged a documentary practice in the service of religious and economic freedom. The earliest settlers wrote primary-source histories, such as Captain John Smith's *Generall Historie of Virginia, New-England, and Summer Isles* (1624) and William Bradford's religiously framed but nonetheless documentary *History of Plymouth Plantation* (1630 – 48). With an aim to draw royal support, investors, or new emigrants, these first histories were partly reports back to England meant to justify and sell the project of colonization, so they included dates, cargo and population numbers, letters of arrangement, terms of contracts, and treaties with Indian tribes; and they were proto-ethnographies, describing the animals, plants, climate, and Indian people of the eastern seaboard.[21]

They are also laced with the language of liberty, whether religious or economic, and sometimes both. In his *History of Plymouth Plantation,* Bradford explains that the New England colonists emigrated so as "to injoye the liberties of the Gospell in puritie with peace,"[22] and Smith, in his colonial writings, argued for a wide freeholder system in the colonies, because "no man will go from hence to have less freedom than here," and he wanted to be able to claim that "[h]ere are no landlords to rack us with high rents, or extorting fines, nor tedious pleas in law."[23] Thomas Hutchinson later confirmed that even in the pious New-England colonies "a fondness for free-holds to transmit to posterity . . . excited so many of the first planters of America."[24]

Yet it is not until the eighteenth century that the language of liberty finds full expression in American histories — and indeed begins to be projected backward on to the settlement period, making liberty the colonists' primary ambition. By the time Macaulay's *History* began to appear (1763), writers across the Atlantic were busily publishing histories of individual colonies that championed their long-standing protection of "*English* Liberty" and "native Right" through the "*English* Form of Government,"[25] such as William Stith's *The History of the First Discovery and Settlement of Virginia* (1747) and William Smith's *The History of the Province of New York* (1757), a language that Jeremy Belknap also developed in his later *History of New Hampshire* (1784–92). Historical arguments circulated back and forth across the Atlantic as regularly as people and goods. These colonial histories wrote back, in effect, to the metropole, "echoing the language we have heard you speak," as John Adams would later write to friends in England in defense of the American revolutionaries (Colbourn 96).

The leading organizers of the American Revolution of course all knew their English history and registered its influence on their thinking, leading H. Trevor Colbourn to conclude that histories of England came to serve as a "mainspring of action" for the Revolution (8). Works of history, especially English history, dominated most library collections, both private and public — and among these, Whig histories were the most popular (Colbourn 10–11). History reading was touted as the guide to enlightened action by men ranging from John Adams, who repeatedly stressed that knowledge and especially historical knowledge was "the road to freedom," to the more democratic thinker Benjamin Franklin, fond of more homely historical analogies — for instance that "Britain was formerly the America of the Germans" and no more than those migrating Germans do "British subjects, by removing into America, . . . lose their native rights" (Colbourn 89; 129–30). Depending on their political leanings, each man had his favorite: Adams admired Bolingbroke's balancing of Tory and Whig principles; Jefferson averred that "as yet no general history [is] so faithful" as Rapin's;[26] and George Washington and Benjamin Franklin favored Macaulay's less derivative, truly documentary *History,* which was generally recognized as the most republican in spirit (Colbourn 87, 127, 153). After the Revolution, like many others, Jefferson recommended that history (as well as the Anglo-Saxon language, one of his own favorite subjects) become a fundamental element of the national school curriculum, for "the study of history will render the people the best protectors of their liberty" (Jefferson 668). His recommended reading list for the University of Virginia included "the Whig historians of England . . . [who] have always gone back to the Saxon period for the true principles of their constitution" (Jefferson 1096) and the ubiquitously cited Tacitus, whom Jefferson calls "[t]he first writer in the world without exception" (quoted in Colbourn 26). This advocacy of history soon issued in "American" national histories.

David Ramsay's *The History of the American Revolution* (1789) and Mercy Otis Warren's *History of the Rise, Progress, and Termination of the American Revolution* (1805) were among the first postrevolutionary histories of the United States.

They can serve briefly here to indicate how, by the turn into the nineteenth century, history was being generated within the racialized frame of the liberty story on the western as well as the eastern side of the Atlantic. Ramsay announces, "The English colonies were from their first settlement in America, devoted to liberty, on English ideas, and English principles. They not only conceived themselves to inherit the privileges of Englishmen, but though in a colonial situation, actually possessed them."[27] He references the early Reformation origins of the Saxon myth in narrating how the Puritans left England to escape persecution and to "have an opportunity without interruption of handing down to future ages the model of a pure church, free from the admixture of human additions" (1:7). Their religious beliefs made them "favourable to liberty, and hostile to all undue exercise of authority" (1:9) since, as he reminds his readers, "They were chiefly Protestants and all Protestantism is founded on a strong claim to liberty, and the right of private judgment" (1:29). Although there were not "yet any well-balanced constitutions in the early periods of colonial history" among New Englanders, "[a] spirit of liberty prompted their industry, and a free constitution their civil right'" (1:17, 20 – 21). In the South too there flourished a "warm love for liberty," in part because the high profits and abundant wealth together with the institution of slavery made the inhabitants "proud and jealous of their freedom" (1:26, 30). Ramsay rejects slavery for the way it affects morals and industry, but in an aside that reinforces the racialization of the freedom legacy, he reports that "Negroes who have been born and bred are so well-satisfied with their condition, that several have been known to reject proffered freedom" — a response that presumably would not occur in a race whose "spirit of liberty" would naturally scoff at such a rejection (1:24).

Like Macaulay, Ramsay draws on the language of heart and sentiment to fashion this liberty spirit as an irresistible internal force precipitating the American Revolution. After the British Parliament's closing of the Boston port, he explains, "a patriotic flame, created and diffused by the contagion of sympathy, was communicated to so many breasts, and reflected from such a variety of objects, as to become too intense to be resisted" (1:122). He later casts this interiorization in more sober, political terms in the course of explaining, in a fascinating formulation, how the Revolution changed people from "subjects to citizens": "a citizen is a unit of a mass of free people, who, collectively, possess sovereignty . . . [and] none have hereditary rights superior to others" so that "[e]ach citizen of a free state contains, *within himself, by nature and the constitution,* as much of the common sovereignty as another" (quoted in Wood, *Radicalism* 169; emphasis added). Although Ramsay eschews hereditary right as a stratifying element with*in* this community, he meanwhile conflates several vocabularies — of sentiment, of nature, and of constitution — to consolidate the special legacy of an Anglo-Atlantic liberty, which assumes a stratifying hierarchy of peoples.

Not surprisingly, then, like Hume and Macaulay, Ramsay emphasizes the importance of reading and writing — of print culture — in the growth of a liberty culture. In accordance with the emergent association of literacy with Anglo-Saxon liberty (an association to which I'll return in chapter 3), Ramsay highlights that, from the beginning, the reach of print combined with geographic distance from authorities in England to "generate ideas in the minds of the Colonists favourable to liberty" (1:29), and so by 1776, "[i]n establishing American independence, the pen and the press had merit equal to that of the sword" (2:319). He concludes that "[a]s literature had in the first instance favoured the revolution, so in its turn, the revolution promoted literature" (2:321). Thus Ramsay, too, positions print culture, of which his own work is part, as central to this history of liberty.

Like Ramsay, Mercy Otis Warren casts colonization as a struggle for liberty that distinguishes the Anglo-Atlantic settlers. She begins with an account of the Puritans, who were persecuted by "the tyranny of the Stuart race," and she even more emphatically states that they left England "not as adventurers for wealth or fame, but for the quiet enjoyment of religion and liberty."[28] She dismisses the role of the Virginia colony (which she says at this stage "scarcely deserved the appellation of a regular colony" [1:10]) and so overlooks the economic substructure of colonization and the crucial support of Virginia men which, as I discussed in chapter 1, made the Puritan colony viable. Also like Ramsay, she critiques both slavery and the initial stealing of land from Indians but quickly passes over these events and later makes denigrating comments about, for instance, the "fierce hordes" that the Puritans faced (1:251).[29]

Invoking the soil and growth metaphors that Macaulay had used, and which by 1804 carried clear racial associations, Warner urges her (predominantly New England) readers to "look back with due gratitude and respect on the fortitude and virtue of their ancestors who . . . planted them in a happy soil" (1:4). She proceeds to explain that the colonists did all they could to avoid revolution, for they were "strongly attached to Great Britain, not only by the impression of ancient forms, but by religion, manners, language, and consanguinuity" (1:99). Yet in the New World they faced "a yoke unknown to their fathers," and so they revolted. Their "hereditary love of freedom," their "manly spirit of freedom" led them to organize with other colonies and finally go to war (1:109). In accord with Ramsay and in a distinct echo of Macaulay, Warren stresses the interior desires that "ought equally to glow in every human breast" as the source of both liberty and histories of liberty (1:iv). Soil, ancestors, heredity, manly spirit, and breasts that shine forth a will to liberty—all of these led to "American freedom" (1:47). The psychological framework of her overall historical analysis, which she lays out in her opening chapter, sets up this implication: she frames her history as a "study of human character" in which a "noble principle implanted in the nature of man" must grapple with "tyranny," "the wanton exercise of arbitrary sway," and those "turbulent passions [that have] depopulated cities" (1:2–3).

Warren herself embodies the workings of this noble principle, for the flame in her breast, her commitment to liberty, leads her, as it did Macaulay, to overcome her "trembling heart" in the face of her transgression as a woman historian —since, she concedes, "there are certain appropriate duties assigned to each sex" (1:iv). She, too, dramatizes the way in which interior dissent overrides exterior prohibitions and so this interior dictates new laws for the polis, in the tradition of both Macaulay and the women protestors of the 1640s. Yet Warren's use of the passive voice and synechdochal self-reference hint at the contortions required to make this claim: "the trembling heart," she says in referring to her decision to write, "has recoiled at the magnitude of the undertaking, and the hand often shrunk back from the task, yet recollecting that every domestic enjoyment depends on the unimpaired possession of civil and religious liberty, . . . the work was not relinquished" (1:iv).

As this last comment indicates, Warren adds another element to her gendered, psychological reconfiguration of the polis from within, for she puts the home as well as the heart in an interactive relation to the political world, on which "every domestic enjoyment depends." Her linking of interiority, domesticity, and political rights not only anticipates the ideological strategies of nineteenth-century feminists but also provides an instance of the newly "privatized" political imaginary identified by Nancy Armstrong, in which stories of agency in the private realm serve as both a rationale and, in novels, an ameliorating substitute for agency in the political realm.[30] Like the other women writers I study here, however, Warren complicatedly uses the idea of race liberty to at once concede and transgress the division between domestic and political. In fact, she applies this model to the "character" of men as well as women when, for instance—in a further strategic feminizing of liberty culture—she praises George Washington and the many French soldiers who, despite their attachment to "the pleasures of domestic felicity," were so "[w]armed by an enthusiastic love of liberty" that they stepped forward to fight in the war of independence (1:234, 375). With such maneuvers Warren includes domesticity, interiority, and herself in the stream of liberty's history, fashioning a place for women in the narrative she is helping to create. Here, race history is doing its liberatory work for the Anglo-Atlantic woman, as we will see it do for Susanna Rowson and Catharine Maria Sedgwick. Indeed, it may be that the racial idea of liberty gains momentum and force in part because it comes to serve Anglo-Atlantic women's freedom agendas.

BY THE TIME the influential, later-nineteenth-century historian George Bancroft came to write U.S. history, he could (serenely) claim that "[t]he Anglo-Saxon mind, in its serenest nationality . . . had made its dwelling place in the empire of Powhatan."[31] Bancroft carries forward the women historians' interiorizing turn as well as the august tone of Hegel's conclusion that "in the Protestant world . . . [t]his is the point which consciousness has attained." Indeed, insofar as, since the English Civil War, the "principle phases" of an English-language print culture were organized around a racialized idea of liberty that allowed an Anglo-Atlantic empire to "realize itself," we might well concede to Hegel (with one small, concretizing addition) that "the History of the [Atlantic] World is nothing but the development of the Idea of Freedom" (454–56). As the next chapter shows, this realization extends into the English-language *literary* imaginary as well—and, as the rest of this book traces, it travels from there into the novels and memoirs written by diverse Atlantic authors.

3 | The Poetics of Liberty and the Racial Sublime

IF HISTORY EXPRESSES a people's growth toward liberty, revived by a racial soil after a ruinous blight, then art and literature (as eighteenth-century theorists concluded) are its flowering. That is, liberty inspires expression as well as governments. Catharine Macaulay closes the preface to her *History of England* with lines from James Thomson's *Liberty,* in which he deems liberty the modern patron of the arts: "And with a strain from thee enrich the Muse: / As THEE alone she serves, her patron THOU, / And great inspirer be!" (emphasis in original). Thomson and Macaulay are simply two among many eighteenth- and nineteenth-century Atlantic writers who cast liberty as the muse of "literature."[1] I argue in this chapter that this muse was a race-muse who, by the end of the century, inspired a new literary history for English-language Atlantic cultures — culminating by the mid-nineteenth century in the idea that "[r]ace is everything: literature, science, art, in a word, civilization, depend on it."[2] As it did for English history, the Saxonist freedom story bestowed on English-language literature a new genealogy, as well as a newly favored aesthetic — that of the sublime.

More than any other literary mode, in both Britain and the United States, the sublime came to be celebrated as liberty's most rare and precious flowering — the highest expression of a free race. Literature became both sign and vehicle of the free "Anglo-Saxon mind, in its serenest nationality," while at the same time the sublime, with its encoding of fear, awe, and, finally, a mastering introjection of an alien world, implicitly registered the violent encounters required for this transcendent serenity.

The Emergence of Literary Nativism

The movement toward a nativist idea of literature was already being prepared in the Reformation, as Richard Helgerson discusses, and at the end of the seventeenth century it began to take distinct shape, as Howard Weinbrot has shown, in the debate between moderns and ancients.[3] Within this latter debate, English-language writers actively made distinctions between classical Greek or Roman styles and English styles and established their own tradition's historical particularity — casting it as peculiarly free and original, as Joseph Roach has also noted.[4] Inspired (or incensed) by Charles Perrault's four-volume study of ancient versus modern culture (*Parallele des anciens et des modernes en ce qui regarde les arts et les sciences* [1688 – 97]) — itself a landmark of the emergent historical, multivolume, and ethnographic consciousness — writers for the next century compared and contrasted Greek and Latin authors with "modern" authors, understood to be "native," writing in the vernacular and naturally molded by English climate and character.

Thus in John Dryden's "Essay of Dramatick Poesie," Neander praises Ben Jonson for avoiding servile imitation of the classics and similarly pronounces Shakespeare "the paradigm of natural English drama."[5] Dryden further points out in his "Answer to Rymer" that "the Climate, the Age, the Dispositions of a People to Whom a Poet writes, may be so different, that what pleas'd the Greeks would not satisfy an English audience" (quoted in Weinbrot, *BI* 162). Likewise, in 1694 William Walsh argues that "as in Physic, so in Poetry, there must be a regard to the Clime, Nature, and Customs of the People" (quoted in Weinbrot, *BI* 155). In these and subsequent decades, in works such as Dryden's *Absalom and Achitophel* and Pope's *Windsor Forest*, writers take up "native" historical subjects that tell tales of English conquerors and liberators. In Dryden's play, the Saxons are cast as noble freedom fighters although they are defeated and appropriately superseded, in Dryden's view, by the Normans. In Pope's poem, after the war in which the Norman conquerors serve as figures for Louis XV, we witness the rising of "Fair Liberty, Britannia's Goddess" (quoted in Weinbrot, *BI* 286 – 87).

By the early eighteenth century, critics and writers began to foreground what they saw as the ancient-classical association between freedom and expressive culture, and they then reassessed classical writers accordingly — sometimes finding their freedom of expression wanting as compared with the modern British authors. Howard Weinbrot has tracked how classicism, specifically Augustanism, came under challenge mainly in relation to this question of freedom in art, although he argues, against the evidence, that most eighteenth-century writers rejected the Gothic lineage as a key freedom legacy.[6] It may be that at midcentury,

Gothicism was mocked as much as it was embraced, but certainly in political discourse the association between freedom and the Gothic legacy ran deep, and, as we'll shortly see, in the latter half of the eighteenth century it informed the literary theories of the sublime that inspired Romanticism. Indeed, it is the very ubiquity of the equation between Saxonist liberty and English arts that made this equation the object of satire. Thus when Samuel Johnson remarks that "the notion of liberty amuses the people of England and helps to keep off the taedium vitae" and he demeans James Thomson's "clamours for liberty," he does so not in dissent from Thomson's narrative of Gothic liberty but rather because of Thomson's clumsy "enumeration of examples to prove a position *which nobody denied.*"[7]

Then, too, despite Johnson's denigration of it, Thomson's long poem *Liberty* had immense influence and stands as the representative mid-eighteenth-century view of an ancient connection between race, liberty, and the arts. As I noted in the introduction, Thomson's poem personifies the figure of Liberty and makes her the narrator of the history of the world. Her history tellingly yields a hierarchy of peoples, crowned by those in which free government fosters free arts and invention. For, as Liberty explains, "MY SPIRIT pours a vigour thro' the soul, / Th' unfettered Thought with Energy inspires" so that free nations are as "Invincible in Arts . . . as in . . . Arms" (2.211 – 14). Thus she begins her story with classical Greece, "LAND OF ARTS" (2.85) where the "Influence of Liberty over all Grecian states" led to their "Vast Superiority" over the Persians and over the "boastful race" of Egyptians (2.8): her gifts of liberty gave them "their Government, their Politeness, their Virtues, their Arts and Sciences" (table of contents, 1.56). She then proceeds to Rome where the "Commonweal [inspired] every Tongue / With fervent Eloquence, *unbrib'd* and *bold*" (1.78 – 79), and after corruption of her reign in Rome she finally arrives in the "NORTHERN NATIONS." Here she cultivates the "bury'd Seeds / Of *Freedom*" that had lain "Long in the barbarous Heart" (3.538 – 39). She "rears to freedom an undaunted Race" (5.71) in which "the gay MUSES raise a nobler strain" and "the SISTER-ARTS . . . knit in harmonious dance" the virtues of liberty (5.667, 684). With nativist partiality, Britain is "My best-establish'd, last / And more than GREECE, or ROME, my steady Reign" (1.316 – 17).

A spate of such liberty poems appeared throughout the eighteenth century, including Thomas Cooke's 1746 *Hymn to Liberty,* which likewise makes liberty the muse of poetry: "To thee the God of Verse shall pay / A grateful and melodious lay" since "His numbers are derived from thee" (quoted in Meehan 2). William Collins's *Ode to Liberty* follows Thomson in emphasizing a mixture of "bloods" yet nonetheless notes that "[i]n Gothic pride" the "fabric" of liberty most endures (quoted in Meehan 77). Literary critics followed suit. Thus Wotton spoke of "the "true Enthusiastick Rage which Liberty breathes into" the true artist, Goldsmith claimed that English taste, "like English liberty, should be restrained only by laws of its own promotion," and Shaftesbury developed his idea of an "antient Poetick Liberty" that "sets us free" — positing an "inward EYE" guided by an "original *native Liberty*" that provides the foundation for moral and aesthetic judgments (quoted in Meehan 6, 9, 38). While not all of these critics mention Gothic or Anglo-Saxon influence per se (as later writers such as Hurd and Percy will), the references to "ancient" and "English" by this time carry strong associations with these lineages.

Even Samuel Johnson participates in this nativist discourse, although his aesthetic loyalties were to higher, classical, and universal "models," rather than to vernacular, soil-nurtured, organic "forms." His investment appears not only in the preface to his edition of Shakespeare, and the choice to make such an edition, but also in his dictionary project. In announcing that "[t]he whole Fabrick and scheme of the English language is Gothick or Teutonick," Johnson fixes in place one cornerstone of the developing literary edifice from which he otherwise dissociated himself. He argues in his preface that this fabric has unfortunately been "deviating towards a Gallick structure and phraseology, from which it ought to be our endeavor to recall it."[8] Johnson stands as an example of how Saxonism had fully infiltrated British values even among the most influential champions of classical traditions.

The Racial Sublime

Most crucially, in the 1760s the long-developing set of associations between race, liberty, and art crystallized around the idea of the sublime, as I have elsewhere discussed at more length.[9] Since the late seventeenth century, translations of Longinus's *On the Sublime* had helped to foster the view that the arts could flourish only in a free society.[10] But it was not until a century later, with the "discovery" of "native" ancient poetry, that this aesthetic theory of the sublime unfolded its full potential within the British context. That is, with the publication nearly simultaneously in the mid-1760s of several powerful texts, the discourses of nativism and the sublime merged to provide the deep loam in which both Romanticism and the gothic novel would grow. In 1762, the publication of James MacPherson's *Poems of Ossian* offered a stirring vision of a profoundly old British literary legacy, and as if by magic that same year Richard Hurd published his *Letters on Chivalry and Romance* — a book that legitimated and even venerated such rude, "native" literary forms, deeming them as sublime as those of classical authors.

The following year, Hugh Blair consecrated "Ossian" as *the* sublime poet in a dissertation which was thereafter appended to most eighteenth-century editions of *Ossian*. Months later Bishop Percy published his *Reliques of Ancient English Poetry* (1764) and argued for the sublimity of the Gothic skalds. These scholars, apprehending the combined power of materials that had been accruing since the seventeenth century — including the developing nativisms of the Scottish and Irish peripheries, as Katie Trumpener has traced — began more vigorously to develop theories of a native poetic tradition.[11]

Just as Anglo-Saxonism had done in the 1640s, so in the 1760s and 1770s the articulation of a native poetic past worked to ease the national identity crisis which Linda Colley attributes in this early imperial period to the hyperextensions of English identity. At first it may seem odd that at the moment when England solidified its empire following the Seven Years' War and the defeat of France in various corners of the globe, the English literati apparently turned inward and became preoccupied with local races. But in fact this coincidence of events confirms the anchoring part played by racial nativism in the Anglo-Atlantic construction of self and empire. For it turns out that the materials gathered by Percy, Macpherson, and Blair allowed the imagining of a youthful yet noble, revolutionary yet imperial nation with just the right Gothic "balance" of battle-fever, melancholic brooding in hoary landscapes, and metaphysical reflectivity on matters of life, death, and freedom. In the tradition of seventeenth-century parliamentary lawyers who had worked to recover an ancient English legal tradition in the Magna Carta and the Common Law, these eighteenth-century scholars now announced that they were unearthing the origins of the ancient English literary tradition.

We see this development in formation in Richard Hurd's *Letters,* which critics since René Wellek have considered key in "the rise of English literary history" and the new "historical point of view."[12] Pitting the "Gothic" against the Greek in literature, Hurd extends the ancients vs. moderns literary debate. He gives the English a new edge by characterizing them as steeped in ancient traditions of their own, especially the "Gothic fables of chivalry."[13] He challenges those who express "perpetual ridicule" of the medieval romances and poetry, claiming that these dark-age "barbarians have their own [philosophy]" (I, 2). And, in fact, "there was a dignity, a magnificence, a variety in the feudal, which the other [the Greek] wanted" (VI, 48). Hurd tinges his discussion with racial overtones, invoking Tacitus (as most writers on the Gothic do), and he echoes the national historians in remarking that the "foundation of this refined gallantry was laid in the antient [*sic*] manners of the German nations" (III, 19).

In Hurd's rhapsodic description, England is not just a piece of land but, as one of the "German nations" under the Saxons, it is a world of quaint "villages" peopled with "Prodigies, Charms, and Enchantments" (VI, 54). It is the soil, birthplace, and legacy of "our forefathers" (VI, 54). It is "enchanted ground, my friend" (VI, 55). This charmed, rough land makes the English "bards . . . more sublime, more terrible, more alarming, than those of the classic fablers" (VI, 55). Enchanted land and inherited customs later shape the character of the great English poets. Shakespeare's "terrible sublime" — "which not so much the energy of his genius, as the nature of his subject drew from him" — is "more poetical for being Gothic" (VI, 55). Like William Mitford and others who follow him, Hurd lionizes Milton and especially Shakespeare as appreciators and inheritors of the Gothic aesthetic, the true "native" poets of England. Although nurtured on the classical writers, "they both appear, when most inflamed, to have been more particularly rapt with the Gothic fables of chivalry" (VII, 56). For the latter have "by their nature and genius, the advantage of the [former] in producing the sublime" (VII, 60). Indeed, the "Gothic language" itself "helped [them] to work up [their] tempests with such terror" (VI, 50).

For Percy, Blair, and MacPherson, the Gothic/Greek ceases to be the crucial opposition. Nor is the French or "Gallic" threat as pressing a presence in these men's minds. Instead, these critics engage in what, in light of Katie Trumpener's work, is probably best understood as a skirmish between British periphery and center, undertaken by way of a debate over the racial genealogies of the poetic sublime. That is, Hugh Blair, James MacPherson, and Thomas Percy vie over which lineage — Scot, Celtic, or Gothic — is most sublimely poetical and therefore the most worthy ancestor for British culture. In these internal polemics race gets worked up into a key term and yoked to a literary identity that draws on Macaulay's rhetoric of the free English spirit planted in native English bodies and that paves the way for Hegel's racial metaphysics.[14]

In his dissertation on Ossian, Hugh Blair helps to spark this debate over racial poetic identities. He announces explicitly that he considers the Scots (of whom, in his account, Ossian is the preeminent bard) to be a Celtic tribe, and thus part of "a great and mighty people" who are "altogether distinct from the Goths and the Teutones."[15] He echoes Hurd's view that the islands of Britain and their conquering history encourage sublimity: "amidst the rude scenes of nature, amidst rocks and torrents and whirlwinds and battles, dwells the sublime."[16] But in prominently contrasting the "Goths" with the Scottish Celtic peoples, to the advantage of the Celts, he gives this discourse a strong polemical turn. Aiming, Blair says, "to discover whether the Gothic poetry has any resemblance to the Celtic or Gaelic," he attempts generosity toward the Goths: although known "for their ignorance of the liberal arts, yet they too, from the earliest times, had their poets and their songs" (92). In ostensibly neutral scholarly fashion, Blair (a professor of rhetoric at Edinburgh) explains that these Gothic poets were called "Scalders" and presents a fragment from the work of the king and scalder Regner Lodbrog. After three full pages of Lodbrog's bloody battle imagery accented by the refrain "the whole ocean was one wound," Blair has prepared us to see that "[w]hen we turn from the poetry of Lodbrog [of the Goths] to that of Ossian [of the Celts], it is like passing from a savage desert into a fertile and cultivated country" (96). For in Ossian we find not only the "fire and enthusiasm of the most early times" but also "tenderness, and even delicacy of sentiment, greatly predominant over fierceness and barbarity" (96).

Blair is aiming to position the Celts as the rightful ancestors of all that is valued in eighteenth-century British culture, modeling through them a kind of emotional Gothic balance but recasting it as Celtic. He goes on to consider the evidence that, in general, the "Celtic tribes" were "addicted in so high a degree to poetry" that they preserved their traditions throughout many invasions and changes of government (98) and to claim that "[t]he two great characteristics of Ossian's poetry are, tenderness and sublimity" (107). Blair is working hard to recuperate the Celts' role in the ancient lineage of the British Isles through his account of their written poetry.

In his preface to *Ossian,* James MacPherson had developed a similar genealogical revision in his celebration of the Scots but, in addition, he seems to apprehend a danger in grouping Britons, Scots, and Celts together — perhaps seeking to distance Scots from the much-maligned Irish — and so he further distinguishes the Highland Scots from these others. He depicts the "Ossianic" culture of the Highland Scots (a figment of his imagination, as it turned out, of course) as a highly isolated one which resisted not only the incursions of the "Saxon race" (70) but also avoided any mixing with the southern Scots and Celts, so that the Highland Scots remained "a different race from the rest of the Britons" (59). As a result, their "language is pure and original, and their manners are those of ancient and unmixed race of men" (59). It is this "most ancient" (74) of European nations and this "more pure" language (75), combined with the secluded "magnificence" of "mountains and hanging woods" (71), that gives rise to the poet Ossian.

Blair's and MacPherson's claims apparently incensed the English bishop Thomas Percy. In his prefaces to the *Reliques of Ancient English Poetry* and to M. Mallet's *Northern Antiquities* (to the title of which he appends "With Incidental Notices respecting our Saxon Ancestors"), Percy virtually reverses Blair's argument. Although he agrees that the Celtic and Teutonic nations "were two races of men *ab origine* distinct," he proceeds to detail the backwardness of the Celts who "do not appear to have had that equal plan of liberty, which was the peculiar honor of all the Gothic tribes."[17] Above all, in an implicit challenge to

Blair and MacPherson, Percy seeks to honor the Goths as the more poetical race. In *Reliques* he is content to comment that poets were admired by "all the first inhabitants of Europe, whether of Celtic or Gothic race; but by none more than by our Teutonic ancestors."[18] But several years later, in his preface to *Northern Antiquities,* he engages openly in debate, pointing out the "fundamental error" in M. Pelloutier's *History of the Celts,* which overlooks "the radical distinction between the Gothic and the Celtic" (*Northern Antiquities* 19). He sharpens his contrast between the two races to the point where he considers the Celts to lack "so much as an alphabet of their own" (*Northern Antiquities* 14). "In this," he concludes, ironically echoing Blair, "the institutions of Odin and the Skalds was [*sic*] the very reverse. No barbarous people were so addicted to writing [as the Goths] . . . no barbarous people ever held letters in higher reverence, ascribing the invention of them to their chief deity, and attributing to letters themselves super-natural virtues" (*Northern Antiquities* 14). Turning Blair's very language against him, Percy seeks to maintain the central position of "our Saxon ancestors" in the increasingly complex mingling of "British" peoples at home and abroad.

As had the reading and writing of history, then, the "addiction to poetry" was beginning by way of these debates to count as important evidence of racial superiority—that is, of a bold attachment to a sublime freedom. By the time William Mitford wrote his *Inquiry into the Principles of Harmony in Language and of the Mechanism of Verse, Modern and Antient* (1804), he could speak of the different principles of "Harmony" experienced by "all the races of mankind in their respective languages" as a popular topic: "In our own country, especially of late years, publications, of which it is either the principal or an incidental topic, have been numerous."[19] Mitford builds on Hurd to determine the formal principles of "native" English poetry and to characterize the "energetic language of our early forefathers" (132), holding that "the form of the English language has hardly in any degree been derived from the French" (367), for despite the Norman-French invasion (a past now pressingly recalled again by contemporary Anglo-French battles) "the genius of the [Gothic] Anglo-Saxon pronunciation at length pre-vailed" (142).

Mitford's unorthodox notion that accentual rather than syllabic verse was native to the British Isles fostered, according to Paul Fussell, the prosodic aspect of the romantic poetic revolution, so that in the following years "trisyllabic substitution bursts into full bloom in the works of Southey, Coleridge, 'Monk' Lewis, Sir Walter Scott, and John Leyden."[20] His theory also helps to reintegrate Saxonist and Celtic lineages and thus, for instance, to confirm a place for Robert Burns, who openly deviates from the syllabic models on the principle that "there is a cer-tain irregularity" in the old Scottish songs, "a degree of wild irregularity" (quoted in Fussell 145). According to Carl Berkhout, by the end of the eighteenth century, "a 'myth' had developed in the English literary world."[21] Though Berkhout does not say it, this rapidly proliferating myth was racial and political as well as poetical. Since that time, in implicitly promoting certain poetic forms as purer and more free, the racialization of literary history has had a subtle yet far-reaching influence on English-language writers and readers — and on the very shape and sound of English-language poetry.

At the level of narrative poetic form, romantic poets such as Wordsworth fashioned a companion practice for this nativist reimagining of the sublime, as I have discussed elsewhere.[22] In the classically sublime narrative sequence, the speaker undergoes a crisis, or has a self-losing vision, by way of an encounter with an ancient, savage landscape or with a ghostly, often foreign or wandering Other, but then, in a subreption figured as sublime, refashions this encounter as the founding experience of a metaphysical self. In *The Recluse,* for instance, Wordsworth narrates his persona's turn from youthful "motions of savage instinct" among "tall trees, black chasms, and dizzy crags" to "Reason," which dictates that his "Voice shall speak" "on Man, on Nature, and on Human Life."[23] In heeding this call, the poem implies, Wordsworth assumes his place as British national poet.

Romantic texts' obsessive rendering of this "sublime turn" or moment of crisis when the self faces the terror of a world beyond its grasp appears, in the novels I study here, as the Atlantic swoon-moment when the subject "falls" and then awakens to become a reasoning citizen, or a slave excluded from this citizenship that is founded on the claim to an interior and balanced freedom. With their transatlantic plots, these novels point us across the ocean, where a parallel vision of the racial sublime arose.

America's Racial Sublime

In his closing praise of English as the language that has "spred in all quarters of the globe" William Mitford hints that this linguistic and literary history is putting wind in the sails of an imperial venture (429). He admonishes his readers: "This speech it becomes us to cherish and preserve; to know its merits, that we may know how to ward it against injury" (430). Although this early-nineteenth-century British intellectual might have considered the United States one of those outlandish places where the English language needed warding against injury, Anglo-Americans were at the same time casting themselves as the youthful, racial renewers of this language.

By the early nineteenth century, U.S. promoters of the arts such as John Hopkinson (author of "Hail Columbia") reiterated the idea that freedom and art grow together. While it is true, he says, that "quietude is necessary to the culture and growth of the arts . . . [p]olitical independence is not less so."[24] Indeed "[a] nation in a state of vassalage cannot excel in them. The mind must be as free as air" (Wood, *Rising* 327). Hopkinson casts the United States as the freest nation, thus best suited for art, folding in along the way key elements of climatic theory that more explicitly racialize this political framework for free art. Concurring with "men eminent in taste and literature" who contend that "particular climates or portions of the earth have a peculiar fitness for the production of genius," he takes as a premise the notion that the arts and sciences "have not flourished beyond the fifty second degree of northern latitude, nor nearer than twenty five degrees to the line" (Wood, *Rising* 323). Northern Anglo-Americans, however, are geographically "placed in a happy medium," and here "the sagacity, ardour, inventive ingenuity of the American character are all calculated to carry us to a high state of perfection in the arts" while "the enterprise of our merchants . . . has extended our commerce to every habitable clime" (323–324). So much good fortune seems to Hopkinson to indicate "more than the ordinary course of human affairs" and indeed "a great design of Providence" (324). This being the case, "Shall we not go on to the more elegant and sublime enjoyments of the human faculties?" (324).

Hopkinson forms part of a chorus of early-nineteenth-century writers who were elaborating the "rising glory" and manifest destiny of America, where vast lands and prosperous commerce supply the scene of a sublime future. In *Inchiquin's Letters,* Charles Jared Ingersoll proclaims unapologetically, "The lien of this 'mighty continental nation' is commercial liberty: not mere political liberty, but positive freedom; geographical absolution from all but the slightest restraints; the inherent and inalienable birthright of this adolescent people, upon the enjoyment of which they entered by a lineal title . . . a heritage as natural as the air they breathe" (quoted in Wood, *Rising* 384). Ingersoll is working rhetorically to attribute an ancient "birthright" of freedom to an "adolescent people" and likewise to make political "title" into a "natural heritage." His maneuvers nicely exemplify John Carlos Rowe's observation that Anglo-Americans' self-image was paradoxically "shaped by a powerful imperial desire and a profound anti-colonial temper."[25] But the history that explains this contradictory self-image predates the American Revolution with which Rowe and other critics begin. It is the longer Saxonist and Atlantic history of the liberty principle that makes resonant Ingersoll's ringing statements, a history that would have given a familiar and natural ring to what are actually rhetorical contortions.

While writers such as Ralph Waldo Emerson and Walt Whitman eschew the grasping tone of such claims, they nonetheless sometimes mirror these rhetorical moves in their visions of the sublime work of (Anglo) "American" literature.

Reading Emerson's essay "The Poet," for instance, we can quickly detect the key words of the Anglo-Atlantic racial imaginary, especially if we consider this essay in combination with his lecture *English Traits*. In the lecture, Emerson first of all quotes Swedenborg's reflections on how "the English nation" harbors an "interior intellectual light" that "derive[s] from the liberty of speaking and writing, and thereby of thinking."[26] He then formulates, de rigueur, his own version of British racial mixture. Here, although he emphasizes the mixture of Norman and Saxon and at first underplays race (which he says "is resisted by other forces" [30–31]), and although he is blunt about the faults of the "broad-fronted, broad-bottomed Teutons" (194), he nonetheless concludes that "it is in the deep traits of race that the fortunes of nations are written" (86). Lecturing to a British audience at the Free-Trade Hall in Manchester, England, Emerson assures them that in England "however derived — whether a . . . mixture of tribes . . . — here exists the best stock in the world" (86). The English have "given importance to individuals" and "by this sacredness of individuals, they have for seven hundred years evolved the principles of freedom" and so they will forever be famous for their "immortal laws, for the announcement of original right which make the stone tables of liberty" (199). The stage is now set for America's entry. Luckily for Americans, as Emerson proceeds to tell his British audience, "the geography of America" means that "we play the game with immense advantage." America's vast expanses inspire the feeling that "there and not here is the seat and center of the British race; and that no skill or activity can long compete with the prodigious natural advantages of that country, in the hands of the same race" (178).

Such is the larger geopolitical stage of Atlantic modernity onto which Emerson very likely felt he was stepping when he wrote "The Poet." For the most part in this text Emerson does not speak directly of race or even of an American literature, instead focusing on "the poet" as a universal figure. He only just hints at Atlantic modernity as the scene of his thinking when he refers to the way this ideal poet "finds a place for the railway" as well as for "fine houses"; and he refers to the United States briefly in conjuring a world where, for the poet, "the belt of wampum and the commerce of America are alike."[27] Not until the very end of the essay does he address the possibility of a new kind of quietly racialized poet in America, as we will see, and then he quickly steps back from this suggestion after a paragraph, self-deprecatingly confessing that "I am not wise enough for a national criticism" ("Poet" 281).

Yet because Emerson *is* wise enough to intuit that myths are best built up implicitly, his essay is not framed as a political or racial call. Instead, it is simply saturated, by way of a liberty language mingled with an imagery of geographic expanse, with the suggestion that the United States plays the literary as well as the commercial "game" with immense advantage. Emerson begins by fashioning the poet as one who continually carries us into "new thought[s]," "new experience[s]," "new relation[s]," and so "new word[s]" ("Poet" 264, 269). If such phrases also conjure the setting of a new world, Emerson doesn't let on that he knows it. He simply reports that in real poetry we sense that "the expression is organic" as it models "the new type which things themselves take when liberated" (273). And he describes how a poet employs an "intellect released from all service" so that, as we approach a true poem, we anticipate that "now my chains are to be broken" (274, 265).

The hint of a "new" geographical horizon for this liberation emerges together with one or two racial cues. The turn begins in the last third of the essay as Emerson suggests that poets inspire "that centrifugal tendency of man, to his passage out into free space, and they help him to escape the custody of that body in which he is pent up" (275).[28] This observation carries him toward his ultimate thesis that "Poets are thus liberating gods" (276). Hereafter the racial cues become more legible. Emerson places his repetition of this resounding phrase at the head of the next paragraph ("The poets are thus liberating gods"), making it the entry point into this example: "The ancient British bards had for the title of their order, 'Those who are free throughout the world'" (277). Emerson adds, "They are free, and they make free" (277).

Although this allusion to ancient British bards is brief, Emerson's subsequent use of the familiar vocabulary of the sublime encodes its racial message. The true poet, he explains, draws us into his vision "with love and terror" and "this perception in him . . . makes the poet or seer an object of awe and terror" (280–81). This is the kind of "genius" for whom America now waits, he finally admits, for "America is a poem in our eyes, its ample geography dazzles the imagination, and it will not wait long for metres" (281). America needs a poet who will recognize in "the barbarism and materialism of the times, another carnival of the same gods whose picture he so much admires in Homer, then in the Middle Age; then in Calvinism" (281). For "as yet unsung" are "our stumps and their politics, our fisheries, our Negroes and Indians, our boats and our repudiations . . . the northern trade, the southern planting, the western clearing, Oregon and Texas" (281). The plural possessive "our" says it all: it ushers in a scenario in which awe and terror get sublimated into a manifest destiny — a vision in which Negro slavery becomes "southern planting," in which the massacre of Indian peoples becomes "western clearing," and in which the bards not only are free but also assume the prerogative to "make others free" — or not. An ancient liberty once more turns imperial and thereby achieves sublimity.

WALT WHITMAN would speak more emphatically of democracy and would more boldly imagine an equal mingling of races in the United States, but he continues the process of racializing freedom and extends the vision of a sublime world-destiny for the United States. In his articulations of a free, "American" poetry, we can feel the profound influence that Emerson's "The Poet" is said to have had on Whitman — as we also feel the profound influence on him of the long-developing liberty discourse that shaped Emerson's own vision. For Whitman, "America is the race of races" for it has that "deathless attachment to freedom," and this attachment gives birth to art, for Americans also have "of all nations at any time upon the earth . . . the fullest poetical nature."[29] Whitman, too, was seduced by an ambitious vision of America's "manifest" destiny as he imagined a sublime westward movement through history, including the final triumphant traversing of the continent which is "by [America's] mighty railroad spann'd" ("Passage to India," 1. line 6).

Whitman is not Emerson, however, and to an important degree his vision of a free America diverges, especially racially. It matters that Whitman's speaker understands racial amalgamation as one telos of this western destiny, as for instance in "Passage to India": "Lo soul, seest thou not God's purpose from the first? The earth to be spann'd, connected by network, / The races, neighbors, to marry and be given in marriage, / The oceans to be cross'd, the distant brought near, / The lands to be welded together" (2. lines 16 – 20). Very few of Whitman's Anglo-American contemporaries would have joined him in his vision of inter-racial marriage, depicted in other poems as well. His explicit imagining of it is of a piece with his "straying" sexual visions.

But "Passage to India" is at the same time a multiracial vision of a cosmic manifest destiny realized by Anglo-Americans. Clearly, first of all, the poem arises within an Atlantic imaginary, insofar as the poem's speaker and his soul "take ship" (8. line 2), and initially the speaker finds that "Struggles of many a captain, tales of many a sailor dead, / Over my mood [steal]" (4. lines 2 – 3). "Passage" is throughout spoken from the Anglo-Atlantic perspective, as it celebrates "the knowledge gain'd, the mariner's compass, / Lands found and nations born, thou born America, / For purpose vast, man's long probation fill'd, / Thou rondure of the world at last accomplish'd" (4. lines 10 – 13). No Indian chief initiates this westward passage and the mourned dead are neither slaves nor tribes but mariners, whose loss gives birth to nations.

And yet other dead do fleetingly appear, although submerged in the poem's final section, as it makes its sublime turn toward transcendence via racial introjection. The first stanza of this final section begins by suggesting that the soul's journey entails a "Passage to more than India! / Are thy wings plumed indeed for such far flights?" Its call to the soul seems to transcend material history and geography. But by the third stanza, the "you" addressed by the speaker is exactly America and its geography — the place to which the soul has traveled:

> Passage to more than India!
> O secret of the earth and sky!
> Of you O waters of the sea! O winding creeks and rivers!
> Of you O woods and fields! of you strong mountains of my land!
> Of you O prairies! of you grey rocks! (9. lines 10 – 14)

Between stanza 1 and stanza 3 in this section there has been a shift, from "you" as the soul to "you" as my American land — which suggests that we need to consider carefully the nature of the "you" in the intervening second stanza, the darkest one of the poem, which seems addressed to the original inhabitants of America. The implications are chilling.

> Passage to you, your shores, ye aged fierce enigmas!
> Passage to you, to mastership of you, ye strangling problems!
> You, strew'd with the wrecks of skeletons, that, living, never reach'd you.
> (9.7 – 9)

If these "aged fierce enigmas" are Indian Americans, who leave behind the wrecks of skeletons, and over whom the poet calls for mastership, then no wonder Whitman ends this line with a muddling of the poem's "you's." And no wonder that the speaker then very suddenly calls for "Passage, immediate passage! the blood burns in my veins! / Away O soul! hoist instantly the anchor! / Cut the hawsers — haul out — shake out every sail!" (9. lines 19 – 21). The poet flees, as the poem flees, such strangling problems. But then the poet transforms this evasion into a sublime launching worthy of those ancient, sea-roaming Saxons: "Sail forth — steer for the deep waters only, / Reckless O soul, exploring, I with thee, and thou with me, / For we are bound where mariner has not yet dared to go, / And we will risk the ship, ourselves and all" (9. lines 25 – 28). Thus has mastership of "you" given way to this sublimely transcendent vision of a "thee and thou." Within the poem's framing logic, this "thee and thou" belongs to one, selfsame Anglo-American "I," or to an Anglo-American "our" that is not so different, after all, from Emerson's vision of "our Negroes and Indians, our boats and our repudiations."

If we may also read Whitman's bold closing lines as a call to embrace a courageous, queer sexuality between thee and thou, then we may see how he shares a strategy with Catharine Macaulay and Mercy Otis Warren, whereby a racial vision underwrites a sexual transgression. Even if with more risky, or racially moderate, or healing intentions, Whitman joins his Anglo-Saxon compatriots in sublimating the violence of American colonization, despite the fact that its latest surge in America's bloody civil war was cupped by Whitman's own nursing hands. The folding-under of this violence fertilizes the freedom vision for Whitman, as the grass "we" tread that continually sprouts again.

Thus did the poetic of the racial sublime on both sides of the Atlantic help to create a compelling vision for the "liberty" narrative, one imbued with risk and prowess, at once freeing and mastering. In the charged air of these poetic visions, Atlantic writers of all kinds, that is, of several "races," eventually generated parallel but antagonistic stories of sublime, racial freedom. In "The Tennessee Hero," for instance, the African American poet Frances Ellen Watkins Harper draws her sublime portrait of a man who won't betray the escape plot of his enslaved comrades: she depicts him as "the noblest of them all" who "stood before the savage throng, / The base and coward crew" of white interrogators while "A tameless light flashed from his eye." For "Though fetters galled his weary limbs, / His spirit spurned their thrall" and "Oh! liberty had nerved his heart, / And every pulse beat true." Following his bold retort that "I know the men who would be free . . . are the heroes of your land," and his refusal to reveal them, "the blows rained thick and fast," but his "monarch soul kept true" even while he met his "death of pain."[30] Rewriting the Oroonoko story while recasting the racialized romantic sublime of her white contemporaries, Harper at once joins and deconstructs the Atlantic literary tradition.

The following pages are less a challenge to this racialized tradition of the sublime, with its real and symbolic deadly swoons, than an invitation to notice how writers have created it and to ask what it has meant to do so — and what it could mean.

II | Founding Fictions of Liberty

Entering Atlantic History

4

Oroonoko, Imoinda, and Behn

OROONOKO, OR THE ROYAL SLAVE (1688) has long been called the first English novel — and for William Spengemann it is the first American novel as well — but its full significance as such is still being discovered.[1] Its significance becomes clearer when we read it beside other Atlantic liberty stories, from *Robinson Crusoe* and Olaudah Equiano's *Interesting Narrative* to *Billy Budd* and *Quicksand*. On my way to doing so, in this chapter I place *Oroonoko* within several convergent genealogies of the English-language novel. *Oroonoko*'s heterogeneous literary sources include courtly romance, historical memoir, colonial ethno-history, classical Greek and Roman fiction, and Restoration drama. I argue that these subgenres merge in Behn's novel to yield, first, its revisionary English history; second, its seminal, Atlantic practices of Africanism and Indianism within a story of liberty and ruin; and third, its marginal-yet-central female narrator, who provides a prototype of narrators to come.

The most important lineage for *Oroonoko* is historical. The text is preoccupied with the violence and treachery of the English Revolution, just as the first early national histories were; in fact, it is contemporary with the late-seventeenth-century "birth" of modern history as a story of struggle against tyranny and lawlessness. *Oroonoko* participates in this refashioning of history, from a Tory point of view. Most strikingly, Behn sets her retelling of history on the Atlantic, structurally situating the national story within the colonial one. As her narrator explains, she writes from and of Surinam, an "obscure" colony where "History was scarce," a place very far from that "part of the World replenished with People and Historians."[2] She writes in the wake of the colonial violence that ultimately ends England's royal power there, for English possession is disrupted by "the *Dutch,* who immediately after [this] time took that Country" (40). Because the Dutch "killed, banished and dispersed all those that were capable of giving the world" the colony's history, her narrator must do the best she can, with her "Female Pen," to compensate for this violent break in history (40). As we will see, this colonial violence and Dutch usurpation not only recall the overthrow of Charles I but also anticipate the dethroning of his second son, James II, who was replaced by the Dutch William and Mary in what came to be called the Glorious Revolution, and which was underway as Behn wrote her novel. The history Behn tells is allegorically national as well as literally colonial, implicitly linking the revolutionary past to the colonial present. And the quest for liberty fails.

Most important, the colonially embedded allegory of English revolutions is encoded within the captive bodies of the "royal slave" Oroonoko and his royal wife, Imoinda. Behn casts Oroonoko as a figure for Charles I, as Laura Brown has shown, yet at the same time through him she publishes the first English-language story of African-Atlantic slave captivity. Her Anglo-Atlantic female narrator (like the author) enters English history at the meeting point of these stories. That is, Behn enters the canon, just as her narrator enters into the act of storytelling, by narrating the experience of ruin that connects Anglo- and African-Atlantic history — or, more precisely, she enters by conflating these Atlantic histories. Like the Saxon-identified revolutionaries of the 1640s, and despite her Tory sympathies, Behn takes power by way of an Atlantic rupture, in the process modeling an Africanist practice for the Anglo-Atlantic authors who follow her.

The reading I offer here is in accord with those that stress Behn's mixed allegiances in the Atlantic's "turbulent modern world" and Surinam's "colonial setting."[3] Yet these accounts, like many others, interpret Behn's text as a protonovel struggling to break free from the rigid, aristocratic romance form that is at odds with its new, modern story.[4] Rather than merely making a faltering turn from romance to history, and from monarchy to modernity, however, the novel seeks to explore the liberty conundrum where these formations meet, and it shrewdly locates the Atlantic as the appropriate setting for doing so. On the Atlantic, Behn forges romance, national history, colonial history, and historical memoir into a narrative of modern subjectivity shaped by the question of free consent, the trope of race, and the drama of rape.

Narrating from the Edge of History:
Behn's Novel Composition

As Margaret Doody establishes in *The True Story of the Novel,* the classical Greek
and Roman tradition of fiction influenced many French romance writers and,
in part via France, early English novelists as well. These classical novels featured
stories of captivity, rape, and escape among high-born characters somehow displaced — either sold into slavery or otherwise exiled from home. Doody tracks
these classical plots and their influence on French and English novels without foregrounding, however, the liberty story at their core. Nonetheless, Doody's scholarship makes clear that — starting with *Oroonoko* — a liberty plot is the English
novel's most salient inheritance, via the French romance, from the classical, narrative tradition.

Behn retools the classical plot within a new narrative structure that borrows
from emerging colonial and national historical forms. As readers have felt, in
Oroonoko the interpolated stories of exotic adventure in Surinam combined with
the high, tragic romance of noble lovers from Africa, as well as the brutal depiction of a colonial slave revolt, make for an oddly hybrid and yet strangely compelling text. We might say that Behn's text "composes" the disparate materials
and encounters of the seventeenth-century Atlantic, a project of bricolage that
recent critics have begun to consider fundamental to the rise of the novel (moving against the grain of traditional criticism from F. R. Leavis to John Richetti,
which has celebrated those who first brought narrative coherence to the genre).[5]
In particular, Ed White has argued that early colonial American histories provide
one set of ur-texts for the genre of the novel. White reads Captain John Smith's
Generall Historie of Virginia (1624) and *True Travels* (1630) as novelistic responses
to the "contradictory ideological projects" and unpredictable encounters with diverse peoples within American colonization. These not-yet-coherent projects and
encounters call forth strategies of Bakhtinian "novelization" that entail, first, a
tapping of available genres (chronicle, anatomy, ethnography) and then a composition of those genres into a loosely coherent narrative. Modeled on such texts, the
novel provides, in White's phrase, "a centripetal genre for the heteroglossia of the
colonial context."[6] I agree. J. Paul Hunter simply describes the process in reverse
when he refers to "the novel's imperialism — its ability to take over features from
other species."[7] No surprise, if the novel is originally the offspring of an imperi-
alizing miscegenation of literary forms. Perhaps exactly because of its hybridity,
Behn's story has lent itself to adaptation in many racialized and contradictory
ways — many of them at odds with Behn's own politics.

Yet Behn also enfolds another form of history writing, one that places her among the many late-seventeenth-century writers preoccupied with the legacy of the English Revolution. She borrows in part from a post–Civil War historical subgenre to which Captain Smith had no access: that of the exile's memoir or "secret" history, made popular by the Earl of Clarendon's *History of the Rebellion* (rebellion in this case referring to the overthrow of Charles I, under whom Clarendon loyally served). As noted in chapter 2, history writing exploded in the later seventeenth-century, most of it brooding in some way on the events of the Civil War and its aftermath — and, by extension, the proper history and limits of liberty. Historical memoirs such as those of Clarendon, Lucy Hutchinson, and Margaret Cavendish participated in this brooding process, although these works have most often been considered by later historians to be personal, partisan, and therefore marginal to or at odds with the development of "objective" modern historiography. Recent historiographers such as Devoney Looser have, however, taken these memoirs more seriously, while the literary critic Robert Mayer has considered them the seedbed of the novel. In *History and the Early English Novel*, Mayer argues that these memoirs' "secret" life histories laid down a pattern for the autobiographical and confessional mode of early novels, which, in his view, Daniel Defoe first successfully adopts, thereby creating the paradigm for later novels.

But, as noted in chapter 2, these accounts look past the political history these memoirs are negotiating and therefore misconstrue the content (of liberty) and the form (of oppositionality) that they bequeath to novels. Accordingly, in Mayer's case, he underestimates Behn's importance in the English-language novel's genealogy. In my view, what's most important for the novel in English about memoir-histories such as Clarendon's is that they construct a certain narrative position, an outside position that is emulated in *Oroonoko*, by which to reframe the historical crisis and liberty discourse of the English Revolution of the 1640s. That is, these memoir-histories tell, from an outside position, an "insider's" story of lineage disruption in the political realm. Clarendon, for instance, was a court member and an apologist for Charles I, but he composed his memoir in exile, during the years of the Interregnum. He wrote initially as a subject defrauded of his English property and rights, and then, when Charles II reclaimed the throne, he published as a privileged insider, whose work drew a large readership. As did other such memoir writers, Clarendon occupied the stance of an eyewitness to English history temporarily exiled to its margins — at once an insider and an outsider.[8]

The conditions creating this positionality deserve some brief attention here. This narrating stance became paradigmatic in the English imagination, I suggest, because of the several radical reversals of power in seventeenth-century England. In sudden and rapid alternations throughout the seventeenth century, Dissenters then Catholics, Parliament-men then Court-members had been purged from public office, imprisoned, scorned, stockaded, exiled, or stripped of estates. By way of their religious and political allegiances, everyone's family had been on the inside, then on the outside. At the end of the seventeenth century, published versions of history clashed and clamored to establish the "true" account against this instability. At the same time, as discussed in chapter 1, the colonies extended this volatility, for in America and the West Indies, the "outside" position was a literal, sociogeographic reality, and yet from this outside position certain "insiders," whether Puritan dissenter or Stuart spy, gained control at the center.

Already, in the middle of the seventeenth century, under Cromwell, this exilic and unstable history had begun to register its effects in literary voice and form. As Trevor Ross points out, just as Puritan censorship and oppression "led Royalists to engage in a highly codified discourse of secrecy and dissimulation," so it also led Cavalier poets toward private publication and coded, ambiguous tropes in their poetry.[9] Abruptly cut off from political power, these poets came to provide a literary realm for the excluded. They fashioned themselves as the true voices of the nation and lamented in privately published verse, "Were not State-Levellers enough! . . . that yet / We must be plagu'd with Levellers of Wit?" and they wondered at the publications of those whose "Prose unhing'd the State" (quoted in Trevor Ross 136–37). In the end, they, too, took up the dissenting discourse of liberty that would ultimately — but not yet — serve to recenter English identity. Only later, in the middle of the eighteenth century, could this outsider-persona be depicted as a settled, country presence — the kind of figure John Barrell traces in his *Wide and Equal Survey of English Literature*: the gentleman-observer who is removed from the fray and who, like Henry Fielding's narrator in *Tom Jones,* surveys the land from the prospect of a Gothic hill and imagines a comic unity among a widely dispersed and newly differentiated people. But in the mid-seventeenth century, this outsider-author remains insurgent and secretive.

Behn writes *Oroonoko* at the end of the seventeenth century, in effect between these two moments, between Interregnum Cavalier poet and Augustan novelist. She is the spy turned novelist under a restored king whose power, however, is under final siege. Increasingly after Behn, novels and histories work in tandem to move English culture past these instabilities. As historians supply pre-histories and post-histories for the unsettling power reversals of the Puritan Revolution, the Restoration, and the Glorious Revolution, so she models the way in which novelists can create stories compelled by rupture — and call them history. She particularly displays how liberty-seeking identity falls apart, so that only the insider-narrator standing nobly on the aggrieved margin can put it back together again in the telling, in a "history." After Behn, eighteenth-century novelists repeatedly titled their texts as "histories," often "secret" histories: *The History of the Nun; The Secret History of Queen Zarah and the Zarazians; The History of Jemmy and Jenny Jessamy; The British Recluse; or, the Secret History of Cleomira, Supposed Dead; Clarissa, or the History of a Young Lady; The History of Tom Jones, A Foundling.* These histories are frequently "secret" histories because they unveil the "insider" story in a plot of liberty and ruin, making private matters public, manifesting them in print, and in the process fashioning the "inside" of a liberty-seeking character. In all these secret histories, as my discussion of Eliza Haywood in chapter 5 will explore, the characters' ontogenetic crises offer a vehicle for the community's phylogenetic refashioning, its re-membering of group identity after rupture.

The narrator who stands on the sidelines of history and witnesses the breakdown of roles and continuity at the same time fills the vacuum created by that breakdown, "composing" and re-anchoring its dispersed persons and events. This is the paradigm Behn begins to put in place. In doing so, she helps to realize what Gerald MacLean deems this period's consolidation of literature's "irreversible authority as a socially constitutive field of public activity."[10] Significantly for the history of English-language narrative, in *Oroonoko* Behn assigns the pivotal insider-outsider position of the narrator to a colonial woman. While Firdous Azim stresses the colonial identity of the narrator and other critics have considered the gendered use that the white female narrator makes of Imoinda,[11] I will be establishing her combination of these positions, paradigmatic for novels to come. Behn initiates a pattern in which the Anglo-colonial woman becomes the figure through whom Atlantic conflicts are negotiated and the African-Atlantic story is absorbed.

Racial Revolution Redux

In *Oroonoko,* this Africanist turn is just getting launched, and Behn's racialization of Oroonoko is complex. Her simultaneous royalization and racialization of him — which has long confused readers aiming to interpret the novel as either abolitionist or colonialist — makes sense when we recognize the novel as a historical meeting point for monarchical and insurgent racial discourses.[12] Behn narrates the transition from an internal, noble-common racial order to a colonial one via the liberty plot prompted by the new Atlantic economy.

To fully understand Behn's portrait of a "royal" slave, and to see the Atlantic

investments of her narrative, we should begin by noting her coded analogy between Oroonoko, the enslaved and murdered African prince, and Charles I, the
imprisoned and beheaded English king. As Laura Brown has established, several
details of the texts establish this analogy.[13] The first hint is the name Behn attributes to Oroonoko once he arrives in Surinam: "Mr. Trefry gave Oroonoko
that of Caesar; which name will live in that Country as long as that (scarce more)
glorious one of the great Roman: for 'tis most evident he wanted no part of the
personal Courage of that Caesar, and acted things as memorable, had they been
done in some part of the World replenished with People and Historians, that
might have given him his due" (40). The name "Caesar" is the code Behn used for
the Stuart monarchs in her other writing, and her application of it here to Oroonoko also implicitly establishes her subscription to the classical, imperial version
of ancient history, against the emergent, nativist one.[14] Standing in for Charles I,
Oroonoko thus represents England's proud connection to power won through
conquering — the Norman-Tory, Roman-associated version of England's claim
to ancient identity. At the same time, Behn echoes the language used in sympathetic Restoration histories and biographies of Charles, revealing the close
connection of her novel to these contemporary historical works, as Brown also
notes. These descriptions feature the "barbarous regicides" who killed Charles
and they characterize Charles as "shewing no fear of death" on the verge of his
execution. Similarly, Behn's text refers to Oroonoko's executioner as a man of
"absolute barbarity" (a "wild Irishman") and it reports that Oroonoko faced his
death "without a Groan, or a Reproach (76–77)." According to these biographies,
Charles's body was cut up and parts of it paraded in the streets; in Behn's story
Oroonoko's body is also dismembered and she refers to the distributed pieces of
his corpse as the "frightful spectacles of a mangled king" (77). In short, as Brown
culls this evidence to suggest, "the sense of momentous loss that Behn's narrative
generates on behalf of the 'royal slave' is the product of a hidden figuration in
Oroonoko's death of the culminating moment of the English revolution" (Brown
58). In telling Oroonoko's story, the narrator works symbolically to renarrate the
story of England's revolutionary past.

Further hinting that a Stuart succession crisis is the subtext for Oroonoko's
story, the Dutch usurpation of Surinam not only alludes to the very contemporary threat in the late 1680s of invasion and usurpation of the Stuart throne by the
Dutch-Protestant Pretender but it also develops as the culmination of a series of
power crises. More than one proper authority has gone missing in this Atlantic
colonialism. The takeover by the Dutch is preceded in the novel by the deaths at
sea of both the narrator's father, who had been designated to become lieutenant-

governor, and also by that of the lord-governor-to-be, who mysteriously never arrives to undo the confusion of authority between the deputy governor Byam and benevolent, powerful plantation owners such as Trefry at Parham House.

These absences and schisms signify the dispersion of inherited authority within a colonial context that will be paralleled, as we will see, in the causes of Imoinda's and Oroonoko's enslavement. These conditions leave an opening for the narrator, the daughter of the drowned governor. She becomes the historian of this colony, she explains, because of the Dutch takeover of Surinam, for if they "had not killed, banished and dispersed all those that were capable of giving the world this great Man's Life, much better than I have done," Oroonoko would not have been left with "only a Female Pen to celebrate his Fame" (40). In other words, the swallowing Atlantic itself and the violence of intra-European colonial competition operate as forces that undermine Stuart succession, enabling the enslavement of African princes and yielding the "daughter's" narrative-insider authority.

The text's alignment of Oroonoko and the Stuarts sheds a different light on the first physical description of Oroonoko, which mingles racist and classical associations. In building her sympathetic account of the noble African Oroonoko, Behn at first assumes a hierarchy of noble over common like that found in England and Europe. Oroonoko is no common Negro but a prince who has "as great a soul, as politic maxims, and . . . [is] as sensible of power as any prince civilized in the most refined schools of humanity and learning, or the most illustrious courts" (8). Distinguishing Oroonoko from other Africans by way of further Caesarian references, she notes that "his nose was rising and Roman, instead of African and flat. His mouth, the finest shape that could be seen, far from those great turned lips which are natural to the rest of the negroes. The whole proportion and air of his face was so noble, and exactly formd, that bating his colour, there could be nothing in nature more beautiful, agreeable, and handsome" (8). This Europeanization of Oroonoko, racist as it is, should not however be read *strictly* as the expression of colonial racism — especially since that racism which is now so familiar to us was only just being born in Behn's day. It follows the traditional European distinction between noble and common and the assumption that in one land there are two races — the ruling and the conquered, the high and the low. As a nobleman, Oroonoko is positioned above "the rest of the negroes," as any Stuart king would be positioned above "the rest of" the English. Behn's emphasis here allows her later to encode the English history in which barbarian "commoners" fail to follow and support their noble king. That is, initially, she is as interested in ennobling Oroonoko as she is in Europeanizing him.

Once Oroonoko becomes a captive in Surinam, however, and as he begins to press for his liberty, the narrator's racial terms shift. While she on the one hand keeps in play his noble attributes, she also gradually aligns him with the "blacks" as distinct from "the Whites" (e.g., 46, 47, 54, 55, 59, 66). To properly track that shift, we must first look closely at the conflicts and the transformations that lead Oroonoko to Surinam: the remaking of him into a modern subject by way of a ruinous and dissenting sexual coupling.

Imoinda's Body and the Deportation of Dissent

Before Oroonoko becomes a slave subject, he becomes a sexual subject. And he becomes a sexual subject at the same time that he becomes a dissenting subject, a virtual Leveller, in fact, by way of his relation to Imoinda. After having married Imoinda illicitly without the king's knowledge, Oroonoko finds that she has been summoned by the king to become the newest royal concubine. Imoinda complies, keeping her marriage a secret while also meeting privately with Oroonoko and eventually consummating their love, violating, on the very grounds of the royal palace, the king's prior claim to her body. When the king learns of her treachery, he sells her into slavery and she ends up in Surinam. Later, in the weakened state that follows from his loss of Imoinda, Oroonoko himself is captured and sent to Surinam.

The question of obedience to a king and the rightfulness of dissent by subjects, catalyzed here by the couple's implicit transgression of the king's prerogative, is an Anglo-Atlantic question, as the couple's final Atlantic destination suggests. In other words, in claiming the right to choose a lover and in placing the value of inner "soul" and love over the king's right to decree and possess, Oroonoko and Imoinda set in motion a modern conflict that has transatlantic sources. Thus although Oroonoko is on the one hand aligned with the Stuart kings, on the other hand he also emblematizes the transgressive activity that brought down those kings. Attending, first of all, to the pivotal role of sex in this transgression, we see why the noble Oroonoko becomes a slave within the logic of Behn's Anglo-Atlantic text. And we see more clearly why gender has a more than symbolic place in the plot of ruin and liberty.

In the first half of the novel in Coramantien, a struggle between Oroonoko and the king is fought over Imoinda's sexual and reproductive body; and a similar struggle catalyzes the violence of the second half, in Surinam. Both struggles concern racial reproduction, but in Coramantien it is a question of royal succession, whereas across the Atlantic it also becomes a matter of slave reproduction. In Coramantien, Imoinda's sexual monogamy is a reigning question. The wretched Oroonoko spends the first half of the novel trespassing on the king's power by seeking out Imoinda to confirm her faithfulness to him and finally to make love to her behind the king's back. As read within England and the colonies, this story would surely resonate with the persistent question of whether there were any limits to a king's rights to the obedience and the "goods" of his subjects, and the extent to which a subject was obligated to obey against heart and conscience. Can disloyalty and dissent be justified? Imoinda and Oroonoko seem to think so and, writing from their point of view, the narrator encourages us to judge the king and sympathize with their disobedience.

Behn quietly keeps this conflict before our eyes, more than once revealing that Imoinda is continually subject to the king's "caresses." She reports explicitly that when Imoinda first arrives in the palace, the servants "(after disrobing her) led her to the Bath, and making fast the Doors, left her to descend. The King, without more Courtship, bad her throw off her Mantle, and come to his Arms" (12). Imoinda "all in Tears, threw herself on the Marble, on the brink of the Bath, and besought him to hear her" (13). Despite her pleading, he "commanded her to lay aside her Mantle, and suffer herself to receive his Caresses" (13). The threat to Imoinda's body drives the risky action of this part of the narrative, as Oroonoko seeks to "learn from *Imoinda's* own mouth" (15) the true state of her virginity. At the same time the narrator seems to hint at the inevitable decline of the old kingly social order by establishing for the reader that the king is impotent (though he "long'd with impatience to behold this gay thing . . . alas! he could not but innocently play" because, as Oroonoko's friends assure him, "the King's Old Age" makes him "uncapable of injuring him with *Imoinda*" [14]). In this way, too, Behn keeps the question of kingly power before us. At this point, the novel seems to offer a Whiggish sympathy for Oroonoko and Imoinda, but eventually the couple's transgression does bring disaster, in the form of deportation across the Atlantic and, ultimately, gruesome death. Thus, as we will see, in the final analysis it may be fair to say that Behn punishes Oroonoko and Imoinda for their "liberties."

This political drama is also a sexual drama because of Imoinda's reproductive role — she reproduces a particular race. Earlier in the story when the king worries about having "disoblig'd" Oroonoko "by the Rape of his Mistress," he is concerned not only because he is no longer "able to defend himself in War" but also because he has "no Sons of all his Race remaining alive, but only this [Oroonoko], to maintain him on his Throne" (26). Oroonoko, for all his tender love, recognizes the same value in Imoinda, so that her pregnancy after their reunion in Surinam makes Oroonoko "even adore her, knowing that he was the last of his great Race" (45). Likewise, when Byam has Oroonoko whipped, he keeps Imoinda safely distant at Parham House, "not in kindness to her, but for fear she should die with the sight, or miscarry, and then they should lose a young Slave, and perhaps the Mother" (67). Thus both the disobedience to kingly power and the accompanying Atlantic exile get played out across Imoinda's sexual body, which stands as the lynchpin of a racialized modern order of things.

In Surinam, Imoinda's desirable body becomes the contested meeting point between two racial orders, as her nobility and natural modesty mingle piquantly (in Behn's rendering) with her Atlantic slave condition. After relating how all the slave men pine after a certain woman slave named Clemene ("no Man, of any Nation, ever beheld her that did not fall in love with her" [42]), Trefry recounts his own attempts to molest this beauty, which are only defeated by her "Modesty" and tears. He then explains that Clemene, who turns out to be Imoinda, keeps herself "so retired, as if she fear'd a Rape even from the God of Day, or that breezes wou'd steal kisses from her delicate mouth" (42). And clearly she has some reason to fear, given Trefry's story of his own efforts: he confesses that he *"entertained her with love so long, as to be transported with my Passion even above Decency, I have been ready to make use of those Advantages of Strength and Force Nature has given me: But Oh! She disarms me with that Modesty and Weeping, so tender and so moving, that I retire"* (42–43, italics in original). We learn that "the Company laugh'd at his Civility to a Slave" (43), and it may be that Behn expects her readers to laugh at this hesitation to use force. Yet nonetheless, structurally, the narration of Imoinda's embattled position forms a refrain in the story.[15] It marks the site where force meets resistance, and common and noble trade places, tellingly achieved via an equivocally racialized woman — noble, African, and aristocratic yet humble, black, and enslaved. In the end, Oroonoko kills Imoinda because, as he explains, he cannot bear to leave "his lovely *Imoinda* a prey, or at least a Slave to the enraged Multitude" (71). Yet at another level his sacrificial murder of her (and indirectly himself) displays the murderous reproduction entailed in the remaking of a racial political order.

It is not simply, then, that Oroonoko's and Imoinda's sexual transgressions stand in for political transgressions. Rather, a sexual plot is implicitly political and racial, as Behn seems to have understood. Along with everything else that this perspicacious text ferrets out, it makes clear that Oroonoko's and Imoinda's sexual "liberties" trouble and yet reconstitute the whole political order.[16] As a result of their implicit challenge to the aristocratic order, Oroonoko and Imoinda become, in effect, racialized Atlantic subjects.

Swooning into Colonial Subjectivity

Behn makes a tableau of the moment when the lovers enter this new order of things — a dramatic swoon moment that recurs in many novels to come. In effect, she narrates the scene of interpellation into modernity. This calling-out entails a dissociative break when, as Behn's narrator puts it, the self "knew not that it had a Being" (43). The swoon's phoenix moment of death follows an Atlantic middle passage — or rather, in Behn's text, it substitutes for that middle passage, the violence of which is left unnarrated and unacknowledged and yet displaced into their near-death fainting at the first meeting in Surinam. Their mutual swoon gives rise to passive, sentimental, sacrificial selves that are re-racialized exactly by way of their modern and domestic love.[17]

When Oroonoko and Imoinda see each other for the first time after their ocean crossings, they exit their bodies. First Oroonoko "saw her Face, her Shape, her Air, her Modesty, and all that call'd forth his Soul with Joy at his Eyes, and left his Body destitute of almost Life: it stood without Motion, and for a Minute knew not that it had a Being" (43). Oroonoko's dissociation from himself (later repeated in his temporary paralysis by the eel) allegorizes what he is undergoing culturally. Significantly, it is only in witnessing the counterpart "death" of Imoinda that Oroonoko reconnects to himself in this new reality: "and, I believe" says the narrator, "he had never come to himself, so oppress'd he was with Over-joy, if he had not met with this allay, that he perceived *Imoinda* fall dead in the hands of Trefry. This awaken'd him, and he ran to her aid, and caught her in his Arms, where by degrees she came to herself" (43–44). Only when Oroonoko sees Imoinda fall dead in the hands of Trefry — under threat once more of a bodily confiscation — does he take up his place as a man — but now as a sentimental, interiorized man — "oppress'd" with this new joy — a man who will be claimed by the English in the same way that Imoinda was once claimed by the king. And only when she is returned to Oroonoko's arms will Imoinda herself awaken within this new order, where her "Modesty" and purity and finally motherhood hold her and Oroonoko in captive place.

This moment has been in preparation ever since Oroonoko first "fell in love" with Imoinda. As the Englishwoman recounts it, from his first sight of her, Oroonoko's love for Imoinda diverges from the custom of his country and partakes of an emergent Western-style, modern love. It is his passion for Imoinda, a certain *kind* of passion for her, that lifts him out of his noble role as loyal and heroic subject within Coramantien and eventually resituates him in his sentimentalized role as slave in Surinam. Tellingly, the narrator's early description of Oroonoko's new passion is circuitous and contradictory.

> as he knew no Vice, his Flame aim'd at nothing but Honour, if such a distinction may be made in Love; and especially in that Country where Men take to themselves as many as they can maintain; and where the only Crime and Sin

with Woman is, to turn her off, to abandon her to want, shame, and misery; such ill Morals are only practis'd in *Christian* Countries, where they prefer the bare Name of religion; and, without Vertue or Morality, think that sufficient. But *Oroonoko* was none of those Professors; but as he had right Notions of Honour, so he made her such Propositions as were not only and barely such; but, contrary to the custom of his Country, he made her Vows, she shou'd be the only Woman he wou'd possess while he liv'd; that no Age or Wrinkles would encline him to change; for her Soul wou'd be always fine, and always young; and he shoul'd have an eternal *Idea* in his mind of the Charms she now bore; and shou'd look into his Heart for that *Idea,* when he cou'd find it no longer in her Face. (10 – 11)

First we learn that honor may have no place in love, but rather vice seems always mingled with love — and this is especially so in Oroonoko's country, the narrator tells us, with its polygamous practices. Then she remarks, however, that this custom may well be superior to those in "Christian countries" where language and intention diverge and monogamous men (unlike polygamous men) will abandon the wife for the mistress, and yet speak of their love for women.

On the one hand, we witness here a reconfiguration of English identity via its colonial encounters, within which there emerges an incipient gender critique, as English customs are now glimpsed from the outside in. The non-European Oroonoko, the narrator assures us pointedly, knew no false divergence between word and deed, speech and act. Yet, on the other hand, those "outside" customs are being absorbed into an English narrative of love. For neither is he a man of his own country when it comes to love, after all: through Imoinda he suddenly understands monogamy, that English practice which the narrator has just outlined as culturally specific. Furthermore, Oroonoko's monogamy, "contrary to the custom of his country," depends on the notion of an unchanging "Soul" (Imoinda's interiority) and an "eternal Idea" (expressed outwardly in Imoinda's face). It is by way of his eternal idea of her essential interiority that she, in turn, has "an eternal Empire over him," as the narrator goes on to say.

The mention of empire is telling — as indeed the whole passage reveals more than it admits — for at this moment not only his notion of marriage practices but also Oroonoko's very philosophy of love and faith becomes English: he becomes a subject of that empire. Fittingly, then, this turn from Coramentien love to Western-style love corresponds to a change in Oroonoko's character as a nobleman, his movement away, that is, from his aristocratic racial identity and toward affiliation with "the rest of the Negroes" — a foreshadowing of his later coalition with "the rest of the Negroes" in their disastrous slave revolt.[18] At first, Oroonoko's gallantry in love is framed as a feature of his high-born, noble-blooded soul. "This prince . . . whose soul and body were so admirably adorned was as capable of love, as twas possible for a brave and gallant man to be; and in saying that, I have named the highest degree of love; for sure, great souls are most capable of that passion" (81). In this sense, Oroonoko's capacity for love appears as a passion that bears testimony to the legitimacy of old notions of noble and common races.

But this changes when Oroonoko meets Imoinda, and it shifts further once Oroonoko hears (falsely) that the king has killed Imoinda.[19] With that news, Oroonoko begins fully to question outward, monarchical, military forms of nobility and adopt an interior, Leveller-ish and Whiggish mode of "noble" self. In fact, his heartbreak leads him explicitly to abandon his investment in the traditional idea of a noble race—and prompts an early swoon that foreshadows his later, Atlantic undoing. Just before he is told that Imoinda is dead (the king thinking this would be easier for Oroonoko to bear), he is poised to enter battle as the heroic general of the king. Learning that he has lost her, he swoons: "he laid himself on a Carpet . . . and remained a good while silent, and was hardly heard to sigh [so that] whatever his greatest Officers . . . cou'd do, they could not raise him from the Carpet, or persuade him to Action and Resolutions of Life; but commanding all to retire, he shut himself into his Pavilion all that day, while the Enemy was ready to engage" (28). When all the chiefs of the army come to him and "implore him to have regard to his Glory," he tells them that "he had now no more business for Glory" and then explicitly rejects the idea and the system of lineal nobility:

> He reply'd, he would not give himself the trouble [of choosing a new leader for them]; but wished 'em to choose the bravest man amongst 'em, *let his quality or birth be what it wou'd*. "For, o my friends!" (said he), "it is not Titles make Men brave or good; or Birth that bestows Courage and Generosity, or makes the owner happy. Believe this, when you behold Oroonoko, the most wretched." (29, emphasis added)

Here Oroonoko's capacity for monogamous love not only depletes his interest in the glories of war and honor but it also compels him to question the validity of distinctions of birth and rank, all in the pursuit of "happiness." Yet, as an African in this new rank-dismantling order, his fate is slavery. Thus this scene prepares and heralds his entry into Atlantic slavery. His mourning and his withdrawal from the field of battle allow the Europeans to trick him onto their boat, leading him to his deathlike swoon and remaking in Surinam, and they ultimately lead to his gruesome death, when his paralysis at the sight of the deceased Imoinda prevents his noble revenge on Byam, so that he is recaptured, dismembered, and burned at the stake in a denouement that Behn's audience apparently considered sublime.

The sentimental nature of Oroonoko's and Imoinda's love — or rather the *notion* of freely chosen, politically untainted love which however entails self-sacrifice — enables the kidnapping of them into the narrative of English history. The very steadfastness and insideness of their love explains, as the narrator casts it, their tolerance of slavery: even though Oroonoko "accus'd himself for having suffer'd Slavery for so long: yet he charg'd that weakness on love alone, who was capable of making him neglect even Glory itself" (47). Indeed, the narrator reports, "Caesar swore he disdained the Empire of the World, while he could behold his *Imoinda;* and she despised Grandeur and Pomp, those Vanities of her Sex, when she could gaze on Oroonoko. He ador'd the very Cottage where she resided, and said, That little Inch of the World would give him more *Happiness* than all the Universe cou'd do; and she vow'd, it was a Palace, while adorned with the Presence of *Oroonoko*" (44, emphasis added). Such a moment prefigures the novelistic paradigm that reaches its climax in *Uncle Tom's Cabin,* where slaves in their "cottages" become the embodiment of a true, free interiority in love. In this light, we can revisit the importance of the question, for Oroonoko, of Imoinda's virginity and reconsider his phrasing of it: "whether she was robb'd of that Blessing which was only due to his Faith and Love" (15).[20] He receives the blessing of her virginity not because of his station or royal manhood but because of his "Faith" — his monogamous, English-styled vow: his emergent Englishness as a man in love, Western-style. In effect, the precariousness and violence of modernity is being reframed as the story of a swooning love. And yet a bodily robbery has occurred.

At the same time, insofar as Oroonoko's embrace of sentimental monogamy and "contractual" marriage undoes him from within and then transforms his racial status, it also apparently allegorizes, for Behn, how the reorganization of culture around liberty and contract leads to chaos, violence, and the end of noble races. His falling in love begins the undoing of the aristocratically noble body by the Atlantic forces of liberty. Behn places the threat of sexual agency and violation at the heart of this allegory of the undoing power of liberty. Through Oroonoko, she reveals how these sexual-political crises create a conflicted, self-dialoguing, feminized, and isolated subject, an outsider to society's traditional codes — and an Atlantic protagonist ready to enter the new racial order of "whites" and "Negroes."

Enter Whiteness

Crucially, Imoinda's and Oroonoko's moment of mutual swooning and interpellation is also the moment when the Anglo-Atlantic female narrator enters the story — now as a participant-observer and not just a reporter.[21] She enters as one all at once drawn by their sentimental love, invested in their quest for liberty, and implicated in their enslavement in the colony. That is, she enters as the vehicle that helps to recast Oroonoko and Imoinda as creatures of a timeless, place-transcending love in which they are simultaneously reborn as enslaved blacks. Behn's sentimentalization of "cottages" and slavery (her contribution to an emerging paradigm) not only elides, for her audience, the true bodily realities of the middle passage and slave experience;[22] it also catapults her readers, through her narrator, into this new order in which Englishness "itself," rather than Stuarts or Protestants or courtly nobles, will come to occupy the center of the story. The narrator is the "white focalizer," drawing readers into a new racial order, fostering their identification with a place far from England while also wedding them to the inside of this emergent, imperial English identity.

The narrator's entry moment is marked by a number of double moves that at once encourage and undercut identification with Oroonoko. Informed by Trefry about the reunion of the lovers, she first of all explains: "I was as impatient to make these Lovers a Visit, having already made a Friendship with Caesar and from his own Mouth learned what I have related; which was confirmed by his *Frenchman* who was set on shore to seek his fortune, and of whom they cou'd not make a Slave, because a Christian; and he came daily to *Parham-Hill* to see and pay his respects to his Pupil Prince" (44). She tells us that her narration proceeds from the authoritative mouth of Oroonoko, although immediately that authority is put into some question when she needs to confirm it by way of the Frenchman. Enfolded in this equivocal move is the crucial point that the Frenchman is unenslaveable though he is merely the tutor of his ambivalently characterized "Pupil Prince," Oroonoko.

A similar concatenation of African/European and noble/common occurs in the subsequent description of Imoinda. The narrator establishes Imoinda's noble lineage, before she learns of her relationship with Oroonoko, when she notes that "we took [her] to be of Quality . . . from her being carved in fine flowers all over her Body" (45). The marks provide a basis for identity with Imoinda as both noble and "native" in her practices (in fact, these markings, we are told, "resemble our antient Picts that are figur'ed in the Chronicles"). But on the other hand, they call for a paragraph of explanation from the narrator and they signify as exotic (taking their place among the narrator's other descriptions of exotica in the fish and animals, and in the customs of Surinam Indians). The description allows her audience to simultaneously claim some exoticism for themselves — in the distant past — and marvel at the lingering exoticism of these Africans. But finally, it is "when we knew Clemene was Imoinda" — the lover over whom Oroonoko has been pining — that they most admire and accept her. Imoinda's status as sentimental love object transcends all exotic or strange differences and brings her into the narrator's circle.

This transitional in-betweenness of the narrator's characterization of Imoinda and Oroonoko (indicating a larger historical transformation) finds its correlative in her ambiguous self-positioning as the mediator of their liberty.[23] Just as we might imagine Behn attempting, by way of her writing projects, to resignify and contain the liberty discourse, her narrator plays the role of she who withholds or condones access to liberty. Most centrally, she reports that she "had assured [Oroonoko] of liberty as soon as the Governour arrived" (44 – 45). Apparently she operates as an empowered representative of the Anglo-Atlantic society who can "assure" Oroonoko of his liberty. Liberty is hers to convey — though not to "the rest of the Negroes," only to these sentimental lovers. The narrator's gender determines this mediating role. She explains that Oroonoko "liked the company of us women much above them men" and so she discourses with him on polite and learned topics (including "the Loves of the Romans" and the "stories of Nuns" as she initiates him into the courtly literary traditions he will also emblematize for her) (46). It is, significantly, within the context of this gender distinction that the narrator speaks of herself as part of an "us": she tells her readers that the women's entertaining and edifying conversations "oblig[ed] [Oroonoko to] love *us* [meaning the women] very well" so that "*we* had all the Liberty of Speech with him, especially myself" (46, emphasis added). As with her history writing, it is her femininity, her very marginality, that gives her the "liberty" to speak where others cannot. Yet this feminine position also, as we'll see, limits her free agency and in this way encourages her hypocrisy, for this womanly subjectivity leads her to move from an "us" aligned with Oroonoko to an "us" aligned against him — providing a pivot, that is, for the new colonial racial order despite all of her feminine sympathy with Oroonoko's displaced nobility.

Quite markedly, in her next few references to "us," something shifts, and underlying the shift is the uncertainty about what constitutes "us."[24] It suddenly becomes unclear whether "us" and "we" mean the nobly identified women or the larger white community — and by extension whether their community includes Oroonoko (and all such African nobles) or excludes him. When the narrator begins to describe Oroonoko's increasing doubts about gaining his liberty, she relates that "we [took it ill that he] should suspect we would break our words with him"

(46). She further tells Oroonoko he should be careful not to give "us a fear of him" because it might "compel us to treat him so as I should be very loth to behold" (46). Here the "us" seems to include the white colonials who would enact the punishment which our narrator — at once part of and separate from them — would not like to behold but would be "compelled" to allow and witness.

It is in the midst of her change in alliance — from a genteel female aligned with Oroonoko to a white aligned with the English men, despite their commonness — that she "strives" to "soften" the language she uses in discussing his captivity. Reading his body language, seeing his interior by way of his exterior, as the emergent "white" woman is so skilled in doing, she tells us, "I perceived he resented that word [confinement], which I strove to soften again in vain" (47). The softening language of a colonial woman helps to elide this shift of racial alliances, from ennobled female to colonizing white. At this point, the narrator's relation to Oroonoko quickly moves from one of perfect intimacy to one of stark dishonesty. Although she reassures him, and he offers his promise of submission and expresses his "entire confidence" in her, she in the very next sentence announces it "no longer convenient to trust him" and openly positions herself against Oroonoko on the side of the white "country who feared him" (48). In the rest of the narrative, she serves as a spy while pretending to be a friend. In other words, she completes the transformation by which genteel English daughter becomes dominant white, and by which noble African becomes enslaved black.

This turn in her relations with Oroonoko arises from the uncertain ground of liberty's relation to authority. That is, her role is prompted by the unsettling of authority in Atlantic modernity, symbolized in the drowning of one governor and the delayed arrival of another. The narrator at once steps into the breach, operating as the agent of liberty, and suffers from a sense of vulnerability, in which (in her view) she could at any moment become "prey" to the disorder unleashed by unauthorized liberty. Thus when Oroonoko leads the slave rebellion, she reports "we were possess'd with extreme Fear, which no Persuasions could dissipate, that he would secure himself till night, and then, that he would come down and cut all our Throats. This apprehension made all the Females of us fly down the River, to be secured" (68).

And yet she implies that the crises of Oroonoko's whipping and the lovers' deaths might have been avoided if she *had* been on the scene, "for I suppose I had Authority and Interest enough there, had I suspected [Governor Byam's cruel intentions]" (68). Nonetheless at a later crisis-moment she again flees, merely because, once Oroonoko is recaptured, half-dead from starvation and grief after his murder of Imoinda, he looks and smells so "ghastly" that "I was persuaded to leave the place for some time, (being myself but sickly, and very apt to fall into

Fits of dangerous Illness upon any extraordinary Melancholy)" (76). Oddly, in this parenthesis and with the narrator's removal of herself, his ordeal of fainting becomes hers.

Africanism is thus launched. When the narrator reappears in the final paragraph of the novella, after her body-collapsing fit, she too reawakens, by way of Oroonoko's story, into the modern order of things — but as a writing subject rather than as a mangled slave-king.[25] She has taken Imoinda's place as the pivot in this turn into a new modern order. As Imoinda unintentionally drew Oroonoko across the Atlantic, so now the narrator holds him there.

On terms she does not wholly choose or endorse, Behn thus enters into modern authorship. In her narrator's closing words, she equivocally marks herself as secondary yet central. The narrator first bemoans the death of "this great Man" and wishes for "a more sublime Wit than mine to write his Praise," and yet she hopes nonetheless that her "pen" can "make his glorious Name to survive to all Ages, with that of the brave, the beautiful, and the constant *Imoinda*" (78). She and Imoinda speak last — or rather she, *through Imoinda,* speaks last:[26] a substitution that further prepares the turn toward an Africanist mode, as confirmed in future versions of the drama that cast Imoinda as a white woman. The Anglo-colonial woman's very removal, in two senses, allows her to colonize the presences of Imoinda and Oroonoko and so to rewrite their Atlantic story as a tale of Caesar's England.

In *Oroonoko,* Behn does after all fashion a *romance* of history. And in this way she begins the work of the Atlantic novel.

5 Rape as Entry into Liberty
Haywood and Richardson

IN "RAPE AND THE RISE OF THE NOVEL" Frances Ferguson argues that rape provided the impetus for the rise of the psychological novel, specifically for *Pamela* and *Clarissa,* which she considers "the first full examples of the psychological novel."[1] According to Ferguson, the indeterminacy of rape prompted the novel's turn to psychology. That is, because rape is a crime owing to its conditions of nonconsent, and because evidence of nonconsent, especially under patriarchy and behind closed doors, is elusive, it can be difficult to prove that a sexual act between adults is rape. Ferguson details how various traditions of law—including Hebrew law, Saxon law, commentaries of and on Edward Coke's *Institutes,* and recent feminist proposals—have attempted and failed, by way of "invariable formulae," to determine the grounds for ascertaining whether an act is rape (92–95). In Ferguson's account, Richardson meant to expose the false ground of the law's search for material "truth" in the trial of rape. She argues that, in the process of exposing this missing ground, Richardson created the mode of the psychological novel.

I suggest we reframe Ferguson's insight about the link between novels and rape. Although the story of rape has provided a vehicle for the novel's psychological plots, Ferguson's account of rape as the origin for these plots begs a question—for if rape has always been a site of indeterminacy about consent, and legal formulae have therefore always been inadequate to it, why, suddenly, does an *eighteenth-century* author turn to "psychology" and make rape a central plot? Why didn't this happen earlier? I propose that the turn inward and to rape arose from a web of political and religious Atlantic conditions. Because the *interior* of the free-born Englishperson had been increasingly fashioned over the previous century as the *source* of the *exterior,* legal order, the question of "consent" had emerged as a central and a psychological question. Meanwhile, given the tumultuous and newly centrifugal dispersion of power, labor, and law in the English-language Atlantic world, the status of consent had become widely indeterminate, for all kinds of subjects. The nature of consent was a continuously pressing question in the polis, capable of provoking unrest, not to mention torture, war, and revolution. To stabilize, legitimize, and yet delimit the subject's rights to representation and, thereby, to consent or dissent, the identity of Englishness had become crucial. At the same time, the spread of print and the uneven censorship of it had allowed stories about nonconsent and the tyrannous violence that suppresses it to be told at all. In this light, the rape story comes to light within and *expresses* rather than causes the crisis of consent, the inward turn, and the increasing instability of the cultural self.

In short, the English-language novel's rape plot has geopolitical sources in Atlantic modernity.[2] In the fiction of Eliza Haywood and Samuel Richardson, the Atlantic is nowhere to be seen; and yet these two authors are innovative fashioners of the interior selves and conflicts over consent spawned by Atlantic modernity — the conditions of which are implicitly embedded in their novels. Following Behn, they develop the ruinous swoon as the scene of interpellation within a treacherous world, and they nativize it for authors to come. Eliza Haywood has recently garnered the critical attention she deserves, but her formative place in the history of the novel becomes clearer when we note how the form of her fiction provides a bridge between Behn and later Atlantic novelists. She crafts a discourse of interior self-dialogue that is narrated from a margin, shaped by continual geographic "removals," and climaxes in a moment of ruin catalyzed by a liberty telos.[3]

Richardson further develops this interiorized liberty drama, placing rape and its swooning aftermath at the center, most especially, of *Clarissa*. First of all, in *Clarissa,* he makes the liberty struggle explicitly native, infusing it with the rhetoric of English birthright. Second, he launches this plot on a more epic scale than had been done, creating a multivolume freedom-seeking subject equivalent to the multivolume histories of freedom-seeking nations. In the process he discovers the full potential of the epistolary form, occasionally used by Haywood, including its capacity for "manifesting" the native self's free interiority. And, perhaps most perspicuously, Richardson stages the Anglo woman's entry into modernity's free, republican order as a trauma shaped by a deadly contest over property with her ambitious brother, himself empowered by the family's new colonial wealth.

Above all, the central insight for which Haywood and Richardson deserve shared credit is that rape encodes and embodies a political story. We find evidence of just how profoundly this political story is an Atlantic story in the political pamphlets I discuss briefly at the start of this chapter. Read together, the pamphlets of the seventeenth-century Leveller Thomas Overton and the eighteenth-century political theorists Thomas Paine and Edmund Burke recall the Atlantic context and the rhetoric of violation that makes the novel's rape plot so resonant.

History Breaks In

In his 1646 pamphlet *The Commoners Complaint: or, Dreadful Warning from Newgate, to the Commons of England, Presented to the Honourable Committee for consideration of Commoners Liberties,* Thomas Overton tries to awaken his compatriots into a liberated consciousness. He writes, as he explains it, so that "(as in a Glasse) every Free-man of *England* may clearly behold his own imminent insufferable bondage and slavery under the *Norman-Prerogative* Men of this Kingdom."[4] He recounts the "Turkish Cruelties" (376) and "barbarous inhumanities" (376) by which these "Prerogative-Butchers" (376), "Prerogative-Porters" (377), and "Prerogative Lordships" (394) of the House of Lords have violated the commoners' "Birth-right, Liberties, and Freedomes" (376). In other words, the Lords' Norman practices are outlandish — they are foreign cruelties inflicted on natives. And over time their power has gotten bolder. The Peers' "barbarous unheard of inhumanities" exceed those "acted by their Norman progenitors" (376). Overton nativizes the fight for freedom — as would pamphleteers and novelists for centuries to come.

Novelists will also repeat his climactic scene of sexualized violence. Overton reaches the pitch of his rage in recalling how the officers used force on his wife when she resisted arrest for aiding the publication of seditious documents (including those of her jailed husband). The "prerogative vassals," he reports, "[broke] open the doore, and [entered] her Chamber," pulled her child from her arms, and finally "dragged" her through the streets to Newgate. On the way, neighbors and strangers called her "*Strumpet* and *vile Whore*" (391), "which dishonourable infamous usage was a sufficient matter to blast her reputation for ever" (391). Overton's description prefigures those scenes of domestic invasion and violation central to novels from Richardson's *Clarissa* to Pauline Hopkins's *Contending Forces*,[5] whose heroines thus emerge as descendants not only of Livy's Lucretia but also of the protesting English women violated by outlandish Stuart-Norman tyranny. Meanwhile, Overton's pamphlet displays the power of print:[6] he enters into print modernity so as to expose its destabilization of persons and reputations, and he simultaneously uses print to gain access to a discourse of race and freedom that counteracts that vulnerability. In other words, he exemplifies the way that print — and especially printed stories of racialized violation — will be both the weapon of individuals against the state and their form of participation in the state, the signature of their racial contract with the state.

In their eighteenth-century pamphlets, Edmund Burke and Thomas Paine wield print in exactly this way. By the time Paine and Burke penned their pamphlets, both the violation story and this print-logic (whereby the very instabilities exposed in a publication are counteracted by this print record) were becoming ubiquitous. Indeed, the power of their writing partly derives from their ability to redeploy these Overtonian tropes that were contemporaneously accruing in gothic and seduction novels. In addition, they bring into view the Atlantic triangle of Europe, America, and Africa that conditions Overton's text. In Paine, we just glimpse the African dimension of this triangle that then becomes more visible in Burke.

Paine and Burke differed, of course, in their views of the French Revolution and of the wisdom of insurgent resistance to the state. In the tradition of William Walwyn, Paine's *Common Sense* particularly debunks the privileging of a "Gothic balance" and of the ancient constitution that Burke will champion, casting the latter as a document that merely defends the "tyrannies" of a "race of kings."[7] Yet both men invoke the "common-sense" association between "ravishment" by such kings and the colonial experience. As Paine tells the story in his American revolutionary pamphlet, the English kings are the invading rapists who threaten to violate — as he oddly puts it — the continent's "mistress": "As well can the lover forgive the ravisher of his mistress, as the continent can forgive the murders of Britain" (99). He goes on to explain that the American continent has become an "asylum" for Freedom, which he figures as a female "fugitive" who is "hunted" around the globe. He insists that on this continent "she" will find safety, for "the domestic tranquility of a nation depends greatly on the *chastity* of what may properly be called NATIONAL MATTERS" (113 appendix, emphasis, italics, and caps in original).[8] Thus, in accord with much of the visual representation of revolutionary America as a violated woman, for Paine the free republic is a chaste polis protected from a race of ravenous kings by the emergent nation's heroic revolutionaries.[9]

In his conclusion, Paine paints an imperial vision for this land in which the nearly raped she-citizen finds asylum, and here, as we will also see is the case in Burke's pamphlet, the nation's untainted legacy acquires buoyancy against the background-horizon of an African-Atlantic world. Highlighting the competitive maritime world in which the as-yet unraped nation pursues its imperial destiny, Paine pronounces that "[s]hip-building is America's greatest pride, and in which, she will in time excel the whole world. The great empires of the east are mostly inland, and consequently excluded from the possibility of rivalling her. Africa is in a state of barbarism" (104). With Africa and the East as backdrop, Paine invokes the vision of an American empire at sea, defeating the British and claiming the world, all on behalf of a threatened national purity.

Writing a few decades later in the wake of the American, French, and Haitian revolutions, in *Reflections on the Revolution in France,* Edmund Burke synthesizes and shrewdly reconfigures the key elements of this narrative of ruin and freedom. By contrast to Walwyn and Paine, he begins by grandly invoking the familiar story of an English "*inheritance from our forefathers*" dating to the Magna Carta and upheld in the Petition of Right. He emphasizes that the English built their revolutions "not on abstract principles 'as the rights of men' but as the rights of Englishmen."[10] "Upon that body and stock," he explains in a language comparable to Catharine Macaulay's, "we have taken care not to inoculate any scion alien to the nature of the original plant" (181), so that English liberty "becomes a noble freedom" with "pedigree" that "inspires us with a sense of habitual native dignity" (185). He reads the French Revolution within these nativist terms, as I've discussed elsewhere.[11] The French, he insists, should have followed the English example and "derived your claims from a more early race of ancestors," for the French "had all these advantages in your ancient states" (187).

As Burke then moves toward his own climactic version of the violation scene, he reveals how another racial attitude is pressing forward this nativist one.[12] Condemning, first of all, the boldness of the French rebels, Burke scolds them for allowing the violence of the Atlantic economy to infiltrate their Frenchness and for choosing "to act as if you had never been moulded into civil society" (187) — for revolting, he says, like Africans. That is, instead of giving their revolution native European pedigree, the French revolutionaries appeared — and were "content to be represented" — like "a gang of Maroon slaves" who presumably have no such "noble" history by which to authorize violence but rather who "suddenly broke loose from the house of bondage" (188). Making a further comparison to colonial racial violence, he depicts the revolutionaries advancing through the streets like "a procession of American savages," with their women acting as "ferocious" as men (226). These protestors allowed an opening, in other words, for identification between Maroon slaves or Indian savages and revolutionary Anglo-Europeans. The latter neglected to nativize the liberty plot so as to fashion the Anglo-

European self *against* the African or Indian other; and so they failed to enclose their northern nation within a history that gives pedigree to violent deeds done in the name of liberty.

Burke is living in the Atlantic triangle, in other words. Much as he condemns the French, he identifies a common "European" ground with them: their freedom, anchored in ancient records, is akin to his — and alien to that of escaped slaves. He is perhaps as unsettled by the potential of French and Haitian revolutions to collapse that European/African difference within the Atlantic economy as he is motivated by English condescension toward France.

His racialization of the French Revolution then frames his sensational account of the violation of Marie Antoinette. It recalls Overton's story, rewrites Paine's Anglo-Atlantic scene of rape, and draws on what were by now the familiar castle scenes of gothic fiction.[13] In his version, after ruthlessly killing the sentinel at Marie Antoinette's bedroom door, "a band of cruel ruffians and assassins, reeking with his blood, rushed into the chamber of the queen, and pierced with an hundred strokes of bayonets and poniards the bed, from whence this persecuted woman had just time to fly almost naked, and through ways unknown to the murderers had escaped" (232). Thus do these French ruffians, who have already been identified with savages and slaves, invade the queen's chamber and violate her bed.[14] As it is Norman barbarism that manhandles Overton's wife so it is African barbarism — if we extrapolate — that violates the queen. In effect what is raped *is* Anglo-European nativeness, most especially its freedom inheritance. In the 150 years between Overton and Burke, Africans and Indians in the Americas have come to replace "foreign" Norman-Europeans as the invasive rapists of the ancient tradition.

Strikingly, Burke closes his pamphlet by imagining himself on a threatened vessel at sea. His comments indicate that he shares Paine's preoccupation with an empire built on sea-power, while they also suggest that Burke's anxiety about the Maroon threat was coupled with an anxiety about Britain's empire at sea, exactly in the face of the Anglo-American will to "excel the whole world" at the art of shipbuilding and imperial expansion. His polemic about the French Revolution comes, he explains, from the pen of a man who perceives that "the equipoise of the vessel in which he sails, may be endangered by overloading it upon one side" and who therefore "is desirous of carrying the small weight of his reasons to that which may preserve its equipoise" (414). With the "weight" of ancient British law and reason, Burke aims to counteract a threatening cargo he has implicitly figured as the African threat in the Atlantic triangle. Paine more arrogantly places that cargo in its proper place, as an African barbarism well secured in the hold, and this Anglo-American confidence and cargo may well explain Burke's sense of lost equipoise on the Atlantic. For the power of African labor and bondage enriching the United States does ultimately threaten the British Atlantic hegemony.

Here is the Atlantic story of *Oroonoko* being reconfigured. In both Paine's and Burke's pamphlets, the native Anglo-European replaces the African as the violated and freedom-seeking subject, even as the African replaces the alien tyrant-king as the violating barbarian. No longer are Africans the first modern subjects (as Behn indicates unintentionally): Anglo-Atlantic peoples are, and they must lead Africans and others into modernity on the sea. While Paine scorns the British and apparently differs from Burke in arguing for the natural rights of man rather than for the rights of Englishmen, these natural rights are implicitly racialized via a habit of thought he shares with Burke. Both men conjure the vision of a racial Atlantic empire pitched against the threat of alien rape. Edmund Burke worries (mistakenly in fact) that the French missed the opportunity to properly reconcile race and modernity under the sign of freedom and so sustain a proper genealogy.[15] But both men's pamphlets work to establish that genealogy and they successfully justify it within a print-rhetoric of liberty. They prefigure the ways that the story of this modernity will be told for years to come—as late as Ian Watt's *Rise of the Novel*—as a traumatic struggle haunted by the threat of "Maroon" rape of "white" women.

Liberty in Motion: Eliza Haywood

Yet to get here, to arrive at Burke's and Paine's (and Ian Watt's) figuring of rape as a story of liberty and race, it's necessary to track the story of rape in fiction after Behn, and therefore to turn to Eliza Haywood. Haywood makes no references to Atlantic colonies, to race in an explicit sense, or to slavery. Yet in her fiction she explores rape as an effect of "liberty" that undercuts "equipoise" in the social contract and that banishes women. She also allows us to glimpse how these conditions send women into the arms of Britishness.

After Aphra Behn, in other words, it is Eliza Haywood who most popularly and incisively exposes the Catch-22's of consent in modernity as expressed in the dynamics of heterosexual seduction or rape. Not only was Haywood among those few authors who "absolutely dominated prose fiction in the decade of the 1720s"; she wrote prolifically throughout the next two decades and in the process set down patterns that canonical authors would follow—in particular, as I'll show in the second half of this chapter, Richardson's novel *Clarissa*.[16] As critics have recently explored, later novelists borrowed numerous motifs and above all the seduction plot from Haywood and other early women novelists, presenting their projects as "reformed" versions of the plot of ruin (a reforming turn that Haywood herself emulated and parodied in her later fiction).[17]

As critics have suggested, the British political landscape of the early eighteenth century, and in particular its climate of dissent under Walpole, fostered Haywood's preoccupation with consent, seduction, and ruin.[18] Walpole's cabinet manipulations, control of the press, interference in city politics, and aversion to foreign and even mercantile war alienated citizens across the spectrum of British politics.[19] It is partly in opposition to Walpole that English subjects both Tory and Whig increasingly rallied, as we've seen, around the ideas of liberty, consent, and dissent. As Melissa Mowry observes, Walpole's maneuvers created a "tense political climate" that "resurrected memories of the civil wars."[20] In this light, Mowry argues, Haywood's licentious plots and protagonists implicitly invoke a discourse dating back to the pornographic publications of the Civil War, which represented political upheaval as an outgrowth of loose or perverse sexuality, so that even her earlier, more strictly sexual stories carry a political resonance for her readers. Likewise, Shea Stuart suggests that in her sexual plots Haywood was probing the contemporary notion of contractual politics.[21] Most clearly in *Eovaai*, through the voice of an editor presenting a translation of a foreign manuscript, Haywood critiques Walpole's "tyranny" and narrates it via the abduction and threatened rape of a female queen.

The question of freedom surfaces throughout Haywood's fiction, always in conjunction with women's response to the double standard in heterosexual relations. In *The History of Miss Betsy Thoughtless*, Haywood not only exposes Betsy to threats of rape but in Betsy's first, unhappy marriage she clearly raises the old questions about disobedience of authority and echoes the old rhetoric of tyranny and yoke. Tortured by the cruelty and infidelity of her husband, Betsy argues that when a husband is "ignorant of the regard he ought to have for his wife, or forgets to put it in practice, he can expect neither affection or obedience" (510). She eventually concludes that "[n]either divine, nor human laws . . . can now compel me any longer to endure the cold neglects, the insults, the tyranny" of this husband and so she begins to consider "easing myself of that heavy yoke" (590). As we saw in chapter 2, Restoration dramatists mocked the analogy between wifely and political dissent, but in the post-1688 atmosphere of tempered monarchy, writers began to probe this analogy more seriously.[22] In 1706, Mary Astell explicitly pointed to the contradiction between support for a balance of power in the state and denial of such a balance in the family: "If Absolute Sovreignty be not necessary in a State, how does it to be so in a Family. . . . *If all Men are born free, how is it that all Women are born Slaves?*"[23] Such questions filled the air in the early eighteenth century, and Haywood's rape stories absorb and digest them.

In the following pages I consider Haywood's seemingly apolitical earlier novellas for the way they use a plot of violation to create a drama about liberty and consent. In these works readers become insiders by way of identification with the uprooted, ruined women who "lose position" and are forced to cultivate private, carefully disguised interiors. By contrast to later reforming writers, including Richardson, she was more interested in how agency, not chastity, was at risk in the new, contractual order of things: her rape plots dramatize how it is women's *desire* — rather than women's virtue — that this new world tricks out of itself. In stories such as *Fantomina* and *The British Recluse,* women seek *entry* into the modern economy but then discover that their entry into *it,* although apparently free, flips over into its entry into *them.* Freedom has a catch, so to speak, and it is a woman. Haywood thus narrates the conditions under which modern persons "join" a "free" society only by undergoing self-alienation while they also all encounter a sexual hailing, which for women *is* the moment of alienation, yet which also marks the moment of their entry into a national identity. Further, Haywood located this interpellation in an unstable world of mobile, monadic subjects cut loose from family — quietly indicating the larger geographical dispersions that condition this story and make rape a fitting trope.

IN *FANTOMINA; OR, LOVE IN A MAZE* (1725), a young woman travels to the city, perceives the freedom with which men speak to prostitutes, desires that freedom, and decides to masquerade, initially, as a prostitute. Thinking to manage her own form of "entry," she soon finds herself entered by force, that is, raped by the man she desires, Beauplaisir; this unhinging of her identity releases her into a subjectivity that is secret, discontinuous, and serial — involving a sequence of masked performances on her part. Thus this violation also yields her creative project of self-fashioning and social mobility: she secretly dons a series of disguises (moving upward across class lines, as maid, widow, heiress) that will give her "liberty" and "Authority over herself" — and allow her to seduce again and again this one man.[24] In the process, Fantomina cultivates an inside and an outside so as to block full invasion of her "interior," while her creator, Haywood, in positioning us behind the disguise, entertains her readers with access to a "secret history" and interiority.

Tellingly, Fantomina's remaking of her identity arises first of all from her social isolation. In this she is like Robinson Crusoe — a similarity overlooked by critics — although the conditions of her isolation exist within the boundaries of England, the home island.[25] The narrator of *Fantomina* tells us explicitly that Fantomina manages her self-remaking project "by making no Person in the World a Confidant in it" (233). She has recently traveled from her country home to the city where she is "a Stranger to the World" and where she stays with an inattentive aunt so that she has "no Body in Town at the Time to whom she is obliged to be accountable for her Actions" (227). It is Fantomina's unusual anonymity, her remoteness from parental authority, and her temporary physical mobility that establish the privacy of her experiences and allow her to test the duplicity of men's conduct. Like Crusoe, she represents the emergent modern person, disconnected from family and community, and the rupture of these bonds teases forth a certain self-dialoguing interiority in her.

The opening of the story traces this emergence of interiority directly to her outsider position. Noting on her first night at the theater how many men ignore the "proper" women and bustle instead round the prostitutes, she expresses her "Contempt" of the men. She finds, however, that she is alone in her response: "But [her friends], either less surprized by being more accustomed to such Sights, than she who had been bred for the most Part in the Country, or not of a Disposition to consider any Thing very deeply, took but little Notice of it. She still thought of it, however; and the longer she reflected on it, the greater was her Wonder" (227). Fantomina's view from outside, prompting an interior disposition to consider things more deeply than her friends, "excited a Curiosity in her to know" about the sexual practices of the men and "in what Manner these Creatures [prostitutes] were addressed." She therefore pursues a kind of sexual ethnography by way of her succeeding orchestration of disguises, recording one man's behavior as it is shaped by his assumption that a woman is a harlot, or a chambermaid, or a widow, or an heiress. From her outsider position and through her several physical "removals" from one place to another, she not only unveils the sexual double standard and the organization of sexuality by class positions; she also exhibits the modern process of securing social membership and gaining a degree of power exactly by traveling outside the mainstream of English life.

But Fantomina's entry into this freer order of things, like Imoinda's and Oroonoko's, will be traumatic. At first, she becomes something alien to herself—when she is raped—and then she wakes up, like Imoinda and Oroonoko, with a new self: a self "in love," who from a position of individual isolation must navigate in a treacherous world. In her rendezvous with Beauplaisir on her first night in the guise of a high-class prostitute, she manages to draw a line at fondling, but on their second evening together, Beauplaisir "let her know, he would not be denied that Happiness the Freedoms she had allowed him made him hope." She "endeavoured to delay" and finally "struggled all she could," but nothing could "[curb] the wild exuberance of his luxurious Wishes, or [make] him in that longing, — that impatient Moment, change the Form of his Address. In fine, she was undone" (230). "After the ruinous Ecstasy was past" Fantomina dissolves in "Tears" and "Distraction," crying "Oh! no, I am undone beyond the Power of Heaven itself to help me!" as well as "many more such Exclamations" (231). This is the moment that commits Fantomina to a continued project of performance — her moment of interpellation and her entry as a secular self (beyond the power of heaven).

Throughout her fiction, Haywood returns again and again and again to this scene of undoing. Her choice of words indicates that freedom is the stake in these scenes, and that agency is confused in this world of freedom. In noting that "he would not be denied that Happiness the Freedoms she had allowed him made him hope," the narrator implies that Fantomina has "allowed" him freedom while at the same time it is he who practices these freedoms, and he can assert that he "will not be denied" this possibility. The confusion is exacerbated by the odd phrasing of "that Happiness the Freedoms she had allowed," which causes the reader at first to halt and wonder where the "Freedoms" fit into the sentence. The ownership and nature of these freedoms is just as uncertain as their grammatical role in the sentence.

This sentence implicitly registers the question that haunts the whole narrative and reiterates that question raised by the historic challenge to English monarchy: it wonders about how it is that natural *freedom* is *granted*. In Fantomina's case, is she, *ab origine,* a freely maneuvering, individual self who metes out freedom to her lover, and so it must be said she causes her own downfall? Or is her involvement in matters of freedom and identity preempted and always already mediated by men's "prerogative," which is backed by physical force, so that she merely gives him (back) the freedom that "he" has, a priori, "allowed" to her? Harriet Jacobs will expose a more radical instance of this same contradiction when she objects, at the end of her memoir, to her friend Mrs. Bruce's agreement to "buy" her freedom for her: "being sold from one owner to another [to gain freedom] seemed too much like slavery."[26] In modernity, Anglowomen and, even more so, all enslaved persons face the Catch-22 that the Putney debaters did: they lack the a priori claim to "rights and liberties" by which they might effectively resist the order that, a priori, denies them those rights and liberties. Haywood was no republican, no dissenter, and not even a Whig; her sympathies were Tory and, like Behn's, her defense of women's sexual agency was of a more rakish, Tory bent.[27] And yet her attunement to women's experience of desire meant that her engagement with the dynamics of "liberty" entailed dissent from men's monopoly of it. Her work clarifies why, like the Putney debaters, like Catharine Macaulay, and in the works of many later writers, protagonists will lay claim to a native identity, a birthright:

in order to interrupt this circularity, to fill in the absent center — and so to establish their "right" to claim the powers of liberty. With this understanding of her work in mind, we can better appreciate the symbolic implications of the fact that Haywood's heroines continue to pursue and desire the men who have forced their "undoing," a pattern that has unsettled feminist readers.[28] I suggest that we see this undoing man as a figure for modernity and accordingly see Haywood's female protagonists' persistent pursuit of him as their determination to "enter" modernity. Haywood portrays sexual, ruined women who willfully meet and ride this powerful, scattering, phallocentric force — this force that simultaneously invades its subjects so as to control them from the inside out and "mobilizes" them in a way that begins to remove them from the bonds of patriarchal kinship and community.

In *Fantomina,* Haywood does other cultural work as well, as she begins to experiment with representing, narratively, the interiority prompted by this social exile. I agree with Helen Thompson that *Fantomina* lends itself to Butlerian readings of performativity, but I would recast Thompson's characterization of an interiorless embodiment and performance in *Fantomina* and instead emphasize that it is precisely interiority that develops, oddly, in tandem with Fantomina's performances.[29] Just after Fantomina is raped, the narrator begins to represent her *in dialogue with herself* — and she relies on parentheses and italics to give written form to this interiorized, dialogical self. Fantomina rationalizes her scheme to continue seeing and masquerading with Beauplaisir in the first self-dialogue in the text: "if he is really (*said she, to herself*) the faithful, the constant Lover he has sworn to be, how charming will be our Amour? — And if he should be false, grow satiated, like other Men, I shall but, at the worst, have the private Vexation of knowing I have lost him; — the Intrigue being a Secret, my Disgrace will be so too" (232). To survive, *with her sexual agency,* in this ostensibly contractual world she has now entered, Fantomina will thus turn inward and her interiority will become dialogical. She will organize her secret self-relation so as to manage the tasks of constructing her relations to the phallocentric public sphere and thereby taking power back from the man who has raped her.

Both alienated and empowered by this means, Fantomina becomes a "she" to herself, as expressed in her costuming of herself as a series of others and in her framing of her maneuvers: "I shall hear no Whispers as I pass, — She is forsaken: — The odious word *Forsaken* will never wound my Ears; nor will my wrongs excite either the Mirth or the Pity of the talking World: — It will not be even in the power of the Undoer himself to triumph over me; and while he laughs at, and perhaps despises the fond, the yielding *Fantomina,* he will revere and esteem the virtuous, the Reserved Lady" (232–33). Fantomina is learning to avoid the fate of Overton's wife. Her self-discourse will displace the world's discourse on her: she will write herself, using her ability to see herself from outside — as what "the talking World" sees — to strategize about her bodily motions in that world. This strategic inner dialogue constitutes her subjectivity and constitutes the novel's story, its print-form entry into the person.

Haywood thus explores the ways that Atlantic modernity carves out an interiority in the subject — and she leaves it a question, perhaps *the* question, as to whether this interiority is found or made and whether it is wholly colonized or wholly colonizable. Building on Haywood, many later novelists explore this interior margin within the subject, seeking to discover whether a self might enter modernity — or rather, become subject to its entry — and yet evade complete, interior colonization. In Defoe's fantastical fictional world, Moll and Roxana always harbor an "excessive" interiority in their roguish, margin-inhabiting lives; they perpetually dodge the invasive determinations of the polis and baffle its claim on both their desires and their property. They embody Cromwell's horror — a hidden interior at odds with the polis, accruing property on the sly. Much later, as we will see, Harriet Wilson will reshape this narrative form to display her more radically appropriated subjectivity and property-in-self, by recounting her interior, first-person autobiographical story mostly in the third person.

In Haywood's novella, Fantomina *temporarily* keeps hold of her secret interior and *temporarily* evades colonization. In the end, however, the ideal of transparency driving a Cromwellian, Protestant modernity strips Fantomina of her disguises and impregnates her with itself; it turns her inside out and makes her the site of its reproduction, for Fantomina as well as for Haywood's readers. That is, Fantomina becomes pregnant. Shortly afterward, her mother finally arrives in town, and she keeps her daughter under "a restraint, little agreeable to [Fantomina's] Humour, and the Liberties to which she had been accustomed" (246). When her pregnancy advances and labor pains begin, the daughter cannot escape unnoticed. The narrator tells us that "had she been at liberty to have acted with the same unquestionable Authority over herself as she did before," she could have remade herself once more (246).

This "liberty" and absolute self-authority are ultimately what Fantomina does not have — like the "Freedoms" that she only apparently has "given" Beauplaisir to exercise. And yet a certain kind of self has emerged in the struggle. The enclosed world of the convent to which Fantomina is finally sent by her mother emblematizes the policing pressure on this interior self, and yet the convent in France also serves as an escape hatch for this interiority, an elsewhere for it to inhabit. That is, this last "removal" of the fallen woman to France suggests that self-alienation and interiorization arise together with exile or deracination — for

Fantomina as for all earlier and later colonial narrators. What Michael Seidel has noted about the links between narration and exile in Daniel Defoe and Joseph Conrad finds early expression in Haywood's fiction.[30]

Meanwhile, our narrator, similarly masked, unidentified, and unfixed, accompanies Fantomina, as we do, on this heterosexual, traveling adventure and creates her own positionality through Fantomina.[31] Via her relation to Fantomina, she can become the anonymous, reflecting self that inducts us into modernity — a position that Haywood herself (a self-supporting and sometimes defamed actress and writer) no doubt came to know quite well as she traveled between Ireland and England. Fantomina and the narrator can indulge Fantomina's (and perhaps the reader's) desire for both the powerful man and his freedom of movement (a desire for phallic modernity, in other words, which might also appeal to some disempowered men) while also cultivating the fantasy of a private self outside him and outside the phallic community.

In all these ways, we can see Haywood transforming within an English setting the fundamental tropes and techniques of the Atlantic novel as initiated by Behn. We see novels-to-be in the making not only in the liberty questions her novels stage but also in the form by which she pursues them.

IN THE BRITISH RECLUSE; or The Secret History of Cleomira, Supposed Dead (1722), Haywood makes this drama felt as a British drama. Here, Cleomira and Belinda tell their stories of "seduction" to each other and in the end discover they have been had by the same man — the same free British order of things. Yet thereafter they themselves exercise "Choice," as the narrator emphasizes in her closing words, when they decide to retire together and live the ideal life of a female "British Recluse."[32] This storytelling frame itself offers a microcosm of the British reading community that is forming, imaginatively, around such tales of ruin, exile, and liberty. Haywood's use of it suggests some awareness on her part, perhaps only unconsciously, of the refashioning of Britishness as a liberty identity, an interiority prompted by ruin and unfolded in the act of telling. Jennifer Thorn and David Oakleaf have each suggested that Haywood's exotic tales construct a modern Britishness, and her use of the frame of translation in texts such as Eovaai likewise seem to indicate her interest in the boundary crossings that underlie nation formation.[33] More implicitly in The British Recluse she fashions identities in which interiority is nationalized and, in the process, an incognito, ruined woman becomes the motor of a "secret" national history in the tradition of Clarendon.

In recounting for Belinda the "History of this Wretch you see before you" (159) so as to explain "the Anguish of my secret Discontent" (172), Cleomira immediately pinpoints a loss of liberty — or perhaps a too-strong desire for liberty, it's not clear which — as the beginning of her troubles. When her father died, she recalls, her mother moved them to the country, and Cleomira experienced a "sudden Change from all the Liberties in the World, to the most strict Confinement" (162). On one exceptional occasion, Cleomira's mother gave her permission to attend a dance, and Cleomira promptly fell in love with "Lysander," thereafter seeking the liberty to embrace him. Whether in spite of or because of her Tory sympathies, Haywood thus participates in the reshaping of "History" as a troubled story of sex and liberty.

As part of this story, we again witness an interior self in formation. We attend Cleomira in her secret reading of missives from Lysander, we witness her hidden maneuvering to avoid the gaze of her mother, and in the end we see her prompted into duplicitous privacy by the libertine's sexual calling-out. As she reports, "I resolved to say nothing to my Mother of what had passed . . . *Love* taught me cunning which before I was a Stranger to; and though I burned with the Desire to be talking something of my adored *Lysander* and vent some Part of the Overflow-ings of my ravished Soul, yet I so well dissembled that at my Return Home I never mentioned the least Syllable which could give Suspicion" (165–66). Suppressed from expression in "syllables" to her mother, her overflowing soul instead finds outlet in the text to which the reader is privy and which makes a private world between the reader and the heroine. We eagerly follow her dissembling attempts to meet Lysander, which fail until finally there arrives a couple, the Marvirs, un-known but apparently friendly, whose motives are at first hidden from the reader as well as Cleomira.

Through their talk of liberty, this wandering, anonymous, duplicitous couple abets the undoing of Cleomira. Mrs. Marvir "was always resenting the Injustice my Mother did me in debarring me from all those Liberties young Ladies in *this Kingdom* are permitted to enjoy" (emphasis added), heightening Cleomira's sense that she suffered "the greatest hardship in the World that I could not have the Freedom of conversing with [Lysander] without all this difficulty . . . till at last, the fears of what they had infused into my Imagination — the Hopes of enjoying my beloved Liberty . . . Made me resolve to do as they advised" (176). She secretly flees her mother's home and makes the Marvirs her legal guardians, explain-ing again that, because of the "unreasonable Restraint she had laid me under . . . I abandoned her only in pursuit of that innocent Liberty" (177). In this tale, the heroine undergoes natal alienation in order to pursue the desires peculiar to "this Kingdom." She is dizzied, the tone implies, perhaps like an entire populace, with ideas of her "beloved Liberty." The tale might thus seem to critique lib-erty — except that in the end it presents two fallen women who epitomize its ideal prerogative, in their "choice" to live apart in their own way in a pastoral setting, as British recluses.

Before we arrive at this ending, however, the story reveals how women's pursuit of liberty is fraught with danger and betrayal because of the a priori "liberties" that men are able to claim. Again, Haywood dwells on the moment of "entry," an entry (ultimately into Britishness by way of a duplicitous, phallocentric British liberty) that the heroine both resists and desires. At their first meeting since the ball, when Lysander takes her in his arms and lays his head against her breast, she "struggled to get free" but "so faintly that he might easily perceive that the Liberties he had taken were not unpardonable" (175). Her similar response in other situations "emboldened him to the taking of greater freedoms than otherwise he would have dared to have attempted" (177). Finally one night he secretly enters her room and "seizing both my Hands, and gently forcing them to encircle his Waist, joined his Lips to mine with too strenuous a Pressure to suffer me to reproach the liberties he took" (177–78). Within an order overrun by liberty, a self can be made and unmade — like Tristram Shandy — in one tick of the second hand, here that "damned undoing minute." And so identity is ruptured.

The "secret history" of liberty is exactly such a series of undoings — leaving the self in need of reconstitution as British.

Haywood particularly seeks phrasing, literally, for the slippery combination of silencing and seducing managed in the syntax of British liberty. Cleomira explains to her friend Belinda, "I *suffered* — or, rather let me say I could *not resist* his proceeding from one Freedom to the other, till there was nothing left for him to ask or me to grant" (178, emphasis in original). Flooded with desire, Cleomira emphatically can "not resist" his "Freedom," so that she has "nothing left" of agency. Her "Person"-ness loses ground against his, and in the aftermath — "the guilty Transport past" — "cold tremblings seized my Limbs — and my Breast heaved no more with Joy but with Horror" (178). I suggest that this horror is not as far removed from that of Joseph Conrad's Marlowe and Kurtz as it might seem — that two centuries of fiction and empire later, the "horror" of Kurtz includes his "liberties" with both his betrothed and his African consort, which the outsider narrator Marlowe turns into his own and his audience's experience of undoing, all reconstituted within the Atlantic frame of race.

Certainly, after her fall, Cleomira epitomizes the wandering and contingent modern self that Conrad's narrators embody, that Wolfram Schmidgen sees in the contemporary work of Fielding, especially *Tom Jones,* and that Richardson will make tragic in *Clarissa.*[34] In Haywood, hereafter, the turning points of Cleomira's story amount to relocations: from her trip out of London to give birth alone, to her wanderings at the crossroads in hopes of a messenger from Lysander (where instead she hears of her mother's heartbreak and death), to her return to London, where "travel" entails both freedom and exile, agency and alienation in search of Lysander, to her cloaked arrival at the boarding house where Belinda and the reader meet her, and finally — after arranging it so that "not a relation or Acquaintance has the least Notion of my being living" — to her country retreat with Belinda. Cleomira is indeed "transported" in both a sexual and a spatial sense.

Cleomira's listener, Belinda (like Haywood's readers), has a history marked by the same tropes of kinlessness, travel, liberty, and unsettled yet expanded interiority. For Belinda, too, as we learn when she then tells her own story of ruin, the "secret history" of Britain creates her experience, a plot of lineage rupture and anguished travel. Her "tranquil State of Life" in the country is first of all disturbed by the death of her mother and father within a year of each other — the death of Filmerite authority and family continuity — and then by a scene of travel that leads to seduction and to further travel, ultimately to London and then to reclusiveness.

The circumstances of Belinda's meeting with the man she knows as Beauplaisir allude multiply to movement. First of all, after her father's death, "not having been at any public Place" for some time, the man she is engaged to marry "needs persuade her to go in his Coach to see a famous Horse-race" where there was "a prodigious Concourse of People" (202). The foregrounding of travel and the figure of racing itself are repeated in the return home, which offers a mini-allegory of the overturning of self in the new world of travel: their drunken coach driver "drove in such a furious Manner . . . that we were overturned" (202). This "overturning" occasions her meeting with the rake Beauplaisir, who is "riding the same way" and offers his servant to drive their coach, so that "[a]ll the time of our little Journey, the obliging Stranger rode by the Coach side, and entertained us with a world of Gallantry" (202). Specifically, Beauplaisir entertains Belinda with an account of his travels. He explains that "having made the Tour of Europe, he thought his Travels would not be complete unless he could be able to give as good an Account of the Kingdom he was born in, as of others; and to that End was proceeding in his Progress, through every County in which there was anything rare or valuable to be seen" (203). In fact, Beauplaisir is escaping (under this pseudonym) from the scandal of his ruin of Cleomira, which suggests that a story of ruin underlies both the Englishman's travel to an elsewhere (including narratively, through ethnography) and his "return home" to his "native" land.

Falling for the world-traveled Beauplaisir and having to hide her feelings from her innocent fiancé, Worthy, Belinda finds the next day that she is "in need of much more Artifice than I was Mistress of to put [Worthy] off without letting him into the Secret" of her feelings (204). She tells herself that her "wishes are at

Liberty to extend themselves wherever they shall find an Object deserving" (211), but she ends up tossed by her new emotions — "My Body restless as my Mind, displeased at everything, uneasy everywhere as I wandered up and down from Room to Room" (208). She too is becoming an interior traveler, an unsettled dissembler; and it is her "inward perturbations" (205) and "racks of Thought" (213) (like Cleomira's earlier) that, in turn, re-ignite the outward motions and the storytelling. When Worthy discovers her feelings, and Beauplaisir flees after severely wounding Worthy in a duel, Belinda, seeking a meeting with Beauplaisir, literally takes to the road: "I had, indeed, so much Anxiety of Mind with everything together that I was not able to stay [home]," and so "ordered the Coach to be got ready and the same Day went to a Relation's" (214). Hereafter Belinda pursues the mobile Beauplaisir, only to be undone and abandoned by him like Cleomira.

Yet this travel and undoing will draw her to Cleomira and thereby allows the narrator's shrewd entry (by print, in place of the phallus) into her protagonists' interiors — providing herself and her audience the pleasures of the phallic polis while also creating a fantasy of escape from this polis. In organizing her novella around the "boarding house" telling of these seductions, Haywood highlights the transient mode of this new history, including of her own act of putting an outcast's secret British history — of bodies demoted, undone, and unanchored — into transportable, transporting print. She crafts a narrative form that captures the "removed" Anglo-Protestant self, whose interior doubleness is made "manifest" in such print, constituting a public of private recluses pursuing choice and liberty.

In the end, as the narrator tells us, "the RECLUSE and [Belinda] took a House about seventy Miles distant from London, where they still live in perfect Tranquillity." Significantly, the question of freedom returns once more at this closure, in the last sentence of the novella: "And where the solitary Life is the effect of *Choice,* it certainly yields more solid comfort than all the public Diversions which those who are the greatest Pursuers of them can find" (224). Cleomira and Belinda practice "their Resolutions of abandoning the World," but the very outpost position of their "choice" draws "the world" of readers to them, via this narrator who can report as if from firsthand knowledge that "they still live" in that house and that reclusive state. Like all emergent modern British subjects, their entry (and our readerly entry into them) entails an undoing removal. Haywood's plot of ruin thus begins to call out a roving, readerly, British interior, and the immense popularity of her fiction testifies to the power of this calling-out. Samuel Richardson learned the lesson well and, as printer and novelist, he joined the project of cultivating this community of British readers.

Clarissa's Civil War

Like Haywood's heroines, Clarissa Harlowe repeatedly finds herself tangled in the Catch-22 of contingent freedom that women particularly face when they try to match their liberty against men's liberties and stumble on the a priori exclusions hidden in the fine print, so to speak, of the discourse of free English agency. Lovelace tells Clarissa that he will give her liberty when she chooses him; but she asks how he can "expect a voluntary favour from one to whom you give not a free choice?"[35] Clarissa's predicament strikingly pinpoints the conundrum of contract.[36] The circle she exposes even supersedes that which she understands, for she remarks that he does not "give" her a choice, as she also earlier asked if he would "permit [her] the freedom" of an English birthright. Her choice depends a priori on his permission: the granting of choice is already a sign that power is in circulation—that, in effect, an uneven distribution of power precedes the contract. As Lovelace later acknowledges to Belford, "She piques herself, thou knowest, and makes it a matter of reproach to me, that she went not off with me by her own consent; but was tricked out of herself" (869).

Tricked out of herself, Clarissa experiences the swoon of all literary swoons, extending over some one thousand pages and hundreds of letters, climaxing after a rape when the heroine finds that she is "no longer what I was in any one thing" and so decrees "Self, be banished from self." If Haywood makes the swoon serial, Richardson makes it epic; and hereafter in the English-language novel it becomes paradigmatic and consistently transatlantic. Although Richardson's novel itself is not directly transatlantic in plot, its influence is spectacularly so, and its concerns are certainly so.

Like Behn, Richardson writes a tragic history of liberty ending in death; but writing in 1740, amid the success of multivolume national histories and the powerful cultural consensus around liberty, he intuits the demand for a temporal and serial scope that will encompass but also enclose and make redemptive history's psychological and revolutionary upheavals. At the same time, he is concerned, as a good stay-at-home Dissenter, with the way upheavals upset the family structure. As it is for Overton, in this novel the central outrage is committed on the home; the violation really begins with the invasion and tyranny of the domestic space—a brotherly tyranny, as I will explore.[37] In Richardson's fiction, we meet women who eschew wild, Haywoodian adventures and instead are securely (if restlessly or unhappily) seated in their birth families—the women whom Moll Flanders judges—who, she says, "place themselves below their common Station, and prepare their own Mortifications, by their submitting so to be insulted by the

Men before-hand" simply because of "the fear of not being Marry'd at all" (119, 121). Richardson's heroine, Clarissa, does not submit quite so easily, but she leaves home only involuntarily.

And yet rape still stalks her and sets her in motion, alone, as well as turning her inward. The phallic aspect of modernity (in plain words, its threat of sexual force) seizes her away from her very home, and it can do so, Richardson makes clear, because this home is divided by a contest for property and authority, wracked by jealousy, greed, and faction. It is a kingdom that "has been shaken," to echo one observer of the English Revolution. The family is specifically factionalized by the dispersal of a fortune, colonial and national. "Our family," reports Clarissa, "has indeed been strangely discomposed — *Discomposed!*" (41, emphasis in original).

The discomposition is created by a historical inheritance — a grandfather's "will" — a lawful legacy that, however, faces challenges from new mercantile sources of riches that gives rise to a brother's jealous power, as I will explore a bit later. In effect, the early offstage duel between Clarissa's brother James and her captor-to-be, Lovelace, foreshadows the contest and the violent "entry" that the grandfather's will provokes.[38] When Lovelace arrives at her home to lure her into his carriage, Clarissa is literally pressed between the competitive brother of the commonwealth and the open force of the monarchy — "expecting," as she says, "a furious brother here, armed servants there" (380). Caught up bodily by Lovelace ("he put my arm under his, his drawn sword in the other hand" [380]), she is part of the property at issue in the transition between these two politico-patriarchal orders. As Lovelace pulls her toward his carriage, Clarissa begins to experience the split that will lead to her first fainting swoon: "I ran as fast as he, yet knew not that I ran . . . my voice, however, contradicting my action; crying No, no, no, all the while" (380). Clarissa will try to resist her position by invoking the *apparently* gender-neutral inheritance of the English birthright of freedom. She is undone, however, by the male prerogative (and specifically the rape laws) that persists in both legacies.[39]

Richardson first of all politicizes his story by implicitly casting Clarissa as a native soul encountering tyranny. Clarissa faces both a lover who fashions himself a "Caesar," as Richardson has Lovelace call himself, seeking "to complete his wishes upon the most potent republic that ever existed," and a father who, as the preface outlines, is "despotic, absolute," and "arbitrary" in pursuing "undue exertion of [his] natural authority" (36 – 37). With "[t]hat *native dignity*" that Anna attributes to Clarissa, Clarissa the freeborn Englishperson valiantly resists (749, emphasis in original). She proclaims, as Sir Edward Coke became famous for doing, that "The LAW shall be my resource . . . The LAW only shall be my refuge" (Lovelace notes that "she spoke the word ["law"] with emphasis" [950]). Not surprisingly, then, Clarissa asks the key Putney Debate (not to mention Shakespearian) question of this history when she presses Lovelace: "Tell me, sir, in so many words tell me, whether it be, or be not, your intention to permit me to quit [this house]? — To permit me the freedom which is my birthright as an English subject?" (934). Clarissa's (and Richardson's) invocation of this birthright discourse ultimately expresses, I believe, an investment in the pride of English culture more than any rebellion against its patriarchy. The novel aspires to be a national allegory *by way of* a woman's violation story.

Richardson makes his novel a national allegory not only through Clarissa's vocabulary of birthright but also by making her a Puritan paragon, committed to good works and noble acts. The Protestant strain in this story finds expression in its parallel to *The Pilgrim's Progress* and in a range of other Puritan tropes, as critics have noted.[40] Clarissa suffers like poor Christian of *The Pilgrim's Progress,* fallen in the Slough of Despond, and she figures herself as a "poor estray [who] has not one kind friend" (566). In making Clarissa a pilgrim, in contrast to Haywood's willfully wandering heroines, Richardson achieves a powerful synthesis, for the figure of "the poor estray" soon becomes ubiquitous in novels in English, including, as Jay Fliegelman has shown, Anglo-American novels.[41] This pattern is most strikingly laid out, as we'll see in chapter 6 in that early, transatlantic novel *Charlotte Temple.* Moreover, and again like sentimental heroines to come, Clarissa's Puritan discipline and good works hold out a model for others: and in this way, too, Richardson fashions her as a figure for Anglo-Protestant history — a one-woman city on a hill. In Anna's wistful sketch of Clarissa after the abduction, or apparent elopement, she writes,

> Your works were shown or referred to wherever fine works were talked of. Nobody [compared to you] had any but an inferior and second-hand praise for diligence, for economy, for reading; for writing, for memory, for learning everything laudable. . . . Everybody almost worshiped you. Envy itself, which has of late reared up its venomous head against you, was awed by your superior worthiness into silence and admiration. . . . Yet, in all this, your sweetness of manner, your humility and affability caused the subscription everyone made to your sentiments. (578)

And all of this is manifested through Clarissa's writing — "shown or referred to wherever fine works were talked of." We become privy to this account of her self-disciplinary works only after her death, via the journal of her daily schedule, indicating how, in the Puritan manner, Clarissa cultivates this aspect of herself in private, without seeking praise or grace but as part of her habitual interiority. She is a *modern* Puritan, the new, virtuous individual whose "native" sensibility and dignity draw everyone's gaze and find their fullest manifestation in print.

A Puritan woman who speaks a Whig language of birthright, Clarissa at the same time embodies a kind of interior Gothic balance. Regal and representative all at once, like the English constitution, she integrates the powers of Lords, Commons, and king. Anna stresses Clarissa's native dignity and Puritan humility, while Lovelace depicts Clarissa "as an empress . . . among her vassals; yet with a freedom from pride and haughtiness," and he imagines them together in a "cavalcade . . . with their satellites and glaring equipages" dazzling "the eyes of the wondering beholders" (534). Free of pride and yet worthy of royalty, Clarissa serves as class-straddling woman, whom Lord M judiciously characterizes as a woman "of standing, and rich, and reputable" (1036). Having risen in part by way of the merchant and interior legacy of individualism, she yet projects the royal and exterior powers of court spectacle. Critics from Leslie Fiedler to Terry Eagleton and John Zomchick have read Clarissa's plight as a negotiation between aristocratic and bourgeois values in the transitional eighteenth century.[42] As Zomchick notes, Clarissa speaks a "hybrid" class discourse, mingling traditional and new values (67). Yet this hybridism, like Shaftesbury's Whiggish Toryism, contributes to the emergent consensus organized around an idea of native liberty.

Particularly through his manipulations of the word "noble," Richardson illustrates the convergence in this period of the royal and the humble, the aristocratic and the common, the materially splendid and the modestly moral — the Tory and the Whig. The shift in the meanings of "noble" reflects the further progress of the transition that we saw in early formation in *Oroonoko* — from a premodern racial order organized around aristocratic "nobility" to a modern, Atlantic racial order, in which race is more quietly embedded, organized around humble, middle-class "nobility." The meaning of "noble" as aristocratic lineage was increasingly infiltrated (just as the power structure was) by broader middle-class and Puritan connotations of "pure or superior character" (as the OED attests in its examples).[43] Thus, for instance, does Immanuel Kant equate the "simple and noble" with the sublime while also measuring national character according to a people's sensitivity to the sublime (the German, English, and Spanish, nations all affiliated with Gothic races, have the highest appreciation for the sublime in his account); and instead of attributing such sensibility to aristocrats, he recommends that "every world-citizen" have access to it and be given opportunity to cultivate it by way of education.[44] The figure of the noble savage, which Behn is sometimes credited with founding in Oroonoko, also contributes to this new formation.[45]

Richardson's novel explores this widening circuit of meanings and participates in the transfer of "noble" from external status to interior sensibility among middling-class citizens, ranging from the wealthy of "good standing" like Clarissa to the humble Pamelas. The first mention of "noble" in *Clarissa* epitomizes its new interiorization. Clarissa is a woman of "noble consciousness" (40): she embodies the psychologically noble, and hereafter others refer to her as a "noble spirit" (128), a "noble creature" (403), "noble-minded," manifesting a "noble expansion of heart" (485) and "noble sincerity" (530). While "her air, her manner, her voice, [are] bewitchingly noble" (646), she unfairly faces a threat to her "noble self-confidence" (450). The word gets joined to the Protestant-Whig emphasis on women's modesty in Clarissa as well, for she is "so generous, so noble, so *discreet*" (979, emphasis added). Thus, the Reverend Arthur Lewen concludes, "to love [Clarissa] is to love virtue, good sense, prudence, and everything that is noble in a woman" (1252). Indeed even Lovelace employs the word's emergent meaning in recognizing "what a noble, what a right spirit has this charming creature" (964). Clarissa embodies a new Protestant nobility, middle-class, modest, and theoretically free.[46]

Most important for the form of Richardson's novel, the rightly noble Clarissa embodies the Atlantic, Anglo-Protestant ideal in her will to transparency: the Cromwellian Puritan dream of an interior fully manifest and the Whig dream of an unmediated relation to the contract.[47] In her prolific letter writing — that is, her will to written transparency — Clarissa carries forward the principle of transparency beyond the comfort level of her immediate community: after the rape, she refuses to cloak what has happened and instead, in the spirit of Overton, she fully exposes her raped interior in writing. While others tell her to conceal her unmarried state and then her "loss of chastity," she refuses to do so, asking: "[W]hy should I seek to conceal that disgrace from others, which I cannot hide from myself?" (985).

In this sense Richardson's full entry into Clarissa's interior expresses his own Puritan longing for "manifestation." The epistolary form of his novel encourages this fantasy of manifestation, promising revelations of hidden interiors in the form of private letters and cultivating a desire for psychological access and free disclosure (by which we are still mesmerized in novels and in reality TV). Although Richardson also teases us with the possibility that we never do penetrate the deepest layers of self, and although he hints that writing often functions as the obfuscation rather than the solid basis of free contract, the very form of his novel structures our desire for the opposite, for unveiling, for knowing the intimate inside via our location on the cultural outside, in dissent from the Harlowes. He seduces his readers with that dream above all by enabling us to participate in a common polity organized around it — as suggested by his own prolific correspondence with his readers and his promotion of the novel as a reproducible commodity.[48]

Thus *Clarissa* also discovers a means for managing a culture's hidden anxiety about women — about women's "free entry" into a "free" modernity — by way of the author's fuller entry into them. In other words, Richardson's full turn inward to depict Clarissa's experience may reflect a will to control more than a transgressive boldness, even if his technique is wonderfully innovative. Like Cromwell at the Putney Debates, Richardson's determination to fathom this character's interior depths also operates, in a Foucauldian sense, as a surveillance of her. Although Richardson creates full sympathy for Clarissa's predicament and although he allegorizes the political conditions for it, he also depicts that predicament within the Anglo-Atlantic terms of patriarchy, property, Protestantism, law, and liberty that create it — and that allow him to contain and redeem it. At this level, Lovelace's invasion of her private self becomes an objective correlative of Richardson's entry into her interiority, forcing her renewed bid to be a member — her request to be taken back into the fold as her father's daughter ("You are my own dear papa, whether you will or not — And though I am an unworthy child — yet I *am* your child" [890]).[49]

But Richardson at the same time incisively identifies the root problem of property that troubles the ideal world of liberty. And, as suggested earlier, he particularly pinpoints the brother's new role in the modern order of property. H. J. Habakkuk notes that in the eighteenth century, as wealth and land increasingly determined political power more directly than royal favor, "[t]he eldest son came to occupy a unique position of authority" as the main inheritor of that wealth and, in turn, as the manager of the political authority in the family.[50] At the same time, as Christopher Hill has discussed, the broader trade economy of eighteenth-century Britain created the ambition among the nouveau riche to acquire and consolidate estates — as Clarissa's male relatives aim to do.[51] Meanwhile, I would add, in the wake of such fiascos as the South Sea Bubble and in the face of the volatility of the transcontinental economy, such sons themselves might well have felt a heightened sense of anxiety and competitiveness. Richardson captures this figure in James Harlowe, who so boldly and violently resists his sister's claim to the liberty of choice, which her "older," grandfatherly inheritance has lent her.

In setting up this family conflict, Richardson narrates the brother-sister problem precipitated by the combined Atlantic forces of a colonial economy and a freedom discourse — which Defoe had already stumbled on, as we'll see in the next chapter, in *Moll Flanders*. That is, the birthright discourse of the English Revolution, interacting with the tradition of inherited, landed property, brings Clarissa into conflict with the new, colonial wealth and the brother who manages it. Clarissa inherits property from her grandfather, the source of whose land and wealth is not precisely specified, allowing space for readers to imagine some illustrious legacy dating from "time immemorial." This landed inheritance, however, detracts from her brother's birthright claims, leaving him to inherit mainly the mercantile, money wealth of his father and the uncles and depriving him of the opportunity to "consolidate" landed wealth and money wealth. Clarissa's inheritance thus threatens his potential for embodying an English Gothic balance rooted in property and (perhaps unintentionally on Richardson's part) exposes the property substructure of the illustrious native tradition. Richardson implicitly spells out how this conflict is ignited on the one hand by a daughter's new access to a discourse of birthright and on the other hand by a brother's new but unstable source of revenue in the colonial economy of Atlantic modernity.

Furthermore—although again implicitly and perhaps unconsciously—Richardson infuses this story with an imagery of barbarism that registers its larger colonial horizon. Suggestively, the text attributes cannibalistic desire to Clarissa's torturers. She faces not only her brother's and sister's "insatiate and devouring" flames of "AVARICE" (1088) but also Lovelace, who prides himself on being a "notorious woman-eater" and whom others refer to (as they do Solmes) as a "savage" or "wild Indian" (1084). Raymond Hilliard reviews this imagery mainly in order to consider the "ritual sacrifice" of Clarissa as a psychological scapegoat for these men, but along the way he usefully documents the contemporary colonialist publications about "primitives" and cannibalism that Richardson would likely have known.[52] He traces the equation of primitive, cannibalistic societies with despotic rulers, slavish subjects, and "absolute tyranny" in both these writings and the novel (1086).

Of course the import of this imagery is unclear, and perhaps equivocal. On the one hand, this set of associations may indicate that Richardson was critiquing middle-class ambition as part of a colonially generated culture of avarice that renewed the threat of tyranny. On the other hand, this imagery renders such consuming avarice as "outlandish"—an attribute of alien, racial others which has unnaturally invaded the British world. Insofar as this second meaning operated, it would have once again subsumed and defamed the African- or Indian-Atlantic subject's story, distorting it to serve the liberty story of the Anglo-Atlantic subject. After all, "cannibalistic" and "barbarian" as James may appear, he is no primitive avatar but rather a creature of the new wealth. And so, even as he apprehends the colonial sources of this story of violation, Richardson also prefigures a future pattern that develops more fully in gothic novels such as *The Monk* and *Wieland*. In those novels, the "barbarian" racialization of "bad" Anglo-Atlantic brothers, like Burke's association of "bad" revolutionaries with "Maroon" slaves, deftly degrades and racializes those colonized "others" who in fact *are* the real but disavowed basis of Anglo-Atlantic "liberties." The power of Richardson's novel no doubt derives in significant part from its braiding together of these several and often contradictory strands of the liberty discourse.

In Clarissa's rape and swoon, Richardson lets the skein unravel utterly. Readers have found themselves "undone" by this rape and its aftermath — powerfully moved as Clarissa's self temporarily splits wide open. In her post-rape incoherence, Richardson dramatizes the self broken and scattered under liberty's centrifugal force. He dwells on the moment of psychotic break over several letters — the break that follows, that is, from the duplicitous pursuit of violation as if it were liberation. During and after the rape Clarissa is "robbed of [her] senses," and for a period she loses her memory (985). Once she begins to recover, she is for a long while incoherent and, as she reports to Anna Howe, "I am no longer what I was in any one thing" — a message that she then rips apart (890). Clarissa's swoon even de-forms the typographical conventions of print itself. Her first writings after the rape are headed not as "Letter 261" and "Letter 262," even though they are addressed to others, but as a series of "Papers" numbered 1 through 10, that constitute a break in the text's numbering sequence. Some of these papers are, as indicated in italics and brackets, "*(Torn in two pieces)*" or "*(Scratched through, and thrown under the table)*" (890). And in the last of them, the print appears vertically or at odd angles in the margin around the text of a poem.

Print itself momentarily breaks and scatters here under the force of violation — and yet this scattering of print manifests, at the same time, Richardson's freedom, as printer, to manipulate it. His freedom enables him powerfully to render Clarissa's lack of freedom. In breaking the linearity of print Richardson not only heightens his reader's awareness of the rape's effects; he also quietly implies that print itself is a shaping condition of both Clarissa's and the nation's story. Not to mention the author's.

The larger Atlantic context of this printer's freedom registers in the final "Paper." In it Clarissa writes a poem in which she imagines that her "freed soul" is dead for a moment, but then, to her dismay, it awakens and returns to her body — as a galley slave. She pictures her soul as a "Fool!" who "resume[s] her broken chain" and so "row[s] the galley here again!" (893). In a margin and aslant, she figures her "misfortunes" as "waves" which "pursue" her, waves of trauma "Which on each other are, / . . . renew'd!" Quite strikingly, like Imoinda and like many black Atlantic protagonists to come, Clarissa swoons and awakens as a slave. Her self-losing, transformational ruin unfolds — in this case only metaphorically — as a traumatic middle passage. Her words resonate exactly within the ruinous, unanchoring experience of blacks on the Atlantic, here subsumed within the story of a pure, Anglo-Atlantic martyr.

As it had in Haywood's texts, and as it will do much more starkly in Harriet

Wilson's *Our Nig,* this undoing gives way to a rhetoric of self-dissociation. Before Clarissa fully "rises" to heaven, phoenix-like, and while still in her lingeringly dissociated state, she repeatedly employs double negatives to express herself, most especially as she confesses her attraction to Lovelace: "At first I saw something in your air and person that *dis*pleased me *not.* Your birth and fortunes were *no* small advantages to you — You acted *not ig*nobly by my passionate brother" (892, emphasis added). She uses ten negatives in the eighteen lines of this post-rape note. Like Fantomina, she has arrived in a circumlocutious modernity and achieved her own dialogical interiority. Accordingly, also like Fantomina, she begins to refer to herself in the third person. She dialogues with herself ("How art thou now humbled in the dust, thou proud Clarissa Harlowe!" [Paper 4, 891]) and speaks to others about herself in third person ("Was it necessary," she writes to Lovelace, "to humble Clarissa Harlowe down to the level of thy baseness?" [912]; and she laments to Anna the passing of "what her Clarissa Harlowe once was" [974]). Exactly through the full penetration of her interior, this total invasion of herself by Lovelace and the novel, Clarissa is simultaneously reduced to and emptied of the public meaning of herself. Her transparency has undone her. She comes to her end in a wreck of a room with "windows dark and double-barred" (1064), where she discovers, "Once more have I escaped — but, alas! I, my *best self,* have not escaped!" (974). We might read her words as a reflection on the Anglo-Atlantic subject, whose pursuit of freedom both entails and draws emotive power from a disavowed slavery.

Such a reading sheds light on the novel's central elision, in spite of all its words: the rape itself. For, as Judith Wilt has noted, we the readers never do witness the actual crime.[53] The night of the rape is a gap in the text; it occurs between letters. Just so, Richardson pulls us powerfully inside this trauma; and yet his narrative occludes the novel's own contract with a Lovelacian modernity, its entry into a colonial and patriarchal modernity by way of this rape plot. Where Haywood reiterated, stylized, and thereby threw into ready relief the moment when force and prior power overcome the terms of contract, Richardson omits that scene and instead embeds its effects in many smaller moments, articulating the problem in psychological, endlessly ramified terms — which, as both Eagleton and Warner show, entangle Clarissa in her own undoing.[54] Although, as Frances Ferguson argues, the novel's psychological turn serves to tell the story of women's rape more fully, historically speaking Richardson's novel also mirrors the equivocations of Anglo-Atlantic culture, insistently reinstalling the heroine in the family and in the identity of Englishness.

Clarissa in fact confesses that she was initially seduced by a belief in the "native" character of Lovelace. At one point she admits to Lovelace, "You seemed frank, as well as generous," qualities which she "believed to be natives of the soil" (892). But it turns out that, like her brother, he too partakes of colonialism's barbarian identities: "You have barbarously and basely conspired against [my] honour" and this behavior "remakes" the Anglo woman, as she points out: "and now you have made me — what is it of vile that you have *not* made me? — " (892, emphasis in original). Lovelace has undone and remade her; he has undone the native self, or rather her belief in it, by exposing to her the madeness of that self. The result is implicitly political — an apparent banishment: "Self, then, be banished from *self*" — but one which ultimately redeems and makes that self heroic (943).

What John Zomchick observes about Clarissa applies to a diverse range of selves in Atlantic modernity: "To be enfranchised as a juridical subject the heroine must undergo alienation from her natal surroundings" (74). Throughout his study, Zomchick astutely notices the narrative patterns dictated by this logic in the law — without, however, giving attention to its Saxonist legacy. Instead he unconsciously echoes this legacy when he characterizes Clarissa's resistance: "Clarissa's will, however, as tenacious as any freeborn Englishman's, forces Lovelace to resort to ever-more arbitrary measures" (89). My reading is meant to step back from this unconscious absorption of the Saxonist legacy that entangles Clarissa and all her readers, so as to avoid simply swooning into it along with her.

Before and after Ian Watt, many a reader has so swooned, on both sides of the Atlantic. As we know, Richardson's novel (or at least an abridged version of it) became deeply embedded in the psyches of American readers, where it was transmuted to allegorize other threatening political "seductions" within the new nation, as for instance when John Adams differently nativized Lovelace as a promiscuous "young rake" called democracy and suggested that "Democracy is Lovelace and the people are Clarissa," that "lovely innocent" who the "artful villain will pursue . . . to her ruin and her death."[55] Adams's comment nicely illustrates not only the influence of *Clarissa* but also more broadly the nexus that the pamphlets of Overton, Paine, and Burke share with the novels of Haywood and Richardson. For many American literary critics, Adams's remark also indicates the overbearing, early influence of the Richardsonian novel on the American novel. This familiar account of an American literature struggling to liberate itself from British influence of course further inscribes the Anglo-Atlantic ur-narrative. More importantly, it overlooks the fact that Richardson's story and the printed text of *Clarissa* are as much shaped by America as America is shaped by Clarissa's story. As the next chapters show, "American" and "British" novels, like African- and Anglo-Atlantic novels overall, form together on the Atlantic.

6

Transatlantic Seductions
Defoe, Rowson, Brown, and Wilson

ODD THAT THE STORY of a kidnapped African prince, or even more so the life experiences of the African-Atlantic writers Olaudah Equiano or Harriet Wilson, should find any kind of fictional corollary in *Moll Flanders* or *Charlotte Temple* or *Robinson Crusoe* or *Wieland*. And yet they do: all these persons and protagonists are cast across the water from family or ancestors, all suffer exile from community, all face poverty, and all endure bodily trauma. And the correspondence makes sense in that, *together,* these figures constituted the economic and socio-political matrix of Atlantic modernity. Their different stories are interdependent; the stories and the lives are interdependent. That is, the texts and lives of Daniel Defoe, Susanna Rowson, and Charles Brockden Brown, as well as those of Wilson and Equiano, arise from a transatlantic economy made viable by the combined activities, gains, and losses of all of them — of the soldiers, sailors, emigrants, ex-convicts, slaves, ex-slaves, slavetraders, wives, mistresses, maids, and prodigal mercantile sons. A quick survey indicates as much. In *Charlotte Temple* (1797), the U.S. nation's first bestseller, the soldier Montraville is called to America to defend Britain's claims; his departure there with Charlotte enables both his ruin of her and his own eventual rise into landed wealth. Crusoe begins his career on a "Guiney" ship and undergoes his famous shipwreck while on a slaving venture, eventually becoming a West Indian island's rich "governor." Moll arrives in Virginia as an exported criminal, that time-honored practice which had initially helped to found the colony and enrich the mercantile new men who then brought the slave trade to it — as well as ultimately offering property to the white bonds-persons set free, as in Moll's case. And, as Houston Baker and others since have noted, even Equiano and his ability to write the *Narrative* ironically depend, as he himself registers, on the "economy of slavery," since as a "free" sailor he often makes his wages on slave ships.[1]

Both the ruin and rise of these Atlantic subjects depend on African-Atlantic labor. Occasionally, in Anglo-Atlantic texts, this fact is indirectly registered, as in the cases of Xury and Friday in *Robinson Crusoe,* or in the unnamed slave woman who inspires "sympathy" in William Wells Brown's *The Power of Sympathy.* In the Africanist maneuvers and moments of these texts, the tribulations of Anglo-Atlantic subjects are silently energized by, and emerge in relief against, the Africans' story of unfreedom. Meanwhile, for African-Atlantic writers from Equiano to Pauline Hopkins and beyond, the story of unfree labor is the text not the subtext, and African bodily ruin is fact, not figure or fiction. To some degree a similar contrast holds between women's and men's works, insofar as the popularity of a strange work like *Charlotte Temple* among American men as well as women may be explained by its ability to allow the displacement onto women of men's sense of loss or anxiety on the Atlantic. In these different and interdependent ways, these texts and writers navigate their ways through the turbulent waters of modernity.

This figurational nexus of Atlantic ruin and liberty may be what most authorizes a reconstitution of the fields of "American" and "British" literature as the field of English-language literature, including (at the least) authors of both African and Anglo descent.[2] This Atlantic pattern constitutes not just a shared imagery but a shared imaginary, or a whole political and emotional economy circuited through race, sex, property, slavery, and print — and wired to the charge of liberty. In this and the next chapter, I juxtapose a diverse set of texts in order to establish the broad contours and intertextual negotiations of this imaginary. As a preface to these readings, I outline here the contours and benefits of this model of English-language literature.

William Spengemann is the first critic to have suggested the need for a paradigm shift toward an "English-language" framework for British and U.S. literature.[3] His work has reoriented mine, although his perspective remains largely Americanist. He would in effect reverse the standard transatlantic story of influence, making America instead of England the catalyst and source for much of modern English-language literature, especially the novel — whereas I see a pressured dialectic among texts embedded in a transatlantic economy.[4] Accordingly, he omits attention to the African dimension of this Atlantic-centered English-language corpus. And yet his fresh angle of vision is salutary. Most usefully for this study, his "Americanist" rereading of John Milton's *Paradise Lost* begins to fathom the depths at which the liberty stories of the Atlantic triangle converge, clash, and enter into dialogue. For Milton's text becomes one of the most important vehicles by which the Puritan, racialized, and Atlantic legacy of the English Civil War enters the allusive structures of modern English-language literature.

As Spengemann points out, Milton's story of Eve's fall is laced with Atlantic allusions. Implicitly, Milton's Satan is a roving Atlantic libertine, the first of many in English-language literature, I'll suggest. That is, Milton casts Satan as the restless seeker "of foreign worlds" (10.441) and in particular "new world[s]" (1.650, 2.403, 4.34, 4.113, 10.257)—a "heav'n on earth" which the fallen angel searches for across the "illimitable ocean" (4.208; 2.892) and where the downcast may "hope to change / Torment with ease" (4.892–93).[5] Milton accordingly fashions Eve as an "advent'rous" woman seduced by this eager Satan and his vision of new-world liberation from God's tyranny. In Spengemann's formulation, Milton meant to discourage the investment in ambitious Atlantic projects and encourage more local and devout goals—or as Spengemann puts it, "the desire for self-government, personal fulfillment, and complete knowledge had to be detached from whatever objects it might set itself"—such as colonizing projects in America or Ireland—"and redirected toward eternal objects . . . set by God" (*New World* 109). *Paradise Lost* appears, in this light, as the Puritan republican Milton's reflection on the Atlantic serpent that helped to corrupt, as I would put it, the Anglo-Protestant revolutionary principle of liberty and so gave way to the censoring Protectorate. Here we begin to glimpse the deep merging of Puritan and Atlantic stories within a troubled liberty plot taken up by both African- and Anglo-Atlantic authors.

In short, Milton's *Paradise Lost* accretes one allusive layer of a developing geo-literary formation—the transatlantic seduction plot. Later writers elaborate on the "fallen" version of the Atlantic story that Milton laid out, sometimes more optimistically transforming it into a *Paradise Found*. Nina Auerbach long ago suggested as much, although not in a transatlantic context, in her study of the "fallen woman" in nineteenth-century British fiction. She argued that, in a Victorian imagination agitated by both religious doubts and global ambitions, the figure of the ruined woman "grafted the doom of Milton's Satan on to the aspirations of his Eve, generating a creature whose nature it is to fall" and yet "whose identity defines itself only in that fall."[6] I would place this pattern next to a similar one visible in the sermons of nineteenth-century American ministers seduced by the "rising glory" prospects of America and inspired to invoke Milton's epic in new ways, casting the American Revolution as the apotheosis of the "fortunate" fall that began with Puritan exodus into the "wilderness."[7] At the same time, Milton's story provides the allusive structure of many African-Atlantic slave narratives and early novels: that of a fall caused by a satanic power but ultimately yielding, in another world if not this one, an awakening rise. In these many ways, then, English-language memoirs and novels enfold this neo-Miltonian logic into their freedom stories.

This framework indicates, furthermore, that the gendered history of novel-writing warrants a transatlantic treatment beyond the standard *Clarissa* reference of most Americanist accounts. If we place American feminist critics' rich work on the early novel beside that of British feminist scholars, we glimpse the possibilities. Julia Stern explores how the first influential American male novelist, Charles Brockden Brown, is "deeply schooled in [Rowson's and Foster's] affective worlds" and so implicitly "declares his allegiance to a native [U.S.] literary tradition in which women figure as important precursors."[8] Stern's account parallels the kind of genealogy recent critics of the British novel have been tracking, as we saw in the last chapter, in their aim to understand Richardson's debt to Behn, Haywood, Manley, and others. If these early British women novelists shaped the work of Richardson, and if Richardson heavily influenced early American novelists, including Brockden Brown, Foster, Hill Brown, and Rowson, as most American critics assume, then it's time to think of all these American authors in relation to Behn, Haywood, and Defoe — as well as Richardson. Three generations of women writers prepared the way for early American novelists — including by registering the fractures of history and thus beginning the cultural work that Stephanie Smith highlights in U.S. sentimental fiction.[9]

Most relevant for this study, when we read early British and early American novels (and the criticism on them) together, we hear their shared political resonances, we glimpse their *trans*atlantic horizons. Again it's worth quoting Julia Stern, one of the most astute and transatlantically oriented critics of the early American novel. She argues that early American novels express an "unprecedented sense of loss" in the "wake of [the American] Revolution" (31). Stern sensitively traces the sense of loss in these texts, but their patterns of loss are in fact fully "precedented," deriving as they do from the discourses and experiences of a much earlier revolution — the English Revolution — and from the entire, unanchoring project of Atlantic colonialism that accompanied that revolution. That is, as we have seen, "republican" questions about authority, community, consent, and liberty arise in the wake of a century of revolutions in England and are embedded in the seduction novel from the beginning in England. These questions are furthermore from the start charged along race, class, and gender lines on both sides of the Atlantic. Both early American fiction and early British fiction are best understood, as Spengemann suggests, as early English-language fiction. And, in the hands of Anglo-writers, both traditions gain force and appeal — not to mention a buying readership — through a disavowed if sometimes fleetingly registered dependence on African labor. If U.S. and British novels diverge, it is not through questions of contract and republicanism or race, nation, and gender — these they share — but rather in the precise accents added to the long history of such questions. Exactly because they do share a set of questions about liberty and identity, and because they work within a racial economy, we can trace in these novels the struggles of seventeenth- and eighteenth-century Atlantic history.

Certainly the correlation of sexual ruin with a spiritual fall as well as a water-crossing trauma constitutes a common narrative structure, I will argue in this chapter, in the novels of Daniel Defoe, Susanna Rowson, William Hill Brown, and Harriet Wilson. In their texts, the Miltonian "fall," which as we've seen also registers the event of a national rupture, finds expression in a near-drowning that leaves the self "at sea," creates a dissociative form of narration, and ushers in troubled republican brother/sister relations. The protagonists' ruin is all at once sexual, spiritual, colonial, and economic. While the racial thrust of this ruin is implicit in Defoe, Rowson, and Brown, in Wilson's text it cuts directly through the grammar of the story, creating a dissociated first- and third-person narrator who both claims and disavows her identity as "our nig." All four of these authors move through the literal or symbolic geography of the Atlantic; and this geography, in turn, links them to the texts with male protagonists I discuss in the next chapter, wherein the plot of a specifically sexual undoing is more subtextual but the Atlantic-induced catastrophe of spiritual, economic, and racial ruin becomes visible and visceral.[10]

The Comedy of Atlantic Contract in Defoe

Moll Flanders and *Roxana,* Daniel Defoe's two novels centered on women protagonists, elaborate the key tropes of the Atlantic imaginary even as they carry forward the subgenre of "secret histories" generated in the late seventeenth century. These two novels merge the mercantile Atlantic story of ruin and redemption Defoe had told in *Robinson Crusoe* with the sexual stories of ruin and recovery being told contemporaneously and with great success by Haywood, while also covertly encoding allegories of English history. In *Roxana,* although the Atlantic does not figure explicitly, the text is nonetheless, we will see, soaked with nautical metaphors, structured by several near-ruinous sea crossings, and fashioned as a secret history of women's "consorting" position in a transatlantic, contractual economy. In *Moll Flanders,* the Atlantic is a central locale and the novel's plot of sexual ruin turns on the separations and reunions structured by its geography. In particular, her Atlantic crossings bring Moll face-to-face with the liberty journey's incestuous effects — that is, its potential to make a man and wife into a brother and sister, equal inheritors of Britain's colonial and cultural capital. In its correlation of Atlantic and sexual ruin and in its incest plot, *Moll Flanders* exerts an influence on early Anglo-American novels that has gone unrecognized, especially in light of critics' habitual references to the influence of Samuel Richardson. I begin here by considering the ways that *Roxana* indirectly negotiates the demands and effects of liberty for Anglo-Protestant women and then turn to Defoe's more explicitly Atlantic female novel, *Moll Flanders*.

In reading these novels, it is useful to bear in mind that Defoe — of a generation younger than Behn and older than Richardson — writes under the influence of England's ruptured succession and religious history. Born in 1660, child of a Dissenter family during the Restoration, and witness as a young man to the Glorious Revolution, Defoe had (like Haywood) directly felt the effects of England's radical changes and its insider-outsider historical vacillations. Accordingly, he works in the tradition of memoir-history tapped by Behn and Haywood, and he deems these two novels "secret histories." Defoe signals the underlying relationship between secret histories, works of fiction, and the discourse of liberty when he "freely" claims that his works are histories. In his preface to *Roxana*, he "takes the Liberty to say, That this Story . . . is not a Story but a History" with a "Foundation" in "Fact" yet for which "it was necessary to conceal the Names and Persons."[11] Similarly the narrator announces that *Moll Flanders* is not one of those "Novels and Romances" but is rather a "private History" with names "concealed" (37).[12] This rhetorical play in which secrecy and "the liberty to say" mingle uncertainly with history and fictionalization restages the founding role of a secret or ruinous history in English novels.

And indeed Defoe's novels encode the secret plots of English history. He carefully sets *Roxana*, for instance, during the Restoration and casts the titular protagonist as a mistress of Charles II fashioned after the real historical courtesan Nell Gwynne, offering at the same time, as I'll argue later, an allegory of women's mediating role in Britain's economic and Protestant future. Likewise, as we will see in chapter 7, Crusoe's island "imprisonment" corresponds in historical time with the decades of the Restoration, simulating the way that Dissenters either experienced exile in their own land or fled to Atlantic colonies, as Michael Seidel suggests; and it ends, as did the Restoration, with this exiled subject's return home and release into "liberty."[13] Moll's Atlantic crossings to the colonies represent the contemporary practice of the transport of criminals and explore this practice as a support for both the sexual and the religious dimensions of Britain's mercantile empire.

By writing these secret histories with historically coded chronologies and doing so in the tradition of those private historical memoirs written in the after-math of the Civil War, Defoe locates his novels within the print legacy of English dissent—religious, sexual, institutional, and Atlantic.[14] This framework helps to make sense of this author who mocked the notion of a "True-Born English-man" (at length, in his poem by that name) but meanwhile extolled British trade and empire as the freest, most civilized traffic on the globe. A close look at his writing indicates that Defoe's manipulations of the rhetoric of history, liberty, and English identity are less ironic than strategic, meant to help consolidate a Dissenter's Whiggish outlook. If we track the historical allusions of his playful-ness we usually find an earnest nationalism impelling it. Thus his poem about trueborn Englishmen, while apparently debunking all lineage myths, works to deflate Stuart lineage claims to the throne and underwrite William's "Whig" ac-cession.[15] Always in this playful but firmly Anglo-Protestant spirit, Defoe cre-ated characters whose plights embody English history and whose lives embody English freedom.

ALTHOUGH THE ATLANTIC is absent in *Roxana*, Defoe obliquely gestures to-ward it as the horizon for this story of a "Protestant whore" and Stuart king's consort who abandons children, corrupts her maid, arranges for the murder of her daughter, and yet emerges as a successful, settled citizen in this property-accruing world. As her life is taking one of its most prosperous turns, Defoe figu-ratively converges the sea-crossing, mercantile, and sexual currents of the plot of ruin. Roxana and her maid, Amy, are journeying from France to Holland, in effect to launder Roxana's wealth in the course of their return to England, when a storm rises. As it threatens to sink the vessel, Amy is "undone" with thoughts of hell for her whoring past and she falls into a "swooning fit"—exactly the vocabu-lary Crusoe uses in describing his experiences of shipwreck (125).

Likewise, the debate over women's freedom is figuratively *navigated* in this novel—that is, rendered in sea tropes—especially in the fifteen-page dialogue between Roxana and "the Dutch Merchant" (significantly named as such). Al-though she loves him, Roxana refuses to marry the merchant because of the loss of control over her property it would entail; the Merchant in turn vows to make no claim on Roxana's money after the marriage. In his nautical parlance, he promises that "you shall be Pilot then, you shall conn the Ship" (151). But Roxana points out that even in making this "offer," he betrays his prior power, as reflected in the fact that "you can take the Helm out of my Hands when you please, and bid me go spin" (151). Implicitly Defoe hints that this new open negotiation between a man and a woman over the terms of the marriage contract arises in a world of navigation—of both seas and mercantile deals.

Throughout *Roxana,* Defoe repeatedly draws attention to the sexual contract as it is negotiated within a rhetoric of liberty, a mercantile economy, and, more obliquely (in the Turkish slave and costume that Roxana receives as gifts), a racialized circuit of slavery.[16] Roxana (originally laid low by marrying a handsome fool incapable of making money who left her destitute with five children) minces no words in naming the systemic problem for women. She points out that "the very Nature of the Marriage-Contract was, in short, nothing but giving up Liberty, Estate, Authority, and every-thing, to the Man, and the Woman was indeed, a meer Woman ever after, that is to say, a Slave" (148). This is the basis on which she continually refuses offers of marriage. As she explains, "I had, perhaps, differing Notions of Matrimony from what the receiv'd Custom had given us of it; that I thought a Woman was a free Agent, as well as a Man, and was born free, and cou'd she manage herself suitably, might enjoy that Liberty to as much Purpose as the Men do; that the Laws of matrimony were indeed, otherwise, and Mankind at this time, acted upon quite other Principles" (147). Under these laws, she points out, "a Woman gave herself entirely away from herself" (147) — just as Clarissa later feels "tricked out of herself" (869). Echoing the circumlocutions by which Haywood characterizes her heroines' encounters with men, Roxana frames her relationship with the Dutch Merchant as one that "admit[s] you to the Liberty I have given you" (151).

Unlike Haywood's heroines, however, Defoe's women are not finally caught by the circularity of the social contract and the duplicitous language of liberty in this economy; instead, they exploit it. Like *Moll Flanders, Roxana* is permeated with talk of liberties and freedoms in ways that give agency to women as well as men, mingling liberty's different meanings. After she has "given the [French] Prince the Last Favour, and he had all the freedom with me that it was possible for me to grant," he in turn "gave me Leave to use as much Freedom with him, another Way, and that was, to have every thing of him, I thought fit to command" (66). In bed with him on a later morning, Roxana reports that "I took the Liberty once, in our Freedoms, to tell him, he was too bountiful" (71). Sexual liberties lead to financial liberties which in turn allow social liberties. Once she has manipulated this chain of liberty connections and garnered its power, she can more safely tell the Merchant that "I valued my Liberty, as I knew my Fortune" and would give neither away (169). Property and personal liberty are repeatedly paired in this novel, an association that reaches straight back to the founding rhetorical maneuvers of the transatlantic economy: "I liv'd a Life of absolute Liberty now; was as free as I was born, and having a plentiful Fortune, I did not understand what Coherence the Words *Honour* and *Obey* had with the Liberty of a *Free Woman*" (171). Her claims could equally well name the subtext of a prosperous colony seeking the right to make its own laws and to refuse taxation without representation. As we'll see below, her "history" as a prostitute who "reforms" herself once she is prosperous encodes the story of England's colonial empire.

Critics have grappled with the apparent disjunction between Roxana's (like Moll's) conversion story and her criminal prosperity, but it needs stressing that the profitability of her liberty quest *enables* her pilgrim's progress. Liberty generates profit, and profit funds redemption. As Defoe's women offer their sexual and thieving liberties for our delectation, they can, within the liberty telos of their fortunate falls, justify, by narrativizing as "progress," the incommensurability of their discourses. Tellingly, the rhetorical mastery of a duplicitous liberty discourse is displayed most strikingly in Roxana's and the Merchant's navigation of the marriage question. In his plea that they marry and make their liaison legitimate, the Merchant ostensibly speaks the voice of reform but in fact only as a move in their chess game. He tells Roxana, "[Y]ou argue for liberty at the same time that you restrain yourself from that Liberty, which God and Nature directed you to take; and to supply the Deficiency, propose a vicious Liberty, which is neither honourable or religious" (157). His circular phrasing deliberately muddles the matter, so that "liberty" becomes that "which God and Nature directed [Roxana] to take." If one is *directed* by God to take the liberty of marrying, is it a free act? To dissent would seem freer. But if this dissent takes the form of "restraining" oneself, is it liberty? The Merchant makes it appear that her dissent (from marriage) is an unnecessary "restraint," and (anticipating Rousseau) that obedience is freedom. No wonder that in such a conversation Roxana likewise equivocates and "*pretended* to argue upon the Point of a Woman's Liberty" (156–57, emphasis added). She, too, is ready to use the terms of liberty and contract in bad faith.

In this dialogue, Defoe creates a tableau of an acutely historical question at this moment in early-eighteenth-century Britain: of whether women, too, will marry the mercantilism that gained new stability in the Dutch merger with England in the Glorious Revolution. The same Dutch that destabilized Behn's colonial economy promise, in Defoe's world, to legitimate it — make it "honourable" — but women's assent is required. In fact, in several ways, Defoe points to the illicit, self-contradicting activities required from women in order to achieve this legitimation of what was in fact a coup d'etat of the old, divine-right order. First of all, Defoe reveals the logic of substitutions shared by the operations of contract, marriage, and money in this Anglo-Protestant mercantile world.[17] As critics have explored, the new money economy, which developed with the founding of the Bank of England in the wake of the Glorious Revolution, rests on an absent center — on credit — and it requires an agreement to dissemble, to allow what is empty to stand for that which is full and substantial.[18] Defoe's *Roxana* not only hints that the marriage contract works analogously (by pretending to promise a woman some material substance via a contract based on her absence, as *feme covert*); but, by fashioning Roxana as a master of such substitutive dissembling, Defoe also implies that illicit sex and proper marriage complement each other within the British money economy. In effect, a Defoian woman is enlisted to circulate widely as a kind of libertine feme covert, or a coinage accruing profit as it travels, who does the work of infiltrating class ranks, channeling noble wealth outward into the money economy, and meanwhile giving piracy, speculation, and embezzlement a comic and Protestant liberty telos. Indeed, as Kimberly Latta suggests in her reading of the figure of Lady Credit in Defoe's *Review of the State of the English Nation,* Defoe's several writings on trade analogously gender as female the figure of debt and thus indicate how women's circulation, licit and illicit, generates credit and therefore profit in the economy. Defoe fashions "Lady Credit" as a powerful strumpet ("her Pimps," says Defoe, "are the brokers, her Cullies the merchants and Tradesmen") and assigns her a necessary role in England's global, mercantile-generated progress.[19] If managed well, her ruinous movements are profitable for the nation.

Roxana's Protestant identity further encourages a reading of her as a vehicle for the national story. As established in the novel's opening paragraph, her childhood recapitulates England's "Whig" history of escape from French tyranny into liberty — by way of a mercantile, water-crossing exile that turns into a permanent profitable settlement: "I was born, *as my Friends told me,* at the City of POICTIERS in the province, or County of POICTOU, in *France,* from whence I was brought to *England* by my parents, who fled for their religion about the Year 1683, when the Protestants were Banish'd from *France* by the Cruelty of their Persecutors" (5). In this light we should recall Roxana's characterization of herself as not just any kind of whore but a "Protestant whore": "tho' I was a Whore, yet I was a Protestant Whore, and could not act as if I was Popish, upon any Account whatsoever" (69). As Alison Conway has discussed at length, Defoe thus casts her as a figure for Nell Gwynne, Charles II's "Protestant" mistress (in contrast to the king's popish female companions), who won the affection of the English public and especially of those who were fearful about Charles's Catholic leanings.[20] As "the Protestant whore," Roxana represents a dissenting insider whose sexual powers might redeem the king.

Thus the story of Roxana allegorizes the promiscuous means by which England achieves its high ends. She is the comic redeemer of the ruin narrative, the commoner-woman who seduces (and soaks) the king, to good ends. Her maneuvers with both French and English royalty play out the geopolitical machinations required for the Anglo-Protestant project. In this light, her spectacular performance in Turkish dress throws into relief her native identity, even as the story of its procurement — by way of a man-of-war that captures a Turkish ship, makes the women slaves, and sells their clothing — registers the warring and patriarchal conditions that attend this project. *Roxana* is accordingly structured by a series of "swoons," in which Roxana herself is repeatedly "overcome" and then reborn by a generous suitor who saves her from the brink of misery in return for a sexual liaison (30, 44, 65). Even as this free Protestant whore sings, "O 'tis pleasant to be free, / The sweetest Mistress is Liberty" (149), Defoe offers an allegory of "bought" liberty as the inherently illicit and unsettling but (re)productive presence behind the proper wife of English, imperial history.

IN *MOLL FLANDERS,* the profitable undoing of an Anglo-Protestant woman directly involves an Atlantic crossing and Defoe more explicitly tracks the colonial engine in this economy of substitutions. As Lou Caton has discussed, Moll's transatlantic "transport" is at once religious and economic — and, I would add, sexual — all of which reshapes Milton's Atlanticizing of the fall into a story of profitable reform. Moll's first Atlantic crossing "ruins" her by revealing she has married her brother, while her later transport as a convict redeems this undoing, converts her to the path of virtue, and brings her into her settled wealth via an inheritance from that same first marriage. Especially insofar as the practice of transporting criminals had since the seventeenth century been framed as a "pardon" from execution generously granted to English "freeborn subjects," this central event of transport nicely gathers all the threads of the Atlantic narrative and offers a pattern for fictions to come.[21] Here, too, then a woman's illicit sexuality allegorizes Britain's free laws, thieving crimes, and colonial prosperity.

More particularly, in the drama of incest that emerges in this Atlantic crossing, Defoe gives early expression to the political subplot that we saw in *Clarissa* and that shapes future fictions of liberty: a brother/sister conflict over inheritance and property. Readers have remarked on the incest in *Moll* but without due attention to its particular form as brother-sister incest, which I believe has political, or "Whig," implications.[22] In *Moll Flanders* and future novels, that is, the liberty struggle often includes a sibling subplot that takes different forms, ranging from fierce antagonism to passionate incest. This brother-sister trouble within what Juliet Flower MacCannell calls "the regime of the brother" surfaces consistently in English gothic novels, early American novels, and early African American novels. We will find it at work in all the novels I consider in this chapter and in most of the novels I treat in this book.

To elaborate, the brother-sister pair expresses a desire to work through the relation of the hetero-erotic to the hetero-political under the reigning sign of liberty and within an economy where everyone theoretically circulates "freely." When women seek a liberty equal to men's and propose to enter the polis on terms equal to theirs, they collide with the heteronormative structures that have defined men's and women's adult relations in hierarchical, strictly sexual terms. To imagine a horizontal (or leveling) relation between men and women that stands beside the sexual one seems to make siblings of sexual partners. This threatening implication gains a purchase partly because of the language of "fraternity" that develops within the emergent, republican regime of the brother — that fraternal polity in which ruling men are no longer obedient sons but competing or cooperating equals. That is, this republican language leaves an opening, linguistically, to the positioning of "sisters," also, as equals to those "brothers." English-language novels usually render the impossibility of this political companionship between brothers and sisters, expressing anxiety about it.

In Moll's case, when her husband turns out to be her brother, and her mother-in-law turns out to be her mother-in-the-flesh who was transported from Newgate to the American colonies, Moll flees in horror, recrossing the Atlantic. My reading of her horror at this Atlantically positioned incest comes closest to Ellen Pollack's understanding of it as a "figure for freedom" (9). Pollack stresses the ways that the incest taboo belongs to patriarchy and organizes its circulation of property: women's export outside the family is "required to create the suprafamilial bonds that make other forms of trade or communication possible" and the "incest-limit" operates thus as the "fulcrum of the text" (9). That is, trade of all kinds depends on women's "marrying-out" and so is supported by the incest taboo. She accordingly reads Moll's repulsion at the discovery that she has married her brother as her conscription into patriarchal and economic norms, at odds with Moll's otherwise unconventional and illicit practices, and she concludes that Moll is thus made to "circulate outside the circuit of her own authority in order for those systems of economic and symbolic exchange to operate" (18). In Pollack's reading, Moll in effect refuses the freedom from patriarchal law that incest represents — and the freedom, I would add, that her mother practiced in her illicit sex.

But Pollack underemphasizes Moll's own agency, her Atlantic maneuverings, in "those systems of economic and symbolic exchange." These systems also belong, in Defoe's rendering (however fantastically), to Moll. In this new, Atlantic world, as monetary or commodity exchange increasingly provides the basis of identity and authority, new conditions attend the pursuits of both men and women. Especially if we consider Moll together with Defoe's gendered figure of Lady Credit in his economic writings, we can see how Moll embodies the freedom to accrue profits by rapid and shifting movements through urban, Atlantic, and colonial spaces. In fact, if women work under cover and largely alone, as Defoe's two heroines do, they may sometimes get the better of men in this system — if they can also avoid pregnancy or child-rearing, a fantasy Defoe allows for his heroines, which is one way his vision diverges from Haywood's otherwise similar world of undercover operators.[23] In this light, it's important to recall that, first of all, following her flight from incest and America, Moll steadily and illegally accrues property and profits in England, which she eventually has shipped to her in Virginia (no less); and, second, once back in Virginia, she thrives by inheriting property from her mother and winning the generous affection of her brother's son, while her brother-husband gradually declines and finally dies.

In rejecting the mingling of husband and brother, Moll merely forbears to acknowledge the new matrix from which she profits, where the circulation of money and goods (uprooted from embedded community and generated now by "individuals") no longer demands the structure of an incest taboo. Here, theoretically, sisters can lounge with brothers, for kinship lines have themselves broken apart and potentially women can contract with any man they choose. The Atlantic dispersal of families — and transport of criminals who, once in the colonies, wear their Newgate brands beneath their wealthy clothes — has in fact created the conditions of anonymity that make possible Moll's incest "mistake." Although it is early in the game of modern capitalism, a woman like Moll can glimpse the radical implications of such a system where everyone circulates "freely." She likes its immediate benefits very well, but, like Defoe, she consciously rejects its breakdown of Puritan family morality. If we can read Defoe's conduct books as expressions of his anxiety about the fracturing pressures on families within an economic system he otherwise condones, we can see that Moll's horror at incest does the same.

Thus in Defoe's female Puritan confession narratives rewritten as the comedy of liberty's equivocations, Moll and Roxana establish themselves by manipulating sexual and colonial economies simultaneously, including in Moll's case an unabashed appropriation of the brother's inheritance. Working mostly alone and pseudonymously, like Haywood's heroines, they reveal only to their readers their secret strategies, identities, and profits. Even when Moll finally reunites with her Lancashire husband and they sail to America, she keeps secrets, and above all money, from him and at one point confesses to wishing that she were free of him to pursue another new identity. Like Haywood's heroines, Defoe's women's interiors emerge from their dissemblance, from their understanding that, in an unstable, contractual world, a split self-relation must substitute for kin-relation as the ground of identity, security, and property.

Along the way Defoe's protagonists subvert Cromwell's hope that this cultivation of an interior could mean perfect transparency between self and socius — for instead it implicitly exposes the will to power of that "Protectorate" dream. And yet insofar as readers (the protagonists' confidants) experience the illusion of transparency, this illusion is upheld, secret power appears accessible, and we seem to become free and prosperous insiders by way of identification with Moll and Roxana as powerful, transgressive yet ultimately reformed outsiders. We, too, become freeborn, righteous, and rich English people.

Innocence Abroad

Susanna Rowson's pair of novels, *Charlotte Temple* and *Lucy Temple,* recast the tale of transatlantic seduction and in the process initiate the readership for "native" U.S. novels. At the origin of *Charlotte Temple* (1797) lies the story of an English father "deprived of . . . liberty," which involves a daughter's near ruin and leads to a granddaughter's utter ruin, enacted on the Atlantic (7). In the sequel, *Lucy Temple,* the great-granddaughter awakens from this legacy of swooning to find herself, like Moll, in an incestuous relation with her brother. Yet by the end of *Lucy Temple,* a world of reformed liberty is born from this crisis (phoenixlike and fortunate), a world in which sisters run pious schools and brothers die nobly in mercantile-colonial battles. In *The Power of Sympathy* (1789) by William Hill Brown, the first novel published in America (but little noticed), the outcome is less sanguine but the crisis is identical: the lovers Harriot and Harrington likewise "awaken" to discover they are siblings via their father's rakish past. Brown furthermore casts the whole sequence in the imagery of shipwreck and sea trauma: Harrington senior, the lovers' rakish but penitent father, feels "like a sailor escaped from shipwreck, who sits safely on shore and views the horrors of the tempest; but as the gale subsides and the waves hide their heads in the bosom of the deep, he beholds with greater concern the mischief of the storm."[24] The brief, pivotal appearance of an African American slave woman in Brown's novel and the fact that the liberty quests in Rowson's later works, although multiracial, are nonetheless led by Anglo-Atlantic women indicate the ways that these liberty plots are forming *racial* identities. It is this dimension of the Atlantic imaginary that Harriet Wilson brings into full view in *Our Nig.*

Critics have productively read early U.S. novels as reflections on the new republican polity in the turbulent postrevolutionary decades in the United States.[25] But in beginning with this postrevolutionary setting and moment, we foreshorten these novels' histories and miss their deepest racial undertones (as well as sometimes misrepresenting early British novels as apolitical).[26] Thus, although Julia Stern illuminates early American novels' psycho-historical substrata when she reads *Charlotte Temple* as a "traumatic *urtext*" that offers a "political subtext and a generic template" for American novels to follow (and my readings of these early novels are indebted to her), the novel's paradigmatic structure becomes even clearer when placed within an older Atlantic history.[27] Stern draws on transatlantic sources in seeing the novel as inflected by both the "haunting Gothicism" of Burke's account of the French Revolution and the dream of "transparency" expressed in Rousseau's vision of society. Yet the longer transatlantic perspective reveals, first, that Gothicism had already been embedded in British novels of seduction (which likely influenced Burke's own rhetoric), and, second, that the vision of a transparent polity was at least as much a Puritan and racialized dream as a primitivist French one, as expressed in Rowson's Christian framing of her tale, signaling her rewriting of Bunyan's *Pilgrim's Progress* and Milton's *Paradise Lost*.[28] In Rowson's pair of novels, *Charlotte Temple* and *Lucy Temple*,[29] this history's continuities and departures are enacted in the explicitly transatlantic plot of rape and liberty.

Rowson herself lived a transatlantic life fully caught up in the Atlantic world's political turmoil. She moved with family across the Atlantic three times, and her experience of not only crossing the Atlantic but also living on both sides of it during the American revolutionary period apparently enabled her to express the visceral and symbolic power of the Atlantic for the emigrants.[30] Like Rowson's other works, *Charlotte Temple* drew little attention in England but was popular in America — very popular. It quickly became the biggest best-seller in the United States until *Uncle Tom's Cabin*. It has seen two hundred editions, and its sequel, published in 1828, went through forty editions before 1900. Charlotte became a kind of cult figure, and her fictional grave a pilgrimage site. Leslie Fiedler considered the novel not a work of literature but a "subliterate myth," and critics have been baffled by its immense popularity (quoted in Douglas viii).

Its popularity very possibly stems from the fact that, while perhaps crude, the myth it narrates — of transatlantic seduction and alienation of the purportedly native self — is a founding one. I concur with Blythe Forcey that *Charlotte Temple* encodes the "nightmare of dislocation, alienation, and abandonment" that "most early Americans" experienced in their "passage from Old World to New" (227), but I would take the argument beyond the question of why Rowson must therefore leave behind epistolary form (which is Forcey's main concern). Much more broadly in American fiction, in the work of authors from Charles Brockden Brown to Nathaniel Hawthorne to Henry James, the American Adam arrives on stage as an Eve, a ruined wanderer of humble yet virtuous origin who, like Clarissa, soon becomes "no longer what I was in any one thing" — a state heightened dramatically by removal across the Atlantic. From this perspective we can see how James Fenimore Cooper—in both his sea fiction and his Natty Bumpo novels—works to masculinize this lone figure, making a freedom-seeking virtue of the protagonist's sea-tossed alienation. In fact, the subgenre of sea-adventure fiction founded by Cooper extends the Atlantic novel's embedded tropes into the central scene of action.[31] In this light, we may glimpse how Melville creates sailor-heroes who descend not only from Cooper's seamen but also, through him, from Cooper's own sources in the exiled woman's story. Such a perspective reorients literary history, bridging the bifurcation of men's and women's traditions as well as British and American ones. As we'll see later, Catharine Maria Sedgwick integrates all these lineages in her epic-historical novel *Hope Leslie.*

Although Rowson wrote *Charlotte Temple* before she wrote either *Reuben and Rachel* or *Slaves in Algiers,* they reveal retroactively that, in crafting Charlotte's story, Rowson is creating a specifically *Anglo*-Atlantic heroine. In these later texts, Rowson imagines multicultural communities and cross-racial freedom quests, and she makes women central and powerful within them, but the Anglo-Atlantic women of "Columbia" ultimately operate as the charmed leaders of these quests, nobly leading dark-skinned women into freedom. These works make clear that in Rowson's imagination the liberty plot structuring her first novel is of Anglo-Saxon derivation; and indeed, as I'll later suggest, its innovative, multigenerational story further fashions this "simple tale" as a corollary to epic, multivolume histories of Anglo-Atlantic liberty, as an allegory of a heroic *history.* Thus Rowson's liberatory gestures in her work, beginning with her first and most popular novel, have white-mystifying effects, though she might have intended otherwise.

In Rowson's foundational novel, her simple heroine Charlotte is seduced within an Atlantic ring of forces. Under the sway of Miss LaRue, a corrupt French teacher at her boarding school, Charlotte begins to be enamored of and eventually agrees to rendezvous with an army officer named Montraville, whose name also hints at French lineage. Thus does Rowson begin with the old Francophobic Saxon-Norman story.[32] Montraville succeeds in his seduction of Charlotte, however, not only with the aid of Miss LaRue but also via the language of America as a land of both loss and promise. First, Montraville persuades Charlotte to meet him regularly because of his imminent departure. He repeatedly reminds her that he will soon "leave my native land"; he emphasizes that they will be "divided by a vast expanse of sea"; and he conjures the possibility that, once he departs, "a few short weeks may terminate my existence; the perils of the ocean—the dangers of war—."[33] Before long he is attempting to persuade her to go to America with him, promising to marry her when they arrive. When she insists that she cannot, out of loyalty to her parents, he confesses his mistaken hope that "you would for my sake have braved the dangers of the ocean, that you would, by your affection and smiles, have softened the hardships of war" (42). Now, with her refusal, he will "welcome the friendly ball that deprives me of the sense of my misery" (43). In the end, as in Clarissa's story, Charlotte meets him once more, with "torn heart," to say goodbye but when she wavers, Montraville offers, "'Let me direct you,' . . . lifting her into the chaise" (48). Charlotte "shrieked, and fainted into the arms of her betrayer" (48).

This French-named seducer has done Satan's new-world work—and the expanse of the Atlantic aids him. In particular, the simple distance of America from England seals Charlotte's fate at the hands of a treacherous French woman and Normanesque man; for not only does Montraville intercept most of the letters she writes to her parents (expressing her wish to return home) but ultimately the "vast expanse of sea" so slows the passage of the one letter that does get sent that her father arrives too late to save her from homelessness and starvation. America—its colonial wars and its distance from a native home—causes Charlotte's death as as well her ruin.

Likewise, the multigenerational structure of this novel would have been likely to entrance American readers who had a strong sense of a generational story line. In fact, Rowson deserves credit for introducing this important innovation to the early English-language novel. Not only does the first novel, *Charlotte Temple*, reach from Mr. Eldridge's middle-age storytelling to the birth of his great-grand-daughter but *Lucy Temple* then moves beyond his death to this granddaughter's coming-of-age. In this pair of novels, the legacy of freedom and reform becomes chronologized across generations (as it also does in *The Power of Sympathy* but more cryptically), and this multigenerational structure signals the novel's role as vehicle of a historical legacy of violation. Meanwhile, it joins the print history that forms a cultural imaginary around this violation. Rowson's introduction of this multigenerational "roots" structure into the novel (together with the idea of a "sequel") predates its use by Sir Walter Scott, and in this sense Rowson first discovers the template for later historical fiction. In *Reuben and Rachel,* she takes this innovation even further, to almost biblical proportions, when she charts ten generations of liberty seekers from Columbus to the American Revolution—anticipating those epic liberty novels I will discuss in part 4.

From this angle, it might be as useful to read Clarissa's many removals in relation to Charlotte's (and Mary Rowlandson's, for that matter)[34] as it is to read Charlotte's in relation to Clarissa's. That is, we can read the trauma of lost or intercepted letters that dooms both women as the fallout of the increased distances and kin separations in this new, yet still male-manipulated, logocentric economy they share. In this and other ways, *Charlotte Temple* is of a piece with British seduction fiction, yet at the same time its story especially appeals to those who have crossed the Atlantic and not returned to England—which perhaps explains why it had more success in the United States.

The starting point of *Charlotte Temple,* as related by her grandfather, Mr. Eldridge, lays out the generational back story for her Atlantic trauma. In a pattern we saw in *Clarissa* and *Moll* and will see again, the brother's launching in this modern world entails, it seems, the sister/daughter's ruin. Indeed, far from evoking a pastoral "green world . . . of the English past" (32) as Julia Stern suggests (that idyll appears briefly in the next generation), the text's originating moment is a scene of violation—when Eldridge is seized from his home and put in prison for a debt forced on him by the near-seducer of his daughter. From the start, that is, Rowson mobilizes the domestic-violation trope laid in Thomas Overton's 1646 pamphlet. The crisis originates by way of a debt incurred when Eldridge borrows money to buy a military commission for his son from an apparent friend of his son's who actually wishes to seduce his daughter.[35] Because he has limited resources for forwarding his son's rise in the world ("I had neither friends nor money to procure him a commission" [10]), and thinking his son's new friend and army comrade has good intentions, Eldridge accepts Lewis's apparently generous offer. But when Eldridge's daughter spurns Lewis, he calls in the father's debt—which Eldridge has no money to pay.

As in Overton's narrative, questions of property underlie this crisis of liberty expressed as a female violation that also unmans the male subject: the sexualized drama of the violation ("they forced open her arms") originates in a lack of property—a state of debt. Violation here is traced to the problem that arises when full "possession" of that original "property"—one's body proper—depends on economic solvency, that is, on the volatile economy of goods, land, and money.[36]

As a result of this problem, Mr. Eldridge's home is invaded, and his women are manhandled and traumatized: "as I was sitting down to supper, unsuspicious of danger, an officer entered, and tore me from the embraces of my family" (11). He sees his wife "faint into the arms of our servant" while his daughter "distracted with her fears for us both, sunk on the floor and endeavoured to detain me by her feeble efforts; but in vain; they forced open her arms; she shrieked, and fell prostrate" (11). Here Eldridge breaks off his narrative, for "[t]he horrors of that night unman me. I cannot proceed" (11). The scene distinctly recalls Thomas Overton's 1646 staging of Norman "barbarities" in his "dreadful Warning from Newgate," which would have been echoing in Rowson's own day in the political pamphlets of Paine, Burke, and others. After Eldridge is dragged to jail, his son confronts and dies in a duel with Lewis, his wife dies in grief, and until he can repay his debts, Eldridge is in confinement, where his daughter (Charlotte's mother-to-be) faithfully visits him. In this new world of fortune seeking, even a benign brother, the plot logic implies, can become an instrument of his sister's and the family's self-loss.

Eldridge narrates these memories, from within his prison and attended by his daughter (and only remaining family member), to a Mr. Temple, whose name invokes the late-seventeenth-century literary and political essayist Sir William Temple, who was among the first to write a book-length study of England's "native" literary tradition. After hearing their story of ruin, Temple pays their debt, liberates Eldridge and his daughter from their prison, and thereafter marries the daughter. This retrospective form of narration of the liberty plot together with her choice of Temple's name suggest some self-consciousness on Rowson's part about the function of literary narrative as an instrument of freedom. She is telling a "native" literary story, and she explicitly conjures the sentimental tropes of Whig identity. Young Mr. Temple's natural benevolence habitually leads him, first of all, to seek out "indigent merit" and "rais[e] it from obscurity" (7). Furthermore, although Mr. Temple is a youngest son and also disadvantaged by the hierarchical distribution of property in primogeniture, he early decides (like Oroonoko) that he will "not sacrifice internal happiness for outward shew" — he will be transparent — and at the same time he will "preserve independence" by handling his small fortune with economy while also marrying "where his heart should direct him": "if I find her in a Cottage, will embrace her with as much cordiality as I should if seated on a throne" (6). This opening frame reenacts the historical tale of humble honesty wronged and liberty usurped but finally redeemed by an "independent" yet "generous" spirit. Appropriately, then, Mr. and Mrs. Temple raise an innocent daughter named Charlotte in honest, English simplicity.

While the scene of violation and the innocent, fresh beginning that follows it would have recalled the American Revolution for American readers, Rowson's tale of Charlotte's subsequent ruin at French hands on the Atlantic would have simultaneously recalled an earlier era and set of transatlantic relations, especially for British readers. In this light it's useful to note that Eldridge, the originally jailed grandfather, serves as a partial frame narrator for Charlotte's story: we begin with his account of his own history; he appears at crucial moments as our focalizer (most significantly as the stricken bearer of the news of Charlotte's elopement); and in the last chapter of this first novel, he is there with his daughter, Charlotte's mother, to receive Mr. Temple (his son-in-law, Charlotte's father) and Lucy (his infant great-granddaughter) on their return from America. His continuing presence operates as the reminder of the novel's origin in that first violation and imprisonment — and implies that the story in this novel is his as much as hers, and accordingly is English as well as American. It is a *generational* transatlantic history.

But then, too, the story is Rowson's. That is, as the usurped Stuart kings and Oroonoko are for Behn, the imprisoned patriarch Eldridge is the authorial daughter's vehicle — the figure and the traumatic past through whom she launches both her story and her future in the United States. Recalling that the situation of a daughter attending a father in jail parallels Rowson's own teenage experience with her father during the American revolutionary years, we can glimpse the subtle ways in which Rowson's novel not only tells the nation's and the patriarch's story but also effects the daughter's emigration to America, as person and author. We may further trace this movement from father's to daughter's story in *Lucy Temple,* written near the end of Rowson's life and published posthumously in 1828, in which the plot becomes more the women's own, although a number of aged and isolated military men populate the background, including the seducer Montraville himself, grown old and depressed and finally devastated by his rake's past. Within this sequel's comic vision in which women learn to manage liberty, the aging male figures recall the violations and wars by which America was won. The shadowiness of their presence suggests that the era of violence is passing now that sensible republican women are actively taking up their roles in the civic world — and on a global scale, as Rowson imagines it in such texts as *Slaves in Algiers.*

In *Lucy Temple,* this new vision is most tellingly indicated in Rowson's handling of the brother-sister incest plot. Here, after the death of her mother and grandparents, Charlotte's daughter Lucy grows up in England in the household of her guardian Mr. Matthews, along with two other adopted daughters. The fates of this brother-free "trio of orphans" provide an anatomy of possible liberty plots for women, and among them Lucy emerges as the new woman: she who survives the storms of seductions past, including the one that nearly ends in her marriage to her brother.[37] Her story unfolds against, on the one hand, the negative example of Mary Lumley, who replays the old seduction history of ruin attendant upon an undisciplined freedom. Mary insists that she is "free to act for herself" (188), but she does not know how to value (as her sister Aura tells her) "this liberty you seem to prize" (185), so she runs off with a man who ruins her, robs her of her inheritance, and abandons her — leaving her notably in an isolated "Gothic cottage" (252) raving madly (in suggestively political terms) about how her "husband the Duke is to be beheaded on Tower Hill to-morrow morning for high treason" (252). On the other hand, Aura Melville embodies the sensible young woman whose happiness stems from her wisdom about the management of liberty (it is she who tries to advise Mary) and whose story moves smoothly toward a conventional happy marriage. Lucy Temple, our main interest, falls in love with a young suitor who seems perfect for her yet who turns out to be the son of Montraville, her mother Charlotte's seducer.

This development suggests that liberty carries the baggage of history and that each generation, however innocent, must cope with it. Yet in Rowson's optimistic vision, Lucy and the young Montraville do so admirably. Young Montraville dies, appropriately, fighting the French (which we learn in a letter from his mother in America, another reminder of the transatlantic world of the story), and Lucy launches a successful school, a "pious undertaking" which "served effectually to divert her mind from harrowing recollections and useless regrets" (240). They thus transcend the "fallen" transatlantic past and herald a new republican future. Whereas Defoe's Moll evaded the implications of incest and transatlantic seduction by way of a life of profitable crime which gave her independence, Rowson imagines a pious version of this evasion and independence — a differently radical version that envisions a woman on her own. Lucy emerges not only successful but active, through her own choices and projects, thus joining an increasing number of other single and independent heroines who appear, for instance, in fiction by Catharine Maria Sedgwick and Lydia Maria Child. What Julia Stern says about incest in *The Power of Sympathy* and *Wieland*, applies equally well to this novel, for here, too, "brothers and sisters long to commingle despite the separation enjoined by custom and law" (6). In Stern's understanding, such stories explore an "incestuous logic to literalize what it means to feel for a fraternal fellow" and thus "proleptically envision a national quarrel" (28).[38] If, as Anne Dalke further argues, incest in early novels such as William Hill Brown's expresses anxiety about "the absence of a well defined social system" and the "ease of social movement" (188) and, in particular, a class anxiety (since many of the "sisters" are also déclassé orphans), then Rowson implicitly thinks her way past class as well as gender "quarrels" in imagining Lucy's success.

Like Lucy, Rowson the author emerges from this fiction as a solvent citizen, an independent Anglo-Atlantic woman who (though married) not only profitably writes fiction, history, plays, and popular song lyrics but also runs her own school, with a curriculum for girls that includes navigation and other men's subjects. By this means she secures her success as a transatlantic woman. Charlotte Temple's passivity served Rowson and her readers well, paradoxically by fashioning their positions as victims rather than agents of the Atlantic economy. And so, for Rowson as for Lucy, Charlotte's exile allows the gift of a better, freer, more prosperous future — as well as a knowledge of "navigation" for Anglo women. In other words, Charlotte's fall contributes to the Atlantic empire by making the Anglo woman's passage into it sentimental and heroic — thus turning Satan's seduction into Eve's redemption.

The Power of Dissociation

By contrast, William Hill Brown's novel *The Power of Sympathy* combines the incest plot with a black/white racial encounter that belies the displacements entailed in this happy and sisterly republican vision. In his story, things fall apart in the face of the "incest" and there is no fortunate rise after the fall. Possibly, the barely glimpsed presence of slavery in the American republic helps to precipitate this bleaker outcome. The highly incoherent or what I'll call the dissociative structure of *The Power of Sympathy* might well derive from its inclusion of those things that novelistic and republican coherence typically excludes.

On the eve of their marriage, Harrington and Harriot learn that in his youth Harrington's father seduced Harriot's mother, his own wife's sister, and then abandoned her. But, unlike Lucy and the young Montraville, when these two sibling-lovers learn of their past, they become paralyzed; they cannot move forward into another history. The novel cannot reconcile sexual love between men and women (especially of different classes) with a "fraternal" political companionship between them. Ultimately, what Harrington at one point calls the democratic empire of virtue takes on a threatening, even obscene aspect. In Brown's novel, no escape hatch is offered. Harriot wastes away in grief and Harrington shoots himself dead.

Other key details encourage a political reading of the incest crisis, as critics have noted.[39] Most strikingly, Brown sets up a parallel between Harrington's progress from rake to proper lover and his conversion from elitist to republican. Harrington initially aims merely to pursue a "scheme of pleasure" with the orphan Harriot because "I am not so much of a republican as formally to wed any person of this class" — a girl who "has no father — no mother — neither is there aunt, cousin or kindred of any degree."[40] But as weeks pass and she resists his schemes, he falls in love with Harriot and accordingly warms to the "democratic empire of virtue" (34). As they plan their covert wedding and he invokes the "native simplicity" of lovers such as they (55), he finally waxes passionate in Oroonokian fashion about how "inequality among mankind is a foe to our happiness" and concludes, "I like a democratic government better than any other kind" (58).

But his attraction to Harriot, read as an attraction to democracy, translates into an incestuous and unacceptable future. Implicitly signaling the Atlantic horizon of this ruinous prospect, the text is awash with sea metaphors. After Harriot's death, Harrington describes his sense of the "[i]mmeasurable gulf" between them, for she is "gone — gone into a far country," and he languishes on the shore, like a female lover: "So on the sea-beat shore, the hopeless maid, unmindful of the storm, bewails her drowned lover" (116, 121). Harrington's cold and avuncular friend Worthy tells him "it is hard, I acknowledge, to buffet the storm. . . . Reason is taken from the helm of life. And nature — helpless debilitated nature — lost to herself and every social duty — splits upon the rocks of despair and suicide" (123). Earlier, Mrs. Holmes has characterized the process of seduction as a "plunge deeper into the sea of dissipation" (100). And in the final lines of the novel, after Harrington has killed himself, Worthy returns to this image from the point of view of one who has survived the storm: "Though a few weeks begin to spread a calm over our passions, yet the recollection of our misfortunes will sometimes cause a momentary agitation, as the ocean retains its swell after the storm subsides" (129). His imagery echoes Harrington senior's remark, after recalling the death of Harriot's mother, whom he abandoned, when he reports feeling "like a sailor escaped from shipwreck, who sits safely on shore and views the horrors of the tempest" (96).

These passages not only draw readers into a familiar Atlantic imaginary of seduction and ruin but they also expose us to the strange and chilling emotional riptide that runs through it. For there is a deep dissociation at the heart of *The Power of Sympathy,* so much so that it might better be called *The Failure of Sympathy.* Brown's novel is contorted by tonal ambivalence, even toward its own heroine and hero, whose story it finally smothers beneath the avuncular sermonizing of their supposed friends. The male protagonist, Harrington (perhaps recalling, as Julia Stern has suggested [22], the seventeenth-century theorist of English history and the Gothic constitution), is himself plagued by ambivalence and nervousness. As he expresses it on the first page of the novel, he is a "strange medley of contradiction: the moralist and the amoroso, the sentiment and the sensibility — are interwoven in my constitution, so that nature and grace are at continual fisticuffs" (31). Likewise is the novel itself a "strange medley," a project of "mixed constitution" — for it purports to be about seduction but no seduction occurs between its main characters.

Furthermore, certain villains do in the end sit safely on shore while the lovers drown — those "worthies" for whom a friend's suicide is merely a "momentary agitation." For it becomes clear that these lovers' deaths might have been averted if it weren't for certain convenient sidesteps taken by the cool-headed circle of well-wishers. First of all, the father of these two lovers never informs them of their relation; it is Mrs. Holmes who finally does, but only quite late, on the day before their marriage. Neither she nor Reverend Holmes says a word as they watch them court each other. As Harrington senior lamely explains: "My heart failed me. Twenty times have I attempted to break the matter to my son — and twenty times have I returned from the task" (102). This crucial failure gets washed under as the narrator ultimately reframes the demise of Harriot and Harrington as a tale about the perils of seduction.

But this "heart failure" that dooms the lovers is also a fault of the lovers themselves, or at least of Harrington junior. Whether or not Brown intended it, he reveals that Harrington suffers what he inflicts, that the republican failure that brings his fall erupts within a larger systemic republican failure — that of slavery. Harrington junior shows himself to be a participant in the republic's economy of rationalized, self-serving denial — despite his Wertherian sentiments and suicide, or perhaps because these are the flip side of that economy. Just as his circle of friends sits safely on shore, unhelpful witnesses to his suffering, so too does Harrington junior, in his encounter first with Harriot and then with a slave woman, literally walk away from their suffering and then reframe it as his own.

In this sequence, Harriot's orphaned predicament is first of all eclipsed by Harrington's egocentric narration of it as his own suffering; and this displacement opens the way to another. As an orphan who gets her living as a companion to a Mrs. Francis, Harriot is treated with little respect. Once Harrington becomes her lover, he sees these slights through new eyes. His insight is the basis for his ostensible conversion to "the democratic empire of virtue." On one occasion when Mrs. Francis "had the insolence to reprimand Harriot in my presence," as Harrington reports it, he is "mortified" (85). His response is center stage: "my heart was on fire — my blood boiled in my veins" and indeed "it is impossible to form an idea of the disorder of my nerves," although he briefly notes that "Harriot's were equally agitated" (85). After Mrs. Francis "saw our confusion and retired," he is left "so completely out of temper," as he explains in a telling choice of words, "that I was forced to follow her example." So, "I kissed the tear from the cheek of Harriot and withdrew to my chamber" (85). He leaves Harriot to cope with her own humiliation while he, in his chamber, can then write, "*I feel that I have a soul*" (85, emphasis in original). He broods on his response to Harriot's suffering as evidence that he is a man of feeling.

This substitution of his trauma and "soul" for Harriot's not only "follows the example" of Mrs. Francis; it also prefigures the next scene, in which his sympathetic response to a slave mother who suffers abuse likewise establishes *his* status as a "man of sensibility" (85). Directly hereafter encountering a slave woman who "had something in her air superior to those of her station," he first of all demonstrates that he knows how to recognize an "air superior," that special, native nobility. Then, as Julia Stern notes (22–26), he works to demonstrate that he can reach across racial and status boundaries, for he actively queries her about the scar on her neck, and she explains that "[i]t is the mark of the whip" (86). Her experience of the whipping actually demonstrates what true sensibility might entail, for she receives the whipping in place of her young son, who had broken a glass tumbler: "I rejoiced," she says, "because I shielded with my body the lash from my child" (86).

The slave mother does exactly what Harrington fails to do: she puts her own body at risk for one whom she loves, while Harrington removes himself bodily from the beloved's suffering and calls the pain his. Nonetheless, in a parallel false substitution, he praises the slave mother's action as if it were analogous to his own act and feels entitled to explain to her that her sympathetic character will make slavery easy for her: "Heroically spoken! . . . May thy soul be ever disposed to sympathize with thy children, and with thy brothers and sisters in calamity. . . . All thy labors will become easy—all thy burdens light, and the yoke of slavery will never gall thy neck" (86). The submerged fantasy here is that the yoke of slavery will never gall *his* neck, if he is simply "disposed to sympathize," which is all he ever shows himself capable of doing, and even barely that. He closes his account with a paragraph beginning "Hail Sensibility!" and ostensibly commenting on the crimes of Mrs. Francis: "Away ye seekers of power—ye boasters of wealth. Ye are the Levite and the Pharisee who restrain the hand of charity from the indigent and turn with indignation from the way-worn son of misery" (86). Although the description of those who "turn with indignation from the way-worn" could describe his own recent actions with Harriot, it is no doubt the next description that is meant to apply to him: "But Sensibility is the good Samaritan who taketh him by the hand and consoleth him and pours wine and oil into his wounds" (86).

In effect, Brown has written an allegory of the "brotherly" republic's use of Anglo-Atlantic and then African-Atlantic women as instruments of Anglo-men's heroism. He exposes the empire in the democratic empire of virtue. In its economy, both "races" of women disappear by being reduced to figures for the man's sensibility. The very leaps of Harrington junior's narrative, the abrupt shifts created by his continual return to himself, have unwittingly revealed the blind spots and displacements of the Anglo-Atlantic regime of the brother. Finally, the deaths of Harriot and Harrington in *The Power of Sympathy* dramatize the fatal fruit of the emotional economy embedded in the property economy: an economy that elides its failures of sympathy and deems warm the cold, disavowed center of its propertied community. In this sense, as in the Anglo-Atlantic polis at large, the slave mother receives the whip even as she undoubtedly does material labor for the Anglo characters in Brown's novel and symbolic labor for Anglo readers and the author.

Narration Undone

Harriet Wilson positions her novel *Our Nig* exactly within this dissociative lapse and Africanist logic in Anglo-Atlantic, English-language narratives. In her story of a biracial daughter abandoned by her white mother and enslaved by a white Northern family, the Bellmonts, for whom she becomes laborer, scapegoat, and catalyst of dissent, not only does Wilson lay out the substitutions of white for black in the republic's economy but she also embeds the dissociative effects of these substitutions in the very grammar of her narrative. Narrating her auto-biographical first-person story through a third-person, omniscient voice, amid small hints that the story is her own, Wilson creates a structural paradigm of appropriation and reverses its operations. She in effect steals the Bellmonts' third-person gaze to dramatize their theft of her body and spirit. Like the slave mother in Brown's novel, Frado (Wilson's name for herself in the novel) endures the abuse from Mrs. Bellmont that the other Bellmonts might have suffered in her absence and she enacts the (republican) rebellions they fear to undertake. Meanwhile, in her third-person telling, Wilson takes up their viewpoint toward herself — thus strangely occupying their position. She inverts the Africanist pattern by simulating the white point of view and practice of surrogacy.

Priscilla Wald has pointed the way toward this reading in her observation that "the discrepancy between the first-person chapter headings and the third-person narration marks the representation of the self as an other — or the recognition of the alterity of the self," concluding that Wilson is writing "a *narrative about* autobiography, *about* what writing for a particular market does to this African-American woman."[41] I build on Wald's interpretation to argue that Wilson in-tuitively displays the Africanist function — economic and political — of even the "free black" in Anglo-Atlantic lives and narratives. It is not strictly that Wilson's third-person narration reveals Frado's internalization of the Bellmonts' racism, nor only that her strategy "trace[s] a process of subjection," in Wald's words — much as I agree with both claims.[42] Using the third-person, omniscient mode and adopting the Bellmont viewpoint as her own, including in moments when family members search for her when she has run away, Wilson at once narrates herself as a missing person and occupies the whites' position to do so. In the novel's two stream-crossing scenes, first with Mary Bellmont and then with the sheep, in which Frado substitutes their near-drowning fall for hers, Wilson also embeds, as we will see, an allegory of her shrewd practice.

Thus it is not quite enough to say that Wilson's story of the seduction, ruin, and betrayal of a heroine "borrows heavily" from the Anglo-American sentimental or seduction novel in order to expose its racialized limits.[43] The exchange between Wilson and this tradition of novels deserves a different description. She is seizing *back* her own story of ruin, labor, and pain from within that tradition whose wide circulation, emotional as well as material, has been fed by her history of ruin — as sharply displayed in William Hill Brown's novel. As I suggested in the introduction, such a project moves beyond even a subtle "mimicry," in Homi Bhabha's sense, or parody, as some readers have suggested about *Our Nig*.[44] In her drama of a "disappearing 'I,'" as Jill Jones characterizes the novel, *Our Nig* offers a meta-story of the Atlantic narrative practices that disappeared the African-Atlantic "I" in the first place.[45] My account of how she does so will focus first on the mother's ruin, which sets up Frado's tale; then on the two sequences in which Frado is lost and others search for her, which clarify the underlying logic of the third-person narration; and finally on two scenes in which Frado narrowly escapes a drowning fall, which establish Wilson's deconstruction of the English-language novel's Atlantic story of seduction, ruin, and freedom.

IMMEDIATELY POSITIONING her readers as distanced, sentimental witnesses to a woman's fall, Wilson opens her story by inviting us to look on at "Lonely Mag Smith! See her as she walks with downcast eyes and heavy heart." As she continues the familiar tale, she registers its Atlantic back story, in the metaphor of Mag's "tiny boat" and in the echoes of Milton's tale of a seducer:

> Early deprived of parental guardianship, far removed from relatives, she was left to guide her tiny boat over life's surges alone and inexperienced. As she merged into womanhood, unprotected . . . there fell on her ear the music of love, awakening an intensity of emotion long dormant. It whispered of an elevation before unaspired to; of ease and plenty her simple heart had never dreamed of as hers. . . . the voice of her charmer . . . seemed like an angel's, alluring her upward and onward. She thought she could ascend to him and become an equal. She surrendered to him a priceless gem, which he proudly garnered as a trophy, with those of other victims, and left her to her fate.[46]

Like Milton's Satan, this whispering "charmer" in the guise of an angel seems to promise a safe landing in a new democratic world of "ease and plenty" where she will "become an equal." So this innocent, wandering seafarer trades the "gem" of her virginity. Asking "[w]ho can tell what numbers" of women like Mag face "a sneering world" after such a "fall," Wilson implies that Mag's experience is paradigmatic. The very conventionality of her language meanwhile tells us that Wilson, like her heroine, is embarking within a tradition, in which she, like her heroine, will navigate the threat of bodily ruin and the loss of an intersubjective voice and presence.[47]

In the rest of her brief account of Mag's undoing, the narrator encapsulates the logic by which sexual ruin leads to economic ruin, which leads to racial ruin. As Carla Peterson observes, Wilson is exploring the "economics of freedom" and in the process tracking, as John Ernest also argues, the intertwining of economic and racial identities."[48] In her account of Mag's entry into the U.S. racial republic organized around property and economic independence, Wilson portrays a mother who is determined, first of all, not to depend on condescending others in this individualist economy, which means that she lives in a hovel in subsistence poverty. When even this home becomes unsustainable, she agrees to marry the "kind-hearted African," Jim, in order "to get [her] living from [him]," but this affiliation pushes her further "down the ladder": "She was now expelled," the narrator explains, "from companionship with white people; this last step — her union with a black — was the climax of repulsion" (15). In the wake of her sexual abandonment, Mag thus not only loses her economic hold but she changes races, joining those at the bottom of the work force. In this low estate, she gives birth to two biracial children, one of whom is Frado — the author — whose story we follow. But when Frado is a toddler, Jim sickens and dies, so Mag and the children move in with his business associate, Seth. Before long, that business fails, so Mag and Seth decide to abandon the two children. Thus at age five Frado is left with the Bellmonts, where she lives as an abused, imprisoned servant until she is eighteen. Those thirteen years constitute most of the rest of Wilson's autobiographical novel, and they unfold the consequences of the mother's ruin.

Scholars have established that Frado's life conforms to the historical facts of Wilson's life, as Wilson hints in her several first-person references.[49] The novel's preface remarks, "My mistress was wholly imbued with *southern* principles" (3, emphasis in original), while the titles of early chapters ("Mag Smith, My Mother," "My Father's Death," and "A New Home for Me") further imply that what follows is an autobiography or autobiographical fiction. Yet this expectation is disrupted and remains so for most of the story. Except for one or two first-person references throughout the rest of the narrative, there is no "I" nor "me" nor "my" nor "we" — only references to Frado, "our nig," "her," and "she" by a third-person storyteller looking on philosophically. While some readers have characterized the first-person references in this otherwise third-person story as "lapses" or deviations, others have explored its complex inscriptions of a split subjectivity.[50] Yet even those critics who stress the latter often nonetheless view the split mainly as a mark of Wilson's struggles or even her "failure" to finally write herself into history. But if we consider the power Wilson seized by way of her third-person narration and the implications she buried in her narrative by simultaneously letting it be known that she is Frado, then we may be led to conclude that this apparently self-erasing doubleness is exactly Wilson's bold achievement. Behind the character Frado, whose "roguish eyes [sparkle] with an exuberance of spirit beyond restraint" (17), we begin to glimpse Wilson, the roguish author.

Wilson's construction of the two separate sequences in which Frado is lost signal the import of her narrational maneuvers. In both cases the reader occupies the viewpoint of those who go in search of her rather than following Frado's (and the author's) own experience of escape or lostness. Wilson has created an omniscient narrator who can and does sometimes follow Frado's point of view: but in these moments of lostness, she chooses not to. The first instance occurs just before Mag abandons her, in a scene which Claudia Tate and Julia Stern have analyzed for the ways in which Wilson's use of the third person allows her to reconstruct her/Frado's relation to her mother in the book's opening chapters (including the years previous to Frado's birth). Tate in particular stresses that, by occupying her mother's point of view in the scene just before Mag and Seth abandon her—when Frado herself wanders off—Frado/Wilson attributes to Mag a worried concern about this long absence, and so imputes a motherly affection toward Frado that otherwise is lacking. In Tate's rich reading, Wilson hereby contributes to the emergence of an enabling maternal discourse in black women's writing.[51]

We can also note, however, that in this construction of the scene, Wilson establishes her independence from her mother: before she is abandoned by Mag, she has herself depart by her own agency in a way that makes Mag feel her absence unexpectedly—in a way that takes control away from Mag. While Wilson is thus imagining and laying claim to affection from her mother she is simultaneously making her mother, and her reader, feel her power—specifically her power to absent herself, to adopt and seize as her own the mother's (and culture's) intention of making her invisible and of denying any relation or social obligation to her. Narrating from the point of view she could not in fact know, while deleting the point of view that is in fact hers, at these moments Wilson shows herself to be more interested in making her absence felt than in making her presence seen. In this light, it is telling that Wilson furthermore has Mag suffer uncertainty about whether Frado has actually run away (or whether she has simply gotten lost: Mag and Seth, we are told, speculate about Frado's absence, fearing that "she had understood their plans [to abandon her], and [she] had, perhaps, permanently withdrawn," so that they "could not rest without making some effort to ascertain her retreat" [19]). Mag cannot tell what degree of agency Frado has exerted within this drama of abandonment, unsettled by the possibility that Frado has understood and usurped her (Mag's) intentions.

This is the situation that Wilson likewise sets up with her reader: we cannot tell whether this third-person "losing" of herself is an exercise of power or a loss of it. Apparently, she has seized the power to lose power, to willfully "abandon" her first-person relation to herself and make that loss a matter of her own choice. Henry Louis Gates Jr. calls attention to the "silences and lacunae" in the text, as signaled when the narrator tells us that "I do not pretend to divulge every transaction in my own life" (preface).[52] I would add that in these comments she also signals her choice-making power as narrator, especially her larger choice to make herself her own lacunae rather than her culture's.

Wilson's narrational choice parallels Harriet Jacobs's sexual choice to lie with Mr. Sands rather than Dr. Flint: both women manage to create the terms for their own casting-out from community and so to manipulate the sexual-racial, woman-reproduced yet woman-erasing matrix of their culture. Paradoxically, through this choice to absent and, in different ways, "abandon" themselves, both women gain the leverage to occupy a certain *place* that, although debilitatingly uncomfortable, extends their power over the history of their displacement.[53] For while Harriet Jacobs lies sick and cramped in her loophole of retreat and Frado wanders cold and hungry in the outdoors on the occasions when she runs away, Linda Brent and Harriet Wilson both establish a viewpoint, literally and symbolically, that allows their absence to be felt and seen: they ensure that readers watch as white families look for them and feel distress at the loss of (the labor of) black women, and at the same time, they ensure that we experience them as writers, occupying the position of "overseer."

Thus this early scene in which Frado turns up missing foreshadows the larger narrational and political logic of her life with the Bellmonts and in the Anglo-American republic. The next crucial sequence that establishes this logic occurs in chapter 4, organized around another moment when Frado runs away, where again we see through the eyes of the whites looking for her.[54] The chapter's turning-point role is signaled in its title: whereas the book's first three chapter titles, as noted, use first-person pronouns ("Mag Smith, My Mother," "My Father's Death," and "A New Home for Me"), the fourth chapter is titled "A Friend for Nig," foreshadowing that in this chapter her first-person presence disappears, under the sign "nig." This disappearance throws into relief Frado's psycho-political anchoring role within the family and, as in the earlier scene with Mag, suggests that

Wilson is again working to register her own, narrational absent-yet-anchoring presence. Early in the chapter, after a particularly harsh beating from Mrs. Bellmont, Frado "jumped up, and rushed from the house, out of sight" (44). She stays away all day, and the rest of the chapter recounts the family dynamics as they argue and search for her until late at night.

All the Bellmont family's submerged conflicts come to the surface as the result of Frado's flight. First, as a direct result of this beating and Frado's flight, an old brother/sister schism, regarding the division of property, emerges in the conversation between John Bellmont and his sister, Aunt Abby. Entering the house "just in time to see the last of [Mrs. Bellmont's] performance" and Frado's flight "out of sight," John and Abby (whose names perhaps allude to the nation's famous Adams couple) then retire together to Abby's separate apartment in the house (44). At this juncture, when John complains of his wife's cruelty toward Frado and mutters that he hopes Frado will run away, Abby asks him, "Why do you have it so, John?" His disingenuous reply that "[w]omen rule the earth" is belied when shortly afterward he turns his "calm, determined eye" upon his wife and countermands her "in a decisive manner" (47). But more telling here is Abby's response to this comment: "I think I should rule my own house, John" (44). "'And live in hell, meantime,' added Mr. Bellmont" before "saunter[ing] out to the barn to await the quieting of the storm" (44–45).

Abby's remark and John's response reverberate within their own relationship as well as bearing on Frado's situation: as the narrator takes this occasion, in the midst of *this* crisis, to explain, Aunt Abby's "sister-in-law had great prejudices against her" because "she did not give her right in the homestead to John, and leave it forever" (45). That is, as Lois Leveen also notes (569), this house *is* in part Abby's and yet she is kept from any "ruling" role in it by John's marriage.[55] As in other Atlantic novels, the sister's claim to property and governing power is thwarted by the brother's dedication to his own comfort. While, for both Abby and Frado, the problem is of Mrs. Bellmont's making, the solution lies within John's power, but he "saunters" away from it and disavows that power. Wildly cruel as Mrs. Bellmont is, here again the real prior condition is one in which he has power over both his sister and his wife, and the latter is always struggling to assert her own strength against his, so that meanwhile John's sister gets displaced to separate quarters.

This (national and familial) sibling conflict is inherited by the young Bellmonts, between sister Mary and the apparently sympathetic, yet collusive, brothers, James and Jack, and Frado becomes the figure through whom it is played out. Earlier, in the scene in which Frado first arrives in the Bellmont family, Wilson sets up the logic of this brother/sister dynamic that here plays out through Jack's and James's brotherly relation to Frado. In apparent solidarity with Frado, when the family is deciding in that first scene whether to "keep" Frado, young Mary Bellmont expresses disgust at the idea of living with her; Jack teases Mary and laughs that she will soon be bragging to her friends of their property as "our nig, our nig." From this moment forward, as Frado becomes "our nig," she also becomes caught in the antagonism between Mary and the brothers. Repeatedly, the brothers embrace Frado (and some critics have seen a sexual subtext in this relationship) exactly against this sister's and their mother's will to power.[56] Although the sister and mother rather than the brother and father become the torturers of Frado, this develops within the already-operative white story of brother-sister competition. Frado is a pawn in their dynamics — as the African-Atlantic person was in the American nation's gendered conflicts (and as Harriet Jacobs, for instance, exposes in her experience with Dr. and Mrs. Flint).

Having hinted at this fraught brotherly relation by which Frado acquires her name as "nig" and further pointing toward it in the title of chapter 4, "A Friend for Nig," Wilson then creates a sequence of events revealing that the brothers, and especially James, maintain their own protected positions and manage their escapes from Mrs. Bellmont at Frado's expense even as they purport to be her protector. Wilson hints at what is to come insofar as Frado departs from visibility just as James arrives for his first visit home since she was abandoned there. In fact, the logic of the events in this chapter covertly implies that his arrival indirectly *catalyzes* her flight. For Mrs. Bellmont's beating of her has been precipitated by his expected arrival: "great exertions" are being undertaken to prepare for it and although "[Frado's] feet were speeding hither and thither so unsparingly," Mrs. Bellmont is dissatisfied with her work (becoming herself now "a trifle fatigued" and "peevish"), so that she begins beating Frado, escalating her violence from boxing on the ears to whipping with a rawhide to knocking her down and kicking her in a frenzy. Shortly after Frado flees, and just after the dialogue between Abby and John reveals the gender fault lines of this world, James arrives. He helps the family to recover Frado and, thereby, to rechannel the family's pain and violence through her.

Several hints suggest that Frado is coming to serve as the surrogate victim, taking the children's place, as both Lois Leveen and Barbara White have suggested, within a history of family conflict and abuse.[57] When James first arrives and hears his mother assert about Frado (in language highlighting that the issue is one of visibility) that "[i]f she makes her *appearance*, I'll take the skin from her body" and "I'll not leave much of her beauty to be *seen, if she comes in sight*" (emphasis added), the narrator tells us that these threats recall James's childhood memories: although "years of absence had erased the occurrences once so familiar . . . he was no stranger to his mother's nature" (46–47). Later, when Frado reports another scene of Mrs. Bellmont's cruel beating and "unrestrained malice," James, we learn, "shut his eyes in silence, as if pained to forgetfulness by the recital" (83–84). The narrator remarks more than once that the children are "accustomed to all phases of indoor storms" (48).

Against this background, James and Jack recover Frado at the end of this chapter, "forcing and coaxing" her back into the house, a house which they and other children then shortly after flee (the next chapter is titled "Departures"). As Priscilla Wald has noted (164), the recovery of Frado reads eerily like the hunting of a fugitive slave. Led by Frado's own dog on the scent, Jack penetrates "far, far into the fields, over walls and through fences, into a piece of swampy land" until, switching into the viewpoint of James, who has fallen behind in the chase, we see Jack reemerge, "coaxing and forcing Frado along with him" (50). Together the brothers "persuaded her to go home with them" (50). Here Wilson makes another telling insinuation: because the third paragraph of the chapter mentions that Fido, the dog, had become the "entire confidant of Frado," we at first may think of Fido as the "friend" of the chapter's title ("A Friend for Nig"), but insofar as Fido leads the brothers to recover this fugitive laborer, these two kinds of "friend" — dog and men — become identified as in fact her hunters. Although back at the house the brothers' pursuit is cast as a rescue, after which they warm her by the fire and feed her dinner, Wilson's inclusion of the dog, the swamp, and their use of bodily force suggests otherwise.

In its final loaded turn, the chapter closes with a conversation between Frado and James that begins their "friendship" even as it signals Frado's substitutional role in the Bellmont home and her unsettling function within the family psyche. At the day's end, James accompanies her to her garret room and asks, "Are you glad I've come home?," which resonates strangely in the wake of the chapter's events and her own forced "homecoming." Frado replies yes, but with a qualification — "if you won't let me be whipped tomorrow" (50). James promises she won't be whipped but, he counsels, "You must try to be a good girl" (50). This prompts Frado's objection that she is whipped even "if I do," especially since "[t]hey won't believe what I say" — and so Wilson reminds us quietly that the power to tell the story is part of what Frado is denied, an element of her missing presence (51). Yet Wilson is telling the story now, as she briefly signals in the religious dialogue that follows. For here Frado's first-person voice gets one of its rare hearings, and James's complacent counsel begins to unravel. Wilson's/Frado's voice for a moment baffles his. Frado asks "who made me so?" and when James answers "God," she asks, "Did the same God that made [your mother] make me?" Again, "yes." Drawing a disruptive conclusion from these seemingly straightforward answers,

Frado shockingly concludes that she "doesn't like [God]" because "he made her white and me black" (51). When she finally asks, "Why didn't he make us *both* white?" (emphasis in original), James lamely responds, "I don't know; try to go to sleep, and you will feel better in the morning" (51). Her "knotty queries" leave him baffled and depressed, so that, in the closing words of the chapter, it was a "number of days before James felt in a mood to visit and entertain old associates and friends" (51). Thus does Wilson follow Frado's recapture with a rare moment of direct speech on her part that leaves James troubled by the return of repressed truths about the family, the nation, and their race-troubled religion.

Despite this brief hearing given to Frado's voice, hereafter she is indeed "captured" by James — seduced by his promises of release and by his Protestant yet racialized freedom narrative for her, all while she is enlisted to meet his increasing physical needs. On more than one occasion, the narrator hints in disjunctively juxtaposed comments that James's various arrivals home expand her workload. In reference to one of his later visits to the family home, she refers to Frado's preparations for "this agreeable increase of the family, this addition to her cares" (67), and in another case she notes that "[t]here had been additional burdens on her since his return" (52). When James turns ill and slowly dies in this "sickening" home, Frado becomes one of his main caretakers (pointedly, in the place of his mother, who feels too weak). The narrator describes the situation equivocally: "With all his bodily suffering, . . . he did not forget Frado. He shielded her from many beatings, and every day imparted religious instructions. No one but his wife could move him so easily as Frado; so that in addition to her daily toil she was often deprived of her rest at night" (76–77). Following the description of Frado's pain, we might at first read "move" in the emotional sense of the word (her ability to "move" him seems to refer to his response to her suffering); but, in Wilson's slippery way, the sentence shifts, like the earlier one, to register her toil and the "bodily suffering" it inflicts on her.

Wilson lets us know that James is a key agent not only of the family's veiled use of Frado but also of its temporal deferral of her freedom. Under the instruction of James and Abby, Frado "became a believer in a future existence" (84); in fact she becomes severely anxious and finally ill under the weight of her "solicitude about the future" (94). Although she serves his material comfort in the present, up until the time of his illness he has continually deferred hers, including by never meeting her request to go and work for him (to cite just one of several such comments, she "begged for one favor only, that James would send for her . . . , the hope she had confidently cherished all these five years" [63]). Instead he continually turns her hope of salvation toward the future, and he implies that her present suffering is in part caused by her own sins of "pertness": he looks forward, he says, to what "she will be" if "the pertness she sometimes exhibited . . . were restrained properly" and if the "elements in her heart . . . were transformed and purified by the gospel" so as to "make her worthy of the esteem and friendship of the world" (74, 69). He imagines that he can carry the white man's burden, as he tells Abby, of making her worthy of a liberty: "When I think of what she might be, of what she will be, I feel like grasping time till opinions change, and thousands like her rise into a noble freedom" (74). To begin her transformation, in conversations with Frado he "combat[s] the notions she seem[s] to entertain respecting the loneliness of her condition and want of sympathizing friends." "I assured her," he reports to Abby, "that . . . in our part of the country there were thousands upon thousands who favored the elevation of her race . . . that she might hope for better things in the future" (75–76).

While I would agree with those critics who believe in Wilson's ultimate conversion to Christianity and see her closing invocations of the Bible as a call for a different, more Christian and communal economy of relationships, I would also argue that Wilson exposes the way that James's spiritualized and racialized freedom narrative for Frado creates Frado's excruciatingly distended investment in hope for "release," as she repeatedly puts it.[58] Wilson implies as much when she cunningly and ironically makes James's death a turning point for the better for Frado (although she initially feels it as the end of hope), after which Frado moves into a secular narrative of freedom. The dissolution of his narrative for her future actually gives rise to a new, stronger Frado in the present: shortly after his death, she "resolved to give over all thought of the future world" and within a page of that resolution, with covert encouragement from Mr. Bellmont, she directly resists Mrs. Bellmont in a way that James never advocated or achieved (104). One day as Mrs. Bellmont raises her whip to beat her for her slow retrieval of wood, Frado shouts, "'Stop, . . . strike me, and I'll never work a mite more for you;' and throwing down what she had gathered, stood like one who feels the stirring of free and independent thoughts" (105). Here, Frado begins her willed entry into secular freedom and takes up the language of independence. By making the prompt for this scene another wood-gathering infraction, Wilson sets this moment against that earlier one in chapter 4 when James's arrival led to her first long absence and the family's upheaval, accompanied at that point by the narrator's abandonment of first-person references until the novel's last chapter.

This rogue narrator inscribes a clue to her practice and her manipulation of the Anglo-Atlantic novel's liberty story in the text's two mirroring "stream" scenes. In the first of these passages, Wilson not only (as Debra Walker King has shown) rewrites a scene from Susan Warner's sentimental and Christian novel *Wide, Wide World;* she also slyly offers an allegory of the substitutional narrative strategy by which she rewrites the racialized Atlantic story of crossing-over and drowning. In Warner's novel, Ellen Montgomery, who like Frado has lost her mother and is at the mercy of oppressive caretakers, at one point is lured by her cruel playmate Nancy into crossing a "brook" by way of "an old log that had fallen across [it]," but when Ellen is almost across and reaches for Nancy's hand "she missed it, — perhaps that was Nancy's fault, — poor Ellen lost her balance and went in foremost" (40 quoted in King). A similar scene occurs in *Our Nig,* when Frado begins to attend school and her naughty pranks and exuberant energy win her many friends, which rouses Mary's intense resentment. In an attempt at revenge, and under the pressure of an overwhelming desire to "use physical force 'to subdue her,' to 'keep her down,'" on the way home from school one day, Mary tries to cause Frado's fall into a brook.[59]

> There was, on their way home, a field intersected by a stream over which a single plank was placed for crossing. It occurred to Mary that it would be punishment to Nig to compel her to cross over; so she dragged her to the edge, and told her authoritatively to go over. Nig hesitated, resisted. Mary placed herself behind the child, and, in the struggle to force her over, lost her footing and plunged into the stream. Some of the larger scholars being in sight, ran, and thus prevented Mary from drowning and Frado from falling. (33)

Inverting Warner's scene, so that the protagonist resists and the torturer falls, Wilson rewrites the story of the African-Atlantic experience as an unwillingness to be "kept down": Nig "resist[s]," and instead Mary "plunges" and nearly drowns while Frado is saved "from falling." Wilson reverses not only the class and Christian logic of Warner's scene but also the Africanist logic by which a black person's ruin serves a white person's (and nation's) rise.[60]

Meanwhile, Wilson remains safely removed from the implications of this scene: in fact it is key that this scene is not only narrated (like all others) in the third person but is also witnessed and later corroborated by whites (the older "scholars"). In the tempest created at home when Mary arrives wet and weeping and claiming that "Nig" pushed her into the stream, these white schoolmates are quoted, undercutting Mary's claims and vindicating Frado. Although Frado afterward receives a severe beating from Mrs. Bellmont for offering her own version of events, Wilson has meanwhile silently told us what her third-person narration accomplishes: through it she *creates and inhabits* white witnesses who testify to her independent spirit and righteous resistance. As third-person narrator, she adopts that "neutral" authority for her own gaze.

In a strikingly parallel scene of a near-drowning for Frado, Wilson even more explicitly places herself and us in the viewpoint of white witnesses. In this instance Frado aims to teach one of the headstrong sheep in the herd a lesson. This greedy sheep always takes food from the other sheep — as whites take the fruit of black labor — and so Frado uses its avarice to "trick" it one day when the herd is grazing in a field "bounded on three sides by a wide stream, which flowed on one side at the base of precipitous banks" (54). Frado positions herself at the edge of one bank with a plate of food to lure the sheep toward her (recalling and signifying on the plate of food with which Jack and James lure Fido into helping them recover Frado). At this moment, Mr. Bellmont and his laborers happen to approach from the opposite side of the field, "unseen by Frado" but seeing her. As they spy her balanced on the edge of the cliff,

> They paused to see what she was about to do. Should she by any mishap lose her footing, she must roll down into the stream and, without aid, drown. They thought of shouting; but they feared an unexpected salute might startle her, and thus ensure what they were anxious to prevent. They watched in breathless silence. The willful sheep came furiously leaping, and ... [j]ust as he leaped for the dish, she suddenly jumped one side, when down he rolled into the river, and swimming across, remained till night. The men lay down, convulsed with laughter at the trick. (54–55)

Here, too, Frado is at risk of a fall and death by drowning, but she arranges it so that a bull-headed animal falls in her place. Meanwhile, whites stand on the side-lines breathlessly and uselessly, since (in an allegory within an allegory of a faulty abolitionism like that of the Bellmont men) they seem to intuit that their intervention may well "ensure what they were anxious to prevent" — Frado's ruin. Yet at the same time Wilson makes theirs the angle of vision through which we once again witness Frado's trickster power (and, by extension, Wilson's, as evident in her creation of these two, seemingly innocuous yet symbolically loaded scenes). Wilson frames her tale of the "shadows" of slavery that reach North within a white gaze and voice that "shadows" her own first-person life — and yet which gaze and voice, as third-person omniscient narrator, she recolonizes.

In coyly re-inserting the first person at the start of the novel's last chapter, Wilson more openly lets us glimpse her seizure of power. Referring to "my narrative," in the text's final paragraph, Wilson then encloses the Bellmonts' lives within her gaze and narration, and she furthermore wields biblical language to do so. The narrator asks, almost as a challenge, "Do you ask the destiny of those connected with her *early* history?" She summarily, almost begrudgingly, gives details about the Bellmonts — which of them is dead and which still living — and then she closes her paragraph and her book: "Frado has passed from their memories, as Joseph from the butler's, but she will never cease to track them beyond mortal vision" (131).[61] Wilson here registers and counters the Bellmonts' failure of vision: they continue in their not-seeing of her while she ceaselessly sees them, even "beyond mortal vision." Her naming of this blindness also overrides it, narratively, insofar as her readers, aligned cunningly with her third-person perspective, can supply the vision missing in the Bellmonts: we see her seeing of them — so her seeing is now, finally, the determinate stance. In fact, far from being the obscured one, here Frado implicitly steps into the role not only of the seer Joseph but also of an omniscient, all-judging God, who can look down upon the Anglo-Atlantic subject's Africanist, moral-existential failure.

Katharine Clay Bassard asks of Wilson's *Our Nig*: "[W]hat are we to make of a black womanhood (in the form of Frado's traumatic 'coming of age' story) that emerges out of a fallen white womanhood? How do we account for our entrance into a black woman's text through white maternity?" (196). Although Brassard never answers her question directly, she does so implicitly when she argues that *Our Nig* rewrites the biblical story of creation, fall, and covenant. If Wilson does indeed join Milton in thus rewriting the biblical story, then she also exceeds him in her refashioning of the Atlantic ur-text of ruin, especially as it habitually positions white women's sexual ruin as a surrogate-story for the violence and losses of all in Atlantic modernity. In entering her black text through a fallen white maternity, Wilson reprises an Atlantic symbology. Like Olaudah Equiano before her and Pauline Hopkins after her, Wilson at once turns this narrative inside out and makes a narrative spectacle of the history that requires this rogue act.

7 Middle-Passage Plots
Defoe, Equiano, Melville

IGNORING HIS FATHER'S ADVICE to settle down comfortably and instead joining a ship's crew at the very start of *The Life and Strange Surprising Adventures
of Robinson Crusoe, of York, Mariner,* Daniel Defoe's young Robinson Crusoe
immediately suffers a sea trauma, prefiguring his life's Atlantic crisis. A storm
rises, the ship threatens to plunge into the sea, and Crusoe feels sure the adventure is his "ruin"; he cries out, "we shall be all undone" before he falls "down in
a Swoon."[1] The other sailors tend to him until he "came to my self" (11–12). In
the book's later, more catastrophic sea storm, Crusoe will face "raging Wave[s],
Mountain-like," and he will be "buried . . . 20 or 30 Foot deep" in one of them,
until finally he is "dash'd . . . against a Piece of a Rock, and that with such Force,
as it left me senseless" (44–45). In graphically depicting this shipwreck, Defoe
crafted what would become a legendary, terrifying scene for the Atlantic liberty
narrative. If Milton created an Atlantic parable, and Thompson, Rousseau, and
Hegel forged the racial epic of a phoenix-people, and novelists from Haywood to
Wilson narrated rape or seduction as the emblematic moment of fall, then in *Robinson Crusoe* Defoe made visceral and literal the oceanic symbology of Atlantic
self-loss. In doing so he brought to the surface a current of fear circulating in the
Anglo-Atlantic social world.

This fear derived not only from the Anglo-Atlantic experience of dislocation
but also from a disavowed social presence — from the African captives crouched
inside the holds or working the decks of such ships: that is, African-Atlantic persons. The degree to which Defoe encoded the instrumentality of this presence in

his novel has gone unnoticed by most critics. Specifically, little attention has been given to two features of the novel. First, Crusoe awakens from both his first and his second "undoing" at sea into the morally corrupt economy of Atlantic slavery, quite directly: immediately after he recovers from his first storm, he decides that he will "set up for a Guiney trader" and his later shipwreck occurs at his setting out for Guinea, to buy slaves for his and others' South American plantations (18). Second, Defoe more than once registers that Crusoe's escapes from his two captivities depend on the skilled agency of his black Atlantic comrades. Perhaps for this very reason, Crusoe's loss and recovery of freedom will be played out against his intention to have slaves rather than be one. That is, in a reversed mirroring of the way Oroonoko and Imoinda awaken from their swoons into a state of modern slavery, Crusoe awakens into slave trading — which does in both cases initially lead to his captivity but ultimately (with the help of others) enables him to become a "governor," a free, prosperous man, and an owner of slaves. Defoe picks up where Behn left off, as he seems to signal in the subtitle of his novel, which locates Crusoe's "un-inhabited Island" somewhere "near the Mouth of the Great River of Oroonoque." He continues the story of the fall, liberation, and rise of the Anglo-Atlantic subject achieved *through* the Atlantic person of color. His novel simultaneously registers and ameliorates the apprehensions attending this instrumental relation of white to black, and this double effect may explain its power for Atlantic readers.

At the end of the eighteenth century, Olaudah Equiano brings this disavowed story to the foreground in his account of captivity and freedom. In *The Interesting Narrative of the Life of Olaudah Equiano, or Gustavas Vassa the African, Written by Himself* (1798), Equiano reclaims the Atlantic plot, implicitly reversing the maneuvers of Behn and Defoe, in which the African slave's story provides the Anglo-Atlantic author's point of entry into history. He reveals whites' dependence on blacks by depicting blacks' heroic seamanship, and he counters the fleeting and apparently random presence of blacks in Anglo-Atlantic texts by revealing a world of African-Atlantic community. Meanwhile, borrowing (back) all the established race and ruin tropes of the liberty story, he employs the Anglo-Atlantic paradigm to effect the entry (in print) of the African-Atlantic subject — including that of the African-Atlantic woman. For, in his account of his relation with his sister, he specifically places the woman's ruin story beside his own.

Because Equiano repeatedly circumnavigated the Atlantic triangle, critics of African American, African, and British culture have by turns claimed him as their own.[2] Indeed, the critical literature on Equiano's text itself reflects Atlantic history in ways that deserve mention, for they bear on my larger argument. In the 1980s, African American critics placed Equiano at the origin mainly of an African American tradition of slave narratives.[3] This placement made and still makes sense, despite the fact that in its own day the text was barely read in the United States as compared to Britain and that Equiano was mostly a passing visitor in the colonies and later the U.S. nation: for it was in the United States that slavery continued as a central economic institution and so yielded a "tradition" of slave narratives. Equiano's *Narrative* does indeed forge some patterns inherent to that tradition, including the complex interplay of literacy and liberty. And, of course, Vincent Carretta's hypothesis that Equiano was born in the United States, if ever confirmed absolutely, would strengthen the claims of this approach (although recent work has raised questions about the hypothesis).[4]

In the next turn in the critical tradition, before Carretta's material came to light, literary critics of African culture began to study the *Narrative* as an early text of Ibo print-literature. They have pointed out that of course American readers would see only the correspondence to American tropes but meanwhile were over-looking patterns that resonated with Ibo tradition and would beckon the African reader. They considered, for instance, the way that notions of "destiny" — which had been understood by earlier critics as part of either Equiano's assimilation or his implicit debunking of Calvinist theology — corresponded with the Ibo idea of the "chi" of each person. They also noted that Equiano's fashioning of himself as a man of military prowess aligned with his narration of his descent from a noble and warrior class in Benin.[5] Regardless of whether Equiano did indeed imbibe these values as a young boy or learned them through his reading, these studies highlight the degree to which Equiano positioned himself between cultures, as a man shaped by multiple traditions.

In a more recent turn, British literary critics have begun to emphasize Equiano's embeddedness in British rhetorical traditions. Adam Potkay has highlighted his use of Anglo-Protestant oratorical and religious forms of address, and Tanya Caldwell particularly emphasizes Equiano's invocation of a British rhetoric of liberty, individualism, and empire. Arguing that postcolonial critics have distorted the reading of Equiano's text by uprooting it from its proper British origins, Potkay and Caldwell propose that his discourse is British rather than African or African American.[6] Noting the parallels between Defoe and Equiano, including their shared rhetoric of British freedom, Caldwell specifically places Equiano in the tradition of Defoe.[7] But she repeats the old Anglo-British appropriation of the African-Atlantic story when she argues that "[t]he Equiano of the entire Interesting Narrative, . . . has after all been formed and educated by the laws, the language, and the habits of English culture, *not* the land of his birth, of which he has no more detailed knowledge than any of his European contemporaries" (266). Unlike other critics who trace a multiplicity of traditions in Equiano's *Narrative,*

Caldwell argues that its frame of reference is exclusively British. She likewise insists that "the *Narrative* shares the world, the experiences, and the language not of Frederick Douglass but of Johnson and Burke, Smith and Defoe" (280). Yet exactly because liberty rhetoric was inflected by colonial trading interests *and* racialized domestic revolutionary movements following its rise during the English Civil War, and discourses of freedom on both sides of the Atlantic were shaped by these developments, there is no neat divide between the liberty language of Johnson and Burke and that of Equiano or Douglass. All of them participate in a liberty language that has racial associations and narratives clinging to it; and indeed the liberty language of Johnson and Burke could have arisen and spread as it did only within an economy that depended on the laboring bodies of Douglass and Equiano. As expressed in Caldwell's exclusive "British/not African or American" formulations, and in her several distortions of Equiano's text to support them,[8] Equiano's insinuation of himself into the forms of Anglo-Atlantic narrative apparently continues to provoke a struggle over his text like that which the slave trade enacted on his body. In my combined reading of *Robinson Crusoe* and *The Interesting Narrative,* I suggest that it is as historically accurate to say that Defoe's novel arises within the terms of Equiano's story as to say the reverse.

These readings lay the ground for a fresh understanding of Herman Melville's *Billy Budd* (1899). Melville's novella offers an allegory for this troubled exchange of African- and Anglo-Atlantic positions, for it frames the Anglo-Saxon's story within the African's and yet also subsumes the African's story within the Anglo-Saxon's. The novella opens with the figure of an African sailor, setting him up as the prototype of what the narrator calls the "Handsome Sailor," but then quickly turns our attention to Billy Budd, the pure-blooded, explicitly "Anglo-Saxon" embodiment of this sailor. In my reading here, Billy's Atlantic — and sexual — undoing covertly plays out the fate not only of a ruined, femininized subject but also of the unnamed African sailor, who sinks into invisibility while Billy sinks to the sound of memorializing story and song. As he does for Defoe in retrospect, Equiano provides the back story of *Billy Budd* a century before Melville wrote it — a situation Melville obliquely acknowledges. These three texts thus join those I have discussed so far in part 2 as founding fictions of a racialized Atlantic liberty.

This Solitary Condition?

In *Robinson Crusoe,* as critics often understand it, Crusoe hears the call of the sea that lures him away from his patrimony and his parents and into the acquisitive, individualistic, mercantile economy.[9] But in leaving his father's home, Crusoe actually follows in his father's footsteps. On second look, his "inheritance," which he explicitly specifies as Anglo-German in origin, is itself the practice of migration and mercantile trade:

> I was born in the Year 1632, in the City of *York,* of a good family, tho' not of that Country, my Father being a Foreigner of *Bremen,* who settled first at *Hull* : He got a good Estate by Merchandise, and leaving off his trade, lived afterward at *York,* from whence he married my Mother, whose Relations were named *Robinson,* a very good family in that country, and from whom I was called *Robinson Kreutznaer;* but by the usual Corruption of Words in *England,* we are now called, nay we call ourselves, and write our Name *Crusoe,* and so my Companions always call'd me. (4)

This German English father—hailing from Bremen, a German port town that prospered within the emergent world-system fed by the Atlantic—"got a good Estate by Merchandise" and then traveled again, from Hull to York. In turning west to seek his own estate and adventure, Crusoe simply emulates his father's entrepreneurial migrations. When he "[breaks] loose" from his parents at age eighteen, with his "thoughts . . . entirely bent upon seeing the world," he proves himself his Anglo-Saxon father's son.

Readers from Karl Marx to Ian Watt have recognized Crusoe as a figure for the emergent "economic man," expressed in his accruing, storing, listing, and distributing goods on his island, and his trading of goods at every opportunity.[10] And, at the same time, for several generations critics have interpreted the novel as a Puritan conversion narrative, a modern *Pilgrim's Progress*—so that what Crusoe at first calls his "Island of Despair" is the equivalent of Bunyan's Slough of Despond, where he suffers from a "Load of Guilt" and "other afflicting Thoughts" and finally develops an interior relation with God and himself (70, 97).[11] More recently, postcolonial critics have highlighted Crusoe's colonizing project, noting, for instance, Crusoe's island reflection that "I might call myself King, or Emperor over the whole Country which I had possession of" and his eventual "possession" of a darker-skinned "savage" for whom "I was absolute Lord and Law-giver" (128, 241).[12]

These different readings all join at the root. The mercantile, colonial, and Puritan narratives merge (in Defoe's text and in the longer rhetorical history) in the story of the modern self's "Forsaken Solitary Condition" (as Crusoe repeatedly refers to it) on the Atlantic (96, 112, 113, 139). This state is the precondition for liberation, prosperity, and salvation. We might say that Defoe's Protestant conversion narrative resacralizes and makes fully Atlantic this ruined, forsaken self that female writers were secularizing and domesticating. In particular, what Defoe's narrative makes quietly clear is that the slave trade — and the African person's body — enables the merging of these stories. The African is the laborer through whom the Anglo-Saxon Protestant on the Atlantic turns loss into profit and captivity into redemption. Because critics have consistently overlooked this element, I will dwell on it.

Long before Crusoe lands on the island, the enabling role that Friday will play in Crusoe's salvation and liberty is prefigured in his relation to his fellow slave under the Moors, Xury (a name that suggests usury and thus the use Crusoe makes of him). Although Crusoe tends to narrate his escape from the Moors as his own singular adventure, he acknowledges in passing that he depends on the guidance and bravery of Xury. On several occasions, Xury keeps them from danger or starvation, seeing a lion on the prowl before Crusoe does (since "his eyes were more about him than it seems mine were" [27]), or suggesting they wait until day to go ashore, which also saves them from the beasts they later see there ("Xury's Advice was good" [24]), and braving the jungle to hunt when Crusoe "did not care to" (26). Yet, in the end, although to win his help in the initial escape Crusoe had told Xury that he would "make you a great Man," one of Crusoe's first profitable transactions on arriving in "the Brasils" is to sell Xury.

Momentarily unveiling the faithless and profiteering logic of the Anglo-Saxons' relation to Africans on the Atlantic, Crusoe reports, "I was very loath to sell the poor Boy's Liberty, who had assisted me so faithfully in procuring my own" (34). The limited extent of his "loathing" to market an African's liberty in order to procure his own is measured a page later when he decides he had "done wrong in parting with my boy Xury" since he could use a slave on his growing plantation (35). Indeed Crusoe soon hereafter once more seeks profit by way of an African's bought liberty when he agrees to lead a slaving venture to Africa to buy slaves both for his own and others' plantations. Like his very first sailing trip, this venture meets a storm and ends in a swoon — in this case one that lands him senseless and leaves him alone on a Caribbean island for twenty-four years, before Friday joins him. But Crusoe ultimately makes this swoon, too, the occasion for gaining a dark-skinned slave and for fashioning himself as a white man who governs.

Quite pointedly, here too the slave sets Crusoe free. It is Friday who informs Crusoe about the presence of Europeans on the mainland (reporting, in a telling detail, that "we save the white Mans from drown" [223]), and Friday who helps him rebuild and steer the ship they will take to the mainland (for, says Crusoe, "I found he knew much better than I what kind of wood was fittest for it" [227]; and then, too, "He was a most dexterous Fellow at managing [the boat]" and so he deserves the credit for their successful launchings [225]). It is Friday who "took his Aim so much better than I," kills the other Caribs, and saves the Spaniard (234). It is Friday who later makes it possible for Crusoe to manage the English pirates whose ship they commandeer to leave the island. Although Crusoe announces that Friday, his father, and the Spaniard "all owed their lives to me," his tale reveals otherwise (241).

Thus does Crusoe carry forward the process incipient in Behn's *Oroonoko*, whereby the "race" that throws into relief the white Christian narrator's liberties is kept a slave for his efforts. Indeed, in a distinct echo of *Oroonoko*, Crusoe describes the man he calls Friday as "very Manly in his Face, and yet he had all the Sweetness and Softness of an *European*" with a "Nose small, not flat like the Negroes" (206). Just as Behn's narrator professes her admiration and friendship for Oroonoko, Crusoe avows a great love between himself and Friday (213). Yet the first word Crusoe teaches Friday in English is "master," and so it is through Friday's "service" that Crusoe manages to become the island's "Governour" (206, 268) and gains "an undoubted Right of Dominion" over his "People" (241).[13]

Even the interior self-dialogue that fills the entire middle of Crusoe's narrative — prompted, like those of the English-language novel's ruined heroines, by his self-losing swoon and subsequent isolation — becomes most probing and illuminating by way of Crusoe's encounters with Friday. He tells us that, as he begins to settle into life on the island, his interior dialogues "made my Life better than sociable, for when I began to regret the Want of Conversation, I would *ask my self* whether thus *conversing mutually with my own* Thoughts, and, *as I hope I may say,* with even God himself by Ejaculations, was not better than the utmost Enjoyment of humane Society in the World" (136). He takes up Bible reading and mingles his thoughts and his text with biblical quotations — a hint that his aloneness is also the basis for another textuality, that which he shares with his readers. And yet, just as this textuality can only be virtual until Crusoe leaves the island, so too does his Protestantism arrive at fruition only in relation to others — to Friday. Crusoe reaches his most complete involvement in Protestantism via his dialogues with Friday. As he begins to "instruct [Friday] in the Knowledge of the true God," he often finds himself "strangely surpriz'd" by and unable to answer Friday's questions (216, 218). He discovers that "in laying Things open to him, I really inform'd and instructed my self in many Things, that either I did not know or had not fully consider'd before; but which occurr'd naturally to my Mind, upon my searching into them, for the information of this poor Savage; and I had more Affection in my Enquiry after Things" (220). The implication is that the Englishman's modern social and religious identity arises in part through questions posed by the Carib — just as his material liberty is achieved by the Carib's labor.

Defoe offers a parable for the way an Anglo-Protestant identity took shape and its imperial wealth accrued by way of these Atlantic encounters, while he also unwittingly displays how narrative and governance work together to reserve these benefits for Anglo-Atlantic subjects *only*. Even at the level of narrative syntax, Defoe's text dramatizes the grammatical contortions entailed in this exclusionary project. We glimpse the elision of Crusoe's dependency on the Carib, for instance, when he reports that, to keep the boat safe during the rainy season, "*I* had stow'd our new Vessel as secure as *we* could" (229, emphasis added). These small movements testify to the larger ways in which Friday is the unwritten navigator of Crusoe's freedom vessel. More broadly, the novel's temporal breaks, halting repetitions, confused dates, conflations of journal and narration, and self-contradictions hint that Crusoe's narrative "I" barely coheres what always threatens to come apart — the project of forging a history out of the ruptures of history, fashioning the exterior world according to the beliefs of an interior ("*to think that this was all my own*" [emphasis added]), and along the way submerging the African-Atlantic presence and the Anglo-Atlantic dependence on it within an individualist "British" liberty story.[14]

In this light we might revise Virginia Woolf's comment that *Robinson Crusoe* "resembles one of the anonymous productions of the race itself rather than the effect of a single mind."[15] Instead it is exactly in its construction of this single "mind" — an isolated, hyperextended Atlantic mind, in motion, afflicted, and in disavowed relation to others — that Defoe's novel most speaks for "the race itself."

Ruin on the Black Atlantic

Like *Robinson Crusoe, The Interesting Narrative of the Life of Olaudah Equiano, or Gustavas Vassa the African, Written by Himself* begins with a rupturing departure from his home and family that leads to his arrival on a "Guiney ship." Like Defoe's, Equiano's *Narrative* offers a meditation on the travails of slavery, trade, and freedom on the Atlantic. Like Defoe's, his *Narrative* accordingly registers a sensibility in motion between two shores, one that furthermore takes shape as a Protestant self-dialogue and conversion. And like Defoe's, Equiano's story includes cross-racial encounters that are at first shocking but later give rise to cross-racial bonds.

These parallels, in turn, throw into relief the fundamental differences between Defoe's and Equiano's texts. Crusoe is never beaten, hung by his waist, or thrown in jail for no cause, while Equiano is repeatedly. Crusoe never faces the threat of slavery based on skin color alone — Equiano does perpetually. Crusoe makes direct profits as an owner of slave plantations and a merchant in slave trading, while Equiano finds work on slave plantations and ships while doing some trading in small goods on the side—and he makes clear that in later life he goes to sea because he needs the money. Equiano is never a slave trader for himself, as Caldwell implies, and even his merchant work is done on the side before and after he is free, while he remains a sailor under the authority of the captain.

But then there is the most important difference: Equiano's story *is* autobiography, and Defoe's is not (a detail Caldwell fails to note in placing them together in this tradition). Friday, the lone footstep, Crusoe's "governorship," and Xury—all are figments of Defoe's imagination. Equiano's black associates and white masters are historical. And even if we acknowledge the gray area between fiction and autobiography, or highlight in Equiano what William Andrews has called the "novelization" of slave narratives, or believe that Equiano was a black born in the southern United States rather than in Benin, we can say safely that Equiano's story represents the historical experience of many (including in large part his own), and Crusoe's isolated life on an island does not.[16] Crusoe's imprisonment is purely literary, and Equiano's is real. In the end, Defoe's story is a fiction of a born-"white" British citizen, and Equiano makes clear that his is not.

But Equiano does insert himself into that free Englishman's story. Not only does he write in English and speak the language of liberty in all its mercantile, imperial, and racial slipperiness, as other critics have noted,[17] but he also enfolds the violation-story of rape that has been its narrative vehicle, and he foregrounds black labor as a material condition for both mercantile wealth and mercantile stories. He flaunts his mastery of the British code, and he unpacks it by choosing to move along its fault lines, to surface its repressions—which is why he might have been perceived as a potential earthquake, as Caldwell at one point suggests (267). We might imagine him as the middle-aged Friday, just as we might imagine Friday to be eventually deemed "free" by Crusoe in some nominal sense but, like Equiano, still at a white man's side and working for wages, shrewdly observing this shipmaster—and probing the racial logic of Atlantic freedom.

Caldwell hears an echo of Defoe's title in Equiano's, since both end "written by himself." More to the point, we should consider Equiano's *doubling* of the author's name on his title page—his inclusion of both his African name Olaudah Equiano and his given British name Gustavus Vassa—as his more pointed signifying on the British tradition. The name "Vassa" would have given white British and American readers pause when paired with that of "Equiano" as well as "the African," in light of their associations of the name "Vassa" with the sixteenth-century "Gothic" liberator of the Swedes from the "Danish Yoke" (as the OED still puts it). Perhaps Equiano even smiled wryly as he published his work on the fiftieth anniversary (1798) of Henry Brooke's play *Gustavas Vasa* (1738). Brooke's play had memorialized Vasa, as Equiano very possibly knew, explicitly casting him as the "Deliverer" of that "Race of hardy, northern sons" in Sweden, "one of those Gothic and glorious Nations, from whom our Form of Government is derived, from whom Britain has inherited those inextinguishable Sparks of Liberty and Patriotism."[18] In Brooke's account, Vasa (as he spells it) restores the Swedes (and therefore, indirectly, the British) to their "Freedom, sacred Freedom." In this way, Equiano sets himself up to be the same kind of deliverer for his own "race."

And yet, as Equiano is careful to report, he had this freedom-fighter's name beaten into him by his master. It is noteworthy that he resisted this name — ("I at that time began to understand him a little, and refused to be called so" [36]) — after having accepted without comment two English names (Jacob and Michael) from previous masters (35). Whether or not the young Equiano was consciously rejecting the white man's joke in naming him Gustavus Vassa, his resistance to the name ironically displays its fitness: he is, after all, fighting for freedom, for rights over his own person. His inclusion of this incident suggests that Equiano was a shrewd teller of the liberty tale. For it allegorizes the contradictions he faces in the land of liberty: he becomes Gustavus Vassa by resisting becoming Gustavus Vassa, and he takes on the name and narrative of freedom *forcibly,* at the hand of a white man. These ironies reverberate again if we place Equiano's story, as autobiographical text, next to Defoe's fantasy. Crusoe can (with Friday) fully orchestrate and gain the freedom of his "subjects" on the island and furthermore position himself as the origin and caretaker of their freedom under the contract they make with him, while Equiano's attempts to be the "Northern liberator" of his fellow Africans are undercut and hemmed in by the very "governors" who have "granted" him freedom.

My point is that Equiano doesn't simply claim affiliation with the British liberty tradition; he narrates the violent force by which he comes to be in a position to do so. At the same time — if we remember that many of his readers would have known Brooke's play and the Gothic associations of Vassa — he presses directly on the racial nerve. He crosses exactly the line which his readers might want to draw between themselves and him but which he, courtesy of his joking master, can use to resist that exclusion. Even his emphasis on his participation in the exploration of the Arctic insinuates that he is the race-equal to that hardy northerner Vassa. Similarly, when he explicitly tracks his Protestant conversion and practices — although like Crusoe he faces a "load of guilt," partly in connection with the slave trade, that compels him — his continual invocation of the Bible to denounce racism and slave-owner cruelty means that he is turning the Christianity of a plantation and mercantile figure like Crusoe back on itself. In the end he works to surpass the everyman status of Crusoe: he is not just a (complicit) mercantile everyman of (corrupted) German name; instead, he carries the original name of Vasa, that heroic challenger of slavery "from whom the British inherited those inextinguishable Sparks of Liberty."

Equiano's text in fact turns the emergent British tradition of fictional autobiography on its head, revealing himself as the shadow behind its narrators, or, in other words, revealing the British narrator (like Defoe's or Behn's) to be a ventriloquist of the African's more radically displaced position. Reprinted eight times in England in the first five years after its 1789 publication, Equiano's popular narrative embodies the way that the cultural as well as the economic capital generated by Africans could accrue — ironically through their stories of liberation — to the British themselves. A close look at the *Narrative* reveals just how astutely Equiano manipulated that tradition in order to place himself, like the Danish Gustavas Vassa, at its origin. In the end, it is not that we need to "grant Equiano the full British voice and British identity" he claimed, as Caldwell suggests (280), but rather that we need to reconfigure our understanding of the conditions creating this British "voice" and recognize how the liberty stories of Defoe and Burke "borrow" from Equiano as much as he "borrows" from them.

MOST GRAPHICALLY AND SIMPLY, Equiano rewrites Defoe's cataclysmic Atlantic storm as perpetual stormings. Equiano in effect takes the swoon and recasts it as a series of everyday, ongoing ontological crises. In contrast to Defoe's apocalyptic "waves, mountains high," for Equiano the sea provides an objective correlative for his psychic and bodily state of "constant alarm," especially in the turbulent surf in the West Indies — even more pointedly so than critics have noted.[19] As he moves from a dialogue with his master about his wish to buy his freedom ("for life had lost its relish when liberty was gone" [88]) to stories of himself and other blacks being kidnapped or defrauded, Equiano remarks: "While I thus went on, filled with the thoughts of freedom, and resisting oppression as well as I was able, my life hung daily in suspense, particularly in the surfs I have formerly mentioned, as I could not swim. These are extremely violent in the West Indies, and I was ever exposed to their howling rage and devouring fury in all the islands" (88).

In the pivot of the phrase "my life hung daily in suspense," Equiano converges the dangers of slavery and sea, and he establishes the pervasive undoing effects of his predicament on the Atlantic. Directly hereafter, he tells of several violent experiences, in which the sea seems to stand in for the violence of the Anglo-Atlantic world, as when "a surf struck us," or the churning waves "tossed" his boat and he "was very near being drowned," or storms "maimed" or "bruised" the sailors — at least some of whom appear to be slaves who fear, on being delayed by the surf, that "we should be used ill for being absent" (88). In closing his account of these experiences and the surf that continually threatens him, Equiano reports that "I and many more often said, and really thought, that there was not such another place under the heavens as this," and then he turns directly from this thought to a description of how "[w]hile we lay in this place, a very cruel thing happened" (89) — a free mulatto man is taken from his wife and child and sold.

The sea thus embodies this ontological undoing that Equiano and all other "negroes" face. Equiano had foreshadowed these world-undoing effects in narrating his arrival on the first slave ship he boards, the one that transports him across the Atlantic — a guiney ship like that on which Crusoe first became a sailor. In that scene, Equiano is overcome by the presence not only of the strange white men running the ship but also of the dejected, chained "black people of every description," so that he is filled with "astonishment," "terror," "horror," and "anguish," and he falls "motionless on the deck" (27). Yet, by contrast to Crusoe's singular swoon and captivity, this will be merely the first of Equiano's sea traumas. And if, in light of Vincent Carretta's argument, we read this moment as Equiano's imaginative reconstruction of such an experience, then the scene further testifies to his shrewd recasting of the tropes of the Anglo-Atlantic narrative of captivity and liberty.

At the same time, in reporting one of his most dramatic shipwreck experiences, Equiano pointedly reverses Defoe's racialized story of agency in *Robinson Crusoe* and in the process proves himself the literal "deliverer" of the Anglo-Saxons. What at first glance appears as merely a self-congratulatory story of Equiano's heroism comes to have a fuller resonance when we read it against Defoe's erasure of blacks on the Atlantic, including skilled action that makes possible Anglo-Atlantic survival and freedom. During one of Equiano's night deck watches he spies a massive crop of rocks, toward which the vessel is being carried by the current. He goes below three times to alert the captain, but the captain first dismisses the threat, then promises to follow Equiano to the deck but doesn't, and finally leaves his cabin only the third time, when it is too late to avoid the rocks. Thus with a dramatic "heave of the swells . . . the vessel struck" and "the sloop was pierced and transfixed among the rocks" (113). Two elements of what follows are key. First, as they consider boarding one of the lifeboats to escape the ship, the captain "ordered the hatches to be nailed down on the slaves in the hold, where there were about twenty in all," explaining that there would be no room for them in the small boat. Equiano feels that "God would punish me for these people's blood," and recalls that this thought "quite overpowered me, and I fainted" (113). Recovering just as the crew is about to obey this order, Equiano rises up to tell the captain "he deserved drowning for not knowing how to navigate the vessel" and then persuades him that they should not nail down the hatches and attempt to flee but should instead huddle on the dry part of the ship until daylight, which they successfully do (113). Equiano's "awakening" from his shipwreck swoon into bold resistance and ethical leadership contrasts with Crusoe's awakening into slave trading and a narrative that veils exactly this African-Atlantic agency.

Second, it is the initiative not only of Equiano but also of the other blacks on the ship that makes it possible for them all to survive. The next day, while other crew members get drunk (ignoring his warnings "as if not possessed of the least spark of reason" — a nice reversal of the lack of reason attributed by whites to blacks), Equiano leads five arduous journeys carrying men and supplies between the ship and the Bahaman island they see five miles off. He emphasizes that "there were only four people who would work with me at the oars, and they consisted of three black men and a Creole sailor ... we had no others to assist us" (114). Thus do we have a miniature of the larger Atlantic freedom story in which whites survive shipwreck and finally achieve freedom from island captivity only by way of the foresight, skill, and labor of blacks. At the same time, Equiano's swoon in the face of the slaves' possible fate in the hold and his sense of entanglement in the captain's cruelty stand in for the larger middle-passage experience of Atlantic blacks. Equiano's awakening and his documentation of the actions of himself and others work discursively to counteract this history. Tellingly, this whole shipwreck episode begins with Equiano's recollection that for three successive nights beforehand he had dreamed of a shipwreck in which he saved the lives of all aboard the ship. He tells us that he had forgotten the dreams until the crisis hit, when it "now returned upon my mind with all its force" — a hint that his action as "deliverer," as he refers to it, is indeed the return of the repressed: that is, the repressed black agency in the reigning fiction of Anglo-Saxon and Danish deliverers (115).

Within this framework, Equiano simultaneously establishes his identification and solidarity with Atlantic blacks. Caldwell claims that Equiano avoids association with other blacks on the Atlantic, describing him as a "lonely wanderer ... [l]ike Crusoe" (270), and she argues that Equiano's psychic identification with British empire "necessarily involves a self-alignment not with but against the 'African brethren'" (268). In fact, however, Equiano repeatedly highlights his affiliations with blacks, recording their shared experiences of being "villainously trepanned and held in bondage" (89). He tells a number of stories of his visits with black friends, particularly stressing the circumstances under which he and his black associates are physically abused, defrauded of money, or taken captive even after they are free.[20] Using the first person plural, he reports that he has "experienced many instances of ill usage, and have seen many injuries done to other

Negroes in *our* dealings with whites. And amidst our recreations, when we have been dancing and merrymaking, they, without cause, have molested and insulted *us*" (85, emphasis added). In one case, he tells of how in Georgia, as he sits "with some Negroes in their master's yard," the master and another white man arrive drunk and take to beating him, "not liking to see any strange Negroes in his yard" (96). "They beat and mangled me in a shameful manner, leaving me dead" so that he lays "quite motionless" until his captain discovers him (96–97). These are events that, to reverse Caldwell's claim, necessarily involve a self-alignment not against but with the "African brethren."

As he records this camaraderie-under-duress, Equiano is also making clear the problematic terms of blacks' potential to find freedom or legal standing on the Atlantic.[21] Again, the point needs stressing in light of Caldwell's argument: in order to defend her claim that Equiano identifies exclusively with the British empire and her equation of Equiano's "dreams of freedom" with those of Robinson Crusoe, she stresses that Equiano cherished England as the only country in which "he [could] be free" (272). But this point obscures Equiano's lack of freedom in the colonies and at sea (where he makes his living). Crusoe could find freedom, in the sense of protection under the law, anywhere English law ruled. By contrast, Equiano repeatedly highlights his exclusion from protection under the law in the British colonies—where, as he says, he "could not by the law get any redress from a white person." This is the case because, he explains, in the West Indies (as in southern American states) "no free Negro's evidence will be admitted in their courts of law" (90)—such as in the story he here tells of "a free mulatto" who is seized and sold "although he showed a certificate of his being born free in St. Kitts" (89).

Indeed, chapter 11, Equiano's last full chapter, consists of one long series of crises in which he suffers abuse from the British, so that his narrative proper ends by emphasizing his "suspended" position as one excluded from full legal rights within the empire and stymied in his pursuit of liberty. This chapter records Equiano's perilous journey on his first return to England after being declared free by his master, on which he repeatedly is kidnapped and beaten by ship captains. One "cruel and bloody-minded" captain, after betraying his promise to give Equiano transport to Jamaica, "vent his fury on me by beating me" (174), while another captain ("my tyrant") resents and claims to doubt Equiano's free status and so hoists him by ropes around his waist "without letting my feet rest on or touch anything" (169). He explains "Thus I hung, without any crime committed ... merely because I was a freeman, and could not by the law get any redress from a white person" (169). Equiano's attachment to England, the island, arises from the "suspension" of his (juridical) person under *British* colonial policy in the West

Indies. Unfortunately he can never stay long in England, since sailoring is the source of his living, so he must continually face violation on board British ships and in British colonies.[22] He praises "old England" as the land of "fair liberty" as a strategic foil, pressing directly on the fault line of its mythology (90).

Furthermore, as Equiano undoubtedly knew,[23] some argued for the withholding of juridical rights from blacks in Britain itself, and they justified their arguments within the language of birthright. One writer for the *London Chronicle*, for instance, insisted that "there can be no just plea for [black Britons] being put on an equal footing with natives whose birthright, as members of the community, entitles them to superior dues."[24] Faced with this kind of racialization of the liberty discourse, Equiano begins to wonder about freedom: "Hitherto I had thought slavery only dreadful, but the state of a free Negro appeared to me now equally so at least, and in some respects even worse, for they live in constant alarm for their liberty; which is but nominal, for they are universally insulted and plundered, without the possibility of redress" (89–90). While his phrasing sometimes feeds the myth of a free England, Equiano's desire to "tread upon English ground" is quite a practical wish for the legal rights of which England herself continually threatened to deprive him in the Caribbean.

In combination with his revised symbology and his reversal of racialized absence and presence, and against this double standard of legal freedom on the Atlantic, Equiano crafts a dialectical intertextuality with English-language narrative conventions. He uses its forms to capture the contradictions of his predicament.[25] In the tradition of English novels since Behn's *Oroonoko*, Equiano begins his *Narrative* by apologizing for himself as a "private and obscure individual" who asks for the attention of his readers. His equivocal claim to insider status as a result of his travels as an outsider both invokes and twists the tradition, as expressed in this sentence:

> I believe there are few events in my life which have not happened to many; it is true the incidents of it are numerous, and, did I consider myself a European, I might say my sufferings were great; but when I compare my lot with that of most of my countrymen, I regard myself as a *particular favorite of heaven,* and acknowledge the mercies of Providence in every occurrence of my life. (4, emphasis in original)

The opening of this sentence could appear in just about any autobiographical eighteenth-century British narrative, fictional or historical, until the phrase "did I consider myself a European." This inkling of something unexpected enlarges when Equiano reveals that the "many" to whom the story's events have occurred are not Europeans at all, as the British reader would have assumed, but kidnapped Africans. Equiano sets up an apparently universalist "many" but quickly reveals what is apparently universalist to be Eurocentric: his experience is *very* common—among Africans. And this African identity, furthermore, fundamentally changes the *meaning* of his experience: what Europeans would consider disastrous he must consider fortunate. He reveals the contingency of political/racial identity, and he uncovers the deep divide in experience between Africans and Europeans veiled by an assumption of universalism.

In opening this broad perspective on how experience can "mean" differently, Equiano establishes his cosmopolitanism, equal to (if not surpassing) that of his readers. He takes up for himself the "free" Anglo-European claim to worldliness and global perspective. This stance sets up his next move, whereby he establishes himself as a Protestant insider exactly because of his outsider position.[26] He must consider himself, he tells his readers, a *"particular favorite of heaven"* who sees "Providence acting" in "every occurrence of my life." And he must do so exactly *because he is an African.*

Equiano makes his difference from Europeans the very pivot of his intimacy with their traditions. Call this English wit or call it African tricksterism—or, rather, understand each of these modes as a function of the encounter between English and African, that is, a function of the colonial economy within which English cosmopolitan wit flourished and African tricksterism found a new object. While British readers must have squirmed under this manipulation from one point of view, their own rhetoric had prepared it—and prepared them for it—from another point of view. Indeed, they were clearly attracted by this contradictory ontopolitical position, as the rapid eight printings of Equiano's text in England seem to attest (while the limited appeal it held in the United States suggests that discomfort overshadowed identification in readers' responses).

After all, it is to the English that Equiano is appealing, in the context of parliamentary debate about the slave trade, and he continues his effort to do so when he then opens his narrative proper, beginning with the subheading of chapter 1, by following the conventions of the ethnographic travel narrative, another staple of English culture by this time:[27] "The author's account of his country, and their manners and customs—Administration of justice—Embrenche—Marriage ceremony, and public entertainments—Mode of living—Dress" and so on. Immediately we see how the insistent bricoleur "I" of Crusoe's narration (the "I" determined to accrue all liberty and property to itself) becomes dispersed, in Equiano, across a we/they construction, an inescapably double "I." His insider-outsider subjectivity gets registered immediately in the grammatical strain between "his country" and "their manners."[28]

This strain continues throughout the chapter as Equiano refers to the people of Benin as both "us" and "them." For the most part, in describing his native kingdom of Benin, Equiano writes in the first-person plural ("As our manners are simple, our luxuries are few"; "blue, which is our favorite color" [7]; "we live in a country where nature is prodigal of her favors" [9]). Yet at key moments, especially when he describes customs relating to sexuality or religion that Europeans would have considered a mark of barbarity and superstition, he slips into third person ("tossing a small quantity of the food in a certain place, for the spirits of departed relations, which *the natives* suppose to preside over *their* conduct and guard them from evil" [8]; "*they* indulge in a plurality [of wives]" [6], emphasis added). In the later chapters, as Equiano narrates his increasing assimilation into Anglo-Atlantic culture, the "us" is a European us, among whom Equiano takes his place as an English shipman battling them, the French — a striking reversal of Behn's shift from an English "us" aligned with Oroonoko to a white "us" aligned against him. A kind of torque thus characterizes the voice of this narrator who is all at once doubly identified with African and European in a perpetual present, and doubly dis-identified ("did I consider myself an European") in a past severed from any present.

Pursuing his manipulation of the codes of Atlantic identity, Equiano establishes a biblical racial genealogy for the Benin people — and a noble origin for the African liberty story. He highlights the "strong analogy" between "the customs of my countrymen and those of the Jews" (16), enumerating the various rituals they share. Most important, his account of this possible racial genealogy climaxes with an appeal for liberty and justice for all Africans, inspired as it is by his own "Love of liberty, ever great" (21). While adopting the principle of racial lineage (and Equiano has also characterized himself as noble, descending from the elite class with the mark of *embrenche*), he belittles those racial arguments based on skin color, hoping "to remove the prejudice that some conceive against the natives of Africa on account of their color. Surely the minds of the Spaniards did not change with their complexions!" At the same time, he invokes the sentimental meanings of noble and speaks the language of sensibility (a sign of superior racial character) when he emphasizes how slavery "depress[es] the mind, and extinguish[es] all its fire and every noble sentiment" (18). Further, he implicitly enfolds the progress narrative of race, when he asks the "haughty European" to recall that "his ancestors were once, like the Africans, uncivilized, and even barbarous" (18).

Thus putting in play the values of both universalism and cultural difference, as well as a timeless idea of "noble sentiment" and a progressivist narrative of the path from barbarism to civilization, Equiano turns the equivocality of the Anglo-European liberty story back upon itself even as, in the process, he establishes himself as a proper citizen of empire. He closes this chapter, cunningly, with Acts 17:26, pronouncing that God "hath made of one blood all nations of men for to dwell on the face of the earth" (18). The Bible serves his race story as well as theirs — an insight that Pauline Hopkins crystallizes, as we'll see, in her novel *Of One Blood*. Thus does Equiano reconfigure race and liberty within "the tradition of Defoe."

Equiano reconstructs this tradition along gender lines as well; he mirrors yet rewrites the gendered ruin at its center by including the story of his lost sister. Here, the woman's ruin is neither redemptive nor allegorical, nor enabling for him as a brother. Rather, the violation of rape hangs over the narrative from the scene in which he parts from his sister to the moment when he buys his freedom, for with this purchase of freedom he hopes to "bid adieu" not only to "dreadful instruments of torture," nor only "to oppressions," and not only "to the angry, howling, dashing surfs" with which he associates these, but also "to the offensive sight of the violated chastity of the sable females, which has too often accosted my eyes" (126–27). Equiano places the woman's ruin *beside* his own, as an intersubjective dimension of his world and a violation more intimate than what he suffers.

In this light, we might understand symbolically as well as literally the fact that Equiano is originally kidnapped for the slave market together with his sister and then, along the road heading west from the interior country of Benin, the two are sold to different owners. Although slavery "captures" them together, it ultimately sets them on divergent paths in which they lose each other as well as themselves. Equiano dwells on the moment when they briefly reunite one last time by chance one night, under the close watch of a master, and his setup of this reunion suggests that it constitutes Equiano's first pivotal moment of self-loss in his experience of slavery.

Interestingly, as Equiano explains it, his brief reunion with his sister occurs because his master sells him in reaction to a female loss — the death of his daughter. Just afterward, at a stop along the new owners' way to the Atlantic slave market, Equiano's group meets with another group of slave traders whose captives include his sister. The encounter at first seems like a substitutional resurrection of the former master's lost daughter and a symbolic return to kin for Equiano as well; yet it turns into his moment of parting from an old self as he enters Atlantic modernity. When he sees his sister, Equiano falls into that unspeaking senselessness that we saw mark the entry moment of Imoinda and Oroonoko: "she gave a loud shriek, and ran into my arms — I was quite overpowered; neither of us could speak, but for a considerable time, clung to each other in mutual embraces, unable to do anything but weep" (23). The next morning, "she was again torn from me forever!" and he explains that he was "now more miserable, if possible, than before" since "the wretchedness of my situation was redoubled by my anxiety after her fate, and my apprehensions lest her sufferings should be greater than mine," including, as he goes on to say, within the clutches of lust of "a brutal and unrelenting overseer" (24). Here is the familiar tableau of unspeakability and self-loss, and it moves Equiano toward his new "alarmed" state in the Anglo-Atlantic world.

And this moment moves him into a highly literary apostrophe to his sister. At this recollection of deepest loss, he disconcertingly becomes a conventional English-language narrator of the story of ruin, here again transforming his experience of utter outsiderness, as a captive slave, into a performance of belonging and mastery, as a narrator.

> Yes, thou dear partner of all my childish sports! thou sharer of my joys and my sorrows! happy should I have ever esteemed myself to encounter every misery for you and to procure your freedom by the sacrifice of my own. Though you were early forced from my arms, your image has been always riveted in my heart, from which neither time nor fortune have been able to remove it; so that while thoughts of your sufferings have damped my prosperity, they have mingled with adversity and increased its bitterness. To that Heaven which protects the weak from the strong, I commit the care of your innocence and virtues, if they have not already received their full reward, and if youth and delicacy have not long since fallen victims to the violence of the African trader, the pestilential stench of a Guinea ship, the seasoning in the European colonies, or the lash and lust of a brutal and unrelenting overseer. (24)

The poignancy of this scene is at once increased and distorted by the fact that Equiano addresses his sister in an English language and sentimental rhetoric she might well not understand or that, at least, is not the language that they would have spoken at their parting—although Equiano implies that such a scene is translatable and universal, transcendent of language or culture. Their innocent bond is at once celebrated and effaced in this literary language that addresses her as "thou dear partner" and refers to rape as a matter of having "fallen victim" to the "lust" of a man. His address to his sister is, in other words, the expression of Equiano as Gustavas Vassa, an African remade and renamed as a hero of the North. Without obscuring the possible actual event of Equiano's momentary reunion with a sister, it is important to note that he narrates it in the familiar sentimental and violation-plot language of "mutual embrace" and prolonged weeping—claiming that language for the events of his own and his sister's lives.

When, shortly after his parting from his sister, Equiano boards one of those "guiney ships" and sees the dejected, chained "black people of every description," he feels that "if ten thousand worlds had been my own, I would have freely parted with them all to have exchanged my condition with that of the meanest slave in my own country" (27). His remark indicates that, indeed, worldness is at stake. An exchange of worlds is taking place. Aghast, "I fell motionless on the deck and fainted" (27). In the very form of his text as well as in his bodily experience of social death, Equiano both disappears and reawakens in the Anglo-Protestant liberty story.

Innocence at Sea

As Equiano disappears, someone else arises in his place. The Anglo-Saxon innocent comes to stand in for the African; his national liberty story repeatedly overscores the slave's — in the process, however, ironically recreating the terms, the possibility, and the readers of the slave's story. While in *Benito Cereno* Herman Melville evokes the layers of race betrayal and the moral, social, and ontological nausea at the heart of these Atlantic displacements, and in *Moby-Dick* he conjures the global scope and maniacal drive of the Anglo-Atlantic enterprise, in *Billy Budd* he quietly creates an allegory of liberty's alibi — the rational order of law — under which seethes a homoerotic battle steeped in race antagonisms. His allegory effects the displacement of the African's story as well as the subsumption of a woman's story even as it signals toward these.

Explicitly, the narrator characterizes Billy Budd as Saxon — a key first point, which signifies much more than critics have recognized. A young handsome man of "free heart" (298), Billy was "[c]ast in a mould peculiar to the finest physical example of those Englishmen in whom the Saxon strain would seem not at all to partake of any Norman or other admixture."[29] He seems, too, to hail from the most noble past of that race for "the ear, small and shapely, the arch of the foot, the curve in mouth and nostril," and "above all, something in the mobile expression . . . indicated a lineage in direct contradiction to his lot" (300). Indeed, it turns out, as Billy tells a ship's officer, that he "was found in a pretty silk-lined basket," and the narrator then more strongly concludes that "[n]oble descent was as evident in [this foundling] as a blood horse" (300).

Like the historical Saxons conquered by Normans (but never in blood), Billy is a noble orphan cut off from his patrimony. His "lily" and "rose" complexion is now hidden by his sailor's tan and his fine hands "dyed to the orange tawny of the toucan's bill" (300). His sailor's "frank manifestations" (301) of feeling arise from his "free heart," and his innocence shows in his "smooth face all but feminine in purity" (299): "To deal in double meanings and insinuations of any sort was quite foreign to his nature" (298). Billy the Anglo-Saxon paragon is hearty, honest, and strong as well as noble and delicate. In sum, "his original constitution aided by the co-operating influences of his lot, Billy in many respects was little more than a sort of upright barbarian" (301) — a pure human embodiment of the Gothic balance of rough freedom and inherited order. Amid the virulence of late-nineteenth-century Anglo-Saxonism, Melville's portrait appears to express a troubled, willful nostalgia for an older, more innocent kind of Anglo-Saxonism.

Nancy Ruttenberg has persuasively argued that, for Melville, Billy embodies the emergent, everyman American poet envisioned by both Whitman and Emerson. She places the climactic scene of Billy's blow to Claggart, which sparks (in the novella's words) a "vocal current electric" among the sailors, beside Emerson's vision in "The Poet" (1844) of a plebian man "balked and dumb, stuttering and stammering" who finally, driven by rage against the insults of life and of "gentlemen," unleashes, in Emerson's words, a "*dream*power . . . by virtue of which a man is the conductor of a whole river of electricity."[30] Yet, as we saw, for Emerson this river of electricity carries a racial charge. In this context it is worth again recalling Emerson's conviction, as expressed in *English Traits* (1856), that "it is in the deep traits of race that the fortunes of nations are *written*."[31] The racial story Emerson tells is an Anglo-Saxon one, beginning with the idea that "[i]n Alfred, in the Northmen, one may read the genius of the English society," and ending with his claim that one now finds the "seat and center of the British race" in the United States (91, 178). If Melville's Billy Budd embodies Emerson's poet of the nation, then he also expresses what Emerson would have understood as the racial patrimony of that poet. Billy is the "Handsome Sailor" as race poet, barbarian yet pure, the vessel of an orphaned yet ancient lineage whose delicacy, I would emphasize, also carries the trace of his ruined mother's history.

And someone else's history as well, as the narrator signals before he begins his story proper. For Billy is not the first instance we meet of the "Handsome Sailor." As readers have noted, before he introduces Billy, the narrator first recalls "a remarkable instance" of such a sailor whom he saw in Liverpool "half a century ago": "a common sailor so intensely black that he must needs have been a native African with the unadulterated blood of Ham — a symmetric figure much above the average height" whose face "beamed with barbaric good humor" (291). If Samuel Otter is right, that in this figure Melville distills into one the several African characters in his life and fiction, then this novella may allow us retrospectively to read the complex, Africanist function served by those earlier figures.[32] Here I will consider the African's place in *Billy Budd*, for he has not as yet received as full a treatment as he deserves, especially with the benefit of Toni Morrison's notion of Africanism.[33] First, this framing of Billy's story indicates Melville's implicit racialization of his protagonist. The "unadulterated" African also oddly evinces a kinship with the northerner Billy in his dress: "a gay silk handkerchief thrown loose about the neck danced upon the displayed ebony of his chest, in his ears were big hoops of gold, and a Highland bonnet with a tartan band set off his shapely head" (291). Both men are gloriously upright barbarians, of ancient innocent stock and "tartan" brotherhood—unraped as yet, we might say, for the African too, when we meet him, is a sailor "ashore on liberty" (291). A similar association appears again, just before Billy's execution, when the narrator compares his comportment to that of a "superior *savage,* so called—a Tahitian, say" (373). And as the language describing the African hints, this ancient innocence in its powerful physical manifestation also casts an erotic power that can—as it does for Clarissa—provoke a fall. "Such a cynosure" says the narrator in turning from the African sailor to Billy, "was the welkin-eyed Billy Budd" (293). The underlying irony is that the very conditions that allow Melville to substitute Billy for the African—their shared Atlantic drama—are also those that promise a heroic fall for Billy and an unsung one for the African.

This will be so in part because Melville makes Billy's impressment into a story about the physical coercion and desire circulating within the order of law and the social "contract" *for* the Anglo-Saxon. Although the African sailor is "ashore on liberty," both his liberty and his place within the order of law that supposedly protects it are deeply compromised by race, as Equiano establishes—whereas the Anglo-Saxon Billy Budd's racial position marks him as the proper protagonist of this story of liberty, law, and contract. Yet Melville does find excessive trouble within this story, and he implies that race as well as gender lies at the root of that trouble.

As the cynosure-figure of the pure barbarian with a naturally honest "original constitution," Billy begins his ship-life on the *Rights-of-Man,* an amiable merchant ship, but he is soon impressed into service on a man-of-war called the *Bellipotent,* so that Melville immediately hints that the contractual rights of man get trumped on the Atlantic by the "law" of colonial war. Meanwhile the text also immediately signals that this tension between two kinds of law will catalyze a sexual fall, as the *Bellipotent's* captain refers to Billy as "my beauty" (296) and the narrator then compares Billy's arrival on the *Bellipotent* to "that of a rustic beauty transplanted from the provinces and brought into competition with the high-born dames of the court" (299). Melville brilliantly compresses the elements of Atlantic narrative. With both blindness and insight, he narrates the way sexual and racial erotics on the Atlantic circulate through the apparently rational structures of the social contract, which is negotiated within the theater of imperial war.

These racial and sexual erotics are played out, of course, between Billy and John

Claggart, the master-of-arms, who causes Billy's fall. The narrator tells us that what "first moved him against Billy" was the sailor's "significant personal beauty" combined with his transparent simplicity "looking out from his welkin eyes as from windows" (327). Claggart appreciates "the charm" of Billy and especially the "moral phenomenon" — or temptation — "presented in Billy Budd" (328). But his response to Billy is also "surcharged with energy" of a certain kind: whenever Claggert's "unobserved glance happened to light on belted Billy" it reveals a "settled meditative and melancholy expression." His eyes become "strangely suffused with incipient feverish tears" and the melancholy even at times "would have in it a touch of soft yearning, as if Claggert could even have loved Billy but for fate and ban" (338).

As does Billy's, Claggart's physical "constitution" explains his character: he is the corrupt French-Norman to Billy's welkin Anglo-Saxon. The "pallor" of his skin below "silken jet curls" (in marked contrast to Billy's "yellow curls" [327]) "seemed to hint of something defective or abnormal in the constitution and blood," even as "a bit of accent" in his speech "suggest[s] that possibly he was not [an Englishman] by birth" (314). Claggart's face, we are told, resembles that of Dr. Titus Oates, fabricator of the Popish Plot under Charles II, and rumors circulate about Claggart that he is originally French, a "chevalier" who volunteered for the king's navy in recompense for some crime against the English. Aboard the *Bellipotent,* his role as policeman puts him "as much in sanctuary" for any past crimes "as the transgressor of the Middle Ages harboring himself under the shadow of the altar" (315).

The text thus draws on Saxon/Norman "race" animosities, teasingly glossing Claggart as the popish French corrupter of innocence whose depravity leads the innocent Anglo-Saxon into crimes against his nature. Claggart's dark-haired, blood-tainted corruption hiding under the cloak of law and order, like his secretive nature overall, stands in opposition to Billy's free heart, blond head, and transparent welkin eyes. By identifying this banned yearning at work in none other than the master-of-arms (the narrator explains that in the age of the cannon, the master-of-arms is mainly "a sort of chief of police" responsible for "preserving order on the populous lower gun decks" [313]), and furthermore racializing as well as sexualizing Claggart's "nature," Melville indicates the entanglement of sexuality and race in the policing of the Atlantic order in the late nineteenth century. In effect, the two races come to a standoff in this world when Claggart accuses Billy of fomenting a mutiny and Billy — nonplussed by Claggart's duplicity and disabled from "free speech" by it — kills Claggart with one impulsive blow. In opening this novella about the "leveling" of Claggart with an *African* "cynosure," Melville places these old Protestant-English and French-Catholic animosities under the sign of race and within the larger history of black-white Atlantic encounters.

He likewise positions homosexual yearning and ruin under that racial sign. Perhaps women, that is, are not the only "sex" whose increased "freedom" to "cruise" threatens them simultaneously with ruin. Perhaps like women, those Claggarts with banned yearnings avoid ruin only by affiliating with the authority of the German-descended Captain Veres of their world, while covertly acting out a "French" clutch of desires. Eve Sedgwick has offered a searingly complete and powerful account of the erotics of the novella, including Captain Vere's enabling and phallic role in the ruin of Billy by Claggart, whereby his position gains hardness, so to speak, via the conflict between the handsome sailor and the melancholy Claggart. I would simply add a racial ground to her reading, the way Melville does in his text. That is, the text's yearning toward a future "after the homosexual" (which, Sedgwick convincingly argues, the novella expresses in its execution of Billy) arises within an Atlantic racial current.[34]

It is this sexual energy of a racial struggle on the high seas that the "handsome" African sailor at "liberty on shore" signals from the start. By transference, the desire of the text is invested not just in Billy but also in the African, as suggested by that "gay silk handkerchief thrown loose about the neck" which "danced upon the displayed ebony of his chest." Via the execution of Billy, the text perhaps aims to purge not just queer but racial desire, specifically the kind of desire that Eric Lott describes in *Love and Theft.* Thus Melville labors, like Edmund Burke, to restore equipoise to the Atlantic vessel as it navigates a sea of troubles.

That Melville also understands his story as a parable of the social contract's troubles is evinced in his emphases on impressment, on the threat of mutiny, and on war as a hidden motor and profit within Atlantic culture, although critics have for decades debated the question of Melville's final "resistance to" or "acceptance of" these legal yet brutal forces.[35] Early in the story, as the small boat carries the impressed Billy from the *Rights-of-Man* to his forced assignment on the *Bellipotent,* the narrator remarks that "officer and oarsmen were noting — some bitterly and others with a grin — the name emblazoned there" (297). At this moment Billy stands and waves goodbye to his old shipmates and adds, "And good-bye to you too, old *Rights-of-Man*" (297). The lieutenant takes Billy's farewell as "a sly slur at impressments in general, and that of himself in especial" (297–98). But Billy has no such intention. As pure descendant of a race of free-hearted men, to whom all "double meanings and insinuations" are "foreign," he willingly submits to the contract that supposedly, by impressing him, protects freedom. Although our narrator seems himself to deal in double meanings — by including, for example, the possibilities of both bitterness and smiles (resistance and acceptance) in the sailors who look on — it is this innocent racial man, the one who submits freely to law, that Melville most calls on us to desire and then to sacrifice — even if he also exposes the manipulations and ambitions of the order to which Billy submits. When faced with execution, Billy implicitly accepts (as Melville himself apparently struggled to do), Rousseau's dictum that the citizen must undergo the "total alienation . . . of himself and all his rights to the whole community."[36]

Thus, the "free" trade economy propelling the good ship *Rights-of-Man* also may entail impressment on the warship *Bellipotent* and slavery in the Americas, a situation that prompts the novella's (and in turn the critics') engagement with the old Putney Debate question about dissent or obedience. The *Bellipotent*'s lieutenant indicates this underlying question when he remarks that he is "delighted to learn that *one* shipmaster at least cheerfully surrenders to the King the flower of his flock, a sailor who with equal loyalty makes no dissent" (296, emphasis in original). Following on his choice of the word "flower," his next question " — But where's my beauty?" — in reference to Billy, suggests that not only Billy but also Claggart and the African will suffer a woman's surrender in this free economy and that the contest will be erotic as well as political. The larger context for the drama of the novel — the recent *Nore* and *Spithead* mutinies in the British Navy in which the mutineers (numbering in the thousands) took over a fleet of ships in protest of impressments and flogging practices — likewise signals that the problems underlying the Putney Debates continue to exert their pressure. Can one "dissent" or in other words withdraw from a contract if the conditions of consent become unacceptable? How is it that a state can force one to die or suffer against one's will for the principle of freedom? How consensually created is this freedom that the state supposedly holds in trust?

Melville's text raises these questions and legitimizes many possible answers, recreating for his readers the edgy, "electric" ground on which Billy, Claggart, and Vere meet, presided over by the African who both defines and is excluded from their contract drama of law and order. In his equivocal, circumlocutory mode of storytelling — what Barbara Johnson reads as Melville's eschewing of fixed grounds for judgment and Brook Thomas as Melville's appeal to readers' moral judgment[37] — the narrator interpellates his readers as eroticized yet frustrated race subjects, knocked off balance by the sacrifices and the banned energies of their contract with state authority. In noting that one of the *Nore* mutineers' main complaints was against the ruthlessness of impressment and disciplinary practices, the narrator calls attention to the coercion of membership in the state as a war machine. Given that in his earlier fiction Melville explicitly exposed and condemned such practices as flogging, we might be led to conclude that he sides with those who look on at Billy's impressments with bitterness. But his narrator just as convincingly evokes the chaos potentially created by dissent and mutiny, as if to warn against the temptation to rebel. Recalling the *Nore* and *Spithead* cases and the mutineers' ritual lowering of the British flag, the narrator remarks that such events were "[m]ore menacing to England than the contemporary manifestoes and conquering and proselyting [*sic*] armies of the French Directory," in fact as dire as "a strike in the fire brigade would be to London threatened by general arson" (303). When the mutineers lowered the flag, they lowered, the narrator says (with equal ambiguity), "the flag of founded law and freedom defined" (303). What do we make of the adjectives "founded" and "defined" attached to law and freedom: are they dissenting qualifiers? or authorizing intensifiers?

Captain Vere is the willing enforcer of the social contract that elides such questions, and Melville offers a similarly equivocal portrait of him. Vere is "allied to the higher nobility," and his military deeds include "gallantry in the West Indian waters" (312).[38] Yet his allegiance to this contract so bound to colonization and war develops not through apparent ambition but thoughtfully, through print: he reads "history, biography, and unconventional writers like Montaigne, who, free from cant and convention, honestly and in the spirit of common sense philosophize upon realities" (312). And he reads with a free heart, apparently: "While other members of that aristocracy to which by birth he belonged were incensed at the innovators [of novel opinion social, political, and otherwise] because their theories were inimical to the privileged classes, Captain Vere disinterestedly opposed them not alone because they seemed to him insusceptible of embodiment in lasting institutions, but at war with the peace of the world and the true welfare of mankind" (312). Yet in light of the climax to which Vere's "principled" conclusions lead, together with passing mention that he "may yet have indulged in the most secret of all passions, ambition" (382), this account of him may suggest that his views are only high-level rationalizations, cleverer than those of other members of the aristocracy but perhaps more deadly for that.

It's worth remembering, however, that although Rousseau's notion of liberty may sound undemocratic to twenty-first-century readers, his idea that the social contract "replace[s] the physical and independent existence we have all received from nature with a moral and communal existence" (*Social Contract* 84) was to Melville and his contemporaries an honorable vision. Accordingly, the narrator makes Vere's case for hanging Billy sound eminently rational. Vere argues that "in receiving our commissions we in the most important regards ceased to be natural free agents" (362). For it is not "Nature," he explains, to which "these buttons that we wear attest . . . our allegiance" but rather "the King" (361). He then elaborates with a paternal metaphor (and a gendering Rousseau would have approved): "We proceed under the law of the Mutiny Act. In feature no child can resemble his father more than that Act resembles in spirit the thing from which it derives — War" (363). Vere further genders this arrangement when he compares any appeal the officers might make to private conscience to that of a "tender kinswoman" who "waylays" a judge about to forestall the execution of her kinsman: "hard though it must be, she must here be ruled out" (362). Thus "private conscience should," he says, "yield to that imperial one formulated in the code under which alone we officially proceed" (362).

The choice of the word "imperial" may be a hint of critique, or may not be. The laws and deeds required in this Atlantic world are not simply protections of communal freedoms but in fact martial support for global dominance in trade and power. As the narrator stresses, the reining in of the mutineers led directly to Nelson's victory over the Spanish and French at Trafalgar (305) — an imperial victory. Vere approves this gendered imperial order, casting it as the demands of a contract, and indeed as a question of consistency with fully legible principles, and the narrator seems to do so as well. Yet the narrator also ferrets out the situation's underlying inconsistencies — including by hinting, perhaps, that Vere does not after all act in strict accordance with the Mutiny Act.[39] Likewise, Vere insists that it is not so much the officers who act to execute Billy as "martial law operating through us" (362), putting the executor at a distance from his act and undercutting the very agency that contract law would seem to confer, even feminizing the officers as mere instruments of law. Yet it is Vere who proceeds virtually single-handedly to condemn and execute Billy. The language of the contract empowers and exonerates him.

Similarly, the agents of war, Melville's narrator emphasizes, often appear in a garb quite innocent — in the guise, that is, of peacemakers and priests. The powerful scene in which Melville displays this fact also clarifies the racial homoerotics gathering such strange bedfellows. At the close of chapter 24, after a beatific vision of Billy in chains, the narrator endeavors to account for the oddity of the chaplain's office with Billy before his execution. "Stooping over, he kissed on the fair cheek his fellow man, a felon in martial law" (372). The chaplain knows, from Captain Vere, that Billy is innocent, yet "marvel not," the narrator tells us, that "the worthy man lifted not a finger to avert the doom of such a martyr to martial discipline" for to do so "would also have been an audacious transgression of the bounds of his function, one as exactly prescribed to him by military law as that of the boatswain" (374). Kiss but don't tell? This upright barbarian made "prone" (370), the Anglo-Saxon martyr, calls forth a kiss exactly in his proneness. To kiss him standing, and rebelling, would be an audacious transgression while to kiss him in his chains is nothing to marvel at.

And yet the narrator does marvel at it, does peek in on this scene, does give us a glimpse of the tenderness circulating under martial law. And even while the narrator seems to explain the secrecy of the chaplain's kiss rather than to cast him as a Judas who betrays desire and freedom, the final sentences of the chapter strike a harsher note: "Bluntly put, a chaplain is the minister of the Prince of Peace serving in the host of the God of War—Mars. As such he is as incongruous as a musket would be on the altar at Christmas. Why, then, is he there? Because he indirectly subserves the purpose attested by the cannon; because too he lends the sanction of the religion of the meek to that which practically is the abrogation of everything but brute Force" (374). This comment sheds light on the lieutenant's early remark that Billy is especially valuable as a "peacemaker" aboard ships and especially as "a fighting peacemaker" (as his famous knock-out capacity attests). Like the chaplain's, Billy's very innocence, his Anglo-Saxon martyrdom, "subserves" the purpose attested by the cannon. Just so does race as a freedom inheritance eroticize and ennoble the violence of colonial empire.

The beatific chapter describing Billy on the eve of his execution furthermore hints that it is women, the "barbarians," and a queer electric yearning that especially suffer ritualistic sacrifice in this racialized economy. Written mostly in the present tense, that is, in its own ritualistic stepping forward from the everyday-past-tense of the text, this chapter asks us to "behold Billy Budd under sentry lying prone in irons in one of the bays formed by the regular spacing of the guns comprising the batteries on either side" (370). The doomed Billy (our race lily) is literally em*bed*ded in the battle structures of his community. In the course of this chapter he will be compared to "a Tahitian" (373) innocently indifferent to the conversion efforts of missionaries, to the first impressive "Angles" encountered by Romans (372), and to a "virgin" oblivious to the evil around her (371)—the latter image recalling an earlier comparison of Billy, when he learns of his final fate, to "a condemned vestal priestess in the moment of being buried alive" (349). Living in "voluntary" submission at the center of this martial world, idealized as its innocent and pure racial essence, desired as its erotic reward, Billy, like Clarissa, must die to redeem its underlying "abrogation of everything but brute Force"—the words which close this beatific chapter.

Which brings us back to the beautiful African "cynosure" with whom the tale opens. A cynosure, indeed. To borrow from the dictionary definition for this word (*The American Heritage,* no less), the African sailor is that "focal point of attention and admiration" which is also "something that serves to guide"—yet guide from behind, as the word's etymology indicates, coming, as it does, from the words for "dog's tail." The African sailor is the dog's tail of this story and of the martial—and lynching—Atlantic economy that it allegorizes. Like Billy Budd, like Haywood's Fantomina, and like Rowson's Charlotte, the African will suffer a fall for his erotically enabling role in modernity. But his story will go untold. Billy's will become a can(n)onical novel.

In this light, we can freshly interpret the narrator's closing comments about the distortion of Billy's tale in the historical record. Comparing newspaper accounts of Billy's story to those histories that "naturally abridge" their accounts of the *Spithead* and *Nore* mutinies (304), the narrator tells us about a weekly paper that records Billy Budd as an "assassin [that] was no Englishman" who brutally stabs the "patriotic" John Claggart (382–83). It's important that the distortion here is specifically of Billy's lineage and Claggart's national allegiance. Melville writes his own tale "by indirection," including perhaps an unconscious reflection on his own effacement of the African sailor's lineage and story. Such substitutions and reversals are necessary, it seems, when one is registering sentiments as "surcharged" as Claggart's and Vere's toward the upright barbarian. In Melville's hand, the liberty story becomes an abridged narrative of the homosocial and racial erotics of Atlantic history.

As we will see in parts 4 and 5, this homoerotic undercurrent likewise just breaks the surface—mostly to be suppressed—in the work of Melville's near contemporaries Pauline Hopkins, Virginia Woolf, and Nella Larsen. Yet a century earlier, in the early gothic narratives to which I turn next, this undercurrent is so submerged as to be absent. The violence of these gothic tales may in fact be a symptom of the effort required to hold those yearnings many fathoms deep—a successful effort. My readings do not, however, work to uncover this possibly submerged queerness in the gothic but instead focus on the violent possession of others that keeps it silent—the race-provoked violence that floods back into the family itself, threatening daughters and sisters with rape in every room of the tyrant's castle.

III | Atlantic Gothic

8 At Liberty's Limits
Walpole and Lewis

IN THE ANGLO-ATLANTIC gothic text, the political violence of the Atlantic appears in traces. These texts transmute the brutal facts of colonization into the wandering figure burdened with a tale of complicity, the sound of distant guns "removing" Indians, the ghostly voice of a biloquist, or satanic compacts sealed in South America. Yet below these fleeting traces, Anglo-Atlantic gothic texts encode the African-Atlantic and Indian American situation whenever they tell the story of interior, bodily possession by others.[1] For even as African-Atlantic and American Indian lives made possible the Anglo-Atlantic world, their appropriated lands and presence haunted the Anglo-Atlantic imagination.

Over the next three chapters, I focus mainly on three gothic texts whose characters are scattered across the Atlantic — *The Monk, Wieland,* and *Of One Blood* — and whose heroines face captivity and violation not just because of but directly by their brothers.[2] In these texts, the brother's possession of a sister (for instance by imprisonment, sexual ruin, or satanic magic) dramatizes the possessive drive of the Atlantic's racial republics.

I stress possession and not just captivity in these narratives (as critics of the gothic have typically done) because "possession" names the economic as well as the psychological matrix from which the brothers operate.[3] That is, the brother's hidden will to property and control embodies the force of an Atlantic economic imperialism that, under the sign of brotherly fraternity, purports to be kindly while greedily seizing the lands, minds, and bodies of others. As is especially clear in these three novels (and we could also add, among classic gothic texts,

The Mysteries of Udolpho), the will to psychic and bodily possession is entangled with fortunes, pitting brothers against sisters, where the brother's desire to possess power, land, money, or authority leads to the possession or ruin of a sister. Paradoxically, these brothers' ambitions threaten race and family ties and yet their ambitions emerge as racial, as expressions of a racial drive for freedom.

At the same time, in this Atlantic modernity, these gothic brothers are often on the defensive. They are faced with a world of mobility, anonymity, and liberty that threatens, even as it spawns, their new power, for it also provokes the agency of their victims and unsettles inherited fortunes. In their sensationalism, the novels express some of the hysteria that these brothers feel as they glimpse the possibility of unprecedented power yet stand on unstable ground. In the brothers' frenzied will to secure control and possession, they commit the "unspeakable" crimes narrated in these texts.[4] Meanwhile, these texts themselves labor to maintain control; and so, even while creating pathos for their terrorized heroines, they work to recontain the heroine's errant desire or mobility.

My arguments here complement those of critics who read the gothic within the political contexts of slavery, imperialism, and revolution, particularly those of Teresa Goddu about American gothic and Cannon Schmitt about British gothic.[5] Foregrounding this political framework instead of the psychoanalytical one used by some critics of the gothic, I would at the same time observe that the gothic's "manifestation" of interior labyrinths by way of castles, ruins, and prisons itself has a political history and as such further elaborates the interior Saxonist-Protestant turn in Anglo-Atlantic subjectivity. The "subjectivization" of the self in English-language modernity, as we have seen, gets narrativized as the liberation of an interior self, expressed in print as well as in art and architecture and operating as adjudicator of sociopolitical relations — all of which constitutes the recovery of a native Anglo-Saxon legacy.[6] Yet this achievement entails violence. The psychic and bodily violations suffered in castle or convent dungeons simulate historical violations, culminating in cataclysmic scenes in which these places burn to the ground. In this sense they play out Rousseau's analogy between the rupture of the person's memory and the state's order, often (though not always) ending with a phoenix rebirth.

This genealogy of the gothic allows us to make much fuller sense of the specifically "gothic" name for this subgenre than has been offered by critics so far.[7] For this genealogy explains the recurring presence of violating "tyrants" as well as the gothic's scenes of revolution and its representations of abject sexual ruin. It allows us to appreciate how, in their ancient barbarian settings, the first British gothic texts work in tandem with those late-eighteenth-century literary historians who were recovering native "barbarian" poetry to fashion the sublimely awed yet other-mastering and freer Anglo-Saxon self. In this light we also better understand why this violent, fantasy-genre of ancient, remote communities immediately took such gripping hold of readers in Atlantic modernity, for its gothic vocabulary would more readily have conjured this whole set of associations.[8] The "narrative force" of gothic novels studied by Peter Garrett, which he argues derives from their self-consciousness about their literary strategies and power, also likely expresses, then, their authors' self-consciousness as bearers of this "ancient" print-sphere story. Accordingly, in many of these stories, writing itself is an instrument of invasion, possession, and kin rupture. As we will see, a racialized violation often finds its opening by way of a book or letter that "enters" the psyche and body and possesses the self. In this sense, gothic narratives tell the story of their own textual power as a practice linked to racial and colonizing power.[9]

Horace Walpole's *The Castle of Otranto* and Harriet Jacobs's *Incidents in the Life of a Slave Girl* serve in this three-chapter section on the gothic as important auxiliaries to my readings, for they formulate the narrative patterns that shaped later Anglo-Atlantic and African-Atlantic gothic novels. Jacobs's text clearly arises in the context of an Atlantic history and economy, and she specifically invokes and reappropriates the gothic tropes that have shaped this story, exposing their factual sources. Meanwhile, even the seemingly remote "crisis in domestic economy" that Christopher Flint identifies in *The Castle of Otranto,* by consensus the first gothic novel, unfolds within the traveling geography and racialized liberty tropes of Atlantic modernity.[10]

Manfred in Modernity

In writing *The Castle of Otranto,* Horace Walpole helped to transfer Saxonist myth from the realms of politics and architecture to that of literature. Son of the Whig leader Sir Robert Walpole and himself a member of Parliament, Walpole explicitly paired what he called his two "Gothic passion[s]" — his devotion to Gothic architecture as flamboyantly expressed in his Gothic mansion at Strawberry Hill ("the castle (I am building) of my ancestors") — and his pleasure in "squabbles in the Wittenagemot" — that is, in Parliament, identified here with the old Anglo-Saxon councils, both of which led him to dabble in antiquarian research.[11] Eventually, Walpole expressed this Gothic passion in *The Castle of Otranto* (1764) — an immediate success, at least in sales. His text marks the most explicit moment of Saxonism's entry into the novel in the later eighteenth century, although its political tropes had been shaping the novel since its inception.

In the first edition of *The Castle of Otranto,* Walpole presented his text as a found manuscript printed in black letter type and translated from the Italian, thus setting up an antiquarian frame which, of course, in the wake of Ossian and accompanied that year by Percy's *Reliques,* linked his tale to these literary-racialist projects. Praising the manuscript's preservation of ancient "manners" in his first preface (6), he encourages his readers to receive it in an ethnographic, nativist spirit. For the second edition, he added the subtitle "A Gothic Story" and in this edition's preface, after confessing his authorship, he invokes "that great master of nature, Shakespeare" as the model for *Otranto*'s combination of the "sublime" and the "naive" (10). The German names of Manfred and the ultimate sacrificial heroine Matilda further point toward the fiction's Saxonist subtext despite the apparently non-Saxon and pre-Protestant settings.[12]

In Walpole's novel, read within this frame, the threat of rape by a tyrant dramatizes the threat of historical discontinuity and creates the pivotal turn by which a new order is ushered in. Manfred belongs to a line of usurpers and lies under a curse on his "race" (24) that threatens to make him the last of his line.[13] In part under the pressure of this curse, Manfred operates by "tyranny," as Walpole names it at least ten times, and at the end of the tale he expresses the hope that "this bloody record be a warning to future tyrants!" (112). Clearly, Walpole invokes the old drama of a struggle against tyranny in his "Gothic story."

And the tyrant threatens rape, as we have seen he often does. When Manfred's son is crushed under a huge armor helmet on the day of his wedding, Manfred's hope for a future for his race appears to be killed as well, but to avoid this fulfillment of the curse he immediately attempts to ravish and marry the son's bride-to-be, Isabella. The implication is that the will to race, or in other words the will to secure kinship bonds in the face of a new free order of things, has become arbitrary and coercive. Its "willed" nature turns race into a gothic "plot." The incestuous hint here signals a future pattern in gothic novels whereby the threat to virtue originates close to home and among kin. When Isabella resists this willed, race-driven violation, Manfred imprisons her. Her savior arrives in the person of an unknown wanderer named Theodore, who eventually turns out to be the lost son of the rightful line of the castle of Otranto and yet who is also imprisoned by Manfred for attempting to help Isabella escape. Having himself recently "obtained ... liberty" from infidel captors in the wars of the Crusades (81), Theodore becomes the key agent in this plot: it is he who ultimately obstructs the rape and reinstalls the proper race through his uncorrupted sensibility — through his will to liberty as well as his simple devotion to "veracity" and "honesty" (32, 53).

Here is the text's — and prototypically the genre's — recuperative turn. One race —a modern, free one, emerging from a long, wandering exile — replaces another, a usurping and tyrannical one, and the result for women is ostensibly a kinder, gentler patriarchy. *The Castle of Otranto* establishes itself as a parable for this Saxonist story when it raises the contractual question that fired all the debates of the English Revolution—when can a people rightfully dissent from their king?—and then fashions the dissenters as the true race representatives. Both Isabella and Theodore practice dissent, invoking the familiar language. Isabella resists not only Manfred but also the command of her own father, Frederic. Although Frederic at first arrives to save her from Manfred, Frederic's resolve is weakened by his desire to marry Manfred's daughter Matilda and therefore to strike a deal with Manfred. Isabella thinks her father is "too pious, too noble, [...] to command an impious deed"—that is, her marriage to Manfred. But when she hears that he does so, she demands to know, "can a father enjoin a cursed act? I was contracted to the son; can I wed the father?—No, madam, no; force should not drag me to Manfred's hated bed" (91). Walpole mingles contractual and natural vocabularies by implying that Isabella refuses, at once, the illegal violation of contract and the unnatural incestuousness of the proposal. Isabella's dissent finds its male counterpart in Theodore's, whose father has commanded him not to interfere further with Manfred's desires. The text explicitly describes his resistance as parallel to Isabella's and as compelled from within: "like Isabella, [Theodore] was too recently acquainted with parental authority to submit to its decisions against the impulse of his heart" (93).

The dissent and finally the marriage of Theodore and Isabella put in place the ancient-yet-new, racial-yet-contractual order. Theodore represents the rightful, ruling race, and his marriage to the dissenting Isabella heralds the new order of the kingdom, substituting for his foreclosed alliance with his true love, Matilda, who has been killed and symbolically ruined in the struggle—by her own father Manfred, who mistakenly (and suggestively) runs a sword through her chest. Theodore and Isabella emerge as the brave modern couple, willing to dissent, although their race-restoring partnership entails the death of a daughter and (for Isabella) symbolic sister. This death falls into that pattern, reaching back to Lucretia and revived in Clarissa's story, by which a woman's ruinous death cleanses history and restores the rightful, more republican order. As in future gothic novels, the figure of a submissive "Matilda" justifies and makes possible the resolution of gothic plots—the daughter/sister-sacrifice catalyzing the gothic's sublime turn into recuperative containment. The question of the woman's dissent and desire raised by Behn and Haywood continues to trouble the modern and "true" racial polis, and gothic plots thus labor at once to represent it and to suppress it—to manage it.

Quaint as Walpole's text appears, it thus tells a modern tale. Its combination of past and present—its projecting of modernity's racial liberty plots onto an ancient scene — is not merely naive nor charming nor merely incidental to the power of the gothic. This combination is shrewd and essential. It installs a sense of progress away from the naive and violent past even as it allows the imaginary fashioning of this past so as to carry its "inheritors" into a "free" future.

The Sister's Discipline and Punishment in *The Monk*

Walpole's tale puts in place some key elements of gothic plots: it allegorizes the historical transformation of the racial order, required by the tyrant-father's aim to violate and realized by the children's act of dissent. Matthew G. Lewis's *The Monk* takes up this story and in addition locates it within a colonial, Atlantic horizon, expressing anxiety about the freeing dissent that this geographical scope makes possible (perhaps anticipating Lewis's own experiences as a colonial plantation owner).[14]

Via two brother/sister pairs and a complicated double plot, Lewis narrates good and bad versions of the liberty quest. Atlantic travel catalyzes the catastrophes of both of these stories, most directly in the "bad" liberty quests of Ambrosio and Matilda, which cause Ambrosio's horrific ruin and the murder of his sister Antonia, but also indirectly in the "good" liberty quests of Raymond and Agnes (the latter of whom is sister to Lorenzo, the lover of Antonia). In Lewis's highly sexualized but conservative vision, which makes a horrifying spectacle of women's power, Atlantic conditions spawn both a salacious will to liberty and (echoing Milton) a deracinated satanic subjectivity. He implies that the proper order can be reinstalled only when women's desire is disciplined.

It is the nobleman Lorenzo's love of the dowryless Antonia that brings into view the colonial origins of the novel's race-troubled, sexual plot. For when Lorenzo presents his wish to marry Antonia (despite her lack of dowry) and describes his expectation that, if his father disinherits him, they can simply "quit Spain" and emigrate to his estate in the colonies, Antonia's mother Elvira relates the story of her own colonial ruin by way of such a marriage. She and her husband had married under similar conditions and had themselves emigrated to Cuba, but this removal ended in disaster: the death by disease of her husband and some of her children, the loss of a son who went away (who turns out to be the corrupt Ambrosio), and Antonia's lack of dowry and proper home. Closing her story of Atlantic ruin, Elvira hands Lorenzo a copy of the poem her husband Gonzalvo wrote on their voyage to Cuba, an expression of classically nativist sentiments. Opening with "FAREWELL, oh native Spain!" the ballad-like poem records Gonzalvo's sudden surge of sorrow as he parts from his homeland and simple "honest" self, and it foreshadows his future losses. Tellingly, Gonzalvo more vividly visualizes the

Spanish "interior" homeland the farther the ship travels and the more indistinct the Spanish shores become: he imagines a "happy swain" in the mountains of Spain whose food is supplied by "native fields" and whose "cottage" holds friends who make him an "honest welcome" in "native accents." Then he bids this world and "all I love, adieu" (despite his wife Elvira's companionship) and anticipates not only the ravages of Indian diseases and animals but also the sense of a lost native past and identity. His ballad ends on a note of keen nostalgia:

> Ah me! How oft will fancy's spells, in slumber,
> Recall my native country to my mind!
> . . . .
> Wild Murcia's vales and loved romantic bowers,
>
> The rivers on whose banks a child I played,
> My castle's antient halls, its frowning towers,
> Each much-regretted wood, and well-known glade;
>
> Dreams of the land where all my wishes centre,
> Thy scenes, which I am doomed no more to know,
> Full oft shall memory trace, my soul's tormentor,
> And turn each pleasure past to present woe.[15]

In the echo of Shakespeare's Sonnet 30 in the last line, Lewis gives us a glimpse of the way he imports "native" authors into this Spanish colonial story to heighten its effects for his English-language readers.[16] As implied by this allusion, in marrying down and sailing away to a colony, Lorenzo would apparently give up his native self, his landed identity — although in fact the text (Monk Lewis's) is helping to fabricate this very nativeness that it depicts as being lost. Significantly, a literary document conveys this nativist lesson.

The trope of displacement from a native home recurs as a catalyst (and plot device) throughout *The Monk*: in the gypsy woman who warns Antonia; in the Wandering Jew who guides Raymond; in the removal of Agnes to Germany, where she begins her series of imprisonment trials; and in the figure of the sleepless and wandering "Bleeding Nun" who comes between Agnes and Raymond. While some of these travels and travelers have good effects (the gypsy and the Jew genuinely offer help from their vantage point as outsiders), the literal wounds and the mournful "wandering" of these symbolic characters express the harm and pain of deracination in this new order of things. Fittingly, the nobleman Raymond sets out to travel in the guise of a merchant so as to widen his knowledge of the world, but this class mask (and difference) must be removed before the noble Agnes can marry him.

At the same time, transatlantic travel, specifically, gives rise to the story of the evil Matilda and Ambrosio. Ambrosio turns out to be Elvira's long-lost son and Antonia's brother, who wandered off from Cuba and became an ambitious Catholic monk in Spain (a portrait which would itself reinforce the anti-Catholic nativism of English-Protestant readers). Ultimately, under the influence of the depraved Matilda, Ambrosio causes the death of his sister Antonia while attempting to rape her, only realizing that she is his long-lost sister as she perishes. This geographically wayward son has become morally wayward.[17] The parents' departure from a native land in pursuit of freedom to marry as they wish has caused their children's sexual ruin as well. Lewis suggests that the apparent escape hatch of the colonies weakens the social order at home, both loosening native bonds and encouraging ruinous sexual agency for both men and women.

Ambrosio's relationship with Matilda is also quite pointedly infected by colonial influences. We are first alerted to the sexual transgressiveness of this story by Matilda's cross-dressing, which allows her entry as a young novitiate into the monastery where Father Ambrosio resides. Dressed as the male Rosario, Matilda seeks Ambrosio's company "with attentive assiduity," while Ambrosio "on his side did not feel less attracted towards the youth[. . . .] no voice sounded so sweet to him as did Rosario's" (67). They quickly develop a friendship with homoerotic overtones.[18] Although Rosario soon reveals herself to be a woman named Matilda (and another young woman gone astray from home), and thus the homoerotic threat fades, the gender trouble continues, for not only does this monk remain sexually entranced by Matilda but she also unsettles Ambrosio's masculinity in another way — by being more "masculine" than he. In his words, she proves most "unfeminine" (234) and indeed makes Ambrosio feel most unmasculine when he "finds himself unable to cope with her in argument; and was unwillingly obliged to confess the superiority of her judgment" (233). He "regretted Rosario, the fond, the gentle, and the submissive; he grieved that Matilda preferred the virtues of his sex to those of her own" (234). For her part, Matilda comes to see Ambrosio as weak — describing his mind as "feeble, puerile, and grovelling, a slave to vulgar errors, and weaker than a woman's" (266). Matilda's and Ambrosio's final crimes are murder and rape, but they arrive at them by way of an illicit and unnatural sexuality.

And by way of a sexual crisis catalyzed by poisonous colonial powers. At the very moment when it seems that Ambrosio might escape Matilda's influence over him, his colonial connections to Cuba symbolically return and give her the final bodily entry point she needs. In the scene in which he persuades Matilda to leave the monastery, she agrees but requests a token of Ambrosio's affection. He picks a rose for her, unaware that coiled within it is "a cientipedro," a poisonous "serpent," which stings him. Lewis appends a footnote explaining that the spider "is supposed to be a native of Cuba, and to have been brought into Spain from that island in the vessel of Columbus" (93). Bitten by this Cuban serpent (symbolically, like his father), Ambrosio becomes deathly ill and swoons — until Matilda sucks the blood from his wound, curing him. This act in turn makes her ill, so that the two surrender to their passion while she is apparently on her deathbed, and then Matilda introduces Ambrosio to her witchcraft so that he may help to save her life. All their other sexual and murderous deeds follow from this bite. In effect, Matilda draws a poisonous, satanic power from Cuban sources that weakens men and foments social chaos.

Lewis thus creates his own version of Milton's story of an Atlantic fall by way of a seductive and satanic "serpent." Ambrosio enters modernity and ultimately ruins his sister via the sting of an ambitious, insatiable woman helped to her ends by satanic, Cuban powers. Given that Cuba is also the place to which Ambrosio's father had emigrated, displaced from his native identity and disrupting his family and inheritance, Lewis implies that coloniality is the original sin in this family's history, a coloniality furthermore fostered by wayward sexual relations with women in both cases. And, as we'll see, after Ambrosio makes a "contract" with the devil for "liberty" from the Inquisition prison, he meets his final demise in South America.

Within the frame of this transatlantic tale of liberty and ruin, Lewis unfolds the story of Agnes (the sister of Antonia's lover, Lorenzo) and her relations with *her* beloved, Raymond. This plot narrates the *reform* of depraved liberty, and the reform is achieved specifically by way of the German legacy of the once-lustful Bleeding Nun, a wandering ghost who turns out to be a native ancestor of Raymond's and who only he can finally put to rest. Tellingly, in the wake of Agnes's sexual tryst with him and by way of her subsequent imprisonment and live burial, Raymond settles the ancestral sexual trouble embodied in the Nun at the same time that Agnes learns to discipline her own errant sexuality.

Agnes herself introduces the tale of the Bleeding Nun, which implicitly unfolds the symbolic genealogy of Agnes's own story. Just after the scene in which Raymond reveals his love for Agnes to her guardian (the Baroness von Lindenberg), and unintentionally provokes the Baroness's jealous wrath, he discovers Agnes drawing a picture of the Bleeding Nun, a tableau-moment that closely juxtaposes three women who suffer the ill effects of their sexual desires — Agnes, the Nun, and the Baroness. At this point Agnes knows only that this nun who is supposed to haunt the Baroness's castle is "a female of more than human stature" who carries a lamp and a dagger, bleeds from a wound in her chest, and terrifies the castle every fifth year on the fifth of May.

What we later learn is that this larger-than-life dead woman who haunts the German castle was, like Agnes, a woman committed at a young age to a nunnery who, however, no sooner discovered "her warm and voluptuous nature" than she "abandoned herself freely to the impulse of her passions" (182). She fled her convent in Spain and traveled to Germany with the then Baron von Lindenberg as his mistress. There she entered a second sexual liaison, with the Baron's younger brother, and together they plotted to murder the Baron, a plot that the narrator of this story (fittingly, the Wandering Jew) tells us she was especially drawn to because he promised to marry her, which the Baron had refused to do (183). A hint of this woman's vulnerability surfaces here, in her need for the security of marriage, although mostly the account emphasizes her "imprudent and abandoned conduct" as not only a "prostitute" but a declared "atheist" (182). Once she kills the Baron in his sleep at the behest of his brother, however, this brother-lover kills her and inherits the barony of Lindenberg, which is exactly what he had "worked up [her passion] to the desired pitch" to bring about. In this story, the "fugitive nun" is guilty of lust, greed, and atheism, but she is also betrayed by these same traits in a man. Her very passion is "worked up" in the plot as the vehicle of property.

Agnes's story parallels the Nun's, for she is destined by her dead and superstitious mother's edict to remain in the convent world in which she has been educated and which, as a good girl, she aims to obey.[19] We learn, however, that, like the Nun, Antonia harbors sexual desire, for she confesses that she early discovered through "a secret instinct" that "she was not born for solitude," and she displays the "freedom of youth and gaiety" by lightly ridiculing some of the convent practices (145) — although she plans to be virtuous. When Raymond tries to persuade her to elope with him, she rejects this as undutiful, and she advises that instead he strive "to gain the affections of those who govern me," but this backfires when instead he attracts the passion of Agnes's guardian, the current Baroness von Lindenberg — who is another lustful woman. Instead of freeing Agnes, the Baroness jealously keeps her "a close prisoner in her chamber" (155) and then returns her to the convent in Spain. Raymond follows Agnes to the convent and in a weak moment she makes love to him, eventually becoming pregnant and being imprisoned by this convent's Domina for her sin. Thus are set in motion the events by which Agnes "shall be restored to liberty" (157).

But the Nun's story is more than a foreshadowing of Agnes's. Most important for the Saxonist coding of Lewis's novel, it turns out that Raymond is actually the one remaining descendant of this nun who haunts the Baroness's German castle. Agnes is in effect caught up in the property plots and ancient wanderings of her Germanic (and implicitly Goth-Spanish)[20] lover, who needs to put to rest this legacy of lustful women. After Raymond's forced separation from Agnes, the Bleeding Nun continues to stalk and haunt him, leaving him utterly overcome and confused — indeed, in a sickened swoon state — until the Wandering Jew explains that he must gather and bury the Nun's (lustful) bones to free himself. Insofar as it turns out that Raymond must lay to rest the bones of a passionate nun before he can save Agnes (or is it the legacy of Aphra Behn and her seminal stories about lustful young nuns, which *Lewis* must put to rest?), the implication is that he and Agnes must construct a chastened Agnes to settle the violent, sexually propelled past and initiate the new kinder, gentler patriarchal order of consenting wives which Agnes will enter.

In initially telling the Nun's story to Raymond and calling herself the "unworthy historian" of the woman's story, Agnes also implicitly offers a metafiction of women's muffled presence in history. She notes that "in all the chronicles of past times this remarkable personage is never once mentioned"; indeed, before her violent demise "she was never known to have existed" (152). This woman enters chronicle only through the story of her betrayal and death, which is thought to have occurred "about a century ago" — about the time that the first seduction novel was written — and since then she has been "shut up" in a room in the castle. While at first this mythical figure showed herself to be "a mighty capricious being" who alternately "howled out the most horrible blasphemies, and then chaunted De profundis" (153) — a regular Moll Flanders — after some time she was made "much more tractable and well-behaved" by an exorcist, for "[s]he was obstinate, but he was more so" (153). In effect, Agnes's story is an allegory of English-language fiction's progress, an unconscious genealogy of women's initially outrageous but slowly tamed presence in the first century of the novel.[21]

Certainly, within Lewis's novel, written in the wake of Richardson's *Clarissa,* the chastening of the heroine is nearly deadly, and it involves a series of swoons narrated in and ultimately redeemed by the language of liberty. In the cruel hands of the domina, Agnes faces increasingly extreme forms of debasement including the forced death of her baby, her own starvation, and a live burial in a crypt of corpses — a symbolic outline of the forms of self-loss that women may suffer in entering this modern form of patriarchy, which echoes what we have seen in *Oroonoko, Clarissa,* and *Charlotte Temple.* Having fainted from the poison administered by the domina's minions (which is actually a sleeping draught, as in the story of her mirror victim in the other liberty narrative, Antonia), Agnes apparently "expire[s] in horror of the past, in fears for the future" (342). But some time later she awakens and finds herself in a locked burial vault "surrounded by the loathsome and mouldering bodies of my companions" — recently dead nuns here but symbolically her sisters in patriarchy — at which point she "despaired of liberty" (386). The domina arrives to tell her that she will descend yet lower and yet further from freedom: "beneath these vaults there exist prisons, intended to receive such criminals as yourself: artfully is their entrance concealed, and she who enters must resign all hopes of liberty" (389).

If we read this warning as a reminder for all women entering the new racial modernity, the domina's comments on appetite are particularly telling: "Food shall be supplied you, but not sufficient for the indulgence of appetite." In response Agnes again "falls senseless" and awakens to find herself in "silence and solitude" attached by a heavy chain to the wall of her prison cell. In this state she "only expected liberty when she [liberty] came [as] the companion of death" (392). Agnes's occasional attendants again urge her to "resign all hopes of liberty" (394). Instead, however, the domina herself is exposed and punished, and a mob burns her convent to the ground. As the convent flames and the still-incarcerated Agnes hears her brother Lorenzo approach amid the burning timbers, she cries out: "Come you to save me, to restore me to liberty, to life and light?" and Lorenzo replies "Be calm! . . . A few minutes will restore you to liberty and the embraces of your friends, from whom you have been secluded" (358). Agnes is thus freed from the fires of passion.

And her liberation leaves her a submissive and yet circumlocutious heroine in the tradition of Fantomina. Returned home and nurtured to health along with her languishing lover Raymond (himself recovering from his encounter with the Bleeding Nun), Agnes tells her tale to him and a circle of friends including her brother Lorenzo. Told to this finally gathered community, her narrative encapsulates the phoenixlike rebirth of the once-conquered yet now-reborn and wealthy race. Yet it also highlights the abruptness of her turn in fortune, creating a sense of the adjacency of captivity, isolation, and living death with "liberty, . . . affluence and ease" — conjuring the incommensurable realities, in short, of the Atlantic world. Meanwhile, as narrator, Agnes herself oddly combines authority and self-subordination. In framing her tale, she appeals to Raymond to

> teach me to bear with fortitude this sudden transition from misery to bliss. So lately a captive, oppressed with chains, perishing with hunger, suffering every inconvenience of cold and want, hidden from the light, excluded from society, hopeless, neglected, and, as I feared, forgotten: now restored to life and liberty, enjoying all the comforts of affluence and ease, surrounded by those who are most loved by me, and on the point of becoming his bride who has long been wedded to my heart, my happiness is so exquisite, so perfect, that scarcely can my brain sustain the weight. (397)

Thus does Agnes's freedom arrive so close on the heels of captivity that it leaves her reeling, a disoriented Atlantic subject.

And, apparently, a submissive one — except that the gender threat that began all the trouble still circulates, in her syntax. The woman's claim to agency at once hides and appears when she admonishes Raymond for seducing her:

> But let not my husband, because he once conquered my virtue, doubt the propriety of my future conduct. I have been frail and full of error: but I yielded not to the warmth of constitution. Raymond, affection for you betrayed me. I was too confident of my strength: but I depended no less on your honour than my own. . . . Still my conduct has been highly blameable. . . . Let me then dismiss the ungrateful subject; first assuring you, Raymond, that you shall have no cause to repent our union, and that, the more culpable have been the errors of your mistress, the more exemplary shall be the conduct of your wife. (397–98)

What a rich and troubled speech. She suggests that Raymond actively conquered her virtue and his honor failed as much as hers to protect them, but it is *her* future conduct that she reassures him about. She calls him to acknowledge her "dependence" on his honor and yet she takes responsibility for her fall ("my conduct has been highly blameable"). And yet, in taking on blame, she also claims the agency expressed in "conduct." In this light we can notice that the whole speech is given as a set of commands ("Let not my husband," "Let me then dismiss") and pivots at every turn on verbs of agency that are, however, qualified by negatives: "let not," "yielded not," "depended no less," "shall have no cause." These phrases at once assume command and negate that control. Although the spirit of the passage is indeed to register Raymond's power over her ("your mistress . . . your wife"), at the purely syntactic level Agnes ambiguously claims power. Indeed, we never do hear Raymond speak directly in this scene.

And yet, Raymond doesn't need to command Agnes, since Agnes is *consenting* to be his subordinate, although she does so actively. In short, Agnes has become a Rousseauian subject, freely denying herself free subjectivity. The taming of desire and the trauma of living death and exile that have conditioned this free "choice" are veiled by the appearance that their "union" is a fair and free contract in which she agrees to trade: "assuring you, Raymond, that you shall have no cause to repent our union, and that, the more culpable have been the errors of your mistress, the more exemplary shall be the conduct of your wife." Her future desire will be repressed in exact proportion to its earlier expression. Her story serves as an object lesson for women who might indulge desire and stray from the good, domesticated liberty path — and for communities whose involvement in colonial emigration might poison their sexuality, loosen their hold on women, and threaten the future of the race.

It is therefore fitting that, just after her speech, in the closing passage of the chapter, we learn that "now Agnes was at liberty to pursue her favourite plan," which is to encourage the marriage of her brother Lorenzo to a young woman (aptly) named Virginia. As with Theodore and Isabella in *The Castle of Otranto*, for Lorenzo and Virginia to marry would be a compromise for both, since Lorenzo's first love was the dead Antonia — but now, for Agnes, it is the "only wish [that] remains ungratified" (397). As she says, once "Antonia's memory is buried in her grave [. . . .] I have nothing more to desire" (397). She says more than she knows, for indeed the death of Antonia embodies the "end" of women's desire in this conservative liberty narrative.

Against the triumph of Agnes's salutary if traumatic entry into liberty, Monk Lewis closes his novel with a spectacle of the final transatlantic horror that results from a lustful woman's quest for liberty. The satanic associations attaching to such a woman and to diseased colonial places are explicitly figured in the final "contract" that Ambrosio and Matilda make with the devil for their liberty (419). As in the closing of the Raymond/Agnes plot, the trope of liberty as telos is unmistakable in this sequence. Having been imprisoned for their witchcraft and for Ambrosio's violation of Antonia, both seek ways to escape their dungeons. As Ambrosio is losing hope and thinking of seeking repentance, Matilda magically appears in his cell to announce that she has "sacrificed all for life and liberty" (408), having made a deal with Satan for the promise of "bliss and liberty" (413). Although Matilda confesses that she did "purchase my liberty at a dear, at a dreadful price," she exults "I am free" (407) and describes herself as "impatient to exercise my newly-gained dominion. I pant to be at liberty" (408). She departs with scorn at his feminine weakness for hesitating to make his own deal with the devil, and, shamed by her, he soon thereafter signs his own satanic contract (419).

This liberty that apparently leads to "dominion" under the sign of a contract in fact leads back to the colonial ruin from which Ambrosio originally issued. The moment he signs his contract with the devil, he is supernaturally transported across the Atlantic to South America, the land that had extended Spanish dominion — but which now faces Ambrosio with a deadly sublime he cannot transcend. Having answered "I do! I do!" to the devil's question, "Do you freely and absolutely renounce your creator and his Son?" Ambrosio suddenly finds himself hanging over "a precipice's brink, the steepest in Sierra Morena" (417). This gothic American scene is complete with "gloomy caverns and steep rocks, rising above each other and dividing the passing clouds" and "the stunning roar of torrents"

(417). Feeling "as yet [. . .] insensible of the blessing of liberty," he demands to be carried to Matilda, but the Daemon tells him that "nothing can restore to you the rights which you have foolishly resigned," that nothing can now "make void our contract," and that he, Satan, in the form of a monstrous daemon, now burns "to possess my right" to send him to his hellish death (417).

Thus may the contract with liberty via Atlantic transport mean a loss of rights to more fiendish forces of possession. And so "darting his talon's into the monk's shaven crown," the Daemon lifts Ambrosio out over the precipice and drops him. He awakens "bruised and mangled" but alive, only to be gouged by birds of prey and insects for days. His earlier "American" bite is recalled in the "[m]yriads of insects" which, as he lays dying at the bottom of this precipice, "fastened upon his sores, darted their stings into his body, covered him with their multitudes, and inflicted on him tortures the most exquisite and insupportable" (420). The self-loss entailed in this transportation to a realm of liberty is also prefigured in the earlier scene, for there too the "wound became so exquisite, that nature was unable to bear it: his senses abandoned him, and he sunk inanimate into Matilda's arms" (92). In the later scene, on the seventh day, in the reverse of creation, a storm drowns him. We are led to assume that Matilda, the lustful man-woman, has suffered a similar colonial fate.

IN THE MONK, Atlantic travel and its accompanying sexual transgression and ambition poison the native Anglo-European. The colonial Atlantic here represents both the breakup of class-based kin structures and the unleashing of female desire, which together spawn the machinations of corrupt brothers. Although all these effects are presumably counteracted by the marriage of women like Agnes who seek proper liberty—that is, the power to give up agency freely—in the process women such as the obedient and pure Antonia will die, by the hand of their very own brothers, who, like Manfred in *Otranto*, plunges a dagger into the breast of his female kin in a fit of sexual desire and social ambition.

This tableau-figure of a dagger in the breast—which also circulates through Lewis's text in the form of the Bleeding Nun—will be conjured repeatedly in gothic fiction, including quite centrally, as we will see in the next chapter, in Charles Brockden Brown's *Wieland*. While such scenes make graphic the bodily violation of Anglo-Atlantic sisters within modernity, they also register, faintly and unconsciously, the effaced ruin of African-Atlantic and Indian-Atlantic persons.

9 | Saxon Dissociation in Brockden Brown

ON THE AMERICAN SIDE of the Atlantic, under the pressures of disavowal, the Anglo-gothic story implodes in Charles Brockden Brown's novel *Wieland* (1798). It is as if Brown set out to encode the whole Anglo-Saxon discourse and register its violent effects, for he offers an eerily precise and apocalyptic allegory of Anglo-Atlantic history, without, however, fully naming its colonial investments. He begins his transatlantic, multigenerational story with a man named Wieland in Germany (named after the influential German poet) who falls from nobility but rediscovers an ancient Saxon literary legacy. The tale then extends through a second-generation son's apprenticed poverty and religious persecution in England, which sends him as a missionary to America. And it culminates in a series of deadly catastrophes, at first apparently removed from colonial violence but finally entangled in it by way of the murderous standoff between the third-generation, republican brother and sister — which is provoked by their probing of the Saxonist-literary legacy. Although some critics have referred in passing to its underlying narrative of European immigration and colonization, and others have noticed its historically allegorical elements, none have taken the full measure of its Saxonist thrust.[1] One or two readers have looked to the "Mohock" voice that Carwin first imitates as a child (as recounted in Brown's *Memoirs of Carwin*) as a key to *Wieland*'s colonial allegory, but only within the larger nativist frame of the novel do such details take on their full significance.[2]

While in *The Monk* the will to possession compels obsessive, flagrantly transgressive action, in Brown's transatlantic, Anglo-Saxonist world those who "possess" merely rationalize, equivocate, and dissociate — until they self-destruct.[3] That is, by way of thought, they distance themselves from the violence on which their colonial comfort and free-thinking conversation rest. Whether consciously or unconsciously, *Wieland* portrays an Atlantic Anglo-Saxon intellectual citizenry that cultivates rational community, accrues property, and performs racial poetry in the midst of genocide, slavery, and war. Yet this propertied world, however rationally theorized by Ireton, Locke, or Smith, establishes itself under the myth of an ancient inheritance whose fictions of gothic violence become, in the end, quite real. The disavowed violence of the republic — symbolized in Carwin's fork-tongued ventriloquism and in the displacement of race battles onto an ancient Saxon manuscript — returns here in the deadly struggle between a free-thinking brother and sister, in a violence that erupts with*in* the (national) family.[4] And thus, in *Wieland,* under a bust of Cicero and on a stage set for the performance of "the first attempt of a Saxon poet" versifying in "wild numbers" a series of "audacious acts, and unheard of disasters," the free, propertied, Anglo-republican self implodes.[5]

Dissociated States

Clara Wieland, the sister in the brother-sister pair at the center of this novel, speaks the Wieland family's violent story like a female ancient mariner, alive yet deadened in the wake of her swoon, the blank-eyed, guilty survivor intoning a horrific tale. Clara wonders, "That I, beyond the rest of mankind, should be reserved for a destiny without alleviation, and without example! Listen to my narrative, and then say what it is that has made me deserve to be placed on this dreadful eminence, if, indeed, every faculty be not suspended in wonder that I am still alive, and am able to relate it" (6). Like Richardson's Clarissa, Clara too had begun as a paragon, "a model worthy of assiduous study" who embodied "the sublimities of rectitude and the illuminations of genius" (133) in both the "felicities of [her] expression" and "the solidity" of "[her] principles" (139). And like the narrator in Behn's *Oroonoko*, this female narrator tells a story about race and murder under colonial conditions which pivots on her own threatened ruin. In putting the story utterly in Clara's hands, we can see Brockden Brown reworking and reflecting on the genre of the novel as it is organized around these sacrificial yet liberty-championing female figures. Accordingly, he arranges it so that a preoccupation with Saxon inheritance provides the entry point for the biloquist-seducer Carwin who will test and sacrifice the free Anglo-Saxon woman and provoke her dissociated voicing.

Brown hints that Clara's story is the nation's as well as her own. Early in the novel, Clara and her brother discuss whether "the picture of a single family [could offer] a model from which to sketch the condition of a nation" (34). If the novel is Brown's sketch of a nation by way of the Wieland family, the nation is in trouble. Not only the brother's murder of his wife and children and his subsequent attacks on Clara but also Clara's account of her "state" as storyteller conjures a traumatic national history that involves "extermination" and threatens "futurity":

> My state is not destitute of tranquility. The sentiment that dictates my feeling is not hope. Futurity has no power over my thoughts. To all that is to come I am perfectly indifferent. With regard to myself, I have nothing more to fear. Fate has done its worst. Henceforth, I am callous to misfortune. I address no supplication to the Deity. The power that governs the course of human affairs has chosen his path. The decree that ascertained the condition of my life, admits of no recall. . . . The storm that tore up our happiness . . . is lulled into grim repose; but not until the victim was transfixed and mangled; till every obstacle was dissipated by its rage; till every remnant of good was wrestled from our grasp and exterminated. (5 – 6)

Only by way of a dissociation equal to Clara's could Brown use the word "exterminated"—and readers in 1798 read it — without being reminded of Native Americans. Since the sixteenth century, the word "exterminate" had denoted the fate of "a people" who were either banished or destroyed (OED), but in North America in the late eighteenth century it would have been most directly and immediately associated with American Indians. As the British observer John Smyth reported in 1784, "nothing is more common than to hear [white Americans] talk of extirpating [the whole race of Indians] totally from the face of the earth, men, women, and children."[6] The sentiment found enactment in national policy during the years Brown was writing the novel, as President George Washington, under pressure from embattled frontier spokespersons, explicitly ordered General John Sullivan to complete "the total destruction and devastation of [Iroquois] settlements."[7] Nor was this an isolated mission. Settler warfare against Indians was of course an established pattern by this time, but it had been exacerbated in the middle of the century by French and then British alliances with Indians against settlers and, most recently, by the mass westward movement of settlers, including veterans of the Revolutionary War who had been paid in grants of land that were sometimes still claimed by tribes. Thus from 1790 to 1796, five-sixths of the federal budget was devoted to war against American Indians on the frontier.[8]

Clara's use of the word "exterminated" makes no direct reference to this history. The very vagueness of its ostensible referent ("every remnant of good") suggests that more is being told here than a woman's or a family's story, while this vagueness also manages to depersonify the exterminating agent — in the form of the "storm" that exterminates — and to make anonymous the figure of the storm's "victim." Likewise, the negatives in these opening sentences obfuscate as much as they divulge, recalling the negatives and circlings in the postrape speeches of Fantomina and Clarissa. How to understand the phrase "not destitute of tranquility"? How *much* tranquility is left to her? Likewise, if it is "not hope," what *is* the sentiment that "dictates" her feeling? Reading carefully, we find that the paragraph's powerful declarations lack content. We learn nothing specific; we learn only what is not. Like the novel's, Clara's state is one of dissociation. The negatives *are* her "state."

Clara's troubled style may well mirror Brown's own double movement of exposure and denial of the exterminations that darken America's past and future. Like the Anglo-Protestant nation, both Clara and Brown have survived "the storm" — in fact, they have found their haunted voices within the storm — but they speak dissociatively and the victims are "removed" from the tale. Clara hints at this implication in one astonishing passage of her narrative. As she recalls her small, free-thinking community's contentment before their tragedy, she notices the distant, enabling conditions for their situation, only to subordinate them: "Six years of happiness had rolled away, since my brother's marriage. The sound of war had been heard, but it was at such a distance as to enhance our enjoyment by affording objects of comparison. The Indians were repulsed on the one side, and Canada was conquered on the other. Revolutions and battles, however calamitous to those who occupied the scene, contributed in some sort to our happiness, by agitating our minds with curiosity, and furnishing cause of patriotic exultation" (29). With an indifference as striking as that of the Holmeses in William Hill Brown's *The Power of Sympathy,* Clara explains that others' calamities contribute to the happiness of those far removed from them. She makes no connection between these calamities and the violence that finally mangles her family, and Brockden Brown himself does so only by this passing mention.[9] Clara embodies the nation's — and the novel's — dissociations in this blanking-out of her relation to the nation's exterminations. While Brown's fiction does not seem after all to realize his intention, as expressed in his preface to *Edgar Huntly,* to fashion a national literature by replacing the "gothic castles and chimeras" of European literature with American scenes and "incidents of Indian hostility," it may well be that the destruction of the Wieland family stands in the place of such incidents.[10]

In fact, in his own dissociative way, Brockden Brown includes two catalysts for this catastrophic plot that *do* link it to the larger social surround of racialized hostilities: the Saxon legacy of the Wieland family and the vaguely Jacobin, Irish-affiliated, ventriloquizing wanderer Carwin. Ultimately, Carwin emerges as a figure for the author, specifically as a *performer* of gothic nativism who dramatizes its dissociative and substitutional function in the colonial project of possession. Carwin's ventriloquizing voice exposes the Saxon's violent proclivities — and in recording this violence, as some critics see it, the republican author calls a nation to recognize its fault lines. Yet at the same time, in telling a gothic tale organized around the romance of the Wieland saga, the novel produces the very Saxonist identity it critiques. In ventriloquizing Anglo-Saxonism, Brown becomes a modern Anglo-American author of it.

The Saxon-Atlantic Genealogy

Clara Wieland begins her story with her family's Saxon genealogy, establishing immediately that her paternal grandfather was a "native of Saxony," born of a "noble" house. Hereafter, each detail of the family history contributes to Brown's racial allegory. To establish the logic and reach of this allegory and provide a foundation for interpreting the novel's gender and racial crises, I offer in this section an extended, Saxonist gloss of the novel.

First, in Brown's rendering, the ancient and noble Saxon enters the modern order by way of a "contract" with the growing merchant class — and ultimately, as for Gonzalves in *The Monk,* this class-transgressive alliance (that in effect replaces the old racial order with the modern, "Germanic" one) yields a story of liberty gone bad, expressed in the ruin of his offspring. But that outcome is two generations hence. In the case of this first modern ancestor, we learn from Clara's account that during vacations at his German college he "employed himself in traversing the neighbouring territory" (6). These ramblings — themselves an element of the modern order of university education he has entered — lead him on one occasion to the city of Hamburg, where he becomes friends with "a merchant of that city." He "speedily contract[s] an affection" for the merchant's daughter and, "in spite of parental menaces and prohibitions," marries her. Hereafter, his noble family treats him as "an absolute stranger," thrusting him forward into modernity.

But as a result, this grandfather discovers his native roots and becomes a translator of ancient Saxon texts that found a new modern tradition. That is, after finding "asylum" in the house of "his new father, whose temper was kind," he manages to earn a small but "independent subsistence" by recovering "works of taste in the Saxon dialect" and arranging them for theater (7). As Clara explains, "My ancestor may be considered as the founder of German Theatre. The modern poet of the same name is sprung from the same family" (7). The ancient Saxon literary works recovered by the grandfather will later catalyze key plot events in the novel even as they do in modern German culture. Modeling his fictional grandfather on the eighteenth-century German poet Christoff Martin Wieland, who is credited with a role in the "revival" of "German" literature, Brockden Brown creates a novel that recapitulates this literary recovery and itself displays the gothic mode — climaxing on the night that Pleyel, Catharine, Clara, and her brother plan to perform an ancient Saxon text.[11] The independence that the grandfather achieves is temporarily lost in the next generation, however, and leads to migration to England, for both he and his wife die young, leaving their only child to "the protection of the merchant" who soon "apprenticed [him] to a London trader" (8). Now the Saxon becomes an Anglo-Saxon, but soon, like the Anglo-Saxons under the Normans, he finds himself oppressed by a tyrant. The London trader turns out to be a "master" of extreme "sternness" who gives him "coarse food," "humble lodging," "sufficient occasions for discontent," and "no opportunities of recreation." He spends all his free time either "pent up in a gloomy apartment" or "traversing narrow and crowded streets" (8). He paces his pre-revolutionary Anglo-Saxon prison-house. Thus "his heart gradually contracted a habit of morose and gloomy reflection" — like that which many attributed to the English (8). This second-generation Wieland has become the alienated yet Anglo-Saxonized citizen, isolated and discontented in an initially oppressive contract with "mercantile service."

But his life takes a transatlantic turn when he undergoes a religious conversion, which eventually leads him to missionary work in America. In characterizing the conversion, Brown continues to piece together an allegory of Anglo-Saxon Protestant subjectivity, freighting his descriptions with suggestive antiquarian and historical details. For Wieland's travel is prompted when one day his "wandering" eyes notice a book that had apparently "lain for years in the corner of his garret, half buried in dust and rubbish" (9). The discovered ancient book gives "an historical account of [the] origin" of the French Protestant dissenting, persecuted, and strict sect of the Camissards which "abounded with allusions to the Bible" (9) — a discovery of true religious origins not unlike those that first drove antiquarian Saxonism and later Puritanism in England. The Camissards, furthermore, attempted active rebellion against the French crown in 1700 but were sorely crushed after four years of fighting — a history resonant with that of religious dissidents in England (Kirkham 87). With his morose heart and in his "bound" condition, Wieland is "in a state peculiarly fitted for the reception of devotional sentiments" and he finds that "the craving which haunted him was now supplied with an object" (9). His "progress towards the formation of his creed [is] rapid" and it raises for him "a thousand scruples" so that he is "alternately agitated by fear and ecstasy" (9). Like a goodly, fretting Puritan he imagines himself "beset by the snares of a spiritual foe, and that his security lay in ceaseless watchfulness and prayer" (10).

This second-generation Wieland thus enters the modern discipline of the body and the project of self-surveillance and conversion work within an Anglo-Saxon Protestant order of things, and this project leads him to a Miltonian rise and fall in America, as Timothy Gilmore argues.[12] What Clara calls his "empire" of religious duty not only "extended itself to his looks, gestures, and phrases. All levities of speech, and negligences of behavior, were proscribed" (10). It also involves him in the emerging Atlantic empire. As with the first religious settlers, Wieland's removal to Pennsylvania is both an exile and an ambition: "[r]esidence in England had . . . become almost impossible, on account of his religious tenets" and "in addition to these motives for seeking a new habitation, there was another of the most imperious and irresistible necessity. He had imbibed an opinion that it was his duty to disseminate the truths of the gospel among the unbelieving nations" (10). Disciplinary empire over the self extends to an "imperious" impulse to incorporate others into that selfsame set of beliefs.

This Saxonist history of downward mobility, religious conversion, and Atlantic missionary work turns out, however, to lead to prosperity. Clara mentions in passing that her father's pilgrimage also enriched him: "the cheapness of the land, and the service of African slaves, which were then in general use gave him who was poor in Europe all the advantages of wealth" (11). Before long, he was able to "dispense with personal labour" (12). Meanwhile, regarding his missionary work, although "the North-American Indians naturally presented themselves as the first objects for this species of benevolence," "a nearer survey of savage manners once more shook his resolution" and "he relinquished his purpose" (11). Once the father is free of personal labor and settled with wife and children, "his ancient belief relative to the conversion of the savage tribes, was revived with uncommon energy," despite the pleading of his wife and family. Yet again he finds that his exhortations were "repelled with insult and derision" and finally "the license of savage passion, and the artifices of his depraved countrymen, all opposed themselves to his progress" (12). Clara suggests that the Saxon's true progress is impeded by those whose savage and depraved natures lack ancient ground, an early hint that she, too, has inherited the Saxon's attitude — not to mention the landed elite's version of it that also separates her from her "depraved [white] countrymen." Sidestepping this obstacle, however, and implicitly in contrast to this shallow savagery, Wieland, her father, not only settles permanently on his ample land but also builds himself a temple. The temple stands as a dwelling amid the Anglo-American sublime, placed as it is "on top of a rock whose sides were steep, rugged, and encumbered with dwarf cedars and stony asperities" and at the edge of a "Precipice . . . Sixty feet above the river which flowed at its foot" (12). Fully returning to his Saxon brooding tendencies, he becomes a recluse, visiting the temple to pray twice a day "unaccompanied by any human being" (13).

Here is the history of American colonization in a nutshell, a history into which Wieland has been led by the original illicit marriage of his father, which broke noble patriarchal rules yet led his ancestor into an antiquarian recovery of an ancient German past, paralleled by the son's conversion to strict Protestantism, which in turn leads him to emigrate with the aim of extending his disciplinary empire. His conversion efforts fail but his settlement at Mettingen becomes permanent and prosperous — except, as we will see, for a mysterious curse. The curse is a troubling decree issued on this sublime spot, a mysterious "command . . . which he had delayed to perform" (14). We never do learn what this command is, but interestingly it involves his knowledge that "the duty assigned to him was transferred [. . .] to another" — which again suggests that the "ease" of this second-generation Wieland is at issue (14). One night he goes out to pray, and a mysterious explosion occurs; the mother finds him naked, bruised, and fatally scorched. He dies, and the mother herself dies shortly thereafter of anguish, so that Clara and her brother are left orphans.[13]

At one level, and in light of the fact that Clara's brother much later begins to replicate the father's moody behavior and finally murders his wife and children and attempts to murder Clara, we can sensibly guess that the "duty" the father has avoided was a shocking, Abraham-like family-murder, which is then "transferred" to his son. Much more speculatively, and at a more embedded level hinted at by Clara's dissociative observations about slavery, land-seizure, war, and "calamity" providing the foundation for her community's "happiness," we might consider that the "transference" of duty that finally ruins father, son, and daughter is the project of colonization itself — that is, prospering via others' labor and losses.

The impression that some sort of dissociation lies at the heart of this undisclosed family curse is reinforced in Clara's way of narrating its aftermath. After closing chapter 2 with the macabre death of her father and opening chapter 3 with the news that the "shock" killed her mother, Clara explains, in her tone of detachment: "My brother and myself were children at this time, and were now reduced to the condition of orphans. The property which our parents left us was by no means inconsiderable" (22). Clara's narration is typical not only in its lack of affect but also in its leap from violence and loss to property. The taking of labor and native land "cheaply" prepares this death that leaves the Anglo-Saxon children orphaned, isolated, and traumatized but "by no means" destitute. They profit from the father's explosive death — perhaps a figure for the American Revolution — so that even his death appears as one of those "calamities of others" that benefit them. "Meanwhile," she continues in her flat voice, the tenderness of their maiden aunt "made us in a short time cease to regret that we had lost a mother" (22).

At Mettingen, these children grow up to form their own small, freethinking community of *philosophes,* as critics have noted.[14] On their safely remote estate, they join with two neighbors and another orphaned girl to discuss all manner of topics, including the interrelations of science and religion. Clara's brother retains the "calvinistic" (28) principles of his father, yet at the same time his mind is "enriched by science, and embellished with literature" (26). He is "conversant with the history of religious opinions, and took pains to ascertain their validity. He deemed it indispensable to examine the ground of his belief, to settle the relation between motives, actions, the criterion of merit, and the kinds and properties of evidence" (25–26). He remains, as she says, "in some respects, an enthusiast, but is fortified in his belief by innumerable arguments and subtleties" (40) — a modern Gothic Protestant. Meanwhile their neighbor Henry Pleyel is a "champion of intellectual liberty, [who] rejected all guidance but that of his reason" (28). Likewise for Clara and Henry's sister Catherine, who eventually marries (and is murdered by) Clara's brother, "our education had been modelled by no religious standard. We were left to the guidance of our own understanding" (24). Hereafter, the temple where their father met his end is "no longer assigned to its ancient use" of prayer but instead there "a thousand conversations took place, pregnant with delight and improvement" (26). It is even graced with a bust of Cicero (26).

The nation comes of age together with this insular community, and thus implicitly does Brockden Brown place the activities of bloodshed, repulsion, and conquering that create the nation alongside — in the same chapter, in fact — its citizens' activities of "long and abstruse deductions from the system of divine government and the laws of our intellectual constitution," developed in "innumerable arguments and subtleties" (40). This enlightened, republican community stands on the Gothic and religious foundation of the father. Allegorically understood, the children's sublimation of the rupture, violence, and shock underlying their condition of ease is emblematic of the governing culture's psychological modus operandi and reminiscent of the facile evasions and disjunctive autobiographies of Defoe's protagonists. Narrator and nation both let slavery and prosperity stand side by side under the banner of liberty — equivocally, dissociatively, and strategically, for these two conditions (orphaned and prosperous) are the twin conditions of Anglo-Atlantic modernity. Clara's prominent habit of speaking in negatives ("a prosperity by no means considerable" or "My state is not destitute of tranquillity") makes a grammar of this tendency to equivocate and thereby to stand implicitly on a negation, to possess others in the wake of self-loss.

Carwin's Sexual Calling-Out

Enter Carwin, the "biloquist," the equivocator, the man of two voices. This man whose voice can seem to be generated "at such a distance" from his material body emblematizes the speech of Mettingen's seemingly ideal community of characters, whose rational republicanism develops at such a distance from the physical battles that make it possible. At one level Carwin may embody the threat of radical Jacobin movements to a landed elite, republican or otherwise, as Nigel Leask and Hsuan Hsu have discussed, and as Brown's sequel, *Memoirs of Carwin*, suggests.[15] In the *Memoirs*, Brown affiliates Carwin with the global movement of the Illuminati, notorious as a secret group that fanned the flames of democratic revolt while, however (according to those who feared them), gathering recruits for a hierarchical, colonial "utopia" where women and indigenous people labor for the ruling "revolutionaries." In these ways, as Hsu emphasizes, Carwin biloquism epitomizes the contradictory combination of revolutionary liberation and colonial oppression in Atlantic republics.

But the racial and sexual contradictions exposed by Carwin's biloquism can also be traced without recourse to the Jacobin threat or to the *Memoirs of Carwin*. Within *Wieland*, Carwin's biloquism very pointedly provokes sexual conflicts within a race-family drama, specifically putting pressure on the relations and trust between men and women. Furthermore, in each instance of Carwin's biloquial antics, the men's and women's attachments to cultural Saxonism create the opening for Carwin's deadly manipulation of them, culminating in the crisis that sends Clara into her traumatized narrational state.

The first intrusion of Carwin hints at these connections: it follows on the heels of the community's discussion about whether "the picture of a single family [could offer] a model from which to sketch the condition of a nation" (34); it directly disrupts their subsequent conversation comparing the sublimity of German and American landscapes; and it creates the first small rift between Clara's brother and his wife Catharine, which foreshadows the gender trouble to come. The comparison is prompted by a letter the group has received from their neighbor Louisa Conway's long-lost father, Major Stuart, who, having fought in the Canadian war after serving first in Germany, now has come to America, discovered the whereabouts of his daughter, and plans to visit her.[16] Oddly, however, in the conversation that ensues from the letter, the group does not explore the wonder of this transatlantic reunion of Germanic-American kin after a long separation (which has involved, we later learn, the mother's ruin), but rather — in the kind of displacement to which Brown accustoms us — they debate the exact details of a sublime American waterfall that the major happened to describe in his letter. As Clara recalls it, the letter

> contained a description of a waterfall on the Monongahela. A sudden gust of rain falling, we were compelled to remove to the house. The storm passed away, and radiant moon-light succeeded. There was no motion to resume our seats in the temple. We therefore remained where we were, and engaged in sprightly conversation. The letter lately received naturally suggested the topic. A parallel was drawn between the cataract there described, and one which Pleyel had seen among the Alps of Glarus. In the state of the former, some particular was mentioned, the truth of which was questionable. (34)

They cannot at first locate the letter to confirm the relation between the two classically sublime waterfalls, and in this sense the scene begins with a search for the *text* that will establish a kinship between the Saxon and the American sublime. When Wieland walks out to the temple to recover the text, he hears the mysterious voice that Carwin ventriloquizes in imitation of Wieland's wife, Catharine. Wieland thinks he hears his wife telling him not to go to the temple in search of this text, but of course when he returns he finds that she has not left the room with the others.

Now there appears a slender thread of doubt in the trust between Wieland and his wife, for when she tells him she has not moved from her indoor location, he questions her claim. Asking the others, "Is it true that Catharine did not follow me," he feels compelled to "deny credit" to her statement or "disbelieve the testimony of my senses" (36). He insists, "One thing is true, either I heard my wife's voice at the bottom of the hill, or I do not hear your voice at present" (36). His menacing fixation on the experience sets his sister Clara thinking about "a shadowy resemblance between [this occurrence] and my father's death" and between his increased "gravity" and her father's. Now we begin to better understand Brown's juxtaposition of the story of a mysterious separation via a middle passage of Louisa and her father (with the mother's ruinous removal from home at its center) and this question of whether Catharine is trustworthy in her claims about having stayed home while her man goes to the temple to probe the nature of America's Gothic inheritance. Louisa's mother was betrayed and defamed by a jealous man — and so too will Catharine and ultimately Clara be. This scene begins to outline the way in which Carwin's ventriloquism will provoke doubts about women's honor and agency in relation to the transatlantic question of a Gothic inheritance.

The next intrusion of Carwin's voice again raises the specter of gender disaffection, and here too the wife apparently countermands the husband's pursuit of liberty-bearing, German-Gothic connections. Pleyel has recently returned from a visit to Germany with the news that, as a result of relatives' deaths in the Prussian wars, the Wieland family's "large domains in Lusatia" have descended to the American line of Wielands, prompting Clara (as narrator) to reiterate, "My ancestors were noble Saxons" (42). Pleyel urges that they all emigrate back to "the Saxon soil, from which he had likewise sprung" (42). It's no coincidence that one of the points of debate about whether to stay or return has to do with which land is the true land of liberty, America or Germany. Henry insists that "the state of manners and government in that country [Saxony], the security of civil rights, and the freedom of religious sentiments" as well as the "field for benevolence" offered by the "servile condition of one class" mean that Saxony is the ideal society for their enlightened community. But Wieland argues that "no spot on the globe" possesses "security and liberty" equal to that of America. Sexuality first surfaces together with this nativist-political theme in that Pleyel reports that he has also fallen in love with a woman repeatedly referred to as "the Saxon lady" (86, 88). It is partly his wish to return to her soon that makes him press his case so urgently.

More important, gender becomes an issue when the letter prompts a discussion between Pleyel and Wieland about whether the women would comply with Wieland's choice were he to decide to return to the Gothic homeland. Wieland avows that before he would return to Germany he would need to be sure that his wife and sister freely concurred, since he is, as he says, their "protector and friend, and not their tyrant and foe." Pleyel then asks, "But when [Catharine] knows your pleasure, will she not conform to it?" Interestingly, Pleyel, the free-thinking secularist and in this sense the more classical republican, expects women's pliant subordination while the stern Wieland follows the demand of consistency in his principles and so upholds the women's right to choose. At this moment, in the ventriloquized voice of Catharine, the two men hear, twice, a "distinct repetition of the same monosyllable, 'No'" (50). Again Carwin mimics the voice of an implicitly dissenting wife. These fabricated moments of Catharine's nay-saying begin to shed light on what otherwise seems arbitrary in Wieland's killing (and perhaps rape, as Clara implies) of Catharine. In effect, through Carwin, Catharine (unwittingly) stands between the men and their inheritance, and for this she will pay the ultimate price.

In the next moment, a woman's lips again foreclose the men's Saxon continuity. Pleyel begins to conclude that, even if the Wielands stay in the United States, he will return to Germany and "fly to [the] presence" of his Saxon lover, but at this juncture "the same mysterious voice exclaims, 'You shall not go. The seal of death is on her lips. Her silence is the silence of the tomb" (51). The Saxon man cannot reunite with the ancestral Saxon woman nor return to his original German-Saxon inheritance. Hereafter, the question of emigrating to reclaim the Saxon legacy is dropped, and Pleyel begins to transfer his affection to Clara, the modern, independent, American Anglo-Saxon woman. Yet this transfer of affection will itself be aborted by his distrust of her, which parallels Wieland's distrust of Catharine. Thus in these several ways do independent and (apparently) dissenting American Saxon women unsettle the claims and decisions of American-Saxon men — and draw out the men's violence and betrayal of them.

Carwin has precipitated, if not caused, all these Mettingen events,[17] so that on the one hand he seems to force into view the freethinking men's latent Gothic conservatism and its fatal effects for women. Yet on the other hand, Carwin also seems to embody the nativist self, and it is this persona to which Clara feels wildly attracted. Carwin appears to her as a "rustic and aukward" [sic] character (57); and during the sublime storm that follows her first encounter with him, after drawing a sketch of his face, Clara "consumed the day in alternately looking out upon the storm, and gazing at the picture" (62). Furthermore, he conjures for Clara her own affiliation with an ancient German lineage, which suggests that women too seek affiliation with an ancient race: for, under the influence of this Gothic scene and countenance, Clara begins to perform some of her "noble Saxon" grandfather's ancient poetry put to music. She sings the ballad of a "German Cavalier, who fell at the siege of Nice" but regrets her choice since "the scenes of violence and carnage" lead her to ruminate on "the horrors of war" (63) — perhaps those horrors that had earlier afforded her community "enjoyment" in conversation. Now these calamities encroach less "happily," although they still attract her oddly, as does the voice of Carwin "in which *force and sweetness were blended*" (59, emphasis added). Carwin arouses Clara's own attraction to the Germanic legacy.

But, in Carwin, this legacy is mere impersonation, and so the novel, consciously or not, casts Saxon identity as a performance, in the Butlerian sense — a self-fashioning that supplements the absent or lost center of the Anglo-Atlantic world and, in doing so, becomes a disavowed vehicle of violence. Characterizing himself as a "native" of America (227), Carwin is above all American in that he is a cultural chameleon, an uprooted individual who adopts native manners as an instrument, paradoxically, of mobility. If, as David Kazanjian argues, Carwin appropriates and masters the "shrill notes" of a "Mohock" voice, he likewise appropriates and mimics whatever other "native" voice will serve his pleasure.[18] We learn, for instance, that Carwin had lived in Spain for three years, during which time "a studious conformity with the customs of the people, had made him indistinguishable from a native, when he chose to assume that character"

(77). He "visited every corner of Spain and could furnish the most accurate details respecting its ancient and present state" (78). He does the same with the Pennsylvania community, precisely studying, mimicking, and disruptively echoing their "native" attachments.[19]

Insofar as Brown seems to have thought of Carwin as a would-be member of the subversive global movement of the Illuminati, we have further grounds for understanding him as an opportunistic racial performer. In this movement, as mentioned, the members pose as benevolent liberators but actually intend violent revolution and at the same time seek colonialist prosperity for themselves. We can read this as a "sketch" of the operations of race in modernity: race is apparently a principle of liberation and the root of a communal bond but at the same time it authorizes the ambitions of an endogamous elite. Carwin adds another twist in that, simply for his own sense of power and amusement, he subverts racial attachment — in the Mettingen community, at least — as much as he promotes it. His behavior suggests that self-serving individualism needs or makes use of racialism when convenient but will just as readily subvert or rewrite it, if convenient. In this light, we may see how Brockden Brown's subtitle signals the emblematic role of Carwin. The novel's full title is *Wieland, or the Transformation: An American Tale,* and in the novel the word "transformation" is emphatically used, in italics, with reference to Carwin, who Pleyel tells us underwent a "*transformation*" in the course of his European travels, from a Protestant Englishman to a Catholic Spaniard. I suggest we understand Carwin's transformative mode as a race-performative mode.

Accordingly, Carwin's culminating acts of native trickery occur in conjunction with the community's plan to perform its racial legacy. Inspired by the arrival of "a new book from Germany," in fact "the first attempt of a Saxon poet," the community plans to gather at the temple and rehearse its epic story. This Gothic text *ab origine* (like those that Brown's near contemporary, Bishop Thomas Percy, was celebrating across the ocean) relates the "exploits of Zisca, the Bohemian hero" set within a "moated fortress" and full of "audacious acts, and unheard of disasters" all expressed "in wild numbers, and with terrific energy" — the product of an "adventurous and lawless fancy" (89). While critics have suggestively read the novel's inclusion of literary texts as its imputation of literature in the breakdown of social relations, none has taken seriously the specifically Saxon content of these texts.[20] Indeed, if we put Brown's interest in Hugh Blair's account of the "primitivist" roots of imagination (a link made by Michael Bell in light of Brown's inclusion of this Saxon text, but the Saxonism of which Bell does not pursue) next to Mark Seltzer's wonderful tracing of the way figures of speech are habitually literalized in *Wieland* — so that metaphoric storms become real storms — we can begin to see how, for Brown, the Gothic imagination of the Anglo-American community might actually translate into Gothic realities, as his novel shows it doing. This content implies that race myths in literature play a role in social breakdown.

But the staged performance of audacious acts never happens because, in effect, the reality takes its place — as Wieland murders his family, Clara is threatened with rape and violence, and Pleyel abandons her to psychological ruin. This Gothic-performance-turned-real is prepared in the weeks leading up to it by Carwin's explicit menacing of Clara's "ancient security," that is, her confident Saxon independence (68–69). Carwin's manipulations draw out the brother's and sister's violent Saxonism, until they finally turn it on each other.

Clara's Gothic Recess

Although readers of *Wieland* have noted its rewriting of the sentimental plot of seduction and have explored the sexual nature of Clara's relations to Carwin, her brother, and Pleyel, few have fully gauged the novel's intense and prolonged treatment of these tangled sexual relations, especially in their political and racial dimensions.[21] Brown writes several key, extended scenes centering on Clara's ambiguously free agency, and he reveals the extent to which both her rise and her fall, her freedom and her ruin, turn on the Gothic interior she carefully protects. Carwin's most elaborate charades are spurred by his desire to challenge Clara's independence in living in a house alone, at some distance from her brother. He invades her private "recesses" in her house and on the estate, and she soon finds that her "ancient security [had] vanished": "that solitude so dear to me, could no longer be endured," for she has lost what she calls the "inviolate asylum" of her independent house (68–69). She has attempted to "closet" the nativist sources of her agency—in a practice similar to Carwin's—and he aims to best her at the maneuver. While in the tale proper Carwin does indeed seem to empty her of this ancient and secure interior, in the end, Clara continues the legacy of Aphra Behn's narrator, for in telling her tale and finally marrying Pleyel she ultimately steps into the "role white women played as authorizing figures" in American colonization.[22]

As with Behn's, Haywood's, and Defoe's narrators as they negotiate their gendered contracts with a racialized sphere of freedom, Clara's narrative circumlocutions obfuscate her agency and desire. When she and Wieland first came of age, Clara explains, "My brother took possession of the house in which he was born," while she chose to live in a small house on the property, "situated on the bank of the river, three quarters of a mile from my brother's" (24). She confesses that she "can scarcely account for my refusing to take up my abode with him, unless it were from a disposition to be an economist of pleasure" — that is, rationing her time with her loved ones. But she also adds that she "was, beside, desirous of administering a fund, and regulating a household, of my own" (24). If she insists on keeping her "desire" to control money and a household in the grammatical position of a "beside," then certainly she will "scarcely" be able to account for her "refusal" to live with her brother. And this veiling serves her desire well.

Clara muddies her motives, and so Brockden Brown confuses the effects of Clara's refusal. On the one hand, her house apart perhaps saves her from her brother's murder of everyone in his household; but on the other, insofar as her independence increases Carwin's opportunities for disrupting both households, which in turn increases the brother's anxiety and perhaps precipitates his murderous impulses, this separation may indirectly cause the family's fatal end. This confusion of effects expresses women's historical conundrum: alignment with a Saxon republican and colonial community allows their movement toward independence but at the same time the "forceful" Gothic attachments and performances of republican men put women at risk from the very legacy that frees them.

Carwin explicitly confesses that he pursued his first trick on Clara to test her seeming character as a "prodigy" within the young nation's world of independent women. As Clara's servant Judith reports, "You took no precautions against robbers. You were just as tranquil and secure in this lonely dwelling, as if you were in the midst of a crowd" (230). Reminiscent of Lovelace's will to test Clarissa's virtue and courage, Carwin now decides "to put this courage to the test" (230). As he reflects, "A woman capable of recollection in danger, of warding off groundless panics, of discerning the true mode of proceeding, and profiting by her best resources, is a prodigy. I was desirous of ascertaining if you were such an one" (230). We might even wonder if he hopes to recruit Clara — if she passes the test — into the cult of the Illuminati. In any case, his first ploy is to simulate the intrusion of two murderers into her closet by propping himself up on a ladder next to her window and ventriloquizing a conversation between the intruders. Although Clara acts calmly at first (for as she too states, she "was habitually indifferent to all the causes of fear" [64]), in the end she flees to her brother's house and faints on his doorstep.

In effect, at this moment — with this fainting swoon — Clara falls into the social order that apparently frees a woman yet simultaneously uses that state of freedom to inculcate fears that make her an instrument of others' ends. Her "ancient security" "vanishes" (68). Her solitude is no longer a retreat from calamities; instead her "bosom was corroded by anxiety, [. . .] visited by dread of unknown dangers" so that "the future was a scene over which clouds rolled, and thunders muttered," for she has been "pushed from my immoveable and lofty station, and cast upon a sea of troubles" (79–80). She tumbles from her "lofty" station as she takes up arms against an Atlantic sea of troubles in this woman's version of a Shakespearean family allegory of nationhood.

Through the imagery of her "recess," Carwin's subversion of Clara's independence is both sexualized and racialized. Interestingly, Clara's servant Judith plays an instrumental role and Brockden Brown thus also re-introduces class as an element in this racial and sexual plot. Carwin has begun a sexual relationship with Judith, and she in turn helps him undermine Clara's confident state in this new political economy—a kind of rewriting of Roxana's loyal Amy. Judith literally provides the ladder for Carwin's first trick (giving him access to the lofty station of Clara's upstairs bedroom), but more significantly, Judith's sexuality gets pitted against Clara's insofar as Judith's "midnight interviews" with Carwin are threatened by another of Clare's independent "singularities": to "leave your bed, and walk forth for the sake of night-airs and starlight contemplation" (232). That is, Carwin calls on his ventriloquizing powers in order to divert the Anglo-Saxon Clara from her brooding, midnight wanderings and to free her outdoor place of retreat for his trysts with Judith.

The description of this retreat is highly erotic; and it is linked—by way of the word "recess"—to the closet where she keeps her father's memoirs, which she also calls a recess and which Carwin also aims to invade. As Clara first describes it, her outdoor retreat is, suggestively, a "recess in [a] declivity" of the river bank, "near the southern verge of my little demesne" (71); alongside a waterfall there is a "slight building, with seats and lattices" over which hangs the "odours" of the cedars and the honeysuckle which "embowered" it. This spot that she repeatedly calls a "recess" (97, 108) is Clara's "favorite retreat in summer," which "[n]o one but myself was accustomed to visit" (108). In Carwin's later and equally suggestive description of this place, echoing Clara's remark, "What recess could be more propitious to secrecy?" (108), he recalls, "No corner of your little domain unites fragrance and secrecy in so perfect a degree as the recess in the bank. The odour of its leaves, the coolness of its shade, and the music of its water-fall, had early attracted my attention . . . here my slumbers were found, and my pleasure enhanced" (232). *This* is the spot that Carwin chooses as the place for his "midnight interviews" with Judith (232). To frighten Clara away from it, he tells her in his ventriloquized and (as Brockden Brown renders it) brother-asssociated voice that this is the only place she is not safe.

The implication, on one hand, is that Clara must shun her own sexuality if she is to be safe in this new double-voiced order of things—and if men are to be allowed to pursue their sexual desires freely and secretly. At the same time, insofar as the recess is equated with her father's papers, the implication is that her "recess" also closets her attachment to the powerful textual legacy of her Saxon male kin, reaching back to her grandfather.[23] This aspect of her "recessed" desire is also indicated in her intent to tell Pleyel of her love on the same night that she will perform the text of the first Saxon poet. Carwin explicitly seeks entry into this kin interior and to the written texts that express it. After being "furnished" by Judith with "curious details of your domestic arrangement," he cannot resist the wish "to examine with my own eyes, the interior of your chamber": "I scrutinized every thing, and pried every where" (234). He eventually finds the key to her indoor recess and "found new scope for my curiosity in your books," especially her diary, containing "the key to your inmost soul" (235). Thus "my knowledge of you was of that kind, which conjugal intimacies can give, and in some respects, more accurate" (234). In particular, on the fatal night of her brother's rampage, Carwin is drawn into her closet especially in pursuit of "something tending to illustrate your character, or the history of your family," especially since "some intimation had been dropped by you in discourse, respecting a performance of your father, in which some important transaction in his life was recorded" (236). Since we know that Clara keeps her Saxon family papers here, Brown implies that Carwin seeks to manipulate her by way of this lineal and literary past.

Not only Carwin but also Henry Pleyel embarks on a quest (itself written, in his case) to take hold of her written interior. Pleyel confesses (in the later scene in which he abandons her) that, after the loss of his Saxon lady, he had begun to study her and record her every move in his journal: "Even the colour of a shoe, the knot of a riband, or your attitude in plucking a rose, were of moment to be recorded. Even the arrangements of your breakfast-table and your toilet have been amply displayed" (140). His list of her traits culminates with her writing: "I have traced you to your home. I have viewed you in relation to your servants, to your family, to your neighbors, and to the world. I have seen by what skilful arrangements you facilitate the performance of the most arduous and complicated duties; what daily accessions of strength your judicious discipline bestowed on your memory; what correctness and abundance of knowledge was daily experienced by your unwearied application to books, and to writing" (139). As in the triangle of Lovelace, James, and Clarissa, writing will be a decisive instrument for the man partly because it is newly in women's hands. Even as she uses it to register herself in the world, to reveal herself intimately in the world, and in this case to maintain her hold on a native lineage, so he will use it to enter her.

Thus does writing emerge as that recessed aspect of Clara that the men most covet and which she must defend (with a penknife!), for these written records are *her* link to the Saxon legacy. In short, Brown stages men's struggle with women over a claim to racial freedom. Indeed, the brother and sister return simultaneously to that Saxon legacy: at the very moment when her brother is committing his bloody deed, Clara enters her room so as to once more "ponder on the turbulent life and mysterious end of my father" by perusing "every relique connected with his fate" in the form of his memoir, "the most useful book in my collection" (95). Clara has returned from her search for Pleyel, who never appeared at the temple to perform his part in the bloody play of the Saxon poet, but now that play will unfold in her and her brother's houses instead.

Yet initially Clara finds herself unable to open the door to her closet-recess. Significantly, although Carwin is the person holding onto the closet door from within, Clara understands the resistance to come from her brother. As critics have noted, Carwin and Wieland become conflated as objects of Clara's fear and desire. On this night, she tries to "exert all my force" to open the door, for the "frantic conception that my brother was within, that the resistance made to my design was exerted by him, had rooted itself in my mind" (101). She tries to dissuade herself from this assumption that her brother might "resist" her "design" in words that recall the conversation between Pleyel and Wieland about his relation to the women ("No," she says to herself, "protection, and not injury is his province" [99]). In this conflation of Wieland and Carwin (a man Clara sometimes desires) the novel reiterates the pattern we have seen in novels of an incestuous brother-sister struggle, which expresses the incursion into the brother-sister relation of a competitive element, felt as a transgressive mingling of political and sexual relations.

The longest sequences of the rest of the novel are composed of Clara's struggles on this night and the later night when her brother escapes from prison and shows up at the house to murder her. Her account of these nights takes the form of a brooding and self-contradictory meditation on her powers of courage and agency. For a total of over forty-five pages, culminating in Wieland's suicide, and especially the last twenty, in which she engages in mortal struggle with him, Clara again and again vacillates over whether to kill herself or kill her brother. She is again and again embarrassed by her inability to do either. In reflecting on her Hegelian brother-sister struggle, she seems to agree that she fails Carwin's test of her capacity for true independence: "Nothing but subjection to danger, and exposure to temptation, can show us what we are. By this test I was now tried, and found to be cowardly and rash" (253). She casts suicide as the virtuous response for a woman whose sexual honor is threatened—at first boasting that she could well end her life, for "I knew how to find the way to the recesses of life, I could use a lancet with some skill, and could distinguish between vein and artery" (221)—and it turns out that she keeps such a lancet in her *closet*, that other container of the "recesses" of her life. Yet after all, when "I stood upon the brink of fate, [when] the knife of the sacrificer was aimed at my heart, I shuddered and betook myself to any means of escape, however monstrous," and so she considers murdering her brother (253). Unlike Walpole's obedient Matilda, Clara resists being sacrificed within the new fraternal order.

When it comes to murdering "the sacrificer" (her striking word for her brother), however, she also repeatedly loses courage. Finally, at the moment when her "hand was ready to inflict death upon the menacer" so that "if my brother had lifted his hand" "[t]his instrument of my preservation [her penknife] would have been plunged into his heart" (254), her brother suddenly "drew back." She, too, then "threw the knife with violence on the floor" (254). She judges herself harshly for this readiness to kill: "Methinks it is too much. I stand aside, as it were, from myself; I estimate my own deservings; a hatred, immortal and inexorable, is my due. I listen to my own pleas, and find them empty and false: yes I acknowledge that my guilt surpasses that of all mankind" (254). When, at her mention of Carwin's name, the brother again moves toward her menacingly, she at first finds that "[o]f self-defense I was incapable. The phrenzy that had lately prompted me to blood was gone" (258), and yet shortly she again "grasped the knife with force" (260). The sequence that follows epitomizes the bizarre and incoherent nature of this vacillating struggle over agency between brother and sister — and the sister's dissociative interjections.

> I felt my left arm within [my brother's] grasp. —
> Even now I hesitated to strike. I shrunk from his assault, but in vain. —
> Here let me desist. Why should I rescue this event from oblivion? Why should I paint this detestable conflict? Why not terminate at once this series of horrors? — Hurry to the verge of the precipice, and cast myself for ever beyond remembrance and beyond hope?
> Still I live: with this load upon my breast; with this phantom to pursue my steps; with adders lodged in my bosom, and stinging me to madness: still I consent to live!
> Yes, I will rise above the sphere of mortal passions: I will spurn at the cowardly remorse that bids me seek impunity in silence, or comfort in forgetfulness. My nerves shall be new strung to the task. Have I not resolved? I will die. The gulph before me is inevitable and near. I will die, but then only when my tale is at an end. (260)

The confusion of her agency and his ("I hesitated to strike. I shrunk from his assault"); the recasting of her hesitation to murder into her hesitation to record her willingness to murder; and the firm reversal of that hesitation: all of these express her "consent" to live and to write a text that expresses her determination to die — which she can only do "when my tale is at an end." These scenes intertwine women's free and independent agency with women's writing, and they place both within the modern yet Gothic contest between women and men. Clara would apparently assert only by choosing death, but in fact she continues to live and to fight so as to resolve freely to die like an independent Anglo-Saxon — and this circumlocution continues, so that the next chapter merely picks up where she left off: "My right hand, grasping the unseen knife, was still disengaged. It was lifted to strike" (261). Again her penknife is lifted yet disengaged.

The Gothic Pen(knife)

The struggle between Clara and her brother offers a kind of tableau of the sexual story embedded in, and shaping, the colonization of the Americas. It reveals the important participation by women in the violence of this colonization, even if partly as a matter of self-defense. Clara spells out this logic dissociatively, burying its full political implications. Her reflections on her brother's way of understanding his murders also nicely describe how acts of colonization get glossed as civilizing projects of "virtue." She remarks with amazement on how he "deemed himself commissioned for this act [of murder] by heaven [and] regarded this career of horror as the last refinement of virtue" (216). She furthermore names the logic by which his love for *her* justifies his violence in that his "implacability was proportioned to the reverence and love which he felt for me" and in fact "the claims of a sister or friend [. . .] were his only reasons for pursuing my destruction" (216). She obliquely references the ethnocentric principle at work as well as the gender fault line in the new republic when she remarks further, "I live not in a community of savages; yet whether I sit or walk, go into crouds, or hide myself in solitude, my life is marked for a prey to inhuman violence; I am in perpetual danger of perishing; of perishing under the grasp of a brother!" (217). Ultimately Clara's story reveals that her brother is the savage by whom she is threatened, although she continues to protect her psyche and her implicated position by displacing this character onto the "savages" whom her father tried to convert.

But Clara does seem unconsciously to apprehend her complicity in Anglo-Saxon men's violent pursuit of liberty. As we saw, she vacillates wildly about whether she should adopt a murderous stance or a suicidal one in the face of this fork-tongued violent order of things. Although it is exactly her powerful identification with her brother — including her pride in not living in a community of "savages" — that makes her part of this order of things, she glimpses this fact in asserting that "the phrenzy which is charged upon my brother, must belong to myself" — an equivocal condition lightly reinforced when a few moments later she "thirst[s] for knowledge and for vengeance" (217) against Carwin, "the intelligence that governed in this storm" (217). If, as I suggested earlier, Carwin's biloquism is indeed the expression of the fault lines in this Gothic republican community, exerting special pressure on its suppressed awareness of the violence that enables its "happiness," then he is truly the "intelligence that governed in this storm" (217) a phrase that also calls up the sea crossing that got them here.

In this light, Clara's self-reflexive comments, which initially, in the scene of threatened murder, seem rather out of place, suddenly take on a broader resonance for her position as an Anglo-American citizen writing a narrative of trauma: "I stand aside, as it were, from myself; I estimate my own deservings; a hatred, immortal and inexorable, is my due. I listen to my own pleas, and find them empty and false: yes, I acknowledge that my guilt surpasses that of all mankind" (254). In effect, the very telling of her story is a confession of guilt — "I will spurn at the cowardly remorse that bids me seek impunity in silence, or comfort in forgetfulness" (260).

Yet Clara finally holds on to *her* authority by way of this story. It turns out that she is free to do at least this much. After a period of convalescence following the traumatic night of her brother's murder of his family and nearly herself, Clara demands to be able to return to her house (despite the admonitions of her uncle and her friends), a desire she links to her commitment to her writing. They are forced, she says, "to consent to my return," for although "[t]hey would have withheld from me the implements of writing," they nonetheless "quickly perceived that to withstand would be more injurious than to comply with my wishes" (268, 265). Clara apparently means to keep the "household" that African labor and Indian land brought into being — and she means to generate her writing from it. She succeeds in securing the consent of others in order to undertake her project of "relating the history of these disasters" (268), until at the end of her account she can exclaim, "[M]y work is done!" (266).

The Saxon woman's work of narrating her ruin paradoxically dramatizes, in other words, her freedom. Brown signals as much, dissociatively so, when he leaps, at the end of his novel, to a period three years later in order to release Clara from the "burden" of this history. We learn through a third-person narrator that Clara has recovered to the point that she feels wholly free to move, both psychically and bodily — for she has traveled back to Europe and lives happily and in "lofty" style — although in order to do so, she has, after all, married that republican doubter of women's virtuous independence, Henry Pleyel.

This last turn reminds us that the author of this story is an Anglo-Atlantic man, ventriloquizing a woman's colonial ruin and freedom. In effect, the closure in marriage is the text's implicit assertion that her writing is actually his, that her story is contained within a Pleyelian republic which requires women's consent to men's racial pursuits as the condition of their freedom. Clara Wieland's power and freedom are in this sense precisely fictional.

But the power that her writing gains for Charles Brockden Brown is historical, factual. Like the Wieland grandfather, he earns a small but "*independent subsistence*" by way of this novel which does indeed fashion an American Gothic replacing the "gothic castles and chimeras" of European literature with an American situation (*Edgar Huntly* 3). As did those of Anglo-European novelists, his production depends on the woman's story of ruin, for her dissociative story emblematizes the history of a nation understood to be reborn from a Gothic struggle over a legacy of freedom. Brown reiterates and revises this story as part of his bid to lead the tradition forward on American soil — and yet equally to reincarnate, as his materials suggest, the German tradition of authorship embraced by the Mettingen community. He does so by invoking the precedent of the historical German poet Wieland;[24] and his allusion to Goethe's *Werther* reinforces the point. Clara stands witness when Wieland is "transformed at once into the *man of sorrows*" (263, italics in original), a characterization realized shortly thereafter when Wieland kills himself.

Brown in effect crafts himself as the carrier of the Anglo-Saxon literary lineage his characters enact. As critics have suggested, Brown also implicitly offers some disturbing judgments about the duplicitous and potentially fatal effects of literature, and I would add that his novel *Wieland* characterizes literature's racial imaginary as one of its key dangers.[25] Yet Brown nonetheless pursues his role as racial performer, working biloquially at one remove from race so as to launch himself in modernity. When African-Atlantic authors in turn take up this Gothic literary legacy, they at once expose its cultural biloquism and articulate their own counteracting version of it.

10 | Dispossession in Jacobs and Hopkins

IN TURNING TO THE African-Atlantic gothic, we see the trope of "possession" from a different angle. In these texts, the world of tortures, swoons, dissociations, and dungeons mimetically represents the conditions of a bodily takeover and the unacknowledged foundations of Anglo modernity's principle of ownership. Reaching from slave narratives through Wilson's *Our Nig* to Toni Morrison's late gothic novel *Beloved*, the African-Atlantic gothic affirms Paul D's observation that when a body is owned by "the men who ha[ve] the guns," *all* of reality appears "possessed," right down to "mist, doves, sunlight, copper dirt, moon."[1] All kinds of ruin — material, bodily, and psychic — follow. Pauline Hopkins strikingly narrates the sexual matrix of this possessive Atlantic ontology in her novel *Of One Blood* — following the path laid out by Harriet Jacobs.

Yet in doing so, these writers face an aporia that, in turn, they enfold into the structure of their texts. They encounter the paradox of writing an African-Altantic gothic text: its already-framed arrival at its own story. For not only are bodies and minds possessed by so-called whites on the Atlantic; and not only are texts themselves part of this propertied economy so that, for blacks, writing becomes (as Henry Louis Gates has observed) "a commodity which they were forced to trade for their humanity."[2] Even beyond all of this, the story line itself is possessed by whites. Already when Harriet Jacobs picks up her pen, the Anglo-gothic has a long tradition on both sides of the Atlantic and is thriving among such authors as Poe and Hawthorne. She and her originary story of captivity, violation, and traumatic escape are already framed.

As a result, for the African-Atlantic writer, the literary gothic is both more real and more surreal than for the Anglo-Atlantic writer. To be in the position of "borrowing" the gothic form from Anglo writers is to revisit the uncanny loss that is slavery. In the end, then, the most gothic dimension of the African-Atlantic gothic text is the writing of it. Harriet Jacobs and Pauline Hopkins respond by symbolically organizing their texts around an unlocatable voice. In both writers, this voice speaks from within the slippery and uncomfortable interrelationships between ruin and agency, possession and freedom, absence and presence, race-mixing and race-solidarity, registering the equivocal Atlantic history of their already overwritten narratives.

Jacobs, the Race Libertine

Harriet Jacobs well understood the gothic legacy shaping both her life and her narrative, and she readily borrowed the language of the literary gothic to tell her (anterior) tale of possession.[3] In her autobiography, *Incidents in the Life of a Slave Girl*, she consistently invokes the gothic vocabulary: in her repeated allusions to Flint as a "tyrant" whose wish is "to conquer";[4] in her references to the Hispano-Gothic Inquisition in association with illicit sexuality ("The secrets of slavery are concealed like those of the Inquisition. My master was, to my knowledge, the father of eleven slaves" [35]); and in her depiction of her hiding place as a "dungeon" (127) or "cell" (144, 148) where, "guiltless of crime," she is "pent up . . . , as the only means of avoiding the cruelties the laws allowed" and where she endures "terrible thunderstorms" (121) and insect infestations. Such references crystallize in her juxtaposition of a reference to the "the land of my birth" and lines from Byron's "Lament of Tasso," which she uses to characterize her homeland as a place

> Where laughter is not mirth; nor thought the mind;
> Nor words a language; nor e'en men mankind.
> Where cries reply to curses, shrieks to blows,
> And each is tortured in his separate hell. (37)

Jacobs imports the imagery of torture, shrieks, and hell, but in contrast to the scenarios of Byron and Monk Lewis in which *separation from* the native land brings a gothic hell, in her story the native land is itself the scene of inescapable torture. At the same time, as will Pauline Hopkins, Jacobs alludes to such texts as Thomas Gray's "Elegy in a Country Churchyard" (191) as she paints the sufferings of "the poor and the lowly" (73) and invokes the idea of "free soil" (187, 193), at once aligning her work with the nativist strain of romantic literature and deconstructing that strain, like Equiano, within the context of Atlantic slavery — by bringing romanticism into direct contact with the historical conditions of its imagining. She likewise manipulates the racialized language of liberty when, for instance, she explains that before the passing of the Fugitive Slave Law she felt at home in Massachusetts ("I relied on her love of freedom, and felt safe on her soil"), but with that law's passage she realizes that she "honored the old Commonwealth beyond her deserts" (187). In speaking of soil, the old commonwealth, and the love of freedom, Jacobs simultaneously rouses her readers' "ancient" associations and reveals the perniciously racialized limits of that legacy.[5]

Jacobs's reworking of the Atlantic story comes into clear view when, near the end of her autobiography, she narrates her journey across the ocean to England. She reports her experience of "pure, unadulterated freedom" in this foreign land (183); and so she conjures the trope of a journey-*into*-freedom-yet-*away*-from home, the primal layer of Puritan-Atlantic narrative. And yet of course her story inverts the Anglo-Atlantic narrative, geographically speaking: she travels not west but east and away from America to freedom. Accordingly, when she returns, her "winter passage" back to America reenacts her African ancestors' middle passage westward into slavery, so that "distant spectres seemed to rise up on the shores of the United States" (183). These specters soon materialize as she learns that her light-skinned son's coworkers have discovered "that he was colored!" and so have driven him away from his job with scorn and abuse. Jacobs concludes, "It is a sad feeling to be afraid of one's native country" (186). Her Atlantic passage in one way repeats history by bringing her into the hands of those same Saxon specters that Equiano described; but in another way her story updates history, for now this land she enters as a slave is her "native" land. Such are the Gothic twists with which Jacobs faces her readers as she turns inside out the layers of Atlantic liberty narratives and takes back the already-appropriated freedom story. In recrossing the Atlantic to come "home," however, she signals that her narrative has boldly recrossed the geographical threshold, and symbolic landscape, where African-Atlantic persons may lose or gain freedom; and she reminds us that her text paradoxically re-occupies the absence that her presence has become within Anglo-Atlantic narrative.

At the heart of this Atlantic abyss that is her home lies Jacobs's struggle against sexual violation within the circle of the family. From the outset, Jacobs establishes that American slavery entails a disturbing intra-kin intimacy and violation. She points out in her opening chapter that her mistress was "the foster-sister of my mother" since "they were both nourished at my grandmother's breast" (2), stressing again a few paragraphs later that her mistress's slaves had "shared the same milk that nourished her" (5) — and yet were kept enslaved by her. In the same passage she notes that her uncle Benjamin was "nearly white; for he inherited the complexion my grandmother had derived from Anglo-Saxon ancestors," a quiet naming of Anglo-Saxons masters' rape of slave women (6). As she recounts, "in that cage of obscene birds," the slaveholder's sons and daughters regularly see their fathers breaking vows and wielding violent authority and likewise see their mothers embittered by this deceit and sexual licentiousness (52). Indeed as Jacobs later wonders, using the framework of Saxon identity while also undercutting it, "who *are* Africans? Who can measure the amount of Anglo-Saxon blood coursing in the veins of American slaves?" (44).

Living under such conditions, Jacobs makes her deliberate "plunge into the abyss" (53). It is key, as Saidiya Hartman and Claudia Tate have pointed out, that she labors to turn her "ruin" into an act of will.[6] Although Jacobs characterizes her sexual "fall" with Mr. Sands as a moment when "the demon Slavery . . . proved too strong for me," she also notes that "calculations of interest" motivated *her decision* to become pregnant by him rather than by Flint (54–55). Although it is not a free choice, this choice to sleep with a white man is a strategic move to possess her own fall into Atlantic modernity against Flint's legalized will to "mastermind" her fall; and, at the metanarrative level, it is a seizing of the ruinous power of Atlantic modernity, including through its stories. Her willed sexual fall prefigures her textual fall into the fathomless waters of representation, the deep danger of writing this realgothik for white readers who bring to it a merely fantastical Anglo-gothic imaginary.

This plunge into ruin occurs explicitly within Jacobs's calling-out of possession. She stresses from the first page of her memoir that slaves' status for whites is one of property, mentioning it three times in her opening paragraph: first when she recalls that she "never dreamed I was a piece of merchandise," next when she remarks that her mother was a "valuable piece of property," and finally when she comments that "a slave, *being* property, can *hold* no property" (5–6, emphasis in original). Her emphasis on the possessed slave's lack of a "holding" power because of his or her possessed "being" hints at the ontological effects of this economy that seizes the very interior of the disenfranchised other.[7] She puts this empty-making structure of possession under strain by always counterpointing it with the soul-rousing rhetoric of liberty and tyranny, as when Dr. Flint "told me I was his property" and she explains that "[m]y soul revolted against the mean tyranny" (27). Likewise, in response to Dr. Flint's declaration "that I was made for his use, made to obey his command in *every* thing; that I was nothing but a slave, whose will must and should surrender to his," she tells us that "I resolved never to be conquered" (18–19, emphasis in original). Jacobs stands poised against the whole order of possession, deploying its very language.

As she takes her plunge in order to counteract her status as possessed object within that order, Jacobs's project thus goes beyond even the dialogical one that William Andrews rightly sees operating in her narrative, for she reveals a fierce existential, bottomless standoff between possession and lack of ground. In this struggle, Jacobs determines that she will possess herself, at least textually, so that in her stead *the master* will become possessed — at least emotionally. For, as she anticipates, her pregnancy leads Mrs. and Dr. Flint into "possessed" states of jealousy and rage exactly because it succeeds in baffling their wills to possess her. Dr. Flint continually appears before her "like a restless spirit from the pit" (77), tortured himself now by the "demon slavery" (82), "rav[ing] and storm[ing] at a furious rate" (97), repeatedly trying to "revenge himself" (110). He fails in his mad desire for possession and revenge, both in the short term (as Andrews notes, he is often reduced to striking Jacobs when what he wants most is to persuade her into docility) and, ultimately, in the long term, since she escapes and he never recovers her, as the fact of this memoir attests.[8] In thus interfering with his "libertine" hold on her, Jacobs loosens the sexual lynchpin of the whole Atlantic system and she plays the part of the mastermind behind the veil.

Yet because the Anglo-Atlantic tradition of print narrative already contains Jacobs's story — and continually reasserts its priority in the world of print, as Teresa Goddu astutely discusses in the context of Harriet Beecher Stowe's relation to Jacobs[9] — Jacobs foregrounds the fact that her resistance must redeploy the powers of print. When she borrows street names and numbers from the *New York Post,* in order to simulate a free place in New York from which she can pretend to write to Flint, she explains that "for once, the paper that systematically abuses the colored people, was made to render them a service" (128). If we substituted "Anglo-Atlantic narrative" for "the paper," the statement would describe the thrust of Jacobs's whole narrative, which borrows from that history of print, formed around Saxonist vocabularies of liberty and tyranny, to render her "people" a service. She need only give the *New York Post* a good shake and there will fall, she suggests, those words that she can appropriate to locate herself, fictionally, in the Northern terrain of freedom.

Yet at the same time this creation of a New York street address from which she writes but where she is not present dramatizes the unlocatable and homeless state of her voice, even her authorship. For her contemporary readers, we should recall, Jacobs was a literal *fugitive* (her whereabouts were concealed from public record and her name was a pseudonym), and for her early-twenty-first century readers she is a textual fugitive, as hinted in the two names of Linda and Harriet by which she still appears in our discussions. Her voice in this sense is a ghostly one, speaking doubly and from nowhere, expressing an illicit freedom.[10] Yet this is the only voice available, she implies, to the writer of the African-Atlantic gothic. This writer *willfully enters* and speaks from the lightless dungeon, in a voice whose pseudonymity is its truth.

Jacobs's final freedom — bought for her by Mrs. Bruce — establishes that she cannot wholly conquer the principle of Saxonist possession that she battles. Hearing that the "bill of sale" is in Mrs. Bruce's hands, she remarks that "the words struck me like blow. So I was *sold* at last! A human being *sold* in the city of New York!" (200, emphasis in original). She confesses in a letter to Amy Post that she preferred the more uncertain freedom she had gained before the money transaction, because "God gave me that freedom," but she understands that she was "obliged to resign my crown, to rid myself of a tyrant" (204). And she also understands that her bill of sale is itself a piece of the print history she has learned to manipulate, as this last reference to crowns and tyrants suggests, for she never ceases to put pressure on white culture's understanding of its history of possession: "The bill of sale is on record, and future generations will learn from it that women were articles of traffic in New York, late in the nineteenth century of the Christian religion. It may hereafter prove a useful document to antiquaries who are seeking to measure the progress of civilization in the United States. I well know the value of that bit of paper; but much as I love freedom, I do not like to look upon it" (200).

Even as she references the whole Atlantic history in which "antiquaries" fashioning new genealogies have played a key part, Jacobs reveals that writing and print are *not* instruments of her freedom — although readers have ever since, and understandably, equated literacy and freedom. What Jacobs makes clear is that exactly this equation — of antiquaries, freedom, and print culture, linked as it is to the theorem that makes writing a function of race — re-imprisons her in the very moment that it frees her. As her choice to write a "fugitive narrative" demonstrates, and as Patricia Williams has so shrewdly explored in *The Alchemy of Race and Rights,* modern property is a paper economy, legal possession depends on print, print legitimizes races, and race-freedom is therefore a written matter that is ugly to "look upon."

When Harriet Jacobs prefaces her memoir, therefore, with the command, "READER BE ASSURED this narrative is no fiction," she shows her cunning as a race-d writer. Her words at once remind her readers of the many "fictions" that begin with just such a disingenuous opening, from *Oroonoko* to *The Castle of Otranto* to *The Scarlet Letter,* and they remind her readers, in another sense, of the historical difference between this narrative and all those novels. The command form of her address presumes a fiction: that she has the freedom — and the status as author — to make this distinction between fact and fiction. In "fictitiously" seizing this ground, she makes her readers feel viscerally the old literary-historical symbiosis of novelistic "fictions" and historical slave "narratives" like her own — what Aldon Nielsen would call the "future-anterior" relation of the latter to the former.[11] In a sense, Jacobs positions herself as the unacknowledged crux, or blind spot, or perhaps what Jacques Lacan understood as the *objet petit a* — the submerged and irretrievable but psychically determining origin — of the African-Atlantic gothic story in Anglo-Atlantic culture.[12] Like Ellison's "invisible man," Jacobs's narrative exposes how an entire written and economic structure depends on her, that is, on her invisible yet "possessed" presence. Or to put it another way, she is the ballast in the bottom of the Atlantic vessel. But to lift herself into view is to sink the boat on which she needs passage. So she speaks the Anglo-Atlantic language of freedom to reveal that it is a race-d fiction.

Hopkins's Gothic Descent

Fifty years later, in the post-Reconstruction era haunted by the terror of lynchings on one side and the monstrosities of an increasingly institutionalized scientific racism on the other, Pauline Hopkins revisits the *mise en abyme* of the African-Atlantic gothic. In her effort to challenge the long history and wide reach of late-nineteenth-century racism, Hopkins crafts a novel that belongs equally to the historical epic and to the gothic, in effect merging the two.[13] Her novel *Of One Blood* shares a globally situated and epic race vision with the works by Sedgwick, Hawthorne, and Eliot that I discuss in part 4 of this study, all of which themselves retain a gothic subtext. But in this work Hopkins keeps the gothic closer to the surface and center of the story — exactly as required by her realgothik historical situation — and so I treat it here in this section on the gothic rather than in the next section on epic-historical fiction. Indeed, in this last and most pessimistic of her novels, Hopkins so flouts the boundaries between romance and science, epic history and gothic fantasy, and, most of all, white and black that she makes race itself into an uncertain shadow. In the end, she leaves her readers with no clear ground for racial community, putting us at the mercy of the Atlantic's abysmal ironies and kinship spirals. Accordingly, she creates a gothic revision of nineteenth-century race-epic that imperils its trajectory toward freedom.

Many critics have explored Hopkins's racial discourse as an equivocal one that seems at once to uphold an essentialist Ethiopianism and to acknowledge a pervasive "amalgamation" at odds with that vision.[14] In her tale of Reuel Briggs's discovery of his royal African lineage and his destiny as king, Hopkins seems to embrace the ideal of a core African identity that persists through centuries and despite diasporic displacement. Yet at the same time, she makes Reuel biracial; and in identifying Telassar as the city he is destined to rule, she links it to an

Anglo-Christian as well as an African cosmology (Telassar also appears in Milton's *Paradise Lost*). If additionally, as one critic suggests, Hopkins's descriptions of Candace the African queen are meant to emphasize that she is a brown-skinned not a black-skinned figure, in several ways the history Hopkins creates is not a pure Ethiopianist one but rather a cross-cultural and biracial one.[15] Then, too, Hopkins's portrait of the African kingdom of Telassar may suggest that Ethiopianism holds as many dangers as Anglo-Saxonism and is not a perfect utopia.[16] And finally, as the structure of Hopkins's novel throws into sharp relief, in the end a woman's life is ruined and sacrificed to attain this Ethiopianist vision. Is Hopkins critiquing or embracing the epic racial vision of Ethiopianism?

I argue that *Of One Blood* refuses to release such a vision from its shadowy gothic foundations even as it strategically pursues an epic revision of race identity. In a key scene in the novel, Reuel wanders the desert all night looking for an entryway into the legendary city of Telassar, listening in despair to "the sound of centuries marching by in the moaning wind and purposeless dust."[17] He suddenly stumbles on a downward path into a chamber "of unknown dimensions" and finds himself face to face with an Ethiopian sphinx amid "rows of pillars flickering drunkenly in the gloom" (544). The scene offers us an image of Hopkins herself, searching and searching for a way out of the "marching centuries" of Anglo-Atlantic history and into some other story. She is especially trying to come to terms with the riddled role of women in this history, as the figure of the sphinx suggests and as also implied by the psychic and bodily violation of Reuel's beloved Dianthe occurring at this very moment on the other side of the Atlantic. In this last scene before her hero discovers his royal African destiny, Hopkins lets us know that she is taking us into a realm of unknowns, riddles, and flickering visions.

In other words, Hopkins is searching, like her hero, for another vision of identity within the modern Atlantic economy of possession, and in the process she fashions Meroe as a powerful match for Anglo-America, the rising power on its Atlantic horizon. As part of her solution, she works to recast the meaning of possession on an epic scale, imagining race as a benevolent pan-psychic intersubjectivity rather than a controlling force, which she traces back to ancient Africa and forward into the future of transatlantic relations. Yet, as does Jacobs, she simultaneously reveals that her already-framed authorship offers an uncertain, equivocal ground for this epic vision.

Race and (En)trance

Hopkins begins her novel by pinpointing the existential crisis precipitated by the Atlantic's "free" economy, even for an apparently white and bright young man with a promising future. *Of One Blood* opens with Reuel Briggs, a Boston medical student, contemplating suicide: "To what use all this persistent hard work for a place in the world — clothes, food, a roof? Is suicide wrong?" (441). He balks at entry into a world where "place" can be gained only by unceasing labor and purchased property. In an uncanny echo of the Putney Debate participant who casts the relation of individual and community as "this Oedipus riddle, this Gordian knot," Reuel feels that "voices and hands seemed beckoning him all day to cut the Gordian knot and solve the riddle of once and whither for all time" (442). Feeling "the loneliness of his position," he reflects (perhaps like Hopkins, who was likely being pressured out of her editorship of *Colored American Magazine* as she wrote this novel) that he occupies no special place, serves no irreplaceable function:[18] "[h]is place in the world would soon be filled; no vacuum remained empty" (441–42). He further crystallizes the dispersed social ontology of modernity insofar as he is a man without relations and without inherited property and identity: he has "no money . . . and apparently no relatives" and none of his friends (or, at first, we the readers) "knew aught of Reuel Briggs's origin" (444). For the modern person embodied in Reuel, entry is bleak and arduous, and the self is utterly alone, while only the choice to exit — by suicide — is truly free.

But another force haunts Reuel — "The Unclassified Residuum," as it is described in the book on mesmeric psychology by Monsieur Binet which in this scene lays open on his desk. This residuum includes the phenomena of "divinations, inspirations, demoniacal possessions, apparitions, trances, ecstasies, miraculous healing," which are "broadcast over the surface of history" (442–43). In Hopkins's novel, the sources of these phenomena turn out to be racial — as is quickly signaled when in the next moment Reuel himself falls into a kind of trance and experiences a vision of his Negro sister, Dianthe, his link to a troubled racial past that ultimately authorizes his mystical powers and makes a race-king of him. This extrapsychic experience eventually leads Reuel back to what he calls the "undiscovered country in" himself (448).

Reuel's turn from alienation to race vision uncannily replays the emergence of racialism within the "free" public sphere two and a half centuries earlier, as expressed in the Putney Debates. Just as in 1647, the "absent center" of the emergent contract polis, threatening "utter destruction" of the kingdom (to recall Ireton's fears), called forth a protective and gendered enclosure of liberty within Saxonism, so here Reuel's position at the fault line of the contract, inspiring thoughts of suicide, provokes a vision of race bonds (a vision catalyzed by a woman's ruin) as antidote to modern alienation.[19] Coming under the power of this historical repetition, Reuel falls "into a dreamy state . . . for which he could not account" until "gradually the darkness and storm [outside] faded into tints of cream and rose and soft moist lips . . . he saw distinctly outlined a fair face framed in golden hair, with soft brown eyes, deep and earnest — terribly earnest they seemed just then — rose-tinged baby lips and an expression of wistful entreaty" (445). The rosy lips and deep entreaty of this vision come to life later that evening when Reuel begrudgingly accompanies Aubrey Livingston, his medical school companion (and, as he'll later learn, his other mixed-race sibling), to hear a "Negro" choir. Reuel discovers that the sublime female soloist of the choir singing "Go Down, Moses" (a song about another wandering race patriarch) has the face of his vision. Seeing and hearing her, Reuel is "carried out of himself" — away from modern suicide and into a modern race quest, transported there by the beseeching voice and face of a violated race woman, which have chased away the Atlantic "storm" (454).

Hopkins certainly had her finger on this inherited plot's pulse, as this scenario suggests. Hereafter, in every dimension of its tangled tale of kinship, violation, and race vision, *Of One Blood* signifies on this plot.[20] In the case of Reuel and Dianthe, first of all, Hopkins makes clear that Dianthe's role is instrumental. Reuel enters a racialized Atlantic modernity via Dianthe, this "fallen sister" of his vision, who turns up again one year later as the victim of a train crash in a strange coma state. When other doctors pronounce her dead, Reuel insists that he can revive her, and when he successfully does so, he wins not only admiration but also several job offers from the Boston medical community — and so is no longer left behind by the free-contract polis. One of these offers leads him on a transatlantic journey to Africa, where he discovers his kingly racial patrimony. Thus Dianthe's catastrophic train journey northward prompts Reuel's heroic Atlantic journey eastward into racial prowess.

But, of course, in this world of freedom, Reuel faces competition from a "brother," in this case Aubrey Livingston, with whom he battles symbolically and sexually over the body of a "sister," the reawakened Dianthe Rusk.[21] Eventually the men learn that they are not only "brothers" insofar as they are medical "colleagues" or U.S. citizens but also in that they are blood siblings with the same parents — and that Dianthe is their actual sister. They have mistaken their blood kinship with Dianthe for a sexual attraction to her — or rather they turn more readily to the empowering heterosexual dynamic than to the "republican" sororial/fraternal one, like the protagonists of the "first American" novels of William Hill Brown and Susanna Rowson. Although Aubrey is apparently the proper white child of Mr. Livingston, he eventually learns that, like Dianthe and Reuel, he too is the child of Mr. Livingston's slave Mira but was secretly substituted, by his African American slave grandmother, for a stillborn white child of Mrs. Livingston. Separated from their mother Mira and from each other when Mira was sold down river by Mr. Livingston, these three children converge in Boston as young adults at the opening of Hopkins's novel, unaware of their kinship.

It's no coincidence that Hopkins alludes early in this novel to Hawthorne's *The Scarlet Letter,* with its similar triangle formed around the woman's troubled relation to race freedom and its similar catalyst in the form of a doctor's covert invasion and sabotage of the relation between a woman and her lover (477). In her retelling of this story, Hopkins foregrounds the competitive game organized around sexuality that these three, like Hester, Dimmesdale, and Chillingworth, enter together in Atlantic modernity. She works both to expose and to reimagine the effects of racialized possession within this world — or, as Reuel describes his project, to unveil the economy of "compensation and retribution carried on in the vast recesses of the human soul" (448).

Traumatic Narration

To do so, Hopkins astutely refashions early-twentieth-century psychology as articulated by William James, Alfred Binet, Sigmund Freud, and others. As several scholars beginning with Thomas Otten have established, Hopkins was reading some of these authors and rethinking their ideas within an Afrocentric context.[22] Not only does her character Reuel refer by name to Binet (author of *On Double Consciousness*) but in her opening scene Reuel echoes the language of William James in James's review of Binet's recent work. These writers were influenced by the lectures of Jean-Martin Charcot Sâltpetrière on hysteria and unconscious states (both Freud and James had studied with him at different times, as Horvitz points out [248]), and they began to experiment with hypnosis as a way of uncovering the etiology of hysteria. Their conclusion that psychological trauma was hysteria's source ultimately led to Freud's connection between childhood sexual abuse and hysteria. Deborah Horvitz argues persuasively that Hopkins would have been familiar with the controversy surrounding Freud's theory, at least through her reading of James (249). With her opening allusions to Binet and James, Hopkins lets her readers know that her novel offers its own, African-Atlantic understanding of trauma and hysteria.

She might have been especially motivated to do so in that, as Athena Devlin has shown, late-nineteenth-century theories of hysteria, hypnosis, and the unconscious were often implicitly racialized, as, for example, in the short stories of Henry James where ancient race "memory" returns to "possess" a character.[23] Hopkins had established in her first novel that she was aware of this troubled mingling of race, memory, and depth psychology, when she had Will Smith refer directly to the story of Dr. Jekyll and Mr. Hyde and furthermore read it as a pro-jection of unconscious white fears (272). In *Of One Blood,* she does the important work of revising these dimensions of psychological theory in the context of At-lantic history. In Hopkins's version, notions of an "undiscovered country" within the psyche work both to narrate African American women's sexual trauma (as I'll consider here) and to imagine a pan-psychic yet still racialized and gendered trajectory for African-Atlantic history that thrives in a "free atmosphere" (468), as I'll discuss in the next section.

Through Reuel's explanation of Dianthe's coma state, first of all, Hopkins anat-omizes black women's rape history in the United States. This history is encoded in Reuel's conclusion that Dianthe "has been long and persistently subjected to mesmeric influences, and the nervous shock induced by the excitement of the [recent train] accident has thrown her into cataleptic sleep" (465). That is, her "subjection" to mesmeric forces had put her in a state of shock before the train accident — itself an image of the injuries attending black travel and uprootedness (and perhaps also sexual force). Therefore, even after her awakening by Reuel she "frequently fell into convulsions, sometimes lying for hours in a torpid state" and when awake she seems to lack any will of her own (474 – 75). "Memory remain[s] a blank" and nothing seems able "to restore the poor, violated mind to its origi-nal strength" (488 – 89). Hopkins thus gives her own portrait of a woman's post-abuse, dissociative condition. If we hear echoes of Clarissa, we need not under-stand them strictly as literary allusions since the two stories are linked at sea-level by Atlantic racial and sexual history. Eventually the novel tracks these "mesmeric influences" to which Dianthe has been "persistently subjected" back to the literal rape of her mother, Mira, for apparently Mira's master, Mr. Livingston, practiced his scientific-mystical experiments on Mira even as he also violated her body and so produced Dianthe as well as her two brothers, Reuel and Aubrey.

While Deborah Horvitz emphasizes the multiplicity of voices and genres that join to fashion this history and to make *Of One Blood* a hysteric's text ("romance, historical romance, allegory, fantasy, and mystery" combine to create "an ex-perimental pattern"),[24] I would stress in addition the self-conscious "framing" mode that Hopkins uses to narrate it and especially to tell the story of Mira. She highlights the embeddedness of this "mesmeric" history in a tradition of representation — and hints at her own difficult position — when she sets up this spectacle of Livingston's hypnosis of Mira, first of all, as a scene of entertain-ment before an audience of white men, Mr. Livingston's curious guests, and then has it narrated, within the novel, by Aubrey, as a childhood memory (before he learns that he is also Mira's son). Through the voice of the unwittingly biracial Aubrey, we are watching a white audience (Aubrey's friends) watch a white audience (Livingston senior's friends) watch this white master's abortive possession of his female slave.

In the symbolic tableau as repeated by Aubrey, Livingston senior hypnotizes Mira and "command[s]" her to "tell the company what you see" (487). Mira remarks that he won't like it, "but if I must, I must" (487). Mira is *compelled* to tell what she sees. She paradoxically enacts agency under compulsion, and it is under these conditions that her potential for second sight—for seeing from behind the veil—finds public expression. Forced to speak, Mira predicts the downfall of both Livingston and the South (soon realized in the Civil War) and the emergence of a communal agency for the "downtrodden": "Your houses shall burn, your fields be laid waste, and a downtrodden race shall rule in your land. For you, captain, a prison cell and a pauper's grave" (487). In effect, Hopkins implies that the master and his white audience(s) compel the speaking of their own downfall and the rise of another "race" via this narrative tradition. Mira's possessed voice serves as the master's performance before his guests and later likewise is made into cocktail-party entertainment by the son Aubrey, and yet both father and son—that is, the whole transatlantic representational economy—are ultimately "betrayed" by this voice.

Mira's position thus crystallizes that of writers such as Hopkins. Her predicament highlights the way that what Saidiya Hartman calls the "coerced agency" of African Americans extends into their authorship.[25] As they work by compulsion within a certain narrative tradition, African-Atlantic authors nonetheless signal the beginning of that tradition's "ruin." Yet insofar as this ruined tradition *contains* the story of liberation, a certain strange investment in it remains. And its vision of a free future for an enslaved race still follows that logic by which, to gain freedom, African Americans are compelled, like everyone else in modernity, to speak in racial terms. What does it mean to seek liberty under a certain race compulsion? Is the voice that tells this story free? Such questions lurk under the surface of this scene and the novel: to whom does this "gothic" voice belong? To whom does this narrative belong? Who possesses it? And is Hopkins's novel a record of liberation if it must still move toward a racial telos? Like Mira, Hopkins herself is at once seizing the voice to tell the downfall of white mastery and yet is compelled to do so in the master's racialized gothic genre.[26] From beginning to end, then, her gothic tale is also a metacommentary on the Atlantic literary gothic.

Transatlantic Trade-offs

As she allegorizes her entanglement in the invasive and gothic history of race possession, Hopkins at the same time spins an alternative vision of possession:

possession as a form of collective association rather than coercive domination — possession as a form of sociality that, furthermore, places men within women's sphere of influence. Thomas Otten and Susan Gillman have both explored Hopkins's "transpersonal" vision as a foundation for her historical and "transcultural" project that is at one level pan-African and yet ultimately offers, Gillman argues, "a syncretic panracial perspective."[27] Meanwhile Kevin Gaines and others have highlighted the imperialist impulses and the contradictions in this racial vision.[28] I will lay stress on the complications that Hopkins faces in mounting this perspective, especially within the context of a racial-patriarchal Atlantic economy that holds in its grasp not only a narrative voice but also the bodies of the ruined women who give rise to that voice.

To explain his ability to revive Dianthe from her deathlike state, Reuel offers (and Hopkins through him) a theory of association or "magnetism" between bodies that is neither hierarchical nor contractual, neither determined from above nor chosen from below, though it requires a "free atmosphere." Because all bodies are sustained by what Reuel calls the "subtile magnetic agent[s]" of the earth's atmosphere, if the form of a person's death has not "injured or destroyed tissue formation or torn down the structure of vital organs, life may be recalled when it has become entirely extinct, which is not [even] so in the present case" (468). For cases such as Dianthe's, he has composed a medicine that reactivates the process by which the "subtile magnetic agent is . . . drawn into the body through the lungs" — salt and oleo resin exposed for several hours in "an atmosphere of free ammonia" — and can revive the seemingly dead person (468 – 69). The requisite of a free atmosphere is telling.

The novel implies that these notions of Reuel's provide a kind of intuitive translation of ancient African knowledge: his ideas about "volatile magnetism" compare to what we later learn about the ancient Meroite notions, which, moreover, seem to enfold an explanation of racial kinship as well, for they explain the energies of human attraction and community. The descendants of Meroe believe in a supreme being as the generative center of all nature, a power which has dispersed parts of itself into humans and now operates in immanent form to draw humans together. In humans, the supreme being manifests itself as an "ever-living faculty or Ego" with "the power of expressing itself to other bodies, with like gift and form, its innate feeling; and by law of affinity, is ever striving to regain its original position near the great Unity" (562). Hopkins's text leaves ambiguous the exact terms of this "law of affinity," in particular the question of whether the phrase "like gift and form" refers to universal-human or specifically racial kinship. The "magnetism" of Reuel, Aubrey, and Dianthe seems, however, to suggest that this kinship is racial, as does Reuel's attraction to the site of Meroe.

Indeed, insofar as we are led to understand Reuel's scientific project as an expression of an ancient African tradition, his entire life's work has been compelled by a racial energy of affinity. Once he has arrived in Africa, "He remembered his mother well. From her he had inherited his mysticism and his occult powers. The nature of the mystic within him was, then, but a dreamlike devotion to the spirit that had swayed his ancestors; it was the shadow of Ethiopia's power" (558). In positioning such apparently white scientific projects as a legacy and revival of a prior African culture, Hopkins reverses the racial chronologies of modernity in the way that black intellectuals were beginning to do at the turn of the century (and as more recently undertaken, for instance, by Martin Bernal in *Black Athena*). Yet at the same time she maintains the racial or inheritance logic of the discourse. Like George Eliot in *Daniel Deronda,* as we'll see, Hopkins's vision seems to sustain the principle of race as, paradoxically, the instrument of the movement toward universal human community.

Hopkins implicitly burrows further into these questions when her text forces Reuel into a series of encounters with the African feminine on his way to Meroe.[29] As Hopkins arranges it, Reuel's experience in Africa pressures him, allegorically, to come to terms with both his homosocial struggle with Aubrey and his divided attachment to what Hopkins figures as the African feminine. The initial late-night descent that leads him to Meroe is, first of all, suggestively gendered. He finds a path "leading down to a well-like depression near the center of the great chamber" (543) and "what was evidently once a tank" (544) — imagery that resonates with William James's description of the "continuum of cosmic consciousness" as a "mother-sea or reservoir" into which "our minds plunge" despite the "accidental fences" that "our individuality builds" (quoted in Gillman 75). James's image of a sea-plunge itself suggests a deep link between Atlantic experience and these raced and gendered theories of the psyche. Hopkins pursues this feminized imagery when, within the dark interior of this tank, Reuel meets "the devilish countenance of the Ethiopian sphinx" and he then encounters "something [. . .] emitting a subtle odor as it moved" so that "he sank upon the ground and consciouess left him" (544).

In effect, Hopkins has reversed the swoon, narrating the man's fall into a gynocentric world rather than the woman's fall into a phallocentric one. Having descended into this dark, scent-filled well, Reuel then awakens among "a singular people, governed by a line of female monarchs, all having the same name, Candace." The monarch is a "virgin queen" who lives in the "inner city" of Telassar, amid a community of virgins from among whom she chooses her successor. To reach this inner city, Reuel must again follow a suggestive path: led by his guide Ai "along a mountain gorge" on a "path straitened between the impending moun-

tain on one side and a rapid sparkling stream on the other," all set in a "romanti-
cally wild, picturesquely beautiful" landscape, he finally arrives at the palace of
the queen, where he walks through "seemingly endless colonnades . . . til [he
comes] to a huge door formed of great winged creatures" (566–67). An "Amazon"
opens the doors, "disclosing the splendour of the royal Presence-chamber" (567)
where the queen lies on "silken cushions" (567). Thus does Reuel descend down
and back into the "chamber" of a female African "presence."

Yet, significantly, although Reuel embraces the feminine world in Africa, he
has abandoned "the feminine," in the form of Dianthe, in the United States. Hopkins sets up an explicitly transatlantic juxtaposition, which suggests some self-
consciousness on her part about the gender sacrifice or substitution entailed in
this reverse middle passage leading to Reuel's recovery of an ancient racial legacy.
In Africa Reuel falls through a hole in the historical world to encounter and move
past the aporia that the feminine has come to represent in a racialized society
(in that a woman exists as an absent presence in the very race-communities she
reproduces). Yet, at the very same time, in America Dianthe is being abducted
and molested by Aubrey, the jealous brother, who is determined to master this
disruptive female (absent) presence. His lust for Dianthe, his will to possess this
woman in Reuel's place, has already led him secretly to sabotage one after another
offer of employment to Reuel, including by suggestions to potential employers
that Reuel is of mixed blood; and Reuel's very journey back to Africa has been
orchestrated by Aubrey, who subverts all job offers except the one that would require Reuel to go to travel to this faraway land for two years (a plot element that
neatly allegorizes the nation's resistance to black employment and the scheme of
repatriating African Americans to Africa, an idea Hopkins rejected).

Hopkins thus hints that Reuel's African destiny, although seemingly radical
in its embrace of a gynocentric world and disruptive in its implications for white
culture, remains circumscribed by the "invisible hand" of apparently white-
Atlantic manipulations. Moreover she deeply, perhaps covertly, embeds in her
text the suggestion that the African American man is complicit in these racialized, homosocial manipulations. For it seems that Aubrey is able to count on
Reuel's commitment to worldly and racial ambition, over and above his loyalty to
a woman and despite her protestations.[30] Hopkins makes clear that Reuel *chooses*
to leave Dianthe and go to Africa against *her* objections. Dianthe insists that
she cares nothing for the economic comfort he says he must provide for her, but
Reuel's aspirations lead him to accept this opportunity and leave her in her weakened state while he goes off to Africa — to search for a hidden city that promises
to reveal the secret and powerful knowledge of an ancient African civilization.

Ironically, Reuel parts from Dianthe to reconnect to a past that she actually carries within her.

In this way, Reuel allows the fatal legacy of possessiveness to reemerge and repeat itself. For it is Reuel's absence that enables Aubrey to exert his mesmeric powers until "the influence [he] had acquired rendered [Dianthe] quiescent in his hands" (597), and Dianthe again "lost her will in another's" (603). Hereafter, Dianthe is lured by Aubrey to the old Livingston plantation where they were all born, and she lives as his prisoner there, returned to her old possessed state. She moves about as if "in another world, unconscious of her own identity," until she stumbles upon her grandmother still living in an outlying hut, from whom she learns the truth of her kinship with Reuel and Aubrey. At this crisis, her memory returns but with it comes madness. She suffers "the torture of [a] soul unmoored" and finally attempts to poison Aubrey, but he instead forces her to drink the potion she has prepared for him. This sequence of events implicates Reuel in the white-identified man's repossession of the African American woman. Reuel is perhaps not so different from Livingston senior, in that he gains social entry by way of his successful "experiments" on the body of a "possessed" woman. That is, via his miraculous awakening of Dianthe, Reuel creates his own opportunity to become a "race man."

A gender critique of the African American man's worldly ambitions (including how they rest on a racial rationale) is circulating here, although so implicitly that it's hard to say whether, or how consciously, Hopkins intended it. Certainly Hopkins starkly juxtaposes these gendered race dramas on opposite sides of the Atlantic, one in Africa open-endedly epic, and the other in the United States foreclosed and tragic. The destruction of Dianthe implies that the pursuit of an Ethiopianist vision entails a troubling repetition of Atlantic race plots. To this extent, Hopkins's story remains gothic and woman-centered: she works to make the exposure of crimes against the African American woman and the redemption of her body the main function of her narrative. One might argue that, by the logic of substitution, in marrying Queen Candace, Reuel cleanses the memory and trauma of his sister/lover Dianthe, transforming the raped and powerless woman into a queenly virgin. Even though Reuel marries Queen Candace, he remarks that she "remind[s] him strongly of his beautiful Dianthe" and when she speaks "it seem[d] to him that Dianthe's own voice [is] breathing in his ears" (568). It would therefore seem an appropriate closure to this rewriting of the middle-passage legacy that, after witnessing Dianthe's death, Reuel sanctions the murder by drowning of his brother-traitor Aubrey.

And yet all of this conforms quite neatly to the old transatlantic plot in which a woman's ruin and captivity launches a man's freedom-seeking identity. Hopkins retains the lineaments of the masculine, racial liberty narrative. The race man must come fully to terms with the powers and violations of the race woman, but he must do so in order to act as the male agent of a renewed racial future. Queen Candace after all "waits the coming of Ergamenes to inaugurate a dynasty of kings" (561), and Reuel turns out to be this Ergamenes. In the end, Dianthe enters the heroic race narrative only by way of her death: she is hailed into the otherworld both by the "disembodied souls of every age" and by "ancient Ethiopia" as a "dying daughter of the royal line" (615). Thus Reuel's entry into his own native and kingly manhood, although entailing a reversal of the middle passage meant to purge the woman's founding Atlantic trauma, does not shake loose of the old Atlantic telos.

The Author's Gothic Entry

Yet at the heart of Hopkins's text there is, as in Jacobs's, a missing ground, a site of substitutions without origin, as expressed in the scene in which Mira's vision of a free future for "her race" is not only spoken under the compulsion of the "other race" but also is represented as racialized performance, in the voice of Aubrey. If such a scenario characterizes Hopkins's own position, as I've suggested, then her generically conventional mode for her vision of a race future merely reminds us that her text is "framed." She speaks before an audience and within a narrative whose terms are not her own but which nonetheless provide her point of entry. It is no accident that Dianthe Rusk is a singer who also makes her first, voiced entrance before an at least partially white audience.

We can hear the vibrato that this predicament creates when, near the end of the novel, Reuel wonders in an aside if the new intercourse between America and ancient Meroe will only bring more violation. Reuel aims to teach "his people all that he has learned in years of contact with modern culture" (including, significantly, Christianity, with its narrative of sacrifice and redemption), but he also wonders, "What will the end be?" of the "mighty nations penetrating the dark, mysterious forests of his native land" (621). The word "native" bears the weight, by this point, of unbearable contradictions.

This quiet vibrato has its structural corollary in Hopkins's final frame for her novel, in which her voice inhabits the transcendent and in this sense indeterminate perspective of God. Her narrator's closing remarks first of all undercut the race-vision she has so carefully elaborated:

The slogan of the hour is "Keep the Negro down!" but who is clear enough in vision to decide who hath black blood and who hath it not? Can any one tell? No not one; for in His own mysterious way He has united the white race and the black race in this new continent. By the transgression of the law he proves his own infallibility: "Of one blood have I made all the nations to dwell upon the whole face of the earth," is as true today as when given to the inspired writers to be recorded. No man can draw the dividing line between the races, for they are both of one blood! (607)

How can Reuel be the heroic regenerator of ancient racial identity within such a dilution of race distinctions? Is this a story that renews a race, or disperses it? A story that frees black women or forfeits them? "Can any one tell? No not one."

Like God, "by the transgression of the law" Hopkins "proves her own" unfixability within the racial story. She once more registers her slippery position in the next and very last paragraph, when she refers humbly to "this *feeble* work" but then praises such humble projects as a repository for divine "*truths.*" She identifies herself with the author of the divine plan in which race becomes a negligible element. Indeed, she ends by diminishing the grandeur of all that the ancient Telassar stands for: "Caste prejudice, race pride, boundless wealth, scintillating intellects refined by all the arts of the intellectual world, are but puppets in His hand, for His promises stand, and He will prove His words, 'Of one blood have I made all race of men'" (621). Although a masculine figure (God) seems to be the agent here, at the same time Hopkins has made "His" words hers, appropriating them for her title and subordinating all of men's possessions (wealth and intellect) to this story that instantiates divine truths. She implies that her apparently essentialist race narrative is the "puppet" *she* manipulates to achieve her exposure of coercive race mixture *and* her historical vision, finally, of healed trauma and an unraced, global unity.

Hopkins's closing words should remind us that, although it is Reuel who finally takes the throne, it is a woman author who puts him there. Yet, if this is so, we must acknowledge as well that it is ultimately *Hopkins* who gains entry through Dianthe. That is, like Reuel, and like many authors before her, Hopkins establishes and authorizes her position in the contract-polis of Atlantic modernity by way of the "mesmerizing" story of Dianthe.

Like Harriet Jacobs, then, in seizing print Hopkins speaks equivocally not only as an African American writing from within a gothic history but as a woman entering the liberty story by way of her own undoing. A gothic tale indeed. And yet also an epic one, which places a long Gothic-Atlantic history within a longer

African one. By way of her gothic yet Africanist epic, Hopkins has turned inside-out the epic tales of the Anglo-Atlantic written by Catharine Maria Sedgwick, Nathaniel Hawthorne, and George Eliot, to which I'll turn next. In bookending my chapters on these three Anglo-Atlantic authors with readings of two of Hopkins's novels — here *Of One Blood* and, at the end of the next section, *Contending Forces* — I imitate Hopkins's inverting of the "frame," in both senses, of Atlantic history.

IV | Liberty as Race Epic

11 | Freedom by Removal in Sedgwick

IN THE NINETEENTH CENTURY, English-language narrators come into their own as mediators of the Atlantic liberty story. Novelists realize the possibilities latent in the narrative stance of Behn's *Oroonoko* and they combine that onlooking stance with the epic scale modeled by historians. Unfolding their stories across many pages and serial installments, they aspire to simulate the broad stream of history through which generations of characters move toward liberty. The "epic" narrators of the four authors I discuss in these next four chapters (Sedgwick, Hawthorne, Eliot, and Hopkins) are typical, in that they stand aside and create continuity across the ruptures and violence of the Anglo-Atlantic legacy. From their sideline position — itself a "free" or objective stance that by now is inherently racialized and to which we saw Pauline Hopkins staking her claim — they chart the motions of the race principle, its Hegelian actualization in history.

These narrators furthermore ground that development in the originating site of a "native spot," as both Nathaniel Hawthorne's and George Eliot's narrators call it. "A human life, I think," says Eliot's meditative narrator in *Daniel Deronda*, "should be well rooted in some spot of a native land."[1] This native spot is the place where "the definiteness of early memories may be inwrought with affection" so as to become a "sweet habit of the blood" and keep the person "rooted" in the face of the "future widening of knowledge" (50). In her novel *Hope Leslie*, on which I focus in this chapter, Catharine Maria Sedgwick likewise speaks of the power of those homes where we develop our "first acquaintance with nature" so that eventually "every familiar object has a history—the trees have tongues, and the very air is vocal."[2] Such sentiments may seem at odds with the characters in these novels who suffer from rootlessness and racial instabilities; but the novels offer to provide imaginatively, in their rhetoric and resolutions, exactly what the characters initially lack. They recuperate for their readers that left-behind or missing native place where "there is a living and breathing spirit infused into nature" (17).

Hawthorne and Hopkins take up more ironic attitudes toward this compensatory native spot, and Hopkins pointedly deconstructs the removals, fabrications, and land seizures veiled by the rhetoric of nativeness. Yet both authors nonetheless invoke its grounding powers. In his introductory, Hawthorne recollects the "deep and aged roots which my family has struck into the soil" and he transfers this attachment to Hester, who returns to Boston after her ordeal apparently because of the "roots which she had struck into the soil."[3] In *Contending Forces* Hopkins similarly begins her story with the "tender ties" that "gave life to every inanimate object" in the Bermuda world of Mr. Montfort, although she simultaneously highlights that he is an emigrant Englishman—not actually a native but rather a colonist supported by a slave economy.[4] Like Eliot and Sedgwick, Hawthorne and Hopkins evoke the gut-level materiality of climate and place that had come to be associated with race, and in doing so they display how race fills an absence and expresses a longing. As they offer imaginary worlds that begin to reconstitute the native homes broken and violated in the gothic story, they accordingly soften the brother/sister property conflict at its core. In short, they call readers forth into a reconfigured romance of the domestic, the sibling, the national, and the native, so as to fashion a racialized individuality that (despite all the turmoil of Atlantic history) feels embodied, communally held, and nationally emplaced. Thus do their novels deserve the name of historical race epics.

Most of the Anglo-Atlantic authors I have discussed so far develop forms of nativism fed subtextually by a disavowed or distorted African-Atlantic subjectivity. By contrast, Sedgwick and Hawthorne, writing during the enactment of Indian-removal policies in the United States, seek instead to enfold the Indian American presence into the Anglo-American freedom story—and in this way imaginatively to remove its threat to that story. As we will see Hawthorne do in *The Scarlet Letter*, Sedgwick sets her novel in the decades leading up to the English Civil War, during the Puritan colonization and Pequot War in New England, and she narrates, with complex investments, how these colonists "took root." In *Hope Leslie*, she creates a heroine who, for Anglo-Atlantic readers, serves to heal the legacy of ruin, in part by recasting the history of radical displacements (experienced by Puritans and by Indians) as the rebellious remaking of the world by young women, under the sign of an Anglo-originated freedom. Along the way,

Sedgwick all at once Anglicizes, ennobles, and "removes" the Pequots. And readers of the novel have sometimes repeated her practice.

Racializing the Indian American

Catharine Maria Sedgwick's narrator attributes to her Pequot (or Pequod, in Sedgwick's spelling) heroine Magawisca a race spirit driven by freedom that, in an apparent paradox, allows her absorption into Anglo-Atlantic history. When, late in the novel, Magawisca is imprisoned for abetting her people in their attacks on the English and then is brought before the court, she tells Governor Winthrop, "My people have never passed under your yoke — not one of my race has ever acknowledged your authority" — but she speaks the Whig language of the "yoke" to make this assertion (302). She responds to questions, the narrator reports, "in the spirit of her race," showing "no surprise, nor emotion of any kind" (302), and yet she closes with Patrick Henry's words, "I demand of thee death or liberty" (309).[5] Magawisca claims a racial purity surpassing that of the English, contrasting her people to "thy mixed race" — and yet Sedgwick figures her race identity in the mode of English revolutionaries, including the interiorized principle of dissent, as when she has Magawisca announce that "the Great Spirit hath *written his laws on the hearts* of his *original* children" (303, emphasis added). Repeatedly in this way, Sedgwick casts Magawisca as adamantly, racially other — Magawisca insists that "the Indian and the White man can no more mingle, and become one, than day and night" (349) — but exactly in the language of the "people" from whom she differentiates herself.

In Sedgwick's rendering, Magawisca's anti-assimilationist stance, in its reinforcement of identity *as* racial, assures Magawisca's assimilation into an Anglo-Atlantic narrative. Renée Bergland rightly remarks, "Native Americans, as a race, are absorbed into the white American mind as an aspect of its consciousness,"[6] but we need to go one step further: it is exactly in fashioning Native Americans *as a race* that such absorption is most fundamentally enacted. Most especially, in shaping the Pequots as a race that demands "liberty," the text makes them its own. With one authorial hand, Magawisca is characterized as proudly other, but with the other she is absorbed into the historical narrative of *English* liberty. Magawisca's resistance to the English "yoke" is continually reassimilated to a narrative of England's triumph over *its* old Norman yoke and French Catholic enemy. In the courtroom scene, for instance, Magawisca enters in "the peculiar costume of her people . . . collar — bracelet — girdle — embroidered moccasins, and purple mantle," and the narrator bothers to tell us that she eschews the English clothing offered her for her court appearance. Yet then the narrator reflects that Magawisca "displayed [her costume] with a feeling resembling Nelson's when he emblazoned himself with stars and orders to appear before his enemies on the fatal day of his last battle" (298). The battle alluded to, of course, is that of Trafalgar in 1805, when the British conclusively defeated the French although Nelson lost his life. Sedgwick doesn't mention it, but Nelson also entered that battle, as Magawisca enters the court, as a one-armed person, having lost the other in a previous battle. Again, exactly in rejecting any affiliation with the English, exactly by proudly costuming herself on the possible brink of death, Magawisca bizarrely emerges as the Nelsonian liberator of the English in their age-old, postcolonial battle with the French. In other key scenes, she will be similarly glossed as a heroic subverter of French, popish forces. Submerged is the more material fact that, indeed, the American colonies and the wealth that stolen land and labor generated *had* placed the English on the world stage and, indirectly, *had* allowed the English to defeat the French at Trafalgar. The Anglicization of Magawisca is merely the necessary discursive aftereffect of that history.

Here is the familiar appropriation, Sedgwick's Indian version of Africanism and Orientalism. Parallel to the function the Jewish Daniel Deronda serves for George Eliot, Magawisca's native "race" provides a dissenting outsider through whom Anglo-Protestant novelists can universalize, or make hegemonic, "their" cultural narrative — thus defeating that dissent even while celebrating it. Furthermore, in rooting the Indian American within Anglo-Atlantic *history,* Sedgwick makes her own novel authoritatively historical. In turn, *Hope Leslie* and its author gain the cultural capital that accrues to such richly allusive, historical texts.

From early in the novel, Sedgwick leavens her story with a yeasty racial language, preparing this appropriation of Magawisca. While critics have understood Sedgwick's inclusion of Magawisca's interpolated account of the Pequot War as a woman-voiced revision of Puritan historiography, and some note the boldness of her celebration of Pequot as well as Pilgrim figures, most have not sufficiently faced the way Sedgwick undercuts the implications of this revision by reenclosing it within racial and Christian frameworks.[7] For, first of all, as Ezra Tawil also points out, in the novel's early chapters Sedgwick infuses all viewpoints with an oppositional racial vocabulary.[8] Visiting Bethel on the day before the attack and just before Magawisca tells her story, Nelema refers ruefully to the "expiration" of "my race," while the narrator tells us that she listened to "the fancied voices of the spirit of her race," and Jennet, as she watches Nelema and Magawisca depart together, deems them "the offspring of a race that are the children and heirs of the evil one" (39, 40, 41). Sedgwick's novel certainly discredits Jennet in the end, but both characters and narrator speak the language of race. Everell is moved, we are told in the narrator's discourse, by Magawisca's story of "those defenceless families of savages, pent in the recesses of their native forests, and there exterminated" (56); and Magawisca's mother's comment that the "blood" of chieftains runs in her children's veins finds an echo in the narrator's closing references in this chapter to the "chieftain of a savage race" who must avenge the "blood of his conquerors" (59). It's not simply a question of whether this racializing of vengeance is essentialist or not; in casting the war as the Indians' race drama, this rhetoric elides English colonization as cause of the war. Likewise, Everell makes repeated references to Magawisca as "noble" and full of "noble feeling" (44, 48, 199). It is her nobility that draws him into cross-racial sympathy with her, yet his affiliation also allows her assimilation into his story *exactly because* he sees her story (like his) as that of a "heroic and suffering people" (56). Furthermore, although Magawisca's motives and actions in saving Everell are repeatedly described as noble, it is Everell whose "brow and hair" take on "an almost supernatural brightness" just before she saves him. Again and again, the noble but simple Pequot serves to heighten Anglo-Protestant heroism. And indeed Judge Samuel Howe, after reading the novel, wrote to thank Sedgwick for her account of the "noble liberality" and "noble character" not of the Pequots but of the Puritan Pilgrims.[9]

Even as the racializing of American Indians "raises" the status of "the savage" to that of a heroic people, it absorbs the Indian into a "noble" English narrative. In turn, the principle of difference embedded in that vocabulary will finally enable the expulsion of the Indian from the land the English want to occupy, yet it will be cast as a "freeing" of Magawisca by the novel's main English characters.

That such absorption is Sedgwick's desire, and not just the colonists,' becomes clear in the Christian framework she builds around her narrative of the Pequot/English war. At a pause in Magawisca's account of it, Sedgwick's narrator steps forward to note how the killing of Magawisca's brother by white colonizers reveals the discrepancy between Christianity's "divine principles" and its practice. She regrets that "instead of always being a medium for the light that emanates from our holy law, [the discrepancy] is too often the darkest cloud that obstructs the passage of its rays to the hearts of heathen men" (53). Yet the narrator maintains allegiance to Christianity as *the* true religion. At the end of Magawisca's account and the chapter, the narrator points to Mononotto's earlier kind acts toward the English as "precious to all those who would accumulate proofs, that the image of God is never quite effaced from the souls of his creatures; and that in their darkest ignorance, and deepest degradation, there are still to be found traits of mercy and benevolence" (59). The Pequots, too, depend on a Christian God—and Sedgwick's Christian narrative—for their movement from savage to noble, heroic race. Indians' naturally degraded state *may* be enlightened by Anglo-Protestant Christianity. The narrator then compares her attitude to

Mungo Park's cherishing of the one beautiful flower "that bloomed in his melancholy track over the African desert" (59), implicitly aligning her perspective with that of an ambitious British colonizer of Africa who appears here, however, as a man carrying the white man's burden.

Sedgwick well understood, though she never fully admitted in print, the ways that her own homestead in America rested on violent dispossession, both territorial and rhetorical. She undoubtedly knew at least the outlines of the history by which various branches of her family had set up Indian mission schools, vying for and winning land grants exactly to house these projects, and then later, when the missions failed under the pressures of conflict, "inherited" the land. She likely knew that the very land on which she grew up had been consolidated through strategic purchases from the few scattered Indians who had not moved west but were unable to maintain their land after having lost spouses or other family, including some who fought on the American side in the Revolutionary War — the war that consolidated the nation and therefore laid the ground for the policies and practices of Indian removal that were under way as Sedgwick wrote this novel.

Although Sedgwick glossed over these facts in the autobiography she wrote for her niece, her novel suggests that she felt the historical ironies. Especially, I propose, through the character of Hope, she implicitly struggles with "the sounds and accents that haunt" this land (to borrow George Eliot's phrase in *Daniel Deronda*, 50). Her awareness of the tragedies and ironies of this "native spot" was no doubt heightened by the fact that members of her family had twice married converted Indians. Indeed, as she was writing *Hope Leslie,* her cousin Harriet Gold was causing a scandal at the mission school in Connecticut run by Sedgwick's uncle by proposing to marry a Christian Indian, Elias Boudinot (ultimately provoking the mob violence led by Harriet Gold's own brother, which forced the couple out of town). Sedgwick eventually attempted to make contact with both this and the Canadian-Indian branches of her family.[10]

And yet, Sedgwick helps to generate the story of "vanishing" Indians, and she does so at the very moment when the question of Indian land rights was being hotly debated, eventually culminating in the Indian Removal Act of 1830. Further, she helps to write it in a powerfully implicit way. As I'll suggest, her feminist desire to bestow the lineage of liberty on her heroines leads her to embrace a race narrative that displaces Indians from the land even as it collapses Magawisca into Hope. The liberalism of her perspective itself "vanished" Indians by framing them within this woman-centered narrative of Anglo-Protestant liberty. We might say that Sedgwick's story sucks the blood out of her Indian American characters, except that it is blood that she, in effect, put into them.

At times, critics of the novel come dangerously close to repeating this absorption, as when one critic approvingly mentions that Sedgwick uses the date of Anne Hutchinson's death for Magawisca's trial without exploring what purpose this Protestant affiliation serves for Sedgwick but instead worrying that highly critical readings of the race politics of Sedgwick's text will "re-vanish" the novel; or another reads Magawisca's "removal" at the end of the novel as the effect of her failure to realize feminist resistance to her father Mononotto's tyrannical masculine politics.[11] Much of the feminist criticism on the novel, as Nina Baym has observed in *American Women Writers and the Work of History*, is impelled by the same attempt to subsume the novel's race politics within a feminist account of it — and, I would add, a liberationist account. This problem in criticism on Sedgwick is in part an extension of the American exceptionalism in Americanist literary studies, discussed earlier. Recent readings of *Hope Leslie* perceptively position it as a pivotal text in the imagining of the nation. Certainly it is that. One common assumption of these accounts, however, is that this republican imagining was being done for the first time, that America was a site of utterly *new* republican narratives and questions, and that Sedgwick's feminism translates readily into a progressive version of these narratives.[12]

It is, however, exactly by way of her freedom discourse, not in spite of it, that Sedgwick's representation of Indian Americans stands shoulder-deep in race politics. I agree with Ezra Tawil that *Hope Leslie* helps to forge the very racial rhetoric from which it also seems to dissent, and perhaps in even more fundamental ways than those Tawil describes.[13] The race rhetoric Sedgwick mobilizes is, in this period, already old (not new, as Tawil argues), and Sedgwick's task is an appropriative layering of racialized vocabularies and conflicts. And yet, oddly enough, as we will see, Sedgwick's novel also seems to tell the story of its own complicity. It signals its own place in cultural history, especially its function as an Atlantic vessel of the sublime English race-narrative.

Undoing the Ruin of Freedom

From the opening pages of the novel, the plight of a freedom-seeking Englishwoman provides the catalyst for Sedgwick's racial-national narrative. She begins her story in the decade before the English Revolution with a letter that lays out the problem of liberty vs. obedience in the context of a sexual plot, and she represents the underlying threat of alienation and anarchy in this conflict. With shrewd literary-historical attunement, Sedgwick invokes both the nativist and the sexual literary legacy: she opens with an epigraph from John Milton's *Comus* — that late-seventeenth-century drama about a fair woman held captive under the sea and threatened with rape by a wily sorcerer, a drama written by a republican author celebrated in Sedgwick's day as a modern reviver of the native tradition. The lines she chooses alert her readers to this legacy: "Virtue may be assail'd, but never hurt, / Surpris'd by unjust force, but not inthrall'd" (5). She immediately establishes that she is telling another story about how tyranny, catalyzed by the powers of the sea, will fail in its coercions yet still unleash a legacy of sexual trauma.

Certainly for Sedgwick, as for Milton, sexual liberty is at stake — so that by the second page of the novel the question — "Liberty, what is it!" — has been raised in a voice of exasperation by the Royalists. Sir William Fletcher, a strident supporter of the king and of a Filmerite worldview, has heard that his nephew, namesake, and heir-to-be has been associating with Puritans and dissenters. In a vehement letter, he tells his brother to "take heed that the boy be taught unquestioning and unqualified loyalty to his sovereign — the Alpha and Omega of political duty" (5), for, too often, "our lads' heads are crammed with the philosophy and rhetoric and history of those liberty-loving Greeks and Romans. This is the pernicious lore that has poisoned our academical fountains. Liberty, what is it! Daughter of disloyalty and mother of all misrule — who from the hour that she tempted our first parents to forfeit paradise, hath ever worked mischief to our race" (6).

Here's the familiar cluster: race-history, liberty, and unruly "Eves." Sir William goes on to vow that "no daughter or guinea of mine shall ever go to one who is infected with this spreading plague" (7), so that William junior, the nephew, will soon be forced to choose between his love for Alice, Sir William's daughter, and his commitment to what the narrator calls the "principles of civil and religious liberty" (8). He decides to leave Alice, choosing the latter. Sedgwick in fact fashions the nephew as the ideal type of a free Englishman. When Sir William first hints at his ultimatum to his nephew, he encounters "the lofty independence of the youth who, from the first, shewed that neither frowns nor favour would induce him to bow the knee to the idols Sir William had served" (7). Indeed, "There was something in this independence that awed the inferior mind of the uncle," and he is thunderstruck when young William Fletcher determines to say farewell to his beloved Alice and follow Mr. Winthrop to the Puritan colony in Massachusetts. It seems that, in the city on a hill, sexual liberty will be sacrificed for (men's) civic and religious liberty.

As young Fletcher prepares to leave Alice and England, the novel's first chapter closes with the now-paradigmatic swoon, a striking tableau of the abandoned woman, set, furthermore, on the verge of an Atlantic crossing. This moment represents the sexual knot that Sedgwick's text will work to undo, the wound it aims to heal — but she will need race as the salve.[14] The "disloyal daughter" Alice disobeys her father and after all appears at the wharf to accompany William;

but she is at the last moment seized by the king's armed men at the order of her father. She is "driven from [William's] sight," and we just glimpse her "last impotent cries," "her beautiful face convulsed with agony, and her arms outstretched towards him" (11 – 12). In this more noble and chaste way, yet still at the hand of a tyrannous man, Alice is undone by liberty. Sedgwick's narrator records that "it was reported for many years after, that she had suffered a total alienation of mind" and afterward "lived in absolute retirement," which the narrator Christianizes in the tradition of *Clarissa* by saying that "if her mind had departed from its beautiful temple, an angelic spirit had entered and possessed it" (12).

"Alienation" that gives way to an "angelic spirit": this could be a description of one of the Atlantic novel's paradigmatic stories. In answer to the question of whether community can be founded on liberty, this and other novels answer yes, if the woman's liberty can first be alienated and then put in line under the banner of race. Sedgwick's closing racial vision in the novel, which separates Indian and Anglo-American, finds its origin, I'll argue, in the gendered alienation entailed in the making of the Anglo-Atlantic woman into a citizen-heroine.

As the narrative proceeds, the agony of Alice falls into the background and yet continues to reverberate as young William Fletcher arrives in the colony and discovers a repetition of unfree conditions, now imposed by the very Puritans who had denounced and fled such conditions. Without specifying exactly who the Puritan leaders put in "shackles," the narrator tells us that Fletcher's "heart sickened when he saw those, who had sacrificed whatever man holds dearest to religious freedom, imposing those shackles on others from which they had just released themselves at such a price" (15). Therefore Fletcher refuses "the offices of honour and trust that were, from time to time, offered to him" and he retires to the "frontier settlement" of Springfield, fixing "his residence a mile from the village, deeming exposure to the incursions of the savages very slight, and the surveillence of an enquiring neighborhood a certain evil" (17). Fletcher's impulse to withdraw, first initiated by the conflict over Alice, now receives fresh impetus from this New World "shackling." At the same time, his community's invasive surveillance moves him into closer relations with the Pequots.

The "alienation of mind" of Alice — symptom of the geographical alienation of Fletcher, now twice removed from his community — represents the unfinished business of the liberty quest, which the novel and the nation will correct. And indeed, insofar as it allows the attack by Mononotto, Sedgwick arranges it so that Fletcher's removal to Bethel, a mile from the town of Springfield and from protection, re-ignites the Atlantic trauma. In this attack, Fletcher loses a second beloved, his New World wife, who then gets replaced, in effect, by the sister and daughter, Hope Leslie, of the alienated (and later drowned) Alice Fletcher. Their presence, Hope's in particular, propels the main events of the novel, resurfacing the connections that will allow Sedgwick's working through of the gender trouble displayed in the swoon.

But the name that Sedgwick gives Fletcher's estate — Bethel — hints at the re-racialization that will be entailed in this working-through. The name expresses Fletcher's underlying alignment, despite his alienation, with the Christian community, in particular its colonial identity founded on a seizure of the land of native others. For Bethel is the place in Canaan where Abraham settled in obedience to God's directive: "Get thee out of thy country, and from thy kindred . . . unto a land that I will shew thee: and I will make of thee a great nation" and "Unto thy seed I will give this land" (Genesis 12.1–2, 7–8). In the biblical story, exile from home actually prompts the work of nation building in another land — implicitly a colonial nation building insofar as it occurs on already-occupied land. Given that the Puritans drew on such biblical analogues to authorize their colonies and in particular identified the Indians with the "native" Canaanites in conflict with Abraham's "seed," Fletcher's choice of name re-involves him in the very "shacklings" and racialized conflicts he seems to eschew — as does his glancing, distorting reference to the "*incursions*" of "savages."

It is possible that Sedgwick meant her readers to note the irony of the name Bethel, but it seems unlikely, considering that throughout her text she approvingly integrates such biblical parallels and allusions. Sedgwick sometimes introduces race as a liberatory term as if it can counteract coercive power, but it subtly reconfigures such power. Accordingly here, Fletcher's dissent and removal from the English community serves paradoxically to position him as its epitome, the embodiment of its spirit. Sedgwick's narrator continues to fashion him in this way, characterizing him as one of the "men of genius — the men of feeling — the men that the world calls visionaries," who, although disillusioned at the discrepancy between their "beau-ideal" and "the actual state of things," manage in their "reclusive" utopias to preserve and pass on the spirit of liberty (15).

Fletcher carries this spirit of liberty into his guardianship, above all, of the "alienated" Alice's daughter, Hope Leslie, and of his own son Everell Fletcher. It is they who will finish this liberty business, resisting gender coercion, repairing the gender rupture by marrying each other, yet, under cover of the "freeing" of Indians, install a new racial order. The plot that issues in this outcome is complicated and requires some description. It begins in earnest when Alice's husband dies, and she decides to emigrate with her two daughters and sister-in-law to Massachusetts. She dies (again, in effect) during the stormy ocean crossing, but bids her children, Hope and Mary, to go to Fletcher's home. When Fletcher goes to Boston to meet them, he arranges for Magawisca, daughter of a Pequot chief, to stay with his son Everell and his wife, while her brother Oneco accompanies him to Boston. On the return, he sends Alice's younger daughter Mary ahead with Oneco, and he follows later with Hope. But in this lag, the Pequots attack the Fletcher homestead, killing his wife and taking Mary and Everell captive. Everell is eventually released from near death and set free by Magawisca (the two have become attached), and he returns home and develops a friendship with Hope Leslie before he is sent off to school in England, all while Mary stays among the Pequots and, as it turns out, marries Oneco. When, seven years later, Everell returns, it happens that he shares a passage with Sir Philip Gardiner, who poses as a Puritan accompanied by his male servant but who is actually a Catholic Royalist traveling with his mistress (who is dressed in a boy's clothing) and hoping to join up with a rakish friend to renew their fortunes. Through Everell, the gothic villain Gardiner gains entry into the Puritan community, which begins to support him as a prospective husband for Hope, although in fact he seeks only to seduce her. The high-spirited Hope scorns him but he manages to interfere in her later efforts to recover her sister and free Magawisca, who has been taken prisoner by the English for her supposed part in Pequot plans to attack the colony.

Sedgwick especially frames Hope as the force of liberty in the Puritan community, the "unruly" daughter of Alice. The community elders see Hope as a "rash and lawless girl," while readers learn — and we are clearly meant to approve — that "her own heart . . . told her that the rights of innocence were paramount to all other rights" (124; also 166). As she intervenes first on behalf of the Pequot woman Nelema and later Magawisca, Hope gets told that she allows herself "too much liberty of thought and word" (189), and the governor tells her that she "dost take liberties unsuitable to thy youth, and in violation of that deference due to the rule and observances of my household" (184). Indeed, it is because Hope Leslie so embodies the principle of liberty that she leaves herself open, as she wanders the streets at night on her freedom missions, to the advances of the lawless Gardiner. But this danger will finally be offset by Everell, son of William, who loves the "unfettered soul" of Hope (294), and by Digby, who defends her as part of "a new spirit in the world" (236).

Through Digby, in fact, the narrator places Hope squarely within the historical narrative that champions "every man's birth-right":

It was but the other day, so to speak, in the days of good queen Bess, as they called her, when, if her majesty did but raise her hand, the parliament folks were all down on their knees to her; and now, thank God, the poorest and the lowest of us only kneel to Him who made us. Times are changed — chains are broken — fetters are knocked off — and the liberty set forth in the blessed word, is now felt to be every man's birth-right. (236)

Digby raises his defense of Hope exactly against those who condemn her New World tendency to "stray" beyond physical bounds and to wander outdoors when she is expected to stay home. He aligns her physical wandering with her moral nobility, for this "straying" is, he says, "the privilege we came to this wilderness world for. . . . Thought and will are set free" (235–36). As we'll see, these correlations between liberty and wandering in relation to Hope signal the importance of land, movement, and colonization for her liberty projects.

Everell, too, embodies the liberty principle. He expresses an "unconstrained freedom" in his manner, and his open dissent erupts (as it did for his father) over a sexual attachment (141). He openly challenges the elders when his father attempts to persuade him to marry Esther — and in the process he displays how the negative terms and effaced interests of the social contract can be turned to advantage and made to serve a visionary-comic ending that looks past the elisions. When Mr. Fletcher sees fit to remind him that "[o]ur individual wishes must be surrendered to the public good" (169), Sedgwick takes the opportunity, through Everell, to set up a perfectly Rousseauian discussion about will and obedience, in which he claims a right to *voluntary* submission. Mr. Fletcher insists that children owe their parents obedience as well as love and reverence, and in response Everell counters that children owe obedience "as far as it can be manifested by not doing what you command us not to do." He speaks in the circular terms and double negatives that always characterize this contractual question of liberty. Further mobilizing the freedom rhetoric used against tyrants, Everell explains that he "wince[s] at the galling of a new yoke," and (from a better position than Clarissa had occupied in relation to her parents) he pressures his father to "admit that my submission has not been less perfect, for being voluntary" (169). The conversation is at this moment interrupted, a sign of the gap on which the contractual balancing act teeters.

Racial Reverb

At several key points, Sedgwick parallels the restless dissent of the younger generation in the colonies with that of the English under Charles I, including their resistance to the threat of Catholicism. The main events are of course contemporaneous with the English Revolution, and she consistently reminds us of the fact. The events of *Hope Leslie* offer a parable of the English Revolution as much as they do a preamble to the American one. Magawisca's "supplementary" role within this drama accords with her role as instrument of an Anglo-Atlantic liberty narrative.

Sir Philip Gardiner embodies the Royalist-Catholic threat; and in Sedgwick's rendering this corrupt force makes women's ruin an instrument of its maneuvers, as revealed in Gardiner's deceitful pursuit of Hope, in his degrading attempt to bribe Magawisca, and in his abuse of his "fallen" concubine, Rosa. In effect, with Magawisca's help Hope will resist this threat and in the process work to save two fallen Catholic sisters, both Rosa and her own sister Mary—whom we should think of also as literary-historical sisters, symbols of the gothic story Sedgwick is redeeming, as hinted in her seeming allusion to the crossing-dressing and secret lover Rosario/Matilda in *The Monk,* who brings the downfall of Ambrosio (here Gardiner).

As Melville does in *Billy Budd* when he implicitly triangulates the French-associated Claggart, the African "cynosure," and the innocent Anglo-Saxon Billy Budd, in this gothic subplot Sedgwick triangulates Gardiner, Magawisca, and Hope. Both texts participate in the making of modern racial formations and hint at how the American project required this double racial negotiation with non-European bodies on the one hand and French ambitions on the other. Positioning Magawisca as the third, crucial if eventually purged term within this plot, Sedgwick creates two tableau confrontations between Magawisca and Gardiner —tellingly, in the jail and the courtroom, those sites of the loss and reclamation of rights. In these scenes, Magawisca exposes Gardiner as a popish seducer of innocent women as well as innocent nations, one who uses poor savages to gain his ends.

First, as we saw in the courtroom, she plays the heroic part of the one-armed Nelson exposing French-Catholic seductions and duplicity, and now we can notice that this exposure climaxes with her revelation of his relation to Rosa. Similarly, in the jail scene, Gardiner reveals his Catholic cross and thereby swears to free her, pretending to sympathize with her as a "noble" maiden who "sigh[s] for the freedom of nature," but when she hesitates to listen to him, he openly confesses that he "doubt[s] the existence" (like Lovelace, or, as Sedgwick says, "like all bad men") of "incorruptible virtue" (268). He then provocatively probes the sore spot of her "strong national pride," as the narrator reports, when he suggests that Everell, who she hopes will speak on her behalf, has abandoned her. She refuses to believe it, insisting on Everell's belief in "the natural equality of all the children of the Great Spirit"—and in the same moment she reinforces the larger racial narrative of progress toward liberty via the Puritans in recalling how Everell had "opened the book of knowledge to her—had given subjects to her contemplative mind, beyond the mere perceptions of her senses; had in some measure dissipated the clouds of ignorance that hung over the forest-child, and given her glimpses of the past and the distant" (276). When Magawisca then rejects Gardiner's offer to help her escape, her racial nobility redounds upon Puritan racial nobility, and she accrues power as a surrogate and Saxonized resister to Catholic tyranny. The point is reinforced when Everell shortly after appears at her jail window and attempts (unsuccessfully) to "achieve her freedom"—a striking formulation (276).

The conflations of Pequot and Protestant in Magawisca's spirit of resistance open the way to her displacement by Hope, exactly insofar as the two heroines face the same gothic-Catholic villain. In a tricky set of substitutions, Sedgwick in effect casts Hope's and Everell's joint freeing of Magawisca, the Pequot, as a corollary to the Puritans' resistance to the popish king. This logic is encoded in Everell's failed attempt to involve Esther, the governor's obedient daughter (to whom he is now betrothed, wrongly thinking that Hope is involved with Gardiner), in the freeing of Magawisca. Esther refuses because, as she explains, no "scripture warrants" this transgression. Everell scoffs at her "slavish obedience to the letter of the law" and instead insists that "there must be warrant, as you call it, for sometimes resisting legitimate authority, or all our friends in England would not be at open war with their king" (292). To liberate Magawisca is, he implies, to stand with Parliament against a tyrant king. Hereafter he learns the truth about Hope—that the nighttime wandering he took as a sign of her involvement with Gardiner was actually part of her attempt to recover her sister Mary—and when she agrees to help him free Magawisca he learns that he can count on her "unfettered soul" (294), willing to transgress rules in the name of a higher principle.

Thus does the disobedience entailed in freeing Magawisca replay the disobedience of Puritans in the English Revolution. And yet of course, historically speaking, to stand with Magawisca is to stand *against* those who side with Parliament against the king, against the Puritan colonists. In Sedgwick's reversal and conflation, the colonists are at once the rebel and the tyrant, just as Magawisca is both Pequot and Puritan. As in the Putney Debates, furthermore, the language that makes the rebel into a patriot strategically mingles the natural and the national. Everell points out to Esther that "[w]ith such a precedent [of our friends in England], I should think that the sternest conscience would permit you to obey the generous impulses of nature" (292). Conforming to the race-liberty tradition, Everell slips between appeals to "precedent" or "warrant," on one hand, and appeals to conscience and the "generous impulses of nature," on the other—between a national liberty and a natural liberty. In the tradition of the debaters, he is seeking a homology between these two formulations but meanwhile playing a shell game—and the end of the novel does the same by implying that each race will realize its natural liberty only by embodying a peculiarly national pride. Sedgwick sets up both a chronological synchrony and a rhetorical-political parallel between the Puritan struggles against the king and Pequot struggles against the Puritans, veiling the contradictions in the parallel.

Yet even as she sets up this parallel, Sedgwick perhaps unconsciously registers its fault lines by indicating how the liberty language is shared by her villain Gardiner and her Puritan hero Everell. During their simultaneous arrival in the colony, Everell celebrates the way that the Puritans "virtually broke the yoke of royal authority, when they left their native land, and shewed what value they set on liberty" (130). Drawing from a similar vocabulary when he later writes to his Royalist friend back home, Gardiner explains that he has come to help Sir Thomas Morton address "all past grievances" and demand "a restitution of his rights" from the colonists who "ejected him from his own territory" in the New World for following the "free tastes of a gentleman" rather than the Puritan codes (207). Perhaps Sedgwick expects her readers to judge Gardiner's mention of grievances and rights as a misuse of the language of liberty, but then how might she have expected her audience to read Everell's comment that the colonists "have a right to enjoy their liberty in peace" since "we have acquired [the land], either by purchase of the natives, or by lawful conquest, which gives us the right to the *vacuum domicilium*"? (131) His invocation of this Latin phrase and specious idea (that American land was a "vacated domicile," not fully settled and cultivated by the Indians and therefore available for the taking, cited by the monarchy and the colonists to authorize their land-grabbing) encapsulates how language veils the violence of this process and reveals that he too, like Hope and our narrator as well as Gardiner, practices the deceptive art of rhetoric in order to lay claim to land. As they close their conversation, Gardiner characterizes himself as a "stranger and a wanderer" and Everell assures him that "[o]f such this country is the natural home," inviting Gardiner to accompany him to the governor's house (131). It's not clear how much Sedgwick means to unravel these tangled skeins of colonial liberty rhetoric, but it certainly is the case that Everell's perception that he and Gardiner speak the same language enables Gardiner's designs on Hope and his interference with the very liberty they celebrate. She reveals the slipperiness of the liberty language even as she uses it.

When Sedgwick has Gardiner explode in his own Atlantic ship, at the very hand of Rosa, the woman he has ruined, so that Hope (and true liberty) can triumph and marry Everell, she clearly means to solidify an opposition between Gardiner and Everell. As Carolyn Karcher points out, in having Rosa begin the fire by tossing her lamp into a barrel of gunpowder (397), Sedgwick alludes to the Jacobin "Gunpowder Plot" of Guy Fawkes in his attempt to explode Parliament; and so she reinforces these historical parallels (xxxi). With the explosion of Gardiner's ship, Sedgwick simultaneously purges the Catholic-French threat to the liberty narrative and absorbs the Indian presence, so as to allow the heroic Anglo-Protestant vision of history to proceed. In the process, she fulfills a deep collective fantasy for her Anglo-American readers.

Landing the Art of Liberty

This fantasy is about land as much as it is about liberty—the two go together. Sedgwick additionally dramatizes the free spirit of her Anglo-Protestant heroine through Hope's relation to land—her wandering, Indian-affiliated tendencies which ultimately make her fit to sponsor English colonization. Especially in chapters 7 and 8, Sedgwick's narrator belies some self-consciousness about Hope's role and Sedgwick's own work as novelist. She reveals that, in effect, Hope is to Sedgwick what Magawisca is to Hope: a figure who enables her own entry into history, writing, and national belonging.

First, it is important to see that Sedgwick's narrator puts into play the substitutional logic of these female relations when she explicitly correlates her own "wandering" movements with those of Hope, signaling the text's "liberties" and its investment in Hope's (and Anglo women's) agency. Apologizing for her abrupt shifts from scene to scene, Sedgwick's narrator explains that "we follow on the trail of our heroine, whose excursive habits have so often compelled us to deviate from the straight line of narration" (320). She thus aligns herself with "this lawless girl" (166), and this correlation just hints at the cultural work of Sedgwick's novel—its mobilizing of gender and liberty to romanticize the "wandering" occupation of other people's lands. As part of this larger project, Hope's relation to the land is made to mirror Magawisca's insofar as Magawisca refers to herself as a "wanderer" and Jennet compares Magawisca to a roving butterfly (40, 39), while throughout the novel Hope is cast as a land-wanderer, with a "[l]ove for exploring hill and dale, ravine and precipice" (126). Hope explains that she likes to "stroll in the garden by moonlight—or to sit and listen to the waves breaking," to which Digby replies that her "heart [was] always linked into such things" (235). Yet this implicit similarity between Hope and Magawisca also underwrites and enables Hope's "liberation" of Magawisca—"back" into the "wilderness"—which will clear the land for herself. Marrying Everell (in the place of Magawisca who saved and loved him), Hope is free to domesticate the native soil that feeds the spirit of liberty. Thus while Hope's transgressive movements might seem merely a way to flout Puritan strictures on women, within an Atlantic framework they take on a more compromised, geopolitical meaning.

Sedgwick lays the ground for Hope's substitutional function in her narrator's early description of these "voluntary exiles," the founders of the colony, who, she tells us, were pilgrims in the true sense of the word, for they gave up their connection with homeland:

> They were pilgrims, for they had resigned, for ever, what the good hold most dear — their homes. Home can never be transferred; never repeated in the experience of an individual. The place consecrated by parental love, by the innocence and sports of childhood, by the first acquaintance with nature; by the linking of the heart to the visible creation, is the only home. There is a living and breathing spirit infused into nature: every familiar object has a history — the trees have tongues, and the very air is vocal. (17)

Ironically, however, Sedgwick makes the colony into just such a native spot. For the first generation of colonists, the trees in the New World, like the people, have no tongues, but this novel will work quite deliberately, through Hope, to make this alien land into a living and breathing home, as authorized by biblical analogues and inspired by the liberty narrative with Hope at its center.

It is above all in the pivotal chapter 8 that Hope's embedded yet central role comes into view — and Sedgwick implicitly tells the story of her own project. In this chapter, in the form of a transatlantic letter to Everell, Hope takes up both discursive power and her role as one who will transform this land into a native spot for the English. The turn from chapter 7 to 8 encodes the rupture and displacement underlying this transformation, for it creates a temporal leap of seven years following Magawisca's heroic rescue of Everell; and it spans the years of Everell's schooling in England, during which Hope comes to replace Everell as the New World offspring (or, as Judith Fetterley notes, as the American Eve substituting for Everell as Adam [496 – 97]).[15] Although *he* was born in Bethel, and she in England, now she writes to him in England from Bethel. While some critics read Hope's letter as a feminist document (so that, in one critic's words, "the objectivity of male-centered 'history' is undermined")[16] the letter simultaneously operates as one of a series of colonialist substitutions, including the substitution of Protestant presence for the Pequot. Sedgwick's setup of this substitution is striking and seems to call attention to itself. Both the spritely playfulness of Hope's letter (in stark contrast to the preceding chapter — and, in fact, adjacent page, on which Magawisca has lost her arm saving Everell) and the description within it of Hope's landscape painting hint at how the story of history is here being crafted, remade, and lightened, with radical excisions from the original. Hope begins by describing a painting she had completed which depicts a boy "sleeping under a birch tree, near a thicket of hazle bushes, and from their deepest shadow peeps a gaunt wolf in the act of springing on him, while just emerging from the depths of the wood, in the background, appears a man with a musket levelled at the animal" (99). We learn later that Digby did indeed discover Everell sleeping under a birch tree, but he mentions no wolf or any act of heroism (100–101). In place of Magawisca's rescue of Everell with no shield or weapon but only her own body, Hope's painting substitutes a white man with a gun saving Everell from a "gaunt wolf"—the latter image seeming to figure the Indian threat to Everell and his community, given that earlier Mr. Fletcher refers to the Pequots as a "wolfish tribe ... displaced from their dens" (21).

Not only does Sedgwick place this revisionist story of Everell's rescue at two aesthetic removes—in a carefully crafted, chapter-long letter that itself begins with an act of ekphrasis—but she also makes this letter an Atlantic vessel, sent back across the ocean from colony to home. As such, the letter stands as an emblem of Anglo-American literature: its substitutional craft and its revisionist work, operating within Atlantic conditions of possibility. It's difficult to know what to make of Sedgwick's seeming exposure of these aesthetic sleights of hand, given that she nonetheless romanticizes, racializes, and justifies colonization. But whatever she intended, this discrepancy is now the gift of her novel. For it provides the opening by which we can enter into the problem—into our readerly entanglement in the misrepresentations of history. Given the combination of details in the second half of the letter, Sedgwick seems to have apprehended that she was telling the story of Hope's initiation into a certain sort of imperial seeing, even if it's less clear that she knew she was telling the story of her own and now to some extent our own imperial vision.

Following her account of the painting, and having created a substitute origin for Everell's survival and future in the colony, Hope participates in the process by which Native American land becomes the Puritan's native spot. Her letter goes on to describe the day that a small party climbed to the top of Mount Holyoke—the day that mountain is christened with its English name by Mr. Holioke. First, in an echo of the narrator's reflections about the home the English Puritans left behind, and displaying her land-sensitive sensibility, Hope recalls that from the top of the mountain she "fanc[ied] these vast forests filled with invisible intelligences" and she "listened to the mighty sound that rose from the forest depths of the abyss, like the roar of a distant ocean, and to the gentler voices of nature, borne on invisible waves of air" (104–5). And then "while I was pondering," Hope explains, the taciturn Mr. Holioke suddenly began to wax historical—and to reeducate her vision: "The Romans ... had their Cenotapha, empty sepulchres, in honour of those who died in their country's cause, and mouldered on a distant soil. Why may we not have ours? And surmise that the spirits of those who have died for liberty and religion, have come before us to this wilderness, and taken possession in the name of the Lord" (104).

The defensive question — why may we not have ours? — tells all: it belies the suppressed knowledge that this soil is not "ours," which in turn calls forth the justifying biblical analogy implying divinely ordained "possession" of it. Mr. Holioke furthermore imagines the valley as an unoccupied site for the "empty sepulchres" of liberty seekers even though, as Hope goes on to explain, "Mr. Holioke and your father were noting the sites for future villages, already marked out for them by clusters of Indian huts" (104). As both comments reveal to a profound degree, not only did the Pilgrims *imaginatively* erase Indians before (and perhaps as a prelude to) killing them but they also arrived at that imagining by reference to Roman, Christian, and English pasts which they then overlaid on the presence of Indian Americans. Repeating the substitutions of Hope's painting, this scene reveals how, through imagination and writing, the English "remove" the Indians.

Yet simultaneously Hope (like Sedgwick) serves as the vessel that carries Indian powers and traditions into an English narrative. Here as elsewhere, Hope attempts to honor Indian practices and presence but she continually faces rebukes which discourage her. She is being disciplined into a certain narrative, as critics have noted, but they do not note that the letter confirms that the discipline has worked. That is, Sedgwick stages a scene of female resistance on this mountaintop that in the end enables Indian erasure. Sedgwick involves Hope in the habit of relegating to the past what is clearly still present. Hope notes that the mountaintop is "strewn with relicts of Indian sacrifices," and then she asks her male elders if "an acceptable service might not have been offered" by the Indians at "the rude altar" near which they stand (104–5). Hope's observation about the "relicts" swirls in contradictory effects: it at once attempts to take up an Indian point of view, relegates Indian practices to the past (via the words "might have been" and "relicts") in spite of the fact that she and her companions are looking at Indian villages, and reconjures the threat of Indian violence in reminding us of Everell's near-beheading at such a site.

Not only is her hypothesis about an "acceptable [Indian] service" severely rejected but the response also contains the threat that Hope could be expelled and aligned with those "others" if she were to continue down such a path of thought. Mr. Holioke "shook his head at me, as if I were little better than a heathen, and said 'it was all worship to an unknown God'" while Mr. Fletcher reintroduces the narrative turn toward "'the time [that] is approaching, when through the vallies beneath, and on this mount, incense shall rise from christian hearts'" (105). Because we are in Hope's point of view, we feel the rebuff of her suggestion as a blow. In response, Hope quickly gets in line, and Sedgwick behind her. Certainly Sedgwick's own closeness to American Indians, through land and marriage, might well have made the threat of a woman's banishment real, especially since as she wrote this novel her cousin Harriet Gold was being expelled from her community for her alliance with an Indian American.

Having had her surmise corrected, Hope quickly changes her approach and tone, playfully offering to underwrite the elders' "conversion" of the land from Pequot to Protestant. She suggests that they christen the spot "Mount Holioke" then and there and that they "let me stand sponsor for it." For this "levity" she is "gently rebuked," but the gentleness belies that this rebuke is actually a cover for their approval, and indeed they allow just that. In short, Hope barters her acquiescence to their erasure of Indian values in exchange for a position of discursive power. Thus does Sedgwick make a liberty-practicing woman the "sponsor" of Anglo-Protestant history—creating a feminine genealogy for the name of an actual mountain still called Mount Holyoke in what is still called the Pioneer Valley in Massachusetts. Hope serves as wry but reeducated agent of colonization, as does Sedgwick in her turn.

Sedgwick indicates the powerful tangle of forces in this education of Hope when she follows it with the crisis in which Hope's *tutor* is bitten by a snake on their descent from the now-christened mountain, an event that invokes powerful Christian imagery. If this scene is a "fall," whose fall is it symbolizing? Hope's, in her seduction by colonial power? Her community's and teachers', in their seduction by the same? Or does it allegorize the fall of Indian Americans, who will soon be exiled from this paradise for their heathen ways? At the same time, in a different frame—the Indian one that Hope a moment ago conjured—perhaps this deadly bite that can only be cured by the Indian woman Nelema suggests a kind of recoil of the Pequot land at this Anglo-Protestant seizing of it—a repulsion of their teaching.

The aftermath of the bite further plays out the powerful and contradictory allegory embedded here and indicates Hope's useful but tricky affiliation with racialized others. For she at first offers to "suck the poison" from Craddock's hand but again is prevented by the men who see this practice as ungodly. The bite festers and so Hope enlists the help of the Pequot healer Nelema. This in turn leads to her first liberty project, for after all the elders imprison Nelema for practicing what, at Jennet's prompting, they come to see as witchcraft (a characterization the text seems to eschew but in fact supports by describing Nelema as "brandish[ing] her wand" and "writh[ing] her body into the most horrible contortions" [108–9]). Hope illegally frees Nelema from prison—with the help of the very Digby who obstructed Hope's attempt to suck the poison. The causal logic of these events reveals implicitly that Hope and Digby free those who after all they have caused to be imprisoned — but the discourse of the text nonetheless casts Hope as the hero.

In "freeing" Nelema, Hope wins the respect of Magawisca and the promise from Nelema that Hope will again see her sister Mary. Hereafter she thus becomes the link between the Indian and the English communities in her "wandering" night meetings, and the catalyst of Sedgwick's revisionary historical text. That is, Hope's liberatory missions provide the motor of Sedgwick's plot and the instrument of Sedgwick's imaginative access to the Pequot community. Hope's "christening" of the native spot creates the ground for Sedgwick's project as national author.

Sedgwick's Sublime

As if she has her finger exactly on the pulse of Anglo-Atlantic self-fashioning, Sedgwick brings her story to a classically sublime climax. She adroitly narrates the culminating moment of this transfer of power from Pequot to Anglo-Protestant in just the terms created by the literary-historical tradition of the sublime.[17] In her account of Hope's reunion with her long-lost sister Mary, Sedgwick manages to combine so many layers of cultural history and literary tropes that the result no doubt affected her nineteenth-century Anglo-Protestant readers as very sublime indeed. This reunion of sisters — Protestant and Catholic — implicitly signals that this novel serves Sedgwick's aim to heal the old, racialized Protestant-Catholic rupture and at the same time to move beyond the story of women's exile and ruin, and so to consolidate the energies of the nation — which, in its westward movement, continued in Sedgwick's own day the Anglo-Atlantic project of empire. This process entails an exchange of the bodies of Hope and Magawisca, issuing in the imprisonment of Magawisca until, in the end, Hope becomes free by freeing Magawisca and replacing her.

The narration of Hope's meeting with her savage/Catholic sister perfectly conforms to the racial sublime as I discussed it in chapter 3. The sequence begins when Hope goes out to one of her favorite native locales on an awesome stormy night to meet her long-lost sister at the shore. As her sister Mary (now renamed Faith) arrives in the canoe, Hope experiences that deep "check" of horror that romantic theorists of the sublime considered the turning point in the sublime experience: "she darted to the brink of the water — she gazed intently on the little bark — her whole soul was in that look. Her sister was there. . . . Hope uttered a scream of joy; but when, at a second glance, she saw her in her savage attire, fondly leaning on Oneco's shoulder, her heart died within her; a sickening feeling came over her, an unthought of revolting of nature" (237). Hope's revulsion and hesitation then cause the lag in time — the sublime moment of suspension as she hesitates to embrace Faith — that allows Hope to be taken captive by Oneco and his father Mononotto in the canoe, while Faith and Magawisca are taken captive on shore by Gardiner and his men.

Hope is thus momentarily overcome, but she finally achieves a sublime mastery of this encounter with a Catholic/savage other as the storm rises on the Atlantic. The narrator first positions us in the canoe gazing at Mononotto, for whom "the sublime powers of nature had no terrors . . . whilst the blasts swept by him, and the lightnings played over him" (248). We do not enter the interior of Mononotto as he takes in the scene, but then in the next sentence, the narration conjures these sublime effects as they register inside a "tremulous, sensitive being." The description suggests that we are turning our attention toward Hope Leslie: "There are few who have not at some period of their lives, lost their consciousness of individuality — their sense of this shrinking, tremulous, sensitive being, in the dread magnificence — the 'holy mystery' of nature" (248). Hope is not cowed by this dread, for as the next sentence announces, she "forgot her fear and danger in the sublimity of the storm" (248). As the narrator pulls back to survey Hope, Mononotto, and Oneco, she Christianizes the movement of sublime recuperation, commenting that "Hope Leslie, her eye upraised, with an instinctive exultation of feeling . . . might have been taken for some bright vision from another sphere, sent to conduct her dark companions through the last tempestuous passage of life" (249). And, we might add, through a final tempestuous passage of history, when the Puritan colony heroically presides over its "dark" companions' last life passage (indeed, Mononotto shortly after dies amid the storm). When the storm subsides, Hope escapes Oneco and is again taken for "a bright vision from another sphere" by the Catholic Italian pirate who will obey her commands and pilot her safely back to the Puritans. Thus the sublime turn is completed: Atlantic mastery is gained over both the Catholic and the savage. With the explosion shortly after of the popish Gardiner's ship, both the Old World and New World forms of barbarity are left behind in the forward progress of the new Anglo-Protestant community.

Hope's swoon follows this sublime triumph. She falls sick and delirious for days. She awakens, however, not as a ruined woman but as a free woman, ready to take up the task for which the novel needs her. And while Hope has been realizing her sublime introjection of an awesome and savage presence, Magawisca has been in prison undergoing a parallel but ultimately disabling introjection of the native English — dramatized, as we've seen in her "noble" spurning of Gardiner, which, however, leads to her "vanishing" exile. In their final act of liberating

Magawisca, Everell and Hope thus free her, above all, into themselves, and they banish her from the history she helps them to found. In one of her last, tricky maneuvers, Sedgwick assigns to Magawisca the task of upholding racial difference and decreeing an unbridgeable difference between the colonists and her people. As Magawisca says goodbye to Hope and Everell and in effect condones Hope's marriage to Everell in Magawisca's place, she remarks that "the Indian and the White man can no more mingle, and become one, than day and night" (349). So she departs. Sedgwick has Magawisca enact her own removal — an odd gift of free agency.

In turning to Esther in the closing lines of the novel, Sedgwick performs once more the move presaged by Aphra Behn in *Oroonoko,* whereby the single English-woman on the sidelines frames the Atlantic story of non-Europeans, as her own vehicle of entry. Noting that Esther never marries because "the current of her purposes and affections had set another way," the narrator tells us that Esther "illustrate[s] a truth": "that marriage is not *essential* to the contentment, the dignity, or the happiness of woman" (371). For it turns out that a single woman who is apparently excluded from history may actually arrange its destiny: "Indeed, those who saw on how wide a sphere her kindness shone, how many were made happier and better by her disinterested devotion, might have rejoiced that she did not '*Give to a party what was meant for mankind*'" (371). Of course the irony is that the work of the Anglo-American Esthers of the land, together with that of the Everells and Hopes, did after all give to a "party" — a race — what was meant for humankind. In closing her novel with these words of Oliver Goldsmith (spoken in Whiggish dissent from Edmund Burke) Sedgwick does so as well, despite her own and Goldsmith's intentions to cast a wider net for liberty than Burke did.

By way of a shrewd synthesis of the elements of the Anglo-Atlantic liberty narrative, Sedgwick completes the transfer of power from Magawisca to Hope, from Hope to Esther, and finally, implicitly, from Esther to herself. For Esther, the *un*fallen yet *un*married Anglo-Protestant woman, is the figure in the book most like Sedgwick. In working to heal the story of women's ruin, Sedgwick locates Esther, herself, and readers who identify with them as the heirs to this legacy of Hope's absorption of Magawisca. She tells us the Anglo-Protestant nation is their creation, their salvation. There's truth in that, and Sedgwick spells it out for us.

Shortly thereafter, in *The Scarlet Letter,* Nathaniel Hawthorne sublimates the fears provoked by this colonial empowerment of Anglo-American women.

12 | "A" for Atlantic in Hawthorne's *The Scarlet Letter*

IN *THE SCARLET LETTER*, colonization just happens, or, more accurately, has just happened. As we have seen, Catharine Maria Sedgwick's novel *Hope Leslie* elaborately narrates the social and psychic process of making an Indian village into a native English spot. Hawthorne eclipses this drama of settlement. Although, like Sedgwick, Hawthorne sets his plot of sexual ruin in the early colonial period of Stuart political crisis and English Civil War, he makes these events a distant backdrop, as remote from his seventeenth-century characters as his nineteenth-century readers. Meanwhile, he recasts Sedgwick's whimsical heroine, Hope Leslie, as a sober, already-arrived and already-fallen woman named Hester Prynne. In beginning from this "already-fallen" moment, Hawthorne keeps offstage both the "fall" of colonization and its sexual accompaniment.

Critics have long noted the offstage locale of Hester's and Dimmesdale's act of passion, but none has noted the novel's elision of the original condition for that passionate act: the transatlantic migration of Hester Prynne *alone*. It is *this* fact that determines Hester's "fall." And if Hester Prynne's journey alone, and into a deeply solitary interiority, emblematizes the exilic effects of Atlantic modernity, Roger Prynne's (aka Chillingworth's) aborted journey into "grievous mishaps by land and sea" and "bond[age] among heathen-folk" emblematizes its violent encounters.[1] But these conditions are placed in the past and only alluded to, so that, as Leslie Fiedler noted, the characters' "whole prehistory remains shadowy and vague."[2] Instead, within the novel, the punishment for adultery becomes the point of origin. In short, in his epic framing of a gothic struggle for liberty,

Hawthorne obscures what we have seen to be the paradigmatic scene of undoing.[3] This way of placing key events at one remove, gestured toward yet submerged, characterizes the novel's historical method and its repressed relation to Altantic history.

At the same time, Hawthorne does implicitly point toward the matter of habitation as key to Hester's fall. He does so, first, albeit indirectly, when he prefaces his story of Hester's "sin" with an account of his own troubled relation to his "native spot," what he calls his "unjoyous attachment to my native town" (11). He more directly sets up a correlation between Hester's departure from home and her loss of innocence (and thus conforms to the Atlantic narrative tradition that merges sexual and colonial seduction) when, as she stands on the scaffold in Boston, Hester looks back to her "village in rural England" where "stainless maidenhood seemed yet to be in her mother's keeping" but which village is now "foreign to her, by comparison" (56). Yet Hawthorne most directly points to the Atlantic coloniality that issues in Hester's fall when his narrator announces that "[Hester's] sin, her ignominy, were the roots which she had struck into the soil" (56). I suggest we take him literally. His words echo those in his "Custom-House Introductory," when he confesses guilt about "the deep and aged roots which my family has struck into the soil" (8). Perhaps, after all, as with Sedgwick, the "sin" with which Hawthorne is most preoccupied is neither adultery nor his ancestors' whipping of adulterous women but rather colonization itself. Hester's "A" is a layered code. Under "adultress" lay the merged meanings of Anglo-Saxon and Atlantic.

Puritan Palimpsest

Criticism on *The Scarlet Letter* makes clear that the novel is a historical palimpsest — with a surface as illegible and in need of translation as the archaic, "gules" A. Not just one but two histories are submerged here, one contemporary with Hester and one with Hawthorne. Or rather, what is ultimately submerged is the deep connection between these two histories — that is, the uninterrupted project of colonization.

Many earlier critics of the novel considered it a mixed critique and expression of American Puritanism, and most of these critics shared Hawthorne's sense of that legacy as *the* cultural origin of U.S. national history. In his 1880 book *Hawthorne*, Henry James helped to establish the identification between Hawthorne and the Puritan tradition, invoking the notion of a racial inheritance when he concluded that *The Scarlet Letter* is utterly "impregnated with that after-sense of the old Puritan consciousness of life" and that indeed the "qualities of his ancestors filtered down through generations into his composition" so that "*The Scarlet Letter* was, as it were, the vessel that gathered up the last of the precious drops."[4] This sense of the book as a racial expression hereafter found an echo in critics from William Dean Howells, who suggests that "Hawthorne was writing to and from a sensitive nerve in the English race that it had never known in its English home," to Carl Van Doren, who sees in Hawthorne "the old Puritan tradition which, much as he might disagree with it on occasion, he had none the less in his blood," to Elizabeth Hanscom in her introduction to the Macmillan edition of the novel, where she concludes that "in his attitude toward life, in his inner thought, [Hawthorne] was bone of the bone, blood of the blood of Puritan New England."[5] By the time of Lloyd Morris's 1928 biography of Hawthorne, *The Rebellious Puritan,* this lineage had become a critical orthodoxy in the form of the idea that Hawthorne "had sought to liberate himself from his origins and environment, but they and not he had determined the character of that effort for emancipation."[6] Building on the notion that Hawthorne's very dissent made him the "child" of Puritan America, early-twentieth-century scholars tracked Hawthorne's knowledge of Puritan sources and studied his ambiguous and shifting allegiances with his main characters as they suffer under and, perhaps, redeem that legacy.

In the later twentieth and early twenty-first centuries, however, an increasing number of scholars place the novel explicitly within the political concerns of the volatile 1840s. These more recent critics call attention to the fact that, in the decade leading up to Hawthorne's writing of *The Scarlet Letter,* the nation was embroiled in conflict over a range of issues — the Indian Removal Act, the annexation of western territories and war with Mexico, the Fugitive Slave Law, the 1848 Women's Convention in Seneca Falls, and the specter (as many felt it) of the European revolutions of 1848. Accordingly they have considered the novel's drama of law, punishment, dissent, and consent as a coded exploration of a citizen's proper response to these matters. In many of these readings, Hawthorne's "vanishing" allusions to Indians, his absence of allusions to slavery, and his "conservative" closure with Hester's final "return" appear as evidence of his investment in what Sacvan Bercovitch deems a liberal process of compromise and consensus, which ultimately advises that obedience to the law, however flawed it may be (even if it meant sending escaped African Americans back into slavery), ultimately sets the nation free.[7] Others have highlighted the same ambiguity earlier critics celebrated, finding in the narrator's sinuous movements and equivocations an invitation to readers to become active interpreters and, by extension, sympathetic, questioning citizens, including of the law.[8]

Rich as these many readings are, in substituting Hawthorne's historical surround for Hester's, they risk overlooking the most deeply historical dimension of Hawthorne's novel — his brooding on the relation between the 1640s and the 1840s. The work of Michael Colacurcio and Laura Korobkin (extending the suggestions of Amy Schrager Lang's scholarship on Anne Hutchinson and Hawthorne) helps to right this imbalance.[9] Colacurcio and Korobkin bring into sharp relief the work of Hawthorne's text in its own historical present exactly by meticulously probing the (non)correspondence between the facts of seventeenth-century Puritan history and the picture of it that Hawthorne creates. While Colacurcio sees Hawthorne quietly indicting the Puritan elders more than we might at first think, and he crucially unveils the troubled coupling of sexuality and governance in the Puritan period, Korobkin argues that Hawthorne softens the portraits and punitive practices of the Puritan rulers in a way that makes more palatable his closing turn — Hester's resubmission to the law. Their arguments are worth close examination since, taken together with scholarship focused on the 1840s, they allow us to place Hawthorne's novel within the history of Atlantic modernity reaching from the seventeenth to the nineteenth century.

Most crucial in Colacurcio's and Korobkin's arguments is their identification of the "constitutional crisis" troubling the colony in the 1640s, the period of the novel's action (Colacurcio 211). Although neither gives any attention to the transatlantic nature of this crisis (whereby the English Revolution and American colonization mutually exacerbated the "constitutional" instabilities in each), their emphasis on Hawthorne's handling of the colonial side lays the foundation for a transatlantic view of Hawthorne's historical work.

Colacurcio takes Hawthorne's misdating of Richard Bellingham's governorship, first of all, as Hawthorne's clue to his readers about the messy, sexual politics lurking behind the Puritan elders' seemingly disciplined and strictly disciplinary visage — behind which lay, in turn, the instability of governance in the colony. It is June 1642 when Hester stands on the scaffold, and Hawthorne — in a rare deviation from his typically meticulous historical accuracy — puts Governor Bellingham on the balcony above her when in fact John Winthrop was the governor in that month, for Bellingham had "been voted out of office, in May 1642, for conduct not so different from Hester's" (Colacurcio 212). At age fifty, Bellingham had secretly married — without banns and without a witness — a twenty-year-old woman who was already betrothed to another man, thereby violating, Winthrop charged, "the constant practice of the country" (quoted in Colacurcio 212). Thus "the demoted 'Governor' Bellingham stood, in June 1642, not as the accuser but as the accused, in a rather tensely central case of sex and constitutionality in the unfolding experiment of Utopian Massachusetts" (Colacurcio 213).

This scandal was one in a series of sexual transgressions with which the colony elders were grappling in the early 1640s, as Colacurcio further documents. During this same summer, as recorded in his journal, Winthrop labored to draw a conclusion about another case of adultery, while, in the previous year, Bellingham had grappled with a shocking case of the two prepubescent daughters of John Humphreys who were repeatedly sexually abused by servants and associates of the father. In documents about the case, Bellingham and Winthrop express no concern about the daughters but are much aggravated over the question of how the case should be decided and punished and the question of whether it amounted to a capital crime (as Winthrop argued, because it involved sexual acts with no promise of "generation" and therefore resembled buggery or sodomy [Colacurcio 214]). It is a symptom, Colacurcio suggests, of the "experiment" in law and punishment under way in the Massachusetts Colony that Bellingham and Winthrop sent out a survey to the congregation's officers asking for views on this matter—and that they combined this question not only with that of how far a magistrate may go in forcing confession from an accused but also with that of how to best maintain "the trade of beaver" (quoted in Colacurcio 216). As Colacurcio wryly remarks, such are the "strangely mixed . . . deliberations" of what Hawthorne calls "that epoch of pristine simplicity." His point reinforces the picture painted by more recent historians of the seventeenth-century Atlantic, which unfurls as an inextricable mesh of religious, legal, sexual, and profiteering interests.

In particular, these unsettling sexual cases erupt against a background of intense wrangling over the political constitution of the colony. The affair of Goody Sherman's pig, to which Hawthorne's narrator humorously refers in passing and which also occurred in the 1640s, is typical in this period of what Korobkin calls "intense attacks on the magistrates' undemocratic authority" ("Scarlet," 9). Buoyed by sympathy from among the lesser colonists, Goody Sherman brought forward a case against a rich merchant, asking compensation for the value of a pig he had mistakenly slaughtered. After more than two years of suits and countersuits, and an astonishing seven days of testimony heard by the nine magistrates and thirty deputies, the deputies supported Mrs. Sherman. But then the magistrates exercised their veto, or "Negative Voice," and the case was decided in the merchant's favor. Recording the resolution of the case in an entry dated June 1642 (the month and year that Hester stands on her scaffold), Winthrop expresses concern over the public's grumbling at the outcome, for "the report went, that [the magistrates'] negative voice had hindered the course of justice, and that these magistrates must be put out, that the power of the negative be taken away" (quoted in Korobkin, "Scarlet" 9). Eventually, Winthrop wrote a defense of the decision and the Negative Voice and in the following year defeated an effort to abolish the Negative Voice. Thereafter, the legislative body operated with an "upper" house of magistrates (allowed a Negative Voice) and a "lower" one of deputies.

Given that this case is offered by Hawthorne's narrator as parallel to the magistrate's interest in Hester's case, Colacurcio concludes that "[s]uddenly Hester seems caught up in the midst of a constitutional crisis," and "the whole crisis seems to take Hester's 'adultery' as its fitting symbol" (210–11). Although "Winthrop had tried hard to keep his sexual cases separate from his political ones," in Hawthorne's treatment "they stand wholly conflated" (211). Indeed, Winthrop himself sensed the difficulty of distinction, since his journal of this period expresses an "exasperated feeling that a whole variety of misunderstandings about 'liberty' are abroad in his land" (Colacurcio 210), manifest in everything from antinomianism to adultery to economic wrangling. Thus do the political conflicts of the 1640s provide the context for "the sex-freedom link in *The Scarlet Letter*" (Colacurcio 188).

I certainly concur that this history helps to explain the powerful "sex-freedom link" in *The Scarlet Letter*. Yet what Colacurcio never sufficiently acknowledges, and Korobkin by contrast explores, is the way that these connections are *buried* in Hawthorne's novel — so much so that no critic before Colacurcio had unearthed them. Colacurcio argues, in light of Bellingham's sexual misconduct and especially the implied indifference to the Humphreys girls' suffering (described, however, in a document Hawthorne might never have seen), that the novel's "famous displacement of Winthrop by Bellingham means to call attention to the fact that . . . the men who judge Hester Prynne do not appear to know what-the-fuck they are talking about" (Colacurcio 216). But if such moral outrage lies at the heart of Hawthorne's substitution, why encode this suggestion so inscrutably? Further, as Korobkin points out, the narrator's reference to the case of the pig comes in a condescending comment (and subordinate clause) that encourages us to see the magistrates' attention to such a trivial case as quaint: "At that epoch of pristine simplicity," the narrator observes, "matters of even slighter public interest . . . than the welfare of Hester and her child" would have been looked into by "statesmen of eminence" — so that indeed "a dispute concerning the property in a pig not only caused a fierce and bitter contest in the legislative body of the colony, but resulted in an important modification of the framework itself of the legislature" (70).

By contrast to Colacurcio, Korobkin avers that, in such wry asides, Hawthorne suppresses rather than exposes the political turmoil of the Puritan community. In fact, she points out that Hawthorne changes much more than the dates of Governor Bellingham's tenure. First, according to the laws of the day, the nature of Hester's punishment would not have been at the discretion of the magistrates — who, in Hawthorne's rendering, appear as mercifully lenient. There would have been a jury, and the jury would have ensured that the magistrates followed the punishment preset for any particular crime — a procedure that had been arranged, after political wrangling, exactly so as to limit the discretion of the magistrates. In the case of adultery, Hester would at *minimum* have been publicly stripped and whipped. Korobkin argues convincingly that Hawthorne excludes a whipping because it would have stirred antislavery sentiment and fed growing dissent about the Fugitive Slave Act in his own day. But her larger point is that Hawthorne is "hard at work rewriting history to improve [the magistrates'] authority and compassion" ("Scarlet" 9). That is, "they may appear cold, distant, cruel, and unfair, and in the short run, they may be so, but the novel as a whole exhibits a powerful underlying faith in the notions of order, authority, and non-participatory law-making which the magistrates represent" (9). In short, while for Colacurcio the details of Puritan history establish that Hawthorne was a closet rebel and woman-sympathizer, for Korobkin they reveal him as an ameliorating apologist for authoritarian law.

It seems clear to me that, in *The Scarlet Letter* at least, Hawthorne stills the volatility and veils the violence of the Massachusetts Puritan community for his readers, even as he may coyly signal their suppressed presence. But for this study, Hawthorne's maneuvers are important not for what they imply about his political beliefs but rather for the way they allow his novel to provide an origin narrative for Anglo-Americans that is cleansed of its colonizing violence. For operating hand in hand with his muffling of political instability in Massachusetts are his suppressions of this colony's involvement in Indian wars and in a transatlantic political crisis that would culminate with a king's beheading in 1649, the same year that Hester's and Dimmesdale's relationship comes to its final crisis and Hawthorne's story-proper ends. As Hawthorne well knew, his story takes place in a colony flanked on one side by the peopled and troubled nation of England and on the other side by the peopled and troubled nations of Indian America, but as we'll see more fully below, he largely de-peoples these adjacent, interlocked communities. His softening of the violence (toward a woman like Hester) within the colony extends into his absenting of the foundational violence among these communities.

Just as Hawthorne lifts the magistrates up onto a balcony and lifts Hester up onto a scaffold — neither of which is historically accurate — so he raises his history up out of the mess of Atlantic maneuvering in 1642 — and, by extension, also keeps it at one remove from what Sacvan Bercovitch characterizes as the "deep cultural anxiety" circulating in the 1840s (*Office* 152). His revisions dissociate his story from colonization as a wrenching, wrangling, and regularly brutal process. Particularly by making remote the island of England from which his troubled history arises, Hawthorne lays out the pattern that enables the exceptionalist approach to American studies. This process of the "removal" of transatlantic history under the cover of an apparent immersion in history begins in his "introductory" to the novel, where he creates a veiled allegory of romance writing as sublimated colonial violence.

Garrison Republic, Native Spot

Hawthorne's "Custom-House Introductory" tells the story of his story, the Alpha-origin of his writing and of Hester's "A," as critics have noted. But it does so at one remove, through a logic of substitution and a rhetoric of exposure and confession that after all veils as much as it reveals. The introductory marks Salem as a native spot that is no longer one and a scene of violence that is no longer one, productively so for Hawthorne's authorship, which rises like a phoenix from that haunted site. His once-removed relation to this violent natality prefigures Hester's removal from her native spot in England while it also narrates such removals as journeys into a native freedom — and, in Hawthorne's case, native writing. That is, even as Hester's cottage stands once-removed from England and on the margins of Boston, and just as Fletcher in *Hope Leslie* erects "Bethel" on the outskirts of Springfield in dissent from colonial hypocrisies about liberty, so also does Hawthorne's account of Salem in the "Custom-House Introductory" initiate a liberty story by way of removal: it begins with a dissenting alienation from community that after all certifies his membership in it. The logic of American dissensus traced by Sacvan Berkovich gains its coherence by way of this nativism.

In a passage that accords well with Sedgwick's and Eliot's accounts of the native spot in every way except their celebrations of it, Hawthorne explains his attachment to his "native town" of Salem as a feeling that is propelled (he repeats) "not [by] love, but instinct" (11, 8, 10):

> The sentiment is probably assignable to the deep and aged roots which my family has struck into the soil. It is now nearly two centuries and a quarter since the original Briton, the earliest emigrant of my name [William Hathorne, in 1630], made his appearance in the wild and forest-bordered settlement, which has since become a city. And here his descendants have been born and died, and have mingled their earthly substance with the soil; until no small portion of it must necessarily be akin to the mortal framework wherewith, for a little while, I walk the streets. In part, therefore, the attachment of which I speak is

the mere sensuous sympathy of dust for dust. Few of my countrymen can know what it is; nor, as frequent transplantation is perhaps better for the stock, need they consider it desirable to know. (8)

Hawthorne here seems to eschew the "natal spot" racialism of "instinct" and criticize the value of human "substance" grown from the "soil" that many other nineteenth-century writers embraced, instead endorsing "frequent transplantation [as] perhaps better for the stock." Yet, at the same time, he keeps racialism intact by maintaining the notion of a "stock" on a path to improvement. In yet another twist, however, by casting his "ancestors" as primordially bound to the soil, he elides the fact that they were of course themselves "transplanted" and that Salem was anything but their "natal spot." In this passage that apparently expresses Hawthorne's valuing of "transplantation" over nativist attachments, he in fact cloaks the transplantation that got his ancestors to Salem. And he meanwhile implicitly lays claim to an originary racial identity. He does so exactly by expressing his desire to leave behind this native spot and original "stock." Like Robinson Crusoe, he is a prodigal son whose tendency to wander and dissent makes him all the more representative and native. His ability to "remove" and so to free himself is the mark of his race — the one step away from simple race identity that, after all, constitutes an always-improving "stock" (and a shrewd author). Thus does Hawthorne set in motion his "transplanting" rhetorical motions.

Hawthorne similarly finesses the coloniality of his story in his subsequent portrait of these forefathers. Readers have long noted that Hawthorne both judges and praises his Puritan ancestors, but he is not simply being judicious. He is carefully managing the "ancestors'" contradictory coupling of liberty and conquest, native simplicity and worldly ambition, exilic isolation and colonial aggression. When he speaks of his "grave, bearded, sable-cloaked, and steeple-crowned progenitor" as a man "of war and peace . . . soldier, legislator, judge" with "all the Puritanic traits, both good and evil," Hawthorne at once registers and smooths over the inherent tension between the qualities of legislator and soldier, and between their conflicting principles of legality and colonization (9). Likewise in the novel, after mentioning that Governor Bellingham had led a regiment in the Pequot War, the narrator remarks, "For, though bred a lawyer, and accustomed to speak of Bacon, Coke, Noye, and Finch, as his professional associates, the exigencies of this new country had transformed Governor Bellingham into a soldier, as well as statesmen and ruler" (73). Much is compacted in the word "exigencies."

Even though Hawthorne makes these passing references to soldiering, neither his story nor his introductory gives any attention to wars between Puritans and Indians; rather, he directs our gaze strictly to intra-community Puritan violence toward religious and moral transgressors like Hester Prynne. That is, Hawthorne decoys any interest in the warring colonial surround exactly by emphasizing the Puritans' "persecuting spirit" toward their own community (9). Thus one ancestor, he admits with seeming openness, "made himself so conspicuous in the martyrdom of the witches, that their blood may fairly be said to have left a stain upon him" — "So deep a stain, indeed, that his old dry bones, in the Charter Street burial-ground, must still retain it" (9). Hawthorne avows that "I, the present writer, as their representative, hereby take upon myself shame for their sakes, and pray that any curse incurred by [. . .] the race [. . .] may now be henceforth removed" (9). He seems unflinchingly to expose ancestral and Puritan violence among a tribe of "Britons" set down in a lonely wilderness.

But of course the "wilderness" was inhabited and the blood soaking the soil was more frequently that of Indians. It is after all because of *this* blood-soaked soil that the Anglo-Saxons' primary "sin, [their] ignominy, were the roots which [they] had struck into the soil" (56). Hawthorne's elision performs a displacement of the violence against Indian Americans in both the seventeenth and the nineteenth centuries. His maneuver is likewise indicated in his quaint use of the word "race," in his wish to "henceforth remove" the curse on his "race." He conjures the word's more archaic, kinship connotations and looks past its contemporaneous saturation by ethnographic, racist meanings. Via such substitutions, Hawthorne does indeed undertake the work of "removing the curse" from his race, but in a different sense than he implies.

At the end of his introductory, Hawthorne completes this equivocal turn by which he simultaneously condemns, cleanses, and lays claim to membership in the Anglo-Atlantic community in confessing its sins with ostensible openness. In the same bantering tone he has used all along to affiliate with while distancing himself equally from his ancestors and their contemporary incarnations in Salem, Hawthorne builds an equivocal relation to the republic that has employed him. In particular he stresses the bureaucracy's emasculating effects, comically fashioning himself as its victim — its "surveyor-king" now "decapitated." In these descriptions, Hawthorne implies his awareness of a long Atlantic history, especially when he adopts "the metaphor of the political guillotine" that recalls not only 1848 and 1789 but also 1649. He playfully takes the role of the decapitated king whose spectacular death unleashes liberty, launches colonial "surveyor" projects, and generates history. Although he seems to affiliate himself with the king beheaded by the republic's uncultured, colonial officers, by the end of the introductory he will have positioned himself as the republic's renewed native man.

To arrive there, he again works through a number of submerged removals, as indicated by his private letters about his loss of position at the custom house.

While in the introductory's published version of his response to his dismissal he uses a revolutionary republican vocabulary, in his private writing he adopted quite a different metaphor for his response to his dismissal, as Renée Bergland has pointed out: that of an avenging Indian. Much of his anger was directed at Charles Upham, a one-time friend who had become leader of the Whig party in Essex County and had actively lobbied against Hawthorne's reinstatement.[10] Writing to Horace Mann, Hawthorne reported that he planned to "do my best to kill and scalp him," which in "The Custom-House" he does so by exposing the corruption in this key institution in Upham's district.[11] In a letter to Longfellow, Hawthorne similarly shares his plans to "immolate one or two of them" (quoted in Woodson 183), and he again invokes Indian-associated imagery in suggesting that the public responded as if he had "burned down the Custom-house and quenched its last smoking ember in the blood of a certain venerable personage" (quoted in Bergland 157). In these fantasies the author himself becomes the "removed" victim, as he suggests again when he identifies himself with a fugitive slave in his comment that "it stirs up a little of the devil within me, to find myself hunted by these political bloodhounds" (quoted in Woodson 183). This is the complex layering of Hawthorne's colonial work: identifying with the removed outsider, taking up the very weapons of that wronged figure, but then usurping the place of that figure. In this way the founding national violence against Indians is submerged into the story of abused *Anglo* "native energy," with Hawthorne as the mock-hero who overcomes this injustice.

The benefits of this substitution are displayed by the fact that Hawthorne's ejection from the custom house ultimately recovers the native man in himself and in turn enables his creation of the novel, *The Scarlet Letter*. He explains that, whatever the custom officer's former bravery on the battlefield or at sea, because the officer ensconced at the custom house "leans on the mighty arm of the Republic, his own proper strength departs from him" (30). In this state, a man may lose his soul's "sturdy force, its courage and constancy, its truth, its self-reliance, and all that gives emphasis to manly character" (30), for he becomes a servant with "the hang-dog look of a Republican official" (26). And yet "[i]f he possesses an unusual share of native energy, or the magic of place do not operate too long upon him, his forfeited powers may be redeemable. The ejected officer [. . .] may return to himself, and become all that he has ever been" (30). Implicitly, of course, Hawthorne is such a man who gets "ejected" and discovers enough "native energy" and "manly character" to "return to" his Anglo-American self and become again "all that he has ever been." While seeming to understand his ejection as a casting out *from* the republic, Hawthorne at the same time reaffirms a republican individualism in which "self-reliance" makes the native man.

Furthermore, within the republic's custom house Hawthorne discovers the native past that regenerates his writing, a past that once more sublimates an Indian presence within his own. Before he loses his post, he spends his time looking through old records kept on the second story of the custom house, regretting the absence of records from the days of Cromwell, which would have "affected me with the same pleasure as when I used to pick up Indian arrow-heads" (23). The parallel signals the American colonist's double origin in a republic turned military protectorate and a deracinated native culture (23), both of which have now become identity-forging pasts for the republican citizen. Although Hawthorne finds no old records, he is nonetheless pleased to find as a substitute (and in Hawthorne's novel, as in Sedgwick's, the logic of substitution, particularly substitution as the work of history, is everywhere) a packet of papers belonging to an eighteenth-century man, Mr. Pue, who is, tellingly, both a surveyor and "local antiquarian."[12] By way of Mr. Pue's papers, Hawthorne gains access to the drama of Hester Prynne and her embroidered scarlet letter, which takes place exactly in the Cromwellian period to which Hawthorne longs to return.

The beautiful red letter at first strikes Hawthorne as "one of those decorations which the white men used to contrive, in order to take the eyes of Indians, — I happened to place it on my breast" (25) — a juxtaposition that, together with his earlier allusion to Indian arrowheads, prefigures, perhaps unconsciously, the full import of his story of the "wild" white colonist, Hester (whose free spirit will be repeatedly compared to that of American Indians). On his chest, the letter burns and it seems to him that the "ancient surveyor" Pue with his "ghostly voice" (who actually was of the eighteenth century but whom Hawthorne now antiquates) exhorts Hawthorne to tell Hester's story: "do this, and the profit shall be all your own! You will shortly need it; for it is not in your days as it was in mine, when a man's office was a life-lease" (26). Indeed. This republic, which first makes Hawthorne dependent and drains all his manly strength, will after all — exactly insofar as it "ejects" him — present him with a native history and an alternative income.

That is, the republic presents him with this letter and manuscript, with this "sign" of a fallen woman whose story will not only replace and "take the eyes" of the Indian but will also thereby accrue a profit "all your own" to the white male author. The allegory Hawthorne writes is undoubtedly deeper than he realizes.

Working-Through Hutchinson

Hawthorne begins his tale of Hester at "The Prison-Door." At this door, we join "[a] throng of bearded men . . . intermixed with women," awaiting the appearance of a fallen woman before the public eye (35). Our gaze is drawn to the legendary rose-bush said to have "sprung up under the footsteps of the sainted Ann Hutchinson, as she entered the prison-door" (36). The mention of the antinomian rebel Hutchinson as the ghost who presides at the prison *door,* a threshold between interior and exterior, calls to mind Michael Colacurcio's comment that "at one primal level, the whole antinomian controversy is about the inner and the outer, the private and the public person," for Hutchinson raised the question of what "our outward works, positive or negative, really reveal about our salvation status" (193). If so, Hawthorne's novel does not simply allude to the antinomian controversy; it *enacts* it in its penetration of uncertain interiors, including here when it moves across the prison-door threshold into Hester's consciousness.

In doing so, the novel also takes up the questions at stake in the "constitutional crisis" erupting at this seventeenth-century moment on *both* sides of the Atlantic, including its sex-freedom link. Hawthorne's crossing of the threshold between outer and inner — like the making public of a free, interior self undertaken in those seventeenth-century printed "manifestations" — has destabilizing effects in America as well as England partly because of its "discovery" of the free or "chosen" interiority of women. Hutchinson's antinomianism is implicitly of a piece, that is, with the early-seventeenth-century assertions of women preachers in England, such as Katherine Chidley, who claimed the possibility of being chosen by Christ as preachers and therefore the freedom to preach, as I discuss in chapter 1. The danger embodied in such women is detectable in Hawthorne's much earlier essay "Mrs. Hutchinson," written nearly twenty years before *The Scarlet Letter.* The essay deserves attention here for the light it sheds on Hawthorne's colony-authorizing portrait of Hester Prynne.

The parallels between the opening of "Mrs. Hutchinson" and the opening of the novel signal their shared involvement in questions of "inner and outer" which, in turn, set up both texts' rewriting, via a wronged woman, of the violence of colonization. In the opening scenes of both, the narration moves from an outdoor, public market to an inside space inhabited by a woman. In the essay, in language much like that Hawthorne will use in the novel, on a "summer evening" we enter the village of Boston where a "crowed of hooded women and of men in steeple-hats and close cropt hair, are assembled," and the narrator guides us to the "thronged doorway" of the building where "we see a woman."[13]

But then, in the essay written twenty years before the novel, we swerve away from that doorway and interior, as if Hawthorne feared where they would take him. And indeed, turning abruptly to his own time, he proceeds to express anxiety about the "portentous signs" indicating that the "domestic race" of "American women" is "relinquishing a part of the loveliness of her sex" (66–67). What are

the portentous signs? The increase in the number of women writers and the critics who praise them. He compares nineteenth-century women writers to Ann
Hutchinson, for just as she threatened ruling men's power, so these women writers who manifest "changes in the habits and feelings of the gentle sex . . . seem
to threaten our posterity" (67). Because "[w]oman's intellect should never give
the tone to that of man," he deplores the "increasing" presence of "ink-stained
Amazons" and the reviewers who promote them. In particular, such "prolific"
women threaten to "expel their rivals," that is, male writers (67). Furthermore, he
"fancies a sort of impropriety in the display of woman's naked mind to the gaze
of the world" — and certainly such a woman should understand that "she is relinquishing a part of the loveliness of her sex" when she does so. Critics have taken
this essay as evidence that, despite its aspect of sympathy, Hawthorne's portrait
of Hester, whom he aligns with Hutchinson, ultimately condemns women's independence, confirmed in his return of Hester to her letter and to the "domestic
race" of American women at the end of the novel.[14]

But it is typical of Hawthorne that he enacts, or rhetorically appropriates, the
"indelicacy" or sin he condemns. In the essay, he violates the modesty he appears
to defend when he conjures the image of a "woman's naked mind" exposed "to
the gaze of the world," and in the opening scenes of *The Scarlet Letter* he will do
so more fully, by taking us into Hester's interior, across the exterior spectacle of
her letter-bearing bosom. Although the probing of interiors may have been a
practice Hawthorne wished to secure for men alone (for he especially objects to
Hutchinson as a woman who "claimed for herself the power of distinguishing"
the true from the false interior), his interest in these interiors nonetheless is a
symptom of the very "changes in the habits and feelings of the gentle sex" that he
feared. Just as the introductory deflates the origins that the novel then proceeds
to raise up on a scaffold and make epic, Hawthorne's digression on women writers in his Hutchinson essay denounces what after all it adopts as its vehicle and
subject, the freethinking woman.

These maneuvers do the work, furthermore, of sublimating another presence
that "threatens our posterity," the earliest antagonists of the nation's origin: the
American Indians. In Hawthorne's imagination, the threat of women and the
threat of Indians merge, insofar as both represent a freedom that could "expel"
Anglo-American men from their dominance in "the field." In closing his essay
with Hutchinson's murder by a "savage foe," Hawthorne allows himself to fantasize how these two threats might cancel each other. Most tellingly, he depicts
this murder through the metaphor of a shipwreck. That is, he installs an Anglo-
American origin-story of sea trauma in the place of an Anglo/Indian battle over
land and in the process purges the threat of both women and Indians:

Her last scene is as difficult to be portrayed as a shipwreck, where the shrieks of the victims die unheard along a desolate sea, and a shapeless mass of agony is all that can be brought home to the imagination. The savage foe was on the watch for blood. Sixteen persons assembled at the evening for prayer; in the deep midnight, their crying rang through the forest; and daylight dawned upon the lifeless clay of all but one. (73)

In this description, Hawthorne does indeed "bring home to the [Anglo-American] imagination" a scene of violence, but it becomes a spectacle of shipwreck rather than of an Indian attack. He merges the Indian threat with the trauma of sea passage at the origin of the Anglo-American narrative, positioning Hutchinson as both catalyst and object of these threats. Hawthorne further remarks on "the tumultuous billows which were left swelling behind [Hutchinson]" after her forced departure from Boston, while at the same time he rhetorically directs the violence of both war with Indian Americans and Atlantic storms against her (73).

Strikingly, this storm imagery surfaces again in Hawthorne's description of his feelings on completing *The Scarlet Letter.* He recalls his powerful "emotions when I read the last scene of *The Scarlet Letter* to my wife, just after writing it — tried to read it, rather, for my voice swelled and heaved, as if I were tossed up and down on an ocean, as it subsides after a storm."[15] If the retaliation by Indians is sunk within an Anglo-American's traumatic passage into colonization, as the essay's closing indicates, then perhaps Hawthorne's storm-tossed emotions on completing the novel also unconsciously register those threatening Indians he works to remove in this foundational text. It seems that, in writing the novel, Hawthorne completes his own Atlantic swoon, achieves a powerful if momentarily destabilizing sublimation of colonial facts, and fully arrives as an Anglo-American male citizen, a "native" author. Not surprisingly, then, as he reports in the same letter, his wife (perhaps under the pressure of serving so many functions at once within this history) goes to bed with a headache.

Interiority as Native History

In *The Scarlet Letter,* Hawthorne more confidently enters the female interior that provides both a vehicle for and a threat to Anglo-Atlantic history. Ultimately it is not only Hester who, as Sacvan Bercovitch puts it in a resonant phrase, "emerges phoenix-like out of the ashes of social stigma" but Hawthorne himself (*Office* 124).

In the novel, Hawthorne has the (manly) confidence to make the rebel woman free and yet keep her alive. In the opening scaffold scene, the female prisoner who emerges, although led by the beadle, shows herself naturally independent since, at "the threshold of the prison-door, she repelled him, by an action marked with natural dignity and force of character, and stepped into the open air, as if by her own free-will" (39). Like many an Atlantic protagonist before her, including Ann Hutchinson, Hester exudes a natural dignity that is the mark of her free self. Indeed her dignity seemed to lift Hester "out of ordinary relations with humanity, and inclos[e] her in a sphere by herself" (40). We are given this image of a free, female self absolutely apart, and then, after several pages (during which the narrator hovers outside her, fixed like the spectators by the scarlet letter and simultaneously piquing his readers' desire to enter her so as to experience that boundary between inner and outer as transparent, as a Puritan-descendant might wish), the narrator finally takes us — not the townspeople — across the threshold into Hester's consciousness, her interior prison and freedom. Impossibly, we witness her aloneness — an image of our own — and so too receive a reassuring image of our interiority as something witnessed, communal, and free.

And native. For this interior is not only "marked with natural dignity and force of character" but it also contains a history, a familiar Anglo-Atlantic history that has become Hester's and the Anglo reader's psychological history.[16] As Hester stands on the scaffold, the narrator makes us privy to her memories of the modest cottage of her childhood "retaining a half-obliterated shield of arms" in her "native village in Old England" (43). With her natural dignity and force of character, she is the effaced, perhaps pre-Norman nobility of English history. And she is the native becoming modern, as is suggested when Hester further recalls "her own face, glowing with girlish beauty" as she traveled, at her coming-of-age, among "the intricate and narrow thoroughfares, the tall, gray houses, the huge cathedrals, and the public edifices, ancient in date and quaint in architecture, of a Continental city; where a new life had awaited her" (43). Her new, traveling life had promised to unfold as a coupling of antiquity and modernity, by way of her alliance to Roger Chillingworth, the "misshapen scholar," a man "well stricken in years, . . . with eyes dim and bleared by the lamp-light that had served them to pore over many strange and ponderous books . . . slightly deformed, with the left shoulder a trifle higher than the right" (43). But this grafting of youth onto an old, antiquarian tree — "feeding itself on time-worn materials" — is a precarious venture, and "like a tuft of green moss on a crumbling wall," not certain to take hold (43).

With this portrait of an ancient/modern alliance, in the form of a January-May marriage, Hawthorne helps to shape another pattern of the Atlantic liberty plot as it unfolded in the nineteenth-century race epic. Like Dorothea in George Eliot's *Middlemarch,* who marries Casaubon, like Hardy's peasant Tess of the

D'Urbervilles, who marries the transatlantic ethnologist Angel Clare, and like Sedgwick's Hope Leslie, who is encouraged to marry an older man who appears to be such a scholar, Hester is a young woman seeking "new life" through an alliance with an antiquarian man, while the man, in turn, seeks a woman who will revive his exiled (Philip Gardiner), directionless (Angel Clare), or flagging (Casaubon and Chillingworth) energies. The men pursue knowledge of an ancient source or claim that will establish their place in the unstable modern world; and they seek women who, as youthful reproducers with a future, will incorporate and carry forward that claim. Repeatedly, these couplings fail, and their failure belies a nineteenth-century anxiety about both the authorizing power of ancient claims and nativism's hold on women, especially women seeking their own future stake — and sometimes their own titles to land, as in the case of Tess. Hester temporarily slips the hold of this duty when Chillingworth never arrives to meet her on the other side of the Atlantic. Instead, through a liaison with a younger New World man, she gives birth to a New World child, who is "wild" as an Indian and yet all the more native and Protestant for that reason, as we will see.

Reading the January-May marriage within this transatlantic frame, we can take Claudia Durst Johnson's interpretation of *The Scarlet Letter* one step further to discover in the novel an embedded trope of colonially appropriated potency.[17] Johnson makes a compelling case for reading Chillingworth as impotent and, in fact, driven to the New World in search of what he calls "herbs of potency," which is what he does indeed learn about from the Indians (87). The narrator explicitly affiliates Chillingworth with the seventeenth-century nobleman Thomas Overbury, whose wife sought to divorce him on grounds of impotence; and the herbs with which Hester associates Chillingworth (nightshade and henbane) were considered cures for impotence (Johnson 599, 602). As Johnson further notes, the narrative of men coming to the New World in search of the fountain of youth — and a new sexual potency — reaches back to Ferdinand of Spain's charge to Ponce de Leon to search out in Florida something to revive "his manly exercises" (Johnson 600). Spanish writers consistently mention that de Leon's goal was to discover "the fountain which turns old men into youths," and several contemporary historians celebrate stories claiming that the waters of the Bimini islands in the Bahamas (which the *American Heritage Collegiate* dictionary still identifies as the "legendary site of the Fountain of Youth") bestowed sexual potency, so that, in one case, an old man "brought home a manly strength" allowing him to "use all the manly exercises" so that "he married again, and begat children" (quoted in Johnson 600).

Hawthorne makes explicit reference to this myth in his story "Dr. Heidegger's Experiment," which tells the tale of three men and a woman who experiment with love elixirs and are inspired to seek out Ponce de Leon's fountain. Following this clue, Johnson tracks the imagery of fountains and pumps in Hawthorne's oeuvre (including the town pump he mentions at the close of his "Custom-House Introductory") to suggest that Hawthorne figures his own writing as a fountain of manliness that takes the place of the withered and impotent fathers of the nation. In other words, Johnson sees Hawthorne's use of this imagery as his claim to a revolutionary son's authorial production within and of the national imaginary. I would simply place this claim within a transatlantic context. That is, the potency Hawthorne garners, as do his characters, is not just national but also colonial, a filching of Indian sources. In this light, Hawthorne's notion that "transplantation is better for the stock" takes on fresh meaning.

By contrast to his youthful essay on Hutchinson, in *The Scarlet Letter* Hawthorne manages to allow this appropriated New World potency to accrue, after all, to a woman. Compelled by her natural dignity and force of character, as well as by "the tendency of her fate and fortunes [which] had been to set her free," this woman "step[s] out into the open air" of the New World and despite her ignominy lives a long life there (136, 40). Hester's native self finds a window of opportunity in the New World. Yet her bold pursuit of freedom must, after all, be contained if it is to spawn the future of the nation. The novel enacts a containment of liberty within her archaic, native interior, at once obscuring the violence of the nation and circumscribing the revolutionary possibilities for women within it.

With all these elements tucked neatly into place, Hester can stand in her raised position as a paragon of the modern Anglo-Atlantic self, implicitly carrying forward the colonizing project with impunity. The novel casts her as a figure of both release and lonely subjectivity in this modernity situated at the seashore:

> Standing alone in the world, — alone, as to any dependence on society, and with little Pearl to be guided and protected, — alone, and hopeless of retrieving her position, even had she not scorned to consider it desirable, — she cast away the fragments of a broken chain. The world's law was no law for her mind. It was an age in which the human intellect, newly emancipated, had taken a more active and a wider range than for many centuries before. Men of the sword had overthrown nobles and kings. Men bolder than these had overthrown and rearranged — not actually, but within the sphere of theory, which was their most real abode — the whole system of ancient prejudice, wherewith was linked much of ancient principle. Hester imbibed this spirit. She assumed a freedom of speculation, then common enough on the other side of the Atlantic, but which our forefathers, had they known of it, would have held to be

a deadlier crime than that stigmatized by the scarlet letter. In her lonesome cottage by the sea-shore, thoughts visited her. (112 – 13, emphasis added)

Stationed at the Atlantic seaboard, Hester travels *in mind* with those who have overthrown both ancient kings and ancient principles. As such she epitomizes the way the world has been "rearranged — not actually, but within the sphere of theory, which was their most real abode" by the freethinkers and scientists of modernity. Like these others, it seems Hester is free mainly in theory. That is, she is free to theorize about freedom in an imaginative world of her own. Yet even while Hawthorne seems to limit the reach of freedom by interiorizing it "within the sphere of theory," he attributes superior potency and heroism to this form of freedom — for, his narrator says, the men who had overthrown "the whole system of ancient . . . principle" were in fact "bolder than" the men of the sword who had toppled nobles and kings. Hester epitomizes this mental boldness — "the world's law was no law for her mind."

At the same time, by way of this characterization of Hester's isolation and specifically *imaginative* freedom, Hawthorne makes the colony a more innocent place than it was and makes freedom a less "levelling" force. In isolating both Hester and the colony, he occludes the active world of transatlantic trade, interloping, and political maneuvering. As we saw in chapters 1 and 2 of this study, the Massachusetts colony was fully involved with events and people in England and on the Continent (we need only recall that these Puritan settlers had first lived in Holland before removing to America). The rebellious events in England rocked the Puritan colony at every turn. In fact, indirectly and sometimes in body, the Puritan colonists were the very men who, by sword and print, were at this moment overthrowing nobles and kings. While Hawthorne may not have had full knowledge of these networks, his text erases them altogether. The narrator not only places all such rebels "on the other side of the Atlantic"; he characterizes "our forefathers" as relatively ignorant of their free thinking: "[Hester] assumed a freedom of speculation then common enough on the other side of the Atlantic, but which our forefathers, had they known of it, would have held to be a deadlier crime than that stigmatized by the scarlet letter." But Puritanism itself entailed "freedom of speculation" in religious as well as legal practice, which is why it was so difficult to draw the line against antinomian innovations — because they were actually extensions of Puritan innovations. And the Puritan freedom of "speculation" was economic and geographical as well as spiritual, legal, and intellectual.

As Milton would have understood, in other words, Hester's New World adultery — far from representing something the "forefathers" could not in their pristine innocence grasp — is of a piece with this speculative venture that searches out and claims possession of New World sources of political, financial, sexual, and (via conversion) religious potency. The fact that Hester comes to live at the center of the community — sewing the official garments of the governor, presiding at births and deaths, drawing the gaze and taunts of children — taken together with the text's hints about colonial politics and corruption that Colacurcio and Korobkin trace, indicates that Hawthorne in fact at some level understood such women's pivotal role in the colony, as embodiments of a "sex-freedom link" requiring carefully contained manipulation.

That is, by making Hester a singular and radically interior self, by quietly *de*-historicizing her and casting her as one who doesn't actually want social membership in this blood-tainted and hypocritical community (she scorned to consider it desirable, and as she later reflects, "In all her intercourse with society, however, there was nothing that made her feel as if she belonged to it" [59]), Hawthorne allows us to embrace her as the rebel-progenitor of "our" community. The same powerful paradox takes hold: as isolated soul she expresses the essence of the race and becomes the avatar of a free community of readers. And, like Hope Leslie, her race essence finds expression exactly insofar as she absorbs and sublimates the "freedom" of American Indians.

Indian-Saxons

It is in fact her ability to live in isolation, to survive in a cottage alone on the shore of a strange continent, with all her freedom interiorized, that makes Hester the most successful colonist and the queenly ancestor of an Anglo-American literary community. Hester long outlives Chillingworth and Dimmesdale, not to mention the governor whose death vigil she keeps — in the book as well as in our imaginations. As the narrator emphasizes, after her public humiliation, Hester remains in her community even though she is "free to return to her birthplace, or to any other European land, and there hide her character and identity under a new exterior, as completely as if emerging into another state of being" (56). But Hester has already emerged into another state of being, and as such, she has power in the colony — not least because this new state of being entails her internalization and sublimation, in Hawthorne's rendering, of Indian powers and presence.

Readers have noted, with varying degrees of critical distance, the novel's affiliation of Hester with Indians, including Leslie Fiedler, who calls Hester "the wildest Indian."[18] As in Sedgwick's fiction, the third figure here in the Atlantic drama is the Indian rather than the African; and it is the Indian's freedom or "wildness" that gets absorbed into the stories of white characters. Hawthorne conjures the possibility that Hester could escape her shame by traveling west, for "the wildness of her nature" is such that it "might assimilate itself with a people whose customs and life were alien from the law that had condemned her" (56). Indeed, the open air of Indian ways and lands inspires her — or at least, Hawthorne borrows the figure of the Indian as a model for Hester's freedom. "Her intellect and heart had their home, as it were, in desert places, where she roamed as freely as the wild Indian in his woods" (136). In Hawthorne's rendering, Hester adopts the Indian perspective on her culture: "For years past she had looked from this estranged point of view at human institutions, and whatever priests or legislators had established; criticizing all with hardly more reverence than the Indian would feel for the clerical band, the judicial robe, the pillory, the gallows, the fireside, or the church" (136). (Meanwhile Hawthorne may also gesture toward the slave economy "holding up" Hester's interior freedom, in his reference to the "iron" arm of the law and in the later comment that "[t]he chain that bound her here was of iron links, and galling her to the inmost soul, but never could be broken" [56].)[19]

And paradoxically, exactly because she adopts the Indian point of view, she is at home as a colonist, so that "[i]t was as if a new birth, with stronger assimilations than the first, had converted the forest-land, still so uncongenial to every other pilgrim and wanderer, into Hester Prynne's wild and dreary, but life-long home" — and in fact "even that village of rural England . . . like garments put off long ago — were foreign to her, by comparison." Hester is an Anglo-Atlantic creature of modernity who could travel if she chose, but she does not do so because "[h]er sin, her ignominy" and her emergence "into another state of being" were "the roots which she had struck into the soil" (56). Much as she seems an outsider to the community, this is not strictly so: "The very law that condemned her — a giant of stern features, but with vigor to support, as well as to annihilate, in his iron arm — had held her up, through the terrible ordeal of her ignominy" (55). As such, she is the paradigmatic figure for the Anglo-nation's future on this land.

While some readers continue to consider the affiliation of Hester with Indians as a mark of her position as a "non-citizen" who "threatens the hegemony" of the Puritan ideology, other recent critics, Renée Bergland most astutely, understand her as one of Hawthorne's vehicles for enfolding Indian presence into his own writing in a way that authorizes his role as national author.[20] Bergland persuasively argues that "the internalization of Native American qualities was central to [Hawthorne's] process of writing" (156). She tracks the process from his observation (laced with resentment) that "no writer can be more secure of a permanent place in our literature than the biographer of Indian chiefs" through his writing of the next two decades in which Indian characters appear as catalyzing specters — exactly during the period in which the policy of Indian removal was put into law and, in Illinois, Florida, and Oklahoma, violently enforced, amid loud voices of dissent in Massachusetts (quoted in Bergland 145). Bergland finds a combination of attraction and repulsion toward Indian "wildness" in these stories, tamed by closing tropes of vanishing Indian presences. Repeatedly, Hawthorne's stories include these presences, beginning with the 1833 tale "The Seven Vagabonds," in which the white narrator's nameless guide is a Penobscot Indian, and expressed most elaborately in "The Old Manse," where the surrounding land is scattered with Indian relics and haunted with Indian presences. In the latter, this felt-presence inspires Hawthorne and his companions to emulate what they imagine as "freeing" Indian ways: "Strange and happy times were those, when we cast aside all irksome forms and straight-laced habitudes, and delivered ourselves up to the free air, to live like Indians" (quoted in Bergland 155). Meanwhile, Hawthorne repeatedly affiliates writing with haunting, as Bergland notes, especially beginning in 1835 in such works as "The Devil in the Manuscipt," "The Haunted Mind," and "The Great Carbuncle."[21]

Bergland further suggests that in *The Scarlet Letter* "each of the main characters is transformed into an Indian, or, at the very least, described as internalizing Indian consciousness," but she does not elaborate (157). I will do so here, tracing how all three main protagonists follow an Atlantic trajectory that brings them from Europe to America and into association with an Indian presence that at least temporarily enhances their quests for freedom — religious, scientific, and sexual. Reverend Dimmesdale had come to what the narrator calls "our wild forest-land" from one of "the great English universities," bringing not only "all the learning of the age" but also "both nervous sensibility and a vast power of self-restraint" — that is, a lively interior operating under the restraint of a properly internalized law (48). Once arrived, he of course makes his regular visits into the forest to redeem Indians — along the way meeting with Hester Prynne — and he eventually comes into association with Roger Chillingworth, who himself arrives in the colony from Europe by way of a detour through captivity and companionship with Indians.

Roger Chillingworth comes from England via Germany to America, where, like Hester and Dimmesdale, he mingles his Old World knowledge with his "potent" New World discoveries. Some colonists imagine that Chillingworth has been "transported . . . bodily through the air" by heaven from "a German university" to work his "cure" upon Reverend Dimmesdale (which Claudia Johnson argues is a potion to induce impotency, 83). He strengthens his scientific powers by combining "knowledge of the properties of native roots and herbs" gained during his "Indian captivity" (82) with the "antique physic" of "European Pharmocopoeia" and his "old studies in alchemy" (51). Appropriately, he first appears in the story as "a white man, clad in a strange disarray of civilized and savage costume," who is "evidently sustaining a companionship with" the man beside him, "an Indian, in his native garb" (43).

Likewise, the apparent "companionship" of Chillingworth and Dimmesdale develops this potently hybrid nativism. These two men share the impulse to invigorate their "civilized" knowledge through encounters with the "savage." In chapter 9, interestingly titled "The Leech," Hawthorne creates a shoreside colonial scene in which these two men's pursuit of an Anglo-Protestant freedom — religious and intellectual — achieves its perfect "transplantation" in a New World wilderness. As Chillingworth and Dimmesdale take "long walks on the seashore" and Chillingworth gathers native "plants with healing balm in them," Dimmesdale finds himself attracted by the "range and freedom of ideas" Chillingworth exhibits as "a man of science" (85). Thus does Chillingworth introduce a "freer atmosphere into the close and stifled study" of Dimmesdale (85). Of course, just as Chillingworth is only "evidently sustaining" a companionship with the Indian, so too with Dimmesdale. And in the end, unlike Hester, both men fail to gain the future they seek in this new world.

As Chillingworth's and Dimmesdale's relationship comes to its crisis, it becomes clear that Hawthorne doesn't simply omit the woman's Atlantic swoon; he belatedly transfers it to his men. He "outs" the men's vulnerability in this process of "transplantation" that merges Indian and Anglo-Saxon nativeness, for the men go down fighting each other over a more powerful woman who keeps possession of "their" child and thereby of the future of the colony. If we bring a postcolonial frame to both Eve Sedgwick's argument in *Between Men* (where she proposes that one key plot in English-language fiction is a romance between men played out over a woman) and Leslie Fiedler's readings of male homoeroticism in American literature, we begin to see how this homoerotic competition arises in *The Scarlet Letter* from a kind of colonial panic in the face of a woman's sexual freedom over which the men have only partial control.[22]

This panic precipitates a moment of collapse in Dimmesdale's native interior. The narrator has already associated Dimmesdale with the native Anglo-Saxon legacy insofar as his "high native gifts" and his "dewy purity of thought" find perfect expression in his voice that sounds "like the speech of an angel" (48) — or perhaps, a sublime Angle, for there was a widespread misconception that the Angles of England first got this name because their blond hair made them look like angels. Further echoing some of the idealized notions about the original Anglo-Saxons, famous for their innocent honesty and brooding meditativeness by contrast to the worldly and corrupt Roman Catholics, the narrator tells us that Dimmesdale's power seems to come from his preference for "seclusion" which "kept [him] simple and childlike" and gave his sermons "a freshness" (48). In other words, this man who comes to do missionary work in the Massachusetts Bay Colony has the soul of the transparent Anglo-Saxon whose words perfectly manifest his heart and mind, apparently. "The only truth, that continued to give Mr. Dimmesdale a real existence on this earth, was the anguish in his inmost soul, and the undissembled expression of it in his aspect" (101).

Dimmesdale's ruinous exposure in his study marks the crisis of this truth as it is tested by the mingling with native Indian powers. When he falls asleep just before Chillingworth enters so as to penetrate to the secret of Dimmesdale's suffering, Dimmesdale has been reading a book in the vernacular — a "large black-letter volume [lay] open before him on the table" (95). In the seventeenth century, Latin texts were printed in *antigua,* while "black letter" print was used for the vernacular; it was closely associated both with the Reformation because of its use for vernacular Bibles and with the "recovery" of "ancient" native identity because of its use in the printing of Anglo-Saxon texts.[23] As when, in chapter 2, we first enter Hester's interior and discover it to be the realm of an ancient past, so our moment of entry into Dimmesdale's interior is betokened by Protestant nativeness in the black-letter book. His "deep, deep slumber" over the book points toward his seduction by the Anglo-Protestant print-dream, the dream of a fully manifested interior and native self (95). Hawthorne's narrator dwells emphatically on "the profound depth" of this sleep which was "all the more remarkable" since usually his sleep is light and "fitful," which also suggests that it might be the effect of native herbs. The possibility seems confirmed by the fact that it is exactly when Dimmesdale's "spirit" had "withdrawn into itself . . . to such an unwonted remoteness" that Chillingworth enters and, in a sexual flourish, "thrust[s] aside the vestment" covering Dimmesdale's heart (95). If Chillingworth has drugged Dimmesdale with a potion drawing on New World herbs, and their powers have, as the narrator suggests, brought into view the "A" on Dimmesdale's chest that reveals him to be an adulterous Anglo-Saxon, then Hawthorne implicitly traces the logic by which a Saxonist "print" nativism finds both expression and exposure through the colonization of American native resources. The swooning sleep unveils the true native man as, after all, a fork-tongued man caught up in a male homosocial dynamic. Hawthorne thus begins to sketch the predicament of the colonial Anglo-American man, including himself.

Pearl is the crystallized essence born of these Anglo-Atlantic desires and travails. Hawthorne not only continually associates her with the sea — "as if a flake of the sea-foam had taken the shape of a little maid, and were gifted with a soul of sea-fire, that flashes beneath the prow in the night-time" (165); nor does he only reiterate that she embodies "the freedom of a broken law" (92); he quietly parallels her entry into the world with the entry of Protestantism. In the last sentences of the chapter bearing Pearl's name as title, Hester recalls the speculations of townspeople that Pearl is one of those "demon offspring" who were spawned through their mother's sin and serve "to promote some foul and wicked purpose" (69). The narrator comments that "Luther, according to the scandal of his monkish enemies, was a brat of that hellish breed," implying that Pearl embodies the radical Protestantism founded by Martin Luther to which these Puritans are the heirs. These Protestants inflict on others and themselves the "scandal" that they at first suffered under in the Reformation, for Pearl was not "the only child to whom this inauspicious origin was assigned, among the New England Puritans" (69).

Thus Pearl too — "born outcast" (65) — is actually a native insider, with both "native audacity" (165) and "native grace" (62). She recapitulates an Anglo-Atlantic Protestant phylogeny in her ontology.[24] In this light, she has "inherited, by inalienable right" what the narrator calls "all this enmity and passion" in her, "this constant recognition of an adverse world, and so fierce a training of the energies that were to make good her cause, in the contest that must ensue" (66). Accordingly she also seems to embody this people's demonlike pursuit of property: "Whenever Pearl saw anything to excite her ever active and wandering curiosity, she flew thitherward and, we might say, seized upon that man or thing as her own property, so far as she desired it; but without yielding the minutest degree of control over her motions in requital" (165).

Not surprisingly, then, although Pearl, too, is associated in her wildness with Indians, she surpasses them and finds stronger affiliation with Atlantic sailors. On the morning of Dimmesdale's Election Day sermon, having captured the strange energy in her mother's air, Pearl runs from one group to another. She "ran and looked the wild Indian in the face; and he grew conscious of a nature wilder than his own" (165). She dwells even longer among the mariners, who recognize a kindred spirit: "she flew into a group of mariners, the swarthy-cheeked wild men of the ocean, as the Indians were of the land; and they gazed wonderingly and admiringly at Pearl, as if a flake of sea-foam had taken the shape of a little maid" (165).

Sex in the Colony

Yet Pearl is above all the offspring of a woman's pursuit of freedom in the colony, and it is in this way that, like Hutchinson, she merges the intersecting New World threats of wild Indianness and sexual transgression. For *The Scarlet Letter* may after all be most fundamentally concerned with the crisis that colonization provokes in Anglo-Atlantic heterosexuality. Certainly, among its other effects, colonization created a margin of possibility for singlehood and other sexual choices for Anglo-women as well as for Anglo-men — a singlehood figured by Sedgwick in the character of Esther and historically evident in Hawthorne's day in the so-called New England marriages of single women who chose to live together (not to mention those scribbling women Hawthorne deplored). Indeed we might say that *The Scarlet Letter* narrates the aftermath of an Atlantic rupture in which each of the main characters becomes an isolated individual with an interiority that precedes and exceeds community membership and so threatens patriarchal coupling. As usual, Hawthorne turns his gaze to what most worries him, for this rupture does in fact seem to bring what, in "Mrs. Hutchinson," he feared would be the end of a "race" of "domestic" Anglo-American women, which occurs by their adoption of an "Indian" freedom, an outcome figured in that essay as the independent woman's "ruin" by Indians and in the novel by Hester's lonely but free and dignified life.

The increased independence of women seems required for colonization, however, and colonization is a project that Hawthorne embraces by "instinct" if not by love. Hawthorne wrestles with this trade-off required by the continuing project of colonization, including in his own day: the implicit exchange wherein Anglo-Atlantic men's hold on Indian lands entails some loosening of their hold on ("Indianized") Anglo-Atlantic women.

In key scenes throughout the novel we can glimpse the ways that Hawthorne's narrator grapples with the transformation of women and the reach of his heroine's freedom, especially insofar as, like Hutchinson, her freedom of thought rivals his. At one point, Hester explores in her mind how the ideal of freedom has implications for "the whole race of womanhood" and she sees the need for "the whole system of society . . . to be torn down, and built up anew" (113). In particular, she touches exactly on the distinction between nature and culture on which the system rests, for, she thinks, "the very nature of the opposite sex, or its long hereditary habit, which has become *like* nature, is to be essentially modified, before woman can be allowed to assume what seems a fair and suitable position" (113, emphasis added). Yet, then too, the narrator tells us, she fears the danger that along the way "she herself shall have undergone a still mightier change; in which perhaps, the ethereal essence, wherein she has her truest life, will be found to have evaporated" (113).

Here is the abyss that opens up under liberty in this colonized land, native only by force and interior fabrication. In this world seeming to offer complete freedom, perhaps eventually no one will have an essential and permanent self. Perhaps we will discover that we have no ultimate bond to, or steady identity within, a community that remains intact over time and despite travel. Perhaps we will find that what seemed "nature" is only "hereditary habit." So, if we "tear down" the hereditary habit, including of "the opposite sex" — which is exactly what Hawthorne has done — we may lose our moorings.

Tellingly, however, it is at this moment that our narrator steps abruptly out of Hester's consciousness to announce that "[a] woman never overcomes these problems by any exercise of thought," having suggested a bit earlier that Hester had already undergone a "sad transformation," in which "some attribute had departed from her, the permanence of which had been essential to keep her a woman" (113, 112). At this point we may wonder if our narrator, more than Hester, is "wander[ing] without a clew in the dark labyrinth of mind" (114) — exactly the labyrinth of a mind that seeks an attribute "the permanence of which had been essential" and yet also unsettles the possibility of that permanence precisely in this restless, "wilderness" seeking. Hawthorne has created a woman who is not one, to echo Luce Irigaray's double entendre, and in the process has created a type of modern identity and community, an ideal that harbors a threat. More than Hester's, he has displayed his own colonial and gender-provoked fumbling before the aporia of liberty.

In response, to steady his hold, Hawthorne imitates Hester's most successful colonial strategy: keeping interiority contained, maintaining a threshold between private and public and only very selectively opening the door to cross it. All his tales ultimately rest on a narrative opacity; they keep the veil over an obscure interiority. On the one hand, his narrators focus on enigmatic characters with the tenacity of Chillingworth, who "strove to go deep into his patient's bosom," and Hawthorne similarly seems to seek what his narrator calls Chillingworth's "power . . . to bring his mind into such affinity with his patient's, that this last shall unawares have spoken what he imagines himself only to have thought" — and so to make public a private agony. Or again, like Chillingworth, he joins his "qualifications of a confidant" to "the advantages afforded by his recognized character as a physician," or man of education (86). Insofar as these phrases suggest an affinity between Hawthorne's practice of writing and Chillingworth's colonial practice of medicine, Hawthorne reveals the degree to which his narration is a bid for power in the colony, addressed to other white, literate men and authorized by his penetration of an illicit woman. This is the American story that Pauline Hopkins rewrites in *Of One Blood* from the African-Atlantic perspective.

Yet Hawthorne also practices a more measured artistry that succeeds where Chillingworth's fails. Dimmesdale collapses under Chillingworth's too-close scrutiny; Hawthorne, by contrast, never takes us over the threshold into Dimmesdale's interior. In the crucial scene in which Dimmesdale falls asleep over his ancient "black-letter" book, Chillingworth thrusts back the vestment and sees, apparently, a sign, but we the readers never do: Hawthorne shows us only the disturbingly gleeful face of Chillingworth as it comprehends what it sees. He shows us, that is, the *desire* to penetrate to the deepest interior, simultaneously heightening and constraining his (and our) desire to see, by keeping that interior cloaked. Similarly with the meteoric sign in the sky, we learn only the townspeople's fully cathected speculations about it. Hawthorne keeps uncertain the reality of the meteor and in the process keeps open the question of God's endorsement or condemnation of Dimmesdale, and, by extension, the degree of his colonial guilt. He *keeps* the secret of these characters' "sin" — the colonial one, that is — and he accordingly does the same for his audience.

In short, by emulating not Chillingworth but the diffident Hester, Hawthorne finds a more effective way to write his way into Atlantic modernity as a man. Like Hester, he successfully renativizes this New England colonial spot and keeps its protective threshold intact. He understands that in founding a native community on stolen soil, one may penetrate and subsume a woman's interior in order to establish and protect a man's. Fictional women may be cast as having a free interiority, and that free interiority may justify colonization; all of which — if distilled into allegory — can accrue to the male author, just as Surveyor Pue promised.

Thus I suggest that we might read the final image of Hester as she returns — an image in which her interior remains inaccessible — as an image of our author, Hawthorne. For after all, as he confesses in his introductory, it is he who must return and plant himself in the New England village, if he is to write a myth of Anglo-American origins. Appropriately, in the novel's final scene, Hawthorne positions us once again at the threshold, on the Atlantic shore, with Hester at her cottage door. We meet her as the figure turning between two worlds, choosing the abode of colonization but whose interior after all remains mostly in shadow. "On the threshold she paused, — turned partly round, — for, *perchance,* the idea of entering, all alone, and all so changed, the home of so intense a former life, was more dreary and desolate than even she could bear. But her hesitation was only for an instant, though long enough to display a scarlet letter on her breast" (176, emphasis added). Her aloneness may be awesome for her, even sublime, perchance — but we won't know. We will know her only through "the letter" — Hawthorne's now instead of hers.

Despite all the deflationary force of the custom house, then, *The Scarlet Letter* reveals Hawthorne forging an epic frame for a gothic history — an epic-historical frame that, however sardonic and ambiguous, will give him and his readers a place to stand outside so as to become masters of that history. The novel's final words remind us once more that this history carries a deeply buried, native interiority. For it closes with Hester's grave's archaic epitaph: "ON A FIELD, SABLE, THE

LETTER A, GULES." Like the half-obliterated shield, this time-effaced yet visibly red print on stone offers an enigma, and "the curious investigator may ... perplex himself with the import" (178). He may in fact write a romance-novel to create its import. The success of such a venture was confirmed by Hawthorne's first readers, who celebrated the novel as the first work of *American* genius. And ever since, the novel has given many readers and critics, including myself, a foothold for their apparent position as outsiders whose allegiance to outsideness authorizes them as members of a free community. Indeed, Hawthorne's charismatic persona as ironist and Salem rebel has placed him in the hallowed halls of founding American authors, next to Emerson, Thoreau, Whitman, and Melville.

But one more closing turn is called for. If "perchance," in our own final tableaus, instead of placing Hawthorne next to these male canonical novelists we place him beside Catharine Maria Sedgwick, we see how literary history ironically replays the drama that novels narrate. Sedgwick has seemed unsuited for the title of rebel American author, given her apparently more accommodating or sentimentalizing attitude toward U.S. history. It's worth considering the possibility that the open realism of her account of colonization required the sentimentality of her rhetoric (a point that may apply to sentimental fiction generally). But in any case, her embrace of a sentimental, marriage-plot dream of race has, in the long run of literary history, failed her, by making her appear conventional. It has, for a century, left her outside the canon — while Hawthorne seems to have established his renegade Anglo-Saxon identity, and so gained his place in the canon, by his apparent dissent from that identity. Of course, no nineteenth-century woman author hoping to find an audience could have afforded this maneuver. If educated Anglo-American men's economic instability in the New World fostered their narrational skepticism,[25] perhaps Anglo women's combined senses of constraint and possibility fostered their narrational conservatism. They needed the conservative slant of the racial myths more than the men, so as to legitimize their authorship. This predicament means that we are forced to read more carefully for the women's subversions — for instance, by placing Sedgwick's marriage plot drama against her narrator's explicit closing statement "that marriage is not essential" for a woman, as instanced in Esther, Magawisca, and the author herself.

Yet in the end, Sedgwick and Hawthorne share an epic Anglo-Atlantic poetics. Both of them craft an individualist race-fantasy of freedom through Anglo-American women — women who have utterly absorbed and in this sense successfully "vanished" the Indians with whom they are affiliated. Together these two authors practice an Indianism that takes its place beside Atlantic Africanism.

13 | Freedom's Eastward Turn in Eliot's *Daniel Deronda*

GEORGE ELIOT'S *Daniel Deronda* (1871) might seem far removed from any specifically Atlantic drama, until we recall that Mirah Cohen suffers a traumatic Atlantic crossing, as the captive of her own father. With this subplot Eliot signals the historical Atlantic core of her British epic. Like Hawthorne and Sedgwick, Eliot depicts an American scene of exile and ruin, briefly yet pivotally. Her novel's movement away from Mirah's — and indirectly Gwendolen's — Atlantic catastrophes, and toward a Mediterranean climax, dramatizes the turn back East of the Anglo-European race epic. In conjunction with this turn, and by way of a liberatory race ideology, here too brothers replace fathers and become "companionate" rulers of women. In this setting, of course, a bitter critique of the new order voiced by a "princess" seems out of place. Although this princess tells her own female tale of a tyrannous "yoke," she endures a defeat required by the republic's story of race liberty.

Eliot's last novel broods on matters that had occupied her since early in her career as a novelist, as evident in *The Mill on the Floss* (1860), which begins with an Atlantic meditation and ends with a brother-sister drowning. In the first paragraph of the novel, Eliot's narrator sits dreaming by the side of the tributary, the Ripple, which, she explains, feeds into the River Floss, which in its turn "hurries on between its green banks to the sea" where "black ships" unload their cargo of wood, spice, and coal and send these back down the river to the inland town of St. Oggs, the setting of her story.[1] Like the river, the narrator imaginatively moves toward the Atlantic, but apparently that ocean marks a limit, for she turns around and flows back from it, delivering the goods to her Anglo-British audience. The closing of this first chapter confirms the Atlantic horizon, and limit, of Eliot's imagination: as it ends, Eliot's narrator suddenly awakens — "Ah, my arms are really benumbed . . . I have been . . . dreaming" — and we realize that the opening vision out toward the Atlantic has all been contained in imagination (55). So in this contained way does the subsequent tale of the dark-skinned Maggie Tulliver, a wild girl attracted to Gypsies and, finally, drowned in this river in the arms of her ruthless (lighter-skinned) brother, allude unconsciously to the Atlantic story hovering at its imaginative limit.

In *Daniel Deronda,* by way of Mirah Cohen and Gwendolen Harleth, this Atlantic story intrudes more noticeably, and then is left behind more definitively, as the figure of the brother rises, and the sister falls. Perhaps the novel's acknowledgment and then transcendence of ruinous Atlantic entanglements is meant to defuse, symbolically, the social-leveling threat of female agency and sibling equality. Certainly in this last novel Eliot seems to narrate the way that men's "brotherly" imperial rise entails the sacrifice of Mirah's and Gwendolen's liberty — although because Eliot has implicated this female liberty in the workings of "bad" empire, especially in the case of Gwendolen, the sacrifice can seem just. Meanwhile, however, Eliot's investment in the notion of an organic, racial progress toward liberty — or in other words the need for a racial brotherhood at the helm of "good" imperial nations — means that Eliot tempers her critique of the new order of brothers. Despite its equally unsavory involvement in bad empire, men's liberty gets preserved and discursively protected. Indeed, in *Daniel Deronda,* the women carry the men's imperial guilt.

In other words, as we saw Pauline Hopkins do in *her* last novel, Eliot in this last of her novels negotiates hard with the conflict between women and race freedom.[2] Both authors shift the emphasis to male and away from female characters in order, it seems, to create a "free," imperial horizon for their communities. But nothing seems to smooth the gender snag in this imperial journey toward race freedom, and the women symbolically or literally drown in it. The epic scope of their final novels — reaching back to antiquity and forward into a grand universal future — at once serves their ambitions to tell a race story and offers them the scope to subordinate the gender crisis provoked by their race affiliations.[3] Hopkins and Eliot thus make "subjects" of women, including themselves, under racial terms — subjects in the empowering as well as the submitting sense. They help to write women's interpellating contract with this racial modernity even as they expose its violent, sexual terms.

Eliot's and Hopkins's novels do not simply compare, of course. Their works share an ocean and a history. Their stories meet — but only just touch and hardly speak — at the Atlantic fault line, held apart (for them and for us) by the modern/colonial formation of difference. And in fact their relation replays the literary as well as the material history of this Atlantic legacy. Eliot's story in effect contains Hopkins's, in the "minority" plot of Mirah, while Hopkins's deconstructs Eliot's from within, as we will see further in chapter 14. Thus it is salutary to read Eliot and Hopkins side-by-side as I will do in this second pair of chapters on nineteenth-century race epic.

Daniel and the Republican Interior

When Eliot chose "the Gothic Abbey" as one key setting for *Daniel Deronda* and made this ancient estate the native spot and founding scene of her male protagonist's "revolutionary shock" in discovering his illegitimate birth, she placed her drama within the long history I have been tracing.[4] The Abbey belongs to Sir Hugo Mallinger, who traces his "origin to a certain Hugues le Malingre, who came in with the Conqueror," and in accord with this French-Norman lineage, the house retains "remnants of [its] old monastic trunk" (204). That is, it contains the trace of a Catholic past, of a pre-Reformation and prerevolutionary period. Yet the property has come to Sir Hugo as a result, nonetheless, of revolutionary changes. For Sir Hugo's ancestors "had the grant" of "the Abbey at Monk's Topping" from King Henry VIII, presumably as a result of Henry's early Reformation seizures of land from monasteries in the 1530s and 1540s after he broke with the Roman Catholic Church, since this break is what put him in the position of "granting" monasteries to nonclergy. The "remnants" of the monastic trunk materialize a historical break as much as they embody continuity.

Like Atlantic modernity itself, that is, Sir Hugo's establishment is created by the cultural and economic ruptures engendered by the Reformation. He is a beneficiary of that shift in property relations that James Harrington, in his groundbreaking history *Oceana* (1656), traced to this sixteenth-century land "redistribution" and which, Harrington argued, was the first, early cause of the events leading to the English Revolution. The Abbey registers in its architecture these violent but prosperous upheavals of English history — a history preserved exactly because Sir Hugo had not attempted to "remedy the mixture of the undisguised modern with the antique — which in his opinion only made the place the more truly historical" (469). Although the Gothic kitchen with its "groined vault" stands out "in perfect preservation" (suggestive of women's preserved and preservative, or reproducing, role in this history), the exterior is "much defaced, maimed of finial and gargoyle" and the "beautiful choir [was] long ago turned into stables, in the first instance perhaps after an impromptu fashion by troopers, who had a pious satisfaction in insulting the priests of Baal" (472). The movement toward "the modern," though it may "preserve" a groined vault, begins in "impromptu fashion by troopers" taking "pious satisfaction" in destruction of this interior. Then, as the more systematic, "improving" process begins in which each "finely arched chapel was turned into a stall," the Abbey provides an objective correlative of the transformations of modernization—and of the effects for women like Gwendolen, who becomes Grandcourt's tamed horse now housed in such a stable (he was "perfectly satisfied that he held his wife with bit and bridle" [744]). The "continuity" of women's condition despite this shift to more modern forms and disciplines finds expression in the fact that there remain, attached to the stable's walls, "four ancient angels, still showing signs of devotion like mutilated martyrs" in a "shadow[y]" scene "untouched by reforming wash" (473).

Sir Hugo's Gothic Abbey thus encodes the religious and sexual back story of Atlantic modernity. As we'll see, the personal revolution that Daniel experiences in the Abbey enacts the interiorization of this history, including its racially marked violence. It is the site for Daniel's discovery of what Jacob Press has understood as the "cut" in his identity, manifested in his circumcised body, that private difference marking him as an illegitimate outsider and which hereafter the novel glosses as a hidden wound.[5]

Yet at first the Abbey appears as Daniel Deronda's safe ancestral home. Here he seems to inhabit that "native spot" where, as Eliot's narrator describes it, "the definiteness of early memories may be inwrought with affection" and "rooted" so that "amidst the future widening of knowledge" a person may sustain "the love of tender kinship for the face of the earth" and "for the sounds and accents that haunt it" since this love becomes "a sweet habit of the blood" (50).[6] The text conjures Daniel's immersion in such a home, showing him "stretched prone on the grass" in its courtyard among sensuous "sounds and accents" at "a moment full of July sunshine and large pink roses shedding their last petals on a grassy court enclosed on three sides by a Gothic cloister" (202). Daniel himself highlights this native spot's "inwrought" effects on him—"I carry it with me," he tells Gwendolen as he draws her attention to the Abbey's architectural details.

This very spot provides the setting, however, for an interior revolution in Daniel's mind about questions of legitimacy—prompted by his reading of republican history, figuratively rendered as a storm at sea, and thereby linked with Britain's tempestuous Atlantic imaginary. First, Eliot casts Daniel's uprooting from this spot as an event at once psychological and historical, the interior absorption of a long-ago set of political upheavals about succession that turn out to mirror his own life. His discovery arises from his reading of Sismondi's *History of the Italian Republics*. Daniel, we learn, is the kind of absorbed, bookish, if beautiful

— might we say Gothic? — young man who already has a "passion for history" at age thirteen. As we've seen, "republican" history, which seeks a form for the modern nation, typically invokes a nativist, soil-nurtured interior that is dedicated to freedom — as was certainly the case in the movement for Italian unification of which Sismondi is writing, and with which Eliot was sympathetic. It is thus fitting that this republican history should be the cause of Daniel's inner awakening and will ultimately lead to his embrace of a racial vision of a Zionist "republic" — Mordecai's exact word, as we'll see, for his ideal Jewish polity.

And yet in this scene what Daniel awakens to — an irony perhaps with more layers than Eliot intended — is the "illegitimacy" underlying this republican history, for his discovery quietly references the illegitimacy not just of popish practices but also of those who first prepared republican history. Although Daniel is reading about Italy and suddenly wondering about popes and their many "nephews," the infrastructure of illegitimacy is reproduced in English Protestant history, as Eliot well knew, even long before the overthrow of Charles I by gentry and commoners. Indeed, his "uncle's" habitation of the Abbey rests, as we've glimpsed, on this "illegitimate" history. For not only land but lineage and succession were tampered with in the course of the Reformation. That is, insofar as Elizabeth I, following in her father Henry VIII's footsteps, played a key role in instituting the Reformation, illegitimacy lay at its root — since she was originally the illegitimate daughter of Henry VIII and Anne Boleyn, made legitimate only after Henry's break with the Church and his marriage to Boleyn. Elizabeth's birth was an important cause of Henry's break with Rome, while the break with Rome, in turn, eventually legitimated her rise to power. And it was of course this Elizabeth who decisively and violently established Protestantism, who actively supported the antiquarian projects that later defined the terms of the English Revolution and the Anglo-Saxon myth, and who further enriched a new line of nobles by continuing the land "redistributions" initiated by her father; and so, indirectly, it is Elizabeth who thereby opened the way to the Puritan-Atlantic English revolution against the Scottish and popish King Charles Stuart I.

Given the Stuart kings' provocative part in this disrupted history of succession and legitimacy in English monarchy, Eliot must have chuckled as it occurred to her to give Deronda a *Scottish* tutor, Mr. Fraser, for it is he who explains the concept of illegitimacy to Deronda in telling him that the popes' and cardinals' "own children were called nephews" since of course "priests can't marry, and the children were illegitimate" (203). Eliot in effect hints — by way of Daniel's discovery — at how illegitimacy lies at the heart of the "Gothic" nation, although ultimately, and possibly in reaction to these embedded facts, she refashions this nation as an organic source and force within the universal movements of history. Yet it will be important that she does so at one remove, resuscitating this organic paradigm through the righteous vision of a minority community's entry into history.

Moving, so to speak, in this deep stream, and perhaps half-consciously, Eliot casts Daniel's first inkling of his own illegitimacy as an interiorized, republican revolution. Daniel feels a "deep blush" — and the threat of a swoon — come over him as "[a] new idea . . . entered his mind, and was beginning to change the aspect of his habitual feelings as happy voyagers are changed when the sky suddenly threatens and the thought of danger arises" (205). Realizing that he has himself been raised as a "nephew" of Sir Hugo, he finds that "[t]he ardour which he had given to the imaginary world in his books suddenly rushed toward his own history" and gave "him something like a new sense in relation to all the elements of his life" (206, 207). Daniel's "reading" of republican history thus tosses him into a rushing current that threatens to become a storm. This rushing history that includes the idea of his own illegitimacy throws him off center like a "[r]evolutionary shock" that "threatened downfall of habitual beliefs which makes the world seem to totter for us in maturer life" (211). His inward habit of living in books eventually reveals to him that an illegitimate yet ultimately empowering law of freedom is "writ" on his breast and will determine all his relations to the world. Like those early, illegitimate Atlantic voyagers, Daniel's journey will set off a series of revolutions that "make the world seem to totter" for an Anglo-Atlantic "us."

In fact his course within this modern history will be shaped by a literal transatlantic passage to America that culminates in a near drowning. The passage, however, will not be his but a woman's, carrying all the effects of racial and bodily ruin. With this in mind, we begin to see that, although most critics consider *Daniel Deronda* a divided novel, falling into English and Jewish halves, everything *is* connected to everything else, as Eliot insisted, for everything is compassed round by the ruinous yet prosperous facts of Atlantic history.

Mirah and the Shedding of an American Interior

Mirah Cohen's journey to America may seem incidental — embedded and subordinated as it is within her short, interpolated recitation of her life. Yet her experience reenacts that of Imoinda, Charlotte Temple, and Equiano's sister: she endures a sexualized middle passage that stands in for the drama of a nation's rupture and republican remaking. Mirah is kidnapped by her father, separated by a trick from her mother and Jewish-religious legacy, and taken across the ocean to America — an experience that culminates twelve years later when her father, after a recrossing of the Atlantic, attempts to prostitute her. As a little girl, she had thought they were only going on a "little journey" but — as Eliot has her explain retrospectively — "we went on board a ship, and got farther and farther away from the land. Then I was ill; and I thought it would never end — it was the first misery, and it seemed endless" (251). Like many before her, she dies symbolically on this journey. One day in America she goes out in search of a synagogue, to reconnect with the severed past, but "I lost myself a long while," and this "losing myself," as she later repeats, in foreign streets means that "[o]ften I wished that I had been drowned" (254–55).

As a result, Mirah becomes an inward-turned, dissenting modern person — and a reader. She begins to make "a life in my own thoughts quite different from everything about me . . . I shrank from all those things outside me into companionship with thoughts that were not like them; and I gathered thoughts very fast, because I read many things" (253). Like the earliest English revolutionaries and Puritans, she begins to fashion her world from the inside out. At the same time she becomes witness to a coarse American world where self is a rootless performance. Moving in the theater circles of her father's friends, she feels that "it was like a sharp knife always grazing me that we had two sorts of life which so jarred with each other" — the glamorous "staged" life, behind which lay the offstage world "with coarse, ugly manners" (253). If Eliot's characterization of these coarse manners expresses a trace of anti-Semitism as well as a fear of America's mixed crowds, this possibility reinforces the point that, through Mirah, Eliot subsumes and reconfigures the "ugly" race dimension of British history, transferred here to America, making America propel the movement back East toward a more heroic racial plot, and purer Semitism.

This movement back toward "home" begins, as Mirah reports, when "[r]ebellious feelings grew stronger in me," and this response will reshape her nation's history as it has the Anglo-British. She is moved to action when her father's coercions begin to include the threat of bodily violation, by encouraging her friendliness toward a count whose "smile went through me with horror" (260). She suspects that "my father was in a conspiracy with that man against me" so that "my heart turned against my father, for I saw always behind him that man who made me shudder" (260). When Mirah's heart turns against her father, the rebellious feelings initiated in America prompt a "revolution," leading the nearly violated British girl to flee to England and, as it turns out, renew her racial destiny and help reproduce a new nation. Mirah's story thus carries traces of an American escaped slave narrative as well as the biblical narrative of Exodus.

Yet Mirah's American story appears in order to be purged, recapitulating the way in which the Anglo-European economy had been forced to shed its investments, economic and psychic, in what became the United States, ameliorated only in part by colonies in Canada and the Caribbean. In relation to the United States, Mirah's story of exile, rupture, and near-ruin is also England's. Eliot's novel marks America as the site in the nineteenth-century Anglo-European imagination of a troubled memory of failure and of coarse, foreign minglings — one that prepares the role of the Mediterranean in Eliot's plotting of *Daniel Deronda*.

In her psychic placement of "America," as in many other elements of her vision of history, Eliot followed the lead of G. W. F. Hegel. Read together, these two authors' comments on "America" bring into view a submerged pattern. At first, both Eliot and Hegel seem to celebrate America's place in world history. In *The Philosophy of History,* Hegel begins by making pronouncements about America that seem to promise extended reflections on it. "America is," he says, "the land of the future, where, in the ages that lie before us, the burden of the World's History shall reveal itself — perhaps in a contest between North and South America. It is a land of desire for all those who are weary of the historical lumber-room of old Europe" (*History* 86). In strikingly similar language, in letters to American and British friends, Eliot referred to America as "that cradle of the future" and again as "the scene of a great future."[7]

For Steve Bamlett, Eliot's phrases provide evidence that she considers America a place of promise, the place outside and beyond, from which she can critique English culture, a source from which she can oxygenate her thinking. He interprets Eliot's refusal to visit America — despite her desire to sell her books there — as the symptom of her need to retain America as an imaginary elsewhere, an enabling figurative presence with which, in order to preserve it as such, she needed to avoid direct contact. In particular she needed her idea of America to remain untainted by actual encounters with what Eliot refers to as the "common American type" and the American nation's "unamalgamated races" (quoted in Bamlett 63). Bamlett points suggestively to midcentury English publications about the interrelation of the American and the British trade economies, such as Edward Gibbon Wakefield's widely read *England and America.* These books helped to build support for the free trade principle in the Atlantic economy — a principle which the *Westminister Review* advocated (Bamlett 54–64). Wakefield figured both the United States and Canada as colonies in the sense that they were sites of emigration from England and of exportation of materials back to both England and her colonies. In this light, Bamlett argues, we can see how America remained a resource for British-colonial material aspirations as well as for a colonial imagination that worked to position all of North America (both the United States and Canada) as serving British interests (including, Bamlett notes, those American readers who might consume the productions of British novelists like Eliot).

I too believe that "America" remains an important element of Britain's nineteenth-century colonial-economic imagination, but I propose that its presence was discomfiting as well as enabling. The United States represented the potential for defeat and loss. We need only recall the well-known eighteenth-century British cartoon titled "Magna Britannia: Her colonies REDUC'D" picturing Britain, after the American Revolution, as a woman with her limbs cut off and scattered on the ground around her.[8] Such images remind us that the Old World imagination had to turn back east from the New World because it was forced back. It was *sent* home. Especially after the American Revolution, the future of North America was no longer simply a British or European future; that future had been usurped by people calling themselves Americans (or, further south, independent Caribbeans and South Americans). Thus the Old World was "reduced" in large part to its eastern commerce and colonial aspirations.

Not surprisingly, then, on closer look, both Eliot and Hegel betray a nervousness about acknowledging America as the land of the future (an apprehension already felt by Edmund Burke, as we saw in chapter 5) — for it is a future in which their nations have little part and over which they have no control, and it is a place where the Germanic spirit of freedom that Hegel idealized was not unquestionably in the ascendancy and the organic, cumulative power of a people steeped in ancient traditions that Eliot cherished was — to white eyes — absent. Thus they both draw back from America directly after they praise it. Eliot concedes that America is the "scene of a great future" as a preface, it turns out, to her epistolary rebuff of invitations to visit from Harriet Beecher Stowe and Elizabeth Stuart Phelps (Bamlett 64). Likewise, in another letter, this time to a compatriot, Eliot refers to America as the "cradle of the future" before adding the caveat "I almost loathe the common American type of character" (quoted in Bamlett 63).

Hegel makes a similar, and more revealing, turnabout. Just after his pronouncements about America, he avers that "as a Land of the Future, [America] has no interest for us here" (*History* 87). "[O]ur concern, "he insists, "must be with that which has been and that which is" (87). "Dismissing, then, the New World, and the dreams to which it may give rise, we pass over to the Old World" (87). This is an odd turn in a philosopher obsessed with telos. Why this sudden unconcern with the future of Spirit? What threat lies coiled in the dreams to which America may give rise?

Immediately following his remarks on America, Hegel directs our gaze to the "three Continents" of the Old World and especially "the Mediterranean," because this region is "the heart of the Old World, . . . it is that which conditioned and vitalized it" (*History* 87). This turn is not as random as it may first seem, for the Mediterranean was emerging as a pivotal region for Anglo-European projects in the East. Yet Hegel also unconsciously acknowledges the uncertainties at this "heart" of the Old World, and the troubled waters of his next descriptions parallel, in effect, Grandcourt's, Gwendolen's, and Daniel's Mediterranean crises. Hegel's phrasing belies the fact that he is moving through a history of ruptures he cannot exit and that, after all, the Old and New Worlds mirror each other. "The Old World," he tells us, "which lies opposite to America, and is separated from it by the Atlantic Ocean, has its continuity interrupted by a deep inlet — the Mediterranean Sea" (*History* 87). Hegel just hints here that, wherever it turns, the "Old World" "has its continuity interrupted," but then in the very next sentence he submerges this hint, pronouncing that "[t]he three Continents that compose [the Old World] have an essential relation to each other, and constitute a totality. Their peculiar feature is that they lie round this Sea" (87). He goes on to detail the ways that "the Mediterranean is the uniting element" of the three Old World continents (87). How is it that the "uniting element" of the Old World is also that which "interrupts" the integrity and "totality" of that world? What better image could one give of what Jacques Derrida worked to reveal: the Anglo-European project to "constitute a totality" was formed around a gap, a deep inlet — which in turn yielded the willful refashioning of interruption as continuity. Hegel's account furthermore reminds us of the materialist ambition underlying this totalizing impulse — the will to territory, and in turn property.

For we should recall that throughout the nineteenth century the Mediterranean was in fact highly contested ground and the site of many battles as European powers struggled to build alliances that would support their trade ambitions and offer safe passage to Asia. British interests were directly threatened by Napoleon's Middle Eastern encroachments, in alliance with Egypt (in 1798 – 99 and again in 1831 – 40), and later Russia's.[9] That is, for England and for Eliot, of course, the Mediterranean basin was the "uniting element" in a most specific material sense: it provided a key part of the overland route to its holdings in India and its trade with Asia.

Most pertinent to Eliot's novel, as some critics have emphasized, the need for a foothold in the Mediterranean stands behind British support for a Palestinian homeland for the Jews.[10] As Eliot's contemporaries knew, the recovery of Palestine "for the Jews," engineered by Britain, would more fully secure the British passageway to India as well as give Britain the security it had lacked for trade, diplomacy, and development in the Mediterranean region and beyond. While both France and Russia had diplomatic ties with Middle Eastern states and justified their incursions by cultivating relations with the region's Catholic and Greek Orthodox "protégé" communities for which they served as advocates, Britain had no such ties or support but only a delicate relationship with the sultans of the Ottoman Empire. By the middle of the nineteenth century, therefore, political motives for emigration of the Jews to Jerusalem began to mingle with the longstanding religious beliefs of British Evangelicals who claimed that God had chosen Britain as the instrument of his plan to return the Jews to the Holy Land, realize their conversion to Christianity, and so prompt the Second Coming of Christ. Thus the seventh Earl of Shaftesbury, an opponent of full Jewish civil rights in England, had begun advocating a Zionist vision in the 1830s and 1840s, implicitly as a solution to the "Jewish problem."

The later-nineteenth-century politicians who took up the idea of a Jewish return to a Palestinian "homeland" avoided pairing it with anti-Semitic sentiments about Jews in England. Instead they tended to ring positive changes on the old Puritan idea of a kinship between the English and the Jews — an idea given renewed expression among such groups as the British Israelites and in such tracts as Edward Hine's *Forty-Seven Identifications of the British Nation with the Lost Ten Tribes of Israel* (1871). The mingling of "liberatory" and pragmatic motives for securing a Jewish homeland is registered in the very titles of such publications as Thomas Clarke's *India and Palestine: or, The Restoration of the Jews, Viewed in Relation to the Nearest Route to India* (1861) and Edward L. Mitford's *Appeal on Behalf of the Jewish Nation in Connection with British Policy in the Levant* (1845). Mitford, a colonial administrator, illustrates the strategic appeal of a British-backed Jewish colony in the Middle East when he points out, for instance, that a Jewish colony "would place the management of our steam communications entirely in our hands" (Levine 48). The colony would, that is, ease the dangers of the Mediterranean – Red Sea passage of travel between Britain and India, since the steamships — whose coal-fueling required frequent stops for replenishment — could then stop at ports unmolested (Levine 48).

As Gary Martin Levine adds, the idea of a Jewish colony became even more compelling during and after the rebellions in India (especially given the need for transporting troops) as well as in the face of an increasingly unstable Ottoman Empire, the one Middle Eastern power with which the English had at least a tenuous alliance (48). Under these conditions, British foreign secretary Lord Palmerston appealed to the Turkish sultan to encourage the "return" of the Jews since, as he wrote in a dispatch to the British ambassador, "It is well known that the Jews of Europe possess great wealth, and it is manifest that any country in which a considerable number of them might choose to settle would derive great benefit," and, he pointed out to the sultan, this renewed wealth and ground of support could "be a check upon any future evil designs of [Egyptian leader] Mehemet Ali or his successor" (Meyer 749). Not surprisingly, most Jews in England (at least before the Russian pogroms of the 1880s) were unenthusiastic about the idea of any such "return" to this unstable region and skeptical about these politicians' motives, preferring to continue the battle for equality of treatment in England.

George Eliot was certainly aware of these matters as she wrote *Daniel Deronda*. As Levine notes, in May 1870 she attended a forum at Oxford organized by the Palestine Exploration Society (founded 1865) and very likely heard the lecture given by Captain Charles Warren of the Royal Engineers (48). The society purportedly had as its goal the mapping of ancient biblical sites, but its crew was dominated by military personnel and surveyors such as Captain Warren. Warren's lecture no doubt drew from the book he was soon to publish, *The Recovery of Jerusalem* (1871), which outlines the strategic wisdom of a settlement of Jews in the Holy Land. More generally, of course, a person as attuned as Eliot to what she called "social philosophy" would be aware of these perspectives on Palestine.[11] Although such British political interests may not wholly account for Eliot's Zionist vision in *Daniel Deronda,* it seems likely that they would have circulated in her mind as a positive by-product of a Jewish "homeland." A close reading of "The Modern Hep! Hep! Hep!" — the last essay in her last published work, *Impressions of Theophrastus Such* — suggests as much.

From Puritans to Palestine: Re-racializing the "Freedom" of English Jews

My purpose in this chapter is not simply to determine the degree of imperial ambition or equivocal philosemitism expressed in Eliot's novel. It is rather to enable a reading of the novel that makes fuller sense of its America-England-Mediterranean circuit and so reveals how Eliot structures her race narrative of liberty along this circuit, both cleaving to and extending the transatlantic patterns initiated by *Oroonoko.* Within this approach we can first of all see that if, after the winning and losing of America, "the Mediterranean is the uniting element" in the Anglo-European imperial imagination, then it is constructed exactly against the further threat of discontinuity and disruption in that region. The subplot by which Mirah's ruinous travels to America turn her back toward a renewed racial-national destiny maps the trade routes, so to speak, of this imagination. And it registers the pressures under which that imagination operated. We glimpse how the English, American, and finally Italian republican revolutions provide more than the imagery for Daniel's interior undoing over a loss of legitimacy. They provide the historical conditions that ultimately led Eliot both inward and eastward in her fiction, toward this crafting of the deeply private, historical imagination of a "Daniel" who becomes the Western founder of an Eastern nation. While inevitably in this discussion I consider the ways in which Eliot privileges Anglo-

Saxon Protestant identities and interests, my main concern is with the way her novel reveals how deeply these patterns are inscribed into *our* English-language imaginations — including a diverse range of "us."

IN "THE MODERN HEP! HEP! HEP!" Eliot renews the old identification, so enabling for British Atlantic history, between the exiled, ocean-crossing Puritans and the exiled, sea-crossing Israelites. As her narrator Theophrastus Such directly points out, "The Puritans, asserting their liberty to resist tyrants, found the Hebrew history closely symbolical of their feelings and purpose."[12] Accordingly, as Theophrastus argues, the "just sympathy and admiration which we give to the ancestors" should also be given to "those brave and steadfast men of the Jewish race who fought and died, or strove by wide administration to resist, the oppression and corrupting influences of foreign tyrants" — especially since, by such resistance they "rescued the nationality that was the very hearth of our own religion" (151). Mirah's American crossing and swoon, especially as it entails the rise of rebellious feelings and culminates in race liberation, carries a trace of this Puritan history and identification.

Significantly, throughout this essay Theophrastus highlights the colonizing privileges that seem to accompany this exilic identity, especially insofar as he compares the Jewish and the Puritan beliefs in themselves as chosen peoples within "a specially divine arrangement" (150). He notes that, like the Israelites, "we have not been noted for forming a low estimate of our selves" (150), so that "[m]any of us have thought that our sea-wall is a specially divine arrangement to make and keep us a nation of sea-kings after the manner of our forefathers, secure against invasion and able to invade other lands when we need them, though they may lie on the other side of the ocean" (150). Clearly, the Atlantic is this ocean and America is this other land. And likewise "it has been held that we have a peculiar destiny as a Protestant people, not only able to bruise the head of an idolatrous Christianity in the midst of us, but fitted as possessors of the most truth and the most tonnage to carry our purer religion over the world and convert mankind to our way of thinking" (150). This comment, of course, erroneously attributes a conversion mission to the Jews, in keeping with what Christina Crosby has established as Eliot's Christianizing of Jewish thought in *Daniel Deronda*.[13] More to the point for my argument, however, it also ambiguously places Jews within a transatlantic and "invading" British frame of reference, that culture whose "tonnage" is the vehicle of its "truth."

In *Daniel Deronda*, Eliot likewise places the Jewish struggle within this frame of reference. As Susan Meyer points out, she more than once casts Mordecai as a heroic American colonizer, as when she compares the rebuff he meets at the Philosophers' Club in response to his Zionist ideas to that of "a missionary tomahawked without any considerate rejection of his doctrines" — even though it is possible, as the narrator remarks, that "his ideas had been as true and precious as those of Columbus" (586).[14] By way of these identifications Eliot achieves a doubly strategic effect. She frames the idea of a Jewish settlement within the Anglo-Atlantic Puritan vision that began as a city on a hill (and had by Eliot's time expanded into a manifest destiny). And yet at the same time she figures the now-cast-off and "ruinous" America as a land of tomahawks left behind for the proper, Eastern unfolding of an Anglo-European future. Her invocation of Columbus as a bearer of true and precious ideas hints at the fact that invasion and empire remain an accepted frame of reference, the schema within which she redefines Anglo-Jews in relation to Anglo-Protestants.

This set of associations begins to explain why Theophrastus broods so much on Britain's identity as a "nation of sea-kings" in an essay ostensibly devoted to Jews as a historical and honorable race. In this chapter, at one level Eliot is working to merge and make complementary two divergent yet equally embedded racial tropes about Anglo-Saxons: the sea-crossing, colonial and the soil-rooted, historical. In the passage Theophrastus approvingly quotes from the Whig historian T. R. Green, Green first exhorts his readers to "know who were our forefathers, who it was that won the soil for us, and brought the good seed of those institutions through which we should not arrogantly but gratefully feel ourselves distinguished among the nations as possessors of a long-inherited freedom" (quoted in "Hep" 145). After this clear reference to the old Anglo-Saxon legacy, Green brings the story forward to its American phase, adding, "These sea-faring, invading, self-asserting men were the English of old time, and were our fathers who did rough work by which we are profiting" (145). Green is working to reconcile Anglo-Saxon tropes of soil and sea here, and he shrewdly allows them ambiguously to come together in that act of "winning the soil," which in its vagueness can include both the soil of England and the soil of America.

In turn, this suggestion of a soil won after a water-crossing invasion prepares the further paralleling of "we English" and "the Israelites," for "[t]here is more likeness than contrast between the way we English got our island and the way the Israelites got Canaan" (150). By way of this shared imagery, Theophrastus can then characterize both Jews and Anglo-Saxons as similarly successful races and in turn imagine for them both a mutually cooperative "part in the comity of nations and the federation of the world" (156). For Theophrastus, and very likely Eliot, it is exactly this self-fashioning — or what he calls "the organized memory of a national consciousness" — that qualifies both England and a Jewish state for such historical roles (162).

We might say that within the choral refrain of the essay's ballad of sea kings, Eliot has Theophrastus compose the romantic melody of racialized, organic nationalism.[15] This organic nationalism will authorize colonial states for both the British and the Jews — or rather, perhaps, for the Jews on behalf of the British. The uncomfortable self-interest underlying the latter scenario may be what prompts Theophrastus explicitly to subsume material motives within a noble, collective identity, as in this remark: "The eminence, the nobleness of a people depends on its capability of being stirred by memories, and of striving for what we call spiritual ends — ends which consist *not in immediate material possession,* but in the satisfaction of a great feeling that animates the collective body with one soul" (146, emphasis added). Tonnage — of cannons and cargo — merely serves the "truth" of a "collective body with one soul." As he proceeds, we can see Theophrastus making lyrical the material violence that transubstantiates this collective body into a sublime Hegelian soul:

> A people having the seed of worthiness in it must feel an answering thrill when it is adjured by the deaths of its heroes who died to preserve its national existence; when it is reminded of its small beginnings and gradual growth through past labours and struggles, such as are still demanded of it in order that the freedom and wellbeing thus inherited may be transmitted unimpaired to children and children's children; when an appeal against the permission of injustice is made to great precedents in its history and to the better genius breathing in its institutions. It is this living force of sentiment in common which makes a national consciousness. Nations so moved will resist conquest with the very breasts of their women, will pay their millions and their blood to abolish slavery, will share privation in all famine and all calamity. (146 – 47)

In addition to the losses fashioned here as the noble deaths of heroes, as labors and struggles, and as the living "force" of sentiment, two turns in the last sentence are particularly telling. First, the core story of *Daniel Deronda* is coiled in the assertion "Nations so moved will resist conquest with the very breasts of their women" — a point to which I'll return.[16]

Second, in the remark that such nations "will pay their millions and their blood to abolish slavery," Eliot begins the crucial turn that carries forward her re-racialization of English Jews. The turn begins as Theophrastus recasts the Anglo-Atlantic "rough work" that instituted slavery ("by which we are profiting") as the Anglo-Atlantic battle against slavery on behalf of others, once Africans, now the Jews.[17] In the wake of this turn, what began as an identification between colonizing Puritans and exiled Israelites becomes an analogy between Negroes and Jews, in which the Jews become a minority and the Anglo-Protestant author becomes their defender.[18] Later in the essay, Theophrastus directly compares the position of Jews to that of Negroes: "As the slave-holders in the United States counted the curse of Ham a justification of negro slavery, so the curse on the Jews was counted as a justification for hindering them from pursuing agriculture and the handicrafts" (151). Likewise Theophrastus compares ridiculous prejudices about Jews to the ridiculous notion that there is "a peculiar odor from the Negro body" and that this is what "determine[s] the question on the side of slavery" (161). An Atlantic discourse about Africans is here feeding an emergent and equally Anglo-enabling discourse of Semitism. Thus in yet another way, the Jews take their place within the American dimension of the British imagination as they also take on status an "other" race. In a maneuver that compares with Catharine Maria Sedgwick's re-racializing of American Indians apparently to champion them but also to "remove" them, Eliot re-racializes British Jews.

In this light we can make new sense of the fact that Theophrastus directly follows Green's celebration of "patriotic affection" with the comment that this affection is what "lifts us above emigrating rats and free-loving baboons" (145). As equivocally hinted in the racial slurs embedded in this statement, just behind "patriotic affection" stands a racial aversion that calls for a separation of races: the rats must emigrate, the baboons be kept at bay. The "lifted" position of "us" depends on this racializing turn.

In fact, Eliot's Theophrastus openly confesses his fears of amalgamation. For although, as he admits, "The tendency of things is towards the quicker or slower fusion of races," we should, he advises, "moderate its course so as to hinder it from degrading the moral status of societies by a too rapid effacement of those national traditions and customs which are the language of national genius — the deep suckers of healthy sentiment" (160). Critical as he is of English exceptionalism, he confesses his agreement with those who feel it would be "a calamity to the English, as to any great historic people, to undergo premature fusion with immigrants of alien blood"; and indeed he is "ready to unite in groaning over the threatened danger" (158). Shortly thereafter comparing the negative sentiments in British culture about the Jews "among us everywhere" to those class feelings about "proletaries" who "elbow us in a thickening crowd," he suggests that "our best course is to encourage all means of improving these neighbors, . . . and of sending their incommodious energies into beneficent channels" (163). The phrase "beneficent channels" echoes the passages that surround it, most especially this one just preceding it, in which Theophrastus wonders whether there may be, "in the political relations of the world, the conditions present or approaching for the restoration of a Jewish state planted on the old ground as a center of national feeling, a source of dignifying protection, a special channel for special energies which may contribute some added form of national genius, and an added voice in the councils of the world" (162–63).

Having just suggested that Jews do have the "organized memory of national consciousness" (162) that fits them to be a nation, and arguing that therefore they are in a position to participate "in that spirit of separateness which has not yet done its work in the education of mankind" (160), Theophrastus thus proposes that Jews can take up their *separate* position, with British support of course, as a racial nation—one that can, as he goes on to add, "constitute a new beneficent individuality among nations" (164). Without referring directly to Palestine or British interests, Theophrastus's allusion to the "old ground" and to the "beneficent" effects of a colony indicates that the Mediterranean political context was on Eliot's mind. Although this vision assigns a noble position to Jews, and I don't believe Eliot meant to underwrite the wish to "elbow out" a "thickening crowd" of Jews, her comment about sending "incommodious energies" into "beneficent channels" at the same time suggests that she understood how the Palestine project could provide the "best course" for thinning out that crowd and thus lessening the animosity of her anti-Semitic compatriots. Certainly such a Mediterranean state would offer a "special channel" and "dignifying protection" for "special energies" that would be beneficent for Anglo-Protestant Britain, just as the "added voice" of such a state in "the councils of the world" would be value-added from a British point of view.

That is, as I will elaborate in the rest of this chapter, in *Daniel Deronda* Eliot is not just comparing Mordecai to colonizers of America. She is strategically redirecting colonial-Atlantic "energies" and rewriting the Atlantic narrative in order (not necessarily consciously) to redeploy it, like Hegel, in the Mediterranean, the scene of a more immediate future. In effect, through Mirah, she recalls the Anglo-Jews from America (with its too-fast movement toward amalgamation) and sends them to Palestine where they will beneficently tip the balance of power in Britain's direction. This interpretation diverges from Neil McCaw's and Christina Crosby's arguments that Eliot's Zionism is actually a recoded British "nationalism" that subsumes Jewishness. Nor do I see Eliot's vision of Jewish emigration to the Mediterranean in the largely anti-Semitic terms that Susan Meyer does. Rather her vision recognizes the potential power and place of English Jews in global politics, as allies of the British. The problem is more an Orientalist, imperial one than an anti-Semitic one, although it does involve racializing the Jews. For Eliot does believe in Britain's world-historical role and she believes in the Jews' crucial place in this history.[19]

Yet while Eliot's attitude about Anglo-Jews is complex and quite rich, her fictional practice in representing Jews is nevertheless analogous to the Africanism operating in other Anglo-Atlantic novels. In her Jewish subplot about Mirah in America, Eliot practices a transmuted, palimpsestic Afro-Jewishism — which as we have seen blends Indian, African American, and Jewish identities — that allows her to recast the Anglo appropriation of the African-Atlantic middle passage as a kind of Jewish middle passage requiring the righteous founding of a Jewish homeland. In this way, just as Xury and Friday actually save Robinson Crusoe while Defoe's text foregrounds the reverse, so here, although it is the Jews who, within the emergent Anglo-Zionist narrative, will "save" Britain in the Mediterranean, the British author appears to redeem and rescue the Jews. It is worth noting tangentially that Europe, in the form of the European Union, is still working on this problem of counterbalancing American power, still ambivalently cultivating a tenuous alliance with Turkey to do so, and at the same time, against and together with Americans, still failing to "make" the Mediterranean the uniting element that would be beneficent for Europe. In her last published texts, Eliot acutely turned her attention to this developing geopolitical situation.

Another Race Republic

All of this takes on further force when we note that, in *Daniel Deronda*, the Eastern Jewish homeland that Mordecai envisions is cast as a republic of liberty and that Eliot explicitly refashions Jews as a freedom-seeking race. As Mordecai puts it, he imagines a "new jewish polity, grand, simple, just, like the old — a republic where there is equality of protection" (594). In his rewritten history of Jewish government, the republican model is the native one, for in "the old" republic the legacy of equality "shone like a star on the forehead of our ancient community, and gave it more than the brightness of Western freedom amid the despotisms of the East" (595).

Indeed, in her portrait of Zionism and Jews, Eliot gathers all the tropes of Anglo-Saxonism. Joseph Kalynomous, the friend of Deronda's grandfather who preserves the family's history and passes it on to Deronda, embodies the freedom-seeking spirit of the Jew. As he tells Deronda, since "we have freedom, I am content" (791). Kalynomous does not seek a Jewish state, for, instead, his freedom-seeking impulses make him a traveling man — "loving to wander, loving transactions, loving to behold all things" — and a brooding man of the sea, "when I am in the East, I lie much on deck and watch the greater stars. The sight of them satisfies me" (791). Indeed, he believes that "[o]ur people wandered before they were driven" (791). Kalynomous might well lead a nation of sea kings. He embodies the venturous, trading side of the free race.

It is Mordecai, on the other hand, with his quest to "restor[e] a political existence to my people," who expresses the soil-rooted, romantic version of racialized nationality that will ground this freedom (875). He believes that, despite disruptions and diaspora, this community's "spirit of sublime achievement" only needs a native spot: "our race," Mordecai predicts, "shall have an organic center" so that, in proper Hegelian form, "the spirit of sublime achievement [shall] move in the great among our people" (595). And he spells out the sentimental, binding role of a race "brotherhood" within the dispersing currents of individualism: "What is the citizenship of him," he asks, "who walks among a people he has no hearty kindred and fellowship with, and has lost the sense of brotherhood with his own race? It is a charter of selfish ambition and rivalry in low greed. He is an alien in spirit . . . [s]haring in no love, sharing in no subjection of the soul" (587). For Mordecai, as for earlier theorists like Thomas Jefferson, the "charter" needs racializing in order to be "bonding."

And for Mordecai this racialized charter, carrying suggestions of a written-down historical record, provides the ground for a culture of contract and "choice." He explains that he discovered his vocation as a visionary Jew when he first began to write in Hebrew. He then points out that "[t]he native spirit of our tradition was not to stand still, but to use records as a seed" (591), setting up written records, and implicitly literacy, as the basis for the freedom to choose: for by such "seeds" does "[t]he life of a people grow," enabling that "strongest principle of growth [which] lies in human choice" (598). In learning Hebrew and entering this print community, Mordecai reports that he felt he had been "released as it were to mingle with the ocean of human existence, free from the pressure of individual human bondage" (601). Here individualism is cast as the bondage from which race frees one. Eliot deftly fertilizes Mordecai's organic and conserving metaphors with the language of "choice." In her portrait, he implicitly upholds the modern, print-disseminated ideology in which race serves to counter possessive individualism, and it is telling that he outlines it as a federation of brothers.

Eliot synthesizes all these elements of the racial vision of freedom in the figure of Deronda. Deronda serves to combine the free spirit of Kalynomous with Mordecai's Hegelian, state-founding, and anti-individualist vision.[20] His Kalynomousian side is expressed in his "boyish love of universal history, which made him want to be at home in foreign countries, and follow in imagination the travelling students of the middle ages" and so to seek out "the sort of apprenticeship to life that would not shape him too definitely, and rob him of that choice that might come from a free growth" (220). At the same time, as Deronda himself observes, he seeks and ultimately finds the "complete ideal shape of that personal duty and citizenship" through his brotherly relation to Mordecai, with whom he affiliates racially and yet by choice (570–71). In addressing Mordecai's demands, he uses the language of consent to balance the racial with the republican, explaining that "my whole being is a consent to the fact [of being a Jew]. But it has been the gradual accord between your mind and mine which has brought about that full consent. It is through your inspiration that I have discerned what may be my life's task. It is you who have given shape to what, I believe, was an inherited yearning — the effect of brooding, passionate thoughts in many ancestors" (819). His desire to realize this (Gothic) balancing act is prefigured in his admiration for the architecture of the Abbey, for he cherishes "the delicate sense which had combined freedom with accuracy in the imitation of natural forms" (475).

In sum, Deronda "consents" to race. And so he signs into modernity. Thus does Eliot, first of all, stir a vision in which "the ancestral life" of a displaced people "lie[s] within them as a dim longing for unknown objects and sensations" and then place this longing at the center of a republic of consent. She is clearly working on the conundrum at the heart of Atlantic modernity. She finds a new, more complicated way to rewrite race as a recuperative power that heals the historical ruptures of republicanism — and America. Helping to carry her nation from West to East, she merges the notions of the Gothic balance, or mixed constitution, with her Jewish racial vision, via the key idea and plot of freedom.

It's no surprise, then, that from the moment Mirah arrives in England, her American experience begins to be recuperated within a Jewish racial narrative of exile and return, in this way giving a "beneficent" turn to Eliot's British-Atlantic story. At first, like a whole cast of protagonists in later-nineteeth and early-twentieth-century English-language novels, Mirah moves toward a drowning suicide. She seems to be the embodiment of a rootless modern soul. When she escapes back to London in search of her family, she finds that the family's old house is gone with no trace of her mother or brother. She feels herself "a lost child taken up and used by strangers. . . . It seemed all a weary wandering and heart-loneliness" (263). On the other hand, however, she identifies her plight with that of "my People [who] had been driven from land to land and been afflicted" (263–64). And so her "mind got into war with itself" about whether this legacy means she should kill herself or not. Mirah is caught in the conundrum of modernity, struggling on the horns of an ideology that makes race a source of both ruin and rebirth, both a drowning and a landing — that is to say, an imaginary that conflates losing land with gaining it.

It is at this moment, as Mirah hovers indecisively between embrace and suicide of the race-d self, poised to "give up" herself by drowning, that Deronda appears in his boat, singing an Italian aria from Rossini's version of the race-vexed drama of Shakespeare's *Othello* (264). Her story at this moment becomes that of a racial nation, once lost now found, like the Italian republics the young Daniel studied

—and like the England that had colonies in America. The allusion to *Othello* implies that, moved by the genius of the native English poet, together Daniel and Mirah will transcend the threat of amalgamation that Shakespeare dramatized and America so clearly embodies. Leaving America, Mirah redirects the rupture of British racial identity and becomes the "preserved" woman who, in reproducing a Jewish republic, will extend the freedom of the British republican empire.

The Imperial Couple and the Crime of Consent

But those women who linger individually, selfishly, resistantly, and racelessly at the margin can threaten this grand unfolding of history. *Daniel Deronda* broods on these women, too. In the case of Gwendolen Harleth, Eliot again works her way through Atlantic history in order to place this errant "spoiled child" in the epic story. Like Mirah's, Gwendolen's drama encompasses the American-Mediterranean circuit of British history. Her trauma begins, in effect, in the West Indies and ends — with a drowning and swoon — in the Mediterranean city of Genoa, birthplace of the republican leader Giuseppe Mazzini. I'll return to this question of setting in the next section. Here I consider the motor of this movement from Atlantic to Mediterranean: the power struggle between the Anglo-Atlantic man and woman, shadowed by a ruinous, interloping sea-captain father, and prompted forward by a colonial financial ruin that makes a casualty of the disinherited Irish-colonial woman, Lydia Glasher.

In the story of Henleigh Grandcourt and Gwendolen Harleth — the woman's name suggestive of her kinship with Defoe's Protestant "harlot," Roxana, who consorts with British power for her own gain — Eliot not only registers and allegorizes the dynamics of British Empire, as critics have noted, but she pointedly places sexuality at the center of Britain's roving imperial history.[21] In particular she exposes how the heterosexual relation — a relation that ostensibly rests honorably on free consent and contract — is in fact structured by a control of property and a coercive "haltering" that gives way to colonial crimes.[22] Eliot aims, I believe, to envision another, beneficent and brotherly kind of inclusion for women.

As the fortunes of Sir Hugo's family rise with the Reformation, those of Gwendolen's family likewise issue, more belatedly, from that historical turn toward a "free" Protestantism. In this case the link is the wealth of the West Indies that began with those seventeenth-century colonies like Bermuda, from which, as we saw in chapter 1, Puritan leaders and merchants financed and leveraged the civil war against Charles I. It is this wealth that eventually filters down to Gwendolen's grandfather, who "had been a West Indian" — "which seemed to exclude further question," given the immense fortunes of sugar and coffee planters of West Indian islands (52). But here too those lands across the Atlantic carry the memory of violent challenges to British preeminence. In 1876, any mention of the West Indies would still have carried a trace of violence and disaster for Eliot's readers, as it would have recalled the 1865 Morant Bay Rebellion, an uprising in Bermuda that was brutally avenged by Governor Eyre, whose actions were in turn hotly debated in England — defended by Carlyle and condemned by John Stuart Mill.

In the novel, Gwendolen's family's Atlantic wealth likewise provokes bitterness and disaster at home. That wealth is first of all depleted after the death of Mrs. Davilow's first husband, as much of it gets squandered by her second husband, notably a sea captain. She is then led by her brother to invest what is left of it in colonial "mines and things of that sort," which ultimately brings complete bankruptcy to Gwendolen's family (274). As Mrs. Davilow's "fortunes" are dependent on what her brother and husband do with her inheritance, so "the family fortune was dependent," as the narrator explains, "[on] conditions of colonial property and banking . . . as [Gwendolen] had many opportunities of knowing" (94). When the investment firm, Grapnell & Co., fails "for a million," and Gwendolen's family is "totally ruined," so is Gwendolen sexually ruined (43). For the bankruptcy leads Gwendolen to accept Grandcourt, just after having nobly rejected him because of his abandonment of Lydia Glasher and their sons. Gwendolen is thus clearly circled round by the empire and its "trade-offs": the failure of colonial speculation after all simply thrusts her, with her possessive desires, back into that same imperial economy, particularly its sexual market of marriageable women who will reproduce the empire's men. Gwendolen's family's "roving," their dispossession — their lack of a "native spot" (the narrator's encomium to which appears exactly in the course of describing this lack of it in Gwendolen's past) — and Gwendolen's displacement arise from colonial economics, which in turn provokes her sexual ruin by driving her into the arms of the imperious Grandcourt.

Embedded here is another allegory of England's losses on the Atlantic — of financial ruin and the loss of native habitation, via empire. Like Mirah, Gwendolen experiences a self-losing entry into her imperial community by way of an Atlantic circuit of "fortunes" that in Gwendolen's case ultimately leaves her prostrate rather than prosperous within empire. Yet, unlike Mirah, Gwendolen has "invested," psychologically as well as materially, in these questionable conditions that "risked too much" (as we are told about Grapnell, "There were great speculations: [the broker] meant to gain. . . . He risked too much" [274]). The novel pointedly introduces us to Gwendolen in a scene of gambling, an activity repeatedly linked to speculative colonial practices. We meet her among the company of gamblers that includes, for instance, a "respectable London tradesman, blond and soft-handed, his sleek hair scrupulously parted" whose play at the table is of a piece with

> a well-fed leisure, which in the intervals of winning money in business and spending it showily, sees no better resource than winning money in play and spending it yet more showily — reflecting always that providence had never manifested any disapprobation of his amusement, and dispassionate enough to leave off if the sweetness of winning much and seeing others lose had turned to the sourness of losing much and seeing others win. (36 – 37)

If gambling and business both entail dispassionately making gain from someone else's loss with the assumed approval of providence, then the colonial market may likewise be a Christian-sanctified form of theft, as the narrator later hints: "It appears that Caribs, who know little of theology, regard thieving as a practice peculiarly connected with Christian tenets, and probably they could allege experimental grounds for this opinion" (246). It is specifically this thieving, gambling economy in which Gwendolen ultimately confesses her participation: "I wanted to make my gain out of another's loss . . . it was like roulette — and the money burnt into me" (757).

But long before this confessional moment, Eliot offers in her portrait of Gwendolen a kind of etymology of the shared roots of freedom and empire that infect the nation's reproductive future (and actually allow Grandcourt's fortune to be diverted to his illegitimate Irish colonial family). Gwendolen's entire impulse is toward freedom, egocentrically and imperially conceived. And she sees her entry into freedom as a passage in a maritime world — her sea journey will be a path to freedom for her, if not for others: "Other people allowed themselves to be made slaves of, and to have their lives blown hither and thither like an empty ship in which no will was present: it was not to be so with her" (69). No middle passage will blow *her* life off course. She "was not going to renounce her freedom, or according to her favourite formula, 'not going to do as other women did'" (168). Gwendolen's delusions arise from her experience within an imperial culture, for she has always been petted and served in her "domestic empire" (71) like a "princess in exile" (53, 71), a "queen in exile" (71). Her "inborn energy of egoistic desire" (71) gives rise to her certainty that she can "conquer circumstance" — although her "passion for doing what is remarkable has an ideal limit in consistency with the highest breeding and perfect freedom from the sordid need of income" (83).

Is this Eliot's wry caricature of the Anglo-Saxon nation's "inborn energy"? The rest of her description in this passage is soaked with literary allusions that would seem to deflate, in any case, the nation's heroic imaginary, its self-fashioning as sublime force that subsumes and transcends its barbarian beginnings, at least in its female version. Gwendolen's inner vision of herself is that of the "genteel romance where the heroine's soul poured out in her journal is full of vague power, originality, and general rebellion, while her life moves strictly in the sphere of fashion" (83) — perhaps a paragon of Western "free" societies. And so "if she wanders into a swamp, the pathos lies partly, so to speak, in her having on her satin shoes. Here is a restraint which nature and society have provided on the pursuit of striking adventure; so that a soul burning with a sense of what the universe is not, and ready to take all existence as fuel, is nevertheless held captive by the ordinary network of social forms" (83). Like Britain's, Gwendolen's "soul burning" pursuit of "striking adventures" that takes its fuel from elsewhere — although "full of vague power, originality, and general rebellion" and led by a transcendent, ship-steering "will" — does not after all, Eliot insists, take her outside the "ordinary." When Gwendolen finally decides to marry Grandcourt she again belies her ambition for a world beyond, as she naively assures herself that "marriage will be the gate into a larger freedom" (159). As the narrator explains, she has "no sense that these men were dark enigmas to her, or that she needed any help in drawing conclusions about them — Mr. Grandcourt at least. The chief question was, how far his character and ways might answer her wishes" (159). Eliot is clearly exposing not only her obliviousness to the possibility that "dark enigmas" might challenge her but also, as Deirdre David noted long ago, the imperial roots of Gwendolen's inflated freedom dreams.

And these fantasies are not just Gwendolen's. They are the counterpart to Grandcourt's. Gwendolen and Grandcourt are attracted to one another exactly by the desire for empire, and both equally misconstrue the freedom it entails. In the figures of the blond Gwendolen and the "white-handed" Grandcourt, Eliot offers a history of racialized English economy and empire as enacted in the power struggles of the heterosexual couple, revealing their "piteous equality in the need to dominate." It turns out that while Gwendolen is planning her new freedom, the "imperious" Grandcourt (654) is reflecting that "[t]o be worth his mastering it was proper that she should have some spirit" (195), since "his pet dogs were not the only beings that Grandcourt liked to feel his power over in making them jealous" (323). He "rules" (655, 656) and is wholly "tyrannical" (665, 783). By his side, she is "brought to kneel," as the narrator starkly points out (365). He is, finally, a colonial power: "If this white-handed man with the perpendicular profile had been sent to govern a difficult colony, he might have won reputation" for he "would have understood that it was safer to exterminate than to cajole" (655). In this light it is crucial that Lydia Glasher was originally the wife of an Irish colonial captain when Grandcourt "conquered" her and it is this colonial woman that Gwendolen herself betrays. In her encounter with Lydia Glasher, Gwendolen is forced into consciousness of the way her entry into marriage—her "woman's life"—is an entry into empire that entails the sacrifice of another woman: "Gwendolen, watching Mrs. Glasher's face while she spoke, felt a sort of terror: it was as if some ghastly vision had come to her in a dream and said, 'I am a woman's life'" (189–90).

Gwendolen's and Grandcourt's common (if mutually exclusive) projects to dominate and willingness to sacrifice others are supported by their communities, as in the case of Gwendolen's uncle, who sees their marriage as an increase of power for the nation. Gwendolen's prospect of a match with Grandcourt "presented itself to [the Rector] as a sort of public affair; perhaps there were ways in which it might even strengthen the Establishment. . . . Grandcourt, the almost certain baronet, the probable peer, was to be ranged with public personages, and was a match to be accepted on broad general grounds national and ecclesiastical" (177). The narrator gestures toward and deflates the "ancient" role of men like Grandcourt: "Such public personages, it is true, are often in the nature of giants which an ancient community may have felt pride and safety in possessing" (177). Thus "there was every reason to believe that a woman of well-regulated mind would be happy with Grandcourt" (177), and Gwendolen's uncle advises Gwendolen that "[m]arriage is the only true and satisfactory sphere of a woman, and if your marriage with Mr. Grandcourt should be happily decided upon, you will have probably an increasing power, both of rank and wealth, which may be used for the benefit of others" (180). Including, of course, Uncle Gascoigne. For, yes, behind Grandcourt stands Gascoigne, Gwendolen's mother's brother and the family ruler. He, too, is ready to make her his instrument of power.

Gwendolen's delusions—and her uncle's maneuvers—allow the beginning of what Sir Hugo later refers to as the "reign of Grandcourt" (864). Under him, Gwendolen lives in an "empire of fear" (479), and her position is compared to that of English subjects under a persecuting crown: she is forced to hide her rebellious feelings "as a Protestant of old kept his Bible or a Catholic his crucifix, according to the side favoured by the civil arm" (655). He can frighten her with a mere look or phrase, for "Potentates make known their intentions and affect the funds at a small expense of word" (322). Insofar as it seeks to stay within the bounds of a "genteel romance," the Englishwoman's dream of liberty has become a "thralldom" (83). Gwendolen eventually boards the yacht in the Mediterranean like a "galley slave" (760). Now she learns, in Hegelian struggle, that "the desire to conquer is itself a sort of subjection" (139).

Eliot's novel thus meditates on the yoking of freedom, empire, and subjection, and it furthermore takes up where Haywood and Defoe left off in probing the sexual contract's entanglement in this Atlantic triangle of forces. As Grandcourt reasons inwardly, their "marriage was a contract": "he had won her by the rank and luxuries he had to give her, and these she had got: he had fulfilled his side of the contract" (732). And Gwendolen herself admits the "truth" of this view: "Her capability of rectitude told her again and again that she had no right to complain of her contract, or to withdraw from it" (665). Not surprisingly, then, the first time Deronda sees them after their marriage he "thought their exchange of looks as cold and official as if it had been a ceremony to keep up a charter" (467). When Grandcourt orders Gwendolen never to see Deronda again, "Grandcourt might have pleaded that he was perfectly justified in taking care that his wife should fulfill the obligation she had accepted," while Gwendolen knows "she could not excuse herself by saying that there had been a tacit part of the contract on her side, namely, that she meant to rule and have her own way" (732).

These last reflections arise, appropriately, as Grandcourt and Gwendolen launch their Mediterranean sailing trip, buoyed by the trappings of empire. Gwendolen finds herself on "the blue Mediterranean dividing her from the world" (an interesting echo of Hegel's language about the Mediterranean), and she is wholly in "the domain of the husband to whom she felt that she had sold herself, and had been paid the strict price so that," the narrator remarks significantly, "he held [her] throttled into silence, collared and dragged behind him to witness what he would, without remonstrance" (669). The closing implication that Gwendolen must be a silent witness to whatever this "white-handed man" might choose to do — this man who might have felt that "it was safer to exterminate than to cajole" if he were "sent to govern a difficult colony" — establishes that her position as his wife is a position within empire, as witness to crimes. Her contract is with this imperial economy. The next sentence hints as much when it asks, "What had she to complain of? The yacht was of the prettiest; . . . the crew such as suited an elegant toy, one of them even having ringlets, as well as a bronze complexion and fine teeth" (669–70). Accordingly, along their journey, Grandcourt points out "a plantation of sugar-canes" for Gwendolen's interest (671).

Additionally, in her description of Gwendolen on the wide expanse of "the blue Mediterranean dividing her from the world," Eliot gathers for the climax her rhetoric of the terrorizing sublime in relation to Gwendolen and empire (and, as we will later see, she will also give it an Orientalist turn). Mordecai's republic and Eliot's Hegelian vision of history in "The Modern Hep! Hep! Hep!" call up the positive, heroic vocabulary of the sublime, which (as we saw in chapter 2) is implicitly racialized (only *some* races have the capacity for sublime experience engendered by vast visions of land and sea and can "channel" the freedom and imperial ambition which that expanse of space conjures). But for Gwendolen, isolation within open spaces terrorizes her. Tellingly, the narrator first mentions Gwendolen's "susceptibility to terror" in the midst of her account of the way the Davilow women depend on "conditions of colonial property and banking" for their livelihood (94). And then the narrator goes on to explain that her fear arises whenever Gwendolen "suddenly feel[s] herself alone" as when, "for example, she was walking without companionship and there came some rapid change in the light. Solitude in any wide scene impressed her with an undefined feeling of immeasurable experience aloof from her, in the midst of which she was helplessly incapable of asserting herself. . . . .but always when someone joined her she recovered her indifference to the vastness in which she seemed an exile" (94–95).

Aloneness within a sudden expansion, or even disappearance, of the spatial referents of identity: this is the individual in modernity. And this modern terror is one symptom of empire. Of course, the earliest and most striking instance in which Gwendolen exhibits this terror occurs during her first tour of Offendene, just after the narrator's reflections on her lack of a native spot, a lack that is itself partly a function of these colonial conditions. When a hinged panel in the wainscot of the drawing-room reveals a painting inside, Gwendolen sees a harrowing image of "the wide expanse" of her future without knowing its reference: "the picture of an upturned dead face, from which an obscure figure seemed to be fleeing with outstretched arms" (56). She insists the panel be under lock and key. The panel later swings open mysteriously, and "the dead face and the fleeing figure" send her into a deathlike frozenness so that "[s]he looked like a statue into which the soul of Fear had entered" (56, 91).

Insofar as we know that this "upturned dead face" prefigures Grandcourt's drowning on the Mediterranean, Gwendolen's wish to keep this ghost of shipwreck and drowning "under lock and key" might express a wish of Eliot's as well. But Eliot does allow the door to swing open, and she allows a glimpse of what Hegel also sees but tries to "pass over": the fact that the turn to the Mediterranean itself comprises a "deep inlet" in world history — for there the crimes of colonization will be repeated, and recloaked. As America had been, the Mediterranean will after all be, as Eliot seems to apprehend, the site of "continuity interrupted," despite its reemergent and ostensible role as "the uniting element." Nonetheless, like Hegel, she will labor to reshape this deadly passage as the triumph of Western liberty amid Eastern despotism.

Eliot at Sea among Race Brothers

Just as Eliot fashioned "the Gothic Abbey" as a palimpsest of a violent British history, so in choosing Genoa as the scene for the drowning of the white-handed

Grandcourt, as well as the revelation of Daniel's Jewish ancestry and, correspondingly, the "confessions" of two wayward race women, she again makes setting a powerfully charged force in her fiction. Landing us in this Mediterranean city, she turns us toward the "heart" of the Old World that will become the bridge to a "freer" Eastern future for Britain. She brings her British story full circuit.

At one level, Eliot seems to have chosen Genoa, as Andrew Thompson argues, for its republican associations. Genoa is the birthplace of Giuseppe Mazzini, leader of the republican cause in Italy in the mid-nineteenth century, as Eliot was aware. During the years when Mazzini was in exile in London, trying to raise money for the fight for a change of regime after the failure of the Roman Republic of 1849, he and Eliot moved in overlapping social circles and on at least one occasion she heard him speak (at a fundraising "Conversazione" at the Freemason's Tavern).[23] Although she did not endorse Mazzini's continuing plans for insurgency (and instead, characteristically, came to support the more gradual unification of Italy under the restored monarchy), she admired his heroism and felt sympathy for his ideals, as Thompson establishes. In *Daniel Deronda*, during the discussion of nationality and assimilation at the Philosopher's Club meeting, Deronda urges the men to "look into Mazzini's account of his first yearning, when he was a boy, after a restored greatness and a new freedom to Italy, which he sought by way of a united nationality" (535). Thompson argues that, by way of this reference and her choice of Genoa, Eliot creates a parallel between Mazzini's and Mordecai/Deronda's national quests.

Yet while Italy's unification as a national republic parallels and prefigures Mordecai's and Daniel's vision of "a new Jewish polity, . . . a republic" where "our race shall have an organic centre" (594), Eliot's crafting of a Jewish republic via Deronda does more than "parallel" an Italian one. And it even does more than fictionalize Moses Hess's idea — although crucial to note here and clearly influential for Eliot — that "with the rebirth of Italy also [begins] the resurrection of Judea" and that in the rebirth of both nations "the history of humankind has become a sacred history . . . a unitary, organic process of development" (quoted in Wohlfarth 207). Important though this Hessian connection between a free Italy and a free Judea is in understanding Eliot's plotting, it does not get at the gender story embedded in Eliot's choice of an Italian setting.

In choosing an Italian location, Eliot also recalls for us the republican history that reaches back to Rome and, most important, to Livy's story of Lucretia. In that story as in Eliot's, the new Mediterranean republic will be born from the ashes of sexual crimes against women. Eliot resurfaces the founding role of women's ruin in this classical republican plot. And yet, in Eliot's version, the crimes appear to be committed as much by the women as by the men who ruin them, and this ambiguity about women's guilt both propels and puts a strain on the national quest she narrates.

In these Genoa scenes, we see Eliot moving in deeply troubled waters. Gender creates a riptide against race, but Eliot labors to channel these vying currents into the broad stream of freedom's epic history. At first glance, it is possible to understand the pair of events that occurs in Genoa as the climax of the novel's two liberty plots, appropriately set in this republican city—for Deronda is liberated into "race" and Gwendolen is released from Grandcourt. As Thompson points out, the novel correlates Gwendolen's "liberation" from Grandcourt in this Mediterranean city with the "liberation" of the Veneto from Austria's occupying forces in 1866, for this is exactly the period when the Grandcourts make their visit. Furthermore, Gwendolen's liberation can also be seen as the revenge of the colonized, the purging of the "exterminating" colonial master. This reading is reinforced when we recall that in the critical moment of Grandcourt's drowning, none of the crew seems to offer help to him, although he calls out repeatedly. Gwendolen makes no mention of the crew, but apparently no member of it steps forward to save him, including the bronze-skinned sailor. So perhaps Gwendolen's release is also, symbolically, the release of the bronze men who serve the imperial vessel.

But another logic is also at work here. Both Daniel's discovery of a racial destiny and Gwendolen's witnessing of Grandcourt's drowning occur, first of all, against a rhetorical backdrop of "Eastern despotism" which quietly brings back into play the binary that casts Western invasions as Western missions of liberation from despotism.[24] This rhetoric instantiates Mordecai's vision of a free Jewish republic that will arise "amidst the despotisms of the East" and will recover the position of the "old republic" of the Jews, as Eliot has Mordecai paint it, which had "shone like a star on the forehead of our ancient community, and gave it more than the brightness of Western freedom amid the despotisms of the East" (595). The description of Gwendolen's subjection to Grandcourt on the Mediterranean repeats this imagery of Eastern despotism. Picturing Gwendolen "throned on her cushions at evening," the narrator wonders "what Moslem paradise would quiet the terrible fury of moral repulsion and cowed resistance" of a woman "captive after this fashion" (670). For Grandcourt, his wife's "protest (kept strictly private) added to the piquancy of despotism" (672). Furthermore, Gwendolen's haremlike captivity seemingly leads her into a barbaric fantasy life, for she is haunted by a "pantheon of ugly idols" and inwardly broods on "the hidden rites of vengeance" she wishes to inflict on her husband (670–71).

On the one hand, Eliot here may be said simply to affiliate Grandcourt with alien tyranny and so Gwendolen rebels in aptly barbaric ways. Or we might attribute to Eliot the desire to expose the fury, antagonism, and violence smoldering within the will to freedom and a "civilized" contract society. Certainly, Eliot casts this marriage as mirroring that which English freedom is thought to oppose: "The brilliant position she had longed for, the imagined freedom she would create for herself in marriage . . . all were immediately before her, and yet they had come to her hunger like food with the taint of sacrilege upon it, which she must snatch with terror" (356). Such is the trade, Eliot seems to hint, that white women have made under British empire — accepting its colonial crimes in return for a promise of comfortable freedom. Yet, by depicting Grandcourt's sailboat as a Moslem harem ruled by a despot, Eliot's rhetoric also reinforces the very opposition between Western freedom and Eastern tyranny that encourages the arrogance of a man like Grandcourt. Eliot's language belies the fact that empire remains the accepted horizon of her novel's events, and her focus on the liberation of the Englishwoman simply reuses the old double-crossing ruse that enlists women in empire. The Anglo-Zionist "republic" of liberty and equality will, it suggests, free women from the Oriental threat of tyrants. And yet the real threat to women is the tyranny of Anglo fathers, husbands, and brothers, to which British culture itself, as the novel also shows, has given rise.

Further, in the logic of this climactic drowning scene on the Mediterranean, Gwendolen's liberating act is cast as her crime; and (appropriately it seems) it entails her financial ruin. In this way, Gwendolen assumes the guilt and becomes the atoning economic sacrifice for the "crude work by which we have profited." While the novel might seem to release Gwendolen, it actually only "forgives" her — behind closed doors, with the brotherly Daniel as her confessor. It merely releases her from the "reign of Grandcourt" into what Juliet Flower MacCannell calls the "regime of the brother," which Jacob Press understands as a homosocial, nationalist brotherhood.[25]

To appreciate the full significance of Deronda's position here, it is necessary to recall the many influential brothers in *Daniel Deronda*. Mrs. Davilow is directed by her brother, the Reverend Gascoigne. Mirah eventually tends to the every need of her brother Mordecai. The Meyrick sisters mend and save so that Hans can go to school. In all these cases, in the absence of proper fathers and husbands, brothers guide, govern, and are served. Within this fatherless order, Deronda emerges as a symbolical and ideal brother. I would place Jacob Press's important reading of the erotic currents in the "marriage" of Mordecai and Deronda within this context, supplementing his account of the masculinist nationalism they symbolically found together. That is, Eliot also traces the effects of this brotherly racialist bonding for the "sisters."

Like the novel's other brothers, Deronda holds the power. He keeps Mirah ignorant of the fact that he has undertaken a search for her brother, leaving himself the option of doing nothing if the brother turns out to be the "wrong" kind of Jew. He believes he can determine what is best for her. Likewise, as Gwendolen begins to tell her sea story to Deronda, she feels the desire to get "nearer to that compassion which seemed to be regarding her from a halo of superiority, and the need turned into an impulse to humble herself more" (694). Under the pressure of this "need," it seems, both of the women fall in love with Deronda, hoping to make a mate out of this superior republican comrade. Deronda, the new race man, plays the role of surrogate brother for both Gwendolen and Mirah, in Mirah's case finally reconnecting her to her blood brother and ensconcing her as his helpmate. In turn, the sisters play an "instrumental" role in the race brothers' founding of a nation.

And it is Daniel who, in Eliot's hands, frames Gwendolen's liberation as her crime. As Daniel reasons it out, "her remorse [for allowing Grandcourt to drown] was the precious sign of a recoverable nature; it was the culmination of that self-disapproval which had been the awakening of new life within her" (695–96). Her witnessing of Grandcourt's drowning becomes a crime requiring feelings of remorse. Thus "Deronda could not utter one word to diminish that sacred aversion to her worst self—that thorn pressure which must come with the crowning of the sorrowful Better" (695–96). The old tropes resurface: the woman's ruin is the "awakening of a new life," and her thorny (Christian) crowning in the Mediterranean world becomes the scene of a nation's redemption. In "forgiving" her sin, brother Daniel proves his ability to be a founder of that nation.

Or rather, in keeping quiet her crime, Daniel keeps clean his mission as brotherly hero and masculine nationbuilder. Gwendolen opens her confession of the events by insisting, "You will not say I ought to tell the world" (689), and she closes by again pleading, "You will not say that anyone else should know?" to which Deronda responds, "Most decidedly not" (698). His answer serves his rather precarious position well, for to be entangled with a woman who might be accused of such a crime could well trouble his relations with Mirah and Mordecai— and more immediately, give his mother cause for bitter laughter at his expense. Lamely, he explains, "There is no injury that could be righted in that way. There is no retribution that any mortal could apportion justly" (698).

And why is this so? Perhaps because to expose publicly the crime that creates Gwendolen's wish for Grandcourt's death — the crime of Grandcourt's cruel treatment of her, of Lydia Glasher, and of his own children — would be to shake the foundations of the imperial republic more deeply than Eliot was willing to do. The white master's bedroom crimes, his "collaring" of her while he does what he will, cannot be adjudicated — they rest on a "prerogative" that must remain the disavowed a priori. This prerogative underlies the position of Daniel as well as Grandcourt and serves the republican order of things as well as the despotic. For, the republican order (despite its claim to universal freedom) likewise requires women's subordination as reproducers of the race and thus belies its principle of consent, as Haywood's Cleomira, Defoe's Roxana, and Richardson's Clarissa understood. It is this contractual pattern of "injury" that cannot be "righted." If he is to inherit the mantle of the father's power of "sovereignty," the brother cannot expose the subordination of women on which it rests.[26]

In other words, different as Grandcourt and Daniel may appear, Deronda's silence actually enables the transfer of power, in effect, from Grandcourt to himself, from tyrant-father to republican-brother, in the project of a renewed racial order. A strange moment in the midst of Gwendolen's narrative of the drowning, in which she identifies Grandcourt with her stepfather, clarifies how Grandcourt represents a violating father and suggests that prior crimes of violation are continued in the story of Gwendolen and Grandcourt. If we consider these hints to be meaningful, we find Eliot signaling, perhaps unconsciously, toward the whole history of women's ruin. Yet it is this history that Deronda, perhaps unthinkingly, is willing to leave untold — taking it as a given that "[t]here is no injury that could be righted in that way. There is no retribution that any mortal could apportion justly." This point suggests, as I'll discuss more fully later, that although Daniel seems utterly to identify with the plight of ruined women, in the end he absorbs that plight as *his* tragedy and, as in the founding of Rome, the origin of "his" republic.

As she recounts her rage at being "forced to go in the boat" with Grandcourt (a phrase she repeats four or five times with slight variation), Gwendolen makes an odd reference to her stepfather, after which he and Grandcourt become implicitly conflated in her use of the pronoun "him." Reporting her sense that, in the boat, "the very light about me seemed to hold me prisoner and force me to sit as I did," she says:

> It came over me that when I was a child I used to fancy sailing away into a world where people were not forced to live with anyone they did not like — I did not like my father-in-law to come home. And now, I thought, just the opposite had come to me. I had stept into a boat, and my life was a sailing away and away — gliding on and no help — always into solitude with *him,* away from deliverance. . . . If it had been of any use I should have prayed that something might befall him. I should have prayed he might sink out of my sight and leave me alone. I knew I had no way of killing him there, but I did, I did kill him in my thoughts. (695)

When we recall that Gwendolen's stepfather was a sea captain, this passage becomes highly suggestive. Given the orientation of the logic of the passage around the reference to the stepfather ("now just the opposite had come to me"), and the ambiguity of the pronoun "him," the implication is that Gwendolen also feared solitude with the stepfather and sought deliverance from "him." Such a hint might begin to explain the high-strung relation between Gwendolen and her mother. That is, the passage's suggestion that Gwendolen had endured a "forced" "solitude with *him,*" her stepfather, might shed new light on Mrs. Davilow's unhappiness and her tremulous indulgence of her taut daughter who "hates" men's lovemaking. And it might also clarify the source of their shared "dread" (more than once referred to), which is perhaps also related to the births of all those additional sisters whose presence so much annoys Gwendolen.[27] The colonially wide "horizon" provoking Gwendolen's "terror" now takes on the coloring of a scene of potential sexual coercion, encircling as it does a situation that "forces [Gwendolen] to sit as I did," a prisoner of the very light. Else why does this sudden reference to the stepfather appear in the midst of her rage toward her husband Grandcourt?

In escaping these two coercive father-figures, however, Gwendolen runs into the arms of a more implicitly and insidiously controlling, if more seductive, brother. For in Deronda's vision, this legacy of coercion becomes Gwendolen's crime, understood as spawning her "worst self," not the men's. Thus, Deronda arrives to guide her, promising not to "forsake" her, another hint that this release will after all mean her self-sacrifice. This confession scene brings to a climax Eliot's fashioning of Deronda as the brother-figure who heralds a new subordinating order for women — justified in the face of the Oriental threat of despotism. This is an order that Eliot seems to have endorsed but the wounding swoons of which she nonetheless fleetingly exposes to view.

Brother as Author

When we recall that Eliot's own brother, Isaac, positioned himself as condemning judge of Marian Evans's free thought and sexually transgressive life, and we recall that the plot of *The Mill on the Floss* ends with the drowning embrace of a brother and sister, we have grounds for speculating that Eliot's investment in these gendered wounds runs deep. We might say that her whole life resists the regime of the brother, while her fiction works to accommodate it. We might propose that she apprehended the threat of feminism to the brotherhood of nations, and loving her nation more than herself (as she suggested all citizens should), she was determined to reconcile woman to race. Thus perhaps do personal lives form the tributaries of empire, the emotional streams of the imperial imagination.

As with other women writers, her solution entailed a double movement: an identification with the brother as race figure and, at the same time, a feminizing of that figure as a kind of tremulous sister. Eliot reaches farthest out in this double movement in those scenes in which Deronda plays the part of confessor and judge to his own mother, the Princess Halm-Eberstein. Hans and Mordecai also play the role of husband/fathers to their own mothers, but Deronda's performance of this role surpasses theirs spectacularly. And perhaps this is the case because, if we understand Eliot to be identifying with Deronda as outsider, in these scenes we witness Eliot placing herself in dialogue, via his dialogues with these women, with her "worst self," her feminine self, her "princess" self — an appellation that the text uses for both Gwendolen and Daniel's mother. In these scenes, we witness Eliot's self-confession — and self-sublimation.

Like Gwendolen, and in that same republican and Mediterranean city of Genoa, Eliot has the Princess confess her "crimes" to Deronda. Yet, by way of this same male-pseudonymous author's pen, the Princess explicitly names the ways that race betrays women's freedom. The Princess enumerates her violent reaction to a father-despot, her refusal to submit, and her refusal, above all, to reproduce the race. She explains that her father "only thought of fettering me into obedience. I was to be what he called 'the Jewish woman' under pain of his curse" (692). Instead "I cared for the wide world. . . . And I wanted to live a large life, with freedom to do what everyone else did, and be carried along in a great current, not obliged to care" (693). She insists that "I had a right to be free. I had a right to seek my freedom from a bondage that I hated" (689). She condemns her father's "iron will. . . . such men turn their wives and daughters into slaves. They would rule the world if they could; but not ruling the world they throw all the weight of their will on to the necks and souls of women" (694). Interestingly, the Princess associates her experience with Oriental coercion: "To have a pattern cut out — 'this is the Jewish woman; this is what you must be; this is what you are wanted for; a woman's heart must be of such a size and no larger, else it must be pressed small, like Chinese feet'" (694).

Appropriately, in rejecting this Oriental coercion, the Princess speaks a Whiggish language. Here Eliot places her within the race narrative insofar as she uses its language of liberty to resist tyranny. Her father had "tyrannized over me" (698). "His yoke has been on me" (726). "It was my nature to resist and say, 'I have right to resist'" (699) because "[m]y nature gave me a charter" (728). The mother's "charter" — which is to perform publicly as an actress — stands off against the son's. Yet, despite her Whiggish language, she is no real race revolutionary, for, in the narrator's rendering, her voice is disconnected from an interior (she exhibits a "double consciousness" and "acted her own emotions" [691]). The implication is that her interior is disconnected from race and therefore is not a true voice.

In response, Deronda states the paradigmatic principle of Atlantic history: the emplacement of the individual within the race, and the interior anchoring of the race within the individual: "The effects prepared by generations," he tells his mother, "are likely to triumph over a contrivance which would bend them all to the satisfaction of self. Your will was strong but my grandfather's trust which you accepted and did not fulfill — what you call his yoke — is the expression of something stronger, with deeper, farther-spreading roots, knit into the foundations of sacredness for all men" (727).

Yet, ironically, it is exactly by way of the woman's story of exile and alienation that Daniel has entered race history. In this way, Eliot offers a metafiction of the work of the transatlantic novel in English. At every turn Daniel enters the stream of history through the text's ruined women. Of course, first of all, the Princess gives birth to him. Then, too, symbolically, the novel opens by entering Daniel's consciousness through the figure of Gwendolen on whom he meditates. And it is initially Deronda's half-conscious awareness of having a "ruined" mother that keeps him in the sideline position, watching from the margin — that role that, in novels, proves any character an insider and aligns him or her with a novel's narrator — and that in this case develops his sensitive consciousness. "His sensibility to the half-known facts of his parentage made him an excuse for lingering longer than others in a state of social neutrality. Other men, he inwardly said, had a more definite place and duties" (220). And so "[h]is early-awakened sensibility and reflectiveness had developed into a many-sided sympathy" (412). Yet because his "diffusive sympathy was in danger of paralyzing in him that indignation against wrong and that selectness of fellowship which are the conditions of moral force," he needs some "external event, or some inward light" that will make him "what he was unable to make himself — an organic part of social life, instead of roaming in it like a yearning disembodied spirit, stirred with a vague social passion, but without fixed local habitation to render fellowship real" (413).

And it is finally through Mirah, another outcast woman, that Deronda enters history; she is the "external event" that gives him an "organic" root in social life. Eliot makes a tableau of the scene in which his encounter with this forsaken woman displays both his prior position of power and the introjection of the woman's story, which gives Daniel the occasion for accepting the mantle of that privilege, culminating in racial leadership. Just before he saves her, Daniel wonders at "the girl-tragedies that are going on in the world, hidden, unheeded," and this in turn raises thoughts about his own "wide-sweeping connections with all life and history" — in particular his uncertain parentage. He slows his boat and he chooses

> a spot . . . where he had a great breadth of water before him reflecting the glory of the sky, while he himself was in shadow. . . . So that he could see all around him, *but could not be seen by any one*. . . . He was forgetting everything else in a half-speculative, half-involuntary identification of himself with the objects he was looking at, thinking how far it might be possible habitually to shift his centre till his own personality would be no less outside him than the landscape, — when the sense of something moving on the bank opposite . . . made him turn his glance." (229 – 30, emphasis added)

This moment of merging with the landscape interestingly brings into view his unconscious relish of his own privileged positionality and vision, buoyed by his boat, "So that he could see all around him, *but could not be seen by any one*." Here is an anatomy of the romantic imagination that in losing itself in the landscape, paradoxically also absorbs that landscape into the self, so that the landscape becomes a site for "his centre" of personality. This self-transcending yet other-absorbing perception is interrupted by "something moving on the bank opposite," but ultimately the interruption (in light of the end of the novel) only brings him back to himself through this other, through Mirah. This sublime Hegelian moment simply enables *his* fuller entry into the "local habitation," and, in turn, into the longer "organic" social life. Fittingly, the scene foreshadows the dynamic of his encounter with his mother (interrupting but also ultimately introjected), for Mirah's distress "stirred a fibre that lay close to his deepest interest in the fates of women — 'perhaps my mother was like this one'" (231).

And yet, as brother-identified, brother-subsuming author, Eliot also achieves her own, most far-reaching social entry through Daniel's introjection of Mirah. For ultimately her novel had material effects that have inscribed her name in Anglo-Jewish history and, quite literally, in the state of Israel, making her text comparable to Harriet Beecher Stowe's *Uncle Tom's Cabin,* a work that Eliot held up as a model of socially productive literature. In the 1880s, *Daniel Deronda* was translated by four Russian Jewish leaders into Hebrew (Meyer, 733) and became widely influential thereafter, even a kind of bible, so to speak, of late-nineteenth-century Zionism, this time as fostered by Jews in the wake of the 1880 pogroms. When, on arriving in Britain from Germany, the early Zionist visionary Theodor Herzl described his notion of a Jewish homeland, he was apparently told by the Chief Rabbi of Britain, Hermann Adler, "That is the idea of *Daniel Deronda*" (Press, 300). Not long after the founding of Israel, a street in Tel Aviv was named after Eliot, and today every major city in Israel has a George Eliot street (Heller, 77).

These streets in the Middle East inscribe a long Atlantic history: for this name by which Eliot "made history" is not her own but a man's. As such it marks her schism with her brother and father and her embrace of a free but ruined woman's life that after all places her at the center of an empire.

14 | Trickster Epic in Hopkins's *Contending Forces*

PAULINE HOPKINS SEEMS well to have understood the Atlantic ur-plot of the novel that turned Eliot and Britain eastward. As her Caribbean-descended character Dora expresses it in *Contending Forces* — unknowingly addressing a ruined woman with a secret over whom another pair of men vies: "I have always felt a great curiosity to know the reason why each individual woman loses character and standing in the eyes of the world. I believe that we would hang our heads in shame at having the temerity to judge a fallen sister, could we but know the circumstances attending many such cases."[1] Hopkins is astute in making explicit this need to "but know" the hidden "circumstances" surrounding the ruinous race-narrative of each individual woman, and in this, her first novel, she identifies them implicitly: the Atlantic slave economy with a key origin in Bermuda (where the novel begins); the desire for transparency between interior and exterior in this duplicitous world in which slavery founds freedom; the brother/sister relation that decides the fate of the "fallen sister"; and the rape that persists, quite literally for African American women, as the traumatic ordeal of entry into this "free" Atlantic modernity.

In the allusiveness of her novels, Hopkins displays full self-consciousness about the literary tradition that has gathered these elements. In *Of One Blood,* she places her African-Atlantic version of the fallen-woman story next to the Anglo-Atlantic version, specifically Hawthorne's. In a key scene of this novel, just before the protagonist Reuel Briggs incautiously reveals his secret desire for Dianthe to his confidant Aubrey Livingston, who, unbeknown to Reuel, is actually his enemy and also desires Dianthe, Aubrey invokes *The Scarlet Letter:* " 'Few things are hidden from the man who devotes himself earnestly and serviciously to the solution of a mystery,' Hawthorne tells us," he says (477). "So Roger Chillingworth," Hawthorne's narrator explains in the passage to which Hopkins refers, "strove to go deep into his patient's bosom, delving among his principles, prying into his recollections, and probing everything with a cautious touch, like a treasure-seeker in a dark cavern. Few secrets can escape an investigator, who has opportunity and license to undertake such a quest." And Hawthorne adds, indicating the private, bodily dimension of such secrets, "A man burdened with a secret should especially avoid the intimacy of his physician" (86). Like Roger Chillingworth, both Reuel Briggs and his enemy Aubrey Livingston are physicians pursuing secrets — intimate, sexual secrets prompted originally by an Atlantic crossing and encoding a communal, historical crisis. In her direct allusion to *The Scarlet Letter,* Hopkins hints at her embeddedness in this Atlantic, nativist tradition of the novel.

And she hints at her investigative work within it. Hopkins "probes" this tradition in order to turn it against itself, practicing a kind of Anglo-ism that reverses the effects of Africanism. She draws from Anglo-Atlantic romance and sentimental modes, quoting Gray and Goldsmith as well as Hawthorne, so as to gloss her story as a tale of the "simple blessings" and "native charm" of humble yet noble folk. This backgrounded Anglo presence serves her development of African-Atlantic identity, apparently. But then Hopkins goes further, in *Contending Forces* as in *Of One Blood,* undercutting both of these nativist maneuvers when the black folk turn out to be part white and the whites part black. In *Contending Forces* (subtitled "A Romance"), she crisscrosses racial genealogies in multiple ways, not only in her mixtures of black and white but also in her minglings of British, Caribbean, Southern U.S., and Northern U.S. characters, not to mention dialect-speaking and standard-English-speaking characters. At every level of her writing, Hopkins embellishes and then trips up the race distinctions of the liberty discourse. She allows into view the gaps, discrepancies, and evasions of its Atlantic formation, sometimes in the very syntax of her sentences.

Recent critics have come to appreciate Hopkins's double-voiced or polyvocal narration, most often in Bakhtinian terms, and the import of such readings expands when they are resituated and adjusted within a broad Atlantic context.[2] In her afterword to John Cullen Gruesser's collection of essays on Hopkins, *The Unruly Voice,* Elizabeth Ammons rightly characterizes Hopkins's fiction as "profoundly experimental," (212) especially in its "Bakhtinian" undercutting of coherence. In applying Bakhtin's arguments to Hopkins, Ammons invokes the notion of the novel as a freedom genre that diverges from the "clearly prescribed, predetermined structure[s]" of lyric and epic: "The novel, in contrast, rebels" because it is "by definition unregulated, even anarchic" (211).

I would rather say that, in returning the English-language novel to its founding Atlantic situation — that of a profoundly contradictory and disruptive colonial contact zone, as argued by Ed White and discussed here in chapter 4 on *Oroonoko* — Hopkins unveils the incoherent conditions prompting the genre's strenuous movement toward coherence, that movement celebrated by novel critics and impressively realized in the works of George Eliot.[3] She makes felt the underlying fractures of social identity within the republican Atlantic order that call forth this will-to-coherence. In fact Hopkins retrospectively helps us to reframe the dialogic structures of the ancient novel as described by Bakhtin. That is, her Bakhtinian methods remind us that such heteroglot and subaltern voicing has developed within a "Western" economy of slavery that reaches back to Greece and then finds renewed, English-language impetus on the Atlantic in the seventeenth century. Hopkins points in this direction by way of her specific borrowings from classical fiction, as discussed by Marla Harris, including, in *Contending Forces*, in her choice of the name "Sappho" for her heroine.[4] This formulation begins to suggest a new genealogy for the novel and for the contributions of authors like Hopkins — a genealogy linked to liberty but much more equivocally than critics have tended to see, and developing in the context of slavery and colonization over a stretch of centuries. Writing as an African American novelist at the dark dawn of the twentieth century, Hopkins creates a fiction of abrupt twists and turns that are themselves representations of a certain roughed-up history and subjectivity. It is this history which necessitates, for her, a return to the novel's core incoherencies or "anarchic" tendencies.

All these strains and incoherencies arise, for Hopkins, from the disavowed crime of rape — as Dora's comments on the fallen sister hint. The text's lovely opening rendering of a native spot in Bermuda quickly unravels into rape, and rape returns just when its legacy appears to be overcome by the engagement of Will Smith and Sappho Clark. Rape circulates in veiled form throughout the novel, in the character of Mabelle the rape survivor, living under the alias Sappho; and it covertly structures the public sphere, Hopkins implies: the raped woman swoons, incognito, at the Coloured American League meeting; and, at the church fair, again incognito, this woman sits "at a distance, keeping strict account of the moneys received" (202). And yet, with supremely shrewd implication, it is through this veiled, raped woman (a channel for "moneys received") that Hopkins develops the racial interiority required for Atlantic freedom.

In one sense Hopkins, too, enters the public sphere of "free" speech and free novel writing through the story of rape, caught in the same contradictions she exposes. In a final trickster twist in her novel's closing tableau, however, in the form of not just one but two Sappho figures, she suggests that some surplus-story remains to be told, a story taken up, as we will see in the final part of this study, by her modernist successors.

Contending with Atlantic Forces

In her first, Caribbean chapter, Hopkins presents us with a series of discursive incoherencies, made up of unsettlingly layered histories:

> Once Bermuda was second only to Virginia in its importance as a British colony; once it held the carrying trade of the New World; once was known as the "Gibraltar of the Atlantic," although its history has been that of a simple and peaceful people. Its importance to the mother country as a military and naval station has drawn the paternal bonds of interest closer as the years have flown by. Indeed Britain has been kind to the colonists of this favored island from its infancy, sheltering and shielding them so carefully that the iron hand of the master has never shown beneath its velvet glove. So Bermuda has always been intensely British, — intensely loyal. (21)

Exactly which "simple and peaceful" people's history lies hidden under the label "Gibraltar of the Atlantic"? With Hopkins as our author, we feel the presence of two peoples, colonizing and colonized, conflated into one. Likewise, there seems to be an embedded double reference in the central image. The "iron hand" of the "sheltering" "master" under the "velvet glove" refers ostensibly to the mother country's governance of the white colonists, but it simultaneously recalls the underlying slave economy of real iron shackles and few velvet gloves. Furthermore, by beginning her colonial narrative with Bermuda and Virginia and emphasizing their linked origins in trade, rather than invoking the heroic Puritan narrative of the New World that is so dear to her New England audience, Hopkins again gestures toward the iron hand and economy of the Atlantic world. These muffled suggestions ripple under the surface of her portrait of Bermuda.

Hopkins's narrator fans these ripples again as she describes the physical island:

> A temperate climate, limpid rivers, the balmy fragrance and freshness of the air, no winter — nature changing only in the tints of its foliage — have contributed to its renown as a health-giving region; and thus Shakespeare's magic island of Prospero and Miranda has become, indeed, to the traveler
>
> The spot of earth uncurst,
> To show how all things were created first.

Mr. Montfort was the owner of about seven hundred slaves. He was well known as an exporter of tobacco, sugar, coffee, onions, and other products so easily grown in that salubrious climate, from which he received large returns. (21–22)

The narrator's abrupt turn from Shakespeare's dream of the Caribbean to the profitable ownership of seven hundred slaves sets up her method for resignifying the literary tradition. She establishes that literary tradition as the lineage *her* story disrupts. Thus if Shakespeare depicted Bermuda to conjure up how all things were created first by God, as his lines suggest, Hopkins recreates this image, with its jarring juxtaposition to Montfort, to trace how all things on this island were created *since* by slaveowners. Whatever the island is "to the traveler," for its seven hundred slaves, its Calibans, it is no doubt precisely a cursed place where these "prosperous" products are anything but "so easily grown." On the Atlantic, she makes us notice, the reality is both, incomprehensibly — fantastic beauty freely available to "the traveler," and the enslavement of hundreds of persons forced to make that beauty bear fruit. And Miranda herself — in this case Montfort's wife — will get caught in this economy as its sexual fetish and reproducer. The paragraph break marks the straddling point of Hopkins's narrative, and she ensures that the narrational gap is felt. No sleek and quiet technique moves us across it. As in Defoe's circumlocutious novels (a comparison that might ease the racialized anxiety over any "flaws" in Hopkins's fiction), Hopkins's style expresses the forced crossings and social ruptures of the Atlantic experience, while (differently from Defoe) exposing the strenuous will to ownership impelling them.

In the preface to her novel, Hopkins had already signaled her awareness of the syntactic torques required by this history. In explaining to potentially skeptical readers that her story "present[s] both sides — lynching and concubinage — truthfully and without vituperation," she pleads "for that justice of heart and mind for my people which the Anglo-Saxon in America never withholds from suffering humanity" (15). First, although we might expect "both sides" to refer to black and white perspectives, on second look we realize that the center of reality has been moved to the African-Atlantic, so that this phrase instead refers to the male and female dimensions of the black experience — the terrorizing of black men through lynching on one side and of black women through rape on the other. This sleight of hand foreshadows the next one in this sentence, the narrator's proclamation that "the Anglo-Saxon in America never withholds [justice] from suffering humanity." If this is so, why is her novel necessary? That is, if Anglo-Saxons in America have never withheld justice, how indeed do American lynching and concubinage exist? Are not Anglo-Saxons, including in the events that follow, the very perpetrators of lynching and concubinage? Or is Hopkins playing here on internal white race divisions, whereby Northern whites considered themselves the liberatory *Saxons,* in particular, as against the depraved Norman- or Celtic-descended whites of the South, so she works one "white" race lineage off against another to enlist a specifically Northern sympathy?[5] Or, if the slippery term is "suffering humanity," and Hopkins means to press directly on the racist assumption that African Americans do not come under the heading of humanity, she undoubtedly discomfits those whites who wouldn't go quite *that* far. In any case, she counts on the schizophrenia of sentimental white American citizens. Whichever reading we choose, we can see that Hopkins suggests that because her readers are Anglo-Saxon they are fated to be the sensitive friends of all humanity; she in effect appeals to racial hubris to trick her white readers into embracing racial equality. A dangerous path, which Hopkins repeatedly treads.

Consider, as a further instance, Hopkins's choice of epigraph for her novel, which likewise manipulates white racial hubris. She quotes an apparently generous pronouncement by Ralph Waldo Emerson — "The civility of no race can be perfect whilst another race is degraded" — but later, in suspiciously similar terms, she describes the motives of white philanthropists

> who gave to the Negro not only because they believed he was wronged, but also because they believed that in great measure his elevation would remove the stigma under which the Southern white labored. For the loyal white man there would be no greater joy in life than to see his poetic dream of superiority to all other governments realized in the "land of the free and the home of the brave." True and loyal son of his country he would sacrifice any race, any principle, to bring about this much-desired consummation; so he contributes money to build up manufacturing interests at the South to his own material disadvantage in the North. . . . .Delusive hope that grasps at shadows!" (243)

Thus does Hopkins expose the racial ambition that underlies racial benevolence or dreams of universal racial "perfection." She belatedly exposes Emerson's desire for "perfect civility" in "his" race as part of a "dream of superiority" for which other races serve as instruments. This delayed subversion of her apparent honoring of Emerson is typical of her trickster method: her deconstructions are covert, operating from the gaps and deferrals in her narrative. These are the means by which she exposes and repeats the bottomlessly appropriative motions of the Atlantic liberty narrative.

Freedom's Colonial Point of Departure

In its rendering of the native spot, the opening Bermuda chapter further displays the gap between racial dream and racist history. The chapter narrates the process of Mr. Montfort's decision to move from Bermuda to North Carolina and his stated intention *eventually* to free his slaves while in the short term protecting his financial interests. The narrator explains that in the late 1790s, with agitation in England to abolish the slave trade and talk of gradual emancipation in the West Indian colonies, Mr. Montfort decides "that he would free his slaves, but in his own way" (23–24). "He was neither a cruel man, nor an avaricious one"—indeed, given the liberal island habit of sometimes acknowledging and financially endowing the mulatto children of slave women, "there might even have been a strain of African blood polluting the fair stream of Montfort's vitality, or even his wife's, which fact would not have caused him one instant's uneasiness" (22–23). But nonetheless, Montfort's motives are simply and pragmatically financial since "like all men in commercial life . . . he lost sight of the individual right or wrong of the matter"—"or" the narrator adds, tipping her hand—"or we might say with more truth, that he perverted right to be what was conducive to his own interests" (22). He would move to the United States "where the institution flourished" and "gradually free his slaves without impoverishing himself; bestow on each one a piece of land, and finally, with easy conscience, he would retire to England and there lead the happy life of an English gentleman of fortune" (24). Montfort will honor this noble principle of freedom for humanity—and get to eat it too—which will make him doubly rich and give him full entry into society as an English gentleman of fortune.

Hopkins establishes "liberty" as the vexed, racialized term in this maneuver. The male community members' comments in this chapter on Montfort's departure are permeated with questions of liberty—not only that of slaves but also that of the "republic" of the United States. Montfort's friends champion a *British* freedom, implying that the American form of freedom is degraded and savage. Trying to discourage him from emigrating, one friend tells Montfort that "for all their boasted freedom, the liberty of England is not found [in the United States], and human lives are held cheaply in the eyes of men who are mere outlaws" (25–26). Another predicts that Montfort will "never be able to accustom [him]self to the habits of a republic" where "the social laws are so different" and he predicts that Montfort will "receive a cold welcome from men of their class" (28–29). Finally the last friend refers to the United States as "the land of savages," conflating lower-class or non-Saxon white with "savage" and repeating the merging of native and colonizer that the narrator enacted regarding the "people" of Bermuda. Taken together, these comments indicate the mingling of race and class fears within the liberty discourse, as Montfort's neighbors racialize their class fears of a more complete democracy. Montfort's willingness to travel to the States seems to suggest that he has a more open-minded view, but it becomes clear that he simply has a more arrogant view: he assumes he can override his new neighbors' opinions and power and free his slaves, despite their objections and laws to the contrary. Although he eventually learns that the Southern U.S. community, acting as a racially defined community, can violently override his individual freedom, here he assumes his English liberty is absolute. He embodies the equivocation embedded in statements like Emerson's, where racial benevolence harbors hubris.

Nonetheless to exercise his liberty, he must, oddly enough, leave his "native" spot; he must after all undergo that deracination that his slaves have already undergone. He joins them belatedly in this free modernity, in which (in Hopkins's wily retelling) his sea-launching, too, will end in captivity and death.

But first Hopkins conjures up the native-spot tableau that we've seen in novels from *The Monk* to *Hope Leslie* to *The Scarlet Letter* to *Daniel Deronda* — only to suggest its fictionality. After his friends attempt to dissuade Montfort from his "proposed exodus" (24) with its biblical overtones, Montfort finds himself reflecting on all the "tender ties" that bind him to the land, including, suggestively, the grave of his little daughter "beneath the flowering trees in the churchyard" (25). In fact, at one point in his reflections, "he almost determined that he would give it all up and remain in this land of love and beauty" (25). Hopkins's narrator dwells on this paradigmatic moment when Montfort's "native" place becomes a living thing that beckons to him:

> To collect his scattered thoughts and calm his mind he turned toward the bay, and stood upon the beach, still allowing the breeze to play about his heated temples. Never before had he appreciated his home so much as now, when he contrasted it with the comparative barrenness of the new spot he had chosen. The water was alive with marine creatures; the sea aflame. The air was full of light-giving insects, incessantly moving, which illumined the darkness and gave life to every inanimate object. . . . Alas! his good angel fled with the darkness and morning found him more determined than ever to go on with his project. (31)

Taking in the beauties of his accustomed "spot," this slave master calms those thoughts so "scattered" by the prospect of removal — the removal required by his freedom-to-profit. Its beauty almost lures him to give up the drive for profit. Yet after all this Atlantic native spot is not really native; it belongs to him by seizure. His real attachment is to the idea of becoming an *English* gentleman "of fortune." Thus Montfort illustrates that in this "incessantly moving" modernity, "Where a man's treasure is, there also is his heart," as one of his more cynical acquaintances remarks (28) — and as Hopkins has already prepared us to notice in her ambiguous portrait of the native spot that operates as a profit-generating, military station controlled by an iron hand.

Both the myth of a native spot and the removal from it for profit have been supported, Hopkins also hints, by the submissive attitude of Montfort's wife — and will culminate in her ruin. The first chapter ends with Montfort's "little family look[ing] through blinding tears at the receding shores of what had been a happy home" and arriving at the North Carolina shore "each longing for the land so recently left behind them, though no word of regret was spoken" (31). No word is spoken for, as Montfort "proudly returned" when one of his friends earlier suggested that he was exposing his wife to inconveniences, " 'She has had her choice, but prefers hardships with me to life without me' " (29). The limited extent of her "choice" in the matter is perhaps implied by the comment that immediately follows, "murmured [by] one who had not yet spoken": " 'A willful man must have his way' " (29).

Montfort's willful way ends in disaster — in a scene that recalls the deeply embedded narrative paradigm reaching back through Burke and Paine to Thomas Overton in England in the 1640s. Once in North Carolina, the combination of his chaste wife's rejections of the libertine Anson Pollock's sexual advances, the concocted rumor that she has "Negro" blood (though Hopkins leaves open the possibility that she might), and Montfort's granting of rights to wage-labor for his slaves lead to a brutal attack on his plantation. Anson Pollock and his men force their way into Montfort's home, shoot him, seize his wife, tie her to a whipping post, lash her, and symbolically, or perhaps literally, rape her — all of which eventually provokes her suicide (significantly, by drowning) and leaves her sons and slaves in the hands of Pollock and his men.[6] In devoting a chapter to this scene of breaking and entering into a home and spectacularly defiling the woman, Hopkins recasts the centuries-old tableau of tyranny's violations — that catalyst of novelistic swoons and the igniting force in the long struggle for liberty. We can place what Debra Bernardi identifies as the trope in Hopkins's fiction of domestic "scenes of invasion" within this longer history as well as within the more immediate history of white acts of terrorism on black homes.[7]

Hopkins's framing of these events not only exposes the hubris in Montfort's individualist yet nativist-British notion of freedom but it also trickily relocates the rape in the house of the master and clearly makes it the effect of a competition among men, including among classes of white men.[8] As Hopkins narrates it, the contradictory combination of a "free" contract economy, ostensibly open to all bodies, and a racist hierarchy that utterly excludes and abuses certain bodies, finds its pressured release, its covert expression, and its symbolic meaning in this fatal violation. It is no coincidence that, in a scene just before Pollock and his men break into Montfort's house, the money nexus of this world appears in the form of Montfort's young son playing on the floor and "building houses" with gold coins under the jealous eyes of Pollock. The boy's complaint that his structures keep "tumbl[ing] down" foreshadows the invasion and sums up Hopkins's rearranged story of Atlantic ruin (48–49).

The Post-Swoon Swerve

Like many race-epic novels, Hopkins's text follows this scene of ruin with a historical leap, as she shifts, between chapters 4 and 5, from this Southern scene to the Northern lives, decades later, of the Montforts' dispersed great grandchildren. *Hope Leslie, The Scarlet Letter,* and *Daniel Deronda* all likewise open with preamble-like, staging chapters (or in Hawthorne's case, a long introduction) that pivot into the novel proper by way of a spatial and temporal leap. In the third chapter of *Daniel Deronda,* Eliot's narrator turns back from the moment when Gwendolen learns of her family's financial ruin (due to disastrous speculation in colonial mines) to her promising arrival one year earlier at Offendene; in *The Scarlet Letter,* Hawthorne crafts an introductory that makes his loss of his custom-house position the catalyst for his recovery of the story of Hester; and, most similar to Hopkins's novel, in Sedgwick's *Hope Leslie,* the Pequot attack on the Fletcher family prompts the leap several years forward to Hope's revisionary letter to Everall. All these swerves narrate the loss of continuity — the break in historical, and ethical, consciousness — that lies at the origin of the free self. And they recuperate this loss within the epic history of a wronged but noble community. In effect, these swerves are narrational swoons, the structural complement to the characters' bodily uprootings and remakings. They at once imitate the ruin's disruptive force and move quickly away from it, sublimating it — thus fashioning the phoenix-like subjectivities and histories that Rousseau imagined.

In writing her version of this swerve, Hopkins catapults us into a sentimentally framed world and establishes a domestic interior, in both senses, for her redemptive, epic text. After chapter 4, titled "The Tragedy," we arrive in the "cozy kitchen" setting of chapter 5, titled "Ma Smith's Lodging-house." Here begins the story of the brown-skinned Smith family (whose mother, we later learn, is the unwitting granddaughter of the Montforts) and a female boarder they take in, the beautiful, mysterious, light-skinned Sappho Clark. The modest yet openly affectionate, working-class Smith family is made up of this kindly mother and two doting children, the son Will, about twenty, and the daughter Dora, about eighteen. The mysterious Sappho soon wins the hearts of both Will and Dora — in Dora's case producing a love that borders on the homoerotic. Dora is engaged to John Langley, a handsome but as it turns out immoral man who also comes to desire Sappho and who turns out to be the descendent of Anson Pollock, who violated Mrs. Montfort, exemplifying slavery's long reach through history. On the eve of Sappho's engagement to the honorable Will Smith, Langley attempts to bribe her into a sexual relation with him by threatening to expose her secret past — for she was the victim of a brutal race-motivated rape, was sold to a brothel, escaped to the North, and now secretly harbors an eight-year-old son. Fearing social rejection, Sappho flees Boston, and three years intervene before she and Will reunite. Dora in the meanwhile has accommodated herself to marriage to another, better man named Arthur Lewis, and the Smith family has uncovered their own hidden history, learning that both they and their rich acquaintance, the Englishman Mr. Withington, descend from the Montforts, which makes the Smiths the surprised inheritors of a large sum of money and of a literal as well as a spiritual nobility.

As critics since Hazel Carby and Claudia Tate have appreciated, Hopkins reshapes this sentimental story to serve the political purposes of her community.[9] My reading here highlights the long literary history in which Hopkins intervenes to do so, including her manipulation of embedded nativist tropes. Her narrational swerve not only places us in a familiar literary world of sentimental domesticity but it makes tricky use of the sentimental vocabulary of humble, noble, and native, ultimately deconstructing its apparently universal but implicitly racial logic.

First, in her preface, Hopkins casts her "little romance" as a "humble tribute" to the friends of humanity, serving her intention to "do all that I can in an humble way to raise the stigma of degradation from my race" (13). In further suggesting that "it is the simple homely tale, unassumingly told, which cements the bond of brotherhood," she completes the familiar maneuver by which expressions of brotherly universalism testify to a humbly noble, native virtue. Appealing to the "friends of humanity everywhere" in her wish to "cement the bonds of brotherhood among all classes and all complexions," she simultaneously reinstates and reaches past divisions of class and "complexion" (13).

Meanwhile — in this same preface in which she sets up the Emerson quote that she will later implicitly deconstruct — Hopkins offers a theory of fiction that reflects her grasp of the historical-cultural work undertaken by this sentimental rhetoric, which cultivates nativism in the service, apparently, of universalist principles. She explains that "[f]iction is of great value to any people as a preserver of manners and customs — religious, political, and social. It is a record of growth and development from generation to generation" (13 – 14). And she places fiction's power beside the work of other "colored" intellectuals in the public sphere, for "[t]he colored race has its historians, lecturers, ministers, poets, judges, and lawyers, — men of brilliant intellects who have arrested the favorable attention of this busy, energetic nation": the novelist's "simple, homely tale, unassumingly told" performs a function equal to theirs (13). In the rest of the novel the narrator repeatedly refers to the kinship of the "human family" (5) and the forces of "natural brotherly love" (254) while simultaneously crafting her narrative of the Smith family and their African American community as a nativist project — for instance by heading her chapters with allusions to such English writers as Goldsmith and Gray who celebrate the natural goodness of "homely joys" and who tell the "short and simple annals of the poor." Clearly, Hopkins understands how fully the "novel of manners" is a race-elaborating form with an implicit historical narrative of "development" driving it.

Her manipulation of the tradition in this way is condensed in chapter 8, "The Sewing-Circle." She opens with an epigraph from Goldsmith: "Yes! Let the rich deride, the proud disdain, / These simple blessings of the lowly train; / To me more dear, / One native charm than all the gloss of art" (141). Here is the familiar discourse of "native charm." Yet it is in this chapter that Mrs. Willis insists that "there is no such thing as an unmixed black on the continent" in response to one woman's mention of a recent lecture, titled "Different Races," that predicted the sterility and demise of the "mongrel" mulatto race (149). If there is no such thing as an unmixed black on the continent, how tell a story of the "native" charms to which Goldsmith's lines refer? What is native?

Hopkins most persistently probes this lacuna in nativist discourse in her manipulations of the word "noble" (which, as we saw in earlier chapters, authors such as Richardson had brought into association with the native, honest, and humble) and in her resolution to the "noble" Smith/Withington story, which exposes a universalist nativism's fundamental incoherence within an Atlantic history of rape and diaspora. First of all, the narrator repeatedly attributes to the Smith family and their associates a native nobleness. Mrs. Willis speaks of the "nobility of the soul" of colored people to support her arguments about equal rights. The educated but humble Will Smith has a "noble head" (181), he manifests a love that is "so good, so noble" (182), and he practices "the natural chivalry of a generous nature" (168). Arthur Lewis likewise displays the "nobleness of a good man's love" (304) as reflected in his ability to "[engineer] all the delicate details of social life with neatness and dispatch" (305). Consistent with what we saw in *Oroonoko*, here the redefinition of "noble" involves a shifting of its referents away from blood, high passion, and military honor toward tender, sentimental devotion and domestic delicacy all operating within a humbly native, domestic scene. Accordingly, in the earnest words of Sappho, the "noblest heritage of a woman" is the love of a noble man (205).

Hopkins's handling of the Withington/Montfort plot employs the domesticating and nativizing of nobility within sentimental discourse, but she makes that discourse serve her reconfiguration of transatlantic kinship. For she not only imports a British sentimental framework into this story of African American community so as to include her community in the Anglo-Atlantic ethos of humble nobility. Ultimately, she also exports an African American genealogy — one which furthermore carries an ambiguous Caribbean lineage — back to England by revealing Mr. Withington to be a man of African American heritage. As she moves us toward the revelation of Mr. Withington's racial lineage, the narrator keeps in play the vocabulary of "noble" and "humble," holding these terms in tension briefly before letting them collapse dramatically into one another. Having come to visit Will Smith, Mr. Withington meets Mrs. Smith and condescendingly praises the "spirits of nobility" that he has discovered in "your race" (373). Impressed by Will Smith's "natural intelligence," he vows that he will return to England and "create sentiment for the [colored] race against its detractors." His gesture is decidedly sentimental. It keeps in place the notion of a colored vs. Anglo-Saxon race while reaching across those racial boundaries to "create sentiment" that bridges them. But Hopkins changes the meaning of this gesture when she reveals that Mr. Charles Montfort-Withington is actually the first cousin of Will's mother.

That is, Mrs. Smith's "homely" (374) tale of her family history reveals that her race is also his race, that his nobility is hers and hers is his, a revelation that flip-flops the meanings of nobility in each case even while dissolving the race differences between these characters and making them transatlantic kin. Hopkins brings her scene to a supremely ironical climax when she tells her reader, "So noble was the nature of this man that he never once thought of the possible ridicule that might come to him through his new kinspeople. He thought only of the tie of blood" (377). His nobility is composed equally of his loyalty to blood ties and his dismissal of blood discourses. Having established the unknowability of blood, or racial identity, Hopkins reconstructs a nobly blood-bonded community.

Ultimately, then, although Hopkins galvanizes the materials of the sentimental tradition in order to provide the nativist credentials for her characters, she deconstructs the purity of that nativism. In the process she not only produces what Lisa Marcus calls a "genealogical revision of America's national family tree" (119) but she also creates, as Lois Lamphere Brown points out, "important European links for her main African American characters" (68) that trouble the text's apparent celebration of a specifically African American community. Hopkins hollows out sentimental language and its accompanying "noble" gesture. She understands how fully the "novel of manners" is a race-elaborating form that she must employ in order to undo — and undo in order to employ.

The Ruined Interior of the Public Sphere

At the same time, Hopkins implicitly confesses that novels *generate* native interiority in their readers, even if they appear only to record it. That is, she anticipates Nancy Armstrong's arguments in *Desire and Domestic Fiction* by nearly a century. She stresses her point by italicizing it: "*No one will do this for us; we must ourselves develop the men and women who will faithfully portray the inmost thoughts and feelings of the Negro with all the fire and romance which lie dormant in our history,* and, as yet, unrecognized by writers of the Anglo-Saxon race" (14, emphasis in original). Although she speaks of faithfully "portraying" this romantic interiority that "lies dormant" in a race — a nice summary of the ostensible project of literature in English from the eighteenth century to the twentieth — she also implies that fiction is exactly the print form that "develops the men and women" who can create such portraits. In a circular economy, then, fiction creates the very authors of the interiority that it purportedly also records. As we saw, in *Of One Blood*, Hopkins drew on the new psychology of Henry James and others to develop and historicize exactly this African American interiority. Here she calls for the development, in effect, of writers who will at once give Negroes depth and make that depth transparent — *and so,* as she adds in a deemphasized, non-italicized clause, "recognizable" to the Anglo-Saxon race.

In her two extended public-sphere scenes in the novel — the American Coloured League meeting on lynching and the church fair — Hopkins pursues this project of going public with a native African American interiority at the same time that she exposes this interior as an already mixed, already violated one, with nothing simple or pure about it. In both scenes, she places Sappho quietly at the center, as the incognito ruined interior of the community.

As did the English in 1642, this community finds itself provoked by illegal violence into a public-sphere textualization of its "interior." In this case, a lynching has prompted the American Coloured League to call a meeting; and here black and white leaders "manifestly" position the crime of rape as the catalyst for their public speech. The accommodationist speakers use rape to justify the white community's lynching of blacks, while ultimately two African American speakers counter this argument — but they likewise position rape as the justification for their outspoken speech and active challenges to whites in the public sphere. Not surprisingly in an author so actively involved in public-sphere performances as she was, Hopkins carefully establishes, first of all, the reach and reality of this community's public-sphere activity.[10] She takes care to document the community's deliberate national mobilization around the news of the lynching via a network of telegrams and a slate of community meetings; and she has Judge Watson open the league meeting by calling for public-sphere action, proclaiming, *"Agitation and eternal vigilance in the formation of the public opinion* were the weapons which broke the power of the slaveholder and gave us emancipation. I recommend these methods to you today, knowing their value in the past" (245, emphasis in original).

Furthermore, not only "like" the English dissenters of the 1640s but indirectly because of them, because of their founding discourse of race-freedom, this community finds its voice by constituting itself as a race with an inner will to freedom, in this case as a "Colored" race. The scene displays what the narrator elsewhere refers to as "the [Negro's] love of liberty, which in its intensity recalled the memory of the New England men" (115) as the speakers invoke the freedom rhetoric that reaches back to the seventeenth century, especially via allusions to the eighteenth-century Anglo-American revolution. Luke Sawyer calls up a scene of interior ruin in order to restate for his community the questions that fired the Putney Debaters and later the American revolutionaries — when is it lawful to break the law? How free is the contract with the state? He asks his audience, "[W] hat do you think the American Colonies would have done if they had suffered as we have suffered and are still suffering?" (262). He reminds them that "[a] tax too heavy placed on tea and things like that, made the American colonies go to war with great Britain to get their liberty" (262). And he directly conjures the narrative of a tyranny-fighting heroism when he recalls "the solemn protest of Patrick Henry, so famous in history . . . 'Gentlemen may cry 'Peace! peace!' But there is no peace!'" (254). As did earlier Atlantic revolutionaries, Sawyer claims the right to battle tyranny because tyranny has already made war on him, specifically by violating the homes and women of the community. Within the tradition and as reinforced by Hopkins's own narrative discourse, these claims vibrate with nativist connotations, which Hopkins now fans to help constitute her "own" insurgent racial community.

But Hopkins also pushes one step further, into the terrain that William Walwyn opened in the 1640s, when finally she has Will Smith declare — at the "Canterbury Club," no less — that "[c]onstitutional equity is a political fiction" (297). Beginning in her preface, as we saw, she has slyly exposed the "fiction" of racial equity, showing it to be an expression of the racial ambition of her white compatriots. Yet at the same time, in that same preface, she has made clear that she understands the power of fictions. She is as interested in creating her own fiction of racial equity as she is in deconstructing the dominant one.

Thus she inserts into the agitated, nativized public sphere of the League meeting a swoon that eventually "manifests" the raped interior of her community.[11] She positions rape as the charged touchstone of all racial communities. Initially, the cry of rape at the League meeting is directed toward the African American community, invoked by the white conservative who denounces the mob law of lynchers but sympathizes with their obedience to "an unwritten law, not peculiar to any section, which demands the quickest execution, in the quickest way, of the fiend who robs a virtuous women of her honor," for this woman now "carries with her a living shame, a living death" (248). A series of other public speakers allude euphemistically yet centrally to the supposed rape of white women by black men. Then a speaker steps forward who was not on the agenda — and he speaks what was also not on the agenda, as does Hopkins in all her fiction: the rape of black women by white men. Luke Sawyer tells the story of the quadroon Mabelle Beaubean, a lovely young woman who, as she reaches adulthood, is kidnapped by her white uncle, then raped and left in a brothel. After three weeks her family finds her "a poor, ruined, half-crazed creature" (260). As Sawyer finishes and he stands "silently contemplating his weeping, grief-convulsed audience," a horrifically sublime awe overwhelms the community, climaxing when "a woman was borne from the auditorium in a fainting condition" (261). As we soon learn, Mabelle is Sappho, the Smiths' boarder and friend, having come to the North to live incognito since her escape; and it is she who faints at the meeting.

Sappho's incognito status within this world is telling. By at first leaving "the woman who fainted" at the League meeting unidentified, Hopkins makes her readers feel the symbolic force of this veiled figure. She defers our access to this woman's interior, her point of view, letting us feel the power of her symbolic meaning as a "woman fainting." Yet for Hopkins and the novel's community, rape is a founding fact, not a founding trope; and through the revelation of Sappho's past, the longstanding literary trope now appears in all its submerged facticity. It becomes the novel's catalyst for delving into characters' interior ruminations. Shortly after this scene, we more fully enter Sappho's consciousness than we have yet done, as she reflects on what her violated past means for her desired future with Will Smith; and throughout the novel, Hopkins takes us into the consciousness of other characters — Ma Smith, Will, Dora, and John Langley — especially insofar as they wonder about the mysterious Sappho's feelings, her past, and her place within their world and fortunes.

Furthermore, Hopkins implies that the legacy of the Atlantic *economy* circulates covertly through Sappho. The coming-to-light of her interior struggles and past trauma brings with it a revelation of the hidden, possessive, and Gothic economy of the Anglo-Atlantic republic. At the League meeting, Luke Sawyer implicitly links rape to the property stakes of race, by juxtaposing his story of Mabelle against his account of the murder of his family by a white mob resentful of his father's business success. Similarly, as Will Smith points out, "If the Negro votes, he is shot; if he marries a white woman, he is shot; if he accumulates property he is shot or lynched" (271). The novel indicates that this economic competition shapes the economy of the African American community as well—as long as its ruined Sapphos are kept incognito. The whole drama of the church fair gains its suspense from the competition between women who vie for the minister's favor, cast aspersions on each other's integrity, honesty, and class positions, and compete over who can bring the most capital to the African American community. Within this scene of emotional and economic competition, Sappho sits, in "a distant corner, . . . keeping a strict account of the moneys received" (202). Hopkins here points to the pivotal "laundering" role of the ruined woman—the services rendered to the community by what Sappho calls her "shipwrecked life." As long as the stories of what Dora calls the "fallen sister" are buried as an embarrassment to the African American community, that community participates in the racialized competition that shipwrecks her. When Hopkins brings to light Sappho's full history and creates in the Smiths a family—and especially a brother—who shun not Sappho but the conditions of her violation, she labors to undo this historical and economic legacy. She establishes that this thing called interiority is not strictly a hidden essence generated purely from within; it is the accretion of a communal history, and it is especially catalyzed by violating acts which, exactly because they are veiled and "secreted," not only constitute a person's interior but also foster a suppressed double consciousness within the community.

It is exactly this *historicized interior* into which the "seer" Madame Frances peers at the Fair and about which she makes predictions. She gives glimpses of selves whose interior depth is a function of temporality, of a long, suppressed history—in other words, selves entangled in a history of crimes and layered by a history of suppressions. Likewise, her power of sight is not a matter of individual prowess but of a communal inheritance that gives access to a historical legacy. As heir to African "occult arts," as the narrator says, Madame Frances has access to the interiors of lives caught up in racial histories (199). She predicts a delayed happiness for the "historically" ruined Sappho and a final doom for John Langley, who turns out to be a descendant of Anson Pollock, the novel's original agent of such ruin. Her fortune-telling coyly makes these fates public, in the form of riddles—a form of veiled expression that resurfaces in the figure of the sphinx in *Of One Blood* and reminds us that Hopkins understood the "Gordian knot" of this interior in its already-appropriated, racialized path to freedom.

In Madame Frances, although Hopkins seems partly to racialize these prophetic powers, her narrator also casts this power of vision as potentially belonging to all who "see" historically.[12] In fact she imagines just such a universal seer at the Fair—an anonymous figure with no race markers attached to him. This seer suddenly comes to understand Sappho's past and position in the community, in particular via the legacy of rape she embodies. We enter his viewpoint—described merely as that of a "learned doctor"—just as his gaze spans out from Sappho and her (also incognito) son Alphonse to the crowd: "Many a thought came into the heart of one learned doctor as he gazed on the child and the beautiful girl, and then upon faces ebony-hued but bright and sparkling with the light of freedom and intelligence. In that moment a cloud passed from before his mental vision, and he beheld in all its hideousness the cankering sore which is eating into the heart of republican principles and stamping the lie upon the Constitution" (202).

This unidentified learned doctor, who might be the African American doctor Abraham Peters but, given the reference to the mental cloud that lifts, is very possibly a white patron, suddenly understands that Alphonse is Sappho's child by a white man and that her case is not unique. He comprehends how this legacy "gives the lie" to republican principles of liberty and creates a cankering sore that lives in the body of a raped black woman—literally and symbolically. At the same moment that he understands himself and this world as arising from this history, he also sees African Americans' interiority, "bright and sparkling with the light of freedom." This moment allegorizes Hopkins's project as laid out in her preface: to make—and make transparent—the wounded yet freedom-seeking interior of the Negro race.

Sisters, Lovers, Brothers, and Mothers

As we've seen, many nineteenth-century epic narratives aim to recuperate a community in the wake of ruin, including by portraying loving republican brothers and envisioning a universalist, benevolent racialism. They also frequently depict a healing of wounds between women—Hope and Esther, Hester and her female neighbors, Mirah and Gwendolyn, and Dorothea and Rosamund. Here, too, Hopkins goes a step further, although very quietly.

In *Contending Forces* Hopkins not only places Ma Smith at the center of her story, as an ideal mother of the community (whereas in many similar novels, mothers die or are largely absent) but she also extends this renewing of female bonds (or is it a fashioning of bonds, required by rupture?) by slipping a homo-erotic subtext into her novel. As I have considered elsewhere, and Siobhan Somer-ville has discussed at length,[13] she does so most pointedly in her depictions of the friendship between Sappho and Dora, whose undercurrent of eroticism is comi-cally mirrored in the subplot of the friendship, jealousy, and "break-up" of Sarah Ann White and Ophelia Davis. At the same time, Hopkins rewrites the identity of the republican brother in a way that makes room for this homoeroticism.

Early in the novel, unknowingly addressing a "fallen sister" in the person of Sappho, Dora remarks, as we saw, that "we would hang our heads in shame at having the temerity to judge a fallen sister, could we but know the circumstances attending many such cases" (101). It turns out that, in the case of this fallen sister named Sappho, Dora not only is sympathetic on principle but she also becomes deeply attached. By way of Dora, Hopkins places the plot of heterosexual ruin directly beside a story of female homoerotic magnetism — and with this latter turn she anticipates modernism, specifically that development Shari Benstock calls Sapphic modernism (which I'll discuss in part 5 in the novels of Larsen and Woolf).[14] But this embrace requires, Hopkins implies, a woman who neither judges nor competes with other women on heterosexual grounds. Certainly Dora is such a woman, notably free of female judgment and jealousy, even when, in the case of John Langley, she has grounds for jealousy. As Dora observes about her-self, she feels remarkably "unsexed" — except toward Sappho, her tellingly named friend. A "glow of mutual interest" lights up the women at their first meeting, and for Dora, Sappho "fills a long-felt want in her life" (98) so that before long "love had taken root in her heart for Sappho" (127).

If we think of Sappho as the silent, ruined, yet resurfacing figure of interiority within the African-Atlantic economy, then, in one striking scene of intimacy between these two women, the text suggests that homoerotic desire, in particular, can foster the remaking of that interior and begin to move the community past its history of ruinous violation. On a stormy winter's day, Sappho "begged Dora to pass the day with her and play company," and Dora "was nothing loathe," so they "locked the door to Sappho's room to keep out all intruders" and they settled in front of the "little stove that gave out a delicious warmth" (117). In Hopkins's delighted rendering, Sappho "lay back among her cushions . . . folded her arms above her head and turned an admiring gaze on the brown face of her friend, who swayed gently back and forth in her rocking-chair, her feet on a hassock, and a scarlet afghan wrapped about her knees" (118). Their conversation turns to marriage, and Dora begins by confessing that, although she likes her fiancé

John Langley, she doesn't feel passion for him. She asks Sappho, "[D]on't you ever expect to marry, and don't you speculate about the pros and cons and the maybes and perhapses of the situation?" (119).

Hopkins then disrupts this conversation with a playful, physical "scramble" between the two women that leaves them "rosy and sparkling" (120). Sappho evades Dora's question by asking about the dessert Dora is just then unveiling, which leads to a "scramble for the pie, mingled with peals of merry laughter, until all rosy and sparkling Sappho emerged from the fray with the dish containing her share of the dainty" (120). This physical tussle for "the dainty," which Hopkins has narrated so sensuously, is suggestively followed by Dora's further admission that she "despair[s] of ever being like other girls" in their desire for men. Pronouncing herself "unsexed," Dora pointedly asks Sappho, "Do you ever mean to marry, or are you going to pine in single blessedness on my hands and be a bachelor-maid to the end?" (121). Notice the tension between pining and blessedness in Dora's question. It is Dora who apparently pines for Sappho, in a position of single blessedness.

But here, too, race reenters to legitimize liberty-seeking interiorities — including the liberties of woman-to-woman intimacy — even though, overall, the book deconstructs race lineage. Just before the afternoon on which Sappho and Dora lock the door of Sappho's room to keep out intruders, the narrator explains that their growing intimacy has been enabled by an atmosphere of Yankee freedom.[15] Dora has watched Sappho become more open to their friendship as Sappho "drank great draughts of freedom's subtle elixir" in the "free air of New England's freest city" (115). Sappho is in turn attracted to Dora, "the energetic little Yankee girl," since indeed, as the narrator now comments, the Negro's "love of liberty [. . .] in its intensity recalled the memory of New England men" (114–15). In effect, Hopkins implies, as did Eliza Haywood in *The British Recluse,* that a discourse of native liberty can underwrite female alliances, and even dalliances.

On the one hand, this implication comes close to making homoeroticism "natural," while on the other hand it "contains" that implication by enclosing it within a racial logic — British, Yankee, or African American — that, ultimately, will always require women's heterosexual conformity so that the native race will be reproduced. And ultimately these two women do marry "race" men. Yet, for a long moment in Hopkins's text, within this racialist protection, the two women can consort sensually. Hopkins's deployment of race rhetoric in this way compares with that of Catharine Macaulay, Mercy Otis Warren, and Catharine Maria Sedgwick, where their race rhetoric serves to justify their female "liberties," even if only provisionally or temporarily. The exotic "scarlet afghan" wrapped about

Dora's knees at the opening of this scene just registers the "exotic" race transgression which, in fact, these liberties threaten to allow.

Hopkins's risks in this realm of female identities are matched in her portrait of these women's closest and shared male associate — Will Smith, who is both Sappho's lover and Dora's brother. In the more enlightened race republic that Hopkins fashions, a brother can display "feminine" sensitivities, and he can affiliate with rather than compete with or dominate sisters — although he may also ultimately substitute for a sister. In one of the other key scenes of intimacy in Sappho's room, as Will and Sappho flirt, the text hints that he is a substitute for Dora. When Sappho discovers Will preparing her morning fire on her return from an early errand, her initial concern turns quickly to laughter as Will turns to face her: "Will had donned one of his mother's kitchen aprons for the protection of his clothing. The bib was pinned well up in front across the broad expanse of shirt bosom; the ample folds of the apron-skirt enveloped his limbs to his ankles; the long strings, crossed in the back, met in front in a huge bow-knot" (172).

As critics have shown, in this and other novels Hopkins shines a revealing light on codes of masculinity and in particular uses cross-dressing to play with gender norms.[16] Her fiction itself is perhaps "crossed in the back." Dressed like his mother, tending to Sappho's comfort in the place of his sister, and playful about his unmasculine appearance, Will emerges as a differently "noble" kind of man. As he banters with Sappho, Will suggests that "I do this for you as I would for Dora" and later proposes that "we play you are my other sister" (174). His erotically charged references to a substitution involving Dora and sisterly play recall the earlier scene of intimacy in this room between Dora and Sappho even as they position him as an unpossessive, republican brother. As characterized by Hopkins, Will is a man whose love of sister and wife is neither at odds with nor a function of his worldly ambitions.

Although Hopkins ultimately directs the love relationships in her novel into strictly heterosexual channels, she nonetheless leaves the ripple of a homoerotic subcurrent. The text's final scene returns us to the Atlantic shore and there lets this ripple surface, for Hopkins doubles the already suggestive name of Sappho, via the body of Dora. In the wake of her breakup with John Langley, Dora has married Arthur Lewis, and, we learn, she has named her baby girl Sappho. This "little Sappho" appears at the center of the novel's closing tableau, along with the maternal figure of the text, Ma Smith. On the deck of a ship stand "Doctor Lewis, Dora, little Sappho, Ma Smith, Will, Sappho — now Will's wife — and little Alphonse" (401). Having come north from the Caribbean, this family heads back to England to enjoy its inheritance, fulfilling the original Mr. Montfort's wish, though not quite in the way he had imagined. They are setting out, in the words of the text's closing epigraph, to "walk this world / Yoked in all exercise of noble end" (401).

Launched on the Atlantic, yoked by way of a noble racial end, prosperously reentering this Atlantic economy that their ancestors helped to build, these characters redirect Atlantic history even as they smuggle a Sapphic passenger into that history's future — and into the texts of Atlantic modernism.

V | Liberty's Ruin in Atlantic Modernism

15 Queering Freedom's Theft in Nella Larsen

LOOKING BACK WRYLY on three centuries, Nella Larsen and Virginia Woolf write metafictions of Atlantic modernity. When Larsen takes Countee Cullen's lines about a speaker "three centuries removed" from Africa as the epigraph to *Passing,* and Woolf embeds allusions to Sir Walter Raleigh in her sea-soaked novels, these authors gesture toward the horizon in which they write. In their novels, they distill Atlantic modernity's elements into potent and stylized form. They at once defamiliarize, demystify, and reenact the killingly sublime vision of racial liberty.

The change we experience in turning from the fiction of Pauline Hopkins to that of Woolf and Larsen may well confirm what Woolf once suggested — that sometime around 1910 human character changed. That year does fall between the publishing dates of Hopkins and those of Larsen and Woolf and certainly *something* has changed. Hopkins published her four novels between 1900 and 1903, and although we can feel her pessimism rising as we move from *Contending Forces* to *Of One Blood,* in none of her novels do we step wholly outside the epic telos of race's liberty plot.

Woolf's first novel, *The Voyage Out* (1915), published a mere twelve years after Hopkins's last novel, opens with an ocean crossing and takes up the Anglo-British side of the Atlantic history Hopkins has narrated. But something goes awry and the rising telos suddenly falls like a phoenix in mid-flight. Our heroine symbolically drowns. No marriage occurs and, accordingly, empire fades rather than appears on the horizon. Likewise, in Larsen's two novels, written two decades after

Hopkins's, the heroines fall and never rise again. End of story. End of freedom. End of the promise of race fulfillment in the republic. In *Quicksand,* Larsen organizes her heroine's demise around an Atlantic crossing and recrossing, and she closes with Helga's slow, sinking fall under the weight of childbirth, after her resigned return to the racial order of things.

A whole fleet of modernist protagonists arrive, after a seaside launching toward freedom, at this dead end in the story of desire, race, and liberty: Jean Rhys's Marya, Kate Chopin's Edna, Henry James's Isabel Archer, E. M. Forster's Adele, Ernest Hemingway's Jake, Gertrude Stein's Gentle Lena, William Faulkner's Quentin, and Zora Neale Hurston's Janie and Teacake (although Janie comes to a hopeful ending, notably with a homosocial bond intact, and it is Teacake who symbolically gets killed by the flood). Drownings sink a remarkable number of these characters, most famously and literally Chopin's Edna Pontellier, yet also many others more figuratively, such as the street-wandering Sasha Jansen in Rhys's *Good Morning Midnight,* whose sneering relatives ask her why she doesn't drown herself in the Seine and who repeatedly imagines herself sinking in a whirlpool.

What gets drowned or lost in these texts is not so much a prelapsarian or virgin self, however, as in the swoons of many earlier novels, but rather a certain sensuous, straying, or queer self.[1] These protagonists' journeys come into conflict with the heterosexually captained mission of race. In Stein's *Three Lives,* Lena crosses the ocean and is guided toward marriage to Herman Kreder (even though he "liked to be with men and hated to have women with them" and even though he divides her forever from the girls who first "made a gentle stir within her"), for marriage is inevitable for every "patient, gentle, sweet, and german" girl; but this marriage slowly kills her, as does Melanctha's involvement with the ambivalent Jeff Campbell, who rejects her wandering, bisexual desires insofar as they deviate from what is "right for a decent colored girl always to be doing."[2] Forster's Adele Quested falls into her swoon after a too-close affiliation with a man of another race, which Susan Stanford Friedman has read as a surrogate for Forster's own cross-racial and homoerotic attachments.[3] Chopin's Edna discovers both the pleasures of intimacy with women and the sensuality of her own body, which she associates with native Mexican and island women, but she drowns herself when she cannot realize her new feelings in her relations with Robert LeBrun. Along with many of these other early-twentieth-century English-language writers, both Larsen and Woolf conjure the prospect of a homoerotic bond, like that which Hopkins hints at between Sappho and Dora. In their pairings of Clare and Irene, Aubrey and Helga, Helen and Rachel, Lily and Mrs. Ramsay, Clarissa and Sally, and Evans and Septimus, they tease out into visibility the erotic possibilities kept (just) below board in Hopkins's fiction. Larsen and Woolf suggest that this bond might give women a mooring outside the brothers' new hegemony. But their novels then narrate the death of that possibility.

It is in *Passing* that Larsen flirts at most length with this race-straying homo-eroticism, as has been amply discussed by critics. Here I focus instead on *Quicksand*, reading it as the back story for *Passing*'s tale of queer desire. Helga Crane's Atlantic crisscrossing in *Quicksand*, impelled by her grappling with modernity's contradictory coupling of freedom and race, and in flight from its attendant disci-plining of sexuality, offers one key to the drama of *Passing*, specifically to the rise and fall of the similarly orphaned, biracial Clare Kendry, whose queer sexuality so attracts the otherwise disciplined Irene Redfield. *Quicksand* likewise provides a framework for reading Larsen's last published story, "Sanctuary," which she was accused of plagiarizing from the British writer Sheila Kaye-Smith. Read next to *Quicksand* and within the history of Atlantic modernity, however, "Sanctu-ary" emerges as Larsen's final encapsulation — and inverted reenactment — of the transatlantic story. With these texts in mind, I propose that we consider Larsen a sort of riptide *Atlantic* modernist. Exactly because she is all at once Scandina-vian, Anglo-American, and Harlem Renaissance writer (as George Hutchinson suggests),[4] she grapples directly with modernity's racial legacy.

Helga's Dilemma

In *Quicksand*, Larsen immediately signals the Atlantic double-cross underlying her fiction. The very name of her protagonist, Helga Crane, alludes to the Ger-manic and marine dimensions of the legacy, as does the name of the school where Helga is teaching when we meet her — Naxos. Not only is it the name of a Greek island of Dionysian affiliations and thereby an erotic struggle but it also suggests "Saxon" scrambled and spelled backwards — a neat naming of Larsen's revision-ary project.[5] The story of "Helga Crane at Naxos" reverses the Saxon story and narrates, without redemption, the fatal disciplining of eros and body within the transatlantic economy of race.

Larsen clearly needed no help from Michel Foucault to chart the regime of the body in modernity, nor to see how this discipline so oddly underpins "free" Western cultures. In her portrait of Helga at Naxos, Larsen displays the absurdity of the way African Americans must be initiated, through bodily discipline, into the freedom and citizenship their labor has already made possible for others and that the "uplift" school of Naxos now belatedly promises them. As Helga ques-tions her role as teacher at the Naxos school, Larsen positions her at a window watching the students assemble for breakfast into "neat phalanxes preparatory to marching in military order."[6] She decides to resign from her teaching position as she observes how "[h]ere and there a male member of the faculty, important and resplendent in the regalia of an army officer, would pause in his prancing or strutting, to jerk a negligent or offending student into the proper attitude or place." Watching "[t]he massed phalanxes [increase] in size and number" until "the goosestep began. Left, right. Left, right. Forward! March! The automatons moved" (12), she concludes finally that she is "utterly unfitted" for Naxos. In this school "[t]eachers as well as students were subjected to the paring process, for it tolerated no innovations, no individualisms" (5).

Yet Helga's comments on individualism collide in this early scene with her invocation of race, displaying how she is caught in the strained yoking of these terms. Larsen does not render Helga simply as the "other" of this implicitly military race culture but as an embodiment of its contradictions. Her predicament finds its most compact expression in her reflections on colorful dress. She indicts the school's "suppression of individuality and beauty," taking its disapproval of color and boldness in clothing as one instance of this suppression.[7] Yet she understands her own love of color as the "inherent *racial* need for gorgeousness, . . . [for] bright colors" (20, 18, emphasis added). Is dress an expression of the individual or the race? Is it unfettered individuality or racial identity that Helga seeks? Freedom from race, or freedom for the race? Noticing that "self-restraint [. . .] was also, curiously, a part of her nature," she recognizes the self abnegation in which she is caught up together with the marching students. It will spur her reactionary Atlantic flights in which she first rejects, then embraces, and then again rejects her racial connections. She, too, is carried by a paradoxically racialized will to individual freedom.

In her travels back and forth across the Atlantic, Helga becomes acutely conscious of the Catch-22 in the culture of freedom. In Copenhagen, first noting the "odd architectural mixture of medievalism and modernity," she observes that "[h]ere there were no tatters and rags, no beggars"—for "begging, she learned, was an offense punishable by law" (75). She reasons that the appearance of settled order and well-bred modernity rests on punitive laws that are justified by the notion of everyone's "duty somehow to support himself and his family" (75). The state apparently feels "bound to give assistance" to the impoverished—yet only, she wryly adds, as help "on the road to the regaining of independence" from the others (75). Helga precisely pinpoints the tension between group and individual in the orthodoxy of Anglo-European modernity: everyone *must* be an independent, propertied *individual* in order to be a member of the *group;* and conversely, one can only be a *group* member by assenting to the *individualist* laws of laissez-faire economy and autonomous self-support.[8] This orthodoxy is the essence of a racial

Saxonism parading as "free" social contract, and it creates the tense marriage of freedom and race for both African- and Anglo-Atlantic persons.

Helga sees that her Harlem circle of friends is also caught in these contradictions, especially through their simultaneous identification and disidentification with race. Helga minces no words—privately—and Larsen none—publicly—when she concludes that Anne and her friends "didn't want to be like themselves. What they wanted, asked for, begged for, was to be like their white overlords" (74). Anne in particular "hated white people with a deep and burning hatred" but "she aped their clothes, their manners, and their gracious ways of living" (48). And conversely, "while proclaiming loudly the undiluted good of all things Negro, she yet disliked the songs, the dances, the softly blurred speech of the race" (48). Larsen unveils the way that Anne and friends appropriate the whites' most shrewd strategy—using race as a way to authorize their escape from race into an ostensibly neutral selfhood and freedom. Like the whites, they do not scrutinize too closely exactly what this supposedly deracialized freedom is. As Negroes they deserve freedom—freedom to be Negroes no longer, to live unraced.

Atlantic Orphan

Helga's insights are forced on her by her "alien" position, which originates in nothing other than her mother's transatlantic journey, which leads her into seduction and abandonment. In enfolding this mother's history into her novel, Larsen positions the old Atlantic plot at the heart of Helga's conflicts.[9] Her mother was a "fair Scandinavian girl in love with life, with love, with passion, dreaming, and risking all in one blind surrender. A cruel sacrifice. In forgetting all but love she had forgotten, or perhaps never known, that some things the world never forgives" (23). Helga's mother becomes the social pariah who, out of "grievous necessity," eventually marries a white man, "for even foolish, despised women must have food and clothing" (23). Scorned by her white stepfamily, Helga leaves them to attend a school for Negroes, which eventually lands her at Naxos. Yet at Naxos, she can no more speak of her white kin than she could, in her white family, embrace her African American heritage. "No family. That was the crux of the whole matter," she realizes in brooding on her sense of distance from everyone at Naxos, including her fiancé, James Vayle, with whom she now ends her engagement (8).

Therefore, when Dr. Anderson, the director of the Naxos school, attempts to persuade her to stay at the school by pointing out that it prizes "a lady" like her with "tendencies inherited from good stock," Helga is "jolted into a rage," and this interview drives her from the school and into her Atlantic wandering—until she ultimately repeats her mother's history, that legacy of Atlantic crossing into racial "ruin" (21). Exactly because Helga is the traveling, excluded figure with "no people" (apparently like Larsen herself), she senses this covert re-race-ing of freedom, including as it works to discipline sexuality within heterosexual, intraracial alliances. Fleeing the school and her fiancé, she takes a traveling job with Mrs. Hayes-Rore, the "race-woman," editing speeches about race and community on a train, ironically — only to arrive in another place where she has no people. When Hayes-Rore takes Helga under her wing and offers to introduce her to Anne Grey and her elite Harlem circle, she does so implicitly on condition that Helga keep her mixed-race identity secret — and that she never mention that she has no known family but white people. Helga's acceptance into this African American community requires her negation of her only known kin. Fittingly, when she settles in Harlem, her home there is not a home but a room in Anne's house. From here, all the way to her last stopping-place in the novel — a return south to a home that turns out to be no home either — Helga is simply a guest in hotels or other people's houses.

After Helga's arrival in New York, the plot of the novel might be characterized as her vacillating movement toward and away from race as a ground of identity, a series of racial reaction-formations in a quest for freedom.[10] In New York Helga feels "that magic sense of having come home" for "Harlem, teeming black Harlem, had welcomed her and lulled her into something that was, she was certain, peace and contentment" (43). In her initial identification with African American community, she feels free of "that tantalizing oppression of loneliness and isolation" and she looks on the "white world" as a collection of "sinister folk . . . who had stolen her birthright" (45). The old language of birthright resurfaces here, just as later Larsen's narrator describes Helga as feeling "yoked" to race. In New York, she relishes a contentment that "she knew sprang from a sense of freedom, a release from the feeling of smallness which had hedged her in, first during her unchildlike childhood among hostile white folk . . . and later . . . among snobbish black folk in Naxos" (46).

Yet, as the next page and chapter announce, "it didn't last, this happiness," for "somewhere, within her, in a deep recess, crouched discontent" (47). In this new city of freedom, she again comes to feel "shut in, trapped" as she discovers that race encloses its landscape as well; so, increasingly "she made lonely excursions to places outside of Harlem" while "a sensation of estrangement and isolation encompassed her" (47–48). She finds especially that she "wanted to be free of this constant prattling of the incongruities, the injustices, the stupidities, the viciousness of white people" (49). It is not only that she is bothered by the "inconsistencies" in her friends who hate but imitate the white world (49) but also that this hatred "stirred memories, probed hidden wounds, whose poignant ache bred in her surprising oppression and corroded the fabric of her quietism" (49). The hidden wound is her double experience of rejection, by white kin and by blacks for having white kin, making her a racial outcast in a world in which race is the ticket to both membership and freedom.

Therefore when the letter from her uncle arrives containing money and suggesting she visit her white aunt in Copenhagen, her sensation is "one of relief, of liberation," for she thinks she can escape this oppression by leaving the United States (54). She realizes abruptly that she had been feeling "boxed up, with hundreds of her race, closed up with that something in the racial character which had always been, to her, inexplicable, alien," and now she wants no longer to be "yoked to these despised black folk" (55). Although she feels "self-loathing" for this last emotion ("'They're my own people, my own people' she kept repeating"), she finds that "[t]he feeling would not be routed" (55). Finally feeling a sharp "necessity for being alone," she concludes that "[s]he was different. It wasn't merely a matter of color. It was something broader, deeper, that made folk kin" (55). Harlem no longer provides her the entry into freedom; instead, "now she was free" in her choice to exit and so throw off this "yoke" of race (54–55). At the very center of Larsen's novel, on board a ship sailing across the Atlantic to Europe, Helga feels a "returned sense of happiness and freedom, that blessed sense of belonging to herself alone and not to a race" (64).

Helga's trip might seem to undo the legacy of the middle passage, following the fantasy that Pauline Hopkins imagines at the end of her 1900 novel *Contending Forces*. But instead of freedom from race, in Copenhagen Helga finds that she is paraded by her aunt and uncle "like a veritable savage" and that their acceptance also depends, ultimately, on their deployment of her racialized, marriageable body to strengthen their ties to the wealthy social order. Suddenly, Helga finds herself "homesick not for America, but for Negroes" (92). Recrossing the Atlantic, she forgives her father his abandonment of her mother and his "surrender to the irresistible ties of race, now that they dragged at her own heart" (92). When she acknowledges that "it was as if in this understanding and forgiving she had come upon knowledge of almost sacred importance" (93), Helga comes as close as she ever will to a Hopkinsian vision of sacred racial bonds. Yet, once in America — though she feels "the appeasement of that loneliness" and how "absurd" it was to think that "other people could liberate her from the ties which bound her forever to these mysterious, these terrible, these fascinating, these lovable, dark hordes" (95) — she also confesses that because of the cruelty and cramping Negroes faced in America, "she couldn't stay. Nor, she saw now, could she remain away." No. Her condition will be forever ambiguous, forever transient: "Leaving, she would have to come back" (96).

Helga is the "race woman" in modernity, in a sense that Mrs. Hayes-Rore might not recognize. Although in the end Helga assumes the more familiar role of "race woman" as maternal reproducer of the race, Larsen hints at the equivalence among all these instrumental, female positions in racial modernity. And she hints that other race-transgressing erotic impulses might underlie Helga's dilemmas.

Queer Ruin

The chapter that precedes and, arguably, most urgently propels Helga's flight to Copenhagen ends on a very queer note. The moment is embedded, furthermore, in the most racially troubled scene in the novel, set in the Harlem cabaret that Helga "half unwillingly" goes to with Anne and her friends (58). In her rendering of this scene, Larsen creates the kind of "break" in consciousness that Ralph Ellison's narrator in *Invisible Man* describes in discussing the effects of jazz on the "invisible" black listener,[11] although Larsen allows us a fuller glimpse than he does of the queer predicaments submerged within it. "Invisibility," Ellison's narrator explains, "gives one a slightly different sense of time, you're never quite on the beat.... Instead of the swift and imperceptible flowing of time, you are aware of its nodes, those points where time stands still or from which it leaps ahead. And you slip into the breaks and look around."[12]

As I have noted elsewhere, when Ellison's narrator slips into one such break in Louis Armstrong's "What did I do to be so Black and Blue?" he discovers in imagination an auction-block scene and the figure of "a beautiful girl the color of ivory pleading in a voice like my mother's as she stood before a group of slave-owners who bid for her naked body."[13] He discovers, as I would put it in this context, an internalized legacy of sexual "ruin," embodied in the girl's ivory skin as well as in the buying of her naked body, linked, in the narrator's mind, to his own mother and lineage. This vision, in turn, provokes him to imagine a further scene of violence — in the form of an aggressive homosocial challenge to the narrator from the slave mother's sons, because his identification with this mother over the fact of ruin threatens her sons, who hate their father and reject the "ruin" that conceived them. As recent critics have suggested, not only the narrator but also Ellison himself is grappling with an ambivalent male homosociality and the threat of queerness lurking in this break.[14]

This constellation of queerness, ruin, and biracial heritage in Ellison's novel retrospectively offers a guide to the cabaret scene in *Quicksand,* where in the midst of a jazz tune, Helga falls into a similar "break." And again here it seems that Larsen negotiates with not only her protagonist's but also her own ambivalent feelings about race in relation to a "ruined," that is, racially mixed and queer, sexuality. In *Quicksand,* the cabaret scene is cast in a provocatively racialized language. Helga "half unwillingly" accompanies Anne and friends to the cabaret, feeling "singularly apart from it all" as they enter the "gay, grotesque" streets of Harlem (58). Although Helga marvels at, and Larsen takes great care to enumerate, the variety of people around her — "sooty black, shiny black, taupe, mahogany, bronze, copper, gold, orange, yellow, peach, ivory, pinky white, pastry white . . . yellow hair, black hair, brown hair; straight hair, straightened hair, curly hair, crinkly hair, wooly hair . . . black eyes in white face, brown eyes in yellow faces, gray eyes in brown faces, blue eyes in tan faces" — the language of savagery also pervades the descriptions. The group is led to their table by "a black giant," served by a waiter "indefinitely carved out of ebony," while people dance "ecstatically to the thumping of unseen tomtoms" and the "savage strains of music" so that Helga later feels on leaving the dance floor that she had "been in the jungle" (59).

All of this is cast as Helga's perception, as that of a woman alienated from her race. And yet as the scene develops, its syntax also suggests the presence of an alienated *author,* a writer who was not only like Ellison in being displaced *by* race but was also unlike him in being displaced *within* race.[15] We can glimpse this attitude as Helga fleetingly loses herself in the jazz band's "jungle" music when she joins her friends on the dance floor. In the midst of Helga's dancing — precisely when Helga is least critical and most lost to the joy of it all — the narrator steps away from her, as if she, too, must take care to stand outside this race-immersion. "For a while, Helga was oblivious of the reek of flesh, smoke, and alcohol, oblivious of the oblivion of other gyrating pairs, oblivious of the color, the noise, and the grand distorted childishness of it all" (59). In noting the reeking smells and the "childishness" that Helga is temporarily overlooking, the narrator provocatively beckons her readers to join her in this condescension. Vacillating, however, like her character-in-flight, the narrator then seems momentarily to merge with Helga's joyful participation, for the prose moves with the rhythms of the music: Helga was "drugged, lifted, sustained, by the extraordinary music, blown out, ripped out, beaten out, by the joyous, wild, murky orchestra" (59). This may be the only moment in the narrative when Helga *and* her narrator shed their vexed sense of double-consciousness. In this here and now, the narrator tells us, "life seemed bodily motion" (59), and Larsen's prose is all verbs.

This "motion" appears on the one hand as the "essence" of a race; but this raciality — as its many-colored surround and its *"orchestra"* playing *"jungle"* rhythms suggest — is on the other hand a manifestation of modernity's racial crisscrossings, also expressed in Helga's nomadic life and pale-brown skin. Motion is the essence of life for Helga (and perhaps for jazz) not because she belongs to a race but because she doesn't, quite. Her continual return to race, like the plot's, like

William Faulkner's or Gertrude Stein's wandering narration, reveals that there is no there, there; yet all the while the fiction of race feeds the motion of modernity (including Stein's racist portraits).[16] Helga leaves the dance floor, dogged by "a shameful certainty that not only had she been in the jungle, but that she had enjoyed it" and so "[s]he hardened in her determination to get away. She wasn't, she told herself, a jungle creature" (59). Thus does this scene begin to move Helga closer to her transatlantic passage.

But this impulse to flee is precipitated most urgently by what follows. When the music begins again and someone asks her to dance, "she declined" and "sat looking curiously about her" as "the crowd became a swirling mass" dancing to the "syncopated jangle" (59). In the midst of this break, in which Helga is not "quite on the beat," as Ellison would put it, she "discover[s] Dr. Anderson sitting at a table on the far side of the room, with a girl in a shivering apricot frock" (60). This girl, Audrey Denney, rivets Helga's attention. After silently nodding to Anderson, Helga begins to turn her eyes away, "[b]ut they went back immediately to the girl beside him, who sat indifferently sipping a colourless liquid, or puffing a precariously hanging cigarette. Across dozens of tables, littered with corks, with ashes, with shriveled sandwiches, through slits in the swaying mob, Helga Crane studied her" (60).

Across a series of obstacles suggestive of sexuality and its "shriveled" aftermath, Helga peers through a slit to fix her attention on Audrey Denney. Through Helga's eyes, the text caressingly details Denney's appearance, lingering over her "softly curving" yet "sorrowful" mouth, her pitch-black eyes "a little aslant . . . veiled by long, drooping lashes," her "pale" and "peculiar, almost deathlike pallor," her "dark hair brushed severely back," and finally the "extreme décolleté of her simple apricot dress show[ing] a skin of unusual color, a delicate, creamy hue, with golden tones": "'Almost like an alabaster,' thought Helga" (60).

Like Helga, Denney herself displays the light-skinned body that signifies both desire and ruin. Audrey's appearance openly queers sexual and racial norms, with slanted black eyes and her peculiar, creamy skin as well as her mannishly brushed-back hair above an alluring décolleté, a mixture of styles that extends into her choice of company, here the gray-eyed African American Anderson, and elsewhere, white people. Helga's dreamy enrapture by this body is sharply interrupted when, in the next sentence, the music stops and Helga's friend Anne arrives at the table "with rage in her eyes" (60). A long, heated conversation between Anne and Helga follows, in which Anne recoils from Helga's observation that "[s]he's lovely" and condemns Audrey Denney as a "disgusting creature" who "ought to be ostracized" because she "goes about with white people" and throws racially mixed parties in which "white men dance with the coloured women" — all of which Anne reports in a voice "trembling with cold hatred" (61). Helga challenges Anne's racial policing of sexuality in a series of questions, speaking "with a slowness almost approaching to insolence," until finally she goes quiet, feeling "it would be useless to tell them that what she felt for the beautiful, calm, cool girl who had the assurance, the courage so placidly to ignore racial barriers and give her attention to people, was not contempt, but envious admiration. So she remained silent, watching the girl" (62). It's worth noting here that Helga's attraction to Audrey parallels Irene's attraction to Clare in *Passing,* both in its sensual magnetism and in its admiration (more grudging in Irene's case) of her boldness in racial transgression. The chapter closes with a long paragraph devoted to Helga's observation of Audrey as she dances with Anderson "with grace and abandon, gravely, yet with obvious pleasure, her legs, her hips, her back, all swaying gently, swung by that wild music from the heart of the jungle" (62). The pleasure is obviously Helga's as well.

That is, Audrey Denney is clearly a charged object for Helga Crane (not to mention Anne or Larsen), a point of cathexis for Helga's "jungle" ambivalence as well as her bodily desire. Audrey's pairing with Anderson is also charged insofar as, for Helga, Anderson is directly associated with those "hidden wounds" of her own biracial past. In fact in the second half of this closing paragraph, Helga's emotion begins to encompass both Denney and Anderson in way that conflates them as objects of her desire. The narrator tells us that she began to feel "a more primitive emotion" as she watched them dance. Neither the exact emotion nor the exact object of it is specified in the description that follows, but the pressing, syncopated syntax builds a moment of racial and sexual panic:[17]

> She forgot the garish crowded room. She forgot her friends. She saw only two figures, closely clinging. She felt her heart throbbing. She felt the room receding. She went out the door. She climbed endless stairs. At last, panting, confused, but thankful to have escaped, she found herself again out in the dark night alone, a small crumpled thing in a fragile, flying black and gold dress. A taxi drifted toward her, stopped. She stepped into it, feeling cold, unhappy, misunderstood, and forlorn. (62)

Thus this chapter ends, and the next one opens with Helga on an ocean liner headed across the Atlantic, "glad to be alone at last, free of that superfluity of human beings, yellow, brown, and black" (63). In escaping these bodies, however, Helga is perhaps also escaping her heart's desire, which takes the "lovely" form of the racially and sexually "superfluous" Audrey Denney.

And indeed Helga is drawn back exactly to this superfluity of queer beings who exceed the proper boundaries. Feeling trapped by race again in Copenhagen, she recrosses the Atlantic and immediately attends a polyracial party where she again meets Dr. Anderson, who still carries the shadow-presence of Audrey Denney. In fact Denney is at the party too, and she again momentarily stands, for Helga, at the center of it. As Helga looks around, she sees African Americans, West Indians, a few white people, and "[t]here too, poised, serene, certain, surrounded by masculine black and white, was Audrey Denney" (99). On this occasion, Helga directly asks to be introduced to this woman so oddly "surrounded by masculine black and white."

But this is the event that never occurs, neither in the chapter nor in the book — not until, in displaced form, it perhaps surfaces in Larsen's next novella, *Passing,* in Irene's "Encounter" and "Re-Encounter" (as the book's first two parts title them) with Clare Kendry. In *Quicksand,* Helga's movement toward Denney is interrupted by two men: first, her old fiancé from Naxos, James Vayle (who, like Anne, condemns the racial mixing at the party), and then, finally, in the last paragraph of the chapter, when some of us might be wondering when Helga will meet Audrey Denney, by Anderson, in a physical collision that leads to Helga's final "ruin," as she calls it (108). It is at the Harlem party that this undoing begins, when Helga steps through a doorway, and

somehow, she never quite knew exactly just how, into the arms of Robert Anderson. She drew back and looked up smiling to offer an apology.

And then it happened. He stooped and kissed her, a long kiss, holding her close. She fought against him with all her might. Then, strangely, all power seemed to ebb away, and a long-hidden, half-understood desire welled up in her with the suddenness of a dream. Helga Crane's own arms went up about the man's neck. (104)

Just when Helga begins to face the fact that her "freeing" transatlantic travel is always in some way a return to race; just as she comes to "[t]his knowledge, this certainty of the division in her life into two parts in two lands" (96); just after she has expressed to James Vayle her lack of interest in marriage and children; and just at the moment when she might approach a "lovely" woman she admires — Robert Anderson kisses her.

She draws away from his forceful embrace as "[s]udden anger seized her" and she "pushe[s] him indignantly aside" to return to the party, but meanwhile she has discovered a well of desire within herself. The wording of the text suggests that she discovers desire as a phenomenon of her own being rather than a desire *for* Anderson in particular. In an echo of the depersonalized description in which "Helga Crane's own arms went up about the man's neck," on the following day she finds herself thinking "not so much of the man whose arms had held her as of the ecstasy which had flooded her" during the long kiss, which is the first of that kind she has experienced (104 – 5). (She explains that she "was used to kisses" during her "mild engagement with James Vayle" but "none had been like that of last night" [105]).

In modernism, such kisses mark the turning point—the deflated, debatable, ambiguous, early-twentieth-century version of the swoon—in the protagonist's voyage out. As Richard Dalloway kisses Rachel Vinrace in *The Voyage Out*, as Rochester kisses Bertha in *Wide Sargasso Sea*, as Adele *says* Aziz kisses her in *Passage to India*, Anderson's kiss reignites an old tainted history, the Gothic racial and sexual core of the liberty plot. At this crisis, one can fairly hear the ghosts rattling their chains or see what Rachel Vinrace dreams as the mocking goblins munching in their wet, dark corners, and what Helga calls the "skeletons that stalked lively and in full health through the consciousness of every person of Negro ancestry in America" (96). These kisses seem to initiate the heroine's discovery of her own desire—but in the end they turn that premonition of "ecstasy" into an experience of violation or ruin. Certainly Anderson's kiss reopens the "wound" of Helga's childhood, that sensation, as she describes it, of being "an obscene sore" in other people's lives, which she repeatedly says Anderson recalls for her (29). When he arranges a clandestine meeting with her after this evening of the kiss, despite her hopes for an illicit affair with him (he is now married to Anne), he simply apologizes for his drunken "mistake." Overcome by "this mortification, this feeling of ridicule and self-loathing," she concludes that she "had ruined everything" (108 – 9).

If this kiss interrupts and displaces the pending encounter with Audrey Denney —the queer figure who has aroused Helga's sensual gaze—then the rest of the novel emerges as a reaction not just to the transgressive encounter with Anderson but also as a reaction to the way Anderson comes between Helga Crane and Audrey Denney. Her kiss-gone-astray and the desire it reveals repeat the crime of her mother's out-of-bounds kiss, but, by way of Audrey Denney, Larsen now subtextually hints that the boundaries at issue are as much those of heteronormativity as they are those of race.

Abandoned to Race

Hereafter, Helga becomes a twentieth-century version of the wandering, ruined self in Atlantic modernity. She feels herself "alone, isolated from all other human beings, separated even from her own anterior existence," with "her staggered brain. . . . [d]istracted, agitated, incapable of containing herself" (109 – 10). She wanders back out into the rainy city that is her alien home. And, as in so many novels, that modern landscape is felt as a drowning world: "Rain and wind whipped cruelly about her, drenching her garments and chilling her body," so that she is already "sopping wet" when "the dark clouds opened wider and spilled their water with unusual fury" until "the streets became swirling waters" and "another whirl of wind lashed her and, scornful of her slight strength, tossed her into the swollen gutter" (110). Larsen ironically deflates not only the ruinous kiss but also the accompanying storm that swamps her.

Bathos is perhaps the best term to describe the tone of these final turns in Larsen's novel, as Helga is taken up by the most "ancient" race community she has yet encountered and consummates a religious conversion that completes her return to race. Not only does the narrator stand back at an ambiguous remove from these "redemptive" scenes but Larsen cinches Helga's conversion, ironically, absurdly, via an act of utterly arbitrary, unabashedly sexual freedom. Entering an urban-storefront revival meeting (a peculiarly modern phenomenon),[18] Helga steps into old, layered time and community ritual that will later culminate in her feeling that "centuries" pass as she lives through marriage and repeated child-labor: "people were singing a song which she was conscious of having heard years ago — hundreds of years it seemed" (129, 134, 111). Surrounded by "a hundred pairs of eyes," she is called out with "Bacchic vehemence" by the crowd of worshippers (111, 113). With her modern, wandering self "so torn, so aching," Helga begins to weep, then to sob "with great racking sobs" (112). The congregation calls out for the conversion of this "pore los' Jezebel!" this "scarlet 'oman," "our errin' sistah" (112). Suddenly feeling she might retch, Helga holds herself very still: "in that moment she was lost — or saved" (113).[19] By leaving the matter of whether Helga is "lost — or saved" undecided, Larsen holds us in a hovering position. The chapter ends with the narrator markedly stepping back from the consciousness of Helga (who becomes a "kneeling girl") to observe that "to the kneeling girl time seemed to sink back into the mysterious grandeur and holiness of far-off simpler centuries" (114). Helga has moved beyond the narrator's access as she returns to the ancient fold — freed into race-community in confessing herself a Jezebel.

Larsen implicitly keeps her attitude of irony in play when she casts Helga's final entry into this ancient community as a moment of an "abandoned" sexual agency. Helped home after her conversion experience by the Reverend Mr. Pleasant Green, "the fattish yellow man" (also a descendant of ruin, as suggested by his skin color), and suddenly realizing that he is attracted to her (he shudders involuntarily with desire when she leans on his arm "to keep herself from falling"), Helga has a flash of insight: "across her still half-hypnotized consciousness little burning darts of fancy had shot themselves. . . . That man! Was it possible?

As easy as that?" She initially rejects this fancy of taking the man to bed: "No. She couldn't. It would be too awful" (115). But then she realizes just how completely free her "lack of family" and her rootlessness have made her: "Just the same, what or who was there to hold her back? Nothing. Simply nothing. Nobody. Nobody at all" (115). So she takes the Reverend home and sleeps with him and the next day marries him. While most critics read this scene as part of Helga's struggle with sexual repression, I see no such struggle against "repression" in Helga but rather a grappling with her *position* as a sexual subject.[20] She equivocally glosses her intention to have him marry her as a manipulative move ("How could he, a naive creature, hold out against her?" [117]), and at the same time a divinely directed entry into a state of grace — for now "she had found some One, some Power, who was interested in her. Would help her" (117). In this act — of being saved by being lost — she thinks perhaps she has finally freed herself into a true community. She goes "home" to the South, but there she will learn that she is from the North, and still a race outsider.

As Larsen makes clear, Helga is free, after all, only to choose race. The lure of freedom keeps snaring her in the trap of race; and race makes her a lost jezebel. In the book's final paragraphs we learn that she has come to despise her husband, and after giving birth to several children by him she finds herself once again overcome with "this feeling of dissatisfaction, of asphyxiation" (134). Although she spends sickly hours in her bed dreaming of "freedom and cities," while a nurse reads Anatole France's fiction about republican polity,[21] the novel's last sentence casts doubt on her fantasy of freedom and the narrator moves out of her consciousness to report its closing words that "she began to have her fifth child" (135).

IN LARSEN'S FICTION, we have traveled a long way (or a "fur piece," as Faulkner's "fallen" and traveling Lena Grove says) from Richardson's *Clarissa*. Clarissa's interiorized character unfolds through letters in a rich intermingling with the epistolary privacy of others; in the end the isolated tragedy of her experience becomes a matter of public record and an occasion for community reconstruction. In Larsen, the (queer) interior, like the future, is left unknowable. Just as, in *Passing*, we never know if Irene pushed Clare, which mirrors the way Irene never gets to the bottom of Brian's, or her own, "affair" with the queer Clare, in *Quicksand*, we never return to the figure of Audrey Denney, and at the close of the novel we are left suspended in Helga's racial predicament, as she is herself.[22] Furthermore, at the ends of both *Passing* and *Quicksand*, Larsen's protagonists are more sharply divided and isolated from community than ever — as with the characters in Toomer's *Cane* or in Faulkner's novels, works also shot through with homoerotic desire and racial violence. Larsen's final, narrational "removal" from her protagonists reinforces their isolation from community even as it represents the community's utter absorption of them.[23]

While Larsen keeps us just outside her community's and heroine's interiors through her use of limited point of view, her novels establish her own stance as critical onlooker, positioned at least partially outside her community. That is, these novels, especially *Quicksand,* adopt a deeply critical stance toward the Harlem community of which Larsen was also a part. In fact, given her acerbic critique of the African American, upper-middle-class community, Larsen might have been surprised at the positive reviews of *Passing* and *Quicksand.* On the contrary, however, these outsiders' stories solidified her role as a Harlem insider. It seems that, as for Hawthorne and Eliot, her authorial acts of defiance proved her embrace of freedom — her transcendence of race, for the race. Thus the tradition's paradoxes had their reward for Larsen, although only momentarily in her lifetime. That is, in Larsen the interior struggle with race-consciousness created a place of narration and has to some extent organized a community of readers around her "freeing," individual voice — exactly the achievement won in the previous three centuries by narrators of history and fiction in their tales of exiles, recluses, and ruptured community. W. E. B. Du Bois found Larsen's novels inspiring for the future of black America; while more recent critics understand her heroines as "powerful, independent" and "resisting subjects."[24] One critic pinpoints the paradox when she remarks that Larsen's *Quicksand* "marks the beginning of greater freedom for self-examination and narrative experimentation in the writing of black American women."[25] Thus once more is the reading and writing of novels bound up with the promise of entry into another, freer future — which nonetheless remains racially defined.

As George Hutchinson points out, insofar as Larsen herself had a mixed lineage and apparently struggled with exclusion from family because of it, when critics deem her a strictly African American writer they recreate the very boundaries she faced and questioned.[26] If she could sit among her twenty-first-century readers, she might challenge any strict racial claims on her legacy. For Larsen was a kind of kamikaze queen of race. With her stark lucidity and honesty, she seems to have been ready to watch herself go up in flames if that's what it took to explode the paradoxes of race and freedom. The fact that her writing career did go up in flames, perhaps through an act of her own, offers a final lens through which to view Larsen's critical Atlantic project.

Rewriting the Theft of Freedom

Instead of *Quicksand* or *Passing*, it was Larsen's ironically titled story "Sanctuary" that "ruined" her. As we know, Larsen was accused of plagiarizing this story from Sheila Kaye-Smith's story "Mrs. Adis," but no one will ever know if Larsen did indeed read Kaye-Smith's story and consciously, unconsciously, or half-consciously take its story for "Sanctuary." In both stories, a man on the run (after shooting someone who catches him stealing) seeks asylum with the mother of a friend; in both cases the flinty mothers reluctantly harbor the men, in both cases for the sake of their sons who have been friends and protectors of the renegade men, as well as out of solidarity with the dispossessed — in "Mrs. Adis" with "poachers" against "keepers" and in "Sanctuary" with Jim as a "po niggah" against his "white folk" pursuers (23). Both stories finally reveal that, in their flight, the renegades have mistakenly shot the sons of the very women who are shielding them. Both mothers choose not to betray their sons' murderers. Though Kaye-Smith's story is set in Sussex County, England, and Larsen's in the U.S. South, both open remarkably similarly, with the men approaching the lonely cottages of the women, looking through the side windows at them before circling back to enter through the door, without knocking — the latter detail emphasized in both.

Given the striking similarities, it's hard to imagine that Larsen had never read Kaye-Smith's story; it seems likely she did and lodged it somewhere in her mind. I am going to proceed as if she did and then later reconfigured it within the U.S. frame of race — with whatever degree of (un)consciousness — rather than try to explain or dismiss this possibility.[27] This approach allows me to give Larsen the credit she deserves for this act of revision, as I understand it to be, for her recasting allows her to offer a piercingly astute anatomy of transatlantic history. Larsen's changes overlay, on Kaye-Smith's story of class in England, the story of race in the United States, encoding the historical interrelation of race and property on the Atlantic. Indeed, to read "Sanctuary" this way makes clear that Larsen was not stealing: she was writing a revisionary history of "stealing."

If we heed the history narrated by Peter Linebaugh and Marcus Rediker in *The Many-Headed Hydra* as well as the colonial history outlined in chapter 1, the characters in these two stories have much in common in terms of material conditions and historical causes, which Larsen implicitly signals in her merging of the two stories. The enclosure of land and the practice of poaching that create the drama of Kaye-Smith's story intersect, in history, with the slave economy that creates the drama of Larsen's. Just as she links the racial mindset of the transatlantic middle classes of Denmark and America in *Quicksand,* so in creating "Sanctuary" Larsen juxtaposes the ruthless policing and impossible predicaments of laborers on both sides of the Atlantic economy. As Linebaugh and Rediker document, the expropriation of common lands in England in the sixteenth and seventeenth centuries, operating together with the turn to a mercantile and manufacturing economy, led to a massive impoverishment and displacement of peasants. These displacements and the wage-labor economy not only were fed by the emergent Atlantic economy but they also found their "outlet," quite literally, in colonization schemes in the Americas, whereby displaced people and petty thieves would be exported as bondservants to the colonies, further laying the foundation for England's own manufacturing and trade wealth. This colonization, in its turn, contributed to the creation of the Atlantic triangle, the slave trade, and the virulent black/white racism of the United States.

Thus the enclosure of commons in England that began the centuries-long war between "poachers" and "keepers" portrayed in Kaye-Smith's text prepares the ground for the racialized drama of theft and displacement in Larsen's story. When Larsen "steals" from an Englishwoman to tell her story, in fact she is stealing back what was long ago stolen — a story of herself initiated in effect by the propertied forces in England that generated the terms of both the original story and her own. Larsen indicates that her story is a later and grimmer symptom of the same modern economy that creates Kaye-Smith's drama when she replaces Kaye-Smith's "great tongue of land [that] runs into Kent by Scotney Castle" with "a strip of desolation . . . between the sea and old fields of ruined plantations." And she signals that this setting has given rise to and given way to the continuing force of modernity when she further places her protagonist's house on this strip and along a road "little used, now that the state has built its new highway a bit to the west and wagons are less numerous than automobiles" (21). Kaye-Smith may be the unfortunate loser in this borrowing, through no fault of her own, but given the ironic twist in Kaye-Smith's story catalyzed by an act of theft, it's possible that Kaye-Smith herself had an inkling of the impossible positions, the irrecoverable losses, the paradoxes of complicity, theft, and compassion created when the principle of ownership reigns supreme. Of course, plagiarism itself — its designation as theft — is likewise an effect of the forces of modernity that make all things property, all art individual, and all claims to common land — or shared printed materials — criminal.

So it's no coincidence that the tale Larsen apparently "steals" is the tale of a marginal woman's attempt to secure freedom for a man of her class/race but which, in the end, in a battle over property, entails her own loss and isolation. The women, these mothers, enable the criminal men's survival, though in doing so they harbor the murderers of their own sons — a kind of reverse-Oedipal drama in modernity, a "Gordian knot," to recall the Putney debater's characterization. Interestingly, in both stories the sons who get shot by their renegade friends are upright citizens who have struck some kind of compromise with the ruthless system that will kill a man for stealing a rabbit or a tire (as the lawmen assure the mothers they will do when the catch the thieves). In Kaye-Smith's story, Mrs. Adis's son is indeed in company with the keepers of Scotney Castle when Crouch shoots and runs, after illegally catching a rabbit; and in "Sanctuary," Annie's son Obabiah is among those who chase Jim for stealing tires. Larsen reinforces this point when the white sheriff condescendingly calls Annie's son "a mighty fine boy" and wishes "they was all like him" (27).

Both Kaye-Smith and Larsen establish this predicament clearly. Initially, before they learn that the renegades have killed their sons, both women accept these men's acts of theft. They agree to hide them from the law in a spirit of solidarity. Mrs. Adis remarks that "shooting a keeper ain't the same as shooting an ordinary sort of man, as we all know, and maybe he ain't so much the worse" — though she will "have it on my conscience for having helped you to escape the law" (122). In Larsen's "Sanctuary," as "a look of irony, of cunning, of complicity passed over her face," Annie Poole finds herself " 'siderin' all an all, how Obadiah's right fon' o' you, an' how white folks is white folks, Ah'm gwine hide you dis one time" (23). Their remarks inadvertently align their sons with the very forces of law that the women are content to subvert. The women's "complicity" is with illegality, while their sons have been loyal to the rule of law that protects property. Thus do these stories return to that question of property that haunts and impels the Putney Debates and the whole matter of the social contract; and Larsen reinserts the Atlantic racializations that have historically extended the monopoly of property.

In the end, both mothers feel the impossibility of the positions they occupy between law and lawlessness, Annie Poole more sharply. In Annie, race loyalty and rage are fused. In Kaye-Smith's story, after Mrs. Adis learns of her son Tom's death and the representatives of the law leave, she simply opens the door of Peter's hiding place in her lean-to and walks away from him without speaking. Notably, Larsen revises this detail, conjuring the intimate violations of African American women entailed in the Atlantic pursuit of liberty.[28] In "Sanctuary," Jim hides by laying "his soiled body and grimy garments between [Annie's] snowy white sheets," over which she then places "piles of freshly laundered linen" (24). Once the sheriff leaves Annie's house, she goes to Jim in her bedroom and speaks with "a raging fury in her voice as she lashed out, 'Git outer mah feather baid, Jim Hammer, an' outen mah house, an don' nevah stop thankin' yo' Jesus he done gob you dat black face'" (27). The "dirt-caked feet" he pushes out from the covers and uses for his final flight from her house leave their physical marks on her bed, as her paradoxical authorizing of her own son's death registers in the fury in her voice.

Perhaps, then, Larsen recognized her story in Kaye-Smith's and performed her own act of expropriation. If so, she daringly, perhaps inescapably, walked the line between truth and lies, fiction and history, and private and common — as her fictionalizations of her own family history indicate. And perhaps her borrowing from "Mrs. Adis" betrays a subconscious wish to see this line dissolve, a kind of haunting by a dream in which the theft of identity she lived privately is made transparent to the public sphere. This seems credible given the hints in her fiction that she well understood the terms offered by a contractual yet racialized society especially to a woman without "people" (and also married to an "unfaithful" husband, as she herself was).

Indeed, in this light, a pattern of suicide in Larsen's fiction takes on new significance. In *Quicksand,* Helga considers but rejects suicide. *Passing* ends with a woman falling to her death from a window, an act that might or might not be suicide.[29] An early short story similarly closes with a man jumping out a window, despairing when he learns of the death of a mistress he has earlier cruelly abandoned. This story is called "Freedom." In the aftermath of her divorce (apparently provoked in part by her husband's infidelity), newspapers carried rumors that Larsen herself fell from a window and broke her leg. Once more we encounter the window to freedom that is no exit.[30]

All these "unfortunate falls" among the lonely and the ruined replay the story of Atlantic modernity that Larsen so adroitly made into fiction. Her final, authorial "bond" with Sheila Kaye-Smith, then, provides a mordant comment on her own, somehow queer, entanglement in this story. And this entanglement also creates her kinship with another British storyteller named Virginia Woolf, a woman likewise immersed in the suicide-inducing waters of Atlantic modernity.

16 | Woolf's Queer Atlantic Oeuvre

These waters were unfathomably deep.
Into them had spilled so many lives . . .

NO OTHER ENGLISH-LANGUAGE novelist's work is as completely flooded with waves, water, wrecks, and drowning as Virginia Woolf's. It seems she lived imaginatively, as she died bodily, in the world's watery currents. The very syntax of her sentences sets us plunging, listing, surging, and sometimes swamps us. Postcolonial readings of Woolf most often consider her in relation to India, sensibly, since it is the most frequently referenced imperial locale in her work, and they give some attention to the South American setting in *The Voyage Out*. If, however, we consider the water tropes in her writing as expressions of the colonial legacy more broadly, we can better plumb the depth of her brooding on things imperial. And on things material and sexual, as they are taken up by Anglo-Atlantic empire and perhaps beckon beyond it. Woolf wrote elegies for the bodies and the sexualities drowned within this empire, forging a queer art implicated in and yet presiding over the end of British empire.

Woolf's novels repeatedly recast the Atlantic story of liberty and ruin. As Larsen does for African-Atlantic modernity, so Woolf writes revisionary parables of Anglo-Atlantic modernity.[1] In *The Voyage Out, Jacob's Room, Mrs. Dalloway, To the Lighthouse*, and *The Waves* — the texts I consider here — Woolf charts the stories of those who drown and those who survive in the British colonial economy. In her first novel, *The Voyage Out*, Rachel Vinrace's literal Atlantic crossing into colonial territory leads at once to her discovery of sexuality and to her death, cast as a drowning. Seaside wandering leads to sexual shock in the very opening of *Jacob's Room*, when Jacob as a young boy happens on a man and woman making love on the beach; and the sea continues to be the scene of sexual awakenings and drownings, including homoerotically charged ones, in this novel that also ends with the lover-protagonist's premature death. Clarissa Dalloway, by contrast, survives the capsizing of her homoerotic desires but stands half-unwilling witness to the "sinking" psychological death of Lady Bradshaw and, most centrally, the suicidal "plunge" of the Shakespeare-loving, war-shattered Septimus, who, in mourning his loss of Evans, feels like "a drowned sailor, on the shore of the world."[2] Mrs. Ramsay dies more figuratively in a storm at sea, after which her son and daughter agree during their belated sea-crossing to "fight tyranny" — in the person of their father — while Lily, the woman artist, stands on a cliff revisiting her love for Mrs. Ramsay and representing the whole drama (93). In *The Waves*, the novel I discuss at most length, the tides that encircle the six characters also carry the native barbarian Percival to his colonial death, signaling, in their ebbing, the faltering of empire at its sublime height. Meanwhile, Woolf implies that this entire story of the rise and fall of empire is being written by a sheltered woman in a walled garden, a garden tended by servants "sweeping, sweeping."

Increasingly in these works, as suggested by the last image, we see Woolf registering her own, the writing Anglo woman's position within the imperial, maritime culture that she critiques. Like other modernists, Woolf eschews the epic stance and instead merges her narrators with her characters' interiors, and, also like other modernists, Woolf signals, via embedded artist figures, her art's witnessing yet implicated position within empire. Woolf develops a form of narration that recasts the Atlantic-Protestant desire to make the inner transparent to the outer world and in the process rewrites the sexual swoon as a drowning of all unraced, unbordered sexuality. While sharing the Puritan desire for transparency or full "manifestation" of the interior (in contrast, for instance, to Gertrude Stein or the communist Dadaists or the "withholding" Nella Larsen), she works to air and thereby dissolve the possessive urge to master the other's presence and body. She explores the encounter between self and other "otherwise," aiming to de-police the surveillance of the interior while still narrating the fugitive possibilities of gay sexuality. Finally, she more fleetingly exposes, as well, by way of the gardeners, servants, and housecleaners who appear in her fiction, how the sexual coercion at the heart of empire installs a hierarchy of labor.[3] I focus here on the Atlantic tropes by which Woolf illuminates the fundamental relationship between race, class, empire, and sexuality; and I consider the narrative powers by which she ambiguously represents and reshapes that relationship.

The Failed Launch; or, Milton Vindicated

When, in *The Voyage Out,* we witness Richard Dalloway kissing Rachel Vinrace in the wake of an Atlantic sea storm on her father's mercantile ship heading to South America for trade, we know that Woolf has set out to retell the English-language novel's founding story. On close look, every detail resonates. The Atlantic crossing associated with a racialized sexual ruin, the American mercantile enterprise of the Flushings, who seek and sell "native" goods, the allusions to Milton's work, the breaking of a female homosocial bond and replacement with a brotherly, bookish, heterosexual one, and the final "drowning" of Rachel all reveal Woolf to be consciously or unconsciously exploring the Atlantic plot.

Like *Quicksand, The Voyage Out* follows the journey of a (virtually) orphaned, uncertain heroine as she wanders the Atlantic and gets taken up by a community whose reproductive mandate for her finally kills her. On the ship the *Euphrosyne,* two brothers and one sister-in-law gather—the other, missing sister-in-law is Rachel's mother, who died when Rachel was a small child (she is also "the one woman Helen called friend" and who Helen suspects of having been bullied by her husband, Helen's brother-in-law). These adults chaperone the motherless daughter Rachel on her visit to an English villa in South America, along the way passing British Navy ships that inspire Richard Dalloway's encomium to British values.

This sea crossing is cast as a launch toward freedom from the outset. On the first morning of their journey, as they all rise together to the deck, Helen exclaims, "Oh, look! We're out at sea!" and the narrator remarks on their state of feeling: "They were free of roads, free of mankind, and the same exhilaration at their freedom ran through them all."[4] Yet shortly after Rachel finds herself alone on deck, and "down she looked into the depth of the sea," imagining the "black ribs of wrecked ships" (27). Insofar as the ship also gets figured as an image of Rachel ("a bride going forth to her husband" in a state "more lonely than the caravan crossing the desert" and on a sea that "might give her death, or some unexampled joy" [19]), the image of shipwreck prefigures Rachel's own fate.

Rachel's symbolic ruin on this journey begins with Richard Dalloway's surreptitious kiss as his wife lies below deck recovering from seasickness after the storm in which they are all temporarily "unmoored" like "atoms flying in the void" (72). Wandering the deck in the wake of the storm, he and Rachel literally collide and then retreat to her room. On cue, just after Dalloway offers to send her Burke's pamphlets on "the French revolution—The American Rebellion," there follows the symbolic sexual fall associated, in the Atlantic imaginary, with these revolutions. The ship lurches, and Dalloway seizes the moment to "kiss her passionately, so that she felt the hardness of his body" after which she "fell back in her chair, with tremendous beats of the heart, each of which sent black waves across her eyes" (76). Rachel afterward vacillates between feeling "a strange exultation" and "a chill of body and mind" (76). Her sleep that night is disturbed by nightmares.

Overdetermined nightmares. Colonial nightmares. Swooning nightmares in which Rachel symbolically dies and then awakens into a "barbarian" surround. She dreams that she is trapped in a vault with "a little deformed man who squatted on the floor gibbering with long nails . . . and the face of an animal. The wall behind him oozed with damp. . . . Still and cold as death she lay, not daring to move, until she broke the agony by tossing herself across the bed, and woke crying 'Oh!'" (77). Awaking from this terrorized, deathlike state, "she felt herself pursued, so that she got up and actually locked her door. A voice moaned for her; eyes desired her. All night long barbarian men harassed the ship; they came scuffling down passages, and stopped to snuffle at her door" (77). She "could not sleep again," but the next day dawns on a calm sea, with the ship "anchored at another shore" as the Dalloways prepare to depart (78). Rachel has arrived in Atlantic modernity.

In conflating, via Rachel's nightmares, the crass actions of Richard Dalloway with the threat of "barbarian men" whose "animal" faces "snuffle" at Rachel's door and "harass" the ship, Woolf reenacts the long Atlantic history of substitutions in which the coercions of colonizing Anglo-Atlantic peoples get reframed, in white people's imaginations, as the threat of the colonized. She follows the logic in which "barbarian men" become the fall guys for Anglo-Atlantic subjects, for the English-proud Richard Dalloways. Instead of choosing to see this reenactment in Woolf as *either* a troubled repetition of this history *or* as a conscious critique of it, I suggest that it is both. Like many other early-twentieth-century writers, Woolf is working within the ubiquitous racial discourse of barbarity, and like some others she is awakening to its violence while at the same time her imagination is infiltrated and shaped by it.

That is, when Woolf invokes images of "barbarian men," which appear throughout her fiction, she is both expressing and critiquing a fear.[5] In particular, the fact that these figures take on characteristics that recall her own memories of sexual violation at the hands of a stepbrother indicates the ways that this fear carries the two interconnected histories we have been considering; it repeats the merging, in the Atlantic imaginary, of the sexual violation of women with the violation of colonized peoples. For in "A Sketch of the Past," Woolf's memory of Gerald Duckworth's molestations is closely associated with "a horrible face — the face of an animal," the latter phrase echoing verbatim her description of the squatting man of whom Rachel dreams (69).[6] Woolf allows her own trauma to find expression within Rachel's colonialist imagery.

Yet in *The Voyage Out*, without wholly escaping her own fears and investments, Woolf also calls explicit attention to the fact that these images are *representations*.[7] First of all, these images of barbarian men are rendered as Rachel's nightmare *projections*, not a narrator's neutral descriptions. More telling is the embroidery that Helen Ambrose works on throughout the novel. Early in their sea passage, we learn that Helen is sewing "a great design of a tropical river running through a tropical forest" where spotted deer "browsed" upon "pomegranates" and "a troop of naked natives whirled darts into the air" (33). The conventional colonialist juxtaposition of innocent deer (eating the fruit associated with the ruined daughter Persephone) against weapon-wielding "native" men in a tropical forest already hints at Woolf's self-consciousness about such images and their bearing on her story.

In case we should mistake her meaning, Woolf explicitly, indeed heavy-handedly, places this artwork of Helen's beside other "texts" of the Anglo-Atlantic world. The first time we see Helen embroidering, she has a philosophy book perched open next to her: "Between the stitches she looked to one side and read a sentence about the Reality of Matter, or the Nature of Good. Round her men in blue jerseys knelt and scrubbed the boards . . . while not far off Mr. Pepper sat cutting up roots with a penknife" (33). Woolf gives a more conscious and satirical version of the dissociated world of Brockden Brown's *Wieland* in which "abstruse" discussions of science and ethics occur amid the "repulsion of Indians," and at the same time she nods toward the element of representation when she places Helen's visual embroidery of naked natives next to these highly intellectual, presumably barbarian-transcending texts.[8] At the same time Woolf includes in this scene both the amateur colonial geographer and botanist Mr. Pepper, whose name conjures Eastern trade, and the men in blue jerseys scrubbing the deck, whose presence establishes the class infrastructure of this colonial economy. These details make manifest Woolf's conscious interest in capturing all the elements of the Atlantic world in which Helen and Rachel are traveling.

Not surprisingly, then, Rachel's journey into heterosexuality also entails a journey upriver where she encounters South American village women whose "faces were an oily brown" and which, to Rachel, "did not look like faces. . . . She owned that she knew nothing about them" (212). Again here, as Rachel owns that she knows nothing about these women, Woolf likewise settles for a representation of their faces as merely "oily brown." At the same time, Woolf implicitly registers the losses, in particular, of potential female relationships across these barriers. This failed encounter with the women directly follows the purging of the homoerotic bond between Helen and Rachel, in which Helen pursues Rachel as she runs off through high grasses, tackles her, and after their charged, laughing tumble, in effect hands Rachel over to Terence Hewitt.[9] As Woolf tells it, Rachel's story is one in which female connections — with South American women as with Helen, and originally with her mother — are prematurely foreclosed by the mercantile and colonial conditions of her life, which ultimately leads to Rachel's death.

Rachel's death by colonial fever reinforces this point. Her delirium brings on hallucinations of threatening barbarian men, as well as of overwhelming waves that pull her under, ending with her sense, at the moment of death, that she is "curled up at the bottom of the sea" (341). Her delirious cry shortly before she dies — "There it falls!" — conjures the whole Atlantic legacy of colonial swooning and ruin (339). The marriage that Rachel and Hewitt had imagined, one of equality and "perfect freedom," turns out to be impossible within "all these barriers" (301, 303). Rachel loses her "war waged on behalf of things like stones, jars, and wreckage at the bottom of the sea," even as the novel begins what will be a key part of Woolf's fictional project: the diving and dredging work that might catalogue these losses.[10] Fittingly, as Rachel dies, Ridley Ambrose paces the terrace quoting John Milton — the novel's perhaps unconscious way of allowing Milton to say, I told you so. By way of this ending, and also in light of references to Milton's *Comus* throughout the novel (Milton's poetic drama about a young woman entranced and held captive in an underwater world by an evil magician), Woolf frames the event of Rachel's Atlantic "drowning" within a "native," Anglo-Atlantic literary legacy.[11]

Queer Elegies: *Jacob's Room*

In Woolf's novels, as just barely hinted in the wrestling-play of Helen and Rachel, ruin on the seas of empire expresses the loss not only of an innocent or unviolated self but also of a certain possibility, a certain other way of being among stones, jars, and bodies that is not thoroughly regulated by racial empire and its brotherly, heterosexual republics — a luxuriously queer way of being. What in *Bordering on the Body* I describe (borrowing Maurice Merleau-Ponty's term) as Woolf's "intercorporeal" vision of bodies-in-the-world also encompasses gay sexual desires — as well as unmoored straight ones and whatever might fall in between. As Woolf herself put it, "Where people mistake is in perpetually narrowing and naming these immensely composite and wide-flung passions."[12] While a number of critics have brought to the surface the plentiful gay or queer currents of Woolf's writing, only Robin Hackett has developed an extended analysis of their turbulent convergence with the tides of empire, focusing mainly on *The Waves*.[13] But even before *The Waves*, in *Jacob's Room* and *Mrs. Dalloway*, Woolf writes elegies for her characters' queer attractions, aiming to capture the breeching and capsizing of these desires within Atlantic empire as well as to acknowledge their merging with empire's oceanic force.

As no one can fail to notice, *Jacob's Room* is soaked with the sea. Reading it is like discovering one of those saturated objects lost at sea that Rachel wished to defend. It begins with Jacob at seaside, narrates his sea crossings and sea storms, sets a pivotal and queerly sexual moment on a boat, foreshadows his death in war as a drowning of soldier-sailors, and, on its penultimate page, merges the sound of the sea with the sound of distant guns just before we learn of Jacob's death, apparently at war. Woolf establishes that she means to probe a little more deeply into the "chasms" in Atlantic history, with its wars, empires, exiles at sea, and capsized desires, when her narrator at one point steps aside to comment:

> The strange thing about life is that though the nature of it must have been ap-
> parent to everyone for hundreds of years, no on has left any adequate account
> of it. The streets of London have their map; but our passions are uncharted.
> What are you going to meet if you turn this corner?
>
> "Holborn straight ahead of you," says the policeman. Ah, but where are you
> going if instead of brushing past the old man with the white beard, the silver
> medal, and the cheap violin, you let him go on with his story, . . . he shows you
> a collection of birds' eggs and a letter from the Prince of Wales's secretary, and
> this (skipping the intermediate stages) brings you one winter's day [with him]
> to the Essex coast, where the little boat makes off to the ship, and the ship sails
> and you behold on the skyline the Azores; and the flamingoes rise; and there
> you sit on the verge of the marsh drinking rum-punch, an outcast from civi-
> lization, for you have committed a crime, are infected with the yellow fever as
> likely as not, and—fill in the sketch as you like.
>
> As frequent as street corners in Holborn are these chasms in the continuity
> of our ways. Yet we keep straight on.[14]

Embedded in the middle paragraph is the old story of sea and empire that touches and shapes all those you might meet around a corner in Holborn—the story of ships and fevers and crimes committed, fill in the sketch as you like. These stories harbor the chasms in "the continuity of our ways," the swoons in our sea crossings.

Woolf's narrator, filling in the sketch, while making us experience one such chasm, leaps abruptly in the next paragraph to the story of a paradigmatic "Helen and Jimmy" and the crisis of Jimmy's refusal to marry Helen. The narrator reports that the community's gossipers, "kind Mr. Bowley and dear Rose Shaw" ("who was re-born every evening precisely as the clock stuck eight"), deplore Jimmy's refusal, for it looms as a threatening chasm in their ways. In a seeming non sequitur (and another textual chasm) the narrator then suddenly turns to the reader and remarks that "if you persist that a command of the English language is a part of our inheritance, one can only reply that beauty is almost always dumb. Male beauty in association with female beauty breeds in the onlooker a sense of fear. Often have I seen them — Helen and Jimmy — and likened them to ships adrift, and feared for my own little craft" (83). These comments imply that, far from embodying "our inheritance" of a sophisticated, articulate civilization, Helen and Jimmy, and their policing admirers, are ships on the loose doing damage. Woolf's prose follows their lurching, crashing movements.

These odd juxtapositions and shifts are typical of *Jacob's Room*. The narrative not only stays behind, so to speak, at the end of a scene to capture what's lost in the chasm — the emptiness of a room from which humans have departed, or the ravaging winds of a sea storm to which sleepers are indifferent — but it also habitually swerves (in a way reminiscent of Pauline Hopkins's disjunctive style) from the trivial matchmaking of the Bowleys and Shaws to the epic destruction of war. Woolf's juxtapositions consistently imply that normative sexuality is at stake in war and its attendant colonial crimes, and that apparently harmless gossip about who should marry whom carries behind it an immense and deadly "force." Thus in another scene, just after the gossipers dissect what they consider Clara Durrant's "alarming" depths of feeling (which might swamp her proper choice of partner) and then coyly refer to Dick Bonamy as a "dark horse" with a "peculiar disposition" (this man who by his own account "couldn't love a woman" [135, 122]), the narrator suddenly turns to the scene of a fleet of battleships on the North Sea:

> At a given signal all the guns are trained on a target which (the master gunner counts the seconds, watch in hand — at the sixth he looks up) flames into splinters. With equal nonchalance a dozen young men in the prime of life descend with composed faces into the depths of sea; and there impassively (though with perfect mastery of machinery) suffocate uncomplainingly together. . . .
>
> These actions, together with the incessant commerce of banks, laboratories, chancellories, and houses of business, are the strokes which oar the world forward, they say. And they are dealt with by men as smoothly sculpted as the impassive policeman at Ludgate Circus. But you will observe that far from being padded to rotundity his face is stiff from force of will, and lean from the effort of keeping it so. When his right arm rises, all the force in his veins flows

straight from shoulder to finger-tips; not an ounce is diverted into sudden impulses, sentimental regrets, wire-drawn distinctions. The buses punctually stop.

It is thus that we live, they say, driven by an unseizable force. They say that the novelists never catch it . . . This, they say, is what we live by — this unseizable force. (136)

Woolf's novel strays out of the reach of exactly this force. At the same time, she "catches" it by stepping back from it and framing its nonchalant drowning of a dozen young men.

And she foreshadows the fact that Jacob's sexuality will be caught up in this deadly force — is already invaded by it — when she depicts him, as he travels through Italy and Greece, reading about slums and the Irish question in the *Daily Mail,* while also wishing for the companionship of his intimate friend Dick Bonamy and thinking about his attraction to Clara Durrant. As he reads, Jacob reflects on the human "gift for illusion" that fills the "superfluous imagination" with romantic ideas about Greece, France, Italy, "and India almost for a certainty," and then suddenly "from being moderately depressed he became like a man who is about to be executed" (120–21). Recalling that "Clara Durrant had left him at a party to talk to an American called Pilchard" and condemning again the "nonsense" of talk and behavior at such parties, he looks up to see an old Greek woman "who refused to budge" for a tram that "rang imperiously" (121). He feels that in this woman's defiant stance "the whole of civilization was being condemned" (121). Immediately, he is engulfed by "this gloom — this surrender to the dark waters which lap us about," falling into a depressed mood which, the narrator remarks, is "a modern invention" (121). Although he momentarily fantasizes going into Parliament and making speeches about the world's problems, he asks, "[B]ut what use are fine speeches, once you surrender an inch to the black waters?" He concludes that an underlying cause for "the ebb and flow [of unhappiness] in our veins" is the combination of "respectability and evening parties," "wretched slums," "the British Empire," and the question of "giving Home Rule to Ireland" (121). Jacob seems here to discern the terms of his interpellation, his calling out into the nonsense of cocktail parties and the glory of heroic parliamentary speeches, which, however, fail to distract him, as they are supposed to, from questioning the slums and coercions and insistently ringing bells of empire. The black waters holding drowned objects and bodies threaten to sink him. And in the end they do.

Yet, before that denouement, Woolf follows another boat and records a flirtatious capsizing in this story of Jacob, evading at least temporarily the unseizable force, skirting its black waters. The boat is not a gunner but a small kayak that carries two men, friends, in this case Jacob and Timmy Durrant (Clara's brother), reading Shakespeare and eating lunch together as they sail to the Scilly Isles to visit Durrant's family. The strokes that "oar" *this* world forward are intimate ones between two men as they strip and swim and sail nude and quarrel over lunch preparations. Woolf hints indirectly at the errant erotic undercurrent propelling their excursion:

> [Timmy Durrant . . .] with a sprout of beard, looking sternly at the stars, then at a compass, . . . would have moved a woman. Jacob, of course, was not a woman. The sight of Timmy Durrant was no sight for him, nothing to set against the sky and worship; far from it. They had quarreled. Why the right way to open a tin of beef, with Shakespeare on board, under conditions of such splendour, should have turned them to sulky schoolboys, none can tell. . . . Ships have been wrecked here. (38)

Although "none can tell" why two young men might become sulky in a scene presided over by Shakespeare (who Jacob places even above the Greeks, and Richard Dalloway in Woolf's next novel deplores for his sonnets that invite us to peep through keyholes), and although Woolf's narrator doth protest (too much) about the possibility that Jacob could be moved by the sight of Durrant, Woolf broadly hints at her gay subtext when she has Jacob undress, swim, and bathe "naked" at the very moment when Shakespeare is knocked overboard, "floating merrily away . . . he went under" (39). The narrator ends her description with a vision of "waves breaking unseen by anyone" and the whole bay rising "to heaven in a kind of ecstasy" (39).

The ecstasy is quickly followed by (postcoital?) sorrow, however, so that "the cottage smoke droops, [and] has the look of a mourning emblem, a flag floating its caress over a grave" (39). In Greece, this "sadness would be routed by strangeness and excitement and the nudge of a classical education" — in other words, a community of male intimacy — but on the Cornish hills, "the chimneys and the coast-guard stations and the little bays with waves breaking unseen by anyone make one remember the overpowering sorrow." "And what can this sorrow be?" the narrator asks. And then answers: "It comes from the houses on the coast. We start transparent, and then the cloud thickens. All history backs our panes of glass. To escape is vain" (40).

A seaside history of coast-guard stations saps the possibility of male intimacy, making ecstasy sorrowful. As the novel unfolds, Jacob will vacillate between straight and gay desires — on the one hand, as he travels, wistfully recalling Clara Durrant and drawn toward the traveling Sandra Wentworth Williams; and on the other hand, thinking always of his friend Dick Bonamy, suppressing impulses to write and tell him to come join him in Greece. Sorrow shadows him throughout his travels and all the way back to England, where, when we last share his consciousness, he has been abandoned in Hyde Park by Bonamy in a huff, for Bonamy suspects his desire for a woman, and meanwhile Jacob has just missed a chance encounter with Clara. In our final direct glimpse of him in the novel, we watch Jacob "[tear] his omnibus ticket to pieces," as if he were abandoning ship, disembarking from the journey under the pressure of his torn desires (152).

Yet he has not escaped, since to escape history is vain. So the novel's penultimate chapter closes with Betty Flanders drawn from her bed in the middle of the night, awakened by a "dull sound, as if nocturnal women were beating great carpets" (154). "The guns?" she asks. No, she concludes, "It is the sea." This conflation of guns and sea reappears throughout Woolf's fiction, especially in *To the Lighthouse*. In *Jacob's Room*, several of the key scenes of Jacob's life take place at sea, and his death, apparently, is by guns at sea, although the novel never tells us this directly. Instead, we simply arrive in the next and final chapter, in the dead Jacob's empty room, where Betty Flanders holds out his shoes to Dick Bonamy, asking, "What am I to do with these?" (155). What to do, the novel leaves us asking, with a young man's empty shoes? With his wandering desires? How tell *this* story of what oars the Atlantic world forward?

Queer Elegies: *Mrs. Dalloway*

Woolf comes closer to telling this story in *Mrs. Dalloway*. Not only does she make the gay currents running through the lives of Clarissa and Septimus more powerful but she catches them up in the undertow of empire by way of the novel's sea tropes and its implicit racialization of queer sexuality. In the story of Clarissa especially, Woolf narrates her own entanglement in the imperial Atlantic imaginary.

In one quiet scene of *Jacob's Room* Woolf anticipates *Mrs. Dalloway*'s imagistic pairing of ships and clocks, the expeditions of empire and the regimes of timekeeping, those pairings that structure the later novel and the lives of its two queer characters, Clarissa Dalloway and Septimus Warren Smith. One night Jacobs's mother and her friend Mrs. Jarvis walk out on to the moor near the remains of an old Roman camp or grave site, and into a moment that, in linking ships and clocks, prefigures the unseizable forces that will capture Clarissa and kill Septimus Warren Smith. The town church looms on the horizon of the moor like "a ship with all its crew aboard," while its bells, chiming every fifteen minutes, "divided time into quarters"; and, as the narrator remarks, it is as if the crew's "tongues join forever in syllabling the sharp-cut words, which forever slice time asunder" (116). It is on this spot, amid these Roman ruins, Betty Flanders recalls, that she has lost innumerable darning needles as well as a garnet brooch, a gift from Jacob. Although the narrator assures us that here, buried in the grass of the Roman camp, "Betty Flanders's darning needles are safe and her garnet brooch," the mention of Jacob's gift foreshadows how, in a world of ships and slicing clocks, Jacob's gifts will remain buried as he himself "goes under" not in a sea-spray of male ecstasy but in a wartime capsizing of gunners.

In *Mrs. Dalloway*, the queer young man survives the war, for a time. Eventually, however, in the form of Big Ben and St. Margaret's chimes, the slicing clocks also rush him to his plunging end. They urge Septimus on to his appointment with Dr. Bradshaw, who "offers help, but desires power," and who strictly schedules his appointments, counting out time like those battleship gunners on the North Sea (100). The booming of Big Ben and the trilling of St. Margaret's likewise keep Clarissa moving forward with preparations for her party and cut short her habitual memories of a gay past. The narrator playfully glosses these ordering clocks as a "couple," with St. Margaret as the hostess figure, following closely on the heels of booming Big Ben. Like Bradshaw's guiding principles, proportion and conversion, this couple orders time, space, and desire for the citizens at the center of empire.

These clocks also express the sea power that buoys British empire and surges through the lives of the characters, as Kaitlin Barry argues.[15] Repeatedly, "the sound of Big Ben *flood[s]* Clarissa's drawing-room" and, following it, St. Margaret's chimes come "flooding and lapping and dancing in on the wake of that solemn stroke which lay flat like a bar of gold on the sea" (117, 128 emphasis added). These same bells send their currents through the "watery gold glow" of Septimus's room as he lies stranded, "bathing, floating, on top of the waves" (141, 139, emphasis added), for Septimus is an "outcast, who gazed back at the inhabited regions, who lay, like a drowned sailor, on the shore of the world" (93). Likewise, these clocks create the floating, bloated element of time in the dead sea life, so to speak, of Dr. Bradshaw's wife, who, with her children grown and gone, sits in a gray car "wedged on a calm ocean, where only spice winds blow" and apparently forever wrapped in grey furs awaits her husband's return from his appointments (94). Lady Bradshaw is a woman who once "caught salmon freely" — once had a more invigorating relation to water and time — but after her marriage she experienced the "slow sinking, water-logged, of her will into his" and so has by now "gone under" into this muffled, waiting world of dead time (101, 100).

As in so many other English-language novels, these flooding and driving currents threaten the characters with sexual ruin; and, following the path opened by *Jacob's Room,* Woolf casts this ruin as a drowning not of innocence or native-ness but of queer desires. From the beginning to the end of the novel, Clarissa's memory of falling in love with a woman presses on her consciousness, if some-times only half-consciously. As readers have noted, she thinks back repeatedly to the moment at Bourton — "the most exquisite moment of her whole life" — when "Sally stopped; picked a flower; kissed her on the lips" and Clarissa feels the world "turn upside down" (35).[16] In effect, for the rest of her life she carefully holds "her treasure," "a present" she had been given by Sally, "wrapped up, and told just to keep it, not to look at it — a diamond, something infinitely precious, wrapped up" (35).

I would highlight, in addition, the hint of racialization that accompanies Cla-rissa's desire, as it does in Woolf's next novel in the character of Lily Briscoe. In this youthful moment of attraction to Sally, Clarissa compares herself to Othello: "Feeling, as she crossed the hall 'if it were now to die 'twere now to be most happy.' That was her feeling, Othello's feeling, and she felt it, she was con-vinced, as Shakespeare meant Othello to feel it, all because she was coming down to dinner in a white frock to meet Sally Seton!" (35). By way of this allusion to Shakespeare, Woolf at once places her novel within the native British tradition of literature and recalls the tradition's stories of ruinous, race-entangled transgres-sion. Associating Clarissa's love with Othello's miscegenous love both reinforces and (like Shakespeare's hero) disrupts the straight lines of British inheritance. Woolf's allusion at one level repeats the strategy whereby racial affiliation (as for Catharine Macaulay) authorizes and protects sexual transgression: here Clarissa and Woolf's text are ennobled for her audience by way of this Shakespearean al-lusion. Yet, at another level, the allusion signals that, like Othello's miscegenous love, Clarissa's gay love threatens racialized Englishness — as is most pointedly expressed in the jealous possessiveness of the empire-complacent Peter Walsh.

In the denouement of the novel, in an anteroom at her party, Clarissa returns to this affiliation with Othello that at once ennobles and exoticizes or African-izes her queer feelings. Immediately after learning from Lady Bradshaw (who stands "balancing like a sea lion at the edge of its tank, barking for invitations" [182] — Woolf's coding is as relentless as the sea itself) — that a young man with shell shock has committed suicide, Clarissa slips away into the little room where the prime minister and Lady Bruton "had been talking about India" (184). Woolf discreetly places Clarissa's desires at the center of empire, behind the closed door of one of its anterooms. In her musing in this anteroom, Clarissa turns directly from Septimus to Shakespeare: she wonders "had he plunged holding his trea-sure? 'If it were now to die, 'twere now to be most happy," she had said to herself once, coming down in white" (184). In this sequence Clarissa becomes the tragic

Moor, now "coming down in white." In the very space of empire's covert consultations, Woolf places perhaps not just one but two secrets, and the second, Africanist one in effect provides cover for the first, queer one, a strategy that Robin Hackett suggests is also at work in *The Waves*.[17] Woolf implicitly explains the need for this double covering when she reminds us of the policing of these desires: Clarissa shudders as she speculates about Septimus, "Suppose he had had that passion, and had gone to Sir William Bradshaw, a great doctor yet to her obscurely evil . . . capable of some indescribable outrage — forcing your soul" (184–85). In Septimus's own affiliation with Shakespeare and in his mourning over Evans, Woolf confirms Clarissa's guess. And in Clarissa's affiliation with Othello, she may confirm a reader's guess that as a queer writer Woolf needs the empire's resources to protect her own transgressions and fears, as we saw in *The Voyage Out,* as we will see again in the following discussion of *To the Lighthouse,* and as is likewise signaled in Woolf's and her Bloomsbury friends' use of blackface in the well-known Dreadnought hoax (in that their subversive, queer joke on empire borrows from empire's own Africanist imaginary).

In other words, Woolf develops Clarissa as the empire's surviving queer, whose complicit and confessional witnessing may in some sense enact Woolf's own position. Perhaps like Clarissa, Woolf feels that "[i]t was her punishment to see sink and disappear here a man, there a woman, in this profound darkness, and she forced to stand there in her [mermaid] evening dress. . . . And once she had walked on the terrace at Bourton" (185). Finally, "with the clock striking the hour, one, two, three," Clarissa concludes that "she did not pity him. . . . She felt glad that he had done it; thrown it away. . . . But she must go back. She must assemble" (186). At least for a time, Woolf must go on writing the novels that ineluctably "assemble" this legacy even as they also deconstruct it.

Queer Visions

Although *To the Lighthouse* has been understood, including by Woolf herself, as an elegy for her parents, when we read it against *Jacob's Room* and *Mrs. Dalloway,* those more legibly queer novels, it appears also as a secret festival of queer vision. By contrast to all her earlier novels, here the queers live on, single yet bonded, standing on high and dry land rather than drowning and intimately if surreptitiously sharing visions about the passing of the heterosexual couple.[18] If the novel is about the death of Woolf's parents, then it also about how that death allows the phoenix-like birth of queer art — anticipating the achievement of Miss La Trobe, the gay artist working behind the scenes and restaging the "pageant" of British history in Woolf's last novel, *Between the Acts.*

Yet the death which allows the birth of this art is not only the gray-eyed mother's. Urmilla Seshagiri argues that Woolf could not have had the novelistic vision embodied in Lily's painting without the encoded, smuggled-in inspiration of "primitive" art, and her case reminds us that, once again, the freedom quests of dissenting or queer, Anglo-Atlantic subjects depend on the "freely" seized resources of empire.[19] While the queers in the novels preside over and bless the sinking of empire that Mrs. Ramsay's death signals, they also inherit from empire the very power to preside, to make the art that positions them thus. Woolf casts the woman artist as not fully seduced, not fully English, not fully heteronormative witness to the demise of the Anglo-Atlantic imperial-freedom project—all in the name of a new freedom plot for such woman artists. A queer story indeed. One that calls for careful consideration, especially as it sheds light on the complicated position of many literary critics who likewise speak on behalf of freedom from within empire's safe harbors.

In *To the Lighthouse,* Woolf again conjures the Atlantic novel's core story. This time she highlights the ruinous death of a mother in the wake of a sea storm and the subsequent journey of a brother-sister pair who feel forced into a "compact" to "fight tyranny to the death."[20] The first section of the novel offers a distilled allegory of women's negotiations and deaths on the Atlantic. In "The Window," Mr. and Mrs. Ramsay's relationship unfolds through their opposed orientations toward an Atlantic horizon and its future. In *Bordering on the Body* I noted that the whole first section of the novel is structured as a struggle between Mr. and Mrs. Ramsay over the naming of the material world—by way of questioning whether the weather will or won't be fine. Here I want to emphasize that they argue especially over the world of the sea, over the question of whether a sea adventure will be possible for the youngest son, James, who Mrs. Ramsay already imagines at the center of the British empire, "all red and ermine on the Bench or directing a stern and momentous enterprise in some crisis of public affairs" (4).

In the life of the Ramsay couple, the swoon is no longer a singular moment of self-loss but rather has become for the wife a habitual, yet oddly satisfying giving-up of herself to her husband in those small daily moments when "the fatal sterility of the male plunged itself, like a beak of brass" into her maternal fecundity (37). After these moments, Mrs. Ramsay is left with "scarcely a shell of herself to know herself by" and she seems "to fold herself together, one petal closed in another" until "the whole fabric fell in exhaustion upon itself" (38). And yet Woolf implies that Mrs. Ramsay also seeks these encounters—in them she feels "the rapture of successful creation" (38). Her desire circulates here, for her feeding of his intellectual ambitions (figured as expeditions to lonely corners of the world) also feeds her desire for the adventures of empire. When alone she herself travels in imagination to "the Indian plains" (62), while the story of the Fisherman's Wife that she reads to James allegorizes her own romance with epic grandeur: this wife, as the husband in the fairy tale reports, "wills not as I'd have her will," and her dissent arises exactly from her desire for him to be "King" — or " 'if you won't be King, I will' " (56). The whole drama comes to its catastrophic end, as Mrs. Ramsay reads it to James, when "a great storm" rises and "houses and trees toppled over . . . and the sea came in with black waves as high as church towers and mountains" (60–61). By way of this tale, Woolf registers Mrs. Ramsay's own ambitions even as she anticipates the crisis in heterosexuality provoked by these imperial dreams.

For the Ramsay's ruling desires do end in a storm that sinks their alliance. In "Time Passes," Mrs. Ramsay dies amid "a downpouring of immense darkness," while the "sea tosses itself and breaks itself" during and nights "full of wind and destruction" (125, 128). So, although the mothers of empire have their "triumph" as Mrs. Ramsay does at the close of the first section of the novel, the Atlantic's ruinous effects triumph in their turn. In the wake of the storm, the sea's roaming airs ("advance guards of great armies" [128–29]) nibble their way into bedrooms — under sheets, perhaps, in the form of a stepbrother's hands — decompose books, crash those imported "china" cups, and unravel the mother's green shawl that had covered the skull in the nursery. These advance guards give way, in turn, to the "silent apparition of an ashen-coloured ship" accompanied by "ominous sounds like the measured blows of hammers dulled on felt" and this conflation of guns and waves, as in *Jacob's Room*, climaxes with the death of a son, imaged as the exploding shell that kills Andrew Ramsay, which also coincides closely with Prue's death in childbirth (133).

In the final section of the novel, after the loss of their mother, brother, and sister, Cam and James Ramsay launch out on their long-awaited, overdetermined journey. As they sit in "anger and silence" because they have now been coerced into this journey that once they desired ("they had been forced; they had been bidden"), they feel themselves "united in their compact to fight tyranny to the death" (164). Cam and James join the long Atlantic project of securing freedom by "compacting" to fight a heroic battle with tyranny. Yet, like all such journeys, this excursion is full of perils and losses, as Woolf signals when she interweaves her narration of it with Macalister's tale of a recent sea storm and shipwreck and at the same time punctures it with Mr. Ramsay's sudden cries that (in Atlantic modernity) "We perished each alone" (164–65).

Woolf furthermore casts this modern journey as a brother-sister expedition in which the brother begins to take the place of the father. Mrs. Ramsay is dead, Mr. Ramsay is old, and James is steering the boat — while Cam endures her brother's anger. Woolf initially invokes Cam's and James's shared sense of freedom at setting out: "with his eye fixed on the sail and on the horizon, [James] steered grimly. But he began to think as he steered that he might escape; he might be quit of it all. They might land somewhere; and be free then. Both of them [Cam and James], looking at each other for a moment, had a sense of escape and exaltation, what with the speed and the change" (165). Yet, in her physical exaltation, Cam is apt to forget the compact, failing to experience the sea wholly as the site of battle and triumph (164). In the silent colloquy between them as the trip continues, Woolf creates a striking cameo of the "sister's" predicament: James scolds Cam "pitilessly," for she "would never resist tyranny to the death," and his thoughts ironically form a tyrant cloud above her so that "Cam now felt herself overcast" (168). Cam "wondered how to answer her father about the puppy . . . while James the lawgiver . . . said, Resist him. Fight him" (168). "And to which did she yield, she thought" (168). She finally reflects, silently addressing James, "you're not exposed to it, to this pressure and division of feeling, this extraordinary temptation" (168–69). Cam looks down into the sea and lets herself be absorbed in the simple sensation of her hand in the current, against the pressure to make the sea into a battleground. Woolf thus encapsulates the sister's conflicted entry into the regime of the brother, or, as she calls it in *A Room of One's Own,* the world of "Arthur's Education Fund."

And up on the cliff, Lily paints and watches this scene with Chinese eyes.[21] And Woolf paints Lily painting and watching. And we can watch them both engaged in acts of encoded representation. At this point in the long history, Woolf seems to have understood, race need hardly be mentioned as a key to the story. The Ramsay men have large foreheads and blue eyes, the young woman artist has Chinese eyes, the old woman cleaning and preserving the house has the name McNab, all while Mr. Ramsay continues reading Walter Scott. The children fight tyranny as they set out on the sea, thinking that when they land they will "be free then." The code is encrypted, an encrypting that Woolf's artistry imitates.

Most important, with clear intention but to complicated effect, Woolf encodes her woman artist as queer and Oriental. Giving the unmarried woman-artist "Chinese eyes," Woolf uses this touch to indicate Lily's position as an outsider who abstractly represents the position of the woman in the Atlantic regimes of the father and brother. As in the work of other modernists such as Gertrude Stein, this Orientalization of the heroine marks her queerness.[22] At the same time, as Urmilla Seshagiri has persuasively argued, in this way Woolf problematically affiliates her own, similarly abstract use of aesthetic form with the stylistic traditions of Eastern and African art, which were at once celebrated and primitivized in Woolf's London milieu, most influentially for Woolf in Roger Fry's theories of art. This affiliation with the aesthetic of "the other" serves Woolf's dissenting purposes; at the same time it entails an imperialist Africanism and Orientalism. These maneuvers take us all the way back to the founding structures of the English-language novel as forged by Aphra Behn. For here again, in empire the cultural outsider proves herself an insider after all, insofar as this outsider's freedom to dissent depends on empire's expansive geography and new wealth as well as the partially "free" (and freely borrowing) aesthetic culture it generates. That is, the very boldness of Woolf's queer framing marks her as one of her nation's proud freethinkers. The point requires more detailed parsing.

Ruth Vanita has carefully traced the gay currents in this novel, not only by exploring Lily's intense love for Mrs. Ramsay but also by considering Lily's bonds with Bankes and Carmichael, both of whose names link them to gayness by way of the historical figure William Bankes (a close friend of Byron's who was twice arrested for homosexuality) and Woolf's fictional author Mary Carmichael, who writes novels about how "Chloe liked Olivia."[23] In Woolf's novel, Bankes imagines his friendship for Mr. Ramsay "like the body of a young man laid up in peat for a century, with the red fresh on his lips" (21), while Augustus Carmichael makes a protégé of Andrew Ramsay and later elegizes his death at war in a book of poems. Lily of course loves Mrs. Ramsay with a feeling that is intensely physical if not sexual, smiling during one of their late-night talks, as she lies in Mrs. Ramsay's lap and hugs her knees, "to think that Mrs. Ramsay would never know the reason of that pressure," and finally wondering how one might become "one with the object one adored" (50–51). For Vanita, this much-discussed, late-night homoerotic moment is only the most visible sign of Woolf's gay subtext.

Building on Seshagiri's and Vanita's arguments, I suggest that Woolf purposefully gathers these queer characters around the central painting of the imperial mother and her republican son, an "avant-garde" painting that abstracts, distances, and distorts these figures by way of the absorbed aesthetic influence of Eastern and African cultures. The very production of Lily's painting, stationed on its easel on a cliff above the sea — interrupted by the motions of the Ramsays and yet an expression of her "being in love" with them, and presided over by the gay presences of Carmichael and Bankes — mirrors the position of Woolf's own Bloomsbury-supported, modernist novel. Around this abstract painting, within this "abstract" novel, that is, the queers stand witness to the passing of an Atlantic heteronormative and racial order of things. Or, rather, they preside over Lily's, and Woolf's, dreamlike *visions* of this passing. The "line, there, in the center" that Lily and Woolf finally draw through that normative order of things at once elegizes and cancels the past, as if both acknowledging a debt and striking it from the books. Yet all the while Lily's and Woolf's freedom to create this art itself garners empire's resources — even as it also depends, as Mary Lou Emery has argued — on the labors of Mrs. McNab and Mrs. Bast.[24]

The purpose of saying so, however, is not so much to deconstruct Lily or Woolf but rather to recognize ourselves — our implicated histories and our liberationist projects — in the mirror that Woolf holds up. On the night of the motherless family's return to the seashore, the sea's infiltrating airs, although scattered by Mrs. McNab ("like a tropical fish oaring its way through sun-lanced waters"), return once more to try to invade the artists' sleep; but, the narrator reports, these artists "said no" to the sea's seductive airs with their incestuously invading fingers, so that in the morning Lily sits "bolt upright" against them, poised to repaint the world (133, 142). By way of Lily's painting, Woolf calls on us to consider, very, very carefully, the historical grounds of our dissent, our art, and our scholarship: that is, our always-already Atlantic pasts.

The Wake of Empire in *The Waves*

In *The Waves*, Woolf focuses directly on the matter of figuration and the legacy of re-presentation, most specifically the cumulative powers of Atlantic metaphors. She begins, again, with the sea, and she returns to the aesthetic of the sublime, imitating and exposing its racialized and imperial ecstasies.[25] She retools this aesthetic that, beginning in the eighteenth century, structured the imperial imagination by symbolically transmuting a ruptured past and peopled world into a mastered terrain made grandly epic and grossly profitable by the labors of possessed bodies. Woolf displays the operations of this sublime poetic through the characters — symbolically, republican brothers and sisters without parents — who organize their imagined community around the native barbarian "figure," in both senses, of Percival. In her sly portrait of Percival, Woolf intervenes in the early-twentieth-century celebrations of legendary folk figures, in which they emerge as the elemental embodiments of racial and national culture, notions which had their roots in that racial romantic imaginary I discussed in chapter 3 — and as hinted by her many allusions to British romantic poems. She allows Percival to operate as the cathected object of the characters' sublimated sexualities, the pivot by which they turn those energies toward a warring, colonizing sense of mastery over all things material and mortal. In the end, Woolf renders Percival as the Derridian supplement, the absent-presence at the origin of Atlantic narratives. In doing so, she draws attention to the bracketed or walled-off center of her own sublime, metaphorical, and imperially situated practice.

Ushered in by the wakening world of the sea in the first interlude, the text proper of *The Waves* begins with a corollary human awakening to physical perception and sensation that, however, undergoes a sexual crisis in the very first chapter — in the form of a kiss.[26] The characters begin in relation to the world of things — "I see a ring. . . . It quivers and hangs in a loop of light," "I hear a sound . . . cheep, chirp; cheep, chirp; going up and down."[27] But then Jinny kisses Louis. And Susan sees her do it and runs off to the woods. And Bernard sees Susan run and sets out after her. And Neville feels abandoned when Bernard leaves him in the woodshed. And Rhoda witnesses the crisis in all these relationships from outside. Her role is to have no role, to define the insiders by way of her excluded, witnessing position. Yet even Rhoda's queerly dreamy, exilic world is, as we will see, recuperated in a language of exotic adventure at sea. The kiss is the beginning of these six children's social lives, the moment of their communal interpellation, the first swoon.

In particular, the kiss heralds their entry into an imperial republic. Eventually we learn that the boy who is kissed is a colonial boy from Australia carrying in his imagination a vision of beasts chained on a beach, and the schoolmate who kisses him is a twirling girl who, as an adult, transgresses sexual norms — never marries and flits from affair to affair. The crisis begins with *these* two. The rupturing kiss is theirs. In a reversal of the encounter between Rachel Vinrace and Richard Dalloway, here the colonial boy swoons under the assertive sexuality of the straying girl. In response, the maternal English girl, Susan, deeply bound to her native spot and father and farmland, objects violently. To placate her, Bernard tells a story — prompted by a glimpse of the woman writer at Elvedon. He spins a narrative of fantasy adventures sought *together* within the walled garden, with the proper English girl and boy exploring side by side in a natural republic of the woods, living a story of innocence lost and redeemed. He soothes her, in effect, by reading her a novel. But meanwhile Neville wants Bernard to remain by *his* side, wants male companionship, wants to share another story. Rhoda watches, lost amid the turmoil and alienated from the sharply gendered ordering of this story-world — drawn instead, as Woolf casts her in drafts of the novel, to a queer and sensual world peopled by amazons and goddesses.[28]

Enter Percival, whom even Rhoda can love in his pure physicality. He is the mythical "barbarian," the ancient figure who might rebuild the ruptured origin-story and carry them all into the future. By way of Percival, "the Oriental problem is solved," as Bernard later puts it (136) — that is, the problem of colonial distension and collapse of community and identity as first figured in the colonial boy's hiding place in the bush and the wandering girl's pursuit and errant kissing of him. Percival will rally and channel these centrifugal energies.

Woolf stresses the pagan, barbarian, and military aspect of Percival, a move consonant with other early-twentieth-century recuperations of the medieval folk figure of Parsifal (such as in Richard Wagner's opera *Parsifal*). Woolf seems deliberately to mimic this figuration, as Larsen does with ancient "Bacchic" rites that catalyze Helga's conversion in *Quicksand*. As Neville observes, Percival is "'remote from us all in a pagan universe'" and "'his magnificence is that of some medieval commander'" (36, 37). He is "'heavy,'" "'clumsy,'" his "'oddly inexpressive eyes, are fixed with pagan indifference upon the pillar opposite'" (36). And yet "'[a] wake of light seems to lie on the grass behind him'" (37). Like those sublime medieval barbarians who inspired, according to Hugh Blair, Richard Hurd, and Thomas Percy, the first "native" poetry, Percival is blind and dumb yet in his wake comes light, comes consciousness, comes writing—comes the subject who sublimates and transmutes that barbarity into the nation's imperial racial identity.

Percival never speaks directly in the text and apparently not much in his fictional life either, and that very dumbness or absence of speech seems an enabling condition for the group formation of the characters: "'Unknown, with or without a secret, it does not matter . . . he is a stone fallen into a pond round which minnows swarm. Like minnows, we who had been shooting this way, that way, all shot round him when he came'" (136). Moreover, Woolf traces how this native English barbarian serves as an organizing vehicle which, when introjected as a figure of the past who launches a modern future, enables the fashioning of non-English peoples into conquered barbarians fixed in the past. As the pagan conqueror-figure who freely leaves England to cross the border into "savage" lands, he allows the introjection of that alien other by his compatriots. As Rhoda envisions it, "since Percival, riding alone . . . advances, the outermost parts of the earth—pale shadows on the utmost horizon, India for instance, rise into our purview. The world that had been shrivelled, rounds itself; remote provinces are fetched up out of darkness; we see muddy roads, twisted jungle, swarms of men, as within our scope, part of our proud and splendid province" (137).

Percival is the barbarian figure whose departure to "there" from the "here" of England creates the meaning of this native "here" and orients all other places toward it. He is the movement outside that constitutes the inside circle of the six characters, grounds the Anglo-Atlantic subject. Once the world is made theirs through him in this way, "'comfort steals over us'" and "'some rapture of benignity'" (137). Thus "'the Oriental problem is solved'"—that problem not only of otherness but also of what constitutes "usness." It is solved by the very traveling figure who creates it (136).

The characters' momentous dinners function as ritual repetitions of this introjection of barbarity for the imperial community. In these scenes, Woolf carefully stages the psychic work of empire, in effect enacting at length the process typically condensed into the swoon moment, whereby the self is remade and ultimately empowered by way of an encounter with (or eating of) an alien world and other.

> "Horns and trumpets," said Rhoda, "ring out. Leaves unfold; the stag blares in the thicket. There is a dancing and drumming, like the dancing and drumming of naked men with assegais."
>
> "Like the dance of savages," said Louis, "round the camp fire. They are savage; they are ruthless. . . . The flames leap over their painted faces, over the leopard skins and the bleeding limbs which they have torn from the living body." (140)

Gathered around Percival or, after his departure for India, in honor of him, they eat flesh — "'we have taken into our mouths the bodies of dead birds'" (292) — while at the same time, as Bernard notes, "'we have destroyed something by our presence . . . a world perhaps'" (232). Woolf makes the Anglo-British into the barbarian cannibals, engaged in epic yet casual destruction of living bodies.

Woolf has Bernard trace their ritual into its next turn, into the imperial triumph. He celebrates, just following the passage quoted above, "'the swelling and splendid moment created *by us* from Percival'" (146; emphasis added) and leads the movement back "'outside'": "'We, too, as we put on our hats and push open the door, stride not into chaos, but into a world that our own force can subjugate and make part of the illumined and everlasting road. . . . The yellow canopy of our tremendous energy hangs like a burning cloth above our heads'" (146). The characters borrow from the savage for the work, and pride, of civilization.

In particular, they fantasize and colonize savagery so as to enter the historical sequence and narrate an acculturated temporality, a movement toward freedom: "'We have proved, sitting eating, sitting talking, that we can add to the treasury of moments'" and so show too that "'[w]e are not slaves bound to suffer incessantly unrecorded petty blows on our bent backs. We are not sheep either, following a master. We are creators. We too have made something that will join the innumerable congregations of past time'" (146). They have achieved the sublimation of a (fictional) barbarity that enables the project of free creation. As Bernard later reflects, "This freedom, this immunity, seemed then a conquest, and stirred in me such exaltation that I sometimes go there, even now, [to the British Museum's world of "pictures," of "Madonnas and pillars"] to bring back exaltation and Percival" (264).

Emigré from colonial Australia, Louis is attuned to "the nightingale who sings among the trampling feet; the conquests and migrations" (218). Yet as colonial subject come to the metropole, whose originary uprooting is signaled in his swoon under Jinny's kiss, he translates the song of the conquered into the speech of free commerce. Now "half in love with the typewriter and the telephone," he has "'inherited a desk of solid mahogany in a room hung with maps . . . [and] helped by my assiduity and decision to score those lines on the map there by which the different parts of the world are laced together'" (167, 218, 168). He guides the ship of empire, feeling that "a vast inheritance is packed in me": "'My shoulder is to the wheel; I roll the dark before me, spreading commerce where there was chaos in the four parts of the world'" (167 – 68). He performs again the sublime turn, the white man's aesthetic burden, carrying forward the "vast inheritance" of a free British past: "'The weight of the world is on our shoulders; its vision is through our eyes'" (169).

The women as well as the men express this competitive and possessive, imperial relation to the world, as when Susan — Woolf's figure for the nativist — boasts that as a mother "'I shall be lifted higher than any of you on the backs of the seasons. I shall possess more than Jinny, more than Rhoda, by the time I die'" (132). She admits even as a young woman that she loves "'with such a ferocity that it kills me when the object of my love shows by a phrase that he can escape'" (132) and so predicts that she "'shall push the fortunes of my children unscrupulously. . . . I shall be debased and hide-bound by the bestial and beautiful passion of maternity'" (132). Woolf hints at how even maternity feeds on an identity of sublimated barbarity, serving a turbulent modernity whose children must ceaselessly pursue "fortunes."

The Heteronormative Turn

This movement through violent sublimation that prepares a transcendent freedom also drives the insistent self-narration noted by Jane Marcus and Patrick McGee, which Bernard describes in imperial terms as "'the incessant rise and fall and fall and rise again'" — echoing the titles of books that narrate the history of empires (297).[29] All the characters express some form of this grasping, willful subjectivity — what Bernard calls "ravenous identity" (143) — fed on an imagined savagery. They all fold an imagery of conquering into their breathless, rhythmic, transporting inner speech. And the urgency of this speech arises from sexual sublimation, both Woolf's and her characters,' as is especially evident in her creation of Rhoda and Bernard.

Woolf's characterization of Rhoda reveals the double impulse of sexual frankness and self-protection operating in her fiction. Rhoda is described in the final version of the novel as "'eyeless,'" like Percival, and like him she is a voyager, an adventurer, her ship "'sails into icy caverns where the sea-bear barks and stalactites swing green chains'" (19). In her child-fantasy, she makes flower petals in a basin into ships at sea and dreams herself as the plunderous proud spirit of Britannia ruling the waves: "'The waves rise; their crests curl; look at the lights on the masthead. They have scattered, they have foundered, all except my ship which mounts the wave and sweeps before the gale and reaches the islands where the parrots chatter'" (19). Yet, based on her study of the drafts, Annette Oxindine shows that these pools replace the pools located, in the first draft, in a grove on a Greek island that provides the setting for Rhoda's fantasies about a girl named Alice whose "lips faded" always as "she was about to kiss her" (quoted Oxindine, 214).

In this light, Woolf subtextually accomplishes two things in her rewriting of these queer waters as the seas of empire. She protects herself from charges of Sapphism — quite real in these years of the active prosecution of homosexuality and the censorship of homosexual publication — and uses a rhetoric of empire to gain this protection for herself, as Robin Hackett differently suggests.[30] At the same time, whether intentionally or not, Woolf's revisions display the ways that this rhetoric, with its romanticization of exilic waifs and its imagery of rebellious adventure, does indeed provide a language that can include even the most alienated spirits within the fold. If it is true that, after Percival's death, Rhoda imagines committing suicide as she stands at the top of a Spanish hill gazing out over Africa (she pictures herself "launch[ing] out over the precipice" and falling until "[r]olling me over the waves shoulder me under . . . dissolving me"), then Woolf also indicates the fatal outcome of this seduction of dreamers and poets by the foreign "heights" of empire, perhaps hinting at her own seduction as a writer (206).

In this light, we can better see how, in her characterization of Bernard, Woolf more openly dramatizes the way that a certain sexuality is naturalized in Anglo-Atlantic empire, and queer sexualities are rolled over and shouldered under. In a sense Bernard is the novel's equivocal Tiresias. He knows both sides of sexuality but ultimately conforms to the heteronormal — and accepts or even at moments feels exulted by the power that this conformity confers on him.

In his youth, Bernard shares Byron, Shakespeare, and moments of intimacy with Neville. After Neville confides to him "a secret told to nobody yet" and asks "whether I am doomed always to cause repulsion in those I love?" Bernard responds, "I too will press flowers between the pages of Shakespeare's sonnets" (88). Yet for Bernard, his night with Neville is merely a phase of his "prodigious booming" in a liberated world. Addressing Neville, he exclaims: "How richly I shall enjoy my youth (you make me feel). And London. And freedom. But stop. . . . You are making some protest . . . 'Do not, in your affluence and plenty,' you seem to say, 'pass me by.' 'Stop,' you say. 'Ask me what I suffer'" (84). Bernard's freedom too readily looks past Neville's suffering, too easily feeds on Neville's desires as merely a rich diversion. Although he acknowledges the problem, Bernard "passes" by Neville anyway: as an adult, Bernard marries and has both children and a mistress, becoming the most "normal" and complacent of the six friends.

Woolf makes the moment of Bernard's wedding engagement a climactic one for the book. His marriage represents an "irrevocable" turning point in their lives, as Susan says; it is the culmination of the opening kiss that sealed their fate as reproductive members of an aggressive, imperial republic: "everything is now set; everything is now fixed. Bernard is engaged. Something irrevocable has happened. A circle has been cast on the waters. We shall never flow freely again" (142). Woolf opens the chapter that contains this turning-point event with telling imagery, as Bernard triumphantly arrives in a feminized London by a phallic train from the north carrying the news of his engagement:

> London lies before me under mist. Guarded by gasometers, by factory chimneys, she lies sleeping as we approach. She folds the ant-heap to her breast.... But we are aimed at her. Already her maternal somnolence is uneasy. ... The early train from the north is hurled at her like a missile. ... men clutch their newspapers a little tighter, as our wind sweeps them, envisaging death. But we roar on. We are about to explode in the flanks of the city like a shell in the side of some ponderous, maternal, majestic animal. ... Meanwhile as I stand looking from the train window, I feel strangely, persuasively, that because of my great happiness (being engaged to be married) I am become part of this speed, this missile, hurled at the city. (111)

The violent effects of Bernard's official induction into heterosexuality within the empire dovetail here with an industrial imaginary of aggressive penetration — penetration that blasts motherly protection. And this martial fantasy life helps to create the reality of war, as the mention of newspapers "envisaging death" suggests. As in *Jacob's Room*, the convergence of sexual, industrial, and martial forces — aimed, in this case, at the maternal — is the yield of a certain, too-complacent freedom that casts a circle on the open waters and is not dependable, or loyal — a "loose wire," as Neville calls Bernard. Thus after Percival's death, Bernard confesses his selfish failure to meet Percival at Hampton Court — although he had said he would — before Percival departed and died.

Woolf makes this voice, Bernard's voice, the reigning voice of the novel. For she is attempting to capture Anglo-Atlantic culture in all its blindness and queerness and to represent its casual founding of one world on the destruction of another.

Fighting Words

In the process, Woolf is exploring what Derrida calls the violence of the letter.[31] Bernard's rhetorical conflation of two kinds of engagement — martial and marital — is mirrored in the novel's interludes, where the world of nature is born within a rhetorical horizon of battle. Although these interludes may seem to conjure the world without humans that Woolf often seeks to depict in her novels, here she reveals all perceptions of nature to be utterly entangled in a warring linguistic imaginary. To understand her project in the interludes, it is necessary first to note how the chapters themselves reveal speech as a mode that anxiously seizes on a naturalized other, seeking to concretize identity, fashion an ostensibly republican community, and veil the impossibility of mastery over materiality and mortality.

Woolf makes clear that the characters' fantasies and self-narrating speech are precipitated by the unspeaking, uncertain, and opaque presence of Percival — the one who will die. Their speech will mystify, make imperial, this youth's death. Early in the book, as the boys leave the "cool temple" where perceptions first cluster round Percival, Neville announces: "'And now let Bernard begin. Let him burble on, telling us stories, while we lie recumbent'" (37). With Percival at the center, mute ("'we all feel Percival lying heavy among us'"), Bernard "'goes on talking'" (38). The very fictionality of Percival's presence in the text is represented in the fact that he says nothing and thus opens the space in which discourse, myth, and imperial narratives proliferate.

Moreover, the speech that results, Bernard's speech, is and must be utterly figural. In fact, as in the interludes that frame the chapters, Bernard's figures are so profuse they become interchangeable, and the logic of centerless substitution is laid bare: "'up they bubble'" Neville tells us, "'images.' 'Like a camel,' . . . 'a vulture.'" The camel is a vulture; the vulture a camel; for Bernard is a dangling wire, loose, but seductive. Yes, for when he talks, when he makes foolish comparisons, a lightness comes over one'" (38). By way of a syntax of substitutions, Bernard makes buoyant the weight of an exotic, camel-inhabited, yet vulture-shadowed world. He masters this different world by giving it sequentiality and making it the origin of a communal narrative for the boys. "'Let him describe what we have all seen so that it becomes a sequence'" (37). Grounded by the *figure* of Percival, Bernard makes sight into sentence, visuality into verbality: dumb, savage nature into culture, history, and community. Meanwhile, for the reader, Percival's mediated and figured presence marks him as nothing other than a site of projections and productions.

The point is reinforced when Percival dies, and empire falters: suddenly, as

Bernard says, "'The place is empty'" (153). "'About him my feeling was: he sat there in the centre. Now I go to that spot no longer'" (153). When they all gather in memory of Percival for the last time — at Hampton Court, favorite residence of English kings since the sixteenth century — Bernard acknowledges how the idea of an ancestral past has functioned as a figure, a structure for negotiating with the unknowable yet coveted world beyond: "'But how strange it seems to set against the whirling abysses of infinite space a little figure with a golden teapot on his head. . . . Our English past — one inch of light. The people put teapots on their heads and say, "I am a King!"'" (227). Bernard's storytelling reveals the infinite regression of that horizon — wherein culture endlessly overlays abyssal time and space while purporting merely to represent nature. His monologues display the process by which culture makes a claim on "reality" and in this way wins the affiliations of its embodied subjects. Yet, even after Percival's death, he continues his sublimating, story-making work.

Woolf implies that all of Bernard's speech — his fictional transubstantiation of the natural world and his substitution of heterosexuality for queer sexuality — has served the Anglo-Atlantic British subject in a quest to master death. At the end of her book, at the close of her vision of empire's end, Bernard asks, "What enemy do we now perceive advancing against us . . . ? It is death. Death is the enemy" (297). Yet even as he admits that this threat that has been structured as social and racial is in fact ontological, Bernard nonetheless takes up the same figurative language that has created a world of young men's and women's premature deaths: "It is death against whom I ride with my spear couched and my hair flying back like a young man's, like Percival's, when he galloped in India" (297). Like Jacob, Bernard never escapes history even though — or perhaps all the more because — he survives its violence. He is the barbarian man, made literate, made figurative. When we read Bernard's closing shout — "'Against you I will fling myself unvanquished and unyielding, O Death!'" — and then we read the last line of the novel, in italics, stating quite simply, *The waves broke on the shore*" we feel the discrepancy between these waves and his weapons. We feel the waves' quietude, their breaking sadness, against the warring force of his speech.

The profusion of metaphors in the novel's interludes, recalling Bernard's stories, indicates that Woolf sought to disclose the logic of these sublimations and substitutions that serve the will to mastery.

The sun had not yet risen. The sea was indistinguishable from the sky *as if* a cloth had wrinkles in it. . . . Gradually the dark bar on the horizon became clear *as if* the sediment in an old wine bottle had sunk . . . Behind it, too, the sky cleared *as if* the white sediment there had sunk, or *as if* the arm of a woman couched beneath the horizon had raised a lamp. (7; emphasis added)

In Woolf's repetition of "as if" and her proliferating similes, she reveals that the very sun's appearance is caught up in metaphoric effects. The effects of a rising, not-yet-visible sun come into view first through something that is not the sun — not only the sea and the sky but in the text a metaphor. The sun appears in *reflection,* in metaphor, before it emerges as visible fact, which inverts the naturalizing narrative order.

And yet as Woolf hints in the third interlude, this "phantom" world of figuration is its own reality: "The real flower on the window-sill was attended by a phantom flower. Yet the phantom flower was part of the flower for when a bud broke free, the paler flower in the glass opened a bud too" (75). And phantom projections create their own material effects — "The looking-glass whitened its pool upon the wall" (75). It is in this world, in which "mirroring" language and materiality are so conflated, that Bernard's fashioning of himself as a missile operates not just as a reflection of but also as contributing cause of those wars and deaths that the newspaper reports — a cause of Percival's rise and fall and of all of the queer and coerced deaths that attend his.

Indeed, the interludes symbolically trace the arc of these lives, in which phantasms have material effects and in which waves become weapons, yet again. The story they spell out is worth following, for they recreate, by way of waves that advance like troops and birds that swoop like bombers, empire's epic and predatory violence. In the first interludes, "force" has not yet arrived. The day dawns as a mingling of light and water, a "fibrous" world where waves "lay rippling and sparkling" so that even the "steel of the knife" appears "liquid" and where recumbent women raising lamps create an "incandescence" that becomes "a million atoms of soft blue" (7, 29). All things are composite and porous and borderless (like those "immensely composite and wide-flung passions" that Woolf celebrates — before people begin, as she goes on to say, "driving stakes through them, herding them between screens" [quoted in Barber 403]). In this hovering first moment, the birds (the interludes' figure for humans) sing without measure or mission, releasing "a strain or two together, wildly, like skaters rollicking arm-in-arm" (29).

But this fibrous, impulsive, and dancing world gives way, slowly at first, to sounds and movements suggesting violence. In the early morning interludes, the waves (like those in *Jacob's Room*) break "like muffled thuds, like logs falling on the shore" (29) and then, more quickly, "drum on the shore like turbaned warriors, like turbaned men with poisoned assegais who, whirling their arms on high, advance upon the feeding flocks" (75), so that, by mid-morning, they pound like "great horses" or "like the thud of a great beast stamping" (150) and with "the energy, the muscularity of an engine which sweeps its force out and in again" (108). The birds now become anxious if beautiful egoists, all "brightly mailed," as they come to sing "in the hot sunshine, each alone . . . with vehemence, as if to let the song burst out of it, no matter if it shattered the song of another bird with harsh discord" (108). "They sang as if the edge of being were sharpened and must cut, must split the softness of the blue-green light, the dampness of the wet earth" — or, like Bernard's train, break open the maternal embrace (109).

By noon, their single voices tuned, the birds begin their monogamous coupling. They "sang passionate songs addressed to one ear only" and "[b]ubbling and chuckling they carried little bits of straw and twig to the dark knots in the higher branches of the trees. Gilt and purple they perched in their garden" (149–50). They build their safe nests. Woolf again indicates the violent effects of this seemingly innocent domesticity when she figures "the girl couched on her green-sea mattress [who] tired her brow with water-globed jewels that sent lances of opal-tinted light falling and flashing . . . like the flash of a falling blade" (148). The metropole-girl's horizon and reach is imperial, so that her bejeweled gaze lights upon "the smooth gilt mosque" and "long-breasted white-haired women who knelt in the river bed"; and it penetrates through the "yellow awnings" of "[s]teamers thudding slowly over the sea" to the "passengers who dozed or paced the deck, shading their eyes to look for land, while day after day, compressed in its oily throbbing sides, the ship bore them on" (149). This is life seen from the center of empire at its pinnacle, and at the midpoint of the book.

Then Percival falls: "His horse tripped. He was thrown" — and so, in Neville's nautical metaphor, "the sails of the world have swung round and caught me on the head" (153). In the accompanying interlude, the birds hesitate in mid-flight. That is, they "paused in their song as if glutted with sound, as if the fullness at midday had gorged them" (165). And suddenly the sea's imperial procession forward is taken aback, so that "some fish, stranded, lashed its tail as the waves drew back" (165–66). The empire falters and begins to withdraw—leaving the colonized world flooded or stranded. In the final interludes, the ebbing of empire's flood becomes a backwashing darkness that casts a pall over the metropole itself: "As if there were waves of darkness on the air, darkness moved on, covering houses, hills, trees, as waves of water wash round the sides of some sunken ship" (236). Even "girls, sitting on verandahs" suffer the flood—"[t]hem, too, the darkness covered" (236–37). In Bernard's last moment of speech, in the deep of night just before dawn, "the canopy of civilization is burnt out. The sky is dark as polished whale-bone" (296).

In the chapters and the interludes of *The Waves*, Woolf narrates the figural turns of empire as a quest for power over death. She makes transparent the sublimating, figurational energy of the imperial self, and in this paradoxical sense she empties its interiority out.

Typography's Queer Sublime

Yet Woolf does not herself escape the figural mode, as she makes abundantly clear, and so she remains tied to the aesthetic economy of imperialism that she exposes. Like Rhoda, she is absorbed by its mythic, binding, Percivalian powers. And at the close of her book, we may be, too. Woolf's sublimely figurative world fills our eyes, draws us in like the inhaling waves even as it tells us we are its project, we are the vessels being filled. She herself recreates a spell of myth; she gives us once more the illusion that culture is nature, destruction is creation, that her images are the world, and that we are in the presence of mimesis, of narrative, of communal history. Though critics labor to separate Woolf from Bernard as cultural narrator and metaphor maker, this task is an impossible one.[32] Woolf shares the speech of figures with Bernard. And with us.

Woolf seems to point toward this identity between herself and Bernard near the end of Bernard's closing monologue. We read, ostensibly in Bernard's voice, that something "'lies deep, tideless, immune, now that he is dead, the man I called "Bernard": the man who kept a book in his pocket in which he made notes —phrases for the moon, notes of features'" (291). This strange turn by which Bernard the narrator becomes the narrator of Bernard hints at the presence of Woolf's voice behind Bernard's. Just as Bernard as a child had peeked over the wall at Elvedon and seen a woman writing, so here we as readers peek over that garden wall and see the woman who sits writing this story of the imperial sublime we have been reading. This woman writer behind the male narrator on the one hand sits apart from his world, commenting on it; but on the other hand she too is a narrator, a figure who, from within a safely walled world, creates history through written words, whose imagery of violence, whose rhythm of vehemence, empowers her text.

Later in Bernard's closing monologue, Woolf again allows herself to become conflated with Bernard and his well-supported, figurative impulses: "'My book, stuffed with phrases, has dropped to the floor. It lies under the table to be swept up by the charwoman when she comes wearily at dawn looking for scraps of paper'" (295). The book is at once Woolf's and Bernard's and *ours* (mine lies open on my desk) — and all will require sweeping up. Bernard and the woman writer at Elvedon and all readers are alike shadowed by the figure of a sweeper. In *The Waves* the sweeper returns whenever the woman writer appears: "'The lady sits between the two long windows, writing. The gardeners sweep'"; "'I see the lady writing. I see the gardeners sweeping'" (17); "'the lady writing and the gardeners with their great brooms'" (192). Like Helen on the Euphrosyne surrounded by working men in blue jerseys, both Bernard and Woolf depend equally on sweepers, on an economy of subordinated labor that is in turn of a piece with empire's violence and sublimations. The book we read, with its introjected, sublimated savagery, belongs to this economy. As woman writer, Woolf lets us know that she speaks a doubled voice, standing at the edge of but not outside the circle of an imperialist sublimity. She reveals that her writing moves along, not beyond, its circumference.

Woolf most strikingly moves along this limit in the structure and typography of her book. Apart from the simple statements "he said" or "she said," all of *The Waves* is in either quotes or italics. There is no "narrator," technically speaking, certainly no transparent narrator who invisibly inhabits and conveys the characters' consciousnesses, as in her earlier novels. In the chapters proper, all is reported in quotation marks, lifted from the characters' internalized dialogues — so that my citations of their words have all had to appear in double quotation marks. These marks remind us that we are reading what the characters thought or said, but not what *is*. Likewise, the interludes — describing sea and sun as the movements of a recumbent woman and charging men with spears — are in italics. The italics render the interludes as imported signs, as traces of an untranslatable foreign world that is covered over with words and type.

Woolf in this most fundamental way calls attention to her text's writtenness. All of it, she tells us, is situated speech, printed speech, historical, projected, interpellated. In this way she reminds us that in reading her book we have entered the world not of nature but of the author. The *phenomenon* the reader encounters in this text is the materiality of print itself, that "phantom" world which nonetheless inhabits the sea's horizon and there achieves its own material effects.

This is a queer literary sublime that claims no transcendence, no dominion, but rather moves in the slippage between one sign and another, makes meaning of the difference between one typography and another, print-manipulations which after all represent the materiality of history. In this "mystical, eyeless book," as she called it, and in the red-streaked evening of the British empire, Woolf reflects on writing's force in the Atlantic world. Working under the sign of literary freedom, she writes a novel without a freedom plot.

Conclusion

FREEDOM SEEMS AN absolute good, a natural value, perhaps one of the few we might deem universal. All good political struggle works to break *free* of oppression and alienation. But this book has shown how freedom itself is weighted with history. Although it seems provocative to say so, at this point it may be the idea of freedom that we need to break free from, at least as it has been forged in the Atlantic individualist imagination.

It's not just that the freedom discourse has emerged within and against systems of domination or slavery. Ironically, the idea of freedom has itself enabled the growth of modern forms of oppression. In Anglophone culture, this peculiar history begins with the second-generation Virginians who invoked freedom to discredit royal monopoly companies and who mingled the idea of freedom with the emergent discourse of freeborn Englishmen, which (to simplify) allowed them to rewrite the economic rules, fund the overthrow of King Charles I, and foster a renewed English turn toward American colonization. As I have tried to show, from this point forward, freedom became the reigning value in national historiography, in literary history, and in Atlantic narratives: all of these tell the freedom story of a *people,* increasingly understood as a race driven by an inherited will to be free. Tapping, as well, into the ancient tropes of Israelites escaping bondage across the Red Sea and of raped Lucretian women prompting the birth of nations, this master narrative of ruin and race-freedom has founded the political imaginary of the English-language Atlantic world. It has given race-souls to subjects and so made heroically free agents of mere laboring individuals.

This history makes especially clear that race, far from being an inappropriately sectarian concern in a Habermasian public sphere of print, has constituted the idea, the content, the location, the capital, and the color of the Atlantic public sphere, by way of its foundational coupling with freedom. Within this world, the powers of race, freedom, and print have been *interproduced,* to borrow a term from Trinh T. Minha.[1] As writing became the sign of a world-historical freedom — a race-freedom once stolen, then seized back, and finally made manifest in print, as the story goes — every printed word in English came to carry some trace of race. "Race is everything," said the British Victorian scientist John Knox, and although in retrospect freedom might appear as the opposite of such determinations, historically the call to freedom has been the call of race. African-Atlantic and Anglo-Atlantic histories and texts have unfolded together in response to this double cell, in a paradoxical yet dialectical interrelation.

Race has thus shaped the Atlantic world — and beyond — through the rhetoric of freedom, and it continues to do so. During his presidency, George W. Bush made perfectly clear that the colonizing powers of the race-freedom narrative are alive and well. To establish the persistence of the tropes I have traced in this study, and to lay the ground for my closing remarks on race, freedom, and Atlantic studies, I will take a moment to track the rhetoric of this U.S. president.

George W. Bush reiterated again and again the master-story of Anglo-Atlantic freedom, invoking all its key terms and giving new evidence of its coupling with colonialist force. Taking words right out of the mouth of Catharine Macaulay and even calling up the phoenix image with which I opened this book, in his 2004 State of the Union address, Bush conjured the universalist ideal in pronouncing that "God has planted in every human heart the desire to live in freedom" so that "even when that desire has been crushed by tyranny for decades, it will rise again."[2] At the same time, he called on the old Anglo-Saxon, transatlantic origin-story, explaining that "the roots of our democracy can be traced to England and its Parliament" and studding his comments with references to the Magna Carta. And he invoked the biblical layer of the palimpsestic Atlantic text of freedom: rousing troops on the warship USS *Abraham Lincoln* with the idea that "wherever you go, you carry a message of hope — a message that is ancient and ever new," he cited Isaiah: "To the captives, 'come out'; and to those in darkness, 'be free.'"[3]

In implicit accordance with the Anglo-centric genealogy of freedom, Bush furthermore assigned the United States a central role in this world-historical epic: "America, in this young century, proclaims liberty throughout the world and to all the inhabitants thereof. Renewed in our strength — tested, but not weary — we are ready for the greatest achievements in the history of freedom" (5). Indeed, he gave full credit for freedom's twentieth-century advance to the United States: "We are the nation that saved liberty in Europe, and liberated death camps, and helped raise up democracies, and faced down an evil empire. Once again, we accept the call of history to deliver the oppressed." We should thus know whom to credit with the fact that, since 1945, as he calculated it in this speech, the world has gone from two dozen to 122 democracies.[4] Repeatedly, Bush placed an American "we" in the position of judging whether this or that "people" could handle freedom, as for instance in the "Final Ultimatum" speech he gave before invading Iraq, when he noted that "we believe the Iraqi people are deserving and capable of freedom," and that "Iraq can become a self-governing nation" (as if it weren't already).[5] Meanwhile he implied that the force of American freedom faced a special challenge in the Middle East, noting that it would be proof that liberty could grow anywhere, "If liberty can blossom in the rocky soil of the West Bank and Gaza."[6]

At the same time, in quiet hints, Bush let it be known that he understood the underlying economic and military compulsions of the freedom epic. "Liberty is the plan of Heaven for humanity" because, he argued, "freedom honors and unleashes human creativity — and creativity determines the strength and wealth of nations." His telling allusion to the wealth and strength of nations mingled, furthermore, with his Hegelian rhetoric of force. Although Bush insisted that "freedom is not determined by some dialectic of history," he nonetheless throughout his presidency repeatedly echoed Hegel's emphasis on the will to freedom as the dialectical "force" of history. In his 2005 inaugural address, he announced, "There is only one force of history that can break the reign of hatred and resentment, and expose the pretensions of tyrants, and reward the hopes of the decent and tolerant, and that is the force of human freedom."[7] Again fashioning the United States as the agent of the "force of human freedom," he called for a "forward strategy of freedom in the Middle East" — or what he elsewhere named the "preemptive action necessary to defend our liberty," supported by a military that is ready to "strike at any dark corner of the world" in the cause of freedom. Thus the 2002 graduating class at West Point learned from him that "history has issued its call to your generation" to "enter this drama" and "serve the cause of freedom." Not surprisingly, then, when Bush announced the creation of the "Homeland Security" office, he conjured a kind of lord-bondsman battle to the death in imagining that "freedom and fear are at war — and freedom is winning."[8]

In his biblical allusions, his references to the wealth of nations, and his sense of history as a forward, force-driven story of freedom, George W. Bush gave ample evidence that the Atlantic master-narrative of freedom flourishes in the twenty-first century. American politicians from both parties, of course, have reiterated this story, as when Senator Carl Levin (Democrat of Michigan) objected in June

2006 to the amnesty plan for Iraqi insurrectionists with the exasperated ejaculation, "For heaven's sake, we liberated that country. . . . We paid a tremendous price. The idea that they should even consider talking about amnesty for people who have killed people who liberated their country is unconscionable."[9] Nor have European politicians left this rhetoric behind. The everywhere-invoked rhetoric of liberty makes clear that, although writers, activists, scholars, and a host of communities have undertaken the task of deconstructing the racialized liberty plot, that plot is surviving their efforts. It continues to do its powerful work in the world, by way of an implicit chauvinism that fundamentally assumes that freedom is every culture's primary value and then deems, for instance, U.S. Anglo-Americans the judges of other peoples' capacity for freedom, and by this means profits one nation at the expense of others.

This legacy of freedom in Atlantic history asks us to think twice about the liberation framework within which many scholarly and activist projects get launched. Might it be that, out of habit, we too readily or too often invoke this word even when other values are more to the point? Freedom is often a necessary and appropriate term — in relation to situations of enslavement, imprisonment, and totalitarian control. But if it is social dignity, or economic justice, or an international politics of mutuality and sustainability that we seek, we misconstrue these when we call them freedom struggles. In literary studies, when we consider the pursuit of freedom the primary aesthetic or political project of authors, we may overlook literature's more sustaining and dialectical movements — not heroically onward and upward, but rather back and forth in call and response within and among readerly communities. That is, in privileging freedom above all we may work against ourselves, for historically the notion of freedom eschews interdependency; it reinscribes a heroic, heteronormative, colonial telos — which implicitly if unintentionally preserves the old racial romance of history.

Indeed, as Orlando Patterson suggests in *Slavery and Racial Death,* it is exactly in the context of race and slavery that we *must* "challenge our conception of freedom and the value we place upon it."[10] With this point in mind we might reconsider, for instance, the rhetoric of Michael Hardt and Antonio Negri in their postmodern rethinking of "empire" and the possibilities for subverting it. Working earnestly to imagine the "multitude" as an "active subject," Hardt and Negri see in the multitude's movements and forms of cooperation a world of "subterranean and uncontainable rhizomes . . . that mark the new paths of destiny."[11] Yet something rings familiar in their story of a revolutionary destiny, especially as these "movements often cost terrible suffering, but there is also in them a desire for liberation that is not satiated except by reappropriating new spaces, around which are constructed new freedoms" (397). It is perhaps not surprising that in this story of freedom that pivots on suffering, with its sexual undertones of desire and "satiation" and its painful "costs," the multitude must once again be streamlined and subsumed within the destiny of a singular "active subject."

Yet, without a freedom telos, how might we narrate our histories and aims? Within what frame for the present and future will we do our work? In the work of all kinds of scholars, what kinds of rhetorical mediations are called for? In her book *Freedom Is Not Enough,* a study of the lessons learned in the U.S. civil rights struggle, Nancy MacLean points in a promising direction. She argues that the rallying call for freedom stops short, that the fight for jobs, houses, health, and dignity requires other values and a different rhetoric. Insofar as "freedom," in modernity's "laissez-faire" economy, also means "good luck pulling yourself up by your bootstraps," the larger goal may not be liberty but *viability,* which after all, as many political scientists, legal studies scholars, and democracy theorists have argued, seems to require a sense of *mutuality and collectivity.*[12] Not just "a multitude" of autonomous agents, but a concerted project of cooperation. Not just shared goals or liberated desires, but mutual recognition and balanced laboring.

In this light we can appreciate anew the salutary thrust of certain feminist and race projects in literary studies. For instance, in the work of Carla Peterson and John Ernst cited in earlier chapters, we are led to see how some of our older stories are already working out this different formulation of economic collectivity and political struggle. These critics help us to see that Harriet Jacobs narrates her escape from slavery not simply as a heroic, individual pursuit of liberty by an "active subject," and not even only as a project requiring a whole village to hide and feed and guide her (although it does), but also as a careful set of negotiations and conversations within this "village," the story of another kind of economy and polis, involving her grandmother's baking business, a white woman's harboring bedroom attic, and black sailors' covert stow-away activities, as well as a series of dialogues, especially with her grandmother when she explains her decision to sleep with a white man and with her readers when she actively questions them about the meaning of her freedom. Harriet Jacobs's path out of slavery entails making that path comprehensible to others, and it establishes a matrix of relations, a complex interdependence. Critics' further attention to the economic and dialogical interdependence expressed in such stories can begin to dislodge freedom's hegemony not only within history but also within our readerly and scholarly imaginations.

And yet such work also implicitly raises questions about how to value freedom's shadow legacy, that of race. Insofar as freedom is joined at the root with race, when we search for sustaining values beyond the freedom narrative, do we also search beyond race? Certainly the framework of race is required to understand English-language literature and the history it encodes. But to what degree will twenty-first-century readers continue to consider that framework their framework and see themselves working strictly within an unbroken continuity of racial community that encompasses the present and future as well as the past? Is it possible that if we historicize our own moment and our own work as carefully as we historicize that of eighteenth-, nineteenth-, and twentieth-century authors, we will see evidence that race is reaching the limits of its enabling powers?

At the end of this study, it appears to me that, the more we read such authors as Pauline Hopkins or W. E. B. Du Bois within the long Atlantic history in which freedom itself is racialized, the more we see that they are beckoning us beyond, at least, the problematic coupling of the heroic and the racial as the only way to produce (a better) freedom. For, after all, this coupling completes the downfall of Dianthe Rusk in *Of One Blood*. Afrocentric as Hopkins's novel appears, does it not tell the story of a heroic quest for African identity across the Atlantic that sacrifices the project of intimacy and healing at home? Does this not sound familiar to women of color who lived through the 1960s U.S. civil rights movement? Hopkins seems to have been the kind of historical seer she so often wrote about. She seems to have anticipated that the contradictory problems she faced, the ones born from the race-freedom legacy, would likewise defeat the Helga Cranes of the world and would continue to trouble us one hundred years later. As did Larsen, she implicitly asked: how achieve public-sphere freedom from race by way of race, that is, by way of a literary and political subjectivity so pervaded by race? How maintain the racial solidarity necessary for survival while resisting the reduction of subjectivity to race? She grappled, as readers have recently done in the wake of Paul Gilroy's book *Beyond Race*, with whether a community can leave race behind when racism still structures the world.

And then, too, there is the question of whether, in the world of capitalist modernity, communities *want* to leave race behind. For, as many Atlantic narratives establish, race has also operated as a supplementary power in modernity, even if phantasmically (in a Lacanian or Derridean sense): its promise of continuous identity across centuries and oceans provides a sense of meaningful community — not to mention material places to work and live — amid capitalism's economic instability and alienated individuality. What would be left after the dissolution of race or ethnic community — what forms of expressivity, worldness, safety, sustainability? Attachment to race community collides, however, with the fact that inequality is deeply embedded in exactly those race-defined neighborhoods and psychic identifications that at the same time sustain us. As long as Anglo-Saxon Protestant whiteness is the gold standard, other identifications will be devalued and double-edged. So, can we truly dis-assemble racial inequality and injustice if we vigilantly preserve, or demand, strict affiliations with race? These are the thorny questions that have plagued writers and thinkers for over a century, the questions that contribute to a contemporary uncertainty about the place of race in our narratives.

One reason it is so difficult to come to a conclusion about these race questions is, of course, that history is uneven in its unfolding. Its dialectics are so much messier than Professor Hegel allowed. Race operates one way here and another there. The unevenness of the playing fields constituted by race, globally and locally, trips us up with every door we lock, channel we change, street we avoid, smile we question; and it puts us back on our heels when, in the midst of all these, we sometimes look across the uneven terrain and see eye-to-eye. Maybe in one room race begins to dissolve, or feel luminous, and you laugh; but walk into the next and it has you by the throat. You feel caught out. You vow not to give up race struggle until it has given up battering you.

Yet still, something is happening in English-language talk about race. And sex has everything to do with it. That is, the embedded race-narrative of heroic freedom that has hewn so closely to a heterosexual plot of Atlantic ruin and redemption has faced the most pressing challenges from queer, gay, lesbian, transsexual, and feminist dissent from sexual norms, as well as from the voluntary undoing of pure race lineage created by biracial and cross-diasporic sexuality and families — black Puerto Rican, Asian Jamaican, Irish African, Anglo–African American. Current scholarship unabashedly turns a light on the heteronormativity coiled in black nationalisms (as in Michelle Stephens's *Black Empire*) or on the homophobic imaginary of young black men in prison (as in Patricia Hill Collins's *Black Sexual Politics*). To the extent that the freedom narrative trailing racial clouds of glory depends on a heterosexual and homophobic plot of ruin and redemption, all such projects will transform our relation to race and freedom both.

ATLANTIC STUDIES and other forms of transnational studies are particularly able to bring such founding master narratives of race, sex, property, and freedom into view and into question. I'd like to close by naming some of the methodological possibilities and practices that this book has clarified for me, especially as they grow out of this kind of transnational approach.

Goods and money — that is, capital — flow around the globe every day and always, but people live in certain places or regions over a duration, even if they seasonally migrate for work or are refugees, exiles, or part of a diasporic community. Indeed, even utterly displaced children and adults live their experiences within and across this placedness of others within villages, cities, nations, and global regions. Transnational studies, as I see it, aims to think through these two facts together: the odd, uneven time-travel of world-system economies and the lived placedness of human lives.

What we might call "regional" transnational studies, including such configurations as the Middle East or, for my purposes, the Atlantic, invites us to think about the global economy in relation to particular communities and their transnational formations, across borders and yet within a certain circumference. This method follows the flow of capital and the interactive dynamics it creates among people(s), and yet it also tracks the regional tilt of these flows and dynamics, of nations in relation, and in clustered relation, as they always are, whether as allies or enemies. Some transnational studies might highlight the former — the global capital flows and the human refugees or migrants they help to create — but the kind I have practiced here centers itself within geographical regions. This regional transnational approach emphasizes cross-border histories, conflicts, and diasporas (within, say, southeast Asia, central Europe, or the Mediterranean) as well as the interproduced discourses that legalize or inscribe these clustered transnational relations. A concentrated focus on such transnational networks of economy and culture (whether indigenous, diasporic, colonial, or national) allows us better to specify the mediating work of expressive forms within a particular region, which in turn can shed light on the larger dialectical interaction of global or "external" economy and local and regional or "internal" culture.

Whether emphasizing global economies or more local, regional cultures and their interdependent formation, the strength of transnational studies lies in its consideration of both global and local dimensions, for the fundamental modern dialectic of economy and culture happens at their intersection. In its attention to this intersection, transnational studies can move us past the question of whether economy or culture provides "the" originary arena of the dialectic that we call history. Culture and economy are utterly inextricable, and this is true exactly because together they *are* the dialectic: people and goods. And while practices of coerced or exploited labor aim to make goods out of people and transfer the profit to others, it is *people* living in certain places who interact in particular ways with this pressure. People and place must in some form be co-original with the capitalist or any other cross-cultural economy — and not reducible to it. Otherwise, there would be no economy.

To better understand this dialectical interlocking of culture and economy, in this study I have situated the "history of the novel in English" in an Atlantic region flooded with race, gender, and class discourses — those discourses that negotiate relations among Atlantic nations as they unfold within a global, capitalist trade economy. From this transnational perspective, the English-language novel clearly emerges as a labor-intensive, mediating form. Viewing the novel regionally rather than strictly racially or nationally, we see the regularity of its underlying narrative formations across different communities, and we comprehend how novels negotiate the anxiety attendant on their place(s) in a newly volatile, distended globe mustering ever greater fire power and travel power, and engendering both higher odds of ruinous exile and larger fantasies of empire. In this light, the novel's will-to-freedom telos can be seen mounting itself and flinging itself, like Bernard at the end of *The Waves*, against a real or imagined threat—the surround of other nations and other people who would equally like to be free masters of their fates. The aesthetic of the sublime, shadowing the novel, tells us this old colonialist, originally Atlantic English-language story, but we have been too nationalist and specialist in our focus to see it.

Once we see all of this, once we read the "English-language novel" rather than strictly the British or American or African American or Indian American or Black British or immigrant novel, we also grasp the extent to which literature encodes that history in which Oliver Cromwell launches both freedom and slavery, and Britain's eastward/southward turn in the nineteenth century occurs in tandem with the United States's westward/southward turn, so that Walt Whitman works under the sign of a passage to India and an Eliotian, Anglo-Jewish Mirah stands both beside and against a Hopkinsian, African American Mira. Thus can regional-transnational literary studies give heft to our account of global-transnational and diasporic histories.

The same dialectical approach can operate in literary-critical methodology. Just as persons, peoples, and nations each occupy and negotiate a place in relation to each other, and insofar as they are not simply empty, interchangeable placeholders within an utterly determined system, so with texts of whatever kind. Our critical practice needs, I think, to attend to each text in its specificity in order to understand both the pressure it exerts in a larger global network and the structured dynamics of that network. A text's gaps, leaps, illuminations, evasions, winks, nods, unveilings, and consolations arise in a here and now, responsive to but not reducible to the patterns of its past or its surround. In fact, a text's peculiarities give us exactly the light we need to read its regional and global surround. A dialectical, transnational literary-critical method entails, in other words, very close reading of individual texts with an eye to the horizon within which each is made and read. By contrast, a practice that quickly scans and summarizes many texts and in *this* way aims at attunement to the constellatory horizon sometimes misses the events that constitute any constellation: the singular entry and effect of each text, author, reader, interaction. Without attending to these singular "events," we are liable to misunderstand both the regional, transnational constellation and its place within a global world-system.

Finally, insofar as this practice of working dialectically between text and constellation, as between transnational and global, heightens our sense of what Jean-Luc Nancy calls the singular-plural of human intersubjectivity, it gives us a glimpse of our own implicatedness, our placedness in this transnational history and world.[13] We are more likely to see how the dialectic encompasses us, whoever we are. We are its story as much as it is ours. Likewise with an Atlantic genealogy of freedom: the genealogy's scope allows us to see that we are its epic story as much as it is ours.

And so the question arises again, especially for those of us still situated in an Atlantic world: what will we do with freedom's racialization of us all, which seems to make us heroes and comrades but by the same logic sets us up to conquer and be conquered? Might it be that if we let go freedom's heroic accents, beginning modestly in our critical writing projects and implicit self-narratives, we will shrink back to size as mere persons forever in encumbered relation? Persons finally naming it together and talking it over? Might that be better than freedom? Or maybe the best kind of freedom?

Notes

Introduction

1. Rousseau, *The Social Contract*, 89. All further references to this work appear in the text.

2. Thomson, *Liberty*. All further references to this work appear in the text.

3. Although Thomson also narrates the mingling of Saxons with Britons on English soil, he clearly points to the Germanic Saxons as the catalyzing force in Britain's recovery of freedom.

4. Hegel, "Philosophy of History" in *Philosophy of Hegel*, 341. All further references to this work appear in the text.

5. In this light, it would be interesting to consider Franco Moretti's argument, in *Way of the World*, about the focus on youth and the structure of *bildungsroman* in the novel.

6. Hartman, *Scenes of Subjection*, 115.

7. See Hartman, *Scenes of Subjection*, 5–10 and throughout. Davis addresses this matter throughout his work. See especially *The Problem of Slavery in Western Culture*.

8. Beginning with Winthrop Jordan, most scholars have considered new encounters between Europeans and Africans, and especially within slavery and the slave trade, the source of racist and racial thinking in Western modernity. See W. D. Jordan, *White over Black*.

9. Gilroy, *Black Atlantic*, 15.

10. These terms allow me more accurately to characterize a range of writers or persons, including both colonial American writers, who are not yet "American" in the conventional, postrevolutionary sense of the term, and writers such as Susanna Rowson or Olaudah Equiano, who move across national identities and borders and yet are understood by themselves and others to have racialized (Anglo or African) Atlantic identities. Additionally, although all the authors treated in this study are writing in English, and could be called "Anglo-Atlantic" in this sense, to adopt this term for all of them would clearly elide the very racialization of freedom and writing that I am addressing.

11. See Morrison, *Playing in the Dark*.

12. This scene shrewdly rewrites, I'll argue in chapter 7, Robinson Crusoe's first "undoing," as he calls it, in his first and foreshadowing sea storm, after which he, too, boards a "Guiney ship," but to become a slaver's seaman rather than a slave.

13. Wood, *Radicalism of the American Revolution*, 173.

14. Baucom, *Specters of the Atlantic*, 6–8.

15. For a full study of this connection, see Melissa Matthes, *The Rape of Lucretia and the Founding of Republics*. Also see Margaret Doody's discussion of rape as a part of a freedom plot embedded in classical Greek novels, although she does not then read English novels

as freedom stories or interpret their seduction plots in these terms (*The True Story of the Novel*, especially 73–81).

16. Livy, *History of Rome*, 73.

17. In historical studies, see especially the work of J. G. A. Pocock and Gordon Wood (see note 20); for application of this analysis to the British novel, see James Thompson, *Models of Value*; Cook, *Epistolary Bodies*; Flint, *Family Fictions*; Zomchick, *Family and Law*; and to the American novel, see Fliegelman, *Prodigals and Pilgrims*; C. Davidson, *Revolution and the Word*; Stern, *The Plight of Sympathy*; Gould, *Covenant and Republic*; and Barnes, *States of Sympathy*.

18. In "Archimedes and the Paradox of Feminist Criticism," Myra Jehlen long ago sketched the possibility that the novelistic heroine's plight stands in for that of the modern citizen. Nina Auerbach has specifically considered the ruined woman as a figuration of the ruined state in Victorian culture in "The Rise of the Fallen Woman." More recently Ros Ballaster in *Seductive Forms*, Amanda Anderson in *Tainted Souls and Painted Faces*, Catherine Gallagher in *Nobody's Story*, and Gillian Brown in *Consent of the Governed* have all considered the ways that the heroine's struggle or "fall" is emblematic, as an increasing number of studies on the novel do, but usually without developing this insight at length. Anderson's *Painted Faces* does so most completely. Also see my fuller discussion and notes in chapters 5 and 6.

19. Brown, *Consent*, 133.

20. See *The Political Theory of Possessive Individualism*, in which C. B. MacPherson traces this social formation to the seventeenth century in a way that prepares and supports my thesis here. Also see Melvin Yazawa, *Colonies to Commonwealth*, for full discussion of the new ideal of "independence" in the American republic which, as Yazawa points out, ultimately implied that "the citizen was on his own" (144). He concludes that, accordingly, "the commitment to republicanism entailed nothing less than the forming of a new identity," disentangled from kinship community, a point that accords with my interpretation of the "swoon" experience in Atlantic narratives. I would add that a parallel discourse of independence circulated in England in the eighteenth century.

21. My suggestions here are in accord with Goldberg's way of understanding how race defines citizenship to the core, with only a slight difference in emphasis. He argues that racialized exclusion from the state is predicated on the presumed "incapacity to fulfill rational and civilized needs and drives, a failure to deliver the goods" (*The Racial State*, 47). But I would note that, underlying this incapacity, according to the liberty plot, is the perceived absence of a drive toward liberty—including the active will to "free" commerce. I also offer a different history for how this logic came into being.

22. See, for instance, Pocock, *The Ancient Constitution and the Feudal Law* and *Virtue, Commerce, and History*; Robbins, *The Eighteenth-Century Commonwealthman*; Wood, *The Creation of the American Republic* and *The Radicalism of the American Revolution*; J. C. D. Clark, *The Language of Liberty* and *Revolution and Rebellion*; Yazawa, *From Colonies to Commonwealth*; and M. Warner, *The Letters of the Republic*. Although the title of Clark's book, *The Language of Liberty*, might suggest a close affinity between our projects, Clark wishes to highlight the ways that this language was driven largely by religious concerns, and he wishes to disconnect the liberty discourse from cultural revolutions related to race,

class, and gender. I would point out, however, that the freedom language of religion was itself implicitly cultural and racial by way of its links to Saxonism.

23. See Horsman, *Race and Manifest Destiny.* For earlier scholarship, see Colbourn, *Lamp of Experience,* and Bernard Bailyn, *Ideological Origins.* For insistent de-emphasis on race in "the language of liberty," see Clark's book by that title. See above, note 22.

24. This is the formulation of Gussman in "Inalienable Rights," 58 – 59. Also see Schuck and Smith, *Citizenship without Consent.* By contrast, in *Empire for Liberty,* Wai-Chee Dimock considers the ways in which liberty as an ideology served imperial ambition, although her focus is not on race as a vehicle for this ideology.

25. Although in "Hybridism and the Ethnicity of the English" (in *Cultural Readings of Imperialism*), Robert Young briefly notes the association between Anglo-Saxon character and "qualities of Protestantism, freedom and liberty," he too quickly reduces this cluster of elements to what he calls "the Saxon supremacist view" and therefore misses the full import of its contradictory racial formation (129 – 30).

26. Poliakov most comprehensively tracks the medieval and modern sources of the notion of superior "Aryan" races, while Kliger, Smith, Adams, Brinkley, and (in the U.S. context) Colbourn focus more narrowly on Anglo-Saxonism. Poliakov's work, together with Kiernan's *Lords of Human Kind,* draws attention to the medieval and early modern conflations of race, class, and nation, where all three categories overlapped and shifted depending on who had most recently conquered whom.

27. See Stephens, *Black Empire,* Weinbaum, *Wayward Reproductions,* and Rice, *Radical Narratives of the Black Atlantic.*

28. Hardt and Negri, *Empire.* See my further discussion of their text in the conclusion.

29. Gardiner, "First English Novel," 204. Warner later makes a similar argument, as I discuss below, and Brown makes an interestingly related one in his account of the "romance" of criticism about the novel. See Brown's "Why the Story of the Origins of the (English) Novel Is an American Romance (if not the Great American Novel)." One could speculate that the Whig sensibility has provided the pulse of all modern scholarship, arising as this scholarship originally does, at least in part, from the work of those seventeenth-century, document-collecting antiquarians whose activities helped to destabilize monarchy. At the same time, more ontologically perhaps, the casting of history in print may work to overcome the experience of a communal loss; and so perhaps scholarship itself always manifests the attachment to a lost past and a desire to reconstitute it. In any case, certainly novel scholarship adopts the language of liberty as if to sustain a threatened tradition.

30. Hazlitt, *Lectures on the Comic Writer,* cited in Warner, *Licensing,* 24. In *Democratic Personality,* Ruttenberg works to detach the freedom impulse from this Anglo-Protestant legacy in arguing that "we can no longer restrict democracy's meaning to a set of sociopolitical or more broadly cultural institutions or procedures grounded in rational (liberal) value" (3). She proposes that the impulse to such expression is "historically realized in an untheorized and irrational practice of compulsive public utterance" (3). While it is the project of my study to establish the print and institutional Atlantic legacy, and while I would argue that this deeply embedded legacy conditions these speech practices, Ruttenberg's study raises the necessary "other" question — about how a possibly "irrational" or perhaps untheorizable "source" interacts dialectically with institutional legacies.

31. Watt, *Rise of the Novel*, 222. All further references to this work appear in the text. For a full, recent reading of Watt's seminal study along different but related lines, see Margaret Reeves, "Telling the Tale of *The Rise of the Novel*."

32. Doody, *Natural Passion*, 11. All further references to this work appear in the text.

33. Cohan, "*Clarissa* and the Individuation of Character," 171.

34. Richetti, *English Novel in History*, 81.

35. Richetti, "Family, Sex, and Marriage in Defoe," 32.

36. McKeon, *Origins of English Novel*, 61.

37. Wenska, "*The Coquette* and American Dream," 244.

38. Chase, *American Novel and Its Tradition*, viii.

39. Lanser, "Befriending the Body," 180.

40. Castle, *Masquerade and Civilization*, 34; and Craft-Fairchild, *Masquerade and Gender*, 3.

41. Gossett and Bardes, "Women and Political Power," 23.

42. Henderson, "Introduction: The Forms of Things Unknown," 5, 18.

43. Hostetler, "The Aesthetics of Race and Gender," 36.

44. Posnock, *Color and Culture*, 6.

45. Chartier, *The Order of Books*, viii.

46. I refer here to Sedgwick's theory in *Between Men*.

47. See Jardine's book, *Gynesis*.

48. Warner, *Licensing Entertainment*, 25. All further references to this work appear in the text.

49. Hazlitt, quoted in Warner, *Licensing*, 22, 24.

50. Taine, quoted in Warner, *Licensing*, 27.

51. See Warner's review essay, "Reading Rape: Marxist-Feminist Figurations of the Literal," *Diacritics* (Winter 1983): 12–32. See also 93 in *Licensing Entertainment*.

52. Warner, *Reading Clarissa*.

53. Gardiner, "First English Novel," 216.

1. Atlantic Horizon, Interior Turn

1. Hare, quoted in Kliger, *Goths in England*, 136–37. All further references to this work appear in the text.

2. Richardson, *Clarissa*, 1073, emphasis added. All further references to this work appear in the text.

3. *London Chronicle*, quoted in Kathleen Wilson, "Citizenship, Empire, and Modernity," 83.

4. King James I, quoted in Brinkley, *Arthurian Legend*, 28. All further references to this work appear in the text.

5. See Kliger, *Goths*, Brinkley, *Arthurian Legend*, and Adams, *Old English Scholarship*, for discussion of how the Reformation in England led to the antiquarian interest in Anglo-Saxons.

6. Parker, quoted in Adams, *Old English Scholarship*, 14. All further references to this work appear in the text.

7. Selden, quoted in Woolf, *The Idea of History in Early Stuart England,* 215. All further references to this work appear in the text.

8. Brenner, *Merchants and Revolution,* 98. All further references to this work appear in the text.

9. For related discussion of the colonies and the movement toward civil war, also see Bliss, *Revolution and Empire.* As Bliss puts it, tobacco and sugar profits "fuel[ed] the sinews of war" (48).

10. See Kupperman, *Providence Island,* 142–43.

11. See Williams, *Capitalism and Slavery* (chapter 1) and, more recently, Linebaugh and Rediker, *Many-Headed Hydra* (chapters 1–4) for an account of white servitude in the West Indies and North America. The economic Atlantic history I outline here in part explains why (as Nicholas Hudson has shown), British conservatives played a key role in the anti-slavery campaigns of the nineteenth century. The Atlantic trade in slaves had interfered with the fortune-making of "greater" British men since its inception.

12. Haller, *Tracts on Liberty,* 3:303. Emphasis in original. All further references to this work appear in the text.

13. Sexby, quoted in Mendle, *The Putney Debates,* 127.

14. For a reprinted selection of these publications, see Raymond, *Making the News,* and for discussion of their nature and effects, see R. C. Richardson, *The Debate on the English Revolution,* and MacGillivray, *Restoration Historians and the English Civil War.*

15. See Thompson, *Media and Modernity,* for an account of the growth of the press and newspapers in these years. All further references to this work appear in the text. Also see the literary scholars Backscheider, *Spectacular Politics,* and Norbrook, *Writing the English Republic,* for discussions of an emergent public sphere in this period.

16. See Wiseman, "'Adam, the Father of All Flesh,'" 134–57.

17. McEntee, "The [Un]Civil Sisterhood," 93–94. All further references to this work appear in the text.

18. See documents compiled in Prall, *The Puritan Revolution,* 134, 129, 134, 127, 128. All further references to this work appear in the text.

19. Underdown, *Freeborn People,* 105. All further references to this work appear in the text.

20. Winstanley, *The Law of Freedom in a Platform,* 22–23. All further references to this work appear in the text.

21. Lyon, *Manifestoes,* 8. All further references to this work appear in the text.

22. Woodhouse, *Puritanism and Liberty,* 20. All further references to this work appear in the text.

23. See Zaret, *Heavenly Contract.*

24. Though Prynne later denounced Cromwell's decision to bring Charles to trial. See Prall, *The Puritan Revolution,* 85–86.

25. Damrosch takes this narration as evidence of the way novels inherit the Puritan traditions of autobiography and godly self-revelation (*God's Plots,* 68), and Bender draws instead on a Foucauldian framework, casting the novel as the literary equivalent of the interiorizing discipline of the panopticon. I suggest not only that the two legacies are interwoven in Atlantic modernity but also that their discourses of transparency are caught up in a racialized

narrative of the subject's remaking and liberation. In my account of novelistic narration in later chapters, I will place more emphasis on the positioning of the exiled or dissenting narrator, who, from outside, claims the most clear-sighted access to this interior law governing both the characters and the community. For other discussions of race in relation to the Foucauldian framework, see Stoler, *Race and the Education of Desire*, and Robyn Wiegman, *American Anatomies*.

26. Hegel, *Philosophy of History*, 10. All further references to this work appear in the text.

27. As Mack has argued in *Visionary Women*, Winstanley himself worked to contain these gender implications (67–73). Also see Mellor, "Were Women Writers Romantics?" for discussion of the ways in which these early women preachers lay the ground for later British women writers, especially 394–97.

28. B. Hill, introduction to *The First English Feminist*, 20. All further references to this work appear in the text.

29. According to Mack, the records suggest that in the 1640s as many as three hundred women spoke in public or private meetings as visionaries and prophets. While women's preaching apparently worried most Independent religious sects, including Winstanley's and Muggleton's, others such as the Quakers—the single largest sect, acquiring over sixty thousand members by 1660—initially fostered and justified women's participation (*Visionary Women* 1; also see appendices, 413–24).

30. Quoted in Rachel Trubowitz, "Female Preachers and Male Wives," in Holstun, *Pamphlet Wars*, 119.

31. Woodhouse, *Puritanism and Liberty*, 444. This work contains the transcript of the Putney Debates. All further references appear in the text.

32. Montesquieu, *Esprit*, 76. All further references to this work appear in the text.

33. Zaret, *The Heavenly Contract*.

34. Linebaugh and Rediker, *Many-Headed Hydra*, 106.

35. Guthrie, quoted in Okie, *Augustan Historical Writing*, 187. All further references to this work appear in the text.

36. Quoted in Wood, *Radicalism*, 305. All further references to this work appear in the text.

37. Kaplan, *Anarchy of Empire in Making of U.S. Culture*.

38. Bailyn, *Peopling of British North America*, 5. All further references to this work appear in the text.

2. Liberty's Historiography

1. Macaulay, *History of England*, xv. All further references to this work appear in the text.

2. Mayer, *History and the Early English Novel*, 15. Also see Braudy, *Narrative Form in History and Fiction*, on historiography and the early novel.

3. Colbourn, *Lamp of Experience*, 74. All further references to this work appear in the text.

4. One might speculate that the soldiers sent by Cromwell to Ireland learned a few things about violence there as well, witnessing both the English army's brutal murdering of peasants and the Irish resisters' desperate measures.

5. Quoted in MacLean, *Culture and Society,* 11–12.

6. Vanbrugh, *Provok'd Wife,* I.1.

7. *The Younger Brother,* I.1.

8. Wood, *Radicalism of the American Revolution,* 13. All further references to this work appear in the text.

9. Hall et al., *Glorious Revolution in America,* 17, 10. These were directions given to Nicolls, the king's agent. All further references to this work appear in the text.

10. Harrington, *Oceana,* 46–47.

11. Paine, *Common Sense,* 69, 77.

12. Sidney, *Discourses Concerning Government,* 479. All further references to this work appear in the text.

13. Swift, "Abstract," 225.

14. Hume, *Essays,* 72. Likewise had Cavalier writers, under Cromwell, been forced "to embrace the opposing principle . . . of freedom," as Trevor Ross has shown in *The Making of the English Literary Canon,* so that the vocabulary no longer belonged to one faction or political vision (134–35).

15. Originally published in French 1707–24. Translated Nicholas Tindal.

16. Hume, *History of England* 1:3. All further references to this work appear in the text.

17. Part 4 of Thomson's poem similarly tells of how the blood of Gothic nations revives England. The "BRITONS" were "Bold" but by the Romans were "enfeeble[d] into slaves" (4. 626, 661) until "deep-blooming, strong, / And yellow-haired, the blue-eyed *Saxon* came" and "the fierce Race / Pour'd in a fresh invigorating Stream, / Blood, where unquell'd a mighty Spirit glowed" (4. 669–75). Although "Rash War" was their "Delight" (4.676), "Wisdom likewise was theirs, indulgent Laws / . . . On which ascends my BRITISH REIGN" for "They brought happy Government along; / Form'd by that *Freedom*" (4.686–92). But the combination of Alfred's "Monkish Dreams" and the invasion of the "haughty Normans" bring down the Saxons, and in the end the "mix'd Genius of these People all" gave rise to the "one exalted Stream" in which "the rich Tide of *English* Blood grew full" (4.725–46). Although mixed, the blood of England is all "Of *Gothic* nations" (4.742), and the Saxon contribution emerges as the most heroic.

18. Gibbon, *Decline and Fall,* 1, chap. 10, 254–55.

19. In the *Philosophy of History,* the ever-dependable Hegel will later spell out the underlying logic of this equation. Contrasting the free states of Europe with the caste-dominated system of India, Hegel claims that there are no proper written histories of India, despite its ancient traditions because "[o]nly in a State cognizant of Laws, can distinct transactions take place, accompanied by such a clear consciousness of them as supplies the ability and suggests the necessity of an enduring record" (61).

20. Macaulay's career thus also reflects the limits of this strategy. Any disenfranchised person's zealous identification with native liberty, if combined with an unconventional practice of agency, can backfire. Macaulay's reputation as a scholar suffered irreparably from her intimacy first with a much older man and then with a much younger man. Thereafter her championing of civil liberty was scurrilously glossed as her pursuit of sexual liberty, most fully in Richard Paul Joddrell's *The Female Patriot: An Epistle from C-t-e M-c-y to the Rev. Dr. W-l-n on Her Late Marriage* The old associations between "ruin" and liberty come easily to hand when a woman calls for liberty. Even now, Macaulay's *History* carries a taint of

unprofessionalism and is held by very few libraries, despite the fact that, unlike Hume's, it uses a significant number of primary documents rather than relying mainly on the work of earlier historians. It seems that if a subject takes his or her dissent too far outside normative boundaries, the contingency of social membership becomes fully visible.

21. See Leder, *Loyalist Historians;* also see Regis, *Describing Early America.*

22. Bradford, *History of Plymouth Plantation,* 382.

23. Smith quoted in Kupperman, *Providence Island,* 145.

24. Hutchinson, quoted in Vaughn and Billias, *Perspectives in Early American History.*

25. Quoted in Leder, *Loyalist Historians,* 138. Italics in original.

26. Jefferson, *Complete Jefferson,* 1094. All further references to this work appear in the text.

27. Ramsay, *History of American Revolution,* 1:27. All further references to this work appear in the text.

28. Warren, *Rise, Progress, and Termination of American Revolution,* 4. All further references to this work appear in the text.

29. Also see Ramsay, 1:2, 24, and Warren 18, 21–22, for additional similar comments.

30. See Armstrong, *Desire and Domestic Fiction.*

31. Bancroft, quoted in Swann, *Nathaniel Hawthorne,* 71.

3. The Poetics of Liberty

1. For full documentation of this eighteenth-century troping of liberty as a muse, see Meehan's *Liberty and Poetics.*

2. Knox, *The Races of Men,* 3.

3. See Helgerson, *Forms of Nationhood,* for discussion of the Reformation period, and see Weinbrot, *Britannia's Issue* and *Augustus Caesar in "Augustan" England* for discussion of the late seventeenth and the eighteenth centuries.

4. See Roach's discussion, throughout *Cities of the Dead,* of this racialized emphasis on origins in British literature. For his treatment of seventeenth- and eighteenth-century British literature, including Dryden, Pope, and others, see especially chapters 3 and 4, 73–178.

5. Quoted in Weinbrot, *Britannia's Issue,* 186. All further references to this work appear in the text as *BI.*

6. See Weinbrot, *Augustus Caesar in "Augustan" England,* for discussion of Augustanism, and see both this volume and *Britannia's Issue* for his argument that the Gothic legacy was universally denigrated.

7. Johnson, quoted in Meehan, *Liberty and Poetics,* 124, 25, emphasis added.

8. Johnson, preface to *Dictionary of the English Language,* n.p.

9. See Doyle, "The Racial Sublime."

10. Longinus was translated by John Hall in 1656, then followed by Boileau's more influential translation in 1674. See the discussion of Longinus's influence in Meehan, *Liberty and Poetics,* 2, and in Monk, *The Sublime.* Also see my analysis of Longinus in "Sublime Barbarians," tracing how the sublime was racialized within an imperial context beginning with Longinus himself.

11. See Trumpener, *Bardic Nationalism,* for an incredibly rich and wide-ranging discussion of nativist aesthetics as they shaped the gothic and romantic novel.

12. Hoyt Trowbridge gives this overview in his introduction to Hurd's *Letters on Chivalry and Romance*, iv.

13. Hurd, *Letters on Chivalry and Romance*, Letter VII, 56. All further references appear in the text with a Roman numeral letter number followed by the page number.

14. One is reminded of Basil Davidson's argument that competition among European nations impelled the slave market and the colonization of Africa. As he shows, Europeans fought one another on African land or water more than they fought any African peoples. African leaders gained market power according to their ability to play European diplomats and generals against each other. See B. Davidson, *The African Slave Trade*.

15. *The Poetical Works of Ossian*, 96. All further citations from both Blair and MacPherson's appended commentaries appear in the text.

16. Hurd, quoted in Monk, *The Sublime*, 68. All further citations appear in the text.

17. Percy, preface to *Northern Antiquities*, 16, 10. All further citations appear in the text as *Northern Antiquities*.

18. Percy, *Reliques of Ancient English Poetry*, Vol. 1, xxxi. All further citations appear in the text as *Reliques*.

19. Mitford, *Principles of Harmony*, 1. All further citations appear in the text.

20. Fussell, *Theory of Prosody in Eighteenth-Century England*, 146. All further citations appear in the text.

21. Berkhout and Gatch, *Anglo-Saxon Scholarship*, 153.

22. See "The Racial Sublime." Sara Suleri has also explored the racial structuring of the sublime in such thinkers as Edmund Burke. For Suleri's discussion, see *The Rhetoric of English India*, especially chapter 2, "Edmund Burke and the Indian Sublime." Also valuable for understanding the structural relationship between imperialism and English literature is Viswanathan, *Masks of Conquest*.

23. Wordsworth, *Poems*, 1:716–17.

24. Hopkinson, quoted in Wood, *Rising Glory of America*, 327. All further citations appear in the text.

25. Rowe, *Literary Culture and U.S. Imperialism*, 3.

26. Emerson, *English Traits*, 27. All further citations appear in the text.

27. Emerson, "The Poet," in *Selected Essays*, 270. All further citations appear in the text as "Poet."

28. Emerson continues here to say that poets also free a man from "that jail-yard of individual relations in which he is enclosed," and in this way he alludes to that paradoxical effect of individualism, which enchains even as it purports to liberate ("Poet" 275).

29. Whitman, *Leaves of Grass*, preface 7, 5. Reprinted in *The Portable Walt Whitman*. All further citations of Whitman are from this edition and appear in the text.

30. Harper, "The Tennessee Hero," in *Heath Anthology of American Literature*, ed. Lauter et al., 2056–57.

4. Entering Atlantic History

1. For a different kind of discussion of the ways that *Oroonoko* comes to inaugurate a race-d tradition of writing, see Aravamudan, *Tropicopolitans*.

2. Behn, *Oroonoko*, 40. All further references to this work appear in the text.

3. For these characterizations, see, respectively, Spengemann, "The Earliest American Novel," 391; and Athey and Alarcon, "Oroonoko's *Gendered* Economies of Honor/Horror," 432.

4. Holmesland, "Aphra Behn's Oroonoko," epitomizes this view in his argument that *Oroonoko* embodies "the uneasy transition, in the late seventeenth century, from an aristocratic, romance-prone ideology towards a more rationalist, progressive age" (57). For discussions sharing this framework to one degree or another, see Brown *Ends of Empire;* Spengemann, "Earliest American"; McKeon, *Origins;* Goreau, *Reconstructing Aphra Behn;* Metzger, "Introduction"; Houston, "Usurpation and Dismemberment"; Moira Ferguson ("*Oroonoko*"); Pacheco, "Royalism and Honor"; and Gautier, "Slavery and the Fashioning of Race."

5. And these critics have accordingly looked askance at those early writers who "failed" to achieve coherence. See, for instance, Richetti's comments in "Histories by Eliza Haywood and Henry Fielding": "Haywood's interesting ambiguity and exposure of ideological contradiction are the result of a lack of full narrative control, of her failure to sustain, with any coherence, her imitation of Fielding's historical approach" (255).

6. White, "Captaine Smith, Colonial Novelist," 510–11.

7. Hunter, *Before Novels,* 58.

8. Spengemann anticipates this point, although without a political context, when he observes that the narrator of *Oroonoko,* as she moves between Surinam and Africa, is "in the game and out of it at once" ("Earliest American Novel," 398).

9. Ross, *Making of the English Literary Canon,* 134–35. In making this point, Ross builds on the work of Potter, *Secret Rites and Secret Writing* and A. M. Patterson, *Censorship and Interpretation.*

10. MacLean, *Culture and Society in the Stuart Restoration,* 13.

11. For a range of discussions of the ways in which Imoinda stands in for the narrator, or the narrator makes use of her as well as of Oroonoko, see Gallagher, *Nobody's Story,* 72–73; Ferguson, "Oroonoko," 353–56; Ferguson, "Juggling the Categories," 169–73; Andrade, "White Skin, Black Masks," 202–8; Ortiz, "Arms and the Woman," 121, 125–26, 133–37; Williams, "African as Text," 5–13; Athey and Alarcon, "*Oroonoko*'s Gendered Economies," 422–24; and Azim, *Colonial Rise of the Novel,* chapter 2, especially 55–60.

12. Most critics acknowledge the text's mixed messages on slavery, yet for discussions that emphasize the abolitionist or anticolonial (and often, correlatively, feminist) attitude of Behn's novel, see Brown, *Ends of Empire;* Goreau, *Reconstructing Aphra Behn;* Chernaik, "Captains and Slaves"; Visconsi, "A Degenerate Race"; Rosenthal, "Owning *Oroonoko*"; and to some degree Ferguson, "Juggling the Categories." For readings that focus on its colonialist attitudes or gestures, see Sussman ("The Other Problem"), Ballaster, *Seductive Forms;* Azim, *Colonial Rise of the Novel;* Andrade, "White Skin, Black Masks"; Moira Ferguson, "*Oroonoko*"; Ortiz, "Arms and the Woman"; Athey and Alarcon, "*Oroonoko*'s Gendered Economies"; and Roach, *Cities of the Dead* (Roach focuses on both Southerne's play and Behn's novel, 152–61). Also see Kaul, "Reading Literary Symptoms," for consideration of colonialist structures in both Behn's text and subsequent versions of Behn's story.

13. See Brown's discussion in *Ends of Empire,* 54–58.

14. See Ortiz, "Arms and the Woman," for a rich discussion of Behn's invocation of classi-

cal imperial plots and tropes—and of the woman's pivotal role in them. Also see Hoegberg's delineation, in "Caesar's Toils," of how Behn's classical networks of allusion make Oroonoko ideologically "captive."

15. For discussions of Behn's treatment of rape in her other writings, see Pacheco, "Rape and the Female Subject in Behn's *The Rover*"; Martin, "Seduced and Abandoned"; and Marsden in "Rape, Voyeurism, and the Restoration Stage."

16. See Ortiz, "Arms and the Woman," for an emphasis on Imoinda's instrumental role in the couple's trouble (134–35).

17. See Rosenthal, "Owning Oroonoko," for a different yet related discussion of Behn's representation of a shift from an old into a new order, which Rosenthal explores in terms of property relations. Likewise, Brown (*Ends of Empire*, 23–63) and Iwanisziw ("Behn's Novel Investment") trace the novel's working-through of the terms of an emergent, mercantile-colonial capitalism.

18. It is interesting to note that the failure of the revolt also arises from gender pressures, insofar as the women discourage their men from participating and, at a crucial moment, the men weaken and retreat.

19. My argument here stands in sharp contrast to that of Holmesland, "Aphra Ben's Oroonoko," 69–70, who continues to see Oroonoko as acting within aristocratic codes.

20. Sussman hints at the text's remaking of the African couple in sentimental terms ("The Other Problem with Women" 229). Also see Starr, "Aphra Behn and the Genealogy of the Man of Feeling," for an early reading of Oroonoko as a sentimental subject, although Starr does not consider the political implications of this characterization.

21. Athey and Alarcon also note this correlation. Their emphasis is not on the coupling moment but more singularly on Imoinda's arrival as it coincides with "the very moment when the white female narrator materializes as a character" ("*Oroonoko*'s Gendered Economies," 432). Azim stresses the narrator's intrusion earlier, in combination with the act of renaming Oroonoko (*Colonial Rise of the Novel*, 55).

22. Spengemann ("Earliest American Novel") and Moira Ferguson ("*Oroonoko*") also read *Oroonoko* as a text that introduces a paradigm for future discourses. Ferguson stresses its slippery combination of colonialist and antislavery notions as they lay a foundation for British colonial ideology, while Spengemann focuses on the novel as a genre, suggestively enumerating a list of characteristics that come into play in this "modern literary form which was devised to deal with the new world that America had made" (413). As I'll discuss in chapter 4, I share Spengemann's interest (as expressed here and in his book *New World of Words*) in the relation between the "new world" and the novel, although within a different framework.

23. In related but different ways, several critics comment on what Holmesland calls the narrator's "mediatory position" ("Aphra Behn's Oroonoko," 60), including Gallagher, *Nobody's Story*; Spencer, *Rise of the Woman Novelist*; Azim, *Colonial Rise of the Novel*; Ballaster, *Seductive Forms*; Andrade, "White Skin, Black Masks"; and Ortiz, "Arms and the Woman."

24. Spengemann ("Earliest," 398, 402–3), M. Ferguson ("Juggling the Categories," 165), Pearson ("Gender and Narrative," 188), Chibka ("Do Not Fear," 522–23), and Athey and Alarcon ("*Oroonoko*'s Gendered Economies," 426) also discuss this pronoun shift.

25. For discussions that connect Behn's narrator's work in *Oroonoko* to the author's turn away from drama and her struggle for position in a world of male authorship and an emergent "readerly" market, see Spengemann, "Earliest American," 404, 409–14; Ferguson, "*Oroonoko*," 353; Carnell, "Subverting Tragic Conventions"; Pearson, "Gender and Narrative," 184–190; and Gallagher, *Nobody's Story,* chapters 1 and 2.

26. See note 11 above for critics who address the narrator's usurping relation to Imoinda.

5. Rape as Entry into Liberty

1. F. Ferguson, "Rape and the Rise of the Novel," 98. All further references to this work appear in the text. Also see note 2 below for studies that consider the seduction or rape plot in the early novel — although, other than Ballaster and Sharpe, surprisingly few critics have made this ubiquitous plot the focus of their discussion.

2. In making this claim, I join the long-running critical discussion about the reasons for the eighteenth-century rise of the novel in English. It's impossible to list the scores of valuable publications on this question. I mention here merely a sampling of those that take up these dimensions of the early novel most broadly and have directly informed my thinking about it. I have loosely grouped the following into feminist, cultural/class, and postcolonial texts, but of course many of them combine several threads of analysis. For largely feminist readings, see Ballaster (*Seductive Forms*), Gallagher (*Nobody's Story*), Spencer, Castle (*Female Thermometer*), Cummings, Flint, Gonda, Todd, Moglen, Cook. For cultural/class readings, see Watt, D. S. Lynch, McKeon, Damrosch, Mayer, Bender, W. B. Warner (*Licensing Entertainment*), Barker-Benfield, Hunter, James Thompson. For postcolonial, see Said (*Culture and Imperialism*), Azim, Laura Brown, Sussman (*Consuming Anxieties*), and, especially pertinent, Sharpe (*Allegories of Empire*). I believe my analysis here adds an underlayer to the story Sharpe tells of how tropes of rape drive the colonial British imagination. From the American side, for feminist readings, see C. Davidson, Stern, Fliegelman; for cultural/class, see Baym (*American Women Writers*), Ruttenberg, M. Warner, Gillian Brown (*The Consent of the Governed*); for postcolonial, see Spengemann (*New World of Words*), Hartman, Bergland.

3. The traveling element of these liberty plots appears in Manley's, Defoe's, and Aubin's fictions as well as in Richardson's *Clarissa* — which might suggest that the picaro strain in the Spanish novel has had such an influence on the English novel not only directly through the works of Cervantes but also indirectly, by way of the Atlantic conditions that these two traditions share. I would like to thank Doris Sommers for the suggestion that, in this context, the influence of Spanish picaro on the English-language novel deserves consideration (correspondence, July 2005).

4. Haller, *Tracts on Liberty,* 3:373. All further references to Overton's pamphlet are from this volume and edition of Haller's *Tracts.*

5. See Bernardi, "Narratives of Domestic Imperialism," 203–24, for discussion of this breaking-in trope in Pauline Hopkins's fiction.

6. On the role of print literature in the shaping of public/private spheres, see Ross, *Making;* Cook, *Epistolary Bodies;* Davis, *Factual Fictions;* MacLean, *Culture and Society in the Stuart Restoration;* Norbrook, *Writing the English Republic;* Mascuch, *Origins of the Individualist Self;* Gillis, *The Paradox of Privacy;* Zomchick, *Family and Law in Eighteenth-century*

Fiction; and Eisenstein, *The Printing Press,* including for consideration of the instabilities of the print order. Also see Nunberg's edited collection of essays on print culture, *The Future of the Book.*

7. *Common Sense,* edited by Isaac Kramnick, 68, 69, 77. All further references are to this edition.

8. For a related reading of these passages in Paine, see Brown, *The Consent of the Governed.* Brown notes the rape imagery in passing (95), but she more centrally highlights this passage as a narrative of parental abuse. Instead, I would directly link the rape image here to her later suggestion that "the situation of women serves as a parable of the impediments encountered by all citizens in the employment of consent" (132). As this last comment indicates, our projects are complementary, although by starting with Locke, Brown begins (like most American literary scholars) too late to take account of the 1640s-era sources of these images. Accordingly, her emphasis on philosophical sources and her vocabulary of "consent" leaves untold a jagged, violent history in which consent is often a belated supplement to an order founded on other grounds.

9. See Richards' discussion of this material in "The Politics of Seduction," 241.

10. *Reflections on the Revolution in France,* edited by J. C. D. Clark, 183 (italics in original). All further references are to this edition.

11. See Doyle, "The Racial Sublime," 26–31. For other discussions of Burke's "ancient constitutionalism," see Dreyer, *Burke's Politics,* and Pocock, "Burke and the Ancient Constitution."

12. For a reading of the rather different way racial discourses inflected Burke's writings on India, see Suleri, *The Rhetoric of English India,* especially chapters 2 and 3. For a broad discussion of the English perception of savagery in the French Revolution, see Bindman, *The Shadow of the Guillotine.*

13. For discussion of Burke's representation of this scene, see especially Furniss, *Burke's Aesthetic Ideology,* chapters 6 and 7. For extended readings of Burke in relation to the Gothic, see Backus, *The Gothic Family Romance,* 89–96; and Kilgour, *The Rise of the Gothic Novel,* 24–31. For an account of Burke in relation to the Saxon revival and the "Gothic" in the political sense of a Whig mythology, see R. J. Smith, *The Gothic Bequest,* 113–26. Smith distances Burke from Saxonism and Gothicism as popular movements but nonetheless tracks the constitutionalist tropes that appear in Burke's work. Also see Conor Cruise O'Brien's introduction to his edition of *Reflections,* for another effort to limit Burke's links with Gothic rhetoric, 42–43. For other key treatments of Burke's rhetoric of revolution, see Blakemore, *Burke and the Fall of Language;* Macpherson, *Burke;* Kramnick, *The Rage of Edmund Burke;* and, a work that emphasizes Burke's alliance with revolutionary movements, Cobban, *Edmund Burke and the Revolt.*

14. Ralph Waldo Emerson makes a similar association when, after 1848, he says the people in Paris and London were "dragged in their ignorance by furious chiefs to the Red Revolution" and contrasts such scenes to the conduct of the American Revolution. Quoted in Bercovitch, *Office of the Scarlet Letter* (148).

15. For discussion of the racializing of revolution in France along lines similar to the English, see Poliakov, *The Aryan Myth;* and also my discussion in *Bordering on the Body,* 37–38.

16. Backscheider and Richetti use this phrase in their introduction to *Popular Fiction by Women,* x.

17. For discussions of intertextual exchanges between Haywood and contemporary male novelists, especially Richardson, see the following: Doody, *A Natural Passion*, 128–51; Warner, *Licensing Entertainment;* Stuart, "Subversive Didacticism"; Flint, *Family Fictions,* especially 207–48; and Nestor, "Virtue Rarely Rewarded." For a study of Haywood's authorship of *Anti-Pamela,* see Brewer, "'Haywood,' Secret History, and the Politics of Attribution." In "Why Look at Clarissa?" Gordon Fulton also reads *Clarissa* against Haywood's fiction for their treatments of the "gaze," but he does not argue that there was any intertextual dialogue between the two authors. For Haywood in relation to the mid-eighteenth-century "reformed" seduction plots and rereadings of her apparent conformity to this trend, see Austin, "Shooting Blanks"; and also Nestor and Stuart. For Haywood as deconstructor of pastoral tropes, see Oakleaf, "'Shady Bowers! and purling streams!'" Also, more generally, see Paula Backscheider's inventory of Haywood's formal innovations, which she suggests were taken up by contemporary and subsequent novelists, in "The Story of Eliza Haywood's Novels." For Haywood in relation to Fielding, see Richetti, "Histories by Eliza Haywood and Henry Fielding." Unlike the other essays cited here, which manage to shed the hegemonic assumptions about fiction that Warner exposes, Richetti disappointingly returns to "coherence" as the standard of good fiction, a standard successfully set, in his view, by Fielding and which Haywood mostly fails to meet. Finally, for a powerful discussion that situates Haywood and her contemporaries within the marketplace matrix, see Ingrassia, *Authorship, Commerce, and Gender in Early Eighteenth-Century England,* especially chapter 3, 77–103.

18. See especially Kvande, "The Outsider Narrator." Also see Bowers, "Collusive Resistance"; Wilputte, "Eliza Haywood's *Frederick*"; Carnell, "It's Not Easy Being Green"; and Wilputte, "The Textual Architecture." For a related account of the "disinterested" gentleman narrator, see Barrell, *English Literature in History.*

19. There are of course many books on the era of Walpole but for a discussion of the animosity he aroused and a reading of Haywood's *Eovaai* in this context, see Beasley, "Portraits of a Monster."

20. See Mowry, "Eliza Haywood's Defense," 645.

21. Stuart, "Subversive Didacticism in *Betsy Thoughtless,*" 559–560.

22. For discussion of the early novel's borrowing from the plots of Restoration drama, see Doody, *A Natural Passion* and Staves, *Players' Sceptres.*

23. "Reflections upon Marriage," quoted in Hill, *The First English Feminist,* 76.

24. *Fantomina,* 246. All further references to this work appear in the text and are from Backscheider and Richetti, *Popular Fiction by Women, 1660–1730.*

25. Defoe scholars have long stressed the "isolation" of his protagonists and have interpreted their circumstances as "selves alone" as a mark of their modern condition, and Christopher Hill long ago considered Clarissa's isolation in relation to Crusoe's (*Puritanism and Revolution,* 381); but few if any Haywood critics have taken stock of this aspect of her fiction.

26. Jacobs, *Incidents,* 225.

27. For Haywood's biography, see Blouch, "Eliza Haywood and the Romance of Obscurity." For attention to her political orientation, see sources listed in notes 17, 18, and 19.

28. See especially Croskery, "Masquing Desire," and Bocchicchio, "Blushing, Trembling, and Incapable of Defense." Also see Ballaster's full discussion in *Seductive Forms*

(170 – 95) — still one of the most subtle readings of desire and sexual politics in Haywood's fiction. In this early study, Ballaster explicitly disconnects Haywood's early fictions from public-sphere politics, but she re-assesses that position in "A Gender of Opposition." Part of my aim is to link Haywood's apparently most apolitical early fiction to public-sphere politics via the term "liberty."

29. See Thompson, "Plotting Materialism." Thompson's wonderful reading brings together a Butlerian and a Cavalier/materialist sense of identity as bodily performance and, I believe, opens up a rich vein for future research. As I suggest above, however, I think the effects for interiority are the opposite of what Thompson claims. Also, for a discussion of Defoe that highlights the structure of "self-dialogue" in a way that can be seen as parallel to my discussion here, see Snow, "Arguments to the Self in Defoe's *Roxana*."

30. See Seidel, *Exile and the Narrative Imagination*.

31. See Ballaster's nuanced discussion of Haywood's shared ground with her narrator in *Seductive Forms,* especially 179 – 95.

32. Citations for *The British Recluse* are taken from Backscheider and Richetti, eds., *Popular Fiction by Women* and will hereafter appear in the text.

33. For readings of tropes of race and lineage in Haywood, see Thorn, "'A Race of Angels,'" and Oakleaf, "The Eloquence of Blood." Both essays focus on the way concerns about reproduction, heterosexuality, and textuality inform Haywood's vocabulary of race and lineage.

34. Schmidgen, *Eighteenth-Century Fiction and the Law.* This mobility and restless circulation in Haywood's early heroines also hints at their involvement in the economic circuits of the period, which Ingrassia (*Authorship*) analyzes at length in Haywood's later fiction.

35. Richardson, *Clarissa,* 939. All further references to this work appear in the text.

36. In addition to Zomchick, *Family and Law,* and Macpherson, "Lovelace, Ltd.," for explicit discussion of *Clarissa* and social contract, see Cook, *Epistolary Bodies,* chapter 3, 71 – 113; and Hinton, "The Heroine's Subjection." For related studies addressing the ways that the social loopholes of language, gender, and sentimental morality undercut Clarissa's struggle to establish herself as a "juridical subject" (in Zomchick's phrase), also see the following: Castle, *Clarissa's Cyphers;* Gordon, "Disinterested Selves"; M. P. Martin, "Reading Reform in Richardson's *Clarissa*"; McKee, "Corresponding Freedoms"; Osland, "Complaisance and Complacence"; and Zias, "Who Can Believe?"

37. For discussion of space in *Clarissa* in terms of its social implications, see Doody, *A Natural Passion,* chapter 8, 188 – 215, which discusses confinement and escape in terms of Clarissa's quest for freedom; and Gillis, *The Paradox of Privacy,* which considers the way letters and spaces both are seemingly private interiors that get invaded and exposed.

38. For two contrasting readings of the law and contract as they help or hinder Clarissa, see, respectively, Zomchick, *Family and Law,* chapter 3, 58 – 80, and Macpherson, "Lovelace, Ltd." Also see Knight, "The Function of Wills in Richardson's *Clarissa*," and note 38.

39. For a full discussion of what Clarissa would have faced in 1741 had she pursued a legal case, see Swan, "Raped by the System." Also useful in this context is Vermillion, "*Clarissa* and the Marriage Act."

40. See Hill, *Puritanism and Revolution,* chapter 14, 367 – 94; Wolff, *Samuel Richardson;* Harvey, "*Clarissa* and the Puritan Tradition"; and Damrosch, *God's Plots and Man's Stories,*

chapter 6, 213 – 62. While Harvey thinks the emphasis on Puritanism in the criticism has been distorting, Wolff and Damrosch trace a subtle Puritan legacy in terms of Clarissa's ethical and interiorized dilemmas in relation to the social world.

41. Fliegelman, *Prodigals*, 145 – 147. And as also suggested by the fact that Mary Rowland-son's Puritan captivity narrative was advertised in the early American edition of *Pilgrim's Progress* (Burnham, *Captivity*, 52).

42. See Fiedler, *Love and Death in the American Novel*; Zomchick, *Family and Law*; and Eagleton, *The Rape of Clarissa*. All future references to Zomchick appear in the text.

43. See my discussion of this word in "The Folk, the Nobles, and the Novel" and "The Racial Sublime."

44. See Doyle, "Racial Sublime," 27 – 28.

45. See the two classic studies, Fairchild, *The Noble Savage*, and Sypher, *Guinea's Captive Kings*.

46. The novel also takes the trouble to mock old or degraded meanings of "noble." Anna deflates the traditional Tory associations of the word in laughing at "the noble lords of the creation in all their peculiarities" (912), while Lovelace consciously mocks the shift in the word's meaning, seeming first to accept its new moral referent but then deflating that association and asserting the importance of birth: "If virtue be the true nobility, how is she ennobled, and how would an alliance with her ennoble, were there no drawbacks from the family she is sprung from" (426). Given Clarissa's special qualities, she could be noble, Lovelace jokes — if only she weren't middle class, a child of a crass, grasping trade family. Clarissa herself identifies the disingenuous uses of "noble" in this transitional moment in the life of the word, whereby aristocratic connotations of generous "noblesse" serve as a cover for mercenary intentions. She notes with disdain that "*the noble settlements* [of Solmes] are echoed from every mouth. *Noble* is the word used to enforce the offers of a man who is mean enough avowedly to *hate*, and wicked enough to *rob* of their just expectations, his own family" (81). In effect, the multiple uses of the word "noble" express the range of conflicting and equivocal forces that Richardson aims to balance and redeem through Clarissa, the properly balanced heir to the English birthright.

47. For a differently framed discussion of Clarissa in terms of this Puritan legacy of "transparency," see especially Damrosch, *God's Plots*, 219 – 28. Also see Hill, *Puritanism and Revolution*, 391 – 92.

48. On Richardson and his work as a printer, which involved him in the *business* of print in all senses, see McKillop, *Samuel Richardson*. For the ways Richardson's involvement in the business of print shaped his fiction and enabled his active promotion of it, see Ingrassia, *Authorship*, chapter 5, 138 – 65, and Turner, "Novel Panic." For one account of the significance of these activities for Richardson's imagination of the (apparently oxymoronic) public interior, see Cook, *Epistolary Bodies*, especially 1 – 30 and 71 – 113.

49. For discussion of the novel's relation to social, gender, and economic pressures on English families in this period, and of Clarissa's ambivalent allegiances under those pressures, see Gonda, *Reading the Daughter's Fictions*, and Flint, *Family Fictions*. Many of the critics cited in note 5 (on contract) also address this issue. For a Lacanian reading of Clarissa's place in the family, see Cummings, *Telling Tales*.

50. Habukkuk, "Marriage Settlements in the Eighteenth Century," quoted in Hill, *Puritanism and Revolution*, 368.

51. See Hill, *Puritanism and Revolution,* especially 368–71.

52. Hilliard, "Clarissa and Ritual Cannibalism." All further references to this essay appear in the text.

53. Wilt, "He Could Go No Further."

54. For a full reading of Clarissa's "no" as an attempt to assert autonomy, see Suarez, "Asserting the Negative," 69, 84. For other readings of Clarissa's combination of passivity and will, which interpret this mingling as strategy on Clarissa's part, see Warner, *Reading Clarissa,* and, more sympathetically toward Clarissa, Eagleton, *The Rape of Clarissa.*

55. "Correspondence between the Hon. John Adams and the late William Cunningham," 19. Quoted in Fliegelman, *Prodigals,* 237.

6. Transatlantic Seductions

1. Baker, *Blues, Ideology, and Afro-American Literature,* 33. Also see Bolster, *Black Jacks,* for discussion of black seamen working on the Atlantic.

2. As the work of Trumpener in *Bardic Nationalism* has made clear, the fullest picture of this English-language, Atlantic nexus would include a number of other communities as well, including the Irish and Scottish (and later in the Caribbean, the Indian and Chinese).

3. Spengemann, *New World of Words,* 109.

4. Much as he debunks American exceptionalism, Spengemann's account remains tethered to an Americanist perspective. For him, the encounter with America is *the* catalyzing moment in the history of modern English-language tradition, not just one important force. When he claims that "the single most important event in the history of the English-language literary tradition, rivaled only by the Norman Conquest, has to be its discovery of the New World" (43), he not only overlooks the impact of later linguistic encounters in the East but he also crucially ignores the effects of the English Reformation. His own evidence indicates the importance of this earlier event, however. Arguing that the exploration by Europeans of America introduced new words into the English language, he chooses words that point instead toward the legacy of the Reformation and the English Civil War — which in turn, I suggest, prepare the way for understandings of America. Spengemann attributes strictly to American Puritans the "invention of words like *independence* to describe the proper allegiance of a congregation to Christ, rather than to the bishops, and *primitive* to denote the original purity from which the church had strayed and to which it must return" (44). Both "independence" and "primitive," as we saw in chapter 1, are Reformation terms — although they do indeed come to have many uses in America. By contrast, the account I offer here begins from that moment when the Reformation meets the New World — in the English Civil War — so as to track how this convergence of forces contributed to the widening tidal wave of an Atlantic liberty discourse.

5. *Paradise Lost* in *The Complete Poetical Works of John Milton.*

6. Auerbach, "The Rise of the Fallen Woman," 30.

7. Fliegelman, *Prodigals,* 266.

8. Stern, *Plight of Feeling,* 21. All further references to this work appear in the text.

9. Smith, *Conceived by Liberty,* 14–25. All further references to this work appear in the text.

10. One could profitably also situate the texts that Traister studies in "Libertinism and

Authorship in America's Early Republic," which center on the "fall" of the libertine himself, beside these texts and within this framework.

11. Defoe, *Roxana*, 1. All further references to this work appear in the text.

12. Defoe, *Moll Flanders*. For a different and suggestive feminist reading of the secrecy trope in *Roxana* and *Moll Flanders*, see Azim, *Colonial Rise*, 71 – 76. For a thorough reading of the fact/fiction matrix in the early English novel, see Davis, *Factual Fictions*.

13. For discussion of Robinson Crusoe and the Restoration, see Seidel, *Exile and the Narrative Imagination*, 29 – 34.

14. Of course, critics have long interpreted Defoe's novels in the light of his Dissenter Protestantism, most especially Starr, *Defoe and Spiritual Autobiography*; Novak, *Defoe and the Nature of Man*; and Damrosch, *God's Plots and Man's Stories*. More recent work that includes attention to Defoe's Protestantism while also clarifying the ways his writing enfolds political and social history includes Westfall, "A Sermon by the Queen of Whores"; Schmidgen, "Illegitimacy and Social Observation"; and Conway, "Defoe's Protestant Whore." Also see Mayer, *History and the Early English Novel*, for consideration of Defoe's narratives in relation to historiography. For the wide range of critics who situate Defoe's work within the rise of mercantile and commodity capitalism, see note 18 below.

15. On this point, see Schmidgen, "Illegitimacy and Social Observation," 135 – 38.

16. See Brown, *Ends of Empire* (146 – 53), and Azim, *Colonial Rise* (80 – 87), for extended analyses of Roxana's "Turkish costume" and the Turkish slave given to her by the French Prince. For discussion of the dramatizations of issues of law and contract in eighteenth-century fiction, see Zomchick, *Family and Law in Eighteenth-century Fiction*, including consideration of Roxana as a character who, after "emptying" herself of affiliations, seeks "a supplement to the contractual processes of accumulation" (54). I suggest that she finds this "supplement" in Protestant Englishness, that is, in herself as "Protestant whore" and thus "mistress of liberty."

17. Critics have remarked on what Richetti calls the "serial factuality" of Moll's and Roxana's mode of being (see Richetti, "The Family, Sex, and Marriage," 24). For other critics stressing the fragmentation, division, or seriality of self in Defoe, see Brown, "The Displaced Self"; Maddox, "On Defoe's *Roxana*"; Laden, *Self-Imitation in the Eighteenth-Century Novel*, especially 55 – 62; Butler, "'Onomaphobia' and Personal Identity"; Snow, "Arguments to the Self"; Warner, *Licensing Entertainment*, 145 – 75; and Thorne, "Providence in the Early Novel." For consideration of this dimension of Defoe's characters in relation to economics, see note 20 below.

18. For more general studies of representations of economy and self in eighteenth-century British fiction that address Defoe's work, see Thompson, *Models of Value*, especially chapter 3, 87 – 131; Bellamy, *Commerce, Morality, and the Eighteenth-Century Novel*, especially 69 – 72; Brown, *The Ends of Empire*, especially chapter 5; and Lynch and Warner, *The Economy of Character*, 31 – 38. For specific studies of Defoe, credit, commodity, and money (in addition to Latta, "The Mistress," and Brown, *Ends of Empire*), see Chaber, "Matriarchal Mirror"; Pollack, "*Moll Flanders*, Incest and the Structure of Exchange"; Hentzi, "Holes in the Heart"; Hummel, "'The Gift of my Father's Bounty'"; Kibbie, "Monstrous Generation"; Flynn, "Nationalism, Commerce, and Imperial Anxiety"; and Schmidgen, "*Robinson Crusoe*, Enumeration, and Mercantile Fetish." Watt of course first fully explored Robinson Crusoe as *homo economicus* in *The Rise of the Novel*, while more traditional studies of De-

foe's economic writings and attitudes can be found in Novak, *Economics and the Fiction of Daniel Defoe,* and Dijkstra, *Defoe and Economics.* Also see Ingrassia, *Authorship.*

19. See Latta, "The Mistress of the Marriage Market," 359. Latta's essay is profitably read together with Brown's discussion in *The Ends of Empire,* especially chapter 5 and pages 153–57. Brown considers additional ways in which Roxana operates as an enabling figure for the violence and machinations of mercantile English culture.

20. Conway, "Defoe's Protestant Whore."

21. See Caton, "Doing the Right Thing with Moll Flanders"; and O'Brien, "Union Jack," 72–73.

22. On incest in Moll Flanders, see Pollack, "*Moll Flanders,* Incest and the Structure of Exchange"; Olsen, "Reading and Righting Moll Flanders"; and Kibbie, "Monstrous Generation," especially 1027–29. All subsequent references to Pollack's essay appear in the text.

23. Critics such as Lois Chaber, "Matriarchal Mirror," and Srivdhya Swaminathan, "Defoe's Alternative Conduct Manual," see positive female networks of support in *Moll Flanders,* which is partly true; but it also seems to me to be countered by the dynamics of feminine abandonment, the system of illicit exchange in which women find their bond, and Moll's self-portrait as a woman who keeps goods, money, and secrets even from those to whom she is closest, including women.

24. Brown, *Power of Sympathy,* 96. All further references to this work appear in the text.

25. The body of critical literature on this topic is large but credit must be given above all to Fliegelman's founding work in *Prodigals and Pilgrims* (1982), and Davidson's equally seminal research in *Revolution and the Word* (1986). Both studies treat the historical context of this fiction with invaluable range and insight, in different ways: Fliegelman does justice to the transatlantic and intellectual sources that inform its "revolution against patriarchal authority" and Davidson unearths its material conditions (in the Marxist sense of production) and clarifies women writers' key role in "the rise of the novel in America." Following their work, two of the most important book-length studies of the republican questions and conditions embedded in early American fiction written by the authors I treat in this section are Stern's *The Plight of Feeling* and Barnes's *States of Sympathy.* For essays treating two or more of these three writers, again in relation to political and usually republican contexts, see Schloss, "Republicanism and Politeness in the Early American Novel"; Gardner, "The Literary Museum"; Tennenhouse, "Libertine America"; Verhoeven, "'Persuasive Rhetorick'"; and Evans, "Rakes, Coquettes, and Republican Patriarchs." In addition, the following list of sources is divided according to which of these three authors they address (Rowson, Brown, or Foster). I include criticism on Foster because the scholarship is pertinent to my discussion as a whole, even though I mention her work only in passing. On Rowson, see Rust, "What's Wrong with Charlotte Temple?"; Epley, "Alienated, Betrayed, and Powerless"; Schöpp, "Liberty's Sons and Daughters"; Ryals, "America, Romance, and the Fate of the Wandering Woman"; Castiglia, "Susanna Rowson's *Reuben and Rachel*"; Forcey, "*Charlotte Temple* and the End of Epistolarity"; Saar, "Susanna Rowson: Feminist and Democrat"; Hansen, "The Sentimental Novel and its Feminist Critique." On Hill Brown, see Barnes, "Natural and National Unions"; Dalke "Original Vice"; Durlson, "Incest and the American Romantic Fictions." On Foster, see Mower, "Bodies in Labor"; Finseth, "'A Melancholy Tale'"; Fleischman, "Concealed Lessons"; Richards, "The Politics of Seduction"; Harris, "Hannah Webster Foster's *The Coquette*"; Fizer, "Signing as Republican Daughters"; Waldstreicher,

"'Fallen Under my Observation'"; Shuffleton, "Mrs. Foster's Coquette and the Decline of the Brotherly Watch"; Hamilton, "An Assault on the Will"; Smith-Rosenberg, "Domesticating 'Virtue'"; and Wenska, *The Coquette* and the American Dream of Freedom."

26. Thus, for instance, Barnes, after acknowledging that early American novels share an interest in "states of feeling" with British novels, implies that they diverge because "[i]n American fiction, however, seduction and sympathy take on decidedly political connotations" (*States of Sympathy,* x). The rich body of scholarship on the British novel and the preceding chapters of this book reveal how the British tradition of seduction novels is itself "decidedly political." Critics likewise deem certain traits "American" without considering how they might be as common in other traditions. Most predictably, critics consider the theme of freedom to be especially "American," as when Wenska in "The Coquette and the American Dream of Freedom," deems freedom "a characteristic, almost obsessive American theme" (244) that has "always engaged the American imagination" and to which, beginning with such novels as *The Coquette,* "our American authors would turn and return" (253). British authors do the same.

27. I admire the integration of psychological, historical, and political elements in Stern's reading of the early novel. It is fruitful to read Stern's book beside Moglen's comparable account of the British novel's narrativization of cultural rupture and gender melancholy in *The Trauma of Gender.*

28. Barton is the only critic to focus mainly on the Christian plotting of Rowson's first novel. In "Narrative Intrusion in *Charlotte Temple,*" Barton highlights Rowson's Christian commitments as expressed through her narrator's homilies and allusions to both *Pilgrim's Progress* and the fall. Barton sees this Christian framework employed as part of Rowson's increasingly feminist agenda.

29. The sequel's original title is *Charlottes' Daughter; or, The Three Orphans,* but the novel was reissued throughout the nineteenth century (after Rowson's death) under the title *Lucy Temple.* For discussion of the publication history of *Charlotte Temple,* see Davidson, *Revolution and the Word,* 17, 75 – 78, on *Charlotte Temple;* and, on both novels, see Douglas's introduction to the Penguin edition containing them both, vii-xvi.

30. Born in England in 1762, at age five Rowson journeyed for three months during winter to meet her father, stationed in New England as a navy officer (her mother had died ten days after her birth and he had been called to America a year later); at age sixteen, in 1778, after three years of tending the family needs while her father was imprisoned as a British officer, she and her family were allowed to return to England in an exchange of prisoners (although Rowson had been friends with James Otis and seems to have sympathized with the revolutionaries); and finally, in 1783, she returned after her marriage to pursue her acting career in Thomas Wignell's new theater company in Philadelphia, eventually joining the Federal Street Theater in Boston in the mid-1790s. Along the way, while working as an actress, Rowson wrote ten novels and six theatrical works as well as poetry, patriotic songs, and, finally, textbooks for the "Young Ladies Academy" she founded. For more information on Rowson's life, see Parker, *Susanna Rowson.*

31. For a rich discussion of Cooper's sea fiction in a transatlantic context, see Cohen, "Traveling Genres."

32. For another discussion of the Francophobia in the novel, see Evans, "Rakes, Coquettes and Republican Patriarchs," 3. For an interesting counterpoint exploration, see Haviland,

"Preciosité Crosses the Atlantic." Haviland documents the influence and popularity of French fiction in the United States. In this light, the anti-French implications of Rowson's names seem as likely to be influenced by her British perspective as by an American one.

33. Rowson, *Charlotte Temple*, 37. Further references appear in the text.

34. For a suggestive transatlantic discussion of Rowlandson in relation to the British sentimental novel, see Burnham, "Between England and America." On Rowlandson's popularity in the revolutionary period, see Castiglia, "Susanna Rowson's *Reuben and Rachel*," 23.

35. No critics have commented at length on the economic origin of ruin in this novel. Cherniavsky ("Charlotte Temple's Debt") does so in passing and Smith Rosenberg ("Domesticating") briefly discusses coquettes and economy (167–69).

36. While Stern, in *Plight*, perceptively reads Charlotte's predicament as the psychopolitical loss of a mother for both characters and readers in this male economy, I would take the allegory further, as a story of women's emblematization of men's own "unmanning" in this unstable world.

37. Rowson, *Lucy Temple*, 145. Further references appear in the text.

38. Also see Barnes's discussion of incest in Brown's and others' novels ("Natural and National Unions"). For Barnes, the incest plot is the symptom of a backward, familial political model rather than a distortion of progressive but threatening possibilities. She interprets it as the logical but problematic expression of the familial model of the nation—one of the many difficulties that such authors were exploring. For Durlson, by contrast, incest in Brown's novel allegorizes "the realization of dreams" in America where nature can freely direct sympathies—which is a vaguely disturbing reading.

39. For readings of incest in Hill Brown's novel, see Barnes, "Affecting," "Natural and Unnatural," and *States*; Dalke, "Original Vice"; Stern, *Plight*; and for the first republican reading of it, Davidson, *Revolution*.

40. Brown, *The Power of Sympathy*, 33–34. Further references appear in the text.

41. Wald, *Constituting Americans*, 168–69 (emphasis in original).

42. For discussion of Frado's internalized racism, see, for example, Wald, *Constituting Americans*, 165–67; West, "Reworking the Conversion Narrative," 4; and Leveen, "Dwelling in the House of Oppression," 575.

43. Most critics have understood this autobiographical novel as Wilson's double revision of slave narrative and sentimental or seduction novel. In relation to the sentimental novel in particular, the phrase "borrows heavily" is from Mitchell, "Her Side of His Story," 8; and the following critics offer discussion of Wilson's influence by and revision of this tradition: Gates, introduction to *Our Nig*; Doriani, "Black Womanhood"; King, "Harriet Wilson's *Our Nig*"; Peterson, "Capitalism, Black (Under)Development, and the Production of the African-American Novel"; Fox-Genovese, "'To Weave It into the Literature of the Country'"; Jones, "The Disappearing 'I'"; Lovell "By Dint of Labor and Economy"; Piep, "Nothing New"; Stern, "Excavating *Our Nig*"; and Foreman, "The Spoken and the Silenced."

44. See, for instance, Tate, *Domestic Allegories*, 39–41, and King, "Harriet Wilson's *Our Nig*," 31–32.

45. For discussion of the text as parody, see especially King, "Harriet Wilson's *Our Nig*"; Tate, *Domestic Allegories*, 39–44; and, on satire, Breau, "Identifying Satire." See Jones, "The Disappearing 'I,'" for a rich discussion of Wilson's novel as a struggle with the novel tradition's founding elements of movement and active agency.

46. Wilson, *Our Nig,* 6. All further references to this work appear in the text.

47. For analysis of the interrelated problematics of voice and body in the text, see C. Davis, "Speaking the Body's Pain," 391–404; R. J. Ellis, "Traps Slyly Laid," 66–71, and "Body Politics," 108–9; and Mullen, "Runaway Tongue" in Samuels, *Culture of Sentiment,* 244–264.

48. See Peterson, "Capitalism," 563, 580 (and also *Doers of the Word* for her full study of this larger topic), and Ernest, *Resistance and Reformation,* 64–80. Readers from Gates forward have remarked on the conditions of economic insecurity emphasized in both the frame and the tale of Wilson's novel. In addition to Peterson and Ernest, see critics cited above for discussion in passing, including Gates, Carby, *Reconstructing Womanhood,* Fox-Genovese, Ernest, Lovell, Piep, Stern, Tate. Also see K. F. C. Holloway, "Economies of Space"; Pratofiorito, "'To Demand Your Sympathy and Aid'"; and Short, "Harriet Wilson's *Our Nig.*" Peterson, Lovell, Fox-Genovese, and Ernest particularly emphasize the ways that Wilson critiques the individualist economy and implicitly calls for what Lovell deems a "sentimental economics" (3) in which community and persons work cooperatively for economic survival. Piep, Tate, and Holloway study Wilson's foregrounding of the "material conditions of literary production" (Piep, 180) and the ways that these affect the form of the novel.

49. For the most recent information about Wilson's biography, see Foreman and Pitts in their introduction to the Penguin edition of *Our Nig* (2004). See also Gates, introduction to *Our Nig;* White, "Our Nig and the She-Devil"; Brassard, "'Beyond Mortal Vision'"; and Gardner, "'The Attempt of Their Sister.'"

50. See Gates in his introduction for this mention of "first-person lapses" (xxxvii), although he also appreciates that Wilson's strategy allows her to "transform her tormenters into objects" (li). Holloway characterizes the novel as "largely monologic" ("Economies of Space," 127). Other critics have closely considered the effects and implications of Wilson's combination of first and third person: see Cole, "Stowe, Jacobs, Wilson," 39, as well as Ellis, Jones, Leveen; Pratofiorito, Wald, Peterson, and Lovell, all cited above. Those readings most closely related to my interpretation here are Peterson (who explores the way Wilson's pronouns create a hybridity that "resists commodification" ["Capitalism, Black (Under)Development, and the Production of the African-American Novel," 567]); Wald (who argues that through the third person Wilson dramatizes "the process of subjection" but in a way that allows her to have "the final word" [*Constituting Americans,* 168–70]); and Jones (who notes that the third-person narration allows Wilson to assume the "illusion of authority" and to assume editorializing privileges without directly implicating herself ["The Disappearing 'I,'" 39]).

51. See Tate, *Domestic,* 33–38, and Stern, "Excavating," 442–45. Near the end of her discussion, Tate also argues that for Wilson this maternal discourse is not simply affectional but also serves strategically as her vehicle for becoming an author. Our readings begin to converge at this point. For other discussions of the representations of motherhood in the text, including debate about whether Wilson ultimately embraces or dismantles the sentimental ideal of motherhood, see Foreman, "The Spoken and the Silenced," 320–23; Ammons, "Afterword," 181–86; Pratofiorito, "To Demand Your Sympathy and Aid," 42; King, "Harriet Wilson's *Our Nig,*" 34–35; and Brassard, "Beyond Mortal Vision," 196–97. I fall on the side of those who emphasize Wilson's critical stance toward Mag, and I would disagree with those (like Tate, *Domestic Allegories,* 33–35) who suggest that Mag simply resembles

the many African American and other desperate parents of her time who placed their children in indentured servitude, for Mag does not place Frado in indentured servitude. She does not make a contract for her daughter: she removes her from the network of her life, not just her home and economic support. That is, Mag *abandons* Frado. In my parlance, she ruins her, furthering the practice of Anglo-Atlantic culture at large — specifically visiting her own experience of ruin, abandonment, racialization, and denial of liberty on her African American daughter.

52. Gates, introduction to *Our Nig,* xxxv.

53. My attention to place and displacement here is indebted to Lois Leveen's suggestive analysis of space, place, and house at the Bellmonts, in "Dwelling in the House of Oppression," informed by material culture studies.

54. Many critics have appreciated the novel, especially in its account of relations between Frado and the Bellmonts, as a rendering of national labor, gender, and racial conflicts in the United States. See Carby, Peterson, Fox-Genovese, Tate, Ernest, Ellis (both), Stern, Leveen, Jones, Lovell, Pratofiorito, and Short, all cited above. My reading has affinities especially with Leveen's and Wald's, who argue, respectively, that Frado's arrival "exposes rifts" in the family mirroring those in the nation (Leveen 568), and that (conversely) her labor and presence preserve the peace in a family and nation that might otherwise come apart (Wald 166–67). If we notice how her "absent presence" structures family and national life, these two seemingly opposite accounts can be reconciled.

55. See Leveen, "Dwelling in the House of Oppression," especially 569–73.

56. See R. C. Johnson, "Said But Not Spoken," for the fullest attention to this possibility. From another angle, Stern suggests in passing that Frado falls in love with the brothers (*Plight of Feeling,* 451). Such suggestions begin to set up a parallel to Moll Flanders's "incestuous" relations with the brothers in her first household. Stern (453) and Leveen ("Dwelling in the House of Oppression," 572) also consider the erotic energy expressed in Mrs. Bellmont's frenzied beatings of Frado.

57. White, "*Our Nig* and the She-Devil," 31–33; Leveen ("Dwelling in the House of Oppression," 572–73.

58. Ernest in particular stresses that Wilson is fashioning a vision of "God's economy" (*Resistance and Reformation,* 5). Tate likewise sees Wilson working toward an integration of political and religiously moral economies (*Domestic Allegories of Political Desire,* 38). West, "Reworking the Early Conversion Narrative," on the other hand, argues against any conversion on Frado's or Wilson's part, and Jones considers the whole drama of Frado's religious struggles merely a device to offer action in a story about a wholly immobilized protagonist, "The Disappearing 'I,'" 4, 13–17).

59. See King, "Harriet Wilson's *Our Nig,*" 40–41, for an account of the additional comparable details.

60. King interprets these two scenes as Wilson's inversion of the "hierarchical oppositions of good and evil and wealth and poverty that is traditional in both the sentimental novel and in nineteenth-century social ideology" (41).

61. For a full reading of the biblical references in the novel, see Bassard, "'Beyond Mortal Vision.'" For discussions of this closing reference to Joseph see Johnson, "Said but Not Spoken," 100–101, and Wald, *Constituting Americans,* 170.

7. Middle-Passage Plots

1. Defoe, *Robinson Crusoe*, 11–12. Further references to this work appear in the text.

2. Equiano, *Narrative of the Life of Olaudah Equiano*, 133. All further references to this work appear in the text.

3. For two influential examples, see Constanzo, *Surprising Narrative*, and Gates, *The Signifying Monkey*.

4. Carretta, *Equiano, the African*, xvi–xvii and throughout.

5. See Samuels, "Disguised Voice in *The Interesting Narrative of Olaudah Equiano*," and Sabino and Hall, "The Path Not Taken."

6. See Potkay, "History, Oratory, and God," and Caldwell, "Talking Too Much English." All further references to these works appear in the text. While critics such as Samuels or Sabino and Hall emphasize Equiano's African legacies over his European ones, they do not pursue an either/or logic as Caldwell does. Samuels stresses the "dual nature of the thematics and characterization of his narrative" and closes by asking that we "not only listen" to the European Vasa "but also to" the African Equiano ("Disguised Voice," 69); and Sabino and Hall ultimately argue simply that Equiano's "acculturation to Anglo-Christian values was highly selective" ("The Path Not Taken," 5). In my discussion, I focus on Caldwell's article, which Potkay draws on, because others have already addressed the unnecessarily either/or logic of Potkay's work. For critiques of Potkay, see Wheeler, "Domesticating Equiano's Interesting Narrative," and Aravamudan, "Equiano Lite."

7. For other critics who combine discussions of Defoe and Equiano, see Aravamudan, *Tropicopolitans*, 275–81; Hinds, "The Spirit of Trade"; and Murphy, "Olaudah Equiano, Accidental Tourist."

8. To support her claim that "[t]he Equiano of the entire Interesting Narrative, . . . has after all been formed and educated by the laws, the language, and the habits of English culture, *not* the land of his birth," Caldwell misrepresents the *Narrative* (266, emphasis added). We are told, first, that Equiano left Africa "as a very young child" at age "eight" and that "he would have been an extraordinary individual to retain unadulterated memories of his first eight years" (269). She goes on to conclude, citing S. F. Ogude's research on Equiano's borrowings from Anthony Benezet's ethnography of Africa, that "the adult Equiano had no more first-hand knowledge of Africa than DeFoe did" (269). But Equiano himself reports that he was eleven (19) and refers more than once to his age in the first years of his captivity. Convinced of "the thoroughly European nature of [Equiano's] mind," Caldwell makes eleven years into eight and implies that any memories need to be "unadulterated" and any knowledge must be "adult" in order to influence the *Narrative*.

Similarly, in her aim to debunk those critics who emphasize Equiano's abolitionist aims or align him with a black Atlantic community, Caldwell insists against ample evidence to the contrary that Equiano eschews any solidarity with blacks, describing him as a "lonely wanderer . . . [l]ike Crusoe" (270). Yet Equiano reports many moments of kinship and affiliation with "black persons" as I discuss later in this chapter.

9. See Watt, *Rise of the Novel*, 65, and Fliegelman, *Pilgrims and Prodigals*, for instance. Fliegelman discusses this opening as a "prodigal son" trope with particular appeal for American colonists in the revolutionary years (69–71). In a different kind of argument, Flint in *Family Fictions* emphasizes Crusoe's family attachments.

10. See Marx, *Capital* 1:169–170, and Watt, *Rise of the Novel,* 60–92. Also see critics cited in note 18 in chapter 6, as well as Hinds, "The Spirit of Trade," and Schmidgen, "*Robinson Crusoe,* Enumeration, and the Mercantile Fetish." For a feminist reading of economics in *Robinson Crusoe,* see Weigman, "Economies of the Body." For pertinent discussions of Defoe's lesser-known texts, see Flynn, "Nationalism, Commerce and Imperial Anxiety in Defoe's Later Works," and O'Brien, "Union Jack."

11. See note 14 in chapter 6.

12. For related postcolonial readings of the novel, see Marzec, "Enclosures," and Wheeler, "My Savage, My Man."

13. In the process, Defoe participates in the fixing of racial meanings that were still unstable at this point, as Wheeler points out — helping to align "savage" and "Moor" with legal and economic statuses and so abetting Anglo-Atlantic projects of trade and ownership ("My Savage, My Man," 828–30).

14. See Brown, "Displaced Self," Snow, "Arguments to the Self," and Marzec, "Enclosures," for other readings of Crusoe's struggle to create a unified "I" in the text.

15. Woolf, "Defoe."

16. See Andrews's arguments about novelization in *To Tell a Free Story.*

17. For a related consideration of Equiano's engagement/entanglement in liberty and rights discourses, see especially Gould, "Free Carpenter," and Kazanjian, "Mercantile Exchanges." Also, in addition to Fichtelberg, "Word Between Worlds," Hinds, "The Spirit of Trade," and Sabino and Hall, "The Path Not Taken," see Aravamudan, *Tropicopolitans,* 247–59. Sabino and Hall interestingly consider Equiano's valuing of freedom as part of his African heritage, although without much discussion or evidence. All these critics consider Equiano's use of this discourse as part of his subversion of his racial identity, overlooking the racialization that plagues all those who take up the liberty discourse.

18. Henry Brooke, *Gustavas Vasa,* Dedication iii–iv.

19. For a related but more general discussion of the sea as the setting for Equiano's crises, see Collins, "Passage to Slavery." Boelhower gives passing rhetorical attention to the "politically turbulent and storm-swept waters of the Atlantic" as the "field of struggles" through which Equiano moves ("I'll Teach You How to Flow," 39, 32).

20. For further examples, see Equiano, *The Interesting Narrative,* 86, 96–97, 121, 123, 126. Carretta's biography *Equiano, the African* also establishes Equiano's alignment with blacks.

21. A number of critics have considered the difficulty Equiano faces in attempting to establish social or legal subjectivity. See especially Hinds, "The Spirit of Trade." Also see Fichtelberg, "Word Between Worlds"; Murphy, "Olaudah Equiano"; Gould, "Free Carpenter"; Chandler, "Originary Displacement"; and Kazanjian, "Mercantile Exchanges."

22. Some recent critics have emphasized the fact that Equiano becomes a "merchant" and does accrue some capital, including by way of the slave trade. But it's important to keep in mind that he remains a wage worker and laborer on ships, not a merchant along for the ride, and he accrues money and goods on the side. Similarly, he works for slave traders and owners but never buys slaves for himself, contrary to Caldwell's suggestion that he becomes a slave trader (271). For other discussions of Equiano's financial projects and maneuvers, see especially Kazanjian, Gould, Fichtelberg, and Chandler, all cited in the previous note. Also see Bozeman, "Interstices, Hybridity, and Identity."

23. See Bugg, "The Other Interesting Narrative," for evidence of Equiano's objections to exactly this threat within England (1472).

24. Quoted in Wilson, "Citizenship, Empire, and Modernity," 83.

25. For related discussions of Equiano's manipulation of English-language narrative conventions, see for instance Gates, *The Signifying Monkey;* Earley, "Writing from the Center or the Margins?"; D. Anderson, "Division Below the Surface"; Pudaloff, "No Change Without Purchase"; Kelleter, "Ethnic Self-Dramatization"; and Bozeman, "Interstices, Hybridity, and Identity."

26. In addition to Potkay, several critics have discussed Equiano's Protestantism. In addition to Fichtelberg, "Word Between Worlds," Hinds, "The Spirit of Trade," and Sabino and Hall, "The Path Not Taken," see Elrod, "Moses and the Egyptian," and Aravamudan, *Tropicopolitans,* especially 233–50, 285–87. For a related discussion of Equiano's stance here, see Kelleter's "Ethnic Self-Dramatization," and his analysis of what he calls "differential universalism," which however leads Kelleter to cast Equiano as more strictly invested in assimilation than I would.

27. For discussion of Equiano's use of ethnographic literary practices, see especially Murphy, "Olaudah Equiano, Accidental Tourist," and also Ogude, "Facts into Fiction," Kitson, "Bales of Anguish," and Constanzo, *Surprising Narrative.* In my view, the fact that he borrows some of his material about Benin from other contemporary travel narratives by whites does not diminish either his own or his audience's sense that he once knew this other land as an insider, that he is reporting from the frontier in the language of the metropole.

28. Murphy considers this pronoun use in passing, although she wrongly remarks that he uses "they" only in describing religious practices. Also see Carretta (*Equiano, the African,* 316) for mention of this pronoun usage.

29. Melville, *Billy Budd,* 299. Further references appear in the text.

30. Quoted in Ruttenberg, *Democratic Personality,* 347, emphasis in original.

31. Emerson, *English Traits,* 86, emphasis added. All further references to this work appear in the text.

32. Otter, *Melville's Anatomies,* 259.

33. Critical discussion of this opening African figure has yet to assess his full significance. Most of those who consider him at all fold him into Billy Budd's story with the same effacing effects that the narrator's brief reference enacts. Browne argued decades ago that the comparison of Billy and the African sailor indicates that Billy is "every race's savior — black, white and in-between" ("*Billy Budd:* Gospel of Democracy," 327–28). He sees no difficulty in Billy Budd the Anglo-Saxon standing in for the freedom struggle of all races, although he acknowledges in an aside that "the black Handsome Sailor is more remarkable than the white, and more nearly represents mankind of the Revolution, as Melville's mention of Anacharsis Cloots demonstrates" (328). Yet Browne, following Melville's lead, relegates this point to a "mention" and nonetheless takes Billy as his protagonist. More recently, Yanella asks, "Is Billy another historical and perhaps representative victim?" and then (only) parenthetically he adds "(Consider the narrator's recollection of the African sailor and his multicultural mates in the book's second paragraph)" (*New Essays on Billy Budd,* 2). Reading the story in the context of contemporary sociological discourses, Mizruchi, "Cataloging the

Creatures of the Deep," equates the Anglo-Saxon and the African sailors as "types" whose purity makes them "anomalies" which must be purged to preserve social regularity. She too thus sets aside the obvious historical divide between them. As I'll argue below, the text may well seek to purge both of these figures but not for the reasons that Mizruchi offers.

Karcher gives the African the most extended treatment in her groundbreaking study of race in Melville's fiction, *Shadow over the Promised Land*. In fact, she concludes her book with a discussion of this sailor, casting him as Melville's "finest — and final — statement about race" (307). But, published in 1980 and not yet in a position to benefit from, in particular, Toni Morrison's critique of "Africanism" in white American fiction, Karcher's book celebrates Melville's racial project for showing that "black and white are identical" (306). Interestingly, Karcher closes her book with a liberty telos of her own, as we've seen other critics do as they tell the stories of novelists: she reports that, as expressed through the African in *Billy Budd,* Melville "has at last become free to dismiss the phantasm of race with complete serenity, and to embrace once again the dark brothers of his youth" (307). Karcher thus doubles Melville's own move: where the African provides Melville with a launching point for his Anglo-Saxon hero, this same figure provides Karcher with a grand finale for her hero, the author. The "freedom to dismiss" that Karcher finally allows Melville names exactly the privilege that racism has allowed Anglo-Americans, for to "dismiss" the phantasm of race "at last" is certainly in itself a race freedom, not to mention a deep impulse compelling many white authors' novels. My point is not to critique the work of Karcher, for in fact it has opened the way to further thinking about this issue. Rather, it is to heighten awareness of the ways that, despite intentions to the contrary, race silently reenters our interpretations via the political unconscious of the liberty plot.

34. Sedgwick, *Epistemology of the Closet*, 91 – 130.

35. For a useful summary of this critical debate, see Milder's introduction to his *Critical Essays*, 3 – 18. Also see Murphy, "The Politics of Reading *Billy Budd*," for a reading of these "resistance vs. acceptance" readings.

36. The phrase is from Rousseau's *The Social Contract*, 60. All further references to this work appear in the text. See Rogin, *Subversive Genealogies,* for a full treatment of Melville's ambivalent relation to his own paternal line and, accordingly, his opposing impulses toward submission and rebellion. Many recent critics likewise see in Melville an ambivalent attitude toward rebellion. See, for instance, Karcher, *Shadow over the Promised Land*; R. S. Levine, *Conspiracy and Romance;* Reynolds, "Billy Budd"; Berthold, "Melville, Garibaldi, and the Medusa of Revolution"; Franklin, "From Empire to Empire"; and Wallace, "*Billy Budd* and the Haymarket Hangings."

37. See Johnson, "Melville's Fist," and Thomas, "Billy Budd and the Judgment of Silence." Thomas's directly engages and dissents from Johnson's deconstructive reading, although I believe he misreads her main claim (that the text forces us to experience the difficulty of judgment), which he understands as a dismissal of the need for judgment.

38. See Cowan, "The Naming of Captain Vere," for an account of the names in *Billy Budd,* especially Captain Fairfax Vere's. Cowan's research suggests that Melville intended to affiliate him and others with earlier dramas of English history.

39. For discussion of the legality of Vere's decision, see Dolin, *Fiction and the Law*, 128 – 31; Douglas, "Discursive Limits"; and Thomas, "Billy Budd and the Judgment of Silence."

8. At Liberty's Limits

1. Recent critical studies have begun to interpret the gothic as a mode that registers this African American history. See especially Winter, *Subjects of Slavery, Agents of Change,* and Goddu, *Gothic America.* For studies that focus less strictly on the gothic but read American literature as "haunted" by the United States' "gothic" history, see Hartman, *Scenes of Subjection;* Bergland, *The National Uncanny;* Brogan, *Cultural Haunting;* and Young, *Haunting Capital.* The gothic themes of possession may also carry at some level the memory of white slavery on the Atlantic practiced most widely in the seventeenth century, as traced by Linebaugh and Rediker in *The Many-Headed Hydra;* but since those practices had mostly ended by the later eighteenth century, the more immediate connotations of bodily possession would have related to non-Anglo persons and to women.

2. Many feminist critics have considered the gothic as a literary mode crafted to expose the violations of patriarchy, including Fleenor, *Female Gothic;* Ellis, *Contested Castle;* Delamotte, *Perils of the Night;* Milbank, *Daughters of the House;* Massé, *In the Name of Love;* Wolstenholme, *Gothic (Re)Visions;* Castle, *Female Thermometer;* Clery, *Women's Gothic.* Nearly all these studies either speak broadly in terms of patriarchy or stress the violations of fathers, overlooking the role of brothers.

3. Although she does not stress the economic connotations of "possession," Kilgour offers related remarks on it in the context of her reading of the Gothic as a deconstruction of individualism. She directly discusses gothic writing itself as an experience of possession (*The Rise of the Gothic Novel,* 167–68). For discussions of the gothic in relation to market and bourgeois economics more broadly, see Clery, *The Rise of Supernatural Fiction,* and Punter, *The Literature of Terror.*

4. With the word "unspeakable" I mean to invoke both Sedgwick's reading of the gothic in *The Coherence of Gothic Conventions*—including her suggestion, made more explicit in *Between Men,* that gay sexuality is part of what cannot be spoken—and Morrison's use of the word in her essay "Unspeakable Things Unspoken," where she addresses the history of race in the United States.

5. Political/historical contextualization of the British gothic usually is made in relation to the French Revolution, which I would in turn place in a transatlantic and imperial context. For imperial readings of the gothic, see Schmitt, *Alien Nation,* and Goddu, *Gothic America,* which provide excellent starting points for Britain and the United States respectively. My aim is to extend such arguments as theirs into a transatlantic "English-language" context. For a broader account including Europe and the Americas, see Monleón, *A Spectre Is Haunting Europe.* Other relevant works include nearly all those that treat the Irish and Anglo-Irish gothic, most especially Backus, *The Gothic Family Romance.* In the U.S. context, see Hartman, *Scenes of Subjection,* and, for treatment of twentieth-century fiction, see Brogan, *Cultural Haunting.* Also see Byron and Punter, eds., *Spectral Readings,* which includes essays on both American and British gothic, although only some of the essays focus on imperialist geography or implications.

6. For an interestingly parallel discussion, see Smith, *Gothic Radicalism,* especially the chapter "History and the Sublime," 59–75. Smith understands the gothic as a subgenre exploring the internalization of the "I" and critiquing it. His study also complements Kilgour's in its focus on the gothic's deconstruction of the individualist order.

7. With the exception of Miles, critics too often dismiss or misconstrue the Germanic racial and related political associations of the term "gothic." See Clery, "The Genesis of 'Gothic' Fiction," and especially Sowerby, "The Goths in History," for the most dismissive accounts. Many critics, like Mighall, continue to miscast the eighteenth-century meanings of "gothic" as largely negative across its variations throughout the century — associated with all things "uncivilized, unprogressive, and 'barbaric'" (*Geography*, xviii). Others simply overlook the relevance of the term's history, as is the case in Schmitt's study, *Alien Nation* — even though this history is particularly pertinent for her arguments. A few studies have come close to appreciating the political and racial meanings of the term but do so incompletely. See, for example, Madoff, "The Useful Myth of Gothic Ancestry"; Baldick, introduction to *The Oxford Book of Gothic Tales*; and Botting, "In Gothic Darkly," 3–14. Baldick accurately maps the "Northern versus Southern, Gothic versus Graeco-Roman" oppositions embedded in the term but misframes the full semiotic network in which these associations are embedded (xii). Similarly, Botting begins to capture what he calls the "heterotopic" meanings of the gothic and gives attention to the revision of aesthetics in the later eighteenth century that revalues the gothic, but he still misses its full political and racial resonance. Kilgour very suggestively includes a chapter titled "The Artist as Goth" in the closing section of her excellent study, but without treatment of the materials I discuss in chapters 1 and 2 of this study (189–217). Miles, "The 1790's: The Effulgence of the Gothic," comes closest to capturing the gothic's genealogy and meanings when he recounts its "Whig" associations; but when he stresses the gothic's change of valence during the French Revolution — after which, he argues, the gothic took on increasingly negative associations and became associated with tyranny (47–49) — he overlooks the continuities carried forward across this shift, specifically, I suggest, by way of the liberty plot and the figure of the tyrant. He also gives no attention to the racial meanings of gothic and the way these situate the gothic text in a broader colonial context.

8. It's important to acknowledge that in the second half of the eighteenth century much of the notice given to "the Gothic" was in the form of sneers and eye-rolling, similar to the attitude toward antiquarianism since the late seventeenth century. But this very ridicule testified to its ubiquity. We might compare it to the status of "new age" beliefs, magazines, and practices in our own time. That is, the sneers themselves reflect the fad's ubiquitousness — everyone seeks to mark it as a "fringe" element of the culture exactly because it keeps taking hold in so many places. "The Gothic" seems to have had a similar pervasiveness. See Baridon in *Exhibited by Candlelight*: "We may smile . . . but snobs are good indicators of the popularity of a movement" (47). As critics have noted, the meaning of the phrase "the Gothic" became so diluted through overuse that it frequently referred simply to "the medieval" or the barbarian or the terrifying. This partly explains why racial valences got buried, for readers then as for critics today.

9. Garrett's discussion of the gothic's self-consciousness as "a social transaction [that] offset[s] its stories of isolated figures" (*Gothic Reflections*, 222) has much in common with Kilgour's similar emphasis in *The Rise of the Gothic Novel*. My study shares their interest in isolated figures and textual self-consciousness, the latter of which I believe reaches its height in African-Atlantic gothic.

10. Characters in gothic novels are often wanderers, as epitomized in Maturin's *Melmouth the Wanderer* and evident in every gothic novel beginning with *Otranto*. Typically, however, critics pay more attention to architecture and inner space than to this outdoor movement.

Mighall, in *A Geography of Victorian Gothic Fiction,* probably gives the most extended attention to outer landscape and movement and does so in relation to history and politics, but in spirit my analysis is closer to Schmitt's *Alien Nation,* which emphasizes how gothic rootlessness travels together with nativism. For the Flint phrase, see *Family Fictions,* 292.

11. *Walpole's Correspondence,* 9, 149 [11 May 1753]. For mention of his antiquarian activities, see Walpole, *The Castle of Otranto,* introduction, viii. Further references are given in the text.

12. See Schmitt, *Alien Nation,* for further discussion of Walpole's ambitions to place his text within a nativist literary tradition, which Schmitt compares to Radcliffe's similar aim, 22–23. Also see Clery's note about the possible historical basis for Walpole's tale, which included a rightful heir named Conrad stranded in Germany during King Manfred's reign (*Rise of Supernatural Fiction,* 117).

13. See Baldick, "The End of the Line," on the trope of "dynastic extinction" in the gothic (147).

14. Lewis later owned a plantation on Jamaica and published the *Journal of a West India Proprietor, Kept during a Residence in the Island of Jamaica* (1834), which shows similar anxiety in its mixture of antislavery and accommodationist sentiment. See Sandiford, "'Monk' Lewis and the Slavery Sublime," for a rich discussion of this ambivalence and of Lewis's treatment of slavery in relation to the sublime.

15. Lewis, *The Monk,* 219–20. All further references appear in the text.

16. In Shakespeare's Sonnet 30 the speaker "with old woes new wail[s] my dear time's waste," "moan[s] the expense of many a vanished sight," and "heavily from woe to woe tell[s] o'er / The sad account of fore-bemoaned moan / Which I new pay as if not paid before." Lewis's closing line echoes Shakespeare's in form but contrasts with it in content, for Shakespeare makes his usual turn when his speaker reflects, "But if the while I think on thee dear friend, / All losses are restored and sorrows end."

17. See Kilgour for a different reading of this drama of family violation in *The Monk,* yet one still linked to the rise of individualism (*The Rise of the Gothic Novel,* 160–63).

18. For discussion of queer sexuality in *The Monk,* see Miles, "Ann Radcliffe and Matthew Lewis," especially 52–54. Also see Rizzo, "Renegotiating the Gothic," for discussion of the way that later eighteenth-century British reviewers and readers "elicit" gothic performances (in writing and in life) from (apparently) homosexual men like Lewis as well as from women.

19. In the light of the gothic's Anglo-Saxon Protestant associations, the use of the convent as a setting in these novels seems to require explanation. I would suggest that gothic texts' convents and monasteries always implicitly reference the Catholic-Norman history of "repression" and lost native rights or beliefs. Appropriately, the novel's liberty plots arise against, and are allegories of, this repression. Likewise, the convent settings of gothic novels allow a redramatization of the Jacobin "threat from within" – so that the threat which Catholicism was said to have offered to the most secret and powerful sources of the Protestant state's integrity and sanctity, even from within the proper (Stuart) family lineage, now gets replayed as a threat to the bodily and psychic interiors of the liberty-seeking, good characters, especially women, in the form of incestuous rape. As such, in their sexual and incest plots these novels replay the trauma of "access" to the "recess," as reflected in the title and

setting of Sophia Lee's wildly popular novel *The Recess* as well as in the Antonia/Ambrosio plot of Lewis's *The Monk*.

20. See Poliakov, *The Aryan Myth*, for an explanation of the Gothic lineage as it was understood to extend into Spain.

21. For a full scholarly treatment of the increasing pressure on eighteenth-century novelists and especially women writers to contain women's agency and create "pure" female characters and plots, see Spencer, *The Rise of the Woman Novelist*.

9. Saxon Dissociation

1. Shirley Samuels refers to the novel as "a history of America" (*Romance of Republic*, 45), Emory Elliot sees it building on the history of "families uprooted" from their homeland (*Revolutionary Writers*, xviii), and David Seed understands its tale of familiacide as an "ideological portrayal of American history as a struggle for freedom" ("The Mind Set Free" 114). Ed White discusses the novel's "spatial geography" mainly to cast the American Wieland homestead as a mediating "German crescent" between "rural subaltern" and urban center (with no attention to "German" per se; 45–46). See subsequent notes for reference to more specific historical readings of the novel.

2. Hsu charts in Carwin's biloquism "an allegorical return of the indigenous peoples expropriated by the settlement and expansion of the colonies" insofar as it begins (as recounted in *Memoirs of Carwin the Biloquist*) through his imitation of what Carwin calls a "Mohock" voice and of Shakespeare's Ariel ("Democratic Expansion in *Memoirs of Carwin*," 148). Working with similar materials in "Charles Brockden Brown's Biloquial Nation," Kazanjian draws a slightly different conclusion. He sees Carwin as a figure whose voice "displaces" (486–87) the voices of indigenous peoples and therefore as part and parcel of Brown's narrative project to "replace the violent history of white settler colonialism with an aesthetic call to incorporate scenes of 'wild' America" (460). Relatedly, Woodard, "Female Captivity and the Deployment of Race," and Leask, "Irish Republicans," consider Carwin the embodiment of a threatening racialized outsider.

3. My analysis of the novel joins those of the many critics who have noted its dissociative or disjunctive mode, although none recognizes the catalyzing role of Saxonism as it produces this fractured world and contributes to the novel's gender and cultural conflicts. See Christophersen, *The Apparition in the Glass;* Samuels, *Romance;* Hsu, "Democratic Expansion in *Memoirs of Carwin*"; Smith-Rosenberg, "Subject Female"; Manning, "Enlightenment's Dark Dreams"; Barnes, "Loving with a Vengeance"; Seed, "The Mind Set Free," and Leask, "Irish Republicans," for interpretations that consider the novel "a study in disjointed perception" (in Christophersen's words, 41) created by the characters' disavowal of their implicated political situation. Scheiber gives the most extended attention to the Catch-22 of gender ideals for women as they create the disjunctions in Clara's behavior and narrative ("'The Arm Lifted against Me'"), although several other critics address gender as well, particularly Samuels (*Romance*), Hinds ("Charles Brockden Brown's Revenge Tragedy" and *Private Property*), and Smith-Rosenberg. More generally, recent Americanist critics read the novel within the "insecure world" (Fliegelman, *Prodigals*, 240) of young republican America, a social milieu troubled by questions of "authority" and "with no markers that

define and fix the self," as Tompkins puts it in *Sensational Designs* (54, 52), and a world that provokes this story of "unfettered individual agency gone awry" (Watts, *Writing and Postcolonialism*, 81); in this world both Lockean rationality (Voloshin, "*Wieland*"; Manning, "Enlightenment's Dark Dreams") and arguments of evidence (Korobkin, "Murder by Madman") lack firm ground. In addition to these critics, for related arguments, see Axelrod, *Charles Brockden Brown;* Hedges, "Charles Brockden Brown and the Culture of Contradictions"; Bell, "Double-Tongued Deceiver"; Barnes, "Loving with a Vengeance"; Ruttenberg, *Democratic Personality;* Levine, *Conspiracy and Romance;* White, "Carwin the Peasant Rebel"; and Elliot, *Revolutionary Writers.*

Christophersen, Smith-Rosenberg, Barnes, White, and especially Hinds give attention to the volatile economic conditions of the postwar nation that underlie the novel's fragmentation, and that, despite the Mettingen community's removed position of privilege, disrupt their world. Yet again, no critic has put due emphasis on the *racialized* "possessive individualism" that embeds the Wielands in those volatile conditions. In this dimension my reading diverges substantially from that of Hinds, who suggests that the novel blasts the Wielands as an "aristocratic" family (and, specifically Clara as an "aristocratic" woman [*Private Property,* 100]). But "aristocratic" is a misnomer that overlooks the Saxonist fall from nobility which Brown takes pains to include; and, more important, it obscures the *colonialist* basis of their prosperity. The "inheritance" that provides the American Wielands' comfort and yet prompts the "suffering visited on the house of Wieland" (Hinds 100) is the colonial land and labor seized by their missionary father from Indians and Africans; its "noble" aspect appears through the cultural materials of racial myth rather than through any landed or monied endowment coming directly through the Germanic family line (which only arrives belatedly).

4. Fleischmann traces a larger pattern of brother trouble for Brockden Brown's and Hannah Foster's female characters in "Concealed Lessons."

5. Brockden Brown, *Wieland,* 89. All further references to this work appear in the text.

6. Quoted in Horsman, *Race and Manifest Destiny,* 112.

7. Quoted in Nobles, *American Frontiers,* 90.

8. See Smith-Rosenberg, "Subject Female," 483, for discussion of the land grants; and see Christophersen, *The Apparition in the Glass,* 12, for this statistic about the federal budget.

9. One of the few critics to comment directly on this remarkable passage, Shirley Samuels (*Romance*), offers a somewhat different reading of it, casting it as part of the novel's "conflation" of national and family violence. She argues that the novel works to undo this conflation by segregating the private/familial from the public/political realm of experience.

10. Brockden Brown, preface to *Edgar Huntly.* All further references to this work appear in the text.

11. On the relation of the novel to the historical poet Wieland, see Frank, "The Wieland Family," and Kirkham "A Note on *Wieland.*" Frank also argues that G. F. Lessing provides a model for Wieland, but his account contains some errors about details in the novel (he confuses two generations of Wieland and, as Kirkham points out, he misrepresents the second-generation Wielands' religious connection to the Camissards [Kirkham 87]). Also see Kanzanjian's discussion of this poet in relation to Kant, "Charles Brockden Brown's Biloquial Nation," 482.

12. For discussions that see Wieland's religious mission as Brown's reconsideration of

the Calvinist-American inheritance, see Gilmore, "Calvinism and Gothicism"; Surratt, "'The Awe-Creating Presence of the Deity'"; Ziff, "A Reading of *Wieland*"; and Manning, "Enlightenment's Dark Dreams." Gilmore explicitly reads the novel as a reprisal of Milton's *Paradise Lost*, a reading which could be fruitfully reframed within Spengemann's suggestion in *New World of Words* that (for Milton) America embodied the seductions of Satan. See my discussion of this thesis in chapter 5.

13. For a rich, culturally situated study of the figure of the orphan in American literature, see Pazicky, *Cultural Ophans in America;* for her discussion of *Wieland,* see 87–89.

14. For analyses that emphasize the conflict between Enlightenment rationality and religious zealotry or human depravity, see Christophersen, Voloshin, Manning, and Korobkin (all cited in note 3); and also Kimball, *Rational Fictions;* Clark, *Language of Liberty;* Ziff, "A Reading of *Wieland*"; and Baridon, "The Gothic Revival."

15. Charles Brockden Brown, *Memoirs of Carwin.* All further references to this work appear in the text. Also see note 2 above.

16. We later learn that the orphan girl Louisa Conway is the product of another transatlantic history of seduction and ruin. Louisa plays a small but apparently symbolic role in the novel, and in fact her full history provides the disjunctive ending of the novel. Here she suggestively attracts Clara's queer side, otherwise submerged within her Gothic drama: Clara explains that she "cannot do justice to the attractions of this girl," that she "often shed tears at her approach, and pressed her to my bosom in an agony of fondness" (30). Perhaps there is yet another untold story here, which would give new significance to the abrupt return to Louisa at the novel's end, but Brown leaves us even fewer clues about this dissociated element than about Indians and Africans. On queerness and Brown more generally see Shapiro, "Man to Man," and Burgett, "Between Speculation and Population."

17. For a careful discussion of Carwin's culpability, see Korobkin, "Murder by Madman." For historical contextualization of this question see Shuffelton, "Juries of the Common Reader."

18. Kazanjian, "Charles Brockden Brown's Biloquial Nation," 462.

19. Carwin's performance even includes a mimicking of contemporary theories of the Gothic kinship of European peoples. In response to Pleyel's comment on the "incongruousness between the religion and habits of a Spaniard, with those of a native of Britain," Carwin replies that Britons and Spaniards draw "from the same fountains of literature, and they speak dialects of the same tongue; their government and laws have more resemblances than differences; they were formerly of the same civil, and till lately, religious, Empire" (83). He thus alludes to the contemporary theorizing of a shared Gothic origin for ancient European manners that fed nativist discourse, even as he proves himself a native of nowhere. See Kliger, *The Goths in England,* for discussion of Spanish Gothicism in relation to English Gothicism.

20. On the role Brockden Brown implicitly assigns to literature, see Bell, "The Double-Tongued Deceiver"; Seltzer, "Saying Makes It So"; Fussell, "*Wieland*"; Ruttenberg, *Democratic Personality,* 211–70; and Jordan, *Second Stories,* 78–97. Also suggestive for this point is Kazanjian's discussion of the parallels between Brown's and Kant's subsumption of the primitive into the "higher" forms of aesthetics, in "Charles Brockden Brown's Biloquial Nation."

21. That is, while Hinds (*Private Property*) focuses on the challenge to Clara as an "aristocratic" woman, and Samuels considers her the key to the novel's constitution of private

and public realms, and many critics discuss the "subtexts" of Clara's thwarted or incestuous desires (for instance, Barnes, Seed, Cowie, Norwood, Wilson, Lyttle), insufficient attention has been paid to the fact that Clara's narration of her physical struggles against what she perceives as rape or murder fills half the book. Scheiber gives the most extended attention to the gender dilemmas that Clara faces.

22. Smith-Rosenberg, "Subject Female," 482.

23. See Scheiber for a different discussion of the importance of Clara's diaries ("'The Arm Lifted against Me,'" 188 – 90).

24. The historical Wieland apparently provides a forerunner for Brown (that is, in Brown's mind) in that Wieland studied Cicero, probed the conflict between reason and passion, created a drama of family homicide (in his epic poem *The Trial of Abraham*), and wrote in a disjointed style.

25. See Bell, "The Double-Tongued Deceiver," especially 145 – 47, and Seltzer, "Saying Makes It So," especially 83 – 86.

10. Dispossession

1. Morrison, *Beloved,* 162. All further reference to this work appears in the text.

2. Gates, "Race," 9.

3. On Jacobs in relation to the gothic, see especially Goddu, *Gothic America,* 131 – 52; Winter, *Subjects of Slavery,* 89 – 91, 126 – 29; Greeson, "Mysteries and Miseries"; and Hamilton, "Dislocation, Violence, and the Language of Sentiment." Greeson treats Jacobs's narrative in relation to the contemporary "urban Gothic," and Hamilton stresses its interweaving of Gothic and sentimental elements. Goddu's argument is most closely related to mine here in that she reflects on the already-written story of gothic American slavery and the problems this raises for African American writers wherein their factual accounts appear as fictional tales (see chapter 6, 130 – 52).

4. Jacobs, *Incidents in the Life of a Slave Girl.* All further references to this work appear in the text. Jacobs uses the word "tyrant" throughout; see, e.g., 19, 27, 42, 55, 55, 55, 101, 204, 42.

5. Several critics have addressed Jacobs's grappling with discourses of freedom — Saidiya Hartman most incisively (*Scenes of Subjection,* 101 – 12). In *Conceived by Liberty,* Smith gives extended attention to Jacobs's refashioning of the discourse of liberty in relation to its individualist and masculinist elements (135 – 59). Tate, *Domestic Allegories,* also tracks Jacobs's revision of the masculine liberty story (26 – 32); Fox-Genovese emphasizes her recasting of its individualism ("To Weave," 37 – 38); and both Doriani ("Black Womanhood," 211 – 12), and Lovell ("By Dint," 1 – 18, 26 – 28) study her foregrounding of the economic foundations of freedom. For related discussions of Jacobs in relation to ideologies of the nation and the republic, also see Ernest, *Resistance and Reformation* (87 – 92) and Berlant, "The Queen of America," 564 – 73.

6. See Hartman, *Scenes of Subjection,* 102 – 12, and Tate, *Domestic Allegories,* 27 – 32, for discussion of Jacobs's practice of sexual "agency." Hartman stresses the impossible terms of Jacobs's efforts to act "freely." For a rich reading of the parallel way in which, at a discursive level, Jacobs "makes use of the erotic power of narration instead of being employed by it," see Sanchez-Eppler, *Touching Liberty,* 83 – 104. Many critics have rightly noted the impossibility of Jacobs's exercising any real choice about her sexuality. See, for instance, Carby,

Reconstructing, 49 – 61; Foreman, "The Spoken and the Silenced," 315 – 19; and Ernest, *Resistance and Reformation,* especially 98 – 108. Like Hartman, Tate, and Sanchez-Eppler, I am emphasizing that Jacobs nonetheless takes action within this situation.

7. For other readings of Jacobs's narrative in relation to matters of property and possession, see Peterson, "Capitalism, Black (Under)Development, and Production of the African-American Novel," 561 – 66; Hartman, *Scenes of Subjection,* 101 – 12; Doriani, "Black Womanhood," 211 – 12; Lovell, "By Dint," 1 – 18, 26 – 28; and Boesenberg, "The Color of Money," 117 – 26.

8. Andrews, *To Tell a Free Story,* 277 – 78.

9. See Goddu, *Gothic America,* 140 – 52. For a related discussion of Jacobs in relation to white women's sentimental fiction and Stowe in particular, see Cole, "Stowe, Jacobs, Wilson," 23 – 37. Almost all critics of Jacobs discuss her relation to conventions of sentimental fiction and are too numerous to mention here.

10. Smith's "Loophole of Retreat" remains one of the best readings of Jacobs's use of writing from this physical hiding place to empower herself. Most other readings, including mine, build on her insights.

11. For definition of this "future-anterior" position of African-Atlantic writing in modernity, see Nielsen, "The Future of an Allusion."

12. For a general summary of the ways that Lacan and psychoanalysis may shed light on these psychodynamic workings of the American gothic, see Savoy, "The Rise of the American Gothic," especially 168 – 71. Unfortunately, like many critics, although Savoy makes passing reference to the historical sources of the American gothic, he leaves these suggestions largely undeveloped; he focuses instead on psychology and on the standard Anglo-American male authors (Brown, Hawthorne, and Poe) with no mention of African American authors' handling of this form. In such critical accounts, what we might call the *petit objet a* at the heart of a Lacanian Anglo-Atlantic "Real" is exactly this missing African American presence.

13. Several critics have fruitfully considered Hopkins's novels as historical and explored her self-fashioning as a historian with an epic and/or Ethiopian vision. See especially Doreski's discussion of the pan-African framework of her project as a "visionary historian" (78), in "Inherited Rhetoric and Authentic History," and also Allen, *Black Women Intellectuals,* and Gaines, "Black Americans' Racial Uplift Ideology." See also Harris, "Not Black and/or White," for useful discussion of Hopkins's use of the ancient classical novel tradition, which, within the context of this study, reinforces the convergence of the modern and the ancient "liberty plots" within a broad historical sensibility and, more specifically, a racialized slave culture. Relatedly, for Hopkins's braiding of epic Judeo-Christian elements into her fiction, see Pamplin, "'Race' and Identity," 174 – 75, and Putzi, "'Raising the Stigma.'" For an excellent account of the ways that Hopkins simultaneously undercuts this epic thrust, see Rohrbach's discussion of "antigenealogy" in her fiction, in "To Be Continued." For related analysis of Hopkins's earlier novel *Contending Forces,* see Campbell, *Mythic Black Fiction,* 31 – 41. In relation to her novel *Winona,* see Patterson, "'Kin' o' Rough Jestice.'"

14. Almost all of Hopkins's critics focus to some degree on her complicated and, by many accounts, compromised racial views of this issue. For discussions most directly treating it, especially in relation to *Of One Blood,* see Carby, Gaines, Harris (all cited above) as well as Otten, "Pauline Hopkins and the Hidden Self of Race"; Gillman, "Hopkins and the Occult"; Wallinger, "Voyage into the Heart of Africa": Nickel, "Eugenics and the Fiction of Pauline

Hopkins"; Stevenson, "Of One Blood, Of One Race"; Japtok, "Pauline Hopkins's *Of One Blood*"; O'Brien, "Race-ing Toward Civilization"; Kassanoff, "'Fate Has Linked Us'"; and Schrager, "Pauline Hopkins and William James."

15. Lewis suggests that Queen Candace is "not recognizably African," a statement he does not elaborate ("Worldview and the Use of the Near-White Heroine," 616) but which may refer to the "bronze" color that Hopkins attributes to Candace. Bost, in "Fluidity without Postmodernism," extends Carby's arguments about the cultural work done by the mulatta figure and places Hopkins together with Harper at the origin of a reconstructing fictional tradition of biracial heroines reaching through Michelle Cliff.

16. Telassar, after all, is, like the United States, a land of riches, a site of advanced technology, and a place of possessing powers. Reuel is drugged and kidnapped by the rulers of Telassar. We learn later that Telassarians can magically call up scenes from across the ocean — their ambitious, scopic power, like that of the Europeans, reaches that far.

17. Hopkins, *Of One Blood*, 544. All further references to this work appear in the text.

18. For discussion of Hopkins's loss of her editorial position at *Colored American Magazine*, see Gaines, *Uplifting the Race*, 439 – 43; Greusser, "Taking Liberties," 5 – 10; Patterson, "Kin' o' Rough Jestice"; Doreski, "Inherited Rhetoric and Authentic History"; and Kassanoff, "'Fate Has Linked Us Together,'" 159 – 60, 176. Kassanoff also suggests, at the close of her essay, that Dianthe Rusk's fate allegorizes Hopkins's experience at the magazine (176).

19. In studying Hopkins's journalistic sketches of "great" men and women, Doreski similarly argues that Hopkins "mediates between the individual heroic soul and the grander racial and cultural tapestry" ("Inherited Rhetoric and Authentic History," 75). Her comparison of Hopkins's labor to that of Ralph Waldo Emerson in his sketches hints at the larger context for this "mediation" that I aim here to establish.

20. Critics have recognized Hopkins's signifying practices, often in Bakhtinian terms, as I discuss in note 2 in chapter 14 on *Contending Forces*. Closest to my emphasis here is Berg's phrase "motivated repetition" in "Reconstructing Motherhood" (5).

21. Schrager also notes this element of brotherly competition that, in the end, betrays Dianthe and operates as part of the larger racial economy. In her argument, given that the "white" brother turns out to be biracial, this element mainly contributes to the novel's destabilization of whiteness ("Pauline Hopkins and William James," 195).

22. Otten was the first critic to do full justice to this dimension of Hopkins's text and her merging of contemporary psychology with Ethiopianism, in "Pauline Hopkins and the Hidden Self of Race." Gillman, Horvitz, and Schrager build richly on this work. For full discussion of this point and a reading of *Of One Blood* as a powerful "hysteric's" text in both form and content, see Horvitz, "Hysteria and Trauma in Pauline Hopkins," especially 249 – 53. For a related, Kristevan reading, see Kassanoff, "'Fate Has Linked Us Together.'"

23. See Devlin, *Between Profits and Primitivism*. For the discussion of James, see 109 – 41.

24. Horvitz, "Hysteria and Trauma," 256.

25. Hartman, *Scenes of Subjection*, 7.

26. See Otten, "Pauline Hopkins and the Hidden Self of Race," 246, 250 – 51, for passing discussion of how Hopkins's use of generic conventions of the gothic and sentimental interact with her handling of racial materials.

27. Gillman, "Pauline Hopkins and the Occult," 65, 70. Otten also explores the interweav-

ing of Hopkins's psychological and racial thought: "the conception of identity Hopkins borrowed from James is put to the work of incorporating collective history within literary character" ("Pauline Hopkins and the Hidden Self of Race," 250). Schrager likewise brings together these two streams of thought, concluding that they converge with biological models to lead Hopkins toward an Ethiopianist racial determinism ("Pauline Hopkins and William James," 199–201).

28. Gaines has outlined the contradictions of Hopkins's vision most fully (*Uplifting the Race*, 433–55), including its Christian dimensions (444–48) and its gender assumptions (434, 450). Gillman gives a more positive account of Hopkins's imperial politics ("Pauline Hopkins and the Occult," 69–72), while Japtock ("Pauline Hopkins's *Of One Blood*," 403–13) and Bernardi ("Narratives of Domestic Imperialism," 215–18) lay more stress on her vexed investment in the empowering effects of what Gaines calls the "civilizationist" rhetoric of imperialism in this period.

29. In a brief aside, Schrager also considers this moment as an encounter with the feminine, linking it to psychoanalytical accounts of a Minoan past and a pre-oedipal stage of development ("Pauline Hopkins and William James," 198). One could profitably read these sequences in relation to Freeman's discussion of the sublime in *The Feminine Sublime*.

30. Both Horvitz ("Hysteria and Trauma," 252) and Schrager ("Pauline Hopkins and William James," 195) remark on Reuel's complicit role in Dianthe's death.

11. Freedom by Removal

1. Eliot, *Daniel Deronda*, 50. All further references to this work appear in the text.

2. Sedgwick, *Hope Leslie*, 17. All further references to this work appear in the text.

3. Hawthorne, *The Scarlet Letter*, 8, 56. All further references to this work appear in the text.

4. Hopkins, *Contending Forces*, 31.

5. In "Anachronistic Imaginings," Insko thoughtfully reads this ventriloquizing use of Patrick Henry as a part of Sedgwick's creative and anachronistic "de-formation of history" (43, 45). Within the larger Saxonist narrative, however, Sedgwick's use of Henry also reinforces a stabilizing historical framework.

6. Bergland, *National Uncanny*, 4.

7. In "Sympathy as Strategy," Nelson notes the discrepancy between this revision and Sedgwick's paean to the first Pilgrims (195–202), and Weierman, "Reading and Writing *Hope Leslie*," offers a more measured account of the revision within the limits of Sedgwick's racial vision, although neither directly addresses Sedgwick's racial and Christian framing of Magawisca's narrative. More typical of critical discourse on the novel is Garvey's "Risking Reprisal," which understands this revision as one of Sedgwick's feminist "risks." In *Covenant and Republic* (chapter 2), Gould focuses centrally on this revision and understands it as Sedgwick's intervention in contemporary politics, though without directly addressing the question of race. In her introduction to the Penguin edition, Karcher gives perhaps the most sustained attention, among feminist readings, to the racial framing. But here, too, the problem gets subordinated. On the one hand, she addresses the question of Sedgwick's racial attitudes by quoting a typical passage and following with a paragraph-long series of questions (for instance, suggesting that Sedgwick raises the question "Is Indian implacabil-

ity due to the unforgivable nature of white crimes or to the 'law of vengeance . . . written in Indian hearts'?" and wondering, "While passionately decrying the failure of Christians to be Christians, is Sedgwick also subtly reaffirming the superiority of the Christians 'rule of forgiveness' to the (alleged) Indian law of vengeance?" (xxviii). But on the other hand, the important force of her questions is weakened by the fact that she has already subordinated them in her approach to the subject. For, earlier in her introduction, she offers the general view that "[i]nstead of accentuating Indian savagery, Sedgwick's narrative works to foster recognition of the two people's common humanity — the prerequisite to preventing racial strife" (xxi). Although such comments importantly acknowledge that Sedgwick was relatively open-minded, they also take for granted the racializing of the situation, and they give Sedgwick credit for "preventing" the very racial strife that her text helps to frame as racial. In a final turn that is typical of feminist criticism on the novel, Karcher concludes, "Despite these obvious limitations, Sedgwick's America does promise far greater freedom" (xxxi). Although she adds "especially for white women," this "especially" euphemistically stands in for "only," if we take full account of the fates of Magawisca and all Pequot women.

8. See Tawil, "Domestic Frontier Romance," 100.

9. Quoted by Karcher in her introduction to *Hope Leslie,* xxxiv. All further reference to this work appear in the text.

10. For this information on Sedgwick's family and her writing about it, see Weierman, "Reading and Writing *Hope Leslie,*" and Kelley "Negotiating a Self." Weierman, in particular, has documented the extended Sedgwick family's connection with Indians, concluding that "there is indeed a direct connection between the arrival of the Sedgwicks and the departure of the Indians" (426).

11. Fetterley begins her essay "My Sister! My Sister!" (on republican sisterhood in the novel) by worrying about the way highly critical readings of the novel's race politics might "re-vanish" the novel and so undo the work of scholars who have recovered it (492). But the word "vanish" troublingly shifts to the white woman author the threat faced by Native Americans (it is the very word Sedgwick puts in Magawisca's mouth to describe the future of the Pequots [*Hope Leslie,* 292]). Overall Fetterley characterizes the novel's race representations mainly as a hitch in its otherwise feminist and egalitarian politics, and all its arguments serve this account. Thus, in identifying the Anne Hutchinson allusion, Fetterley is quick to note that "supporters of Hutchinson" refused to engage in the hostilities against the Pequots (513) without addressing why it serves Sedgwick's purposes to frame Magawisca as a dissenting white woman. As I will note later, Fetterley and I share the view that Sedgwick is rewriting the old plot of women's ruin within the liberty story and is locating a place for women in the republic — but, in my reading, she creates a place only for Anglo-Protestant women. Also see Maddox's study, *Removals,* in which she reads Magawisca's "vanishing" as a symptom of her failure to join the white women like Hope who rebel against patriarchal authority, implying that Magawisca stays loyal to the "atavistic" call of racial patriarchy while Hope (and Sedgwick) commit themselves to a liberatory, nonpatriarchal, and pluralistic future (105–8). Although Maddox's reading ends with an apparent critique of Sedgwick's racial politics, it is shot through with suggestions that Magawisca misses her chance to join "white civilization and all it has to offer," including alliance with "the white women and children who are her intellectual peers and natural allies" (106, 105). For another feminist-liberatory account, see Castiglia, who places *Hope Leslie* in the captivity-narrative

tradition as "a tale of liberation, uniquely woman-centered" and which expresses women's desire for "the freedom to enter the world" ("In Praise of Extra-vagant Women," 3). Other critics who take this approach include Bardes and Gossett, *Declarations;* Ross, "(Re)Writing"; Susan Harris, "Limits of Authority"; and Singley, "Catharine Maria Sedgwick's *Hope Leslie.*" Several critics do foreground the novel's "conflicted" racial representations. Nelson, "Sympathy as Strategy"; Karafilas, "Catharine Maria Sedgwick's *Hope Leslie*"; Ford, "Inscribing"; Matter-Seibel, "Native Americans"; and Weierman, "Reading and Writing *Hope Leslie*" offer carefully balanced readings of the race and gender politics, seeing "complicity" with the impulse of removal despite Sedgwick's dissent from the terms of the Indian Removal Act. Only a few, such as Baym (*American Women Writers and the Work of History*) and Tawil ("Domestic Frontier Romance"), however, centrally highlight how Sedgwick's subordination or erasure of Indians *serves* her liberatory frame for white women—making her text accommodationist rather than radical.

12. Higonnet stands out as an exception insofar as she argues that American women writers should be read in an international context, especially within the transnational preoccupation with questions of "political authority" ("Comparative Reading," 19). Susan Harris makes passing reference to the English Civil War as background to the novel's questions about obedience to authority (274, 276). Tawil also acknowledges the continuity between the British novel's earlier seduction plots and Anglo-American women's domestic frontier narratives, but he suggests that the U.S. American texts "gave the sentimental heroine a racial identity that, strictly speaking, she had not possessed" ("Domestic Frontier Romance," 118). I'm arguing that the racialization process had begun with the inception of the novel and included the earliest British heroines. For Americanist republican readings of *Hope Leslie,* see, for instance, Bardes and Gossett, *Declarations of Independence;* Maddox, *Removals;* Singley, "Catharine Maria Sedgwick's *Hope Leslie*"; Garvey, "Risking Reprisal"; Gould, *Covenant and Republic;* Fetterley, "My Sister!"; and Karafilas, "Catharine Maria Sedgwick's *Hope Leslie.*" Although Brown, in *The Consent of the Governed,* does not discuss *Hope Leslie,* her approach is typical in implying that American writers politicize, in the context of republicanism, the British tradition of apolitical seduction novels: "The early American novel's preoccupation with female experience recapitulates a primary interest of the British novel: the exploration of interiority through the case of a woman. American novels bring to the representation of individual experience a different context"—one focused, as she spells out, on questions of "the consent of the governed" (13). As we've seen in earlier chapters, these questions were present from the beginning in seduction novels on both sides of the Atlantic.

13. Tawil persuasively argues that Anglo-American men's and women's frontier romances "not only shared a fundamentally similar racial ideology but also worked together to produce it" ("Domestic Frontier Romance," 100). Also see Ashwell, "Savagism and its Discontents," for another reading that demystifies Sedgwick's racial politics. In contrast to critics who see her racial representations (of miscegenation, for example) as risky, Ashwell emphasizes the bolder representations of "mixed blood" relations and characters in literature by William Apes and Elias Boudinot, the latter married to Sedgwick's cousin Harriet Gold. Of course some Indian Americans, including "mixed" persons such as William Apess, were themselves appropriating this rhetoric in arguing for Indian sovereignty, as when Apess argues that the Mashpees had over generations formed a government "suited to the spirit and

capacity of freeborn sons of the forest" (quoted in Bergland, *Uncanny*, 113). This adoption of a racialized liberty rhetoric among some Indian Americans testifies once more to its unavoidable ubiquity for those who attempted to "enter" the nation and the battle for rights.

14. Fetterley likewise notes that Sedgwick aims to rewrite this plot of ruin, although as I discuss in note 11, she sees Magawisca simply as one of the "sisters" forwarding this revision, rather than (as I would see it) one of the useful but discarded tools of it.

15. Fetterley, "My Sister," 496–97.

16. Castiglia, "In Praise of Extra-vagant Women," 12.

17. See my discussion and notes on the sublime in chapter 3.

12. "A" for Atlantic

1. Hawthorne, *The Scarlet Letter,* 44. All further references to this work appear in the text.

2. Fiedler, *Love and Death,* 131.

3. Hawthorne was an avid reader of the gothic early in his career and of course this novel may also be described as gothic in its dark tone and tropes of imprisonment and possession. See Lundblad, *Nathaniel Hawthorne and the Tradition of Gothic Romance,* who argues that "Gothic romance formed an important substratum of Hawthorne's productions" (95). Also see Fiedler, *Love and Death,* for discussion of Hawthorne's attachment to the gothic (and especially the links of this novel to Lewis's *The Monk*). In my view, Hawthorne carefully contains the gothic here via his narrative mode: that is, I believe that the careful historicism and the frame of the novel—both its Custom-House Introductory and its intrusive narrative voice—create a retrospective distance from his material that places the text within the epic mode of the nineteenth-century novel. Yet clearly Hawthorne's internalization of gothic tropes is part of his process of working through the events of Atlantic history. For another suggestive angle on the racialized materials that Hawthorne folds into his fiction, see Luedtke, *Nathaniel Hawthorne and the Romance of the Orient* and Irwin, *American Hieroglyphics.* In my argument here, I will mainly emphasize Hawthorne's "gothic" subsumption of the haunting Indian American presence in his fictional and real worlds.

4. Quoted in Scharnhorst, *The Critical Response to Nathaniel Hawthorne's "The Scarlet Letter,"* 79.

5. Other critics who made similar suggestions include Schneider, *The Puritan Mind* (1930), Winters, *Maule's Curse* (1938), and of course, Mathiessen, *American Renaissance* (1941). For Howells, see Scharnhorst, *The Critical Response,* 102; for Van Doren, see Scharnhorst, 140; for Hanscom, see Scharnhorst, 146. Munger interestingly dissents to some degree and in the process spells out the underlying tension between race and individualism: he agrees that Hawthorne is an "unweaned child of his native land" and yet, he adds, "there is more in him that offsets Puritanism than identifies with it. In fact, it outdid itself, as has continually happened, and created in Hawthorne an individualism that separated him from itself. A system whose central principle is individualism cannot count upon holding together its own adherents. It is by its own nature centrifugal, though none the worse for that; it makes a man the denizen of the heavens rather than of his mundane sphere. But the way is long, and at great cost is it trod" (quoted in Scharnhorst, 127–28).

6. Quoted in Lundblad, *Nathaniel Hawthorne and the Tradition of Gothic Romance,* 10.

7. See Bercovitch, *The Office of the Scarlet Letter.* Most readings of Hawthorne acknowledge the ambiguity of voice and position in his work, but for critics who align him most fully with a traditionalist orientation, see, for instance, Leverenz, "Mrs. Hawthorne's Headache"; Jehlen, "The Novel and the Middle Class in America"; Fleischner, "Hawthorne and the Politics of Slavery"; Reynolds, *European Revolutions,* 79–96; Madsen, "'A' for Abolition"; Brown, "Hawthorne, Inheritance, and Women's Property"; Gussman, "Inalienable Rights"; Maddox, *Removals;* Korobkin, "The Scarlet Letter of the Law"; and Bergland, *The National Uncanny.* Also noteworthy is Barlowe's study of the ways that some Hawthorne critics have perpetuated this conservatism by failing to cite the work of female Hawthorne scholars. See *The Scarlet Mob of Scribblers.* All further references to these works appear in the text.

8. For critics who acknowledge Hawthorne's conservative gestures of containment but nonetheless consider his shifting narrative voice and/or his romance form an expression of his investment (even if partly unconscious) in subversion, see, for instance, Carton, *The Rhetoric of American Romance;* Hutner, *Secrets and Sympathy;* Bell, *Hawthorne and the Historical Romance;* Millington, *Practicing Romance;* R. S. Levine, *Conspiracy and Romance;* Budick, *Engendering Romance;* Cagidemetrio, *Fictions of the Past;* Thomas, "Citizen Hester"; Bellis, *Writing Revolution;* and Berlant, *The Anatomy of National Fantasy*—although Berlant perhaps gives equal emphasis to Hawthorne's double impulses to subvert and conserve. All further references to these works appear in the text.

9. See Colacurcio, *Doctrine and Difference,* 180–225; Korobkin, "The Scarlet Letter of the Law"; and Lang, *Prophetic Woman.* All further references to these works appear in the text.

10. Woodson, "Hawthorne, Upham, and *The Scarlet Letter,*" 186–87. All further references to this work appear in the text.

11. Quoted in Bergland, *The National Uncanny,* 157.

12. See Jehlen's *American Incarnation,* for a full contextualization of the work of surveying and its shaping presence as a trope in American literature.

13. "Mrs. Hutchinson," in *Centenary Edition of the Works of Nathaniel Hawthorne,* 68–69. All further references to this work appear in the text.

14. Bell was among the first to stress this point, in *Hawthorne and the Historical Romance of New England,* 173–80. Fryer, Davis, Lang, and Cocalis all stress the ambivalence expressed in Hawthorne's affiliation of Hester with Hutchinson, while Colacurcio underplays Hawthorne's critique of Hutchinson and women writers and mainly sees the connection as an expression of Hawthorne's endorsement of both. See Fryer, *Faces of Eve,* 72–76; Davis, "Another View of Hester and the Antinomians" 189–98; Lang, *Prophetic Woman,* 1–13, 188–89; Cocalis, "The 'Dark and Abiding Presence,'" 254–55; and Colacurcio, *Doctrine and Difference,* 177–204.

15. Quoted in Stewart, *Nathaniel Hawthorne,* 95.

16. Newberry's *Hawthorne's Divided Loyalties* is perhaps the only study that stresses Hawthorne's imaginative attachment to and evocations of Old World England. He notes that "Hawthorne regularly surrounds Hester, Pearl, and Dimmesdale with Old World motifs . . . to emphasize positive historical and cultural continuities" (173). His material reinforces my emphasis on the transatlantic codes of the novel, although Newberry's sense of the import of these connections is quite different from mine.

17. Johnson, "Impotence and Omnipotence," 549–612. All further references to this work appear in the text.

18. Quoted in Bloom, *Hester Prynne*, 69.

19. Several scholars have discussed the novel's links to slavery and slave narratives. For discussions focused on historical material and Hawthorne's attitude toward slavery, see Fleischner, "Hawthorne and the Politics of Slavery"; Korobkin, "The Scarlet Letter of the Law"; Madsen, "'A for Abolition.'" For discussions linking Hawthorne's text to slave narratives, see Dukats, "The Hybrid Terrain of Literary Imagination"; and Cocalis, "The 'Dark and Abiding Presence.'"

20. For the former view, see, for instance, Gussman, "Inalienable Rights," and Bergland, *The National Uncanny*.

21. The association of a haunted artistry with Indians also finds expression, Bergland notes, in Hawthorne's persistent imagery of burning-red jewels such as the carbuncle, an imagery borrowed from an Abenaki storytelling tradition. Bergland establishes that Hawthorne's "mysterious women" are most strongly associated with "rich red ornaments," including Hester's embroidered scarlet letter (154). Bergland's material further clarifies how, through women, Hawthorne achieves a "sublime turn" toward "romance" in his transmutation of awe and repulsion toward Indians into aesthetic mastery.

22. For readings of homoeroticism in the novel, see Derrick, "A Curious Subject of Observation and Inquiry"; and Kilcup, "'Ourself behind Ourself, Concealed.'"

23. For discussions of the cultural meanings of "black letter" print, see Mish, "Black Letter," and Newton, *Deutsche Schrift*." Mish tracks the seventeenth-century shifts in the use of black-letter print, while Newton reviews these and, in addition, traces its rising and falling fortunes up to its revival in early-twentieth-century Germany, under the sway of "volk" ideology (although, interestingly, Hitler happened to dislike black letter and so resisted the proposed change to blackletter for official documents).

24. Tate has suggestively compared Frado in Harriet Wilson's *Our Nig* to Pearl (*Domestic Allegories*, 45). Especially when we recall that New Englanders Wilson and Hawthorne were contemporaries and consider that Wilson might well have read Hawthorne's much-discussed novel, it is interesting to view Wilson's novel as a rethinking of Hawthorne's. For she too tells the story of a woman's fall that yields a wild child while also making the mother an outcast.

25. A number of critics have considered the crisis in vocation for "middle-class" men in the nineteenth-century United States. For discussions of male authorship in particular, see Brodhead, *The School of Hawthorne*, and Newbury, *Figuring Authorship in Antebellum America*. For consideration of Hawthorne's own crisis of vocation and his formulation of the terms of authorship, see, for a psychological reading, Crews, *The Sins of Fathers*; for a class reading, Gilmore, "Hawthorne and the Making of the Middle Class"; and, for gendered readings, Johnson, "Impotence and Omnipotence," and Egan, "The Adultress in the Market-Place."

13. Freedom's Eastward Turn

1. Eliot, *The Mill on the Floss*, 53. All further references to this work appear in the text.

2. The entanglement of race and gender/sexuality in *Daniel Deronda* has long been a theme in interpretations of the novel. Critics grapple with the discrepancy between the Princess's (Daniel's mother's) exposure of the imprisonment of women by race ideologies

and the novel's apparent replication and approval of that imprisonment in the stories of Gwendolen and Mirah. For studies directly focused on these questions, and in particular on the way that Eliot's constructions of Jewishness and Englishness intersect with her handling of gender identities, see David, *Fictions of Resolution;* Gallagher, "George Eliot and *Daniel Deronda*"; Crosby, *Ends of History;* Chase, "The Decomposition of Elephants"; Meyer, "'Safely to Their Own Borders'"; Carroll, *Dark Smiles;* Levine, *Merchant of Modernism;* Cheyette, "White Skin, Black Masks"; Heller, "Jews and Women in George Eliot's *Daniel Deronda*"; Hirsch, "Women and Jews in *Daniel Deronda*"; Andres, "Fortune's Wheel in *Daniel Deronda*"; Ward, "Zion's Mimetic Angel"; Lovesey, "The Other Woman in *Daniel Deronda*"; Gates, "'A Difference of Native Language'"; and Press, "Same-Sex Union." Other relevant studies that explore the troubled interlocking of race and gender in Eliot's writing include McKay, "Race and Myth"; Nord, "'Marks of Race'"; and Haynie, "The Illegitimacy of the Colonial Entrepreneur." Without mentioning race at all, John Goode, "'The Affections Clad with Knowledge,'" fruitfully tracks the difficulty Eliot seems to encounter whenever her heroines venture into the public realm; the implications of his account are amplified when we recall the degree to which the public sphere was racially conceived. Also see Henry, *George Eliot and the British Empire,* for information about Eliot's direct involvement in empire, including through investment in colonial stocks and Lewes's sons in Africa.

3. For related suggestions about Eliot's use of epic scale in her fiction, see Gates, "'A Difference of Native Language,'" who specifically understands the epic as a form that might contain gender contradictions (703), and Knoepflmacher who argues that "the residue of [Eliot's] Puritan idealism prompted her to infuse historical actuality with a teleology of epic proportions," in *George Eliot's Early Novels* (21). Of course, in connection with the influence of biblical and Protestant narrative patterns on Eliot's vision, Carpenter's study is indispensable (*George Eliot and the Landscape of Time*). For a rich discussion of Eliot's mixing of genre, specifically realism and romance, in relation to the novel's Jewish plot, see Levine, *Merchant,* 37–52.

4. Eliot, *Daniel Deronda,* 211. All further references to this work appear in the text. Useful in this connection are two older studies of Eliot that read her in relation to the novel tradition: Doody, "George Eliot and the Eighteenth-Century Novel," considers Eliot's debt to eighteenth-century women novelists, and Wilt, in "Steamboat Surfacing," places Eliot among those novelists implicitly constructing British identity by way of references to Walter Scott. Neither study speaks of race directly but each in different ways further establishes the embeddedness of Eliot's fiction in the long Atlantic story.

5. See Press, "Same-Sex Union," for a full consideration of the question of Daniel's circumcision (first raised by Chase in "Decomposition") and for a queer and compelling reading of the relation between Daniel and Mordecai.

6. Many critics have commented on this "native spot" passage. For readings that similarly understand it within Eliot's organic national and racial vision, see Semmel, *George Eliot and the Politics of National Inheritance,* and Cohen, "From Home to Homeland." From another angle, Sudrann understands Eliot's invocation of the native spot that her characters lack as of a piece with her retelling of ancient stories of exile ("*Daniel Deronda* and the Landscape of Exile").

7. Quoted in Bamlett, "The Scene of a Great Future," 63, 64. All further references to this work appear in the text.

8. For discussion of this image, see David, *Rule Britannia,* 6.

9. See Meyer, "'Safely to Their Own Borders,'" 748.

10. For discussion of this historical background, see Meyer, "'Safely to Their Own Borders'"; Levine, *Merchant of Modernism;* and Cheyette, "White Skin, Black Masks," as well as Brandabur, "George Eliot's *Daniel Deronda* and the Making of Modern Israel," and Wohlfarth, "*Daniel Deronda* and the Politics of Nationalism." My account here is indebted to these scholars. Also useful are Baker, *George Eliot and Judaism,* and Rose, *From Palmerston to Balfour.* Meanwhile, of course, the question of how to read Eliot's representation of Jewishness in the novel has long been a point of critical debate. Since the novel's publication, many readers, perhaps most famously F. R. Leavis, have objected to the "takeover" of the novel by its "Jewish part." For full discussion of this legacy of response, see Johnson, "F.R. Leavis." For other discussions of Eliot's treatment of Judaism (and in some cases Palestine) in the novel, in addition to Meyer, Brandabur, Levine, Cheyette, and Wohlfarth, see the following (listed in chronological order of publication): Said, *The Question of Palestine,* 92; David, *Fictions of Resolution,* 147–81; Christiansen, "The Identity of Klesmer"; Crosby, *Ends of History,* 12–43; Nubhai, "Metafiction and Metaphor"; Baumgarten, "Seeing Double"; Lesjak, "Labours"; A. Anderson, *Powers of Distance;* Levine, *Merchant of Modernism,* 37–52. All further references to these works appear in the text.

11. See Eliot, "Prospectus," 5.

12. "The Modern Hep! Hep! Hep!" is the last chapter of *Impressions of Theophrastus Such* (this citation, 150). All further references to this work appear in the text.

13. See Crosby, *Ends of History,* 27–42.

14. See Meyer's discussion, "'Safely to Their Own Borders,'" 751.

15. The fullest discussions of Eliot's investment in an organic and racial version of nationalism are in Semmel and Wohlfarth (both cited above) and McCaw, *George Eliot and Victorian Historiography.* Also see Lesjak, "Labours"; Brantlinger, *Fictions of State,* 178–82; Rosenberg "George Eliot"; Arkush, "Relativizing Nationalism"; Malcolm, "'Grand and Vague'"; and A. Thompson, "Giuseppe Mazzini."

16. Meyer likewise takes note of the way this image expresses the position of women within Eliot's vision of empire ("'Safely to Their Own Borders,'" 755–56).

17. First Theophrastus must set aside the "Red Indians" that prompted the rough work of colonization. Setting up his analogy for the Indians, Theophrastus begins (like Hawthorne) by seeming to deflate English pride and expose English acts of violence, when he reminds his readers that "[t]he men who planted our nation were not Christians" but rather "worshipped Odin, massacred Britons, and were with difficulty persuaded to accept Christianity" (145–46). Moving directly from this past to American invasion, he goes on to point out that "Red Indians, not liking us when we settled among them, might have been willing to fling such facts in our face" (146). As perhaps Palestinians might, in 1875. Theophrastus seems here to enter the point of view of the colonized and put the English "invasions" on trial, but as it turns out he does so only to run roughshod over such twists, for the Red Indians "were too ignorant, and besides, their opinions did not signify, because we were able, if we liked, to exterminate them" (146). In a wonderful instance of the paradigmatic gesture we also saw operating in Hawthorne, Eliot uses irony to gloss an act of violence as an exposé of violence.

18. Also see Cheyette's different but related discussion of Eliot's identification between Jews and blacks, which he reads next to Fanon's discussion of these two communities

("White Face," especially 110–13). Watson also points in this direction in "Jamaica, Genealogy, and George Eliot."

19. Meyer's important early essay on these issues has been relegated to a footnote and too quickly dismissed, in my view, by such critics as Amanda Anderson ("George Eliot and the Jewish Question," 120) and Carolyn Lesjak ("Labours of a Modern Storyteller," 41). Meyer carefully considers and substantiates the gender, nationalist, and imperialist strains of Eliot's vision. Yet I do see less of anti-Semitism ("a certain distaste for the Jews" ([750]) in Eliot's vision; I believe her treatment of Jews mostly reflects her deep investment in an ostensibly liberatory racialism. Her portrait of the Cohen family arises as much from her class biases as from racial ones, although of course the two are hard to separate.

20. See Anderson, "George Eliot and the Jewish Question," 123–32, and Arkush, "Relativizing Nationalism," for discussions of how Deronda's vision differs in important degrees from Mordecai's.

21. David long ago noticed the imperial vocabulary in Eliot's portrait of this couple (*Fictions of Resolution*, 177–81). Several critics have remarked on it since, including Meyer (735–36), Linehan, "Mixed Politics," and Andres, "Fortune's Wheel."

22. For complementary discussions of *Daniel Deronda* as a novel about property, freedom, and inheritance, see Nunokowa, *Secret Life of Property*, 77–99; Gallagher, "George Eliot and *Daniel Deronda*," 46–50; Tucker, *A Probable State*, 33–79; and Wohlfarth, "*Daniel Deronda* and the Politics of Nationalism," 198–99.

23. For further details, see Thompson, "Giuseppe Mazzini and George Eliot's *Daniel Deronda*," 103.

24. While Wohlfarth (like Schaffer, whom he quotes) here considers Eliot to be expressing a grand vision that unites West and East against despotism, which Jews would mediate ("*Daniel Deronda* and the Politics of Nationalism," 207), clearly such "uniting" would be done on the West's "free" terms and in support of its trade ambitions.

25. See MacCannell, *Regime of the Brother*, and Press, "Same-Sex Unions." Also see my discussion of MacCannell's term in the introduction.

26. For a reading of "sovereignty" within modern English law and its double-crossing of women's rights, as well as a brief but suggestive treatment of the expression of these problems in Victorian fiction, see Petch, "The Sovereign Self," 410–15.

27. For a different, Freudian reading of this scene see David, *Fictions of Resolution* (201–2). Like most critics, David still places Gwendolen in the position of immature child. For a different orientation toward Gwendolen, closer in spirit to mine here, see Tromp, *The Private Rod*, chapter 5, and especially 229–39. Tromp is one of the few critics, perhaps the only one, to take seriously the "dread" Gwendolen feels toward men. Of course Eliot discourages our sympathy with Gwendolen and the narrator links her skittishness more often to her spoiled position within empire than anything else. Tromp nonetheless sees Eliot as giving a searing portrait of abuse within marriage. I am stressing the few hints in the text that this dread has its roots in a sexually abusive father-daughter relationship.

14. Trickster Epic

1. Hopkins, *Contending Forces*, 101. All further references to this work appear in the text.
2. On *Contending Forces*, specifically, see Cassidy and his remarks on Hopkins's "dou-

bly masked double-voicedness" in relation to racial discourses ("Contending Contexts," 663–64); Rohrbach, who speaks suggestively in terms of Hopkins's "literary sampling" ("To Be Continued," 484) and so positions Hopkins's practices as precursor to the practices of contemporary music; and Berg, who applies Henry Louis Gates's notion of racial signifying as "motivated repetition" to Hopkins ("Reconstructing Motherhood," 134–38). Also, on *Of One Blood*, see Gillman ("Pauline Hopkins and the Occult," 60–64), Kassanoff ("Fate Has Linked Us," 174–76), and Horvitz ("Hysteria and Trauma," 256–57); on *Winona*, see Beam ("The Flower of Black Female Sexuality," 71–74) and Ammons ("Afterword," 211–19); and on *Hagar's Daughter*, see Bost ("Fluidity without Postmodernism," 678). On the dialogical nature of Hopkins's fiction in its representation of dialect and class, see Brooks ("Mammies, Bucks, and Wenches," *Unruly*, 119–157). Also see note 15 in chapter 10 for critics who discuss the related issue of Hopkins's polyvocal or contradictory handling of race.

3. See for instance, Richetti's comments in "Histories by Eliza Haywood and Henry Fielding": "Haywood's interesting ambiguity and exposure of ideological contradiction are the result of a lack of full narrative control, of her failure to sustain, with any coherence, her imitation of Fielding's historical approach" (255). See chapter 3 of the present volume for a summary of White's argument.

4. See Harris, "Not Black and/or White," 375–90. Also see my discussion in chapter 4 of the influence of classical plots on early novels.

5. For analysis of these vying racial genealogies played out between Northern and Southern whites, see Hanlon, "The Old Race are Old Gone." Relatedly, for two rich discussions of Hopkins's awareness of and intervention in regionalized identities of race, see Knadler, *Fugitive Race*, 62–70, and Sawaya, "Emplotting National History," 73–87.

6. See Carby's reading of the whipping scene as a figurative rape (*Reconstructing Womanhood*, 132). Also see Marcus for an extended reading of it as Hopkins's rewriting of U.S. history and genealogy ("'Of One Blood,'" 119–24). For other analyses of Hopkins's central concern with the legacy of rape, see Gunning (*Race, Rape, and Lynching*, 96–107), Horvitz ("Hysteria and Trauma"), Putzi, "Raising the Stigma," and McCullough, "Slavery, Sexuality, and Genre."

7. Bernardi, "Narratives of Domestic Imperialism," 204. Bernardi usefully considers this trope as doubly signifying African Americans' historical experience of violation and their developing investment in a U.S. imperial imaginary.

8. For rich treatment of the intertwined dynamics of class, masculinity, and race in this novel, see McCoy, "Rumors of Grace." Also see McCann, "Bonds of Brotherhood," for exploration of class in relation to gender (801–11). For related discussions of masculinity and/or class in Hopkins, see Nerad, "'So Strangely Interwoven'"; O'Brien, "Race-ing toward Civilization" (especially 124–28); Brown, "'To Allow No Tragic End'" (50–70); Knadler, *Fugitive Race*, 59–84; and, more tangentially, Beam, "The Flower of Black Female Sexuality," 89, and Rohrbach, "To Be Continued," 487.

9. See Carby, *Reconstructing Womanhood*, 128–44, and Tate, *Domestic Allegories of Political Desire*, 161–65.

10. For discussion of Hopkins's journalism and other activities, see especially Greusser, "Taking Liberties," 98–118; Gaines, "Black Americans' Racial Uplift Ideology"; Gillman, "Pauline Hopkins and the Occult"; and Doreski, "Inherited Rhetoric and Authentic History."

11. For a related reading of Sappho's swoon as an adaptation of the tradition of melo-drama, see McCann, "'Bonds of Brotherhood,'" in which he suggests that in this moment Sappho's body "is repossessed by the past" and becomes "a vessel of history" (791), through which the community negotiates its balancing of class positions and of the competing needs of individuals and the race.

12. The narrator suggests that Madame Frances's powers may derive from ancient African ancestors (placing her as the heir "of the occult arts which were once the glory of the freshly imported African"), but she also frames this suggestion as what others "supposed" and she glosses the inserted poem about an African "princess" with a face like a sphinx as a "quaint conceit" (199, 201).

13. See Doyle, "The Folk, the Nobles, and the Novel," and Somerville, *Queering the Color Line*, 77–100. Also see Randle, "Mates, Marriage, and Motherhood." For a compelling read-ing of Hopkins's treatment of women's sexuality in *Winona*, see Beam, "The Flower of Black Female Sexuality."

14. For arguments that Sapphism shapes the content and form of white women's mod-ernist texts, see Laity, "Decadence and Sapphic Modernism," and Benstock, "Expatriate Sapphic Modernism."

15. See Sawaya, "Emplotting National History," for informative discussion of Hopkins's use and revision of the notion of New England's tradition of freedom. She does not, how-ever, connect this rhetoric to the text's homoerotic liberties.

16. See McCoy ("Rumors of Grace") on her depictions of class-inflected white masculin-ity; Brown on Will Smith as an unconventional figure of black masculinity ("'To Allow No Tragic End,'" 64–69); and see Ammons ("Afterword," 217–18) and Somerville (*Queering the Color Line*, 100–107) on cross-dressing in *Winona*. Somerville also gathers suggestive material about the contemporary resurgence of interest in the Greek poet Sappho, including suggestions of an African lineage for her (85–87).

15. Queering Freedom's Theft

1. The most extensive recent studies of gay or lesbian sexuality in English-language modernism include Boone, *Libidinal Currents*, Hackett, *Sapphic Primitivism*, and Meese, *(Sem)erotics*.

2. *Three Lives*, quoted as follows: 177, 180, 172, 208.

3. See Friedman's essay, "Paranoia, Pollution, and Sexuality."

4. In deconstructing the way criticism reinstalls race, Hutchinson notes that we could also call Larsen a "Scandinavian modernist" ("Subject to Disappearance," 185).

5. A number of critics have commented on the name Naxos, as an anagram for Saxon and as a hint of sexual struggle, but Hutchinson has provided the fullest reading of the latter through close consideration of the original Ariadne story, which involves both "miscege-nation" and the abandonment of a woman. See Hutchinson, "Subject to Disappearance," 179–80; Hostetler, "The Aesthetics of Race and Gender in Nella Larsen's *Quicksand*," 38; and Gray, "Essence and the Mulatto Traveler," 265.

6. Larsen, "*Quicksand*" and "*Passing*," 5. All further references to this work appear in the text.

7. For discussion of color and dress in the novel, see Barnett, "'My Picture of You is, after

All, the True Helga Crane,'" 575; DuCille, *The Coupling Convention,* 94; Gray, "Essence and the Mulatto Traveler," 263; Rhodes, "Writing Up the New Negro," 191; and Roberts, "The Clothes Make the Woman." None of these critics notes the contradiction in Helga's desire for color as it is both individualist and racial.

8. Carby (*Reconstructing Womanhood,* 168–75) and Rhodes offer readings that complement mine here, Carby suggesting that the novel captures "the full complexity of the modern alienated individual . . . embedded within capitalist social relations" (170), and Rhodes reading it as "a critique of the capitalist division of labor that necessitated the invention of racial difference" ("Writing Up the Negro," 184). In "Nella Larsen's *Moving Mosiac*" Esteve develops a different and valuable reading of Larsen's interest in modernity, reflected in Larsen's representations of crowds and anonymity.

9. For the most relevant discussions of Larsen's novel as a racialized revision of the classic sexual plot, see Barbeito ("Making Generations"), Kaplan ("Undesirable Desire"), and Sisney ("The View from the Outside"). Kaplan, in particular, understands this revision as an engagement with citizenship questions. She implicitly signals the relationship to liberty and gives a parallel interpretation of Helga's conflicts when she mentions that Helga seeks "freedom from identity" as well as recognition of her "complex identities" (165). In "Phantasmatic Brazil," Nunes likewise reads the novel as concerned with citizenship, as coded in its references to Brazil. I aim to highlight the longer, transatlantic history of these concerns.

10. Clemmen, "Nella Larsen's *Quicksand,*" and Gray, "Essence and the Mulatto Traveler," also study the vacillating movement of the novel. Gray especially emphasizes the European dimension of this movement and suggestively argues that "racial indeterminacy and indeterminacy of geographical 'place' become one question" (259).

11. See Moten, *In the Break,* for a powerful set of meditations on this aesthetic and ontology of "the break."

12. Ellison, *Invisible Man,* 8.

13. Doyle, *Bordering on the Body,* 9.

14. See Robinson, "The Other Invisibility in Ellison's *Invisible Man,*" and Ferguson, *Aberrations in Black.*

15. Dittmar, in "When Privilege Is No Protection," likewise notes that Larsen expressed ambivalence about blackness in this scene, wishing both "to affirm and castigate" it (147). But most discussions of this scene attribute ambivalence to Helga, not to Larsen: see Esteve, "Mosaic," 278; Monda, "Self-Delusion and Self-Sacrifice in Nella Larsen's *Quicksand,*" 27–28; Rhodes, "Writing Up," 192; Silverman, "Nella Larsen's *Quicksand,*" 610; Wall, *Women of the Harlem Renaissance,* 100.

16. For discussions of Stein's racism, especially in *Three Lives,* see Saldivar-Hull, "Wrestling Your Ally"; Cohen, "Black Brutes"; Silverman, "Nella Larsen's *Quicksand,*" Peterson, "The Remaking of Americans"; and Doyle, "The Flat, the Round, and Gertrude Stein."

17. See Smith, *Lesbian Panic,* for analysis of recurring scenes of sexual panic in twentieth-century British fiction.

18. See Esteve's discussion of this phenomenon, "Nella Larson's *Moving Mosaic,*" 279–80.

19. Johnson reads this scene as Helga's "Kohutian" loss of self ("The Quicksands of the Self," 258), but Larsen here pointedly baffles any clear conclusions.

20. Critics seem to conflate Helga Crane with Irene Redfield, assuming that she makes the same sublimating trade-off between sex and security that Irene does. She doesn't

though — from the moment she flees Naxos, she refuses this trade. For readings that assume Helga is grappling with psychological "acceptance of her sexual self" (Carby 169), see Carby, *Reconstucting;* Monda, "Self-Delusion," 23; Rhodes, "Writing Up the Negro," 190; Silverman, "Nella Larsen's *Quicksand,* 612; and McDowell, "That Nameless . . . Shameful Impulse," 141.

21. For a neat reading of this allusion, see Hutchinson ("Subject to Disappearance," 190).

22. See Carr for a critique of the way critics have essentialized Irene's gay desires using a depth/surface model in which they see Irene as "repressing" her true, homoerotic desire for Clare. Carr argues that such readings fail to queer the text because they keep the essentializing categories of gay and straight intact. I would agree that Larsen implicitly insists on the unknowability of interiority or desire and I would emphasize that she does so in resistance to the Atlantic legacy of subjectivization in which interiority carries the "true content" of race and sexuality. I do not, however, assume that the notion of self as having interiority or depth is, in itself, naive or untenable. First of all, Larsen herself follows a depth model insofar as she renders moments when her narrator makes us privy to feelings that her characters deny. Second, many modern Atlantic subjects also experience themselves within this depth model, exactly because the legacy of Atlantic modernity has had lasting material and psychological effects. See Carr "Paranoid Interpretation, Desire's Nonobject, and Nella Larsen's *Passing,*" 282 – 95. On Brian Redfield as queer, also see Blackmore, "'That Unreasonable Restless Feeling,'" and Basu, "Hybrid Embodiment and an Ethics of Masochism." Butler gives some attention to Brian's channeling role in Irene's desire for Clare. See her chapter on Larsen, "Passing, Queering," in *Bodies That Matter,* 167 – 186, and especially 176, 179.

23. For a related reading of style in Larsen's novels (as practicing a "holding back"), see Dittmar, "When Privilege Is No Protection," 145. Also see Butler, *Bodies That Matter,* 174, for brief attention to Larsen's portrait of Irene within a pattern of "withholding."

24. Williams, "Nella Larsen," 165 – 66.

25. Hostetler, "The Aesthetics of Race and Gender," 36.

26. For accounts of Larsen's life and discussion of Larsen's different accounts of her past, see Davis, *Nella Larsen, Novelist of the Harlem Renaissance,* and, more recently, Hutchinson, *In Search of Nella Larsen.* Also see Hutchison, "Subject to Disappearance," 185, for his comments on this point. See Haviland, "Passing from Paranoia to Plagiarism," for further discussion of Larsen's family relations.

27. Johnson, "The Quicksands of the Self," and Haviland, "Passing from Paranoia to Plagiarism," also analyze "Sanctuary" as plagiarism, combining psychoanalytic approaches with an analysis of Larsen's relationship to the social and racially inflected category of "authorship." Their account of the historical context of Larsen's story does not extend beyond the general categories of race and gender.

28. Haviland reads this revision psychoanalytically, as expressing Larsen's anger at the effects of her mixed-race parentage, although since she frames this rage as directed primarily at Larsen's *white* mother for abandonment, her account requires some unpersuasive contortions ("Passing from Paranoia to Plagiarism," 304).

29. For a compelling reading of suicide in Larsen and in others, see Ryan, "The Intentional Turn."

30. For this reading of windows in Faulkner's *Light in August,* see Doyle, "The Body against Itself," 354.

16. Woolf's Queer Atlantic Oeuvre

1. See Allan, "The Death of Sex and the Soul in *Mrs. Dalloway* and Nella Larsen's *Passing*," for another comparison of Larsen and Woolf. Allan mostly stresses their common interest in the story of suppressed lesbianism and the homophobic surround that shaped both of these novels.

2. Woolf, *Mrs. Dalloway*, 93. All further references to this work appear in the text.

3. For pertinent discussion of Woolf's representations of laboring women, see Emery, "Robbed of Meaning," 217–34; Levy, "'These Ghost Figures of Distorted Passion'"; Rosenfeld, "Links into Fences"; and Dobie, "This Is the Room that Class Built." For a broad and useful study of the pivotal role of servant figures in British fiction, see Robbins, *The Servant's Hand*.

4. Woolf, *The Voyage Out*, 27. All further references to this work appear in the text.

5. My understanding of this double impulse in Woolf is most in accord with that of Hackett, *Sapphic Primitivism*, in her reading of the links between imperialism and lesbianism in *The Waves*. Hackett sees imperialist imagery as "one aspect of the structure of Woolf's own imagination" (61).

6. See DeSalvo, *Virginia Woolf*, for full consideration of the effects of sexual abuse on Woolf's life and fiction. For more literary discussion of this dimension of Woolf's imagination and in particular as it pervades this novel (though not in relation to colonialist imagery), see Shelton, "'Don't Say Such Foolish Things, Dear,'" 224–48; Swanson, "'My Boldness Terrifies Me'"; and Rado, *The Modern Androgyne Imagination*, 150–52.

7. For other readings of Woolf's treatment of colonial discourse in this novel, see Phillips, *Virginia Woolf against Empire*; Wollaeger, "Woolf, Postcards and the Elision of Race"; and Montgomery, "Colonial Rhetoric and the Maternal Voice."

8. For a related discussion, see Bradshaw, "Vicious Circles," which traces Woolf's implicit critique in this novel of metaphysical theories of the state, especially those of Bernard Bosanquet.

9. See *Bordering on the Body* for my earlier consideration of this scene. For fuller discussion than mine, either here or in *Bordering on the Body*, of the homoerotic current in Helen's relation to women and to Rachel in particular, see Smith, *Lesbian Panic*, 18–34.

10. Woolf, *Melymbrosia*, 210.

11. Haller traces the allusions to *Comus* in "The Anti-Madonna in the Work and Thought of Virginia Woolf."

12. Quoted in Barber, "Lip-Reading," 403.

13. See Hackett, *Sapphic Primitivism*, 60–83. Jane Marcus, of course, led the way for lesbian readings of Woolf's oeuvre, beginning with *Virginia Woolf and the Languages of Patriarchy*, and critics too numerous to list have since uncovered an impressive array of textual patterns and allusions, as well as contextual materials, that establish just how queer Woolf's fiction is. The essays and bibliography in Barrett and Cramer's collection *Virginia Woolf* provide an excellent representation of past and current work on Woolf and queer or lesbian sexuality. Much of the biographical work on Woolf and, relatedly, studies of her roman à clef *Orlando* also focus on this dimension of her creativity. See the bibliographies in the *Modern Fiction Studies* special issues on Woolf: 38.1 (Spring 1992) and 50.1 (Spring 2004). For an emphasis similar to mine on the sensual intersubjectivity that Woolf characterizes as a

part of queer feeling, see Barber, "Lip-Reading." In Barber's words, Woolf "finds or cathects in gay characters a mode of joyful experimentation with being" (405).

14. Woolf, *Jacob's Room*, 82. All further references to this work appear in the text.

15. Barry, "Clarissa Dalloway."

16. See Smith, *Lesbian Panic* (41–64, 66–67), and Barrett, "Unmasking Lesbian Passion," for two of the richest, most sustained readings of lesbian desire in the novel.

17. See Hackett, *Sapphic Primitivism,* for a careful unearthing of the colonial African rhetoric circulating in Woolf's drafts and revisions of *The Waves* (60–83).

18. In "Entering a Lesbian Field of Vision," Weil makes a related point, although her emphasis is less on art than on social vision, when she suggests that in *To the Lighthouse* the reader enters "a lesbian field of vision" (241) and by the end "begins to see like a lesbian" (257). See Barber, "Lip-Reading," and also Cramer, "Pearls and the Porpoise," for parallel discussions of Eleanor and Nicholas as queers in *The Years,* who, they suggest, preside over the novel as a whole. Cramer sees *The Years* as an elegy for "what possibilities [of queer sexuality] remain unfulfilled" (224). Barber's reading also implicitly traces the language of freedom running through Eleanor's speech, although he sees no special significance in it except as part of a desire for sexual liberation.

19. Seshagiri, "Orienting Virginia Woolf," 58–84.

20. Woolf, *To the Lighthouse,* 164. All further references to this work appear in the text.

21. See Laurence's discussion of this Orientalization of Lily's vision in *Lily Briscoe's Chinese Eyes.*

22. On Stein, see Alfey, "Oriental Penetration," 405–16.

23. Vanita, "Bringing Buried Things to Light."

24. See Emery, "Robbed of Meaning," for full discussion of Mrs. McNab's enabling function in Lily's project.

25. For a rather different reading of the sublime in this novel, see Rado, *Modern Androgyne Imagination,* especially 171–77. Rado focuses especially on Rhoda as a figure dramatizing the "failed sublime" of the "androgyne." Our readings intersect insofar as she sees Bernard as one who practices a kind of "psychic imperialism" which, as I'll also suggest, "appropriates experiences of both sexes for his own use" (174). Our readings diverge, however, in that Rado sees the figure of the lady writing as a trope for Woolf, the author, as outsider, excluded from and critical of this sublime project. As I argue later, I believe that through this figure of the lady writing Woolf implicates herself in the imperial sublime that she also critiques.

26. For another reading of the kiss as central, see Moon, "The Two Kisses."

27. Woolf, *The Waves,* 9. All further references to this work appear in the text.

28. See Oxindine, "Rhoda Submerged." All further references to this work appear in the text.

29. Both Marcus ("Britannia Rules *The Waves*") and McGee ("The Politics of Modernist Form") discuss this narrative rhythm, although they disagree about Woolf's relation to it. See note 32 below. Also see Doyle, "Sublime Barbarians in the Narrative of Empire," from which this part of the chapter developed.

30. Hackett's reading in *Sapphic Primitivism* focuses mainly on Rhoda and Woolf's association of her with blackness, primitive "natives," corruption, and degeneracy. Hackett sees, as I do, a form of Africanism operating in this novel, whereby colonial figures serve

to narrate white and especially sexually deviant identity. Hackett emphasizes the loose-ness of these associations in the novel (82–83), while I argue that Woolf undertakes a more total restructuring, exposure, and repetition of the imperial aspect of the Anglo-Atlantic imagination.

31. See "Violence and Metaphysics."

32. Marcus ("Britannia Rules *The Waves*") argues that Woolf distances herself from both Bernard and the lady at Elvedon, and more generally, in *Virginia Woolf against Empire*, Phillips assumes that Woolf has critical control over her colonial representations. My view is closer to that of McGee, Wollaeger, and especially Hackett, who tend to see her entangled in her own colonial tropes—although I put more emphasis on Woolf's self-consciousness about this entanglement than these other critics.

Conclusion

1. Minh-ha, 198.

2. 2004 State of the Union Address. *Whitehouse.gov*, http://www.whitehouse.gov/news/releases/2004/01/20040120-7.html (accessed July 9, 2007).

3. "President Bush Announces Major Combat Operations in Iraq Have Ended," May 1, 2003. *Whitehouse.gov*, http://www.whitehouse.gov/news/releases/2003/05/20030501-15.html (accessed July 9, 2007).

4. 2006 State of the Union Address. *Whitehouse.gov*, http://www.whitehouse.gov/news/releases/2006/01/20060131-10.html (accessed July 9, 2007).

5. "Final Ultimatum, Delivered to the Nation, Washington, D.C., March 17, 2003." *Vital Speeches of the Day* 69.12:354–56.

6. "Call For New Palestinian Leadership, Delivered in the Rose Garden, Washington, D.C., June 24, 2002." *Vital Speeches of the Day* 68.19:578–80.

7. Inaugural speech, January 20, 2005. *Whitehouse.gov*, http://www.whitehouse.gov/news/releases/2005/01/20050120-1.html (accessed July 9, 2007).

8. For the first three phrases quoted here, and also "forward strategy," see "Freedom in Iraq and the Middle East: Delivered to the 20th Anniversary of the National Endowment for Democracy, United States Chamber of Commerce, Washington, November 5, 2003. *Vital Speeches of the Day* 70.4, 98. For the reference to "preemptive action," see Bush's West Point speech, "A Just and Peaceful World: Delivered at the United States Military Academy, West Point, New York, May 29, 2002," *Vital Speeches of the Day* 68.16, 515. For the reference to "freedom and fear," see his founding "Homeland Security" speech, 2002. See the "Vital Speeches" website in note 5 above. Accessed through Academic Search Premier.

9. Borzou Daragahi. "Iraq Plan Includes Amnesty," *Chicago Tribune*, June 26, 2002, sec. 1, 22.

10. Patterson quoted in Hartman, *Scenes of Subjection*, 115.

11. Hardt and Negri, *Empire*.

12. See MacLean, *Freedom Is Not Enough*.

13. Nancy, *Being Singular Plural*.

Bibliography

Accomando, Christina. "'The Laws Were Laid Down to Me Anew': Harriet Jacobs and the Reframing of Legal Fictions." *African American Review* 32.2 (Summer 1998): 229–45.

Adams, Eleanor N. *Old English Scholarship in England from 1566–1800.* New Haven, Conn.: Yale University Press, 1917.

Alfey, Shawn. "Oriental Penetration: Gertrude Stein and the End of Europe." *Massachusetts Review* 38.3 (1997): 405–16.

Allan, Tuzyline Jita. "The Death of Sex and the Soul in *Mrs. Dalloway* and Nella Larsen's *Passing.*" In *Virginia Woolf: Lesbian Readings,* edited by Michele Barrett and Patricia Cramer, 95–113. New York: New York University Press, 1997.

Allen, Carol. *Black Women Intellectuals: Strategies of Nation, Family, and Neighborhood in the Works of Pauline Hopkins, Jessie Fauset, and Marita Bonner.* New York: Garland Publications, 1998.

Ammons, Elizabeth. "Afterword: *Winona,* Bakhtin, and Hopkins in the 21st Century." In *The Unruly Voice: Rediscovering Pauline Hopkins,* edited by John Cullen Gruesser, 211–20. Urbana: University of Illinois Press, 1996.

Anderson, Amanda. "George Eliot and the Jewish Question." *Yale Journal of Criticism* 10.1 (1997): 39–61.

———. *The Powers of Distance: Cosmopolitanism and the Cultivation of Detachment.* Princeton, N.J.: Princeton University Press, 2001.

———. *Tainted Souls and Painted Faces: The Rhetoric of Fallenness in Victorian Culture.* Ithaca, N.Y.: Cornell University Press, 1993.

Anderson, Douglas. "Division Below the Surface: Olaudah Equiano's *Interesting Narrative.*" *Studies in Romanticism* 43 (Fall 2004): 439–460.

Andrade, Susan Z. "White Skin, Black Masks: Colonialism and the Sexual Politics of *Oroonoko.*" *Cultural Critique* 27 (Spring 1994): 189–214.

Andres, Sophia. "Fortune's Wheel in *Daniel Deronda:* Sociopolitical Turn of the British Empire." *VIJ: Victorians Institute Journal* 24 (1996): 87–111.

Andrews, William. *To Tell a Free Story: The First Century of Afro-American Autobiography, 1760–1865.* Urbana: University of Illinois Press, 1986.

Aravamudan, Srinivas. "Equiano Lite." *Eighteenth-Century Studies* 34.4 (2001): 615–19.

———. *Tropicopolitans: Colonialism and Agency, 1688–1804.* Durham, N.C.: Duke University Press, 1999.

Arkush, Allan. "Relativizing Nationalism: The Role of Klesmer in George Eliot's *Daniel Deronda.*" *Jewish Social Studies: History, Culture, and Society* 3.3 (1997): 61–73.

Armstrong, Nancy. *Desire and Domestic Fiction: A Political History of the Novel.* New York: Oxford University Press, 1987.

Ashwell, Gary. "Savagism and Its Discontents: James Fenimore Cooper and His Native American Contemporaries." *American Transcendental Quarterly* 8.3 (September 1994): 211–27.

Astell, Mary. *The First English Feminist: Reflections upon Marriage and Other Writings.* Edited by Bridget Hill. New York: St. Martin's Press, 1986.

Athey, Stephanie, and Daniel Cooper Alarcon. "*Oroonoko*'s Gendered Economies of Honor/Horror: Reframing Colonial Discourse Studies in the Americas." *American Literature* 65.3 (September 1993): 415–43.

Auerbach, Nina. "The Rise of the Fallen Woman." *Nineteenth-Century Fiction* 35.1 (1980): 29–52.

Austin, Andrea. "Shooting Blanks: Potency, Parody, and Eliza Haywood's *The History of Miss Betsy Thoughtless.*" In *The Passionate Fictions of Eliza Haywood: Essays on her Life and Work,* edited by Kirsten T. Saxton and Rebecca P. Bocchicchio, 259–82. Lexington: University Press of Kentucky, 2000.

Axelrod, Alan. *Charles Brockden Brown, an American Tale.* Austin: University of Texas Press, 1983.

Azim, Firduos. *The Colonial Rise of the Novel.* New York: Routledge, 1993.

Backscheider, Paula R. *Spectacular Politics: Theatrical Power and Mass Culture in Early Modern England.* Baltimore: Johns Hopkins University Press, 1993.

———. "The Story of Eliza Haywood's Novels." In *The Passionate Fictions of Eliza Haywood: Essays on her Life and Work,* edited by Kirsten T. Saxton and Rebecca P. Bocchicchio, 19–47. Lexington: University Press of Kentucky, 2000.

Backscheider, Paula R., and John J. Richetti, ed. *Popular Fiction by Women, 1660–1730: An Anthology.* New York: Oxford University Press, 1996.

Backus, Margot Gayle. *The Gothic Family Romance: Heterosexuality, Child Sacrifice, and the Anglo-Irish Colonial Order.* Durham, N.C.: Duke University Press, 1999.

Bailyn, Bernard. *The Ideological Origins of the American Revolution.* Cambridge, Mass.: Harvard University Press, 1992 [1967].

———. *The Peopling of British North America.* New York: Vintage, 1988.

Baines, Barbara. "Ritualized Cannibalism in 'Benito Cereno': Melville's 'Black-Letter' Texts." *ESQ: A Journal of the American Renaissance* 30.3 (1984): 163–69.

Baker, Houston. *Blues, Ideology, and Afro-American Literature: A Vernacular Theory.* Chicago: University of Chicago Press, 1984.

Baker, William. *George Eliot and Judaism.* Salsburg: Institut fur Englische Sprache und Literatur, Universitat Salsburg, 1975.

Baldick, Chris. "The End of the Line: The Family Curse in Shorter Gothic Fiction." In *Exhibited by Candlelight: Sources and Developments in the Gothic Tradition,* edited by Valeria Tinkler-Villani, Peter Davidson, and Jane Stevenson, 147–57. Amsterdam: Rodopi, 1995.

———. Introduction to *The Oxford Book of Gothic Tales.* New York: Oxford University Press, 1993.

Ballaster, Ros. "A Gender of Opposition: Eliza Haywood's Scandal Fiction." In *The Passionate Fictions of Eliza Haywood: Essays on her Life and Work,* edited by Kirsten T. Saxton and Rebecca P. Bocchicchio, 143–67. Lexington: University Press of Kentucky, 2000.

———. *Seductive Forms: Women's Amatory Fiction, 1684–1740*. Oxford: Clarendon Press, 1992.

Bamlett, Steve. "The Scene of a Great Future: George Eliot, America, and Political Economy." In *America in English Literature*, edited by Neil Taylor, 49–77. London: Roehampton Institution of Higher Education, Southlands College, 1980.

Barbeito, Patricia Felisa. "'Making Generations' in Jacobs, Larsen, and Hurston: A Genealogy of Black Women's Writing." *American Literature* 70.2 (June 1998): 365–95.

Barber, Stephen. "Lip-Reading: Woolf's Secret Encounters." In *Novel Gazing: Queer Readings in Fiction*, edited by Eve Kosofsky Sedgwick, 401–43. Durham, N.C.: Duke University Press, 1993.

Bardes, Barbara, and Suzanna Gossett. *Declarations of Independence: Women and Political Power in Nineteenth-Century American Fiction*. New Brunswick, N.J.: Rutgers University Press, 1990.

Baridon, Michel. "The Gothic Revival and the Theory of Knowledge in the First Phase of the Enlightenment." In *Exhibited By Candlelight: Sources and Developments in the Gothic Tradition*, edited by Valeria Tinkler-Villani, Peter Davidson, and Jane Stevenson, 43–56. Amsterdam: Rodopi, 1995.

Barker-Benfield, G. J. *The Culture of Sensibility: Sex and Society in the Eighteenth Century*. Chicago: University of Chicago, 1992.

Barlowe, Jamie. "Rereading Women: Hester Prynne-ism and the Scarlet Mob of Scribblers." *American Literary History* 9.2 (Summer 1997): 197–225.

———. *The Scarlet Mob of Scribblers*. Carbondale: Southern Illinois University Press, 2000.

———. "Response to the Responses." *American Literary History* 9.2 (Summer 1997): 233–37.

Barnard, Philip, Mark L. Kamrath, and Stephen Shapiro, eds. *Revising Charles Brockden Brown: Culture, Politics, and Sexuality in the Early Republic*. Knoxville: University of Tennessee Press, 2004.

Barnes, Elizabeth. "Affecting Relations: Pedagogy, Patriarchy, and the Politics of Sympathy." *American Literary History* 8.4 (Winter 1996): 597–614.

———. "Loving With a Vengeance: Familicide and the Crisis of Masculinity in the Early Nation." In *Boys Don't Cry?: Rethinking Narratives of Masculinity and Emotion in the U.S.*, edited by Milette Shamir and Jennifer Travis, 44–63. New York: Columbia University Press, 2002.

———. "Natural and National Unions: Incest and Sympathy in the Early Republic." In *Incest and the Literary Imagination*, edited by Elizabeth Barnes, 138–55. Gainesville: University Press of Florida, 2002.

———. *States of Sympathy: Seduction and Democracy in the American Novel*. New York: Columbia University Press, 1997.

Barnett, Pamela. "'My Picture of You is, After All, the True Helga Crane': Portraiture and Identity in Nella Larsen's *Quicksand*." *Signs* 20.3 (Spring 1995): 575–600.

Barrell, John. *English Literature in History, 1730–80: An Equal Wide Survey*. New York: St. Martin's Press, 1983.

Barrett, Eileen. "Unmasking Lesbian Passion: The Inverted World of *Mrs. Dalloway*." In *Virginia Woolf: Lesbian Readings*, edited by Michele Barrett and Patricia Cramer, 146–64. New York: New York University Press, 1997.

Barrett, Michele, and Patricia Cramer, eds. *Virginia Woolf: Lesbian Readings.* New York: New York University Press, 1997.

Barry, Kaitlin. "Clarissa Dalloway: Surviving the Flood of British Empire." Essay written for English 200H, University of Massachusetts, Amherst, Fall 2004.

Barton, Paul. "Narrative Intrusion in *Charlotte Temple:* A Closet Feminist's Strategy in an American Novel." *Women and Language* 23.1 (Spring 2000): 26–32.

Bar-Yosef, Eitan. "Christian Zionism and Victorian Culture." *Israel Studies* 8.2 (2003): 18–44.

Bassard, Kathleen Clay. "'Beyond Mortal Vision': Harriet Wilson's *Our Nig* and the American Racial Dream-Text." In *Female Subjects in Black and White: Race, Psychoanalysis, Feminism,* edited by Elizabeth Abel, Barbara Christian, and Helen Moglen, 187–200. Berkeley: University of California Press, 1997.

Basu, Biman. "Hybrid Embodiment and an Ethics of Masochism: Nella Larsen's *Passing* and Sherley Anne Williams's *Dessa Rose.*" *African American Review* 36.3 (Fall 2002): 383–401.

Baucom, Ian. *Specters of the Atlantic: Finance Capital, Slavery, and the Philosophy of History.* Durham, N.C.: Duke University Press, 2005.

Bauer, Ralph. "Between Repression and Transgression: Rousseau's *Confessions* and Charles Brockden Brown's *Wieland.*" *American Transcendental Quarterly* 10.4 (December 1996): 311–29.

Baumgarten, Murray. "Seeing Double: Jews in the Fiction of F. Scott Fitzgerald, Charles Dickens, Anthony Trollope, and George Eliot." In *Between "Race" and Culture: Representations of "the Jew" in English and American Literature,* edited by Bryan Cheyette, 44–61. Stanford, Calif.: Stanford University Press, 1996.

Baym, Nina. *American Women Writers and the Work of History, 1790–1860.* New Brunswick, N.J.: Rutgers University Press, 1995.

———. "Passion and Authority in *The Scarlet Letter.*" *New England Quarterly* 43 (1970): 209–30.

Beam, Dorri Rabung. "The Flower of Black Female Sexuality in Pauline Hopkins's *Winona.*" In *Recovering the Black Female Body: Self-Representations by African American Women,* edited by Michael Bennett, Vanessa D. Dickerson, and Carla L. Peterson, 71–96. New Brunswick, N.J.: Rutgers University Press, 2001.

Beaseley, Jerry C. "Portraits of a Monster: Robert Walpole and Early English Prose Fiction." *Eighteenth-Century Studies* 14.4 (1981): 406–31.

Behn, Aphra. *Oroonoko, or The Royal Slave.* New York: W.W. Norton, 1973.

———. *The Younger Brother, or, the Amorous Jilt.* London: Printed for J. Harris, 1696.

Bell, Michael Davitt. "The Double-Tongued Deceiver: Sincerity and Duplicity in the Novels of Charles Brockden Brown." *Early American Literature* 9.2 (September 1974): 143–63.

———. *Hawthorne and the Historical Romance of New England.* Princeton, N.J.: Princeton University Press, 1971.

Bellamy, Liz. *Commerce, Morality, and the Eighteenth-Century Novel.* New York: Cambridge University Press, 1998.

Bellis, Peter J. *Writing Revolution: Aesthetics and Politics in Hawthorne, Whitman, and Thoreau.* Athens: University of Georgia Press, 2003.

Bender, John. *Imagining the Penitentiary: Fiction and the Architecture of Mind in Eighteenth-Century England*. Chicago: University of Chicago Press, 1987.

Bennett, Michael, and Vanessa D. Dickerson, eds. *Recovering the Black Female Body: Self-Representations by African American Women*. New Brunswick, N.J.: Rutgers University Press, 2001.

Benstock, Shari. "Expatriate Sapphic Modernism: Entering Literary History." In *Rereading Modernism: New Directions in Feminist Criticism*, edited by Lisa Rado, 97–121. New York: Garland, 1994.

Bercovitch, Sacvan. *The Office of the Scarlet Letter*. Baltimore: Johns Hopkins University Press, 1991.

——. *The Rites of Assent: Transformations in the Symbolic Construction of America*. New York: Routledge, 1993.

Berg, Allison. "Reconstructing Motherhood: Pauline Hopkins' *Contending Forces*." *Studies in American Fiction* 24.2 (Autumn 1996): 131–50.

Bergland, Renée L. *The National Uncanny: Indian Ghosts and American Subjects*. Hanover, N.H.: University Press of New England, 2000.

Berkhout, Carl, and Milton Gatch, eds. *Anglo-Saxon Scholarship: The First Three Centuries*. Boston: G. K. Hall, 1982.

Berlant, Lauren. *The Anatomy of National Fantasy: Hawthorne, Utopia, and Everyday Life*. Chicago: University of Chicago Press, 1991.

——. "The Queen of America Goes to Washington City: Harriet Jacobs, Frances Harper, Anita Hill." *American Literature* 65.3 (September 1993): 549–75.

Bernardi, Debra. "Narratives of Domestic Imperialism: The African American Home in the Colored American Magazine and the Novels of Pauline Hopkins, 1900–1903." In *Separate Spheres No More: Gender Convergence in American Literature, 1830–1930*, edited by Monika M. Elbert, 203–24. Tuscaloosa: University of Alabama Press, 2000.

Berthold, Dennis. "Melville, Garibaldi, and the Medusa of Revolution." In *National Imaginaries, American Identities: The Cultural World of American Iconography*, edited by Larry F. Reynolds and Gordon Hutner, 104–38. Princeton, N.J.: Princeton University Press, 2000.

Bindman, David. *The Shadow of the Guillotine: Britain and the French Revolution*. London: Published for the Trustees of the British Museum Publications, 1989.

Blackmer, Corinne E. "The Veils of the Law: Race and Sexuality in Nella Larsen's *Passing*." *College Literature* 22.3 (October 1995): 50–67.

Blackmore, David. "'That Unreasonable Restless Feeling': The Homosexual Subtexts of Nella Larsen's *Passing*." *African American Review* 36.3 (Fall 1992): 475–484.

Blair, Hugh. "A Preliminary Discourse and Dissertation on the Era and Poems of Ossian." Appended to James MacPherson, trans., *The Poetical Works of Ossian*. Boston: Crosby and Nichols, 1863.

Blakemore, Steven. *Burke and the Fall of Language*. Hanover, N.H.: Published for Brown University Press by University Press of New England, 1988.

Bliss, Robert M. *Revolution and Empire: English Politics and the American Colonies in the Seventeenth Century*. New York: Manchester University Press, 1990.

Bloom, Harold, ed. *Hester Prynne*. New York: Chelsea House, 1990.

Blouch, Christine. "Eliza Haywood and the Romance of Obscurity." *SEL* 31.3 (Summer 1991): 535–52.

Bocchicchio, Rebecca P. "'Blushing, Trembling, and Incapable of Defense': The Hysterics of *The British Recluse*." In *The Passionate Fictions of Eliza Haywood: Essays on her Life and Work,* edited by Kirsten T. Saxton and Rebecca P. Bocchicchio, 95–114. Lexington.: University Press of Kentucky, 2000.

Boelhower, William. "'I'll Teach You How to Flow': On Figuring out Atlantic Studies." *Atlantic Studies* 1.1 (2004): 28–48.

Boesenberg, Eva. "The Color of Money." In *Black Imagination and the Middle Passage,* edited by Maria Diedrich, Henry Louis Gates Jr., and Carl Pedersen, 117–26. New York: Oxford University Press, 1999.

Bolster, Jeffrey W. *Black Jacks: African American Seamen in the Age of Sail.* Cambridge, Mass.: Harvard University Press, 1997.

Boone, Joseph. *Libidinal Currents: Sexuality and the Shaping of Modernism.* Chicago: University of Chicago Press, 1998.

Bost, Suzanne. "Fluidity without Postmodernism: Michelle Cliff and the 'Tragic Mulatta' Tradition." *African American Review* 32.4 (Winter 1998): 673–89.

Botting, Fred. "In Gothic Darkley: Heterotopia, History, and Culture." In *A Companion to the Gothic,* edited by David Punter, 3–14. Malden, Mass.: Blackwell Publishers, 2000.

Bowers, Toni. "Collusive Resistance: Sexual Agency and Partisan Politics in *Love in Excess*." In *The Passionate Fictions of Eliza Haywood: Essays on her Life and Work,* edited by Kirsten T. Saxton and Rebecca P. Bocchicchio, 46–68. Lexington: University Press of Kentucky, 2000.

Bozeman, Terry S. "Interstices, Hybridity, and Identity: Olaudah Equiano and the Discourse of the African Slave Trade." *Studies in the Literary Imagination* 36.2 (Fall 2003): 61–71.

Bradford, William. *History of Plymouth Plantation.* New York: Knopf, 1952.

Bradshaw, David. "Vicious Circles: Hegel, Bosanquet, and *The Voyage Out*." In *Virginia Woolf and the Arts: Selected Papers from the Sixth Annual Conference on Virginia Woolf,* 183–91. New York: Pace University Press, 1997.

Brandabur, Claire A. "George Eliot's Daniel Deronda and the Creation of Modern Israel." *Gombak Review: A Journal of Language and Literature* 5.1 (2001): 34–50.

Brantlinger, Patrick. *Fictions of State: Culture and Credit in Britain, 1694–1994.* Ithaca, N.Y.: Cornell University Press, 1996.

Braudy, Leo. *Narrative Form in History and Fiction.* Princeton, N.J.: Princeton University Press, 1970.

Braxton, Joanne M. "Harriet Jacobs' *Incidents in the Life of a Slave Girl*: The Re-Definition of the Slave Narrative Genre." *Massachusetts Review* 27.2 (Summer 1986): 379–87.

Breau, Elizabeth. "Identifying Satire: *Our Nig*." *Callaloo: A Journal of African American and African Arts and Letters* 16.2 (Spring 1993): 455–65.

Brenner, Robert. *Merchants and Revolution: Commercial Change, Political Conflict, and London's Overseas Traders, 1550–1653.* Princeton, N.J.: Princeton University Press, 1993.

Brewer, David. "'Haywood,' Secret History, and the Politics of Attribution." In *The Passionate Fictions of Eliza Haywood: Essays on her Life and Work,* edited by Kirsten T.

Saxton and Rebecca P. Bocchicchio, 217–39. Lexington: University Press of Kentucky, 2000.

Brinkley, Roberta. *Arthurian Legend in the Seventeenth Century*. Baltimore: Johns Hopkins University Press, 1932.

Brodhead, Richard H. *The School of Hawthorne*. New York: Oxford University Press, 1986.

Brogan, Kathleen. *Cultural Haunting: Ghosts and Ethnicity in Recent American Literature*. Charlottesville: University of Virginia Press, 1998.

Brooke, Henry. *Gustavas Vasa, the Deliverer of His Country*. London: R. Dodsley, 1739.

Brooks, Kristina. "Mammies, Bucks, and Wenches: Minstrelsy, Racial Pornography, and Racial Politics in Pauline Hopkins's *Hagar's Daughter*." In *The Unruly Voice: Rediscovering Pauline Hopkins*, edited by John Cullen Gruesser, 119–57. Urbana: University of Illinois Press, 1996.

Brown, Charles Brockden. *Edgar Huntly; or Memoirs of a Sleepwalker*. Kent, Ohio: Kent State University Press, 1984.

———. *Wieland* and *Memoirs of Carwin the Biloquist*. New York: Penguin, 1991.

Brown, Gillian. *The Consent of the Governed: The Lockean Legacy in Early American Culture*. Cambridge, Mass.: Harvard University Press, 2001.

———. "Hawthorne, Inheritance, and Women's Property." *Studies in the Novel* 23.1 (1991): 107–18.

Brown, Homer O. "The Displaced Self in the Novels of Daniel Defoe." *English Literary History* 38.4 (December 1971): 562–90.

———. "Why the Story of the Origins of the (English) Novel Is an American Romance (If Not the Great American Novel)." In *Cultural Institutions of the Novel*, edited by Deirdre Lynch and William B. Warner, 11–43. Durham, N.C.: Duke University Press, 1996.

Brown, Laura. *The Ends of Empire: Women and Ideology in Early Eighteenth-Century English Literature*. Ithaca, N.Y.: Cornell University Press, 1993.

Brown, Lois Lamphere. "'To Allow No Tragic End': Defensive Postures in Pauline Hopkins's *Contending Forces*." In *The Unruly Voice: Rediscovering Pauline Hopkins*, edited by John Cullen Gruesser, 50–70. Urbana: University of Illinois Press, 1996.

Brown, William Hill. *The Power of Sympathy*. In *"The Power of Sympathy" and "The Coquette"* [by Hannah W. Foster], edited by William S. Osborne. New Haven, Conn.: College and University Press, 1970.

Browne, Ray B. "*Billy Budd*: Gospel of Democracy." *Nineteenth Century Fiction* 17.4 (March 1963): 321–37.

Budick, Emily Miller. *Engendering Romance: Women Writers and the Hawthorne Tradition, 1850–1990*. New Haven: Yale University Press, 1994.

———. "We Damned-If-You-Do, Damned-If-You-Don't Mob of Scribbling Scholars." *American Literary History* 9.2 (Summer 1997): 233–37.

Bugg, John. "The Other Interesting Narrative: Olaudah Equiano's Book Tour." *Publication of the Modern Language Association* 121.5 (2006): 1424–42.

Burgett, Bruce. "Between Speculation and Population: The Problem of 'Sex' in Thomas Malthus's Essay on the Principle of Population and Charles Brockden Brown's *Alcuin*." In *Revising Charles Brockden Brown: Culture, Politics, and Sexuality in the Early Republic*, edited by Philip Barnard, Mark L. Kamrath, and Stephen Shapiro, 122–48. Knoxville: University of Tennessee Press, 2004.

Burke, Edmund. *Reflections on the Revolution in France.* Edited by J. C. D. Clark. Stanford, Calif.: Stanford University Press, 2001.

Burnham, Michelle. "Between England and America: Captivity, Sympathy, and the Sentimental Novel." In *Cultural Institutions of the Novel,* edited by Deirdre Lynch and William B. Warner, 47–72. Durham, N.C.: Duke University Press, 1996.

———. "Loopholes of Resistance: Harriet Jacobs' Slave Narrative and the Critique of Agency in Foucault." *Arizona Quarterly* 49.2 (1993): 53–73.

Butler, Judith. *Bodies that Matter: On the Discursive Limits of "Sex."* New York: Routledge, 1993.

Butler, Mary. "'Onomaphobia' and Personal Identity in *Moll Flanders." Studies in the Novel* 22.4 (1990): 377–91.

Byers, John R. Jr. "A Letter of William Hill Brown's." *American Literature: A Journal of Literary History, Criticism, and Bibliography* 49.4 (January 1978): 606–11.

Byrd, Alexander X. "Eboe, Country, Nation and Gustavus Vassa's *Interesting Narrative." William and Mary Quarterly* 63.1 (January 2006): 123–48.

Byron, Glennis, and David Punter, eds. *Spectral Readings: Towards a Gothic Geography.* London: Macmillan, 1999.

Cagidemetrio, Alide. *Fictions of the Past: Hawthorne and Melville.* Amherst: University of Massachusetts Press, 1992.

Caldwell, Tanya. "'Talking Too Much English': Languages of Economy and Politics in Equiano's *Interesting Narrative." Early American Literature* 34 (1997): 263–82.

Campbell, Jane. *Mythic Black Fiction: The Transformation of History.* Knoxville: University of Tennessee Press, 1986.

Carby, Hazel V. "The Politics of Fiction, Anthropology, and the Folk: Zora Neale Hurston." In *History and Memory in African American Culture,* edited by Genevieve Fabre and Robert O'Meally, 28–44. New York: Oxford University Press, 1994.

———. *Reconstructing Womanhood: The Emergence of the Afro-American Woman Novelist.* New York: Oxford University Press, 1987.

Carnell, Rachel. "It's Not Easy Being Green: Gender and Friendship in Eliza Haywood's Political Periodicals." *Eighteenth-Century Studies* (1998–99) 32.2: 199–214.

———. "Subverting Tragic Conventions: Aphra Behn's Turn to the Novel." *Studies in the Novel* 31.2 (1999): 133–51.

Carpenter, Mary Wilson. *George Eliot and the Landscape of Time: Narrative Form and Protestant Apocalyptic History.* Chapel Hill: University of North Carolina Press, 1986.

Carr, Brian. "Paranoid Interpretation, Desire's Nonobject, and Nella Larsen's *Passing." PMLA* 119.2 (2004): 282–95.

Carretta, Vincent. *Equiano, the African: Biography of a Self-Made Man.* Athens: University of Georgia Press, 2005.

Carroll, Alicia. "'Arabian Nights': 'Make Believe,' Exoticism, and Desire in *Daniel Deronda." Journal of English and Germanic Philology* 98.2 (April 1999): 219–38.

———. *Dark Smiles: Race and Desire in George Eliot.* Athens: Ohio University Press, 2003.

———. "The Giaour's Campaign: Desire and the Other in *Felix Holt, the Radical." Novel: A Forum on Fiction* 30.2 (Winter 1997): 237–59.

Carton, Evan. *The Rhetoric of American Romance: Dialectic and Identity in Emerson, Dickinson, Poe, and Hawthorne.* Baltimore: Johns Hopkins University Press, 1985.

Cassidy, Thomas. "Contending Contexts: Pauline Hopkins's *Contending Forces*." *African American Review* 32.4 (Winter 1998): 661–72.

Castiglia, Christopher. "In Praise of Extra-vagant Women: *Hope Leslie* and the Captivity Romance." *Legacy* 6.2 (Fall 1989): 3–16.

———. "Susanna Rowson's *Reuben and Rachel*: Captivity, Colonization, and the Domestication of Columbus." In *Redefining the Political Novel: American Women Writers, 1797–1901*, edited by Sharon Harris, 23–42. Knoxville: University of Tennessee Press, 1995.

Castle, Terry. *Clarissa's Ciphers: Meaning & Disruption in Richardson's "Clarissa."* Ithaca, N.Y.: Cornell University Press, 1982.

———. *The Female Thermometer: Eighteenth-Century Culture and the Invention of the Uncanny.* New York: Oxford University Press, 1995.

———. *Masquerade and Civilization: The Carnivalesque in Eighteenth-Century Culture and Fiction.* Stanford, Calif.: Stanford University Press, 1986.

Cateau, Heather, and S. H. H. Carrington, eds. *Capitalism and Slavery Fifty Years Later: Eric Eustace Williams—A Reassessment of his Work.* New York: Peter Lang, 2000.

Caton, Lou. "Doing the Right Thing with Moll Flanders: A 'Reasonable' Difference between the Picara and the Penitent." *College Literature Association Journal* 40.4 (1997): 508–16.

Chaber, Lois A. "Matriarchal Mirror: Women and Capital in *Moll Flanders*." *PMLA* 97.2 (March 1982): 212–26.

Chandler, Nahum Dimitri. "Originary Displacement." *boundary 2* 27.3 (2000): 249–86.

Chard, Joan M. "'A Lasting Habitation': The Quest for Identity and Vocation in *Daniel Deronda*." *George Eliot Fellowship Review* 15 (1984): 38–44.

Chartier, Roger. *The Order of Books: Readers, Authors, and Libraries in Europe between the Fourteenth and the Eighteenth Centuries.* Translated by Lydia Cochrane. Stanford, Calif.: Stanford University Press, 1994.

Chase, Cynthia. "The Decomposition of the Elephants: Double-Reading *Daniel Deronda*." *PMLA* 93.2 (1978): 215–27.

Chase, Richard. *The American Novel and its Tradition.* Garden City, N.Y.: Doubleday, 1957.

Chernaik, Warren. "Captains and Slaves: Aphra Behn and the Rhetoric of Republicanism." *The Seventeenth Century* 17.1 (April 2002): 97–107.

Cherniavsky, Eva. "Charlotte Temple's Debt Remains." In *Discovering Difference: Contemporary Essays in American Culture*, edited by Christoff K. Lohmann, 35–47. Bloomington: Indiana University Press, 1993.

Cheyette, Bryan. *Constructions of the "Jew" in English Literature and Society: Racial Representations, 1875–1945.* New York: Cambridge, 1995.

———. "White Skin, Black Masks: Jews and Jewishness in the Writings of George Eliot and Frantz Fanon." In *Cultural Readings of Imperialism: Edward Said and the Gravity of History*, edited by Keith Ansell-Pearson, Benita Parry, and Judith Squires, 106–26. New York: St. Martin's Press, 1997.

Chibka, Robert L. "'Oh! Do Not Fear a Woman's Invention': Truth, Falsehood, and Fiction in Aphra Behn's *Oroonoko*." *Texas Studies in Literature and Language* 30.4 (1988): 510–37.

Christiansen, Rupert. "The Identity of Klesmer in *Daniel Deronda.*" *George Eliot Fellowship Review* 17 (1986): 84–85.

Christophersen, Bill. *The Apparition in the Glass: Charles Brockden Brown's American Gothic.* Athens: University of Georgia Press, 1993.

Clark, David Lee. *Charles Brockden Brown: Pioneer Voice of America.* Durham, N.C.: Duke University Press, 1952.

Clark, J. C. D. *The Language of Liberty: Political Discourse and Social Dynamics in the Anglo-American World.* New York: Cambridge University Press, 1994.

———. *Revolution and Rebellion: State and Society in England in the Seventeenth and Eighteenth Centuries.* Cambridge: Cambridge University Press, 1986.

Clasby, Nancy Tenfelde. "Being True: Logos in *The Scarlet Letter.*" *Renascence* 45.4 (Summer 1993): 247–56.

Clemmen, Yves W. A. "Nella Larsen's *Quicksand*: A Narrative Difference." *College Literature Association Journal* 40.4 (June 1997): 458–66.

Clery, E. J. "The Genesis of 'Gothic' Fiction." In *The Cambridge Companion to Gothic Fiction,* edited by Jerrold E. Hogle, 21–39. Cambridge: Cambridge University Press, 2002.

———. *The Rise of Supernatural Fiction, 1762–1800.* Cambridge: Cambridge University Press, 1995.

———. *Women's Gothic: From Clara Reeve to Mary Shelley.* Tavistock: Northcote House in association with the British Council, 2000.

Cobban, Alfred. *Edmund Burke and the Revolt against the Eighteenth Century: A Study of the Political and Social Thinking of Burke, Wordsworth, Coleridge, and Southey,* 2nd ed. London: Allen and Unwin, 1960.

Cocalis, Jane. "The 'Dark and Abiding Presence' in Nathaniel Hawthorne's *The Scarlet Letter* and Toni Morrison's *Beloved.*" In *The Calvinist Roots of the Modern Era,* edited by Aliki Barnstone, Michael Tomasek Manson, and Carol J. Singley, 250–262. Hanover, N.H.: University Press of New England, 1997.

Cohan, Steve M. "Clarissa and the Individuation of Character." *ELH* 43.2 (Summer 1976): 163–83.

Cohen, Margaret. "Traveling Genres." *New Literary History* 34.3 (2003): 481–99.

Cohen, Milton. "Black Brutes and Mulatto Saints: The Racial Hierarchy of Stein's "Melanctha." *Black American Literature Forum* 18.3 (Fall 1984): 119–21.

Cohen, Monica. "From Home to Homeland: The Bohemian in *Daniel Deronda.*" *Studies in the Novel* 30.3 (Fall 1998): 324–54.

Colacurcio, Michael. *Doctine and Difference: Essays in the Literature of New England.* New York: Routledge, 1997.

Colbourn, H. Trevor. *The Lamp of Experience: Whig History and the Intellectual Origins of the American Revolution.* Chapel Hill: University of North Carolina Press, 1965.

Cole, Phyllis. "Stowe, Jacobs, Wilson: White Plots and Black Counterplots." In *New Perspectives on Gender, Race, and Class in Society,* edited by Audrey T. McLuskey, 23–45. Bloomington: Indiana University Press, 1990.

Collins, Janelle. "Passage to Slavery, Passage to Freedom: Olaudah Equiano and the Sea." *Novel: A Forum on Fiction* 39.1 (Fall 2005): 209–23.

Constanzo, Angelo. *Surprising Narrative: Olaudah Equiano and the Beginnings of Black Autobiography.* Westport, Conn.: Greenwood, 1987.

Conway, Alison. "Defoe's Protestant Whore." *Eighteenth-Century Studies* 35.2 (2002): 215–33.

Cook, Elizabeth Heckendorn. *Epistolary Bodies: Gender and Genre in the Eighteenth-Century Republic of Letters.* Stanford, Calif.: Stanford University Press, 1996.

Cowan, S. A. "The Naming of Captain Vere in Melville's *Billy Budd.*" *Studies in Short Fiction* 21.1 (Winter 1984): 41–46.

Craft-Fairchild, Catherine. *Masquerade and Gender: Disguise and Female Identity in Eighteenth-Century Fictions by Women.* University Park: Pennsylvania State University Press, 1993.

Cramer, Patricia. "'Pearls and the Porpoise': *The Years* — A Lesbian Memoir." In *Virginia Woolf: Lesbian Readings,* edited by Michele Barrett and Patricia Cramer, 222–40. New York: New York University Press, 1997.

Crews, Frederick. *The Sins of Fathers.* New York: Oxford University Press, 1996.

Crosby, Christina. *Ends of History: Victorians and the "Woman Question."* New York: Routledge, 1991.

Croskery, Margaret Case. "Masquing Desire: The Politics of Passion in Eliza Haywood's *Fantomina.*" In *The Passionate Fictions of Eliza Haywood: Essays on her Life and Work,* edited by Kirsten T. Saxton and Rebecca P. Bocchicchio, 69–94. Lexington: University Press of Kentucky, 2000.

Cummings, Katherine. *Telling Tales: The Hysteric's Seduction in Fiction and Theory.* Stanford, Calif.: Stanford University Press, 1991.

Dalke, Anna. "Original Vice: The Political Implications of Incest in the Early American Novel." *Early American Literature* 23.2 (1988): 188–201.

Damon-Bach, Lucinda, and Victoria Clements, eds. *Catharine Maria Sedgwick: Critical Perspectives.* Boston: Northeastern University Press, 2003.

Damrosch, Leopold Jr. *God's Plots and Man's Stories: Studies in the Fictional Imagination from Milton to Fielding.* Chicago: University of Chicago Press, 1985.

David, Deirdre. *Fictions of Resolution in Three Victorian Novels: "North and South," "Our Mutual Friend," "Daniel Deronda."* New York: Columbia University Press, 1981.

———. *Rule Britannia: Women, Empire, and Victorian Writing.* Ithaca, N.Y.: Cornell University Press, 1995.

Davidson, Basil. *The African Slave Trade.* Boston: Back Bay Books, 1980.

Davidson, Cathy. *Revolution and the Word: The Rise of the Novel in America.* New York: Oxford University Press, 1986.

Davis, Brion David. *The Problem of Slavery in Western Culture.* New York: Oxford, 1988 [1966].

Davis, Cynthia. "Speaking the Body's Pain: Harriet Wilson's *Our Nig.*" *African American Review* 27.3 (Fall 1993): 391–404.

Davis, Lennard. *Factual Fictions: The Origins of the English Novel.* New York: Columbia University Press, 1983.

Davis, Sarah. "Another View of Hester and the Antinomians." *Studies in American Fiction* 12.1 (Autumn 1984): 189–98.

Davis, Thadious. *Nella Larsen, Novelist of the Harlem Renaissance: A Woman's Life Unveiled.* Baton Rouge: Louisiana State University Press, 1994.

Defoe, Daniel. *The Fortunes and Misfortunes of the Famous Moll Flanders.* New York: Penguin, 1989.

———. *The Life and Strange Surprising Adventures of Robinson Crusoe, of York, Mariner.* New York: Oxford University Press, 1972.

———. *Roxana, the Fortunate Mistress.* New York: Oxford University Press, 1964.

Delamotte, Eugenia C. *Perils of the Night: A Feminist Study of Nineteenth-Century Gothic.* New York: Oxford University Press, 1990.

Derrick, Scott. "A Curious Subject of Observation and Inquiry: Homoeroticism, the Body, and Authorship in Hawthorne's *The Scarlet Letter.*" *Novel: A Forum on Fiction* 28.3 (Spring 1995): 308–26.

Derrida, Jacques. "Violence and Metaphysics." In *Writing and Difference,* translated by Alan Bass, 79–152. Chicago: University of Chicago Press, 1978.

DeSalvo, Louise. *Virginia Woolf: The Impact of Childhood Sexual Abuse on Her Life and Work.* New York: Ballantine Books, 1989.

Devlin, Athena. *Between Profits and Primitivism: Shaping White Middle-Class Masculinity in the United States, 1880–1917.* New York: Routledge, 2005.

Diehl, Joanne Feit. "Re-Reading the Letter: Hawthorne, the Fetish, and the (Family) Romance." *New Literary History* 19.3 (1988): 655–73.

Dijkstra, Bram. *Defoe and Economics.* New York: St. Martin's Press, 1967.

Dimock, Wai-Chee. *Empire for Liberty: Melville and the Poetics of Individualism.* Princeton, N.J.: Princeton University Press, 1989.

Dittmar, Linda. "When Privilege Is No Protection: The Woman Artist in *Quicksand* and *The House of Mirth.*" In *Writing the Woman Artist: Essays on Poetics, Politics, and Portraiture,* edited by Suzanne W. Jones, 133–54. Philadelphia: University of Pennsylvania Press, 1991.

Dobie, Kathleen. "This is the Room that Class Built: The Structures of Sex and Class in *Jacob's Room.*" In *Virginia Woolf: A Centenary Celebration,* edited by Jane Marcus, 195–207. Bloomington: Indiana University Press, 1987.

Doherty, Thomas. "Harriet Jacobs' Narrative Strategies: *Incidents in the Life of a Slave Girl.*" *Southern Literary Journal* 19 (Fall 1986): 79–91.

Dolin, Kieran. *Fiction and the Law: Legal Discourse in Victorian and Modern Literature.* New York: Cambridge University Press, 1999.

Doody, Margaret. "George Eliot and the Eighteenth-Century Novel." In *George Eliot: Critical Assessments,* vol. 4, edited by Stuart Hutchinson, 15–39. East Sussex, England: Helm Information, 1996.

———. *A Natural Passion: A Study of the Novels of Samuel Richardson.* Oxford: Clarendon Press, 1974.

———. *The True Story of the Novel.* New Brunswick, N.J.: Rutgers University Press, 1996.

Doreski, C. K. "Inherited Rhetoric and Authentic History: Pauline Hopkins at the *Colored American Magazine.*" In *The Unruly Voice: Rediscovering Pauline Hopkins,* edited by John Cullen Grusser, 71–97. Urbana: University of Illinois Press, 1996.

Doriani, Beth Maclay. "Black Womanhood in Nineteenth-Century America: Subversion and Self-Construction in Two Women's Autobiographies." *American Quarterly* 43.2 (June 1991): 199–222.

Doubleday, Neal Frank. "Hawthorne's Hester and Feminism." *PMLA* 54.3 (September 1939): 825–28.

Douglas, Ann. Introduction to *"Charlotte Temple" and "Lucy Temple,"* by Susanna Rowson. New York: Penguin, 1991.

Douglas, Lawrence. "Discursive Limits: Narrative and Judgment in *Billy Budd.*" *Mosaic* 27.4 (December 1994): 141–60.

Doyle, Laura. "The Body against Itself in Faulkner's Phenomenology of Race." *American Literature* 73.2 (June 2001): 339–64.

———. "The Body Unbound: A Phenomenological Reading of the Political in *A Room of One's Own.*" In *Virginia Woolf Out of Bounds,* edited by Jessica Berman and Jane Goldman. New York: Pace University Press, 2001.

———. *Bordering on the Body: The Racial Matrix of Modern Fiction and Culture.* New York: Oxford University Press, 1994.

———. "The Flat, the Round, and Gertrude Stein: Race and the Shape of Modern(ist) History." *Modernism/Modernity* 7.2 (April 2000): 249–72.

———. "The Folk, the Nobles, and the Novel: The Racial Subtext of Sentimentality." *Narrative* 3.2 (May 1995): 161–86.

———. "The Racial Sublime." In *Romanticism, Race, and Imperial Culture, 1780–1834,* edited by Alan Richardson and Sonia Hofkosh, 15–39. Bloomington: Indiana University Press, 1996.

———. "Sublime Barbarians in the Narrative of Empire." *Modern Fiction Studies* 42.2 (Summer 1996): 323–47.

———, ed. *Bodies of Resistance: New Phenomenologies of Politics, Agency, and Culture.* Evanston, Ill.: Northwestern University Press, 2001.

Doyle, Laura, and Laura Winkiel, eds. *Geomodernisms: Race, Modernism, Modernity.* Bloomington: Indiana University Press, 2005.

Dreyer, Frederick A. *Burke's Politics: A Study in Whig Orthodoxy.* Waterloo, Canada: Wilfrid Laurier University Press, 1979.

Dubois, W. E. B. *The Souls of Black Folk.* New York: Penguin, 1996 [1989].

DuCille, Ann. *The Coupling Convention: Sex, Text, and Tradition in Black Women's Fiction.* New York: Oxford University Press, 1993.

Dukats, Mara L. "The Hybrid Terrain of Literary Imagination: Maryse Condé's Black Witch of Salem, Nathaniel Hawthorne's Hester Prynne, and Aimé Césaire's Heroic Poetic Voice." In *Order and Partialities: Theory, Pedagogy, and the "Postcolonial,"* edited by Kostas Myrsiades and Jerry McGuire, 325–40. Albany: State University of New York Press, 1995.

Durlson, J. "Incest and the American Romantic Fictions." *Studies in the Literary Imagination* 7.1 (1974): 31–50.

Eagleton, Terry. *The Rape of Clarissa: Writing, Sexuality, and Class Struggle in Samuel Richardson.* Oxford: Blackwell, 1982.

Earley, Samantha Manchester. "Writing from the Center or the Margins? Olaudah Equiano's Writing Life Reassessed." *African Studies Review* 46.3 (December 2003): 1–16.

Easley, Alexis. "Authorship, Gender, and Identity: George Eliot in the 1850s." *Women's Writing* 3.2 (1996): 145–60.

Eberly, David. "Woolf and Gay and Lesbian Modernism." In *Virginia Woolf: Themes and Variations: Selected Papers from the Second Annual Conference on Virginia Woolf,*

Southern Connecticut State University, New Haven, June 11–14, 1992, edited by Vara Neverow-Turk and Mark Hussey. New York: Pace University Press, 1993.

Egan, Ken Jr. "The Adultress in the Market-Place: Hawthorne and *The Scarlet Letter.*" *Studies in the Novel* 27 (1995): 26–41.

Eisenstein, Elizabeth. *The Printing Press as an Agent of Change: Communications and Cultural Transformations in Early Modern Europe.* New York: Cambridge University Press, 1979

Eliot, George. *Daniel Deronda.* Edited by Barbara Hardy. New York: Penguin, 1978. [1967].

———. *Impressions of Theophrastus Such,* edited by Nancy Henry. Iowa City: University of Iowa Press, 1994.

———. *The Mill on the Floss.* New York: Penguin, 1985.

———. "Prospectus of the *Westminster and Foreign Quarterly Review.*" In *Selected Essays, Poems, and other Writings* by George Eliot, edited by A. S. Byatt and Nicholas Warren, 3–7. New York: Penguin, 1990.

Elliot, Emory. *Revolutionary Writers: Literature and Authority in the New Republic, 1725–1810.* New York: Oxford University Press, 1982.

Ellis, Kate Ferguson. *Contested Castle: Gothic Novels and the Subversion of Domestic Ideology.* Urbana: University of Illinois Press, 1989.

Ellis, R. J. "Body Politics and the Body Politic in William Wells Brown's *Clotel* and Harriet Wilson's *Our Nig,*" In *Soft Canons: American Women Writers and Masculine Tradition,* edited by Karen L. Kilcup, 99–122. Iowa City: University of Iowa Press, 1999.

———. "'Traps Slyly Laid': Professing Autobiography in Harriet Wilson's *Our Nig.*" In *Representing Lives: Women and Auto/Biography,* edited by Alison Donnell and Pauline Polkey, 65–76. New York: St. Martin's Press, 2000.

Ellison, Ralph. *Invisible Man.* New York: Vintage Books, 1995.

Elrod, Eileen Razzari. "Moses and the Egyptian: Religious Authority in Olaudah Equiano's *Interesting Narrative.*" *African American Review* 35.3 (2001): 409–25.

Emerson, Ralph Waldo. *English Traits.* Cambridge: Harvard University Press, 1966.

———. "The Poet" in *Selected Essays,* edited by Larzer Ziff, 259–84. New York: Penguin, 1982.

Emery, Mary Lou. "'Robbed of Meaning': The Work at the Center of *To the Lighthouse.*" *Modern Fiction Studies* 38.1 (Spring 1992): 217–34.

Emmitt, Helen V. "'Drowned in a Willing Sea': Freedom and Drowning in Eliot, Chopin, and Drabble." *Tulsa Studies in Women's Literature* 12.2 (Autumn 1993): 315–32.

Epley, Steven. "Alienated, Betrayed, and Powerless: A Possible Connection between *Charlotte Temple* and the Legend of Inkle and Yarico." *Papers on Language and Literature* 38.2 (March 2002): 200–222.

Equiano, Olaudah. *The Interesting Narrative of the Life of Olaudah Equiano, or Gustavas Vassa, the African Written by Himself.* Boston: Beacon Press, 1969.

Ernest, John. *Resistance and Reformation in Nineteenth-Century African-American Literature: Brown, Wilson, Jacobs, Delaney, Douglass, and Harper.* Jackson: University Press of Mississippi, 1995.

Esteve, Mary. "Nella Larson's *Moving Mosaic:* Harlem, Crowds, and Anonymity." *American Literary History* 9.2 (Summer 1997): 268–86.

Evans, Gareth. "Rakes, Coquettes and Republican Patriarchs: Class, Gender, and Nation in Early American Sentimental Fiction." *Canadian Review of American Studies* 25.3 (1995): 41–62.

Fairchild, Hoxie Neale. *The Noble Savage; A Study in Romantic Naturalism.* New York: Russell and Russell, 1961.

Ferguson, Frances. "Rape and the Rise of the Novel." *Representations* 20 (Fall 1987): 88–112.

Ferguson, Margaret. "Juggling the Categories of Race, Class, and Gender: Aphra Behn's *Oroonoko.*" *Women's Studies* 19 (1991): 159–81.

Ferguson, Moira. "*Oroonoko*: Birth of a Paradigm." *New Literary History* 23.2 (1992): 339–59.

Ferguson, Roderick A. *Aberrations in Black: Toward a Queer of Color Critique.* Minneapolis: University of Minnesota, 2003.

Fetterley, Judith. "My Sister! My Sister!: The Rhetoric of Catharine Sedgwick's *Hope Leslie.*" *American Literature* 70.3 (September 1998): 491–516.

Fichtelberg, Joel. "Word between Worlds: The Economy of Equiano's *Narrative.*" *American Literary History* 5.3 (1993): 459–80.

Fiedler, Leslie. *Love and Death in the American Novel.* New York: Criterion Books, 1960.

Finseth, Ian. "'A Melancholy Tale': Rhetoric, Fiction, and Passion in *The Coquette.*" *Studies in the Novel* 33.2 (Summer 2001): 125–59.

Fizer, Irene. "Signing as Republican Daughters: The Letters of Eliza Southgate and *The Coquette.*" *Eighteenth Century: Theory and Interpretation* 34.3 (1993): 243–63.

Flanders, Jane. "The Fallen Woman in Fiction." In *Feminist Visions: Toward a Transformation of the Liberal Arts Curriculum,* edited by Diane Fowlkes and Charlotte S. McClure, 97–109. Tuscaloosa: University of Alabama Press, 1984.

Fleenor, Julianne, ed. *The Female Gothic.* Montreal: Eden Press, 1983.

Fleischman, Fritz. "Concealed Lessons: Foster's Coquette and Brockdon Brown's 'Lessons on Concealment.'" In *Early America Re-explored: New Readings in Colonial, Early National, and Antebellum Culture,* edited by Klaus H. Schmidt and Fritz Fleischman, 309–48. New York: Petersburg, 2000.

Fleischner, Jennifer. "Hawthorne and the Politics of Slavery." *Studies in the Novel* 23.1 (1990): 514–33.

———. "Mastering Slavery." *Journal of the Early Republic* 18.4 (Winter 1998): 748–50.

Fliegelman, Jay. *Prodigals and Pilgrims: The American Revolution against Patriarchy.* New York: Cambridge University Press, 1982.

Flint, Christopher. *Family Fictions: Narrative and Domestic Relations in Britain, 1668–1798.* Stanford, Calif.: Stanford University Press, 1998.

Flynn, Christopher. "Nationalism, Commerce, and Imperial Anxiety in Defoe's Later Works." *Rocky Mountain Review of Language and Literature* 54.2 (2000): 11–24.

Forcey, Blythe. "*Charlotte Temple* and the End of Epistolarity." *American Literature: A Journal of Literary History, Criticism, and Bibliography* 63.2 (June 1991): 225–41.

Ford, Douglas. "Inscribing the 'Impartial Observer' in Sedgwick's *Hope Leslie.*" *Legacy* 14 (1997): 81–92.

Foreman, P. Gabrielle. "The Spoken and the Silenced in *Incidents in the Life of a Slave Girl* and *Our Nig.*" *Callaloo* 13.2 (Spring 1990): 313–24.

Foreman, P. Gabrielle, and Reginald H. Pitts. Introduction to *Our Nig* by Harriet Wilson, xxxv–xlx. New York: Penguin, 2005.

Foster, Hannah. *The Coquette.* In *"The Power of Sympathy"* [by William Hill Brown] *and "The Coquette,"* edited by William S. Osborne. New Haven, Conn.: College and University Press, 1970.

Fox-Genovese, Elizabeth. " 'To Weave It into the Literature of the Country': Epic and the Fictions of African American." In *Poetics of the Americas: Race, Founding, and Textuality,* edited by Bainard Cowan and Jefferson Humphries, 31 – 45. Baton Rouge: Louisiana State University Press, 1997.

Frank, John G. "The Wieland Family in Charles Brockden Brown's *Wieland.*" *Monatshefte* 42 (1950): 347 – 53.

Franklin, H. Bruce. "From Empire to Empire: Billy Budd, Sailor." In *Herman Melville: Reassessments,* edited by A. Robert Lee, 199 – 216. London: Vision Press, 1984.

Freeman, Barbara Claire. *The Feminine Sublime: Gender and Excess in Women's Fiction.* Berkeley: University of California Press, 1995.

Fryer, Judith. *The Faces of Eve: Women in the Nineteenth Century American Novel.* New York: Oxford University Press, 1976.

Fulton, Gordon. "Why Look at Clarissa?" *Eighteenth Century Life* 20.2 (May 1996): 20 – 32.

Furniss, Tom. *Edmund Burke's Aesthetic Ideology: Language, Gender, and Political Economy in Revolution.* New York: Cambridge University Press, 1993.

Fussell, Edwin Sill. "*Wieland:* A Literary and Historical Reading." *Early American Literature* 18 (1983 – 84): 171 – 86.

Fussell, Paul, Jr. *Theory of Prosody in Eighteenth-Century England.* New London, Conn.: Connecticut College, 1954.

Gaines, Kevin. "Black Americans' Racial Uplift Ideology as 'Civilizing Mission': Pauline E. Hopkins on Race and Imperialism." In *Cultures of United States Imperialism,* edited by Amy Kaplan and Donald E. Pease, 433 – 55. Durham, N.C.: Duke University Press, 1993.

———. *Uplifting the Race: Black Leadership, Politics, and Culture in the Twentieth Century.* Chapel Hill: University of North Carolina Press, 1996.

Gallagher, Catherine. "George Eliot and *Daniel Deronda:* The Prostitute and the Jewish Question." In *Sex, Politics, and Science in the Nineteenth-Century Novel,* edited by Ruth Bernard Yeazell, 39 – 62. Baltimore: Johns Hopkins University Press, 1986.

———. *Nobody's Story: The Vanishing Acts of Women Writers in the Marketplace, 1670 – 1820.* Berkeley: University of California Press, 1995.

Gardiner, Judith Kegan. "The First English Novel: Aphra Behn's Love Letters, the Canon, and Women's Tastes." *Tulsa Studies in Women's Literature* 8.2 (Autumn 1989): 204.

Gardner, Eric. " 'This Attempt of Their Sister': Harriet Wilson's *Our Nig* from Printer to Readers." *New England Quarterly* 66.2 (June 1993): 226 – 246.

Gardner, Jared. "The Literary Museum and the Unsettling of the Early American Novel." *English Literary History* 67.3 (2000): 743 – 71.

Garrett, Peter K. *Gothic Reflections: Narrative Force in Nineteenth-Century Fiction.* Ithaca, N.Y.: Cornell University Press, 2003.

Garvey, Gregory T. "Risking Reprisal: Catharine Sedgwick's *Hope Leslie* and the Legitimation of Public Action by Women." *American Transcendental Quarterly* 8.4 (December 1994): 287 – 98.

Gates, Henry Louis. Introduction to *Our Nig, or, Sketches from the Life of Free Black,* by Harriet Wilson. xi – lix. New York: Vintage Books, 1983.

————. *The Signifying Monkey: A Theory of African-American Literary Criticism.* New York: Oxford University Press, 1988.

————, ed. *"Race," Writing, and Difference.* Chicago: University of Chicago Press, 1986.

Gates, Sarah. "'A Difference of Native Language': Gender, Genre, and Realism in *Daniel Deronda*." *ELH* 68.3 (2001): 699–724.

Gautier, Gary. "Slavery and the Fashioning of Race in *Oroonoko, Robinson Crusoe,* and Equiano's *Life*." *Eighteenth Century: Theory and Interpretation* 42.2 (summer 2001): 161–79.

Gerzina, Gretchen. "Mobility in Chains: Freedom of Movement in the Early Black Atlantic." *South Atlantic Quarterly* 100.1 (2001): 41–59.

Gibbon, Edward. *The Decline and Fall of the Roman Empire.* Book 1. London, 1846.

Gillis, Christina Marsden. *The Paradox of Privacy: Epistolary Form in "Clarissa."* Gainesville: University of Florida Press, 1984.

Gillman, Susan. "Pauline Hopkins and the Occult: African-American Revisions of Nineteenth-Century Sciences." *American Literary History* 8.1 (Spring 1996): 57–82.

Gilmore, Michael T. "Calvinism and Gothicism: The Example of Brown's *Wieland*." *Studies in the Novel* 9.2 (Summer 1977): 107–18.

————. "Hawthorne and the Making of the Middle Class." In *Discovering Difference,* edited by Christopher Lohmann, 88–104. Bloomington: Indiana University Press, 1993.

Gilroy, Paul. *Black Atlantic: Modernity and Double Consciousness.* Cambridge, Mass.: Harvard University Press, 1993.

Goddu, Teresa A. *Gothic America: Narrative, History, and Nation.* New York: Columbia University Press, 1997.

Goldberg, David Theo. *The Racial State.* Malden, Mass.: Blackwell Publishers, 2002.

Goldsmith, Meredith. "Shopping to Pass, Passing to Shop: Bodily Self-Fashioning in the Fiction of Nella Larsen." In *Recovering the Black Female Body: Self-Representations by African American Women,* edited by Michael Bennett and Vanessa D. Dickerson, 97–120. New Brunswick, N.J.: Rutgers University Press, 2001.

Gonda, Caroline. *Reading the Daughter's Fictions, 1709–1834: Novels and Society from Manley to Edgeworth.* New York: Cambridge University Press, 1996.

Goode, John. "'The Affections Clad with Knowledge': Woman's Duty and the Public Life." In *George Eliot: Critical Assessments,* vol. 4, edited by Stuart Hutchinson. East Sussex, England: Helm Information, 1996.

Gordon, Scott Paul. "'Disinterested Selves': *Clarissa* and the Tactics of Sentiment." *English Literary History* 64.2 (Summer 1997): 473–503.

Goreau, Angeline. *Reconstructing Aphra Behn: A Social Biography of Aphra Behn.* New York: Oxford University Press, 1980.

Gossett, Suzanne, and Barbara Ann Bardes. "Women and Political Power in the Republic: Two Early American Novels." *Legacy: A Journal of American Women Writers* 2.2 (1985): 13–30.

Gould, Philip B. *Covenant and Republic: Historical Romance and the Politics of Puritanism.* New York: Cambridge University Press, 1996.

————. "Free Carpenter, Venture Capitalist: Reading the Lives of the Early Black Atlantic." *American Literary History* 12.4 (2000): 659–85.

Gray, Jeffrey. "Essence and the Mulatto Traveler: Europe as Embodiment in Nella Larsen's *Quicksand.*" *Novel: A Forum on Fiction* 27.3 (Spring 1994): 257–70.

Greeson, Jennifer Rae. "The 'Mysteries and Miseries' of North Carolina: New York City, Urban Gothic Fiction and *Incidents in the Life of a Slave Girl.*" *American Literature* 73.2 (June 2001): 277–309.

Greusser, John. "Taking Liberties: Pauline Hopkins's Recasting of the Creole Rebellion." In *The Unruly Voice: Rediscovering Pauline Hopkins,* edited by John Cullen Gruesser, 98–118. Urbana: University of Illinois Press, 1996.

Gunning, Sandra. *Race, Rape, and Lynching: The Red Record of American Literature, 1890–1912.* New York: Oxford University Press, 1996.

Gussman, Deborah. "Inalienable Rights: Fictions of Political Identity in *Hobomok* and *The Scarlet Letter.*" *College Literature* 22.2 (June 1995): 58–80.

Hackett, Robin. *Sapphic Primitivism: Productions of Race, Class and Sexuality in Key Works of Modern Fiction.* New Brunswick, N.J.: Rutgers University Press, 2004.

Haight, Gordon S. *George Eliot: A Biography.* London: Clarendon Press, 1968.

Hall, Michael G., Lawrence H. Leder, and Michael G. Kammen, eds. *The Glorious Revolution in America: Documents on the Colonial Crisis of 1689.* Chapel Hill: Published for the Institute of Early American History and Culture and Williamsburg, Va., by the University of North Carolina Press, 1964.

Haller, Evelyn. "The Anti-Madonna in the Work and Thought of Virginia Woolf." In *Virginia Woolf: Centennial Essays,* edited by Elaine K. Finsberg and Laura Moss Gottlieb. Troy, N.Y.: Whitston, 1983.

Haller, William, ed. *Tracts on Liberty in the Puritan Revolution, 1638–1647.* Volume 3. New York: Columbia University Press, 1933.

Hamilton, Cynthia S. "Dislocation, Violence, and the Language of Sentiment." In *Black Imagination and Middle Passage,* edited by Maria Diedrich, Henry Louis Gates Jr., and Carl Pedersen, 103–16. New York: Oxford University Press, 1999.

Hamilton, Kristie. "An Assault on the Will: Republican Virtue and the City in Hannah Webster Foster's *The Coquette.*" *Early American Literature* 24.2 (1989): 135–51.

Hanlon, Christopher. "The Old Race Are All Gone': Transatlantic Bloodlines and Emerson's English Traits." Forthcoming in *American Literary History* 19.4.

Hansen, Elaine Tuttle. "Ambiguity and the Narrator in *The Scarlet Letter.*" *Journal of Narrative Technique* 5.3 (September 1975): 147–63.

Hansen, Klaus P. "The Sentimental Novel and its Feminist Critique." *Early American Literature* 26.1 (1991): 39–54.

Hardt, Michael, and Antonio Negri. *Empire.* Cambridge, Mass.: Harvard University Press, 2000.

Harrington, James. *The Commonwealth of Oceana.* Edited by J. G. A. Pocock. New York: Cambridge University Press, 1992.

Harris, Marla. "Not Black and/or White: Reading Racial Difference in Heliodorus's *Ethiopica* and Pauline Hopkins's *Of One Blood.*" *African American Review* 35.3 (Fall 2001): 375–90.

Harris, Sharon. "Hannah Webster Foster's *The Coquette.*" In *Redefining the Political Novel: American Women Writers, 1797–1901,* edited by Sharon Harris, 1–22. Knoxville: University of Tennessee Press, 1995.

Harris, Susan K. "The Limits of Authority: Catharine Maria Sedgwick and the Politics of Resistance." In *Catharine Maria Sedgwick: Critical Perspectives*, edited by Lucinda L. Damon-Back and Victoria Clements, 272–85. Boston: Northeastern University Press, 2003.

Hartman, Saidiya V. *Scenes of Subjection: Terror, Slavery, and Self-Making in Nineteenth-Century America*. New York: Oxford University Press, 1997.

Harvey, A. D. "*Clarissa* and the Puritan Tradition." *Essays in Criticism: A Quarterly Journal of Literary Criticism* 28 (1978): 38–51.

Haviland, Beverly. "Passing from Paranoia to Plagiarism: The Abject Authorship of Nella Larsen." *Modern Fiction Studies* 43.2 (Summer 1997): 295–318.

Haviland, Thomas P. "Preciosité Crosses the Atlantic." *PMLA* 59.1 (March 1944): 131–41.

Hawthorne, Nathaniel. "Mrs. Hutchinson." In the *Centenary Edition of the Works of Nathaniel Hawthorne*, Volume 23, edited by Thomas Woodson et al., 66–73. Columbus: Ohio State University Press, 1994.

———. *The Scarlet Letter*. A Norton Critical Edition. New York: W.W. Norton and Company, 1988 [1961].

Haynie, Aeron. "The Illegitimacy of the Colonial Entrepreneur in George Eliot's *Felix Holt*." *Victorian Newsletter* 100 (Fall 2001): 26–31.

Hazlitt, William. *Lectures on the Comic Writer*. London: John Templeman, 1841.

Hedges, William. "Charles Brockden Brown and the Culture of Contradictions." *Early American Literature* 9.2 (September 1974): 107–42.

Hegel, Georg W. F. *The Philosophy of Hegel*. Edited by Carl J. Friedrich. New York: Random House, 1953.

———. *The Philosophy of History*. Translated by John Sibree. New York: Dover Press, 1956. [1899].

Helgerson, Richard. *Forms of Nationhood: The Elizabethan Writing of England*. Chicago: University of Chicago Press, 1992.

Heller, Deborah. "Jews and Women in George Eliot's *Daniel Deronda*." In *Jewish Presences in English Literature*, edited by Derek Cohen and Deborah Heller, 76–95. Montreal: McGill Queen's University Press, 1990.

Henderson, Stephen. "Introduction: The Forms of Things Unknown." In *Understanding the New Black Poetry, Black Speech, and Black Music as Poetic References*. New York: William Morrow, 1973.

Henry, Nancy. "Ante-Anti-Semitism: George Eliot's Impressions of Theophrastus Such." In *Victorian Identities: Social and Cultural Formations in Nineteenth-Century Literature*, edited by Ruth Robbins and Julian Wolfreys, 65–80. New York: St. Martin's Press, 1996.

———. *George Eliot and the British Empire*. Cambridge: Cambridge University Press, 2002.

Hentzi, Gary. "Holes in the Heart: *Moll Flanders, Roxana,* and 'Agreeable Crime.'" *boundary 2* 18.1 (1991): 174–200.

Herbert, T. Walter. "Response to Jamie Barlowe." *American Literary History* 9.2 (Summer 1997): 230–32.

Higham, John. "Indian Princess and Roman Goddess." *Proceedings of the American Antiquarian Society* 100.1 (1990): 45–79.

Higonnet, Margaret R. "Comparative Reading: Catharine M. Sedgwick's *Hope Leslie*." *Legacy* 15 (1998): 17–22.

Hill, Bridget, ed. *The First English Feminist: Reflections upon Marriage and Other Writings*. New York: St. Martin's Press, 1986.

Hill, Christopher. *Puritanism and Revolution*. New York: Schocken, 1958.

Hilliard, Raymond F. "Clarissa and Ritual Cannibalism." *PMLA* 105.5 (October 1990): 1083–97.

Hinds, Elizabeth Jane Wall. "Charles Brockden Brown's Revenge Tragedy: *Edgar Huntly* and the Uses of Property." *Early American Literature* 30.1 (1995): 51–70.

———. *Private Property: Charles Brockden Brown's Gendered Economics of Virtue*. Newark: University of Delaware Press, 1997.

———. "The Spirit of Trade: Olaudah Equiano's Conversion, Legalism, and the Merchant's Life." *African American Review* 32.4 (1998): 635–47.

Hinton, Laura. "The Heroine's Subjection: Clarissa, Sadomasochism, and Natural Law." *Eighteenth-Century Studies* 32.2 (1999): 293–308.

Hirsch, Pam. "Women and Jews in *Daniel Deronda*." *George Eliot Review: Journal of the George Eliot Fellowship* 25 (1994): 45–50.

Hodges, Elizabeth Perry. "The Letter of the Law: Reading Hawthorne and the Law of Adultery." In *Law and Literature Perspectives*, edited by Bruce L. Rockwood and Robert Kevelson, 133–68. New York: Peter Lang, 1996.

Hoegberg, David E. "Caesar's Toils: Allusion and Rebellion in *Oroonoko*." *Eighteenth Century Fiction* 7.3 (April 1995): 239–58.

Hogle, Jerrold. *The Cambridge Companion to Gothic Fiction*. New York: Cambridge University Press, 2002.

Holloway, Karla F. C. "Economies of Space: Markets and Marketability in *Our Nig* and *Iola Leroy*." In *The (Other) American Traditions: Nineteenth-Century Women Writers*, edited by Joyce W. Warren, 126–42. New Brunswick, N.J.: Rutgers University Press, 1993.

Holmesland, Oddvar. "Aphra Behn's *Oroonoko*: Cultural Dialectics and the Novel." *English Literary History* 68 (2001): 57–79.

Holstun, James, ed. *Pamphlet Wars: Prose in the English Revolution*. London: Frank Case, 1992.

Hopkins, Pauline. *Contending Forces*. New York: Oxford University Press, 1988.

———. *Of One Blood. Or, the Hidden Self*. In *The Magazine Novels*. New York: Schomburg Library, 1988.

Horsman, Reginald. *Race and Manifest Destiny: The Origins of American Anglo-Saxonism*. Cambridge, Mass.: Harvard University Press, 1981.

Horvitz, Deborah. "Hysteria and Trauma in Pauline Hopkins' *Of One Blood; or, The Hidden Self*." *African American Review* 33.2 (Summer 1999): 245–60.

Hostetler, Ann E. "The Aesthetics of Race and Gender in Nella Larsen's *Quicksand*." *PMLA* 105.1 (1990): 35–46.

Houston, Beverle. "Usurpation and Dismemberment: Oedipal Tyranny in *Oroonoko*." *Literature and Psychology* 32.1 (1986): 30–36.

Howells, William Dean. *Heroines of Fiction*. New York: Harper and Brothers, 1901.

Hsu, Hsuan L. "Democratic Expansion in *Memoirs of Carwin*." *Early American Literature* 35.2 (2000): 137–56.

Hudson, Nicholas. "From 'Nation' to 'Race.'" *Eighteenth-Century Studies* 34.4 (2001): 559–76.

Hume, David. *David Hume: Essays, Moral, Political, and Literary.* Edited by Eugene F. Miller. Indianapolis, Ind.: Liberty Classics, 1985.

———. *The History of England.* Volumes 1–6. London: T. Cadell, 1841.

Hummel, William E. "'The Gift of My Father's Bounty': Patriarchal Patronization in *Moll Flanders* and *Roxana*." *Rocky Mountain Review of Language and Literature* 48.2 (1994): 119–41.

Hunter, J. Paul. *Before Novels: The Cultural Contexts of Eighteenth-Century Fiction.* New York: W. W. Norton, 1990.

Hurd, Richard. *Letters on Chivalry and Romance.* Edited by Hoyt Trowbridge. Los Angeles: William Andrews Clark Memorial Library, 1963. Publication No. 101–102 [orig. 1762], Letter I, 2.

Hutchinson, George. *In Search of Nella Larsen: A Biography of the Color Line.* Cambridge, Mass.: Belknap Press of Harvard University Press, 2006.

———. "Nella Larsen and the Veil of Race." *American Literary History* 9.2 (Summer 1997): 329–49.

———. "*Quicksand* and the Racial Labyrinth." *Soundings: An Interdisciplinary Journal* 80.4 (Winter 1997): 543–71.

———. "Subject to Disappearance: Interracial Identity in Nella Larsen's *Quicksand*." In *Temples for Tomorrow: Looking Back at the Harlem Renaissance,* edited by Genevieve Fabre and Michel Feith, 177–92. Bloomington: Indiana University Press, 2001.

Hutchinson, Stuart, ed. *George Eliot: Critical Assessments.* East Sussex, England: Helm, 1996.

Hutner, Gordon. *Secrets and Sympathy: Forms of Disclosure in Hawthorne's Novels.* Athens: University of Georgia Press, 1988.

Ingrassia, Catherine. *Authorship, Commerce, and Gender in Early Eighteenth-Century England: A Culture of Paper Credit.* Cambridge: Cambridge University Press, 1998.

Insko, Jeffrey. "Anachronistic Imaginings: *Hope Leslie*'s Challenge to Historicism." *American Literary History* 16.2 (Summer 2004): 179–207.

Irwin, John T. *American Hieroglyphics: The Symbol of the Egyptian Hieroglyphic in the American Renaissance.* Baltimore: Johns Hopkins University Press, 1983.

Ito, Akiyo. "Olaudah Equiano and the New York Artisans: The First American Edition of the *Interesting Narrative of the Life of Olaudah Equiano*." *Early American Literature* 32.1 (1997): 82–101.

Ives, C. B. "*Billy Budd* and the Articles of War." *American Literature: A Journal of Literary History, Criticism, and Bibliography* 34.1 (March 1962): 31–39.

Iwanisziw, Susan B. "Behn's Novel Investment in *Oroonoko*: Kingship, Slavery, and Tobacco in English Colonialism." *South Atlantic Review* 63.2 (1998): 75–98.

Jackson, Tommie L. "The Sado-Masochistic Dynamic in Harriet Jacobs' *Incidents in the Life of a Slave Girl,* as Illuminated by Sartre's *Being and Nothingness* and Chancer's *Sadomasochism in Everyday Life*." *Official Journal of the Southern Conference on Afro-American Studies* 20.2 (Fall 2001): 57–67.

Jacobs, Harriet. *Incidents in the Life of a Slave Girl, Written By Herself.* Edited by Jean Fagan Yellin. Cambridge: Harvard University Press, 1987.

Japtok, Martin. "Pauline Hopkins's *Of One Blood,* Africa, and the 'Darwinist Trap.'" *African American Review* 36.3 (Fall 2002): 403–15.

Jardine, Alice A. *Gynesis: Configurations of Woman and Modernity*. Ithaca, N.Y.: Cornell University Press, 1985.

Jefferson, Thomas. *The Complete Jefferson*, assembled and arranged by Saul K. Padover. Freeport, N.Y.: Books for Libraries Press, 1969 [1943].

Jehlen, Myra. *American Incarnation: The Individual, the Nation, and the Continent*. Cambridge, Mass.: Harvard University Press, 1986.

———. "Archimedes and the Paradox of Feminist Criticism." In *Feminist Theory: A Critique of Ideology*, edited by Nannerl O. Keohane, Michelle Rosaldo, and Barbara C. Gelpi, 189–216. Chicago: University of Chicago Press, 1982.

———. "The Novel and the Middle Class in America." In *Ideology and Classic American Literature*, edited by Sacvan Bercovitch and Myra Jehlen, 125–44. Cambridge: Cambridge University Press, 1986.

Johnson, Barbara. "Melville's Fist: The Execution of Billy Budd." *Studies in Romanticism* 18 (1979): 567–99.

———. "The Quicksands of the Self: Nella Larsen and Heinx Kohut." In *Female Subjects in Black and White: Race, Psychoanalysis, Feminism*, edited by Elizabeth Abel, Barbara Christian, and Helene Moglen, 252–265. Berkeley: University of California Press, 1997.

Johnson, Charles S. "The Rise of the Negro Magazine." *Journal of Negro History* 13.1 (January 1928): 7–21.

Johnson, Claudia Durst. "Impotence and Omnipotence in *The Scarlet Letter*." *New England Quarterly* 66.4 (1993): 594–612.

Johnson, Claudia L. "F. R. Leavis: The 'Great Tradition' of the English Novel and the Jewish Part." *Nineteenth Century Literature* 56.2 (2001): 199–227.

Johnson, Ronna C. "Said But Not Spoken: Elision and the Representation of Rape, Race, and Gender in Harriet E. Wilson's *Our Nig*." In *Speaking the Other Self: American Women Writers*, edited by Jeanne Campbell Reesman, 96–116. Athens: University of Georgia Press, 1997.

Johnson, Samuel. Preface to *Dictionary of the English Language*. New York: AMS Press, 1967.

Jones, Jill. "The Disappearing 'I' in *Our Nig*." *Legacy: A Journal of American Women Writers* 13.1 (1996): 38–53.

Jordan, Cynthia. *Second Stories: The Politics of Language, Form, and Gender in Early American Fictions*. Chapel Hill: University of North Carolina Press, 1989.

Jordan, Winthrop D. *White Over Black: American Attitudes Towards the Negro, 1550–1812*. Chapel Hill: University of North Carolina, 1968.

Judd, Catherine A. "Male Pseudonyms and Female Authority in Victorian England." In *Literature in the Marketplace: Nineteenth-Century British Publishing and Reading Practices*, edited by John O. Jordon and Robert L. Paten, 250–68. Cambridge: Cambridge University Press, 1995.

Kamrath, Mark. "*Eyes Wide Shut* and the Cultural Poetics of Eighteenth-Century American Periodical Literature." *Early American Literature* 37.3 (2002): 497–536.

Kane, Patricia. "The Fallen Woman as Free-Thinker in *The French Lieutenant's Woman* and *The Scarlet Letter*." *Notes on Contemporary Literature* 2.1 (January 1972): 8–10.

Kaplan, Amy. *The Anarchy of Empire in the Making of U.S. Culture*. Cambridge, Mass.: Harvard University Press, 2002.

Kaplan, Carla. "Undesirable Desire: Citizenship and Romance in Modern American Fiction." *Modern Fiction Studies* 43.1 (Spring 1997): 144–69.

Karcher, Carolyn. Introduction to *Hope Leslie, or Early Times in the Massachusetts,* by Catharine Maria Sedgwick. New York: Penguin, 1998.

———. *Shadow over the Promised Land: Slavery, Race, and Violence in Melville's America.* Baton Rouge: Louisiana State University Press, 1980.

Karafilas, Maria. "Catharine Maria Sedgwick's *Hope Leslie:* The Crisis between Ethical Political Action and the U.S. Literary Nationalism in the New Republic." *American Transcendental Quarterly* 12.4 (December 1998): 327–44.

Kassanoff, Jennie A. "'Fate Has Linked Us Together': Blood, Gender, and the Politics of Representation in Pauline Hopkins's *Of One Blood.*" In *The Unruly Voice: Rediscovering Pauline Hopkins,* edited by John Cullen Gruesser, 158–81. Urbana: University of Illinois Press, 1996.

Kaul, Suvir. "Reading Literary Symptoms: Colonial Pathology and the Oroonoko Fictions of Behn, Southerne, and Hawkesworth." *Eighteenth-Century Life* 18.3 (1994): 80–96.

Kazanjian, David. "Charles Brockden Brown's Biloquial Nation: National Culture and White Settler Colonialism in *Memoirs of Carwin the Biloquist.*" *American Literature: A Journal of Literary History, Criticism, and Bibliography* 73.3 (September 2001): 459–96.

———. "Mercantile Exchanges, Mercantile Enclosures: Racial Capitalism in the Black Mariner Narratives of Venture Smith and John Jea." *CR: The New Centennial Review* 3.1 (2003): 147–48.

Keating, AnaLouise. "Interrogating 'Whiteness,' (De)Constructing 'Race.'" *College English* 57.8 (December 1995): 901–18.

Kehler, Dorothea. "Hawthorne and Shakespeare." *American Transcendental Quarterly* 22 (1974): 104–5.

Kelleter, Frank. "Ethnic Self-Dramatization and Technologies of Travel in *The Interesting Narrative of the Life of Olaudah Equiano.*" *Early American Literature* 39.1 (2004): 67–82.

Kelley, Mary. "Negotiating a Self: The Autobiography and Journals of Catharine Maria Sedgwick." *New England Quarterly* 66 (1993): 366–98.

Kelley, Robin D. G. "How the West Was One: The African Diaspora and the Re-Mapping of U.S. History." In *Rethinking American History in a Global Age,* edited by Thomas Bender, 123–47. Berkeley: University of California Press, 2002.

Kibbie, Ann Louise. "Monstrous Generation: The Birth of Capital in Defoe's *Moll Flanders* and *Roxana.*" *PMLA* 110.5 (1995): 1023–34.

Kiernan, V. G. *Lords of Human Kind: Black Man, Yellow Man, and White Man in an Age of Empire.* Boston: Little, Brown, 1969.

Kietzman, Mary Jo. "Defoe Masters the Serial Subject." *ELH* 66.3 (1999): 677–705.

Kilcup, Karen. "'Ourself behind Ourself, Concealed—': The Homoerotics of Reading in *The Scarlet Letter.*" *Emerson Society Quarterly* 42.1 (1996): 1–28.

Kilgour, Maggie. *The Rise of the Gothic Novel.* New York: Routledge, 1995.

Kimball, Arthur. *Rational Fictions: A Study of Charles Brockden Brown.* McMinnville, Oregon: Linfield Research Institute, 1968.

King, Debra Walker. "Harriet Wilson's *Our Nig*: The Demystification of Sentiment." In *Recovered Writers/Recovered Texts,* edited by Dolan Hubbard, 31–45. Knoxville: University of Tennessee Press, 1997.

Kirkham, E. Bruce. "A Note on *Wieland*." *American Notes and Queries* 5.6 (February 1967): 86–87.

Kitson, Peter. "'Bales of Living Anguish': Representations of Race and the Slave in Romantic Writing." *English Literary History* 67.2 (2000): 515–37.

Kliger, Samuel. *The Goths in England: A Study of Seventeenth and Eighteenth Century Thought.* Cambridge, Mass.: Harvard University Press, 1952.

Knadler, Stephen. *The Fugitive Race: Minority Writers Resisting Whiteness.* Jackson: University of Mississippi Press, 2002.

Knight, Charles A. "The Function of Wills in Richardson's *Clarissa*." *Texas Studies in Literature and Language* 11 (1969): 1183–90.

Knoepflmacher, U. C. *George Eliot's Early Novels: The Limits of Realism.* Berkeley: University of California Press, 1968.

Knox, Robert. *The Races of Men.* Philadelphia: Lea and Blanchard, 1850.

Korobkin, Laura Hanft. "Murder by Madman: Criminal Responsibility, Law, and Judgment in *Wieland*." *American Literature: A Journal of Literary History, Criticism, and Bibliography* 72.4 (December 2000): 721–50.

———. "The Scarlet Letter of the Law: Hawthorne and Criminal Justice." *Novel: A Forum on Fiction* 30.2 (Winter 1997): 193–217.

Kramnick, Isaac. *The Rage of Edmund Burke: A Portrait of an Ambivalent Conservative.* New York: Basic Books, 1977.

Kupperman, Karen Ordahl. *Providence Island, 1630–1641.* New York: Cambridge University Press, 1993.

Kvande, Marta. "The Outsider Narrator in Eliza Haywood's Political Novels." *Studies in English Literature* 43.3 (Summer 2003): 625–43.

Laden, Marie-Paul. *Self-Imitation in the Eighteenth-Century Novel.* Princeton, N.J.: Princeton University Press, 1987.

Laity, Cassandra. "H. D. and A. C. Swinburne: Decadence and Sapphic Modernism." In *Lesbian Texts and Contexts*, edited by Karla Jay and Joanne Glasgow, 217–40. New York: New York University Press, 1990.

Lang, Amy Schrager. *Prophetic Woman: Anne Hutchinson and the Problem of Dissent in the Literature of New England.* Berkeley: University of California Press, 1987.

Lanser, Susan S. "Befriending the Body: Female Intimacies as Class Acts." *Eighteenth-Century Studies* 32.2 (1998–99): 180.

Larsen, Nella. *Quicksand* and *Passing.* New Brunswick, N.J.: Rutgers University Press, 1986.

———. *An Intimation of Things Distant: The Collected Fiction of Nella Larsen*, edited by Charles R. Larson. New York: Anchor Books, 1992.

Latta, Kimberly S. "The Mistress of the Marriage Market: Gender and Economic Ideology in Defoe's *Review*." *English Literary History* 69 (2002): 359–83.

Laurence, Patricia. *Lily Briscoe's Chinese Eyes: Bloomsbury, Modernism, and China.* Columbia: University of South Carolina Press, 2003.

Lauter, Paul, et al., eds. *Heath Anthology of American Literature*, vol. 1. Third edition. New York: Houghton Mifflin, 1998.

Lawrence, Douglas. "Discursive Limits: Narrative and Judgment in *Billy Budd*." *Mosaic: A Journal for the Interdisciplinary Study of Literature* 27.4 (December 1994): 141–61.

Leask, Nigel. "Irish Republicans and Gothic Eleutherarchs: Pacific Utopias in the Writings of Theobold Wolfe Tone and Charles Brockden Brown." *Huntington Library Quarterly* 63.3 (2000): 247–67.

Leder, Lawrence H., ed. *Loyalist Historians*. New York: Harper and Row, 1973.

———. *Historians of Nature and Man's Nature: Early Nationalist Historians*. New York: Harper and Row, 1973.

LePore, Jill. "*The Scarlet Letter/Pocahontas*." *American Historical Review* 101.4 (October 1996): 1166–68.

LeRoy-Frazier, Jill. "'Reader, My Story Ends With Freedom': Literacy, Authorship, and Gender in Harriet Jacobs' *Incidents in the Life of a Slave Girl*." *Obsidian III* 5.1 (Spring/Summer 2004): 152–61.

Lesjak, Carolyn. "Labours of a Modern Storyteller: George Eliot and the Cultural Project of 'Nationhood' in *Daniel Deronda*." In *Victorian Identities: Social and Cultural Formation in Nineteenth-Century Literature*, edited by Ruth Robbings, Julian Wolfreys, and James R. Kinkaid, 25–42. New York: St. Martin's Press, 1996.

———. *Working Fictions: A Genealogy of the Victorian Novel*. Durham, N.C.: Duke University Press, 2006.

Leveen, Lois. "Dwelling in the House of Oppression: The Spatial, Racial, and Textual Dynamics of Harriet Wilson's *Our Nig*." *African American Review* 35.4 (2001): 561–80.

Leverenz, David. "Mrs. Hawthorne's Headache: Reading *The Scarlet Letter*." *Nineteenth Century Literature* 37.4 (1983): 552–75.

Levine, Gary Martin. *Merchant of Modernism: The Economic Jew in Anglo-American Literature, 1865–1939*. New York: Routledge, 2003.

Levine, Robert S. *Conspiracy and Romance: Studies in Brockden Brown, Cooper, Hawthorne, and Melville*. New York: Cambridge University Press, 1989.

Levy, Heather. "These Ghost Figures of Distorted Passion." *Modern Fiction Studies* 50.1 (Spring 2004): 31–57.

Lewis, Matthew G. *Journal of a West India Proprietor, Kept During a Residence in the Island of Jamaica*. New York: Negro Universities Press, 1969 [1834].

———. *The Monk*. New York: Grove Press, 1952.

Lewis, Vashti Crutcher. "Nella Larsen's Use of the Near-White Female in *Quicksand* and *Passing*." In *Perspectives of Black Popular Culture*, edited by Harry B. Shaw, 36–45. Bowling Green, Ohio: Bowling Green State University Popular Press, 1990.

———. "Worldview and the Use of the Near-White Heroine in Pauline Hopkins's *Contending Forces*." *Journal of Black Studies* 28.5 (May 1998): 616–27.

Lindgren, Margaret. "Harriet Jacobs, Harriet Wilson and the Redoubled Voice in Black Autobiography." *Obsidian II* 8.1 (1993): 18–38.

Linebaugh, Peter, and Marcus Rediker. *The Many-Headed Hydra: Sailors, Slaves, Commoners, and the Hidden History of the Revolutionary Atlantic*. Boston: Beacon Press, 2000.

Linehan, Katherine Bailey. "Mixed Politics: The Critique of Imperialism in *Daniel Deronda*." *Texas Studies in Literature and Language* 34.3 (Fall 1992): 323–46.

Livy. *The Early History of Rome*. Volume I. Translated by Audrey de Sélincourt. Introduction by R. M. Ogilvie. New York: Penguin, 2002.

London, Philip W. "The Military Necessity: *Billy Budd* and Vigny." *Comparative Literature* 4.2 (Spring 1962): 174–86.

Lovejoy, Paul E. "Autobiography and Memory: Gustavus Vassa, alias Olaudah Equiano, the African." *Slavery and Abolition* 27.3 (December 2006): 317–47.

Lovell, Thomas B. "By Dint of Labor and Economy: Harriet Jacobs, Harriet Wilson, and the Salutary View of Wage Labor." *Arizona Quarterly* 52.3 (1996): 1–32.

Lovesey, Oliver. "The Other Woman in *Daniel Deronda*." *Studies in the Novel* 30.4 (1998): 505–20.

Luedtke, Luther S. *Nathaniel Hawthorne and the Romance of the Orient*. Bloomington: University of Indiana Press, 1989.

Lundblad, Jane. *Nathaniel Hawthorne and the Tradition of Gothic Romance*. New York: Haskell House, 1964.

Lynch, Deirdre Shauna. *The Economy of Character: Novels, Market Culture, and the Business of Inner Meaning*. Chicago: University of Chicago Press, 1998.

Lynch, Deirdre Shauna, and William B. Warner, eds. *Cultural Institutions of the Novel*. Durham, N.C.: Duke University Press, 1996.

Lynch, James V. "The Limits of Revolutionary Radicalism: Thomas Paine and Slavery." *Pennsylvania Magazine of History and Biography* 123 (July 1999): 177–200.

Lyon, Janet. *Manifestoes: Provocations of the Modern*. Ithaca, N.Y.: Cornell University Press, 1999.

Lyttle, David. "The Case against Carwin." *Nineteenth Century Fiction* 26.3 (December 1971): 257–69.

Macaulay, Catharine. *The History of England from the Accession of James I to the Elevation of the House of Hanover*. London: Edward and Charles Dilly, 1763–83.

MacCannell, Juliet Flower. *The Regime of the Brother: After the Patriarchy*. New York: Routledge, 1991.

MacGillivray, Royce. *Restoration Historians and the English Civil War*. The Hague: M. Nijhoff, 1974.

Mack, Phyllis. *Visionary Women: Ecstatic Prophecy in Seventeenth-Century England*. Berkeley: University of California Press, 1992.

MacLean, Gerald, ed. *Culture and Society in the Stuart Restoration: Literature, Drama, History*. Cambridge: Cambridge University Press, 1995.

MacLean, Nancy. *Freedom Is Not Enough: The Opening of the American Workplace*. Cambridge: Harvard University Press, 2006.

MacPherson, C. B. *Burke*. New York: Oxford University Press, 1981.

———. *The Political Theory of Possessive Individualism*. New York: Oxford University Press, 1962.

MacPherson, James, trans. *The Poetical Works of Ossian*, including "A Preliminary Discourse and Dissertation on the Era and Poems of Ossian" by Hugh Blair. Boston: Crosby and Nichols, 1863.

Macpherson, Sandra. "Lovelace, Ltd." *English Literary History* 65.1 (1998): 99–121.

Maddox, James H. "On Defoe's *Roxana*." *English Literary History* 51.4 (Winter 1984): 669–91.

Maddox, Lucy. *Removals: Nineteenth-Century American Literature and the Politics of Indian Affairs*. New York: Oxford University Press, 1991.

Madoff, Mark. "The Useful Myth of Gothic Ancestry." *Studies in Eighteenth-Century Culture* 9 (1979): 337–50.

Madsen, Deborah L. "'A for Abolition': Hawthorne's Bond-Servant and the Shadow of Slavery." *Journal of American Studies* 25.2 (August 1991): 255–59.

Majumdar, Santanu. "Memory and Identity in Wordsworth and in George Eliot's *Middle-march*." *Critical Review* 36 (1996): 41–61.

Malcolm, David. "'Grand and Vague': Why Is *Daniel Deronda* about the Jews?" *George Eliot Review: Journal of the George Eliot Fellowship* 29 (1998): 33–45.

Manly, William M. "The Importance of Point of View in Brockden Brown's *Wieland*." *American Literature* 35.3 (November 1963): 311–21.

Manning, Susan L. "Enlightenment's Dark Dreams: Two Fictions of Henry Mackenzie and Charles Brockden Brown." *Eighteenth Century Life* 21.3 (1997): 39–56.

Marcus, Jane. "Britannia Rules *The Waves*." In *Decolonizing Tradition: New Views of the Twentieth-Century British Literary Canon,* edited by Karen R. Lawrence, 136–62. Urbana: University of Illinois Press, 1992.

———. *Virginia Woolf and the Languages of Patriarchy.* Bloomington: Indiana University Press, 1987.

Marcus, Lisa. "'Of One Blood': Reimagining American Genealogy in Pauline Hopkins's *Contending Forces*." In *Speaking the Other Self: American Women Writers,* edited by Jeanne Campbell Reesman, 117–43. Athens: University of Georgia Press, 1997.

Margolies, Edward. "The Image of the Primitive in Black Letter." *Midcontinent American Studies Journal* 11.2 (1970): 67–77.

Markovits, Stefanie. "George Eliot's Problem with Action." *Studies in English Literature* 41.4 (Autumn 2001): 785–803.

Marks, Patricia. "'Red Letters' and 'Showers of Blood': Hawthorne's Debt to Increase Mather." *American Notes and Queries* 15.7 (March 1977): 100–105.

Marsden, Jean I. "Rape, Voyeurism, and the Restoration Stage." In *Broken Boundaries: Women and Feminism in Restoration Drama*, edited by Katherine M. Quinsey, 185–200. Lexington: University Press of Kentucky, 1996.

Martin, Mary Patricia. "Reading Reform in Richardson's *Clarissa*." *Studies in English Literature 1500–1900* 37.3 (Summer 1997): 595–614.

Martin, Wendy. "Seduced and Abandoned in the New World: The Fallen Woman in American Fiction." In *The American Sisterhood: Writings of the Feminist Movement from Colonial Times to the Present*, edited by Wendy Martin, 257–72. New York: Harper and Row, 1972.

Marx, Karl. *Capital*, Volume I. Translated by Ernest Mandel. New York: Vintage Books, 1976.

Marzec, Robert. "Enclosures, Colonization, and the Robinson Crusoe Syndrome: A Genealogy of Land in a Global Context." *boundary 2* 29.2 (Summer 2002): 129–56.

Mascuch, Michael. *Origins of the Individualist Self: Autobiography and Self-Identity in England, 1591–1791.* Stanford, Calif.: Stanford University Press, 1996.

Massé, Michelle. *In the Name of Love: Women, Masochism, and the Gothic.* Ithaca, N.Y.: Cornell University Press, 1992.

Mathe, Sylvie. "The Reader May Not Choose: Oxymoron as Central Figure in Hawthorne's Strategy of Immunity from Choice in *The Scarlet Letter*." *Style* 26.4 (Winter 1992): 604–33.

Mathiessen, F. O. *American Renaissance: Art and Expression in the Age of Emerson and Whitman.* New York: Oxford University Press, 1941.

Matter-Seibel, Sabina. "Native Americans, Women, and the Culture of Nationalism in Lydia Maria Child and Catharine Maria Sedgwick." In *Early America Re-Explored: New Readings in Colonial, Early National, and Antebellum Culture,* edited by Klaus H. Schmidt and Fritz Fleischman, 411–40. New York: Peter Lang, 2000.

Matterson, Stephen. "Shaped by Readers: The Slave Narratives of Frederick Douglass and Harriet Jacobs." In *Soft Canons: American Women Writers and Masculine Tradition,* edited by Karen L. Kilcup, 82–96. Iowa City: University of Iowa Press, 1999.

Matthes, Melissa. *The Rape of Lucretia and the Founding of Republics: Readings on Livy, Machiavelli, and Rousseau.* University Park: Pennsylvania State University Press, 2000.

Mayer, Robert. *History and the Early English Novel: Matters of Fact from Bacon to Defoe.* New York: Cambridge University Press, 1997.

McAndrew, Elizabeth, and Susan Gorsky. "Why Do They Faint and Die? — The Birth of the Delicate Heroine." *Journal of Popular Culture* 8 (1974): 735–45.

McCann, Sean. "'Bonds of Brotherhood': Pauline Hopkins and the Work of Melodrama." *English Literary History* 64.3 (Fall 1997): 789–822.

McCaw, Neil. *George Eliot and Victorian Historiography: Imagining the National Past.* New York: St. Martin's Press, 2000.

———. "'The Most Ordinary Prompting of Comparison'? George Eliot and the Problematics of Whig Historiography." *Literature and History* 8.2 (1999): 18–33.

McCoy, Beth. "Rumors of Grace: White Masculinity in Pauline Hopkins's *Contending Forces.*" *African American Review* 37.4 (Winter 2003): 569–81.

McCullough, Kate. "Slavery, Sexuality, and Genre: Pauline Hopkins and the Representation of Female Desire." In *The Unruly Voice: Rediscovering Pauline Hopkins,* edited by John Cullen Gruesser, 21–49. Urbana: University of Illinois Press, 1996.

McDowell, Deborah E. "'That Nameless . . . Shameful Impulse': Sexuality in Nella Larsen's *Quicksand* and *Passing.*" In *Black Feminist Criticism and Critical Theory,* edited by Joe Weixlmann and Houston A. Baker Jr., 139–67. Greenwood, Fl.: Penkevill, 1988.

McEntee, Ann Marie. "The (Un)Civil Sisterhood of Oranges and Lemons: Female Petitioners and Demonstrators, 1642–1653." In *Pamphlet Wars: Prose in the English Revolution,* edited by James Holstun, 92–111. Buffalo: State University of New York Press, 1992.

McGee, Patrick. "The Politics of Modernist Form: Or, Who Rules *The Waves?*" *Modern Fiction Studies* 38.3 (Autumn 1992): 631–50.

McKay, Brenda. "Race and Myth: The Spanish Gypsy." *George Eliot Review: Journal of the George Eliot Fellowship* 26 (1995): 53–60.

———. "Victorian Anthropology and Hebraic Apocalyptic Prophecy: 'The Lifted Veil.'" *George Eliot-George Henry Lewes Studies* 42/43 (September 2002): 69–92.

McKay, Nellie. "Black Women's Autobiographies — Literature, History, and the Politics of Self." *Hurricane Alice* 3.4 (Summer 1986): 8–9.

McKee, Patricia. "Corresponding Freedoms: Language and the Self in *Pamela.*" *English Literary History* 52.3 (Fall 1985): 621–648.

McKeon, Michael. *The Origins of the English Novel, 1600–1740.* Baltimore: Johns Hopkins University Press, 1987.

McKillop, A. D. *Samuel Richardson: Printer and Novelist.* Chapel Hill: University of North Carolina Press, 1936.

McLendon, Jacquelyn Y. *The Politics of Color in the Fiction of Jessie Fauset and Nella Larsen.* Charlottesville: University Press of Virginia, 1995.

Meehan, Michael. *Liberty and Poetics in Eighteenth Century England.* Dover, N.H.: Croom Helm, 1986.

Meese, Elizabeth. *(Sem)erotics: Theorizing Lesbian: Writing.* New York: New York University Press, 1992.

Mellor, Anne K. "Were Women Writers Romantics?" *Modern Language Quarterly* 62.4 (December 2001): 393–405.

Melville, Herman. *Billy Budd and Other Stories.* New York Penguin, 1986.

Mendle, Michael, ed. *The Putney Debates of 1647: The Army, the Levellers, and the English State.* Cambridge: Cambridge University Press, 2001.

Menke, Richard. "Fiction as Vivisection: G. H. Lewes and George Eliot." *English Literary History* 67 (2000): 617–53.

Metzger, Lore. Introduction to *Oroonoko* by Aphra Behn. New York: Norton, 1973.

Meyer, Susan. *Imperialism at Home: Race and Victorian Women's Fiction.* Ithaca, N.Y.: Cornell University Press, 1996.

———. "'Safely to Their Own Borders': Proto-Zionism, Feminism, and Nationalism in *Daniel Deronda*." *English Literary History* 60.3 (Autumn 1993): 733–58.

Mighall, Robert. *A Geography of Victorian Gothic Fiction: Mapping History's Nightmares.* New York: Oxford University Press, 1999.

Mignolo, Walter. *Local Histories/Global Designs: Coloniality, Subaltern Knowledges, and Border Thinking.* Princeton, N.J.: Princeton University Press, 2000.

Milbank, Alison. *Daughters of the House: Modes of the Gothic in Victorian Fiction.* New York: St. Martin's Press, 1992.

Milder, Robert, ed. *Critical Essays on Melville's Billy Budd, Sailor.* Boston: G. K. Hall, 1989.

Miles, Robert. "Ann Radcliffe and Matthew Lewis." In *A Companion to the Gothic*, edited by David Punter, 41–57. Malden, Mass.: Blackwell Publishers, 2000.

———. "The 1790's: The Effulgence of the Gothic." In *The Cambridge Companion to Gothic Fiction*, edited by Jerrold Hogle, 41–62. New York: Cambridge University Press, 2002.

Miller, Derek. "Daniel Deronda and Allegories of Empire." In *George Eliot and Europe*, edited by John Rignall, 113–22. Aldershot, England: Scholar, 1997.

Miller, Quentin. "'A Tyrannically Democratic Force': The Symbolic and Cultural Function of Clothing in Catharine Maria Sedgwick's *Hope Leslie*." *Legacy* 19.2 (2002): 121–36.

Millington, Richard. *Practicing Romance: Narrative Form and Cultural Engagement in Hawthorne's Fiction.* Princeton: Princeton University Press, 1992.

Milton, John. *Paradise Lost. The Complete Poetical Works of John Milton.* Edited by Douglas Bush. Boston: Houghton Mifflin, 1965.

Minh-ha, Trinh T. *When the Moon Waxes Red: Representation, Gender, and Cultural Politics.* New York: Routledge, 1991.

Mish, Charles. "Black Letter as a Social Discriminant in the Seventeenth Century," *PMLA* 68.3 (1953): 627–30.

Mitford, William. *Inquiry into the principles of Harmony in Language and of the Mechanism of Verse, Modern and Antient.* London: T. Cadell and W. Davies, 1804.

Mizruchi, Susan. "Cataloging the Creatures of the Deep: 'Billy Budd, Sailor' and the Rise of Sociology." *boundary 2* 17.1 (Spring 1990): 272 – 304.

Moers, Ellen. *Literary Women.* Garden City, New York: Doubleday Books, 1976.

Moglen, Helen. *The Trauma of Gender: A Feminist History of the English Novel.* Berkeley: University of California Press, 2001.

Monda, Kimberly. "Self-Delusion and Self-Sacrifice in Nella Larsen's *Quicksand.*" *African American Review* 31.1 (Spring 1997): 23 – 39.

Monk, Samuel. *The Sublime: A Study of Critical Theories in Eighteenth-Century England.* Ann Arbor: University of Michigan Press, 1960 [1935].

Monleón, Jose B. *A Spectre Is Haunting Europe: A Sociocultural Approach to the Fantastic,* Princeton, N.J.: Princeton University Press, 1990.

Montesquieu, Charles. *Esprit du Loi.* Translated and edited by Anne M. Cohler et al. New York: Cambridge University Press, 1989.

Montgomery, Nick. "Colonial Rhetoric and the Maternal Voice: Deconstruction and Disengagement in Virginia Woolf's *The Voyage Out.*" *Twentieth-Century Literature* 46 (2000): 34 – 55.

Moon, Keith. "The Two Kisses: Human Sexuality in Virginia Woolf's *The Waves.*" *AUMLA: Journal of the Australasian Universities Language and Literature Association* 70 (1988): 321 – 35.

Morgan, Winifred. "Gender-Related Difference in the Slave Narratives of Harriet Jacobs and Frederick Douglass." *American Studies* 35 (Fall 1994): 73 – 94.

Morris, David B. "Gothic Sublimity." *New Literary History* 16.2 (1985): 299 – 319.

Morrison, Toni. *Beloved.* New York: Knopf, 1987.

———. *Playing in the Dark: Whiteness and the Literary Imagination.* New York: Random House, 1992.

———. "Unspeakable Things Unspoken: The Afro-American Presence in American Literature." *Michigan Quarterly Review* 28.1 (Winter 1989): 1 – 34.

Mortimer, Anthony. "The Early Regional Novel: Notes Towards a Theory." *Anglistentag 1980 Gissen: Tagungbeitrage und Berichte im Auftrage des Vorstandes,* edited by Herbert Grabes, 211 – 25. Grossen-Linden: Hoffmann, 1981.

Moten, Fred. *In the Break: The Aesthetics of Black Radical Tradition.* Minneapolis: University of Minnesota Press, 2003.

Mower, Christine Leiren. "Bodies in Labor: Sole Proprietorship and the Labor of Conduct in *The Coquette.*" *American Literature: A Journal of Literary History, Criticism, and Bibliography* 74.2 (June 2002): 315 – 44.

Mowry, Melissa. "Eliza Haywood's Defense of London's Body Politic." *Studies in English Literature* 43.3 (Summer 2003): 645 – 65.

Mullen, Harryette. "Runaway Tongue: Resistant Orality in *Uncle Tom's Cabin, Our Nig, Incidents in the Life of a Slave Girl,* and *Beloved.*" In *The Culture of Sentiment: Race, Gender, and Sentimentality in Nineteenth-Century American Literature,* edited by Shirley Samuels, 244 – 64. New York: Oxford, 1992.

Murphy, Geraldine. "Olaudah Equiano, Accidental Tourist." *Eighteenth-Century Studies* 27.4 (Summer 1994): 551 – 68.

———. "The Politics of Reading *Billy Budd.*" *American Literary History* 1.2 (Summer 1989): 361–82.

Nancy, Jean-Luc. *Being Singular Plural.* Translated by Robert D. Richardson and Anne E. O'Byrne. Stanford, Calif.: Stanford University Press, 2000.

Nelson, Dana. "Sympathy as Strategy in Sedgwick's *Hope Leslie.*" In *The Culture of Sentiment: Race, Gender, and Sentimentality in Nineteenth-Century American Literature,* edited by Shirley Samuels, 191–202. New York: Oxford University Press, 1992.

Nerad, Julie Cary. "'So Strangely Interwoven': The Property of Inheritance, Race, and Sexual Morality in Pauline E. Hopkins's *Contending Forces.*" *African American Review* 35.3 (Fall 2001): 357–73.

Nestor, Deborah J. "Virtue Rarely Rewarded: Ideological Subversion and Narrative Form in Haywood's Later Fiction." *Studies in English Literature, 1500–1900* 34.3 (Summer 1994): 579–98.

Newberry, Frederick. *Hawthorne's Divided Loyalties: England and America in Hawthorne's Works.* London: Associated University Presses, 1987.

Newbury, Michael. *Figuring Authorship in Antebellum America.* Stanford, Calif.: Stanford University Press, 1997.

Newman, Simon P. "Reading the Bodies of Early American Seafarers." *William and Mary Quarterly,* 3rd ser., 55.1 (January 1988): 59–82.

Newton, Gerald. "*Deutsche Schrift:* The Demise and Rise of German Black Letter." *German Life and Letters* 56.2 (April 2003): 183–204.

Nickel, John. "Eugenics and the Fiction of Pauline Hopkins." *American Transcendental Quarterly* 14.1 (March 2000): 47–60.

Nielsen, Aldon Lynn. "The Future of an Allusion: The Color of Modernity." In *Geomodernisms: Race, Modernism, Modernity,* edited by Laura Doyle and Laura Winkiel, 17–30. Bloomington: Indiana University Press, 2005.

Nobles, Gregory. *American Frontiers: Cultural Encounters and Continental Conquest.* New York: Hill and Wang, 1997.

Norbrook, David. *Writing the English Republic: Poetry, Rhetoric, and Politics, 1627–1660.* New York: Cambridge University Press, 1999.

Nord, Deborah Epstein. "'Marks of Race': Gypsy Figures and Eccentric Femininity in Nineteenth-Century Women's Writing." *Victorian Studies* 41.2 (Winter 1998): 189–99.

Norwood, Lisa West. "'I May Be a Stranger to the Grounds of Your Belief': Constructing Sense of Place in *Wieland.*" *Early American Literature* 38.1 (2003): 89–122.

Novak, Maximillian. *Defoe and the Nature of Man.* New York: Oxford University Press, 1963.

———. *Economics and the Fiction of Daniel Defoe.* Berkeley: University of California Press, 1962.

Nower, Joyce. "The Traditions of Negro Literature in the United States." *Negro American Literature Forum* 3.1 (Spring 1969): 5–12.

Nunes, Zita. "Phantasmatic Brazil: Nella Larsen's *Passing,* American Literary Imagination, and Racial Utopianism." In *Mixing Race, Mixing Culture: Inter-American Literary Dialogues,* edited by Monika Kaup and Debra J. Rosenthal, 50–61. Austin: University of Texas Press, 2002.

Nunokawa, Jeff. *The Afterlife of Property: Domestic Security and the Victorian Novel*. Princeton: Princeton University Press, 1994

——. "Eros and Isolation." *English Literary History* 69 (2002): 835–60.

Nubhai, Saleel. "Metafiction and Metaphor: Daniel Deronda as Golem." *George Eliot Review: A Journal of the George Eliot Fellowship* 25 (1994): 39–44.

Nunberg, Geoffrey, ed. *The Future of the Book*. Berkeley: University of California Press, 1996.

O'Brien, Colleen C. "Race-ing toward Civilization: Sexual Slavery and Nativism in the Novels of Pauline Elizabeth Hopkins and Alive Wellington Rollins." *Legacy* 20.1–2 (2003): 118–33.

O'Brien, Conor Cruise. Introduction to *Reflections on the Revolution in France*, by Edmund Burke. New York: Penguin, 1986.

O'Brien, John. "Union Jack: Amnesia and the Law in Daniel Defoe's *Colonel Jack*." *Eighteenth-Century Studies* 32.1 (1998): 65–82.

Oakleaf, David. "'Shady Bowers! and purling streams! — Heavens, how insipid!': Eliza Haywood's Artful Pastoral." In *The Passionate Fictions of Eliza Haywood: Essays on her Life and Work*, edited by Kirsten T. Saxton and Rebecca P. Bocchicchio, 283–299. Lexington: University Press of Kentucky, 2000.

——. "The Eloquence of Blood in Eliza Haywood's *Lasselia*." *Studies in English Literature* 39.3 (1999): 483–98.

Ogude. S. E. "Facts into Fiction: Equiano's Narrative Reconsidered." *Research in African Literature* 13.1 (Spring 1982): 31–43.

Okie, Laird. *Augustan Historical Writing: Histories of England in the English Enlightenment*. Lanham, Md.: University Press of America, 1991.

Olsen, Thomas Grant. "Reading and Righting *Moll Flanders*." *Studies in English Literature* 41.3 (Summer 2001): 467–81.

Omer-Sherman, Ranen. "Emma Lazarus, Jewish American Poetics, and the Challenge of Modernity." *Legacy* 19.2 (2002): 170–91.

Orban, Katalin. "Dominant and Submerged Discourses in the *Life of Olaudah Equiano* (or Gustavas Vassa?)." *African American Review* 27.4 (1993): 655–64.

Ortiz, Joseph M. "Arms and the Woman: Narrative, Imperialism, and the Virgilian *Memoria* in Aphra Behn's *Oroonoko*." *Studies in the Novel* 34.2 (Summer 2002): 119–140.

Osland, Dianne. "Complaisance and Complacence, and the Perils of Pleasing in *Clarissa*." *Studies in English Literature, 1500–1900* 40.3 (Summer 2000): 491–509.

Otten, Thomas J. "Pauline Hopkins and the Hidden Self of Race." *English Literary History* 59 (1992): 227–56.

Otter, Samuel. *Melville's Anatomies*. Berkeley: University of California Press, 1999.

Overton, Thomas. "The Commoners Complaint: or, Dreadful Warning from Newgate, to the Commons of England, Presented to the Honourable Committee for Consideration of Commoners Liberties" [1646]. In *Tracts on Liberty in the Puritan Revolution, 1638–1647*, volume 3, edited by William Haller, 373–395. New York: Columbia University Press, 1933.

Oxindine, Annette. "Rhoda Submerged: Lesbian Suicide in *The Waves*." In *Virginia Woolf: Lesbian Readings*, edited by Michele Barrett and Patricia Cramer, 203–21. New York: New York University Press, 1997.

Pacheco, Anita. "Rape and the Female Subject in Behn's *The Rover*." *English Literary History* 65.2 (1998): 323–45.

Pacheco, "Royalism and Honor in Aphra Behn's Oroonoko." *Studies in English Literature* 34.3 (1994): 491–506.

Paine, Thomas. *Common Sense*. Edited by Isaac Kramnick. New York: Penguin, 1986.

Pamplin, Claire. "Race and Identity in Pauline Hopkins's *Hagar's Daughter*." In *Redefining the Political Novel: American Women Writers, 1797–1901*, edited by Sharon M. Harris, 169–83. Knoxville: University of Tennessee Press, 1995.

Parker, Patricia L. "*Charlotte Temple*: America's First Best Seller." *Studies in Short Fiction* 13 (1976): 518–20.

Parker, Patricia L. *Susanna Rowson*. Boston: Twayne, 1986.

Patterson, Annabel M. *Censorship and Interpretation: The Conditions of Writing and Reading in Early Modern England*. Madison: University of Wisconsin Press, 1984.

Patterson, Anita. "Jazz, Realism, and the Modernist Lyric: The Poetry of Langston Hughes." *Modern Language Quarterly* 61.4 (2000): 651–82.

Patterson, Martha H. "'Kin' o' Rough Jestice Fer a Parson': Pauline Hopkins's *Winona* and the Politics of Reconstructing History." *African American Review* 32.3 (Autumn 1998): 445–60.

Pazicky, Diana Loercher. *Cultural Ophans in America*. Jackson: University Press of Mississippi, 1998.

Pearson, Jacqueline. "Gender and Narrative in the Fiction of Aphra Behn." *The Review of English Studies* 42.165 (1991): 40–65.

Peele, Thomas. "Queering Mrs. Dalloway." In *Literature and Homosexuality*, edited by Michael J. Meyer, 205–21. Atlanta: Rodopi, 2000.

Percy, Bishop Thomas. *Northern Antiquities; or, an Historical Account of the Manners, Customs, Religion and Laws, Maritime Expeditions and Discoveries, Language and Literature, of the Ancient Scandinavians. With Incidental Notices respecting our Saxon Ancestors*. Translated by M. Mallet. London: Henry G. Bohn, 1847. [1770].

————, ed. *Reliques of Ancient English Poetry*. Volume 1. London: James Nisbet, 1858 [1765].

Perreault, Jeanne. "Mary Wollstonecraft and Harriet Jacobs: Self Possessions." In *Mary Wollstonecraft and Mary Shelley: Writing Lives*, edited by Helen M. Buss, D. L. Macdonald, and Anne McWhir, 99–112. Waterloo, Ont.: Wilfrid Laurier University Press, 2001.

Person, Leland S. "A for Affirmative Action?" *American Literary History* 9.2 (Summer 1997): 226–29.

Petch, Simon. "The Sovereign Self: Identity and Responsibility in Victorian England." In *Law and Literature*, edited by Michael Freeman and Lewis Andrew, 397–415. Oxford: Oxford University Press, 1999.

Peterson, Carla L. "Capitalism, Black (Under)Development, and the Production of the African-American Novel in the 1850s." *American Literary History* 4.4 (Winter 1992): 559–83.

————. *Doers of the Word: African American Women Speakers and Writers of the North, 1830–1880*. New York: Oxford University Press, 1995.

————. "The Remaking of Americans: Gertrude Stein's 'Melanctha' and African American Musical Traditions." In *Criticism and the Color Line*, edited by Henry B. Wonham, 140–57. New Brunswick, N.J.: Rutgers University Press, 1996.

Pettengill, Claire. "Hannah Webster Foster (1758–1840)." *Legacy: A Journal of American Women Writers* 12.2 (1995): 133–41.

Phillips, Kathy J. *Virginia Woolf against Empire*. Knoxville: University of Tennessee Press, 1994.

Piep, Karsten H. "'Nothing New Under the Sun': Postsentimental Conflict in Harriet E. Wilson's *Our Nig*." *Colloquy: Text Theory Critique* 11 (May 2006): 178–94.

Pocock, J. G. A. *The Ancient Constitution and the Feudal Law: A Study of English Historical Thought in the Seventeenth Century*. New York: Cambridge University Press, 1987.

———. "Burke and the Ancient Constitution: A Problem in the History of Ideas." *Historical Journal* 3 (1960): 125–43.

———. *Virtue, Commerce, and History: Essays on Political Thought and History, Chiefly in the Eighteenth Century*. New York: Cambridge University Press, 1985.

Poliakov, Leon. *The Aryan Myth: A History of Racist and Nationalist Ideas in Europe*. Translated by Edmund Howard. London: Chatto and Windus Heinemann for Sussex University Press, 1974.

Pollack, Ellen. "*Moll Flanders,* Incest and the Structure of Exchange." *Eighteenth Century* 30.1 (1989): 3–21.

Posnock, Ross. *Black Writers and the Making of the Modern Intellectual*. Cambridge: Harvard University Press, 1998.

Potkay, Adam. "History, Oratory, and God in Equiano's *Interesting Narrative*." *Eighteenth-Century Studies* 34.4 (2001): 601–14.

Potter, Lois. *Secret Rites and Secret Writing: Royalist Literature 1641–1660*. New York: Cambridge University Press, 1989.

Prall, Stuart E. *The Puritan Revolution: A Documentary History*. Gloucester, Mass.: Peter Smith, 1973.

Pratofiorito, Ellen. "'To Demand Your Sympathy and Aid': *Our Nig* and the Problem of No Audience." *Journal of American & Comparative Cultures* 24.1–2 (Spring–Summer 2001): 31–48.

Press, Jacob. "Same-Sex Unions in Modern Europe: *Daniel Deronda*, Alneuland, and the Homoerotics of Jewish Nationalism." In *Novel Gazing,* edited by Eve Kosofsky Sedgwick, 299–329. Durham, N.C.: Duke University Press, 1997.

Pudaloff, Ross J. "No Change Without Purchase: Olaudah Equiano and the Economies of Self and Market." *Early American Literature* 40.3 (2005): 499–527.

Punter, David. *The Literature of Terror: A History of Gothic Fictions from 1765 to the Present Day*. London: Longman, 1980.

Putzi, Jennifer. "'Raising the Stigma': Black Womanhood and the Marked Body in Pauline Hopkins's *Contending Forces*." *College Literature* 31.2 (2004): 1–21.

Rado, Lisa. *The Modern Androgyne Imagination: A Failed Sublime*. Charlottesville: University Press of Virginia, 2000.

Ragan, Barbara M. "Harriet Jacobs and Molly Horniblow: Self-Reliance among Black Women Ancestors in *Incidents in the Life of a Slave Girl*." *Middle Atlantic Writers Association Review* 12.2 (December 1997): 80–86.

Ramsay, David. *The History of the American Revolution.* Volumes 1–2. New York: Russell and Russell, 1968.

Randle, Gloria T. "Mates, Marriage, and Motherhood: Feminist Visions in Pauline Hopkins's *Contending Forces.*" *Tulsa Studies in Women's Literature* 18.2 (Fall 1999): 193–214.

Rapin de Thoyras, Paul. *The History of England.* Trans. Nicholas Tindal. London: James, John, and Paul Knapton, 1732–47.

Raymond, Joad, ed. *Making the News: An Anthology of the Newsbooks of Revolutionary England, 1641–1660.* New York: St. Martin's Press, 1993.

Redinger, Ruby V. *George Eliot: The Emergent Self.* New York: Knopf, 1975.

Regis, Pamela. *Describing Early America: Bartram, Jefferson, Crevecoeur, and the Rhetoric of Natural History.* DeKalb: Northern Illinois University Press, 1992.

Reid, Margaret. "From Revolutionary Legends to *The Scarlet Letter:* Casting Characters for Early American Romanticism." In *Comparative Romanticisms: Power, Gender, Subjectivity,* edited by Larry H. Peer, 59–80. Columbia, S.C.: Camden House, 1998.

Reynolds, Larry J. "Billy Budd and American Labor Unrest: The Case for Striking Back." In *New Essays on Billy Budd,* edited by Donald Yanella, 21–48. New York: Cambridge University Press, 2002.

———. *European Revolutions and the American Literary Renaissance.* New Haven, Conn.: Yale University Press, 1991.

Rhodes, Chip. *Structures of the Jazz Age: Mass Culture, Progressive Education, and Racial Discourse in American Modernism.* New York: Verso, 1998.

———. "Writing Up the New Negro: The Construction of Consumer Desire in the Twenties." *Journal of American Studies* 28.2 (August 1994): 191–207.

Rice, Alan. *Radical Narratives of the Black Atlantic.* New York: Continuum, 2003.

Richards, Jeffrey H. "The Politics of Seduction: Theater, Sexuality and National Virtue in the Novels of Hannah Foster." In *Exceptional Spaces: Essays in Performance and History,* edited by Della Pollock, 238–57. Chapel Hill: University of North Carolina Press, 1998.

Richardson, R. C. *The Debate on the English Revolution.* New York: St. Martin's Press, 1977.

Richardson, Samuel. *Clarissa; or, The History of a Young Lady.* New York: Penguin, 1985.

Richetti, John. *The English Novel in History, 1700–1780.* New York: Routledge, 1999.

———. "The Family, Sex, and Marriage in Daniel Defoe's *Moll Flanders* and *Roxana.*" *Studies in the Literary Imagination* 15.2 (1982): 32.

———. "Histories by Eliza Haywood and Henry Fielding." In *The Passionate Fictions of Eliza Haywood: Essays on her Life and Work,* edited by Kirsten T. Saxton and Rebecca P. Bocchicchio, 240–58. Lexington: University Press of Kentucky, 2000.

Rizzo, Betty. "Renegotiating the Gothic." In *Revising Women: Eighteenth Century "Women's Fiction" and Social Engagement,* edited by Paula Backscheider, 58–103. Baltimore: Johns Hopkins University Press, 2000.

Roach, Joseph. *Cities of the Dead: Circum-Atlantic Performance.* New York: Columbia University Press, 1996.

Robbins, Bruce. *The Servant's Hand: English Fiction from Below.* New York: Columbia University Press, 1986.

Robbins, Caroline. *The Eighteenth-Century Commonwealthman*. Cambridge, Mass.: Harvard University Press, 1959.

Roberts, Kimberly. "The Clothes Make the Woman: The Symbolics of Prostitution in Nella Larsen's *Quicksand* and Claude McKay's *Home to Harlem*." *Tulsa Studies in Women's Literature* (1997): 107–30.

Robinson, Angelo. "The Other Invisibility in Ellison's *Invisible Man*." Conversations in the Community, Graduate English Conference, University of Massachusetts, Amherst, May 1998.

Roder-Bolton, Gerlinde. "'A Binding History, Tragic and Yet Glorious': George Eliot and the Jewish Element in *Daniel Deronda*." *English: The Journal of the English Association* 49.195 (Autumn 2000): 205–27.

Rogin, Michael. *Subversive Genealogy: The Politics and Art of Herman Melville*. New York: Alfred A. Knopf, 1983.

Rohrbach, Augusta. "To Be Continued: Double Identity, Multiplicity and Antigenealogy as Narrative Strategies in Pauline Hopkins' Magazine Fiction." *Callaloo* 22.2 (Spring 1999): 483–98.

Rose, Norman, ed. *From Palmerston to Balfour: The Collected Essays of Mayir Vereté*. Portland, Ore.: Frank Cass, 1992.

Rosenberg, Brian. "George Eliot and the Victorian 'Historical Imagination.'" In *George Eliot: Critical Assessments*, edited by Stuart Hutchinson, 237–45. East Sussex, England: Helm Information, 1996.

Rosenfeld, Natania. "Links into Fences: The Subtext of Class Division in *Mrs. Dalloway*." *LIT: Literature Interpretation Theory* 9 (1998): 139–60.

Rosenthal, Laura. "Owning *Oroonoko*: Behn, Southerne, and the Contingencies of Property." *Renaissance Drama* 23 (1992): 25–38.

Ross, Cheri Louise. "(Re)Writing the Frontier Romance: Catharine Maria Sedgwick's *Hope Leslie*." *College Literature Association Journal* 39 (1996): 320–40.

Ross, Trevor. *The Making of the English Literary Canon from the Middle Ages to the Late Eighteenth Century*. Montreal: McGill-Queens University Press, 1998.

Rousseau, Jean-Jacques. *The Social Contract*. Translated by Maurice Cranston. New York: Penguin, 1977.

Rowe, John Carlos. *Literary Culture and U.S. Imperialism: From the Revolution to World War II*. New York: Oxford University Press, 2000.

Rowson, Susanna. *Charlotte Temple*. New York: Oxford, 1986.

———. *Charlotte Temple and Lucy Temple*. New York: Penguin, 1991.

Rozakis, Laurie. "Another Possible Source of Hawthorne's Hester Prynne." *American Transcendental Quarterly* 59 (1986): 63–71.

Rust, Marion. "What's Wrong with Charlotte Temple?" *William and Mary Quarterly* 60.1 (January 2003): 99–118.

Ruttenberg, Nancy. *Democratic Personality: Popular Voice and the Trial of American Authorship*. Stanford, Calif.: Stanford University Press, 1998.

Ryals, Kay Ferguson. "America, Romance, and the Fate of the Wandering Woman." In *Women, America, and Movement: Narratives of Relocation*, edited by Susan Roberson, 81–105. Columbia: University of Missouri Press, 1998.

Ryan, Kathleen O. "The Intentional Turn: Suicide in Twentieth-Century U.S. Literature by Women." Ph.D. dissertation, University of Massachusetts, 2000.

Saar, Doreen Alvarez. "Susanna Rowson: Feminist and Democrat." In *Curtain Calls: British and American Women and the Theater, 1660–1820,* edited by Mary Anne Schofield and Celia Machesky, 231–46. Athens: Ohio University Press, 1991.

Sabino, Robin, and Jennifer Hall. "The Path Not Taken: Cultural Identity in *The Interesting Life of Olaudah Equiano.*" *MELUS* 24.1 (1999): 5–19.

Said, Edward. *Culture and Imperialism.* New York: Knopf, 1993.

———. *The Question of Palestine.* New York: Vintage Books, 1992.

Saldivar-Hull, Sonia. "Wrestling Your Ally: Stein, Racism, and Critical Practice." In *Women's Writing in Exile,* edited by Mary Lynn Broe and Angela Ingram, 181–98. Chapel Hill: University of North Carolina Press, 1989.

Sale, Maggie. "Critiques from Within: Antebellum Projects of Resistance." *American Literature* 64.4 (December 1992): 695–718.

Samuels, Shirley. *The Culture of Sentiment: Race, Gender, and Sentimentality in Nineteenth-Century America.* New York: Oxford University Press, 1992.

———. *Romance of the Republic: Women, the Family, and Violence in the Literature of the Early American Nation.* New York: Oxford University Press, 1996.

Samuels, Wilfred D. "Disguised Voice in *The Interesting Narrative of Olaudah Equiano.*" *Black American Literature Forum* 1.2 (1985): 64–69.

Sanchez-Eppler, Karen. *Touching Liberty: Abolition, Feminism, and the Politics of the Body.* Berkeley: University of California Press, 1993.

Sandiford, Keith. "'Monk' Lewis and the Slavery Sublime: The Agon of Romantic Desire in the Journal." *Essays in Literature* 23.1 (1996): 84–88.

Savoy, Eric. "The Rise of the American Gothic." In *The Cambridge Companion to Gothic Fiction,* edited by Jerrold Hogle, 167–88. New York: Cambridge University Press, 2002.

Sawaya, Francesca. "Emplotting National History: Regionalism and Pauline Hopkins's *Contending Forces.*" In *Breaking Boundaries: New Perspectives on Women's Regional Writing,* edited by Sherrie A. Inness, 72–87. Iowa City: University of Iowa Press, 1997.

Saxton, Kirsten T., and Rebecca P. Bocchicchio, eds. *The Passionate Fictions of Eliza Haywood: Essays on her Life and Work.* Lexington: University Press of Kentucky, 2000.

Scharnhorst, Gary. *The Critical Response to Nathaniel Hawthorne's "The Scarlet Letter."* New York: Greenwood, 1992.

Scheiber, Andrew J. "'The Arm Lifted against Me': Love, Terror, and the Construction of Gender in *Wieland.*" *Early American Literature* 9.2 (September 1991): 173–94.

Scheick, William J. "Literature to 1800." *American Literary Scholarship* (1999): 223–41.

Scheiding, Oliver. "'Plena Exemplorum est Historia': Rewriting Exemplary History in Brockden Brown's 'Death Of Cicero.'" In *Revisioning the Past: Historical Reflexivity in American Short Fiction,* edited by Bernd Engler and Oliver Scheiding, 39–50. Trier, Germany: Wissenschaftlicher, 1998.

Scheuermann, Mona. "The American Novel of Seduction: An Exploration of the Omission of the Sex Act in *The Scarlet Letter.*" *Nathaniel Hawthorne Journal* 8 (1978): 105–18.

Schloss, Dietmar. "Republicanism and Politeness in the Early American Novel." In *Early America Re-explored: New Readings in Colonial, Early National, and Antebellum Cul-*

ture, edited by Klaus H. Schmidt and Fritz Fleischman, 269–90. New York: Petersburg, 2000.

Schmidgen, Wolfram. *Eighteenth-Century Fiction and the Law.* New York: Cambridge University Press, 2002.

———. "*Robinson Crusoe,* Enumeration, and the Mercantile Fetish." *Eighteenth-Century Studies* 35.1 (2001): 19–39.

———. "Illegitimacy and Social Observation: The Bastard in the Eighteenth-Century Novel." *English Literary History* 69 (2002): 133–66.

Schmidt, Klaus H., and Fritz Fleischman, eds. *Early America Re-explored: New Readings in Colonial, Early National, and Antebellum Culture.* New York: Petersburg, 2000.

Schmitt, Cannon. *Alien Nation: Nineteenth Century Gothic Fictions and English Nationality.* Philadelphia: University of Pennsylvania Press, 1997.

Schneider, Herbert. *The Puritan Mind.* New York: H. Holt, 1930.

Schöpp, Joseph C. "Liberty's Sons and Daughters." In *Early America Re-explored: New Readings in Colonial, Early National, and Antebellum Culture,* edited by Klaus H. Schmidt and Fritz Fleischman, 309–48. New York: Petersburg, 2000.

Schrager, Cynthia D. "Pauline Hopkins and William James: The New Psychology and the Politics of Race." In *The Unruly Voice: Rediscovering Pauline Hopkins,* edited by John Cullen Gruesser, 182–210. Urbana: University of Illinois Press, 1996.

Schuck, Peter H., and Rogers M. Smith. *Citizenship without Consent: Illegal Aliens in the American Polity.* New Haven, Conn.: Yale University Press, 1985.

Sedgwick, Catharine Maria. *Hope Leslie, or Early Times in the Massachusetts.* New York: Penguin, 1998.

Sedgwick, Eve Kosofsky. *Between Men: English Literature and Male Homosocial Desire.* New York: Columbia University Press, 1985.

———. *The Coherence of Gothic Conventions.* New York: Arno Press, 1980.

———. *Epistemology of the Closet.* Berkeley: University of California Press, 1990.

———, ed. *Novel Gazing: Queer Readings in Fiction.* Durham, N.C.: Duke University Press, 1993.

Seed, David. "The Mind Set Free: Charles Brockden Brown's *Wieland.*" In *Making America, Making American Literature,* edited by Tobert A. Lee and V. M. Verhoeven, 105–22. Amsterdam: Rodopi, 1996.

Seidel, Michael. *Exile and the Narrative Imagination.* New Haven, Conn.: Yale University Press, 1986.

Seltzer, Mark. "Saying Makes It So: Language and Event in Brown's *Wieland.*" *Early American Literature* 13 (1978): 81–91.

Semmel, Bernard. *George Eliot and Politics of National Inheritance.* New York: Oxford University Press, 1994.

Seshagiri, Urmilla. "Orienting Virginia Woolf: Race, Aesthetics, and Politics in *To the Lighthouse.*" *Modern Fiction Studies* 50.1 (Spring 2004): 58–84.

Shapiro, Stephen. "'Man to Man I Needed Not to Dread His Encounter': *Edgar Huntly's* End of Erotic Pessimism." In *Revising Charles Brockden Brown: Culture, Politics, and Sexuality in the Early Republic,* edited by Philip Barnard, Mark. L. Kamrath, and Stephen Shapiro, 216–51. Knoxville: University of Tennessee Press, 2004.

Sharpe, Jenny. *Allegories of Empire: The Figure of Woman in the Colonial Text.* Minneapolis: University of Minnesota Press, 1993.

Shelton, Jen. "'Don't Say Such Foolish Things, Dear': Speaking Incest in *The Voyage Out.*" In *Incest and the Literary Imagination,* edited by Elizabeth Barnes, 224–48. Gainesville: University of Florida Press, 2002.

Short, Gretchen. "Harriet Wilson's *Our Nig* and the Labor of Citizenship." *Arizona Quarterly: A Journal of American Literature, Culture, and Theory* 57.3 (Autumn 2001): 1–27.

Shuffelton, Frank. "Mrs. Foster's Coquette and the Decline of the Brotherly Watch." *Studies in Eighteenth Century Culture* 16 (1986): 211–24.

———. "Juries of the Common Reader: Crime and Judgment in the Novels of Charles Brockden Brown." In *Revising Charles Brockden Brown: Culture, Politics, and Sexuality in the Early Republic,* edited by Philip Barnard, Mark. L. Kamrath, and Stephen Shapiro, 88–114. Knoxville: University of Tennessee Press, 2004.

Sidney, Algernon. *Discourses Concerning Government.* London: J. Darby, 1704.

Silverman, Deborah. B. "Nella Larsen's *Quicksand*: Untangling the Webs of Exoticism." *African American Review* 27.4 (Winter 1993): 599–614.

Singley, Carol. "Catharine Maria Sedgwick's *Hope Leslie*: Radical Frontier Romance." In *The (Other) American Traditions,* edited by Joyce E. Warren, 39–53. New Brunswick, N.J.: Rutgers University Press, 1993.

Sisney, Mary F. "The View from the Outside: Black Novels of Manners." In *The Critical Response to Glora Naylor,* edited by Sharon Felton and Michelle C. Loris, 63–75. Westport, Conn.: Greenwood, 1997.

Smith, Andrew. *Gothic Radicalism: Literature, Philosophy and Psychoanalysis in the Nineteenth Century.* New York: St. Martin's Press, 2000.

Smith, Lisa Herb. "'Some Perilous Stuff': What the Religious Reviewers Really Said about *The Scarlet Letter.*" *American Periodicals: A Journal of History, Criticism, and Bibliography* 6 (1996): 135–43.

Smith, Patricia Juliana. *Lesbian Panic: Homoeroticism in Modern British Women's Fiction.* New York: Columbia University Press, 1997.

Smith, R. J. *The Gothic Bequest: Medieval Institutions in British Thought, 1688–1863.* New York: Cambridge University Press, 1987.

Smith, Stephanie A. *Conceived by Liberty: Maternal Figures and Nineteenth-Century American Literature.* Ithaca, N.Y.: Cornell University Press, 1994.

Smith, Valerie. "Loopholes of Retreat: Architecture and Ideology in Harriet Jacobs's *Incidents in the Life of a Slave Girl.*" In *Reading Black, Reading Feminist,* edited by Henry Louis Gates Jr., 212–26. New York: Meridian, 1990.

Smith-Rosenberg, Carroll. "Domesticating 'Virtue': Coquettes and Revolutionaries in Young America." In *Literature and the Body,* edited by Elaine Scarry, 160–84. Baltimore: Johns Hopkins University Press, 1988.

———. "Subject Female: Authorizing American Identity." *American Literary History* 5.3 (Autumn 1993): 481–511.

Snow, Malinda. "Arguments to the Self in Defoe's *Roxana.*" *Studies in English Literature* 34.3 (Summer 1994): 523–36.

Somerville, Siobhan. *Queering the Color Line: Race and the Invention of Homosexuality in American Culture.* Durham, N.C.: Duke University Press, 2000.

Sowerby, Robin. "The Goths in History and Pre-Gothic Gothic." In *A Companion to the Gothic,* edited by David Punter, 15–26. Malden, Mass.: Blackwell Publishers, 2000.

Spencer, Jane. *The Rise of the Woman Novelist: From Aphra Behn to Jane Austen.* New York: Blackwell, 1986.

Spengemann, William. "The Earliest American Novel: Aphra Bern's *Oroonoko.*" *Nineteenth-Century Fiction* 38.4 (March 1984): 384–414.

———. *New World of Words: Redefining Early American Literature.* New Haven, Conn.: Yale University Press, 1994.

Stanford Friedman, Susan. "Paranoia, Pollution, and Sexuality: Affiliations between E. M. Forster's *Passage to India* and Arundhati Roy's *The God of Small Things.*" In *Geomodernisms: Race, Modernism, Modernity,* edited by Laura Doyle and Laura Winkiel, 245–61. Bloomington: Indiana University Press, 2005.

Starr, G. A. "Aphra Behn and the Genealogy of the Man of Feeling." *Modern Philology* 87.4 (May 1990): 362–72.

Starr, George S. *Defoe and Spiritual Autobiography.* Princeton, N.J.: Princeton University Press, 1965.

Staves, Susan. *Players' Scepters: Fiction of Authority in the Restoration.* Lincoln: University of Nebraska Press, 1979.

Stein, Gertrude. *Three Lives.* New York: Vintage Books, 1936 [1909].

Stephens, Michelle Ann. *Black Empire: The Masculine Global Imaginary of Caribbean Intellectuals in the United States.* Durham, N.C.: Duke University Press, 2005.

Sterling, Laurie. "Paternal Gold: Translating Inheritance in *The Scarlet Letter.*" *American Transcendental Quarterly* 6.1 (March 1992): 15–30.

Stern, Julia. *The Plight of Feeling: Sympathy and Dissent in the Early American Novel.* Chicago: University of Chicago Press, 1997.

Stevens, Laura M. "Transatlanticism Now." *American Literary History* 16.1 (2004): 93–102.

Stevenson, Pascha. "Of One Blood, Of One Race: Pauline E. Hopkins' Engagement of Racialized Science." *College Literature Association Journal* 45.4 (June 2002): 422–43.

Stewart, Randall. *Nathaniel Hawthorne: A Biography.* New Haven, Conn.: Yale University Press, 1948.

Stoler, Ann Laura. *Race and the Education of Desire: Foucault's History of Sexuality and the Colonial Order of Things.* Durham, N.C.: Duke University Press, 1995.

Stone, Deborah. "Sex, Lies, and *The Scarlet Letter.*" *American Prospect* 21 (Spring 1995): 105–9.

Stout, Janis P. "The Fallen Woman and the Conflicted Author: Hawthorne and Hardy." *American Transcendental Quarterly* 1.3 (1987): 233–46.

Stuart, Shea. "Subversive Didacticism in Eliza Haywood's *Betsy Thoughtless.*" *Studies in English Literature* 42.3 (Summer 2002): 559–75.

Suarez, Michael F. "Asserting the Negative: 'Child' Clarissa and the Problem of the 'Determined Girl.'" In *New Essays on Samuel Richardson,* edited by Albert J. Rivero, 69–84. New York: St. Martin's Press, 1996.

Sudrann, Jean. "*Daniel Deronda* and the Landscape of Exile." *English Literary History* 37.3 (1970): 433–55.

Suleri, Sara. *The Rhetoric of English India*. Chicago: University of Chicago Press, 1992.

Surratt, Marshall N. "'The Awe-Creating Presence of the Deity': Some Religious Sources for Charles Brockden Brown's *Wieland*." *Papers on Language and Literature: A Journal for Scholars and Critics of Language and Literature* 33.3 (Summer 1997): 310–24.

Sussman, Charlotte, *Consuming Anxieties: Consumer Protest, Gender, and British Slavery, 1713–1833*. Stanford: Stanford University Press, 2000.

———. "The Other Problem with Women: Reproduction and Slave Culture in Aphra Behn's *Oroonoko*." In *Rereading Aphra Behn: History, Theory, and Criticism*, edited by Heidi Hunter, 212–33. Charlottesville: University Press of Virginia, 1993.

Swaminathan, Srivdhya. "Defoe's Alternative Conduct Manual: Survival Strategies and Female Networks in *Moll Flanders*." *Eighteenth-Century Fiction* 15.2 (January 2003): 185–206.

Swan, Beth. "Raped by the System: An Account of Clarissa in the Light of Eighteenth-Century Law." In *1650–1859: Ideas, Aesthetics, and Inquiries in the Early Modern Era*, vol, 6, edited by Kevin L. Cope, 113–29. New York: AMS Press, 2001.

Swann, Charles. *Nathaniel Hawthorne: Tradition and Revolution*. Cambridge: Cambridge University Press, 1991.

Swanson, Diana L. "'My Boldness Terrifies Me': Sexual Abuse and Female Subjectivity in *The Voyage Out*." *Twentieth Century Literature: A Scholarly and Critical Journal* 41.4 (Winter 1995): 284–309

Swift, Jonathan. "An Abstract of the History of England." In *Prose Works*, Vol. 10. London: 1879–1908.

Sypher, Wylie. *Guinea's Captive Kings: British Anti-Slavery Literature of the Eighteenth Century*. New York: Octagon Books, 1969.

Szirotny, June Skye. "George Eliot's *Spanish Gypsy*: The Spanish-Moorish Motif." *Annual Notes Quarterly* 16.2 (Spring 2003): 36–46.

Tate, Claudia. *Domestic Allegories of Political Desire: The Black Heroine's Text at the Turn of the Century*. New York: Oxford University Press, 1992.

Tawil, Ezra M. "Domestic Frontier Romance, or How the Sentimental Heroine Became White." *Novel: A Forum on Fiction* 32.1 (Fall 1998): 99–124.

Taylor, Douglas. "From Slavery to Prison: Benjamin Rush, Harriet Jacobs, and the Ideology of Reformative Incarceration." *Genre: Forms of Discourse and Culture* 35.3–4 (Fall–Winter 2002): 429–47.

Tennenhouse, Leonard. "Libertine America." *Differences: A Journal of Feminist Cultural Studies* 11.5 (1999–2000): 1–28.

Thomas, Brook. "Billy Budd and the Judgment of Silence." In *Literature and Ideology*, edited by Harry R. Garvin and James M. Heath, 51–78. Lewisburg, Pa.: Bucknell University Press, 1982.

———. "Citizen Hester: *The Scarlet Letter* as Civic Myth." *American Literary History* 13.2 (Summer 2001): 181–211.

Thompson, Andrew. "Giuseppe Mazzini and George Eliot's *Daniel Deronda*." *Quaderni del Dipartimento di Lingue e Letterature Straniere Moderne, Universita de Genova* 6 (1993): 101–11.

Thompson, Helen. "Plotting Materialism: W. Charleton's *The Ephesian Matron*, E. Haywood's *Fantomina,* and Feminine Consistency." *Eighteenth-Century* 35.2 (Winter 2002): 195–214.

Thompson, James. *Models of Value: Eighteenth-Century Political Economy and the Novel.* Durham, N.C.: Duke University Press, 1996.

Thompson, John. *The Media and Modernity: A Social Theory of the Media.* Stanford, Calif.: Stanford University Press, 1995.

Thomson, James. *Liberty, The Castle of Indolence and Other Poems.* Oxford: Clarendon Press, 1986.

Thorn, Jennifer. "'A Race of Angels': Castration and Exoticism in Three Exotic Tales by Eliza Haywood." In *The Passionate Fictions of Eliza Haywood: Essays on her Life and Work,* edited by Kirsten T. Saxton and Rebecca P. Bocchicchio, 168–193. Lexington: University Press of Kentucky, 2000.

Thorne, Christian. "Providence in the Early Novel, or Accident if You Please." *Modern Language Quarterly* 64.3 (September 2003): 323–47.

Tompkins, Jane. *Sensational Designs: The Cultural Work of American Fiction, 1790–1860.* New York: Oxford University Press, 1985.

Traister, Bryce. "Libertinism and Authorship in America's Early Republic." *American Literature* 72.1 (March 2000): 1–30.

Tromp, Marlene. *The Private Rod: Marital Violence, Sensation, and the Law in Victorian Britain.* Charlottesville: University Press of Virginia, 2000.

Trubowitz, Rachel. "Female Preachers and Male Wives: Gender and Authority in Civil-War England." In *Pamphlet Wars: Prose in the English Revolution,* edited by James Holstun, 112–33. Portland, Ore.: F. Cass, 1992.

Trumpener, Katie. *Bardic Nationalism: The Romantic Novel and the British Empire.* Princeton, N.J.: Princeton University Press, 1997.

Tucker, Irene. *A Probable State: The Novel, the Contract, and the Jews.* Chicago: University of Chicago Press, 2000.

Turner, James Grantham. "Novel Panic: Picture and Performance in the Reception of Richardson's *Pamela.*" *Representations* 48 (Autumn 1994): 70–96.

Ulla, Haselstein. "Giving Her Self: Harriet Jacobs' *Incidents in the Life of a Slave Girl* and the Problem of Authenticity." In *(Trans)Formations of Cultural Identity in the English-Speaking World,* edited by Jochen Achilles and Carmen Birkle, 125–39. Heidelberg: Carl Winter Universitatsverlag, 1998.

Underdown, David. *A Freeborn People: Politics and the Nation in Seventeenth-Century England.* Oxford: Clarendon Press, 1996.

Vanbrugh, John. *The Provok'd Wife: A Comedy as it is Acted at the Theatres-Royal in Drury-Lane and Covennt-Garden.* London: Printed for Richard Wellington at the Dolphin and Crown in St. Paul's Churchyard: and William Lewis at the Dolphin in Great Russell Street Covent Garden, 1709.

Vanita, Ruth. "Bringing Buried Things to Light: Homoerotic Alliances in *To the Lighthouse.*" In *Virginia Woolf: Lesbian Readings,* edited by Michele Barrett and Patricia Cramer, 165–79. New York: New York University Press, 1997.

Vasquez, Mark. "'Your Sister Cannot Speak to You and Understand You as I Do': Native American Culture and Female Subjectivity in Lydia Marie Child and Catharine Maria Sedgwick." *American Transcendental Quarterly* 15.3 (September 2001): 173–90.

Vaughn, Alden T. and George Athan Billias, eds. *Perspectives on Early American History: Essays in Honor of Richard B. Morris.* New York: Harper and Row, 1973.

Verhoeven, W. M. "'Persuasive Rhetorick': Representation and Resistance in Early American Epistolary Fiction." In *Making America/Making American Literature: Franklin to Cooper,* edited by A. Robert Lee and W. M. Verhoeven, 123–64. Atlanta: Rodopi, 1996.

Vermillion, Mary. "*Clarissa* and the Marriage Act." *Eighteenth-Century Fiction* 9.4 (July 1997): 395–412.

Visconsi, Elliot. "A Degenerate Race: English Barbarism in Aphra Behn's *Oroonoko* and *The Widow Ranter.*" *ELH* 69.3 (2002): 673–701.

Viswanathan, Gauri. *Masks of Conquest: Literary Studies and British Rule in India.* New York: Columbia University Press, 1989.

Voloshin, Beverly. "*Wieland:* Accounting for Appearances." *New England Quarterly* 59.3 (September 1986): 341–57.

Wald, Priscilla. *Constituting Americans: Cultural Anxiety and Narrative Form.* Durham, N.C.: Duke University Press, 1995.

Waldstreicher, David. "'Fallen under My Observation': Vision and Virtue in *The Coquette.*" *Early American Literature* 27.3 (1992): 204–18.

Wall, Cheryl. *Women of the Harlem Renaissance.* Bloomington: Indiana University Press, 1995.

Wallace, Robert K. "*Billy Budd* and the Haymarket Hangings." *American Literature* 47.1 (March 1975): 108–13.

Wallinger, Hanna. "Voyage into the Heart of Africa." In *Black Imagination and the Middle Passage,* edited by Maria Diedrich, Henry Louis Gates Jr., and Carl Pederson, 203–14. New York: Oxford University Press, 1999.

Walpole, Horace. *The Castle of Otranto.* New York: Oxford University Press, 1996.

———. *Horace Walpole's Correspondence,* compiled by Edwine M. Martz. Volume 9: 149 [11 May 1753]. New Haven: Yale University Press, 1983.

Walser, Richard. "Boston's Reception of the First American Novel." *Early American Literature* 17.1 (Spring 1982): 65–74.

Walter, Krista. "Surviving the Garret: Harriet Jacobs and the Critique of Sentiment." *American Transcendental Quarterly* 8.3 (September 1994): 189–210.

Ward, Bernadette Waterman. "Zion's Mimetic Angel: George Eliot's *Daniel Deronda.*" *Shofar: An Interdisciplinary Journal of Jewish Studies* 22.2 (2004): 105–15.

Wardrop, Daneen. "'What Tangled Skeins Are the Genealogies of Slavery!' Gothic Families in Harriet Jacobs' *Incidents in the Life of a Slave Girl.*" *Literary Griot* 14.1–2 (Spring–Fall 2002): 23–43.

Warner, Michael. *The Letters of the Republic: Publication and the Public Sphere in Eighteenth-Century America.* Cambridge, Mass.: Harvard University Press, 1990.

Warner, William B. "The Elevation of the Novel in England: Hegemony and Literary History." *English Literary History* 59.3 (Fall 1992): 577–96.

———. *Licensing Entertainment: The Elevation of Novel Reading in Britain, 1684–1750.* Berkeley: University of California Press, 1998.

———. *Reading "Clarissa": The Struggles of Interpretation.* New Haven, Conn.: Yale University Press, 1979.

Warren, Mercy Otis. *The History of the Rise, Progress, and Termination of the American*

Revolution: Interspersed with Biographical, Political, and moral Observations, Volumes 1–3. Boston: Manning and Loring, 1805.

Watson, Timothy. "Jamaica, Genealogy, George Eliot: Inheriting the Empire after Moran Bay." *Jouvert: A Journal of Postcolonial Studies* 1.1 (1997): http://social.chass.ncsu.edu/jouvert.

Watt, Ian. *The Rise of the Novel.* Berkeley: University of California Press, 1957.

Watts, Edward. *Writing and Postcolonialism in the Early Republic.* Charlottesville: University Press of Virginia, 1998.

Watts, Steven. *The Romance of Real Life: Charles Brockden Brown and the Origins of American Culture.* Baltimore: Johns Hopkins University Press, 1994.

Weierman, Karen Woods. "Reading and Writing *Hope Leslie*: Catharine Maria Sedgwick's Indian 'Connections.'" *New England Quarterly* 75.3 (September 2002): 415–43.

Weil, Lise. "Entering a Lesbian Field of Vision: *To The Lighthouse* and *Between the Acts.*" In *Virginia Woolf: Lesbian Readings,* edited by Michele Barrett and Patricia Cramer, 222–58. New York: New York University Press, 1997.

Weinbaum, Alys Eve. *Wayward Reproductions: Genealogies of Race and Nation in Transatlantic Modern Thought.* Durham, N.C.: Duke University Press, 2004.

Weinbrot, Howard. *Augustus Caesar in "Augustan" England: The Decline of a Classical Norm.* Princeton, N.J.: Princeton University Press, 1978.

——. *Britannia's Issue: The Rise of British Literature from Dryden to Ossian.* Cambridge: Cambridge University Press, 1993.

Wenke, John. "Melville's Indirection: *Billy Budd,* the Genetic Text, and 'the Deadly Space Between.'" In *New Essays on Billy Budd,* edited by Donald Yannella, 114–44. New York: Cambridge University Press, 2002.

Wenska, Walter P. Jr. "*The Coquette* and the American Dream of Freedom." *Early American Literature* 12 (1977–78): 243–55.

Wesley, Marilyn. "A Woman's Place: The Politics of Space in Harriet Jacobs' *Incidents in the Life of a Slave Girl.*" *Women's Studies* 26.1 (1997): 59–72.

West, Elizabeth J. "Reworking the Early Conversion Narrative: Race and Christianity in *Our Nig.*" *MELUS* 24.2 (Summer 1999): 3–27.

Westfall, Marilyn. "A Sermon by the Queen of Whores." *Studies in English Literature* 41.3 (Summer 2001): 483–97.

Wheeler, Roxann. "Domesticating Equiano's Interesting Narrative." *Eighteenth-Century Studies* 34.4 (2001): 620–624.

——. "My Savage, My Man: Racial Multiplicity in *Robinson Crusoe.*" *English Literary History* 62.4 (1995): 821–61.

White, Barbara. "*Our Nig* and the She-Devil: New Information about Harriet Wilson and the Bellmont Family." *American Literature* 65.1 (March 1993): 19–52.

White, Devon. "Contemporary Criticism of Five American Sentimental Novels, 1970–1994: An Annotated Bibliography." *Bulletin of Bibliography* 52.4 (December 1995): 293–305.

White, Ed. "Captaine Smith, Colonial Novelist." *American Literature* 75.3 (September 2003): 487–513.

——. "Carwin the Peasant Rebel." In *Revising Charles Brockden Brown: Culture, Politics, and Sexuality in the Early Republic*, edited by Philip Barnard, Mark L. Kamrath, and Stephen Shapiro, 41–59. Knoxville: University of Tennessee Press, 2004.

White, Paula K. "Puritan Theories of History in Hawthorne's Fiction." *Canadian Review of American Studies* 9.2 (Fall 1978): 135–53.

Whitford, Kathryn. "'On a Field, Sable, the Letter "A," Gules.'" *Lock Haven Review* 10 (1968): 33–38.

Whitman, Walt. *The Portable Walt Whitman.* Edited by Michael Warner. New York: Penguin, 2004.

Wiegman, Robyn. *American Anatomies: Theorizing Race and Gender.* Durham, N.C.: Duke University Press, 1995.

———. "Economics of the Body." *Criticism* 31.1 (Winter 1989): 33–51.

Williams, Andrew P. "The African as Text: Ownership and Authority in Aphra Behn's *Oroonoko.*" *Journal of African Travel Writing* 5 (1998): 5–14.

Williams, Bettye J. "Nella Larsen: Early Twientieth-Century Novelist of Afrocentric Feminist Thought." *College Language Association Journal* 39.2 (December 1995): 165–78.

Williams, Eric. *Capitalism and Slavery.* Chapel Hill: University of North Carolina Press, 1994. [1944].

Wilputte, Earla A. "Eliza Haywood's *Frederick, Duke of Brunswick-Lunenburgh.*" *Studies in English Literature, 1500–1900.* 41.3 (Summer 2001): 499–514.

———. "The Textual Architecture of Eliza Haywood's *Adventure of Eovaai.*" *Essays in Literature* 22.1 (Spring 1995): 31–44.

Wilson, Harriet. *Our Nig, or Sketches from the Life of a Free Black.* New York: Vintage, 1983.

Wilson, James D. "Incest and American Romantic Fiction." *Studies in the Literary Imagination* 7.1 (1974): 31–50.

Wilson, Kathleen. "Citizenship, Empire, and Modernity in the English Provinces, c. 1720–1790." *Eighteenth-Century Studies* 29.1 (1996): 69–96.

Wilt, Judith. "Double-Reading *Daniel Deronda.*" *PMLA* 93.5 (October 1978): 1012–14.

———. "He Could Go No Further: A Modest Proposal about Lovelace and Clarissa." *PMLA* (January 1977): 19–32.

———. "Steamboat Surfacing: Scott and the English Novelists." *Nineteenth-Century Fiction* 35.4 (March 1981): 459–86.

Winstanley, Gerrard. *The Law of Freedom in a Platform,* edited by Max Radin. San Sutro: California State Library, 1939.

Winter, Kari J. *Subjects of Slavery, Agents of Change: Women and Power in Gothic Novels and Slave Narratives, 1790–1865.* Athens: University of Georgia Press, 1992.

Winters, Yvor. *Maule's Curse: Seven Studies in the History of American Obscurantism: Hawthorne, Cooper, Melville, Poe, Emerson, Jones Very, Emily Dickinson, Henry James.* Norfolk, Conn.: New Directions, 1938.

Wiseman, Susan. "'Adam the Father of All Flesh': Porno-Political Rhetoric and Political Theory in and after the English Civil War." In *Pamphlet Wars: Prose in the English Revolution,* edited by James Holstun, 134–57. London: Frank Cass, 1992.

Wohlfarth, Marc E. "*Daniel Deronda* and the Politics of Nationalism." *Nineteenth-Century Literature* 53.2 (September 1998): 188–210.

Wolff, Cynthia Griffin. *Samuel Richardson and the Eighteenth-Century Puritan Character.* Hamden, Conn.: Archon, 1972.

Wolfreys, Julian. "The Ideology of Englishness: The Paradoxes of Tory-Liberal Culture and National Identitiy in *Daniel Deronda.*" *George Eliot – George Henry Lewes Studies* 26 (September 1994): 15 – 33.

Wollaeger, Mark. "Woolf, Postcards, and the Elision of Race: Colonizing Women in *The Voyage Out.*" *Modernism/Modernity* 8.1 (2001): 43 – 75.

Wolstenholme, Susan. *Gothic (Re)Visions: Writing Women as Readers.* Albany: State University of New York Press, 1993.

Wood, Gordon S. *The Creation of the American Republic, 1776 – 1787.* New York: Norton, 1972.

———. *The Radicalism of the American Revolution.* New York: Knopf, 1992.

———. *The Rising Glory of America, 1760 – 1820.* New York: Brazillier, 1971.

Woodard, Maureen L. "Female Captivity and the Deployment of Race in Three Early American Texts." *Papers on Language and Literature: A Journal for Scholars and Critics of Language and Literature* 32.2 (Spring 1996): 115 – 46.

Woodhouse, A. S. P. *Puritanism and Liberty: Being the Army Debates (1647 – 9) from the Clarke Manuscripts with Supplementary Documents,* 3rd ed. London: Dent, 1986.

Woodson, Thomas. "Hawthorne, Upham, and *The Scarlet Letter.*" In *Critical Essays on Hawthorne's "The Scarlet Letter,"* edited by David B. Kesterson, 186 – 87. Boston: G. K. Hall, 1988.

Woolf, D. R. *The Idea of History in Early Stuart England.* Toronto: University of Toronto Press, 1990.

Woolf, Virginia. "Defoe." In *Common Reader I.* New York: Harcourt Brace Jovanovich, 1953 [1925].

———. *Jacob's Room.* New York: Penguin, 1992.

———. *Melymbrosia.* Edited by Louise A. DeSalvo. New York: New York Public Library, 1982.

———. *Mrs. Dalloway.* New York: Harcourt Brace Jovanovich, 1985 [1925].

———. *To the Lighthouse.* New York: Harcourt Brace Jovanovich, 1981 [1927].

———. *The Voyage Out.* New York: Harcourt Brace Jovanovich, 1948 [1920].

———. *The Waves.* New York: Harcourt Brace Jovanovich, 1959 [1931].

Wordsworth, William. *The Poems,* volume 1, edited by John O. Hayden. New York: Penguin, 1988.

Yanella, Donald, ed. *New Essays on "Billy Budd."* New York: Cambridge University Press, 2002.

Yazawa, Melvin. *From Colonies to Commonwealth: Familial Ideology and the Beginnings of the American Republic.* Baltimore: Johns Hopkins University Press, 1985.

Yellin, Jean Fagan. "John S. Jacobs' 'A True Tale of Slavery' and Harriet Jacob's *The Deeper Wrong: A Brother's Story.*" In *Monuments of the Black Atlantic: Slavery and Memory,* edited by Joanne M. Braxton and Maria I. Diedrich, 53 – 58. Munster: LIT, 2004.

Young, Hershini Bhana. *Haunting Capital: Memory, Text, and the Black Diasporic Body.* Hanover, N.H.: University Press of New England, 2006.

Young, Robert. "Hybridism and the Ethnicity of the English." In *Cultural Readings of*

Imperialism: Edward Said and the Gravity of History, edited by Keith Ansell-Pearson, Benita Parry, and Judith Squires, 127–150. New York: St. Martin's Press, 1997.

Zaret, David. *The Heavenly Contract: Ideology and Organization in Pre-Revolutionary Puritanism.* Chicago: University of Chicago Press, 1984.

Zias, Heather. "'Who Can Believe?': Sentiment vs. Cynicism in Richardson's *Clarissa.*" *Eighteenth-Century Life* 27.3 (Fall 2003): 99–123.

Ziff, Larzer. "A Reading of *Wieland.*" *PMLA* 77.1 (March 1962): 51–57.

Zim, Rivkah. "Awakened Perceptions in *Daniel Deronda.*" *Essays in Criticism: A Journal of Literary Criticism* 36.3 (1986): 210–34.

Zomchick, John P. *Family and Law in Eighteenth-Century Fiction: The Public Conscience in the Private Sphere.* New York: Cambridge University Press, 1993.

Index

British culture, 80–86; Macaulay's nativist rendering of, 71–73; property principles in, 53–55, 118, 136, 140–41; Putney Debates, 29, 48–56, 137; in rape narratives, 127–28, 136–37; republican and contract-state's enfolding of, 12–14, 51, 54–56; Saxonist narratives of, 2–5, 13–14, 27–32, 40–41, 457n24; Whig views of, 19–20, 32; white women writers' rhetoric of, 9, 10–11, 59, 67, 77–78, 112–13, 115

Black Athena (Bernal), 269

Black Atlantic, 5

Black Empire (Stephens), 451

Black Sexual Politics (Collins), 451

Blair, Hugh, 83, 84–86, 244–45, 433

Boleyn, Anne, 335

Bolingbroke, Lord (Henry St. John), 66–67, 70, 74, 461n14

bonded labor, 12

"Bonds of Brotherhood" (McCann), 500n8, 500n11

Bordering on the Body (Doyle), 418, 427

"Boston Declaration of Grievances," 63

Botting, Fred, 483n7

Boudinot, Elias, 282, 493n13

Bradford, William, 73

Brenner, Robert, 33–34

Brent, Linda, 174

Brinkley, Roberta, 14, 58

"Britannia Rules *The Waves*" (Marcus), 505n29, 506n32

British Recluse, The (Haywood), 125, 130–34, 388

Britons, 27–28

Brooke, Henry, 191–92

Brooks, Kristina, 499n2

brother-sister plots, 10–13, 386; in W. H. Brown's *The Power of Sympathy*, 166–69, 474n38; in Defoe's *Moll Flanders*, 155–57; in Eliot's *Daniel Deronda*, 331–33, 360–67; in gothic novels, 215–17, 220, 232–35, 249–51, 482nn3–4; in Hopkins's *Contending Forces*, 369–70; in Hopkins's *Of One Blood*, 262, 263, 264–65; in Rowson's *Lucy Temple*, 164–65; the "unspeakable" in, 216, 482n4; in Woolf's *To the Lighthouse*, 428–29; in Woolf's *The Waves*, 431–32

Brown, Charles Brockden, 7, 145, 148, 159,

457n29; *Memoirs of Carwin*, 231, 240; Native Americans' extermination and, 234–35; *Wieland*, 231–53, 487n20, 488n24

Brown, Gillian, 11, 467n8, 493n12

Brown, Laura, 103, 473n19

Brown, Lois Lamphere, 381–82

Brown, William Hill, 22, 158, 165, 166–70, 234

Browne, Ray B., 480n33

Brutus (Lucius Junius Brutus), 9

Bunyan, John, 137, 159

Burgett, Bruce, 487n16

Burke, Edmund, 119–20, 144, 159, 463n22; apprehensions about British ascendency of, 122–23, 339; on maroons and Indians, 121–22; racialist freedom rhetoric of, 121–23; on rape and race, 122; *Reflections on the Revolution in France*, 121–23, 141, 467nn12–13

Burns, Robert, 86–87

Bush, George W., 446–48

Byron, George Gordon, Lord, 256

Caldwell, Tanya, 185–86, 191–93, 195–96, 478n6, 478n8

Calverts of Maryland, 36, 61

Cane (Toomer), 407–8

Carby, Hazel, 379, 500n6, 502n8

Carlyle, Thomas, 352

Carpenter, Mary Wilson, 497n3

Carr, Brian, 503n22

Carretta, Vincent, 185, 194

"Case of the Army Truly Stated, The," 48–50

Cassidy, Thomas, 499n2

Castiglia, Christopher, 492n11

Castle, Terry, 17

Castle of Otranto (Walpole), 217–20

Caton, Lou, 155

Cavendish, Margaret, 100

Celtic legacy, 82–86

Cervantes, Miguel de, 466n3

Characteristics (Shaftesbury), 22

Charcot Sâltpetrière, Jean-Martin, 265

Charles I, king of England, 27–30, 61; historiography of, 64, 70; *Oroonoko* analogies to, 103–4; overthrow and execution of, 33, 37, 47, 98, 103, 310, 335, 445;

Parliament dissolved by, 32, 35. *See also* English Civil War

Charles II, king of England, 59–60; colonial fealty sought by, 61–62, 461n9; historiography of, 64; liberty rhetoric used by, 62; Navigation Acts and, 61; Protestant mistress of, 150, 154

Charlotte Temple (Rowson), 7, 10, 21, 137, 145–46, 165–66; as allegory of heroic history, 160, 161–62, 164; Anglo-specificity of, 160; economic contexts of seduction in, 162–63, 474n36; Mr. Eldridge as narrator of, 161–64; political context of, 158–59, 162–63; popularity of, 159–60, 474n29; swoon moment in, 8

Chartier, Roger, 18

Chase, Richard, 17

Cheyette, Bryan, 498n18

Chidley, Katherine, 46–47, 313

Child, Lydia Maria, 165

Chopin, Kate, 394

chronotopes, 4

Cities of the Dead (Roach), 5, 462n4

citizenship, 14; racialized notions of, 11–12, 456n21; transition from subject to, 75–76

civil rights movement, 450

Claiborne, William, 34–35

Clarendon, Earl of (Edward Hyde), 100

Clarissa, or the History of a Young Lady (Richardson), 6, 7; brother in, 10, 136, 141; colonial contexts of, 137, 141–42; domestic setting of, 135–37, 470n49; epistolary form in, 118, 137–38, 139, 142; in history of the novel, 18–19, 144; individualism of, 16; isolation and interiority of, 137–38, 139–40, 468n25, 470n46; as national allegory, 137–40, 470n41; property and law in, 118, 136, 139–42, 362, 469nn36–39, 470n49; rape in, 20, 28–29, 117–19, 135–36, 142–44, 471n54; savagery in, 141–42; struggle against tyranny in, 18–19; swoon moment in, 135–36; traveling elements of, 132, 466n3

Clark, J. C. D., 456n22

Clarke, Thomas, 341

classical legacies: in Augustanism, 80–81, 462n6; in rape narratives, 9, 99, 358–59, 445, 455n15

Clemmen, Yves W. A., 502n10

Clery, E. J., 483n7, 484n12

Cohan, Steven, 16

Coherence of Gothic Conventions, The (Sedgwick), 482n4

Coke, Edward, 31, 117, 136–37

Colacurcio, Michael, 304–7, 313, 320, 495n14

Colbourn, H. Trevor, 14, 58, 74

Coleridge, Samuel Taylor, 86

Colley, Linda, 83

Collins, Patricia Hill, 451

Collins, William, 81–82

colonialism. *See* English colonies in America; imperialist narratives

Colonies to Commonwealth (Yazawa), 456n18, 456n20

Color and Culture (Posnock), 17–18

Colored American Magazine, 263

Commoners Complaint, The (Oberton), 119–20

Common Sense (Paine), 65, 120–21

Commonwealth of England, 32, 53, 73

community: imagined, 68; individualism vs., 10–14, 456n18, 456nn20–21; Rousseau on, 1–2, 11–12, 22, 207, 480n36; social contract and, 50–56, 118, 140–41, 206–9, 207

Comus (Milton), 283–84, 418

Conceived by Liberty (Smith), 488n5

Conrad, Joseph, 130, 132

Consent of the Governed, The (G. Brown), 467n8, 493n12

"Contending Contexts" (Cassidy), 499n2

Contending Forces (Hopkins), 8, 119, 274, 490n20; authorial maneuvers in, 369–72, 378–80; classical legacy of, 371; codes of masculinity in, 332–33, 389, 500n8, 501n16; colonial setting of, 278–79; competing freedom values in, 375–78; economics of colonization and slavery in, 372–74; epic-narrational swerves in, 378–82; female homoeroticism in, 386–90, 501nn13–16; Madame Frances's historical vision in, 385–86, 501n12; mixed racial genealogies in, 370–71, 380–82; native spot in, 278, 371, 375–78; polyvocal narration of, 370–71, 386, 499n2; public-sphere scenes in, 382–86; rape and communal history in, 9, 371–72,

"Dislocation, Violence, and the Language of Sentiment" (Hamilton), 488n3

Dittmar, Linda, 502n15

divine right doctrine, 31–32

"Dr. Heidegger's Experiment" (Hawthorne), 317–18

Dr. Jekyll and Mr. Hyde (Stevenson), 266

Domestic Allegories (Tate), 488nn5–6

"Domestic Frontier Romance" (Tawil), 492n11, 493nn12–13

Doody, Margaret, 16, 99, 455n15, 469n37, 497n4

Doreski, C. K., 489n13, 490n19

Dorislaus, Dr., 31

Douglass, Frederick, 186

Doyle, Laura, 418, 427, 501n13, 505n29

Dryden, John, 80

Du Bois, W. E. B., 14, 17–18, 56, 408, 450

Duckworth, Gerald, 416–17

Durlson, J., 474n38

Eagleton, Terry, 138, 143

economics of liberty: in American colonies, 4, 21, 61, 410; in brother-sister possession narratives, 215–17, 482nn3–4; in English Civil War, 37–38, 40–43, 44, 445; globalization and, 15; in gothic narratives, 215–17, 231–32, 255–56, 258–60, 267–72, 482n1, 482n3, 485n3; in Hopkins's *Contending Forces*, 372–74, 385; Overton's views of, 162; property and race in, 51–55, 118, 139–42, 152–57, 175–76, 469nn36–39, 470n49, 472nn17–18, 473n23, 476n48; Protestant influence on, 4, 21, 32–36, 51, 53, 61, 153–54, 410; in seduction narratives, 162–63, 474n36; sexual contracts in, 152–54, 362, 472n17, 473n19; slavery as basis for, 237–40, 251–53, 378; slave trade in, 3, 184, 186–88, 190–91, 479n19, 479n22; for women, 118, 153–54, 472nn17–18

Edgar Huntly (C. B. Brown), 234

Eighteenth-Century Fiction and the Law (Schmidgen), 469n34

eighteenth-century literature, 483n8; ancients vs. moderns, 80–81, 83–84; Blair's treatise on Ossian, 83, 84–86; C. B. Brown's *Wieland*, 231–53; W. H. Brown's *The Power of Sympathy*, 146, 158, 166–70;

Celtic visions in, 82–86; Defoe's *Robinson Crusoe*, 5–6, 8, 145–46, 149–51, 183–90; Defoe's *Roxana* and *Moll Flanders*, 149–58; Equiano's *Interesting Narrative*, 97, 184–86, 190–202; Haywood's *Fantomina* and *The British Recluse*, 123–34; Hurd's *Letters on Chivalry and Romance*, 82–84, 86; Lewis's *The Monk*, 220–29; liberty poems, 81–82; MacPherson's *Poems of Ossian*, 82–86; Percy's *Reliques*, 84–86; racialization of the sublime in, 82–87; rape narratives in, 117–44, 466n2; Richardson's *Clarissa*, 10, 18–19, 28, 135–44; Rowson's *Charlotte Temple*, 158, 164; Spanish picaro influence on, 118, 466n3; Walpole's *Castle of Otranto*, 215–20

"Elegy in a Country Churchyard" (Gray), 256–57

Eliot, George, 269, 277–79, 333–37, 352–55, 361–65, 453; epic scope of, 497n3; Hegelian ideas of, 338–40, 356–57; literary forebears of, 358–59, 497n4; literary legacy of, 371; *Middlemarch*, 316; *The Mill on the Floss*, 331–32, 363; "The Modern Hep! Hep! Hep!," 342, 343–47, 356–57, 498n12, 498n17; political context of, 340–42, 358–60; Semitizing of Britain's Jews by, 345–51, 498–99nn16–19; Zionist vision of, 340–48, 366–67, 498n10. *See also Daniel Deronda*

Elizabeth I, queen of England, 335

Elliot, Emory, 485n1

Ellison, Ralph, 14, 261, 400–401, 402

Elstob, Elizabeth, 64

Elstob, William, 64

Emerson, Ralph Waldo, 22, 55, 463n28, 467n14, 490n18; Hopkins's deconstruction of, 374, 379–80; racialized American everyman of, 89–90, 203; racialized sublime in, 88–90; Whitman influenced by, 91

Emery, Mary Lou, 431

empire. *See* imperialist narratives

"Emplotting National History" (Sawaya), 501n15

Ends of Empire, The (Laura Brown), 473n19

England and America (Wakefield), 338

"England's lamentable Slaverie" (Walwyn), 41–42

English Civil War, 1, 4, 9, 13, 21–22, 30–31; American liberty narratives of, 471n4; anti-Normanism of, 55; Atlantic context of, 32–38; Diggers's communal vision in, 40–41, 52, 54; economic basis of, 36–37, 40–43, 44, 445; historiography of, 63–73; land distribution in, 333–34; Levellers' rhetoric of freedom in, 40–43, 44, 47, 52; Long Parliament, 36, 38; memoir-histories of, 100; newspapers and public sphere in, 38–43; Petition of Right, 32; political context of, 38–43; politicization of people in, 60, 460n4; portrayal in *Liberty* of, 2–3; Protestantism in, 43–48, 333–34; Putney Debates, 29, 48–56, 71, 263; Saxon origin stories in, 27–28; Sedgwick's *Hope Leslie* as allegory of, 288–92; Star Chamber abolished during, 36, 38; *State Tracts, 1660—1687*, 58; tropes of national rebirth in, 2–3, 5, 455n3; women's activism in, 39–40, 46–48. *See also* Saxonist legacy of freedom

English colonies in America, 7, 12, 32, 41, 55, 93, 338; Bermuda colony, 35; British crown opposed by, 34–38; Calverts of Maryland, 36, 61; historiography of, 73–78; Massachusetts Bay Colony, 33, 61, 304–8; mercantile colonialism of, 4, 21, 34, 61, 237–40, 410; New Hampshire, 62; New York, 61, 62; Saxon notions of freedom in, 58, 60–63; slave trade in, 35–36, 237–40; violence of land acquisition in, 251–53, 281–83, 290–91; Virginia settlements, 33–35, 76, 445; West Indian colonies, 35–36, 351–52, 372. *See also* imperialist narratives; United States

English-language frameworks, 146–49, 451–54, 471n2, 471n4

English Traits lecture (Emerson), 89–90, 203

"Entering a Lesbian Field of Vision" (Weil), 505n18

Eovaai (Haywood), 124, 130, 468n19

epic narratives, 22; Eliot's *Daniel Deronda*, 331–67, 497n3; gendered alienation of citizen-heroines in, 285–86; Hawthorne's *The Scarlet Letter*, 301–29; Hopkins's *Contending Forces*, 369–90; native spots in, 277–78, 292–97, 302, 308–12, 333–35, 352, 357, 371, 375–78, 497n6; race principle in, 277–79; racialization of transplanted English stock in, 309; racialized Native Americans in, 6, 278–83, 286, 491n7, 492n11, 493n13; Sedgwick's *Hope Leslie*, 277–99; swooning swerves in, 378–82

Equiano, Olaudah, 6, 22, 145, 182, 184–86, 455n10; Caldwell's views of, 185–86, 191–93, 195–96, 478n6, 478n8; economic activities of, 146, 197, 479n22; English name of, 191–92; literary forebears of, 193–95, 197–98, 478n6; notions of liberty of, 28–29, 479n17; Protestantism of, 198, 480n26; racialized double standard in, 184, 196–202, 479n17, 479n21, 480n25, 480n27; sister of, 200–201; on *Zong* massacre, 9. *See also Interesting Narrative of the Life of Olaudah Equiano*

Ernest, John, 172, 449, 477n58

"Essay of Dramatick Poesie" (Dryden), 80

"Essence and the Mulatto Traveler" (Gray), 502n10

Ethiopianism, 261–62, 271–72, 489nn13–14, 490nn15–16, 490n22, 490n28

ethnographic travel narratives, 198–99, 480n27

European Union, 348

Evans, Isaac, 363

Evans, Marian. *See* Eliot, George

Exclusion Crisis (1678—81), 60

exile narratives, 5–6, 145; African labor in, 146, 149; W. H. Brown's *The Power of Sympathy*, 166–70; Cooper's sea-adventure fiction, 160; Defoe's *Moll Flanders* and *Roxana*, 149–58; Miltonian "fall" in, 146–49, 155; nautical metaphors in, 149, 151, 158; political contexts of, 150–51, 158–59; racialized ruin in, 149, 158–59; Rowson's *Charlotte Temple* and *Lucy Temple*, 158–66; sexual ruin in, 149–50; transatlantic framework for, 146–49; Wilson's *Our Nig*, 170–82. *See also* shipwreck and sea trauma narratives

Eyre, Edward, 352

Fantomina; or, Love in a Maze (Haywood), 125–30, 469n29

brother-sister subplots in, 215–17, 220, 232–35, 249–51; Brown's *Wieland*, 231–53, 487n20, 488n24; convent and monastery settings in, 224, 484n19; feminist readings of, 482n2; Hopkins's *Of One Blood*, 255–56, 261–74; Jacobs's *Incidents in the Life of a Slave Girl*, 217, 255–61; Lewis's *The Monk*, 220–29; Morrison's *Beloved*, 255; possession in, 215–17, 231–32, 255–74, 482n1, 482n3, 485n3; psychological theory in, 265–67, 269, 382, 489n12, 490n22, 490n27; ridicule of, 483n8; Saxonist legacy of, 216, 217, 219, 231–32, 235–40, 483n7, 485n3; subjectivization of interior self in, 216, 482n6; tale of the Bleeding Nun, 223–25, 229; threats of rape in, 218; trope of displacement and colonial ruin in, 220–23, 228–29, 231, 235, 237, 245–51, 483nn9–10; Walpole's *Castle of Otranto*, 217–20

Gothic Radicalism (Smith), 482n6

Gothic Reflections (Garrett), 483n9

Gothic Scalders, 85–86

"Goths in History, The" (Sowerby), 483n7

Goths of England, The (Kliger), 55

Gould, Philip B., 491n7

Gray, Jeffrey, 502n10

Gray, Thomas, 256, 370, 380

"Great Carbuncle, The" (Hawthorne), 322

Green, T. R., 344, 346

Greeson, Jennifer Rae, 488n3

Gruesser, John Cullen, 370–71

Gunpowder Plot, 291–92

Gussman, Deborah, 457n24

Gustavas Vasa (Brooke), 191–92

Guthrie, William, 55

Gwynne, Nell, 150, 154

gynesis, 19

Habakkuk, H. J., 140

Hackett, Robin, 418–19, 426, 504n5, 505n30, 506n32

Hall, Jennifer, 479n17

Hall, Michael, 63

Hamilton, Kristie, 488n3

Hamor, Ralph, 34

Hanscom, Elizabeth, 303

Hardt, Michael, 15, 448–49

Hardy, Thomas, 316–17

Hare, John, 27

Harper, Frances Ellen, 93

Harrington, James, 21–22, 57, 65–66

Harris, Marla, 371, 489n13

Harris, Susan K., 483nn11–12

Hartman, Saidiya, 3, 258, 267, 488nn5–6

"Haunted Mind, The" (Hawthorne), 322

Haviland, Beverly, 503nn27–28

Hawthorne (H. James), 302–3

Hawthorne, Nathaniel, 6, 8, 159, 265, 277–79, 301, 313, 319–20, 323–25, 327; Atlantic swoon of, 315; colonial history of conquest elided by, 302–3, 309–11; custom house dismissal of, 310–12; "The Custom House Introductory," 302, 308–12, 378, 494n3; "Dr. Heidegger's Experiment," 317–18; gothic tradition of, 255, 494n3; interiorization of self of, 315–16, 328–29; literary legacy of, 329, 369–70, 496n25; "Mrs. Hutchinson" essay, 313–15, 318, 326; on Native Americans, 314–15, 321–22, 496n21; political context of, 303–8, 310–11, 494n7, 495n8, 495n19. *See also Scarlet Letter, The*

Hawthorne's Divided Loyalties (Newberry), 495n16

Haywood, Eliza, 22, 102, 119, 137, 144, 464n5, 469n33, 500n3; *The British Recluse*, 130–34, 388; consent, seduction, and ruin emphasized by, 123–25, 143, 362, 468n28; *Fantomina*, 125–30; isolation and interiorization of characters of, 126, 128–34, 468n25; literary forebears of, 118; literary legacy of, 123–24, 148, 150, 467n16; political context of, 127, 131, 468n19; traveling element of, 118, 130, 131–33, 466n3, 469n34

Hazlitt, William, 16, 20, 457n30

Hegel, G. W. F.: on America, 338–40; on documentary approach to historiography, 461n19; on freedom as motor of history, 57–58, 78; on revolution and rebirth, 2–3, 4, 7; on universality of freedom, 46, 183, 451

Helgerson, Richard, 80

Hemingway, Ernest, 394

Henderson, Stephen, 17

Henry, Patrick, 279, 383, 491n5

Henry VII, king of England, 65

Henry VIII, king of England, 30, 65, 333, 335

Herzl, Theodor, 366

Hess, Moses, 358

Hickes, George, 64

Higonnet, Margaret R., 493n12

Hill, Christopher, 140, 468n25

Hilliard, Raymond, 141

Hine, Edward, 341

Histoire d'Angleterre (Rapin), 67–69

Historical and Political Discourse of the Laws and Government of England (Bacon), 40

historical race epics. *See* epic narratives

"Histories by Eliza Haywood and Henry Fielding" (Richetti), 500n3

historiography in England, 60–62, 74–77; by American colonists, 73; Bolingbroke's Country-Tory formulation, 66–67, 70, 461n14; documentary approach to, 58–59, 64–65, 70, 73, 461nn19–20; English Civil War in, 64, 70; Gothic balance of English parliamentary monarchy in, 57–58, 63–73, 120–21, 138; Harrington's *Oceana*, 65–66; Hegel's views of, 57–58, 78; Hume's moderating view of Saxonist liberty, 68–70; interiorization of liberty through reading of, 67–68, 72; Macaulay's embodiment of liberty, 70–73, 84; memoir-histories, 58–59, 100; on rape and sexual violation, 120–23; Rapin's shaping of Saxonist identity, 67–68; Saxonist legacy of freedom in, 64–73, 216–17; "secret" inside-outside perspectives of, 100–102, 464n8; serial form of, 67–69; *State Tracts, 1660–1687*, 58; Whig and Tory versions of, 63–73; by women, 72–73

historiography in United States, 73; exceptionalist approach to, 61, 283, 308, 471n4; Macauley's impact on, 74, 76; political contexts of, 120–21; Ramsay's use of Saxon liberty narratives, 74–76; Warren's gendered interiority and domesticity, 76–78

"History, Oratory, and God" (Potkay), 478n6

History and the Early English Novel (Mayer), 100

History of England from the Accession of James I (Macaulay), 70–73, 79, 84, 121, 461n20

History of England (Hume), 68–70

History of Miss Betsy Thoughtless, The (Haywood), 123–24

History of New Hampshire (Belknap), 74

History of Plymouth Plantation (Bradford), 73

History of the American Revolution, The (Ramsay), 74–76

History of the Celts (Pelloutier), 86

History of the First Discovery and Settlement of Virginia, The (Stith), 74

History of the Italian Republics (Sismondi), 334–35

History of the Province of New York, The (Smith), 74

History of the Rebellion (Clarendon), 100

History of the Rise, Progress, and Termination of the American Revolution (Warren), 74–75, 76–78

History of Tithes (Selden), 31

Hobbes, Thomas, 43

Holmesland, Oddvar, 465n19, 465n23

Hope Leslie (Sedgwick), 17, 160, 493n12; as allegory of English Civil War, 288–92; Christian alignment of, 281–82, 286, 295–99, 491n7; epic-narrational swerve in, 378; liberty principle in, 283–92, 494n14; marriage in, 288, 299, 326, 329; narrator of, 283, 292; native spot in, 277–78, 286, 292–97; racialized Native Americans in, 6, 278–83, 286, 491n7, 492n11, 493n13; struggles for sexual liberty in, 283–88; sublime climax of, 297–99; swoon moment of, 284–85, 298–99; "vanished" Indians of, 281–83, 295–96, 298–99, 491n7, 492n11

Hopkins, Pauline, 6, 7, 8, 119, 146, 182; authorial position of, 255–56, 262, 273–74, 369–72, 378–80; Bible cited by, 200; *Contending Forces*, 274, 277–79, 332–33, 369–90, 490n20; as editor of *Colored American Magazine*, 263, 490n18; as historical writer, 261, 489n13; literary forebears of, 369–70, 371; literary legacy of, 499n2; *Of One Blood*, 255–56, 261–74, 327, 369–70, 450, 489–90nn13–16

Hopkinson, John, 87–88
Horsman, Reginald, 13–14
Horvitz, Deborah, 265, 266, 490n30
Howe, Samuel, 280
Howells, William Dean, 303
Hsu, Hsuan, 240, 485n2
Hume, David, 1, 22, 59, 64; on Arthurian
    legends, 70; on Gothic balance of
    England's parliamentary monarchy,
    66–67; *History of England*, 68–70
Humphreys, John, 305, 306
Hunter, J. Paul, 99
Hurd, Richard, 82–84, 86, 433
Hurston, Zora Neale, 394
Hutchinson, Anne, 283, 304, 312–16, 325–
    26, 492n11, 495n14
Hutchinson, George, 395, 408, 501nn4–5
Hutchinson, Lucy, 100
Hutchinson, Thomas, 73
"Hybridism and the Ethnicity of the En-
    glish" (Young), 457n25
Hymn to Liberty (Cooke), 81

Illuminati movement, 240, 244, 246
imagined community, 68
immigrant narratives, 7
imperialist narratives, 5, 56; Africanism
    in *Oroonoko*, 97–98, 102–5, 115, 464n12;
    of George W. Bush, 446–48; of colonial
    speculation and bankruptcy, 352–57; eco-
    nomic basis in slavery of, 98, 237–40, 242,
    251–53, 372–74, 463n14; Eliot's Zionist
    vision, 340–48, 359–60, 498n10; martial
    law of the sea in, 209–10; modern order
    of property in, 53–55, 118, 139–42; na-
    tive literary traditions in, 83, 87; post-
    modern rethinking of, 15, 187, 448–49;
    of rape, 118–19, 466n2, 467n8; trope
    of displacement and colonial ruin in,
    220–23, 482n5; violence of colonization
    in, 104–5, 251–53, 281–83, 290–91, 302–3,
    307–8; in Woolf's queer visions, 426–43,
    504n5, 505n18, 505n25, 505n30, 506n32.
    See also Africanism; English colonies in
    America; Native Americans; slavery
Impressions of Theophrastus Such (Eliot),
    342, 343–47, 498n12, 498n17
"Inalienable Rights" (Gussman), 457n24
incest, 10; in W. H. Brown's *The Power of*

Sympathy, 166–70, 474n38; in Defoe's
    Moll Flanders, 155–57; in Rowson's *Lucy
    Temple*, 158, 164–66; in Woolf's novels,
    416–17
Inchiquin's Letters (Ingersoll), 88
Incidents in the Life of a Slave Girl (Jacobs),
    217, 255–61, 449, 488n3, 488nn5–6
indentured servitude, 35, 410, 459n11
independence. *See* Atlantic imaginary of
    racialized freedom
India and Palestine (Clarke), 341
Indianism, 6, 278–83, 286, 491n7, 492n11,
    493n13. *See also* Native Americans
Indian Removal Act (1830), 282, 303, 492n11
individualism and autonomy, 16–17;
    of Hawthorne's self-reliance, 311–12;
    in memoir writing, 58–59; republi-
    can brotherhood vs., 10–13, 456n18,
    456nn20–21; Rousseau on, 11–12, 22, 207;
    in social contract, 50–56, 118, 140–41,
    206–9
Ingersoll, Charles Jared, 88
"Inherited Rhetoric and Authentic
    History" (Doreski), 489n13
"In Praise of Extra-vagant Women"
    (Castiglia), 492n11
Institutes (Coke), 117
*Interesting Narrative of the Life of Olaudah
    Equiano* (Equiano), 97; as autobiogra-
    phy, 191–93, 197–98, 478n8; Benin de-
    scribed in, 199–200, 480n27; Bible cited
    in, 200; dangers of the sea in, 193–95;
    literary antecedents of, 184–86; loss nar-
    rated in, 201–2; popularity of, 193; racial-
    ized double standard in, 184, 196–202,
    479n17, 479n21, 480n25, 480n27; rape
    narrative in, 200–201; slave trade in,
    190–91, 479n22; swoon moment in, 7–8,
    194–95, 201–2
interiorization of liberty, 43; in Defoe's
    Moll Flanders and *Roxana*, 129; Fou-
    cault's interiority of modern power,
    45; of Hester Prynne, 312–20; in his-
    toriography of American Revolution,
    74–78; in Hopkins's *Contending Forces*,
    371, 382–86; in Hopkins's *Of One
    Blood*, 265–67, 269, 490n22, 490n27; in
    Macaulay's historiography, 70–73; mod-
    ern self in, 132–34; through printing,

publishing, and reading, 44–45, 67–68, 72, 76, 459n25; in rape narratives, 126, 128–30, 130–34, 137–38, 468n25, 469n29, 470n46; Winstanley's nativist views of, 45–46; women's demonstrations of, 46–48. *See also* Protestantism

intertextuality. *See* dialectical intertextuality

Invisible Man (Ellison), 261, 400–401

Iraq, 447

Ireton, Henry, 50, 51–55

Irigary, Luce, 327

Irish colonization, 37

Italian Revolution, 358

Jacobs, Harriet, 6, 8, 127, 174, 176, 489n9; authorship of gothic of, 256–57; fugitive status and pseudonym of, 259–60; *Incidents in the Life of a Slave Girl*, 217, 255–61, 449, 488n3, 488nn5–6; sexual violation and agency of, 258–59, 488n6

Jacob's Room (Woolf), 413–14; critique of imperialism in, 418–21; Jacob's vacillating sexuality in, 421–23; narrative shifts and juxtapositions in, 419–21; pairing of ships and clocks in, 423–24

"Jamaica, Genealogy, and George Eliot" (Watson), 498n18

James, C. L. R., 14

James, Henry, 159, 265–66, 302–3, 382, 394

James, William, 265, 269, 490n27

James I, king of England and Scotland, 4, 29–33

James II, king of England, 59–62; dethroning of, 98; Oxford decree, 60

Jardine, Alice, 19

Jefferson, Thomas, 61; on England's parliamentary tradition, 65; on Rapin, 67, 74; Tacitean sympathies of, 69

Jehlen, Myra, 456n18

Jews: in Eliot's works, 498n10; Semitizing of, 345–51, 498–99nn16–19; Zionist visions and, 340–48, 358, 366–67

Jocelyn, John, 30

Johnson, Barbara, 207, 480n37, 503n27

Johnson, Claudia Durst, 317–18, 322

Johnson, Samuel, 81, 82, 186

Jones, Jill, 171

Jonson, Ben, 31, 80

Jordan, Winthrop, 14, 455n8

Joyce, James, 48

Kaplan, Amy, 56

Kaplan, Carla, 502n9

Karcher, Carolyn, 291–92, 480n33, 491n7

Kaye-Smith, Sheila, 7, 409–12

Kazanjian, David, 243, 485n2, 487n20

Kiernan, V. G., 457n26

Kilgour, Maggie, 482n3, 482n6, 483n7, 483n9, 484n16

King, Debra Walker, 179, 477n60

Kliger, Samuel, 14, 55

Knoepflmacher, U. C., 497n3

Knox, John, 446

Korobkin, Laura, 304–7, 320

Lacan, Jacques, 261, 489n12

"Lament of Tasso" (Byron), 256

Lang, Amy Schrager, 304

Language of Liberty, The (Clark), 456n22

Larsen, Nella, 7, 17, 414, 450, 501n4, 503n26, 504n1; critical outsider view of, 408; "Freedom," 7, 412; *Passing*, 393–95, 403, 404, 407–8, 412, 502n20, 503n22; *Quicksand*, 394–408, 412; "Sanctuary," 7, 395, 409–12, 503nn27–28

Latta, Kimberly, 154, 473n19

Laud, William, 31

Leask, Nigel, 240

Leavis, F. R., 99

Lectures on the Comic Writer (Hazlitt), 457n30

Letters on Chivalry and Romance (Hurd), 82–84, 86

Leveen, Lois, 175, 176–77, 477n56, 477nn53–54

Levellers, 40–43, 44, 47, 52, 119

Levin, Carl, 447–48

Levine, Gary Martin, 341

Lewis, Matthew G., "Monk," 86, 220–29, 256; colonial connections of, 484n14; literary forebears of, 225–26

Leyden, John, 86

Liberty (Thomson), 2–3, 69, 79, 81, 455n3, 461n17

liberty discourses. *See* Atlantic imaginary of racialized freedom

Licensing Entertainment (Warner), 19–20

410. *See also* economics of liberty; English colonies in America

Meyer, Susan, 343–44, 347, 498n10, 498n16, 499n19

Middlemarch (Eliot), 316

middle passage, 7–8, 195, 257, 272, 399

Mighall, Robert, 483n7, 483n10

Mignolo, Walter, 5

Miles, Robert, 483n7

Mill, John Stuart, 352

Mill on the Floss, The (Eliot), 331–32, 363

Milton, John: James II's banning of books by, 60; parable of Atlantic fall by, 146–49, 171, 182, 183, 223, 237, 283–84, 415, 418, 486n12; *Paradise Lost*, 146–49, 171; Saxonism of, 60, 84; Spengemann's transatlantic reading of, 155

Min-ha, Trinh T., 446

"Mistress of the Marriage Market, The" (Latta), 473n19

Mitford, Edward L., 341

Mitford, William, 84, 86–87

Mizruchi, Susan, 480n33

Moby Dick (Melville), 202

Modern Androgyne Imagination (Rado), 505n25

"Modern Hep! Hep! Hep!, The" (Eliot), 342, 343, 356–57, 498n12, 498n17

modernist narratives, 5, 22; fall of protagonist in, 393–95, 405–8, 502n8; in Larsen's novels and short stories, 393–412; nativism of, 55–56; racialized homoeroticism in, 393–95, 400–405, 423, 425–26, 429–31, 501n1, 502n15, 505n18, 505n25, 505n30, 506n32; reversals of Saxon story in, 395–97; swoons in, 394–95, 405, 416; in Woolf's novels, 8, 393, 405, 413–18, 413–43

modern liberal nation-state, 14–15

Moglen, Helen, 474n27

Moll Flanders (Defoe), 10, 21, 135–36, 145–46, 158; Atlantic Ocean in, 149–50; incest and liberty in, 149–50, 155–57, 165, 473n23; interiority in, 129; political context of, 150; property in, 140, 150, 155–57, 472n17, 473n23

Monk, The (Lewis), 7, 141, 215; sexual transgressions in, 222–29, 484n18; tale of the Bleeding Nun, 223–25, 229; trope of dis-

placement and colonial ruin in, 220–23, 228–29

Monmouth's Rebellion (1685), 60

Montaigne, Michel Eyquem de, 208

Montesquieu (Charles-Louis de Secondat), 52

Morant Bay Rebellion (1865), 352

Morris, Lloyd, 303

Morrison, Toni, 14; on Africanism, 6, 19, 203–4, 480n33; *Beloved*, 255

Mowry, Melissa, 124

"Mrs. Adis" (Kaye-Smith), 409–12

Mrs. Dalloway (Woolf), 413–14, 419, 422, 423–26

"Mrs. Hutchinson" (Hawthorne), 313–15, 318, 326

Murphy, Geraldine, 480n27

Mutiny Act, 209

mutuality and collectivity, 449

"Mysteries and Miseries" (Greeson), 488n3

Nancy, Jean-Luc, 454

Napoleon, 340

"Narratives of Domestic Imperialism" (Bernardi), 500n7

Nathaniel Hawthorne and the Tradition of Gothic Romance (Lundblad), 494n3

National Covenant, 53

nation-states, 14–15

Native Americans, 3, 14; Charles II's use of liberty rhetoric on behalf of, 62; conversions and intermarriage of, 282, 493n13; in epic narratives, 278–79, 320–25; extermination of, 233–35; Indianism and "vanished" Indian, 6, 279–83, 295–96, 298–99, 329, 491n7, 492n10, 492n11; missionary work with, 237; representation of wildness in *The Scarlet Letter*, 320–25; in vision of manifest destiny, 90, 344; Warren's racialized views of, 76; Whitman's calls for mastership of, 92. *See also* gothic narratives

nativism. *See* birthrights and racial inheritance

Natty Bumpo series (Cooper), 160

Natural Passion, A (Doody), 469n37

Navigation Acts, 61

Negri, Antonio, 15, 448–49

queer sexuality, 22, 451; in Eliot's *Daniel Deronda*, 497n5; in Ellison's *Invisible Man*, 400–401; female homoerotic magnetism, 387–89; in gothic narratives, 211, 482n4, 484n18; imperial basis of, 426–43, 504n5; in Larsen's *Quicksand*, 400–405, 502n15; in Lewis's *The Monk*, 222, 484n18; in Melville's *Billy Budd*, 202–11; in modernist narratives, 393–95, 501n1, 502n15, 503n22; Sapphic modernism, 387, 501n14, 501n16; in Whitman's "thee and thou," 92–93; Woolf's imperialized and racialized vision of, 423, 425–26, 429–31, 505n18, 505n25, 505n30, 506n32; in Woolf's *Jacob's Room*, 418–24; in Woolf's *Mrs. Dalloway*, 419, 423–26; in Woolf's *To the Lighthouse*, 426–31, 505n18; in Woolf's *The Voyage Out*, 8, 393, 405, 417–18; in Woolf's *The Waves*, 419, 442–43

Quicksand (Larsen), 7, 97, 393, 408, 412; conflicts with Saxon orthodoxy in, 394–97, 405, 501n5; Helga's quest for racial freedom in, 397–400, 405–7, 502nn9–10; Helga's racial alienation in, 405–7, 502n8, 502n20; Naxos school, 395–97, 501n5; racialized homoeroticism in, 400–405, 502n15

"Quicksands of the Self, The" (Johnson), 503n27

race: in literary history, 15–21, 79–93; nation conflated with, 14; in readings of gender and sexuality, 6–10; value and power of, 23, 446–54. *See also* African-Atlantic narratives of freedom; Africanism; Saxonist legacy of freedom

race epics. *See* epic narratives

racialism, 7–8, 15; anti-Normanism, 55; birthrights and racial inheritance, 2–5, 9–11, 13–14, 19–20, 40–41, 457n24; Ethiopianism, 261–62, 271–72, 489nn13–14, 490nn15–16, 490n22, 490n28; of Gothic balance of English parliamentary monarchy, 71–73; Indianism, 6, 278–83, 286, 491n7, 492n11, 493n13; Orientalism, 359–60, 364–65, 429–31; in protection of property, 51–56; racialized American everyman,

89–90, 202–4, 210, 480n33; racialized homoeroticism, 393–95, 400–405, 423, 425–26, 429–31, 502n15, 505n18, 505n25, 505n30, 506n32; Semitism, 345–51, 498–99nn16–19; of transplanted English stock in epic narratives, 309; whiteness, 3, 6, 12, 14, 309, 450–51. *See also* Africanism; Saxonist legacy of freedom

racialized sublime, 79; in American arts, 87–93; in Eliot's *Daniel Deronda*, 356–57; in English poetry, 82–87, 462n6; in Sedgwick's *Hope Leslie*, 297–99; in Woolf's *The Waves*, 431–35, 442–43, 505n25

racial uplift, 9

racism, 5, 13–15. *See also* Africanism; race; racialism

Rado, Lisa, 505n25

Rainborough, Thomas, 40

Raleigh, Walter, 393

Ramsay, David, 59, 67, 74–76

"Rape and the Rise of the Novel" (Ferguson), 117–18

rape narratives, 29, 466n2; African-Atlantic narratives of, 7, 8, 9, 372–74; birthrights and native freedoms in, 127–28; as catalyst for racial uplift, 9; classical legacies of, 9, 99, 119, 358–59, 455n15; of enslaved women by white masters, 258–59, 266–67, 372–74; in Equiano's *Interesting Narrative*, 200–201; figurative rape, 500n6; in gothic narratives, 218; Gwendolyn's consent in, 351–57, 359–62; Haywood's preoccupation with consent in, 123–34, 143, 362, 468n28; in Hopkins's *Contending Forces*, 9, 371–72, 377–78, 384–86, 500nn6–7; interiorization of liberty in, 126, 128–40, 469n29; lynching in, 382–83; political contexts of, 119–23, 124, 467n8, 468n19; Richardson's interiorized *Clarissa*, 20, 28, 117–19, 135–44. *See also* seduction narratives

Rape of Lucretia and the Founding Republics, The (Matthes), 455n15

Rapin-Thoyras, Paul de, 1, 67–69, 74

reading: of history, 74; interiorization of liberty through, 67–68, 72, 76; of vernacular Bibles, 43–44, 324, 496n23. *See also* printing and publishing

Southey, Robert, 86
Sowerby, Robin, 483n7
Spanish picaro influence, 118, 466n3
Specters of the Atlantic (Bauman), 8
Spelman, Henry, 31
Spencer, Jane, 485n21
Spengemann, William, 97–115, 146–49,
   464n8, 465n22, 471n4
Spithead mutiny, 207–8, 211
Star Chamber, 36, 38
States of Sympathy (Barnes),
   473–74nn25–26
State Tracts, 1660—1687, 58
"Steamboat Surfacing" (Wilt), 497n4
Stein, Gertrude, 48, 394, 402, 414, 429
Stepan, Nancy, 14
Stephens, Michelle, 14, 451
Stern, Julia, 148, 473n25; on Brown's *The
   Power of Sympathy*, 167, 169; on incest,
   165; on psycho-historical basis of novels,
   158–59, 474n27; on Rowson's *Charlotte
   Temple*, 158–59, 162, 474n36; on Wilson's
   Our Nig, 173, 476n51, 477n56
Stith, William, 74
Stoler, Ann Laura, 14
Stowe, Harriet Beecher, 259, 339, 366,
   489n9
Stuart, Shea, 124
Stuarts, 4, 335; historiography of, 63–73;
   persecution of Puritans by, 32, 76. *See
   also* English Civil War
Subjects of Slavery, Agents of Change
   (Winter), 482n1
"Subject to Disappearance" (Hutchinson),
   501nn4–5
sublime, 79, 92–93, 462n6. *See also* racial-
   ized sublime
"Sublime Barbarians in the Narrative of
   Empire" (Doyle), 505n29
Suleri, Sara, 463n22, 467n12
Sullivan, John, 233
Sussman, Charlotte, 465n20
Swedenborg, Emanuel, 89
Swift, Jonathan, 57, 66
swoon moments, 2, 6, 51; in Behn's
   Oroonoko, 107–11, 465n17, 465nn20–21;
   in C. B. Brown's *Wieland*, 246–47;
   classical legacies of, 9; in Defoe's
   Robinson Crusoe, 8, 151, 183, 188; in

Defoe's *Roxana*, 155; in Eliot's *Daniel
   Deronda*, 336, 343; in Equiano's
   Interesting Narrative, 194–95, 201–2;
   in Hawthorne's *The Scarlet Letter*,
   323–24, 327–28; in Haywood's fiction,
   126–27, 132; in Hopkins's *Contending
   Forces*, 371, 384; in Hopkins's *Of One
   Blood*, 269–72; in Larsen's *Quicksand*,
   405–7; in MacCannell's regime of
   the brother, 10–13, 155; in middle passage, 7, 195; in modernist narratives,
   394–95, 405; in political pamphlets,
   119–23; racialized sublime in, 87, 93; in
   Richardson's *Clarissa*, 135, 142–44; in
   Rowson's *Charlotte Temple*, 162–63; in
   Sedgwick's *Hope Leslie*, 284–85, 298–99;
   of shipwreck and sea trauma, 8, 151, 183,
   188, 194–95, 201–2; in Woolf's *Jacob's
   Room*, 419; in Woolf's *To the Lighthouse*,
   427–28; in Woolf's *The Voyage Out*, 416;
   in Woolf's *The Waves*, 434. *See also* rape
   narratives
"Sympathy as Strategy in Sedgwick's *Hope
   Leslie*" (Nelson), 491n7, 492n11

Tacitus, 67, 74, 83
Taine, Hippolyte, 20
Tainted Souls and Painted Faces
   (Anderson), 456n18
"Talking Too Much English" (Caldwell),
   478n6
Tarquin and Lucretia, 9, 119, 358–59, 445,
   455n15
Tate, Claudia, 173, 258, 379, 477n58,
   488nn5–6, 496n24
Tawil, Ezra, 280, 283, 492n11, 493nn12–13
Temple, William, 163
"Tennessee Hero, The" (Harper), 93
Tess of the D'Urbervilles (Hardy), 316–17
Testimonie of Antiquities, A, 30
Thirty Years War, 38
Thomas, Brook, 207–8, 480n37
Thompson, Andrew, 358, 359
Thompson, Helen, 128, 469n29
Thompson, John, 35, 459n15
Thomson, James, 2–3, 4, 69, 79, 81, 183,
   455n3, 461n17
Thomson, Maurice, 34–37
Thorn, Jennifer, 130, 469n33

Waves, The (Woolf), 10, 413–14; authorial positioning in, 435, 442–43, 505n29; Bernard's desire for heteronormative freedom in, 435–43, 453, 505n25; figurative speech and interludes in, 435, 438–42; imperial racialized sublime in, 434–43, 505n25, 505n30; Percival as mythic English barbarian in, 431–34; Percival's death in, 438–42; queer sexuality in, 419, 442–43; racialized sublime in, 431–35, 442–43, 505n25; swoon moments in, 434
Weber, Max, 53
Weierman, Karen Woods, 491n7, 492nn10–11
Weil, Lise, 505n18
Weinbaum, Alys, 14
Weinbrot, Howard, 80–81
Wellek, René, 83
Wenska, Walter, 17, 474n26
West Indian colonies, 35–36, 351–52, 372
"What Did I Do to Be So Black and Blue" (Armstrong), 400
"When Privilege Is No Protection" (Dittmar), 502n15
Whig views of history, 2, 16–18, 21, 40, 457nn29–30; American Revolution influenced by, 74; birthright narratives in, 19–20, 32; Exclusion Crisis (1678—81), 60; historiography of England's Gothic balance in, 63–73, 138, 483n7; Petition of Right, 32; Stuarts condemned in, 64. *See also* Saxonist legacy of freedom
White, Barbara, 176–77
White, Ed, 99, 371, 485n1, 486n3
"White Face" (Cheyette), 498n18
white indentured servitude, 35, 410, 459n11
whiteness, 3, 6, 12, 14, 309, 450–51
Whitman, Walt, 22, 91–93, 203, 453
Wide, Wide World (Warner), 179–80
Wide and Equal Survey of English Literature (Barrell), 101
Wide Sargasso Sea (Rhys), 405
Wieland, Christoff Martin, 236, 253, 486n11, 488n24
Wieland, or the Transformation: An American Tale (C. B. Brown), 7, 10, 141, 145–46, 165, 215; Carwin's biloquism in, 231, 240–49, 252, 485n2, 487n19; Clara's

betrayal and abandonment in, 241, 245–51; Clara's dissociated narration in, 232–35, 238–39, 240, 485n3; Clara's free agency in, 245–53, 487n21; as colonial allegory, 231, 239–40, 242, 251–53, 485nn1–2; economic basis of liberty in, 237–40, 251–53, 485n3, 486n9; possession in, 231–32, 485n3; Saxon genealogy in, 231–32, 235–40, 242–45, 485n3; sexual betrayal in, 240–51; swoon moment in, 246–47
William of Orange, 63, 98, 151. *See also* Glorious Revolution
Williams, Patricia, 260
William the Conqueror, 27
Willis, John, 8
Wilson, Harriet, 22, 129, 145, 158; Christian conversion of, 179, 477n58; literary forebears of, 496n24; *Our Nig*, 170–82, 474n43
Wilt, Judith, 143, 497n4
Windsor Forest (Pope), 80
Winstanley, Gerard, 40–41, 45–46, 460n27
Winter, Kari J., 482n1
Winthrop, John, 304–6
witchcraft, 47
Wohlfarth, Marc E., 499n24
Wollaeger, Mark, 506n32
women, 60; in African-Atlantic narratives, 184–87; agency of, 17, 18–19, 227–28, 245–51, 485n21, 487n21; Clarissa's birthright of freedom, 10, 28–29, 118, 136–37, 140, 469n37; complicity in violence of colonization of, 251–53, 281–83, 292–97, 299, 320, 328–29, 366–67; domestic roles of, 123–24, 173–74, 476n51; Eliot's ambiguity about, 358–59; "fallen," 147–48; female bonds in Hopkins's *Contending Forces*, 386–90, 501nn13–16; Hawthorne's condemnation of women writers, 314; historiography by, 71–73, 76–78; interior freedom and witchcraft of, 46–48; Macauley's enthusiastic accounts of liberty, 72–73, 461n20; MacCannell's regime of the brother, 10–13, 155; negotiation of Anglo-colonial conflicts by, 102; in patriarchal gothic novels, 218–19; preaching, speaking, and activism of, 39–40, 46–48, 123–24, 313, 460n27;

property ownership by, 118, 153–54, 472nn17–18; racialization of virtue of, 19; racial maneuvering by Anglo-Atlantic female writers, 9, 10–11, 59, 72–73, 77–78, 112–13, 115; ruined heroines and states, 456n18. *See also* brother-sister plots; feminist readings; rape narratives; seduction narratives; sexual transgressions

Wood, Gordon, 7–8

Woolf, Virginia, 8, 394, 504n1; images of barbarian men of, 416–17, 431–34; imperialist visions of, 414, 426–43, 504n5, 505n25, 505n30, 506n32, 515n18; interiorized narrations of, 414, 419–20; *Jacob's Room*, 413–14, 418–24; *Mrs. Dalloway*, 413–14, 419, 422, 423–26; plot of heteronormativity of, 435–43, 453, 505n25; queer sexuality explored by, 414, 417–23, 425–26, 429–31, 504n13, 505n18; queer sexuality racialized by, 423, 425–26, 429–31, 505n25, 505n30, 506n32, 515n18; racialized sublime of *The Waves*, 431–35, 442–43, 505n25; on *Robinson Crusoe*, 190; ships and clocks paired by, 423–24; "A Sketch of the Past," 416–17; *To the Lighthouse*, 413–14, 423, 426–31; *The Voyage Out*, 8, 393, 405, 413–18; *The Waves*, 10, 413–14, 431–42

Wordsworth, William, 87

Wotton, Henry, 82

Yanella, Donald, 480n33

Yazawa, Melvin, 456n18, 456n20

Years, The (Woolf), 505n18

Young, Robert, 14, 457n25

Younger Brother, The (Behn), 60

Zaret, David, 53

Zionist vision, 340–48, 347, 358, 366–67, 498n10

Zomchick, John, 138, 144, 469n38

Zong massacre, 8, 9

Laura Doyle is a professor of English
at the University of Massachusetts.

Library of Congress Cataloging-in-Publication Data
Doyle, Laura (Laura Anne)
    Freedom's empire : race and the rise of the novel in
atlantic modernity, 1640–1940 / Laura Doyle.
        p. cm.
Includes bibliographical references and index.
ISBN 978-0-8223-4135-2 (cloth : alk. paper)
ISBN 978-0-8223-4159-8 (pbk. : alk. paper)
    1. American fiction — History and criticism.   2. English
fiction — History and criticism.   3. Race in literature.
4. Liberty in literature.   5. Modernism (Literature)
I. Title.
PS371.D69 2008
823'.009355 — dc22   2007033638